Basic Drama Projects

Perfection
Learning®

Editorial Director Julie A. Schumacher
Senior Editor Gay Russell-Dempsey
Illustrations Mike Aspengren
Picture Research Lisa Lorimor
Permissions Meghan Schumacher, Oliver Oertel
Text Writers Sheri Reda, Education Specialist, Chicago, Illinois
        Lisa Dillman, Playwright, Teacher, Education Writer, Chicago, Illinois
Handbook Writer Ric Averill, Composer, Playwright, Drama Program Director for Lawrence Arts Center,
        Lawrence, Kansas
Design Herman Adler Design, Evanston, Illinois

Acknowledgments
Text Credits

Excerpt from "The Actor's Nightmare" by Christopher Durang from *Christopher Durang Explains It All for You.* Copyright ©1982 by Christopher Durang. Reprinted by permission of Grove/Atlantic, Inc.

Excerpt from *After Cages* by Cin Salach. Copyright ©1996 by Cin Salach. Reprinted by permission of Tia Chucha Press.

Excerpt from *Blood Wedding* by Federico Garcia Lorca. Translation by James Graham-Lujan and Richard L. O'Connell, from *Three Tragedies.* Copyright ©1947 by New Directions Publishing Corp. Reprinted by permission of New Directions Publishing Corp.

Excerpt from *Blithe Spirit* by Noël Coward. Copyright ©1941 by Noël Coward. Reprinted by permission of Alan Brodie Representation Ltd. 211 Piccadilly, London W1V 9LD.

(Acknowledgments continued on page 624)

Copyright © 2009 by Perfection Learning® Corporation
1000 North Second Avenue
P.O. Box 500
Logan, Iowa 51546-0500
Tel: 1-800-831-4190 • Fax: 1-800-543-2745
perfectionlearning.com

13 14 15 16 17 18 RRD 18 17 16 15 14 13
[hardback] ISBN-13: 978-0-7569-1640-4
[hardback] ISBN-10: 0-7569-1640-2
[paperback] ISBN-13: 978-0-7891-6175-8
[paperback] ISBN-10: 0-7891-6175-3

Basic Drama Projects

8th Edition

Projects

by Fran Averett Tanner, Ph.D.
College of Southern Idaho, Twin Falls, Idaho

Perfection
Learning®

Review Board

The Editors are indebted to the following teachers for their help in creating this book and for their tireless efforts on behalf of theatre students around the country.

Jeanne Averill
Drama Teacher
Lawrence High School
Lawrence, Kansas

Tracy Boylan
Drama Teacher
La Salle-Peru Township High School
LaSalle, Illinois

Deborah Clark
Drama Teacher
Hollywood Hills High School
Hollywood, Florida

Robert Kallos
Drama Teacher
The Galloway School
Atlanta, Georgia

Andrea Kidd
Drama Teacher
Dr. Michael M. Krop High School
Miami, Florida

Elaine Malone
Drama Teacher
The Galloway School
Atlanta, Georgia

Carmen McElwain
Drama Teacher
Plano, Texas

Kim Rubinstein
Professor of Theatre Arts
Northwestern University
Evanston, Illinois

Nan Zabriski
Professor of Theatre Arts
De Paul University
Chicago, Illinois

Student Actors

We would also like to thank the following student actors for their help in making the photographic images in this book lively and instructive.

Emmett Adler	Lauren Gray
Max Adler	Yasmeen Kheshgi
Stephon Albert	Christa Koskosky
Gail Amornpongchai	Lizzie Laundy
Paige Azuma	Henry Marcus
Calvin Baptiste, Jr.	Mghnon Martin
Bryan D. Blaney	Tatyana Pramatarova
Peter Bloom	Alex Rosenfield
Elaine Coladarci	Isaac Simpson
Amanda Georgantas	Eileen Spangler
Alex Goode	Hilary Ubando

Additional thanks go to Lost Era Costumes, Chicago, Illinois, for their generous help in costuming; Joe Silvestri of Lake Forest Academy for allowing use of theatre space and student models; Shauna Thieman of Western Michigan University Theatre Department, Lee Ann Bakros from the Des Moines Community Playhouse, and Christina Faison of North High in Des Moines, Iowa, for the use of photographs from their productions.

Welcome to Drama Class!

We think you're going to enjoy your stay!

Basic Drama Projects offers you just what the name suggests: projects that provide an introduction to theatre basics. Basics that are engaging, challenging, creative, and fun. Here are hands-on, action-packed assignments—from improv and character development to writing and directing to creating props and planning set designs.

Success in this class will not necessarily lead to a starring role on Broadway or a career in costume design or sound engineering. Instead, it is a place where you can tap into your own creativity, gain self-confidence, and experience working collaboratively with others. You will discover that working in the theatre almost always means being part of a team.

This is a class where teamwork and dependability aren't just words—they are tools of the trade. And as you gain a broader theatre background, you will also develop other skills. You will learn to become a critical listener and viewer—qualities that will serve you well no matter where your future takes you.

Unit
Five

Unit Seven

Exploring Theatre History 398

Unit Eight

Unit One

Begin with the Basics

Chapter 1 Warm Up

Actors relax and warm up in order to be alert and responsive as they perform. Warm-ups help increase the actor's ability to direct the nervous energy that arises before going onstage. By relaxing and warming up before a performance, you too can prepare your voice and body for the strenuous work ahead.

Project Specs

Project Description You and a partner will create and perform a two- to three-minute warm-up routine using techniques and exercises learned in class.

Purpose to learn techniques that help increase flexibility, body control, relaxation, and vocal articulation

Materials loose-fitting, comfortable clothing; a list of the elements in your routine or the Warm Up Activity Sheet your teacher provides

Theatre Terms
adrenaline
articulation
pliable
professionals
routine
stage fright
vocalizing

On Your Feet

To begin exercising clear speech, or **articulation,** try to say one or more of the following tongue twisters rapidly without mispronouncing any words:

- Two teamsters tried to tag twenty-two keys.
- She makes a proper cup of coffee in a copper coffee pot.
- Red leather, yellow leather, red leather, yellow leather (repeat)
- Would Wheeler woo Wanda while Woody snoozed woozily?

The Actor Prepares

Like all disciplined **professionals,** good actors make what they do look effortless. They seem to inhabit the characters they play. Their bodies, minds, voices, and emotions are their tools, and they use them expertly to create the effects they desire. Some actors undergo rigorous physical training to maximize their capabilities onstage. Some do not. However, all serious actors warm up before rehearsals and performances. They know that they will need to be alert and responsive to stage directions, other actors, and their own physical, mental, and emotional needs.

Actors who warm up become alert and physically prepared for the demands

of acting. They also direct the normal nervous energy that arises before a performance. Instead of spiraling into fright, actors who loosen up can put increased energy into the demands of their roles and of the play at hand.

Actors are often called upon to perform very vigorous movement, such as dancing, fighting, or wrestling. Singing, yelling, and other **vocalizing** may also be called for. If you learn these skills and practice them as part of your everyday **routine,** your voice and body will become strong, **pliable,** or adaptable, and disciplined. As a bonus, you will always be ready and qualified for that physically demanding, once-in-a-lifetime role.

Why Warm Up?

Just as athletes do not take to the court or the field without doing warm-up exercises, neither do actors. The warmups help you in a number of ways: they relax you, they help clear your mind, and they prepare you to use your voice and body effectively. In other words, they take the nervous energy that arises naturally and put it to work as you portray your character on stage. Additionally, these exercises will build confidence and expand your range of communication and movement. Gaining mastery over your body's expressive ability can be exhilarating. It also helps you appreciate the work of those actors who make it look easy.

Actors warm up before a performance.

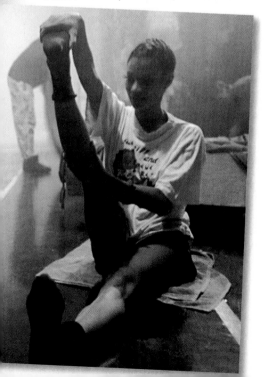

The following warm-up routines will prepare you physically and vocally for the stage—and for the demands of everyday life.

Relaxation Techniques

- With feet apart in a comfortable balance, stretch up tall. Then bend over like a rag doll, collapsing quickly and loosely from the waist with your relaxed arms and hands dangling to the floor. Keep your arms, hands, and head completely relaxed. Slowly rise up, keeping relaxed. Repeat.

- Breathe in as your teacher or director counts to eight. Take a deep breath, bringing air in through your nose, then into your throat, your chest, and your lungs. Feel your middle expand as your breath fills your body. Then breathe out slowly through your mouth to the count of eight. Repeat several times.

- With your neck relaxed and your chin close to your chest, slowly move your head to the left, back to the front, to the right, and up. Then reverse the rotation. Be sure to move very slowly and cautiously. Keep your neck relaxed, letting your head slowly roll like a dead weight in a socket.

- Lie quietly on your back. Close your eyes and make your mind a blank slate. Chase all thoughts away, concentrating only on relaxing your body. Listen to the rhythm of your heartbeat as, one at a time, you relax every part of your body—from your toes, to your legs and arms, and up to your head. Feel your body melt into the floor. Remain in this relaxed position for a few moments before you begin your warm-up exercises.

Warm-up Exercises

- Swing your relaxed arms in large circles, one at a time.

- Lie on your back and tuck in your knees, holding them to your chest with your hands. Roll gently from side to side. Do this ten times.

The rag doll: Stretch and collapse gently.

- Sit on your ankles, keeping your back straight. Stretch up, with your arms extended, as high as you can go. Keep your body straight. Do this four times.

- Use your entire body to draw huge numbers, from one to ten, in the air. Use as much space as you can. Bend, stretch, and travel around the room as you write. Do this for about three minutes.

- Play "imaginary jump rope." By yourself or with two partners (to hold the imaginary rope), jump an imaginary rope until you are tired. You might want to try using a few different rhythms, changing your jumping pattern accordingly—alternating feet together and feet apart, and so on.

- Lie on your back and then extend your entire lower body into a shoulder stand, placing your hands on your back and your elbows on the floor. Stay in this position for a count of twenty. Next, roll your legs back and over your head, letting your feet drop to the floor. Keep your legs straight. Only go back as far as is comfortable. Then unwind until you are flat on your back again. Repeat.

- Stand with your feet slightly apart. Begin to shake your hands. Shake them more and more vigorously. When your teacher yells, "Freeze!" stop all movement. Then begin to tense the same muscles in your hands. Repeat this exercise several times. Be sure you stop shaking the moment you hear, "Freeze!"

- Stretch your tongue. Try to touch the tip of your tongue to your nose. Don't be discouraged if you can't do it—only one in 1000 people can. It's the stretch, not the parlor trick, that counts. Repeat several times.

Be careful to keep your back straight as you do this exercise. Do not overdo it.

Here's How
To Do the Rhythm Hop

Can't walk and chew gum at the same time? Doing the rhythm hop can help. It takes a little time, attention, and some practice to learn, but it gets easier as you do it.

- With your weight on your left foot, hop once, while pointing your right foot out front. Extend your arms out in front of you and clap your hands. Hop a second time, with your right foot extended out to the right and your arms extended out to the sides.

- Hop on your left foot a third time, and bring your right foot down to the left foot. Also put your arms down at your sides. Next, shift your weight to your right foot and repeat the process.

Do the rhythm hop 10 to 20 times rapidly. Eventually, you will be able to perform this exercise while chanting rhymes or song lyrics.

Vocal Exercises

- Smile! Smile with great exaggeration, letting your teeth show and drawing your lips as tightly as possible. Say "eeeee." Then exaggerate a pucker and say "ooooo." Repeat these two motions and sounds ten times in quick succession. Then add consonants to create sound combinations such as "me-moo," "tee-too," "bee-boo," gee-goo," and "lee-loo."

- Begin a slow yawn and make the sound "ahhhh" as you exhale. Remember the open quality of the sound you are making. Aim for it in all your speech.

- Open wide. Open your mouth as wide as possible. Say "ahhh" as you exhale. Now close your mouth, saying "oooo" as you exhale. Repeat "ahhh-oooo" several times. Take care to open your mouth as wide as possible.

- Read the rhyme below with clarity and emphasis. Start off slowly, then increase your speed as you read it two more times.

To sit in solemn silence in a dull dock
In a pestilential prison with a life long
  lock
Awaiting the sensation of a short
  sharp shock
From a cheap and chippy chopper
  on a big black block.
    —W.S. Gilbert from *The Mikado*

PREPARE

Work Out Your Warm-up Routine

Your teacher will assign you a partner or ask you to find a partner for this project. Have your partner read the various routines and exercises described on the previous pages while you follow the directions for doing them. Then you do the same for your partner. Repeat the exercises until you feel comfortable doing them all.

Together, decide whether you will use both physical and vocal elements to create your routine. Next, order the elements you will include for your two- to three-minute routine using a list or the Activity Sheet your teacher provides.

Plan how you will present the routine to the class: Will one of you instruct the class while the other demonstrates the routine? Will you both demonstrate the routine while you give instructions?

You may want to use music to accompany your routine. If you do, be sure the music has the appropriate rhythm and tune for what you are trying to achieve.

When you have completely worked out your routine, time it to be sure it is no longer than three minutes and no shorter than two minutes. Practice at least five times before you actually present your routine.

PRESENT

Be the Instructor

When your turn comes, stand still for a second with your partner and take a deep breath, bringing air into your lungs. Introduce yourselves to the class and then present your routine. Encourage your classmates to join in the routine. Have fun, smile, and harness all that nervous energy!

When you are finished, pause and then quietly leave the playing area. Remember to maintain a sense of physical and vocal control from the time you leave the playing area until you return to your seat.

Theatre Journal

Make a list of the things you do in your everyday life that could help prepare you for performing on the stage. Examples might be singing in the chorus or playing basketball. Write a short explanation of the ways in which these activities help you both physically and emotionally.

CRITIQUE

Compare Two Warm-up Routines

As you watch your classmates' warm-up routines, take notes as to how well the routines are presented. Use a scale of 1 to 5, with 5 being "outstanding" and 1 being "needs much improvement." Ask yourself questions such as those below as you evaluate the routines.

- Were the instructions clear and easy to do?

- Did the instructors speak clearly?

- Was the routine the correct length?

- Was the routine effective in warming up and relaxing the participants?

- How would you use this routine to warm up for a performance?

Compare how well two separate pairs of presenters created and presented their routines. Write a paragraph explaining the reasons for the scores you gave.

Spotlight on

Stage Fright

According to a nationwide survey, speaking in front of others is the number one fear of Americans. We experience **stage fright**–dry mouth, shaky knees, trembling hands, sweaty palms, and queasy stomach–because we suspect we won't do well. Minor stage fright can be helpful to a performer because it releases extra **adrenaline,** a chemical our bodies produce to help us deal with unfamiliar situations. The surge of adrenaline provides the performer with increased energy, enthusiasm, and animation. A heightened sense of awareness is useful to the actor, but uncontrolled stage fright can derail a performer. Below are a few tips for managing stage fright.

Be Prepared. When we are prepared we automatically feel more comfortable and confident. If you find your hands are shaky or your mouth is dry, take a moment to remind yourself that you know exactly what you're doing.

Use Good Posture. Good posture provides a strong base for movement and vocal production. Your good posture will give the audience an impression of confidence–and it just might make you feel more confident yourself!

Breathe. Don't forget to breathe! Inadequate breath can lead to a shaky voice and a feeling of physical insecurity. If necessary, take a couple of deep breaths to ground yourself before you begin speaking.

Give Yourself Time. Remember that most people who experience stage fright usually warm up after a short time. The more public speaking you do, the easier it becomes.

Additional Projects

1 Say "ahhhhh." Sustain a comfortably pitched tone. Then create variations by increasing the volume, decreasing the volume, and bringing the volume back to start. Repeat with pitch: make the sound higher in pitch, then lower in pitch, then bring it back to start.

2 With a partner, carry on an animated conversation in gibberish or a pretend "foreign language," using only nonsense or invented words. If you find it difficult to make up words or sounds, use the syllables "da-da-shoon" repeatedly. Sincerely try to communicate through this new language.

3 Say a sentence such as "Now is the time," or "There goes the last one," in each of the following ways: sternly, eagerly, worriedly, soothingly, shyly, drowsily, angrily, sadly, and happily.

4 Blow yourself up. Imagine that you are a balloon. You can be completely inflated with three large inhalations. Expand in three stages, until you are completely expanded, like a balloon. Ask a partner or classmate to "pop" you. Then deflate as a balloon might.

5 Form a circle with seven or more classmates. Hold hands with the people on each side of you and do not let go. Begin weaving under and around the arms and legs of the other people in the circle. Once you are tangled to the point that no one can move any further, try to untangle yourselves. Do not, under any circumstances, let go of the hands you are holding, but stop the moment anyone becomes uncomfortable.

6 Memorize part of Biff's monologue from *Death of a Salesman* by Arthur Miller found in Unit Eight. Imagine that Biff is doing sit-ups or bouncing a ball during the scene. Then perform the movements of this activity while speaking the lines from the scene. Allow the words to accompany the movement. If you prefer, memorize a monologue of your own choosing and work out your own activity to accompany it.

Chapter
2 Observation

Acting is said to be the study of human behavior. So, in addition to their own memories and imaginations, actors must depend on their powers of **observation.** As an actor, you must become aware of how other people feel, move, speak, think, and behave. You must be able to recall what you observe, and use it to build believable characters.

Project Specs

Project Description For this assignment, you will give a detailed one- to three-minute description of an object.

Purpose to learn the skills of observation and recall

Materials a list of the characteristics of your chosen object or the Observation Activity Sheet provided by your teacher

Theatre Terms
conscious
observation
recall
sense memory
spontaneous
subconscious
visualize

On Your Feet

To test your powers of observation, look around the classroom and choose an object, such as a poster, and quietly observe it for one minute. Concentrate on the colors, shapes, printed words, and textures. Also pay attention to how the item makes you *feel*. Now close your eyes and try to re-create the object in your mind. Now, without looking at the object, write down every detail you remember. Compare what you have written to the object. Did you miss anything?

Getting Specific

Someone once said that only through the specific can we reveal the universal. This is true in the arts, and it is especially relevant in the theatre, where actors are called upon to create believable characters and situations in front of an audience.

As an actor you must become a keen observer—a student of the world around you. That's because to portray any character believably, you have to create a complex and specific human being made up of hundreds of key details.

That might sound difficult, but using your powers of observation can help. You can start off with something slightly less complicated than a human being— an inanimate object.

Karen Allen in a recent production of *The Glass Menagerie.*

Plays are often about people's relationship with their possessions—or their relationship with *other* people's possessions. In Tennessee Williams's play *The Glass Menagerie,* a painfully shy young woman named Laura seeks refuge from the outside world in her collection of delicate glass animals. When playing this character, an actor must have a specific *relationship* with the members of the tiny glass menagerie. After all, if the figurines mean nothing to Laura, they won't mean much to an audience either.

Alan Cumming, as Hamlet, focuses on the skull of Yorick in the 1993 London production.

PREPARE

Your Observations and Impressions

In this assignment you will describe a familiar object and provide your impressions and feelings about it from your **sense memory** —in which you use all five senses to recapture an experience. You should describe the physical object in detail and also reveal to your audience what the object means to you.

Suppose, for example, that you decide upon a treasured toy from your early childhood. Using your powers of observation, you will **recall** or re-create this item in such a way that your audience will **visualize** the object you describe. But you can also share other details and memories, such as how you felt when you first saw the toy or what it meant to you at a particular time in your life. Perhaps the toy makes you feel sad that you are no longer as carefree as you once were. Or it might amuse you to think about a time when the toy was an important part of your life.

You can choose any object—but make sure it's one that means something to you or meant something to you in the past. In order to describe your object so that your audience will actually be able to see it, ask yourself the following questions and keep a list of your answers:

- What does the object look like?
- How does it smell?
- How does it feel?
- How does it/might it taste? (if applicable)
- How does it sound?
- What does it remind me of?
- What makes it important to me?

Suggestions for Objects

- a piece of jewelry
- a photograph
- an article of clothing
- a trophy or plaque
- a piece of art
- a musical instrument

A Test Run

Set a timer for three minutes. Rehearse describing your chosen object and its impact on you. This is not a scripted activity, so you do not have to memorize what you will say. Because the object has personal meaning for you, the words to describe it should be **spontaneous**. Stay within the one- to three-minute time limit.

Theatre Journal

Look at the list you have made about your chosen object. Write a paragraph about a day in your life that includes this object. Describe what the object looked like then. Be specific. Describe it in physical detail, but as you write, also pay attention to the feelings going on inside you. If you find you can go on for more than a paragraph, do so.

Here's How
To Improve Your Sense Memory

You look at thousands of things every day without really *seeing* them. You can improve your powers of observation by using a few simple techniques.

1 **Relax.** Don't strain to focus on the details you think you're most likely to remember. Instead, try to look at the world around you with fresh eyes.

2 **Observe in segments.** For instance, if you look at an object, an ornate vase for example, you might focus on its outline, then the color, the texture, the weight, and the way it feels to the touch. Notice the associations that you make. Let your observation take in not only what your eyes tell you, but also what your other senses reveal. These associations can be very important for later recall.

3 **Use your journal** to record your impressions and observations. This gets you into the habit of paying attention to what you notice—and what you don't. Writing down what you observe can help you hold it in your **conscious** mind as well as in your **subconscious**—the part of the brain just below your awareness—so you can use it later. You can write about almost anything: what you saw on a walk, what a chocolate shake tastes like, what the air smells like after a rainstorm, and so on.

PRESENT

Describe Your Object

When your name is called, hand in your list or Activity Sheet and walk to the playing area.

Begin by telling the audience what your chosen object is. This can be a simple, objective statement, such as "I'm going to describe my trumpet."

As you begin your presentation, remember to keep your body relaxed and to breathe deeply to avoid excessive nervousness. Don't hurry. Concentrate on specifics. Don't worry that you're not including everything. Speak naturally and try to be completely truthful. After all, you are talking about something you know very well.

When you have finished, ask the audience if they have questions about the object you've just described. Set a limit of three questions. Afterward, thank your audience and return to your seat.

CRITIQUE

Evaluate a Classmate's Description

Choose one of the descriptions presented in class to evaluate. Think about both the successful and unsuccessful aspects of your classmate's performance. Your evaluation should be based on a scale of 1 to 5, in which 1 is equal to "needs much improvement" and 5 is equal to "outstanding." Your evaluation should answer these questions:

- How did the person involve all five senses in the description of the object?
- Did you believe that the object meant something specific to the person?
- Could you visualize the object?
- Was any one sense emphasized while another was ignored?

Write a paragraph defending your scoring.

Spotlight on

Peer Evaluation

Peer evaluation, the act of looking critically at the work of your classmates, is beneficial to the evaluator as well as to the performers. When you critique the work of your peers, you have the opportunity to compare your work to that of others whose performance level is similar to your own. You will also participate in an exchange of ideas as you communicate your point of view, and your insights may have an impact on another's work. When your peers evaluate you, you gain worthwhile information regarding your work as well as a number of ideas for growth and improvement.

An effective peer evaluation often tells the performer what you understand to be the purpose or meaning of the work, what you enjoyed, what was especially effective or well done, and anything that confused or disturbed you. If possible, conclude with a final comment about the work as a whole.

It is very important to remember that when you are evaluating your classmates you should maintain a positive, but objective, attitude. Keep an open mind—give your classmates the benefit of any doubt—and try not to be overly critical. Remember, you are all beginners, and no performance will be perfect. State any suggestions for improvement in an even, upbeat manner, and never say anything that would unnecessarily hurt someone's feelings.

Additional Projects

1 A simple action, when analyzed in minute detail, can be hilarious. Describe a familiar action, such as eating an orange, sharpening a pencil, or washing your hair. See yourself performing the action. Describe it in as much detail as you can.

2 Write a one-page monologue in which a character uses observation and recall to describe a specific moment from the distant past.

3 Play "Who am I?" Divide into two teams. On small strips of paper, each person in the class will write down the name of a different well-known actor or musician. Put all the names in a bag or container. A member of the first team draws a name out of the hat and tries to describe that person's physical characteristics, vocal quality, and facial expressions to his or her teammates. The object is for the teammates to guess the name on the paper through descriptions and impressions—but *without* any biographical information. If a team member guesses the name within one minute, that team gets to take another turn. If no one on the team guesses correctly within the allotted time, the name goes back in the hat, and the other team takes its turn.

4 Work with a partner to play the "mirror game." Stand face to face about one foot apart. Choose which of you will be the leader. This person will initiate movements, which the other person will mirror. In other words, the follower will perform the exact same gestures as if seeing himself or herself in a mirror. If the leader's left hand goes into the air, the follower makes the same gesture but uses the right hand. Work together for several minutes. By observing each other very closely, you should be able to create a very convincing mirror image.

5 Read the scene between Nora and her husband in *A Doll's House* by Henrik Ibsen, found in Unit Eight. Consider what Nora has observed about their relationship, and write a short summary.

Harpo Marx and Lucille Ball play "the mirror game."

Theatre **Then** and **Now**

Stanislavski's System/ The Actors Studio

The Stanislavski System

Russian actor, director, teacher, and author Konstantin Stanislavski (1863-1938) co-founded the Moscow Art Theatre, which was regarded during his lifetime as one of the world's greatest theatre companies. But he is best remembered for creating a type of theatre training that influenced generations of actors around the world, a program known as the Stanislavski System. Through experimentation he came to believe that even those who were not born with artistic genius could achieve great acting.

One of Stanislavski's main concepts was that the actor who uses imagination as well as sense memory to recall experiences will be able to substitute them for those of the character—thus achieving believability. The script's reality or truthfulness becomes secondary to the emotional reality of the actor. It all depends on what Stanislavski called the "magic if." The actor must try to answer the question "What would I do *if* I were ..." Thus, the actor is not forced into trying to believe that he or she is the person

"Live truthfully in imaginary circumstances."

—Stanislavski

in these actual circumstances but rather what he or she would do given the same situation.

Stanislavski's system had the following goals:

1. to make the external behavior—movement and voice—natural and convincing
2. to know and carry out the *objectives* or inner needs of a character
3. to make the life of the character onstage continuous, with a past and a future, and a life in between the scenes onstage
4. to commit to action (behaving in ways to get characters' objective) and reaction (listening and responding to the other characters)

Stanislavski's system, based on the actor's own experience and emotions, helped create an onstage reality that revolutionized the theatre. He later cautioned against adapting his system, however, without accounting for the differences in the actors' cultural backgrounds and artistic sensibilities.

The Actors Studio

Stanislavski and his company took the American theatre world by storm when the Moscow Art Theatre performed in New York City. Among the American admirers Stanislavski won over were actors from the famed Group Theatre (1931–1941). When three members of the Group (Cheryl Crawford, Robert Lewis, and Elia Kazan) decided to create an actor training center in 1947, the basis of the program was the Stanislavski System. They called this training center the Actors Studio. In 1952, Lee Strasberg took over as head of the program, which he ran for the next thirty years. During that time Strasberg refined, developed, and branched out from Stanislavski's ideas. Strasberg's new technique would eventually become known simply as "The Method."

The Actors Studio still exists today. It is administered by the New School in New York City. It offers a three-year graduate training program in playwriting, acting, and directing. It is also the subject of the popular cable television show *Inside the Actors Studio*.

The Distinguished Alumni of the Actors Studio

Alec Baldwin
Marlon Brando
James Dean
Robert De Niro
Shirley MacLaine
Marilyn Monroe
Paul Newman
Sidney Poitier

Vivien Leigh and Marlon Brando in the film adaptation of Tennessee Williams's *A Streetcar Named Desire*.

Chapter
3 Pantomime

You face your audience with an important message, but you must communicate without words! By using **pantomime**—gestures, body movement, and facial expressions—you can get your ideas across quite well. You need not be an accomplished mime to be an actor, but training and practice in the art of pantomime will certainly help.

Project Specs

Project Description For this assignment, you will prepare a one- to three- minute pantomime of an activity.

Purpose to develop actions that are believable to both actor and audience

Materials a 50- to 100-word outline of your pantomime or the Pantomime Activity Sheet your teacher provides

Theatre Terms
body language
clown white
mime
pancake makeup
pantomime

On Your Feet

To begin your study of pantomime, think of a way you can express to a partner the following ideas without saying a word:

"Everything is OK."
"Please, help me out here."
"Don't say another word!"
"I haven't a clue."

Street mimes perform
for passersby.

PREVIEW

Make-believe and Acting

The basis of acting is literally a matter of "make-believe." It requires the ability to pretend—an ability that nearly everyone possesses to some degree. You can probably recall the fun you had as a child playing a game in which you were a heroic astronaut or a professional athlete. Your pleasure was great because you gave yourself over completely to the game. You were believing.

The belief that a child brings to pretending is similar to the belief that an actor must bring to a part. Like children playing make-believe, actors must become the characters they play. This is a difficult task because, unlike children who enjoy the unrestrained freedom of play for its own sake, actors must

communicate to an audience. In order to make an audience believe, the actor must believe!

The Basics of Pantomime

Mime is one of the oldest forms of theatre—the dramatic art of representing life through expressive movements of the body and face. The English word *mime* comes from the ancient Greek *mimos,* meaning to imitate or to mimic. *Pantomime* usually refers to the mimed dramatic sketch as a whole. The actor performing a pantomime must communicate without words, using precise gestures and exact movements to convey ideas. Like all actors, the mime's objective is to make the audience believe in the world he or she is creating. As you learn the basic techniques of mime, you will feel your body becoming your instrument. Your timing, coordination, and reflexes improve. This in turn helps you communicate better in your personal life. You will also come to appreciate the importance of nonverbal communication and **body language**—how body positioning and movement reflect thoughts and feelings.

Try It on for Size

On the following pages are just a few of the many techniques employed by students of the art of pantomime. Take the time to study the images carefully, thinking about the instructions as they relate to the pictures. Then practice these movements yourself.

The Chest

The chest is an essential element in all movement in pantomime. It harbors the body's center of gravity and is often the moving force behind emotion.

The Face and Head

The face is unique; it is what identifies us to others. We can communicate a lot with just a little effort of the facial muscles—a subtle downturn of the mouth to show displeasure or the angry flair of the nostrils. While these small facial movements speak volumes, learning how to control them may not be easy. The mime must learn to do just that, however, in order to tell his or her story. A mime often wears **clown white,** a kind of white makeup, to highlight the face and its movements.

This mime stands with chest expanded. This connotes pride, sophistication, nobility, or confidence.

If the chest is pushed forward more dramatically, aggressiveness and determination are suggested.

The chest is now curved inward, indicating weakness, old age, shyness, or exhaustion.

This mime's open and upturned lips, wide eyes, arched brows, and raised head indicate happiness—or sometimes surprised delight.

A down-turned mouth, narrowed eyes, with the head thrust forward, can indicate anger or threat.

With the mouth in a straight line, eyes wide, eyebrows arched, and head raised and to the side, the mime appears to be listening, attentive, or curious.

Here's How
To Use White Makeup

Although it is not essential that you wear clown white to perform pantomime, the white, along with the black that outlines the eyes and brows, helps the audience focus on your face.

1 Dip the sponge in water, squeeze, then rub it into the white pancake makeup.

2 Apply the white over your face, excluding the lips. Gently blot the face to remove any streaks.

3 Apply red grease pencil or paint to lips.

4 Apply black grease pencil or paint to the area above eyebrows, above and below the eyes, and around eyes for emphasis.

5 Fill the sock with baby powder and tap your face to set the makeup. Brush away excess powder.

The Makeup Kit

- White **pancake makeup**
- Small sponge
- Makeup brush
- Black grease pencil or paint
- Red grease pencil or paint
- Baby powder
- White athletic sock
- Small painter's brush

The Legs and Feet

We walk, run, hop, jump, sit, stand, and even lie down using our legs and feet. We jiggle them when nervous or bored and stamp them when we are angry or upset. Have you ever noticed that when you are impatiently waiting for someone you tap your foot in irritation? And when you are excited or happy about something your feet almost dance? The mime can express character and personality through movement of the legs and feet just as with the face and chest. Try to imitate a few of the poses below.

One leg crossed over the other with the body leaning indicates a relaxed, casual, and sometimes, arrogant personality.

Feet turned in or one leg bent behind the other indicates a shyness or timidity.

Feet apart and legs straight show strength and confidence. Add a head held very high with the hands on the hips and you create a feeling of scorn, threat, or contempt.

The Arms and Hands

Never underestimate the power of the arms, hands, and fingers in conveying emotion or telling a story. Mimes create invisible walls, stroke, caress, or push away using hands and arms. The joints of the elbow, wrist, and hand give the mime the flexibility to manipulate invisible objects. Practice the hand positions used in the photographs, combining them with various face, body, and leg movements.

Palms up often indicate acceptance, pleading, or sympathy.

Clenched fists indicate anger, threat, or forced control.

Palms down show rejection, demanding, denial, or fear.

PREPARE

Visualize and Focus on Your Pantomime

In this assignment you will need to focus all of your attention on your pantomime. This means that you must see the situation and objects in your mind's eye and work within that imaginary setting until it becomes believable to you.

Suppose that you choose bowling for your pantomime. You must "see" the alley, see where the balls are stored, and where you fill out your score sheet. You must visualize the action of bowling: wiping your hands on the towel; picking up the ball as you walk up to the starting line. Begin your approach on the proper foot. Feel the weight of the imaginary ball as you swing it back and then forward. Feel its size, shape, and texture. Then feel the release of the ball, and watch it travel down the alley or gutter. Follow through with your reaction. Make everything you do believable. Remember, in this assignment you are doing the action in your own person, not as a character in a play. Be the real you. Your teacher and classmates will be observing how true your actions are to the situation.

Suggestions for Pantomimes

- Play a computer game.
- Build a campfire.
- Row a boat.
- Go fishing.
- Eat a meal.
- Clean your room.
- Play a sport.
- Prepare a meal.
- Build something.
- Get ready for school.

Work through the following steps to prepare your pantomime.

1 **Think of an action** you want to pantomime. Choose an activity that you have performed in real life many times. Make your selection quickly. Spend your time in preparing the action rather than in choosing it. See the suggestions at the left.

2 **Outline each step** in the action. Divide each main step into smaller actions until you have a complete series of movements. Remember that your purpose is a well-planned action that is believable. Visualize your surroundings. Then think about the action and see it. If you cannot recall the exact action, perform the action or observe someone else doing it. Record the details and movement. If you need to refresh your understanding of observation, recall, and sense memory, reread Chapter 2, pages 14–15.

Theatre Journal

Observe someone participating in the activity you have chosen to pantomime. Watch carefully and record the steps in the activity in a numbered list.

PRESENT

Perform Your Pantomime

Begin your presentation with a short, well-worded introduction to awaken audience curiosity. Then present your pantomime. Take your time and include each detail. If you are immersed in the task at hand, intent on doing the action in a believable way, you will not be worried about what the audience thinks of you.

At the conclusion of your scene, pause, give a slight bow, and then quietly leave the playing area. Remember, you cannot make an audience believe in something you do not believe in yourself.

CRITIQUE

Evaluate a Classmate's Pantomime

Imagine that you are a drama critic and write a short review of a classmate's pantomime. Include strong points as well as areas that could be improved. Use a scale of 1 to 5, with 5 equaling "outstanding" and 1 equaling "needs much improvement." Review Peer Evaluation on page 16 for further help.

Ask yourself these questions:

- Was the pantomime well planned?
- What important details did the actor include or leave out?
- How did the actor make you believe in the dimensions of the imaginary objects used?
- What did the actor do to help you believe that he or she was actually engaged in this action?

Write a short explanation of how you arrived at the score you gave.

To pantomime an action, first visualize it step by step.

Additional Projects

1 Using an imaginary rope, play tug-of-war. Teams of equal number should stand in front of each other in a line, facing a similarly positioned team. In your mind, see and feel the rope. Pull together as hard as you can to take the rope from the other team. Be careful that the rope does not stretch. If one side gets the advantage the other side must give. Make the game so believable to you, that at the end of it, you feel tired from the strong physical exertion.

2 In a one- to two-minute scene, make believable your efforts to escape from a place where you are trapped—perhaps a cave or an elevator. Visualize the area in which you are trapped. Then use your whole body in trying to escape. Strain, grunt, claw, climb, and dig. Make yourself and your audience believe your endeavors. Continue your efforts until your teacher calls, "Cut."

3 Play "Statues" with a group of classmates. Each person takes a turn dancing freely about the room until someone calls, "Stop!" The dancer then freezes into a statue that shows a specific emotion, such as anger, pain, fear, or joy. The others must guess the feeling being expressed. If people have trouble determining the emotion, try to discover the reason, and rework the statue until it fully captures the emotion being expressed.

4 Play the game of "changing ball toss." Make a large circle with your classmates. Toss around an imaginary ball. Start with a basketball, then switch to a tennis ball, then a bowling ball, a golf ball, a ping-pong ball, and so on. Your reactions should be very different depending on the kind of ball you are catching.

5 Read all the stage directions for *The Drummer* by Athol Fugard, found in Unit Eight. Use pantomime to tell the entire story.

Master of the Craft
Marcel Marceau

Marcel Marceau is undoubtedly the most famous mime in the world. He usually performs on a bare stage with few or no props. The clown white makeup he wears highlights every subtle facial expression. Marceau has the ability to make his audience feel what his character is feeling and to see the imagined world that he creates.

Marceau's interest in pantomime began when he was quite young. He would imitate with gestures anything that captivated his imagination. His admiration for such silent screen artists as Charlie Chaplin and Buster Keaton inspired his pursuit of silence as a profession.

In his essay "The Poetic Halo," Marceau said this about his profession: "When the actor-mime sustains his dramatic action with the inspiration of his thought, the sensitive response he induces is the echo of his soul, and the gesture becomes a silent inner song."

His most famous pantomimes include "The Cage," "Walking Against the Wind," and "In the Park."

In 1947, Marceau created Bip, the clown who has since become his most famous and most beloved character.

Theatre **Then** and Now

This male actor portrays a woman in a Kabuki play.

Kabuki of the 1600s

Probably the best known drama form of traditional Japanese theatre is Kabuki. In the early 17th century a female dancer named O-kuni is said to have developed a new form of dance and drama popular with the people. When she danced in the dry river beds of Kyoto, the capital, O-kuni caused a sensation, and soon she had many imitators. From this Kabuki was born.

Another early form of Kabuki, seldom performed today, was a simple silent performance that lasted no longer than ten minutes—much like a short pantomime. Over the years, Kabuki became more and more elaborate, stylized, and intricate. Eventually women were banned from Kabuki performance

and certain men became specialists in portraying women. To this day only males perform traditional Kabuki.

Traditional Kabuki performances are distinctive for the elaborateness of their costuming, makeup, and staging. Costumes are highly stylized and colorful, and the traditional white makeup and elaborate hairstyles help create Kabuki's richness.

Actors on a traditional Kabuki stage.

Kabuki Interpretations Today

Kabuki has taken an interesting turn in the last twenty years or so in its partnership with such Western drama classics as *Macbeth* and *Medea*. Western plays with strong, universal themes lend themselves well to Kabuki interpretation. Pageantry, nobility, pride, revenge, and bloodshed are common elements.

The artist and teacher Shozo Sato earned international acclaim for producing Kabuki versions of Western classics, including *Kabuki Medea, Kabuki Faust,* and *Kabuki Othello.* He also produced the operas *Madame Butterfly* and *The Mikado* in the Kabuki style. Sato's *Kabuki Medea,* performed by the Berkeley Repertory Theatre, won the Hollywood Drama Critics Award for best theatrical production. His productions of *Macbeth* and *Medea* both received several Joseph Jefferson awards, given for Chicago theatre.

In 1991, nineteen American students toured Japan as members of Sato's production of *Achilles: A Kabuki Play*. The tour marked the first time actors from the United States had performed a Kabuki drama in Japan, where the form was born. Their two-week tour included the village of Damine, where Kabuki has been part of the religious ritual for more than three centuries.

Sato's productions have also been performed in Europe and the Middle East and continue to be popular throughout the world.

Kabuki acting is highly symbolic and rhythmic.

Chapter
4 Improvisation

One of the most demanding things an actor can be called upon to do is to **improvise**—to make up the words in the **dialogue** and the action while playing out a scene. No lines to learn, no planned movement, just you (and your fellow actors) going wherever your imagination leads you.

Project Specs

Project Description You and a partner (or partners) will perform a three- to five-minute improvisation.

Purpose to learn introductory improvisation skills in order to develop concentration and focus

Materials a 50- to 100-word sentence outline of your group improvisation or the Improvisation Activity Sheet your teacher provides

Theatre Terms
collaboration
dialogue
ensemble
etiquette
improvise
set

On Your Feet

To practice working with a partner, play a round of "Who am I?" with your classmates as the audience. Your partner will decide what kind of person he or she wants to play without telling you. For example, he or she might play a traffic cop arresting you for speeding or a babysitter looking after you, the child. Based on how your partner acts toward you, you must guess who that person is and try to respond accordingly.

PREVIEW

Yes, and . . .

Improvisation means acting without a script. It means creating a scene on the spot that you and your fellow actors—the **ensemble**—compose together. Improvisation requires a great deal of **collaboration** and trust. You must share ideas, believe that your partners will support you, and work together to create something all your own.

Most of our actions in daily life are improvised, since real life rarely offers a script. Sometimes we have expectations about what's going to happen next, but no one ever knows for sure. In real life, those who want to make the best of things enjoy their good fortune and learn from ill luck. They embrace life's surprises. They say "yes" to life.

Successful improvisers say "yes, and. . ." They embrace a situation or comment presented to them and react to it, add to it, and make it into a character or scene. In doing this, they exercise their creativity, their mental and emotional flexibility, their trust for one another, and their capacity for concentrating on the task at hand. When they're faced with a problem onstage, they use their wits to solve it.

When actors who are adept at improvising work with a script, they know how to embrace it and make the imaginary world their own. They also know how to work with and respond to their fellow actors. An effective improviser is also an effective actor.

Members of The Second City improvise a skit suggested by an audience member.

Basic Rules of Improv

Some improvisation scenes begin with a plot suggestion. Others begin with an idea for a character. All improvisations depend on the following rules:

- Always remain open to your partner(s), the plot, and your own ideas.
- Listen carefully and respond to your partner(s) onstage.
- Show, rather than tell how you feel.
- Take chances! Don't be afraid to fail.
- Trust yourself and your partner(s).

PREPARE

Commit to the Reality of Improv

This assignment will require that you respond naturally and immediately to any suggestion that pops into your mind or the mind of your partner(s). You will need to commit to the reality of an imaginary circumstance no matter how silly or impossible it seems.

Suppose, for example, that you and your partner or team are building a fire. One of your improv partners says, "I'm getting freezer burn from this fire!" Don't argue about whether freezer burn is possible; it already has happened. Your partner said it, so it's true. Instead of denying the idea, put yourself in a world where freezer burn from a fire is possible—or even common. Respond to your partner's predicament.

This does not mean you can't ever argue in an improvisation. You can blame your partner for getting freezer burn. You can berate your partner for bringing you to Jupiter in the first place. You can claim that your injury or problem is even worse than your partner's. You must, however, buy into your partner's reality. No matter what, you must remain "in the scene."

Easing into It

Unfortunately, there's no such thing as "easing into it"! You'll have to jump in with both feet. How do you make sense out of a leap into the void? These tips can help orient you:

- Remember that trust in the team is essential. Your improv partners will enter any reality you propose. They will believe your characters are real. They will build on the plot you imagine. You are not alone.

- You can develop a character from a gesture, a voice, an expression, a piece of clothing, and so on.

Career Focus

The Improv Group

If you are an aspiring actor, improvisation can hone your skills. If you want to be a doctor, lawyer, teacher, executive, sales rep, or any other person who deals with the public, improv can help you relax, be self-confident, and have a sense of humor about yourself.

Some improv groups will accept students with little or no experience. Students and professionals alike may improvise together in workshops. Those who develop their skills may be invited onstage in a showcase, or as part of the improv cast.

Does your local improv group demand experience? Start a group of your own and rent a space when you're ready to perform.

- You can develop an activity—and spark a plot idea—by finding a new use for an everyday object, such as turning a pot into a helmet or an umbrella into a baseball bat.

- You can open dialogue by repeating a cliché, a line from a poem, or a bit of slang.

- After you have developed a scene, or even part of a scene, you can retain, or **set,** the parts of the scene that were effective. Then you can do the scene again with your partner, letting new ideas come to the surface. Again, set the material that works. Eventually, the material that is set gives you a framework in which to perform.

- Your scene, once you set it, will have the familiarity of a memorized script. But refrain from setting the scene in stone. Go ahead and improvise words, phrases, and new moments in any scene—even one that is "finished."

PRESENT

Perform an Improvisation

When your names are called, hand in your outlines or Activity Sheets, then with your partner or partners walk to the playing area. Be aware that it is perfectly normal to be nervous. Trust your partners to help you, try to relax, and enjoy the moment. When you have finished your improvised scene, turn to the audience and ask, "What happens next?" Take a suggestion and continue the improvisation for another minute.

When you are finished, pause and then bow politely before leaving the playing area.

Two students improvise a game of baseball.

CRITIQUE

Evaluate Your Classmates' Improvisation

Choose one of the improvisations presented in class and evaluate it. Use a scale of 1 to 5, with 5 being "outstanding" and 1 being "needs much improvement." Ask yourself these questions:

- In what way did the actors remain true to the improvisational principle of "yes, and. . ."?

- How did the performers display trust and acceptance?
- How did the performers build on each other's suggestions?
- How well did the performers listen and respond to each other?
- How did the partners show, rather than tell, their feelings?
- In what way did the performers keep you interested in the outcome of the scene?

Write an explanation of how you arrived at this score.

Spotlight on

Audience Etiquette

The real-time immediacy of live theatre makes it a special event. When you are in the audience, your behavior affects the enjoyment of those around you. To be a courteous audience member, follow the rules of **etiquette** below.

- Show respect for the actors and other audience members by dressing appropriately.
- Arrive early to be seated and to read your program. After the curtain is up, most theatres will not seat people until a scene break, so latecomers miss part of the show. If you are allowed to enter late, you inconvenience those already seated.
- ALWAYS turn off your cell phone and the beeper on your watch or pager. Alarms not only disturb those around you but distract the actors as well.
- Remove your hat so that those seated behind you can see.
- NEVER put your feet on the back of the seat in front of you.
- Do not talk during the performance—not even a whisper. Save it until intermission.
- Do not take food or drink into the theatre. NEVER unwrap candy or gum during a performance.
- Don't leave during the play except in an emergency, and don't leave at the end until the house lights are turned on. It is bad manners to slip out early.
- Applaud the performers at the end of the play as they take their bows, but reserve a standing ovation for the truly outstanding performance.

Additional Projects

1 Form a discussion panel with four or more classmates. Have each participant represent the line of clothes of a particular designer, a magazine in a publishing house's stable, or a piece of furniture in a housewares store. Each improviser should adopt the personality of the item represented. The teacher or a classmate can serve as the moderator, asking various panel members questions, which they must answer in character.

2 Host a party for strange and unusual superheroes, such as Yapping-Dog Man, Backwards Girl, or Bionic Bellower. The host should be a superhero, too. Have each superhero guest arrive at the party individually and reveal who he or she is. Once all the players have arrived, the host should announce that he or she needs them to solve a world problem. Have the group find a way the superheroes can collaborate to solve the problem.

3 Bring to the front of the class an everyday object, such as a tennis racket, a paper bag, or a broom. Take turns with your classmates, one by one, finding a new use for the object. Then display that use for the class. Remember that you should not be limited by the actual name or function of the object. You imagination can make it anything you want it to be.

4 Read the scene between Argan and Louison in *The Imaginary Invalid* by Molière found in Unit Eight. With a partner, improvise another scene in which Argan tries to extract information from Louison.

Theatre Then and Now

Improvisation in the 1500s

Commedia Dell'arte

Developed in Italy from pantomimes that may have been remnants of ancient Roman comedy, *commedia dell'arte* (comedy of art) was flourishing in the middle 1500s. It was a highly improvised comedy performed in the streets for the masses. A company, consisting usually of seven men and three women, would improvise action, dialogue, song, and dance around a familiar plot—one that usually involved love and intrigue. Actors had to be clever and inventive to keep the plot moving, and an athletic, agile body was necessary for the fights, acrobatic stunts, and dances that were required.

Commedia dell'arte is still performed around the world with many of the stock characters that were familiar to 16th-century Italians. A few of the most famous characters are the clever, witty, and mischievous Harlequin; the flirtatious and pretty Columbine; Pantalone, the gullible father; and Pierrot, the clown.

This recent performance of *Scapin* is based on Molière's adaptation of a *commedia dell'arte* play.

Pierrot, the clown, is often lovelorn and moody.

Improvisation Today

The Second City

In 1955, a group of students, musicians, and actors rented a storefront attached to a bar. They fashioned a house and stage that featured a few nondescript chairs. And they called themselves the Compass Players.

The Compass Players wanted to try something no one else was doing. They wanted to improvise scenes from thin air. So they walked on stage and whipped up sketches about mothers and daughters, husbands and wives, dating, taxes, social issues, and anything else that came to mind. Sometimes, they were hilarious. Sometimes they were terrible. No one—not even the actors—knew what would happen next.

Audiences loved the thrill of watching actors in process. And so, the idea caught on and led to the creation of the most successful improv group to date—The Second City, named after the city in which it was born, Chicago, Illinois.

In 1959, The Second City opened a sort of low-rent cabaret in the seedy Old Town neighborhood in the heart of Chicago. To the clink of people eating and drinking, the actors improvised dozens of scenes. Some were ideas they had worked out themselves, in advance. Others were spontaneous. Still others were based on suggestions from the audience. Thus, each evening was a brand-new collaboration. The concept was a smashing success.

The Second City today.

In the 1970s and 1980s John Belushi, Gilda Radner, Jane Curtin, Dan Akroyd, Bill Murray, and many others learned their craft at The Second City. They continued improvising on TV's "Saturday Night Live," paving the way for other TV improv shows, such as "Who's Line Is It Anyway?" The Second City is still a thriving theatrical event as well as a well-respected school in Chicago, with branches in Toronto, Cleveland, Detroit, and Los Angeles.

Unit One Review

PREVIEW

Examine the following key concepts previewed in Unit One.

1 Which relaxation technique works best for you? Why?

2 Why it is important for actors to warm up before a rehearsal or performance?

3 How does observation help you as an actor?

4 If you were to play a character devoted to a pet, how would speak to, touch, and talk about that pet? Give examples.

5 How is a child's game of make-believe similar to an actor playing a role?

6 What is the mime's objective?

7 Without using words, indicate that you are angry about something.

8 How is improvisation like real life?

9 Why is it important to say "Yes, and . . ." in improvisation?

PREPARE

Assess your response to the preparation process for projects in this unit.

10 Was it easier to prepare with a partner you chose or one that your teacher chose for you? Why?

11 When working with a partner, how did you decide which tasks you would take on and which your partner would be responsible for?

12 Were you able to fully utilize all five senses when using your sense memory? Which senses seemed easier to call upon and why?

13 What techniques did you use to visualize your pantomime project?

14 Did you find it more difficult to prepare for your pantomime or your improvisation project? Why?

PRESENT

Analyze the experience of presenting your work to the class.

15 Were you able to have fun while presenting your warm-up routine? Why or why not?

16 In describing your object, were you able to help your audience see it clearly? Did you forget any important elements?

17 Were you able to become fully immersed in the pantomime you presented, or did you lose focus? What did you find distracting? How did this feel?

18 When the audience gave a suggestion for continuing your improvisation, were you able to do this to your satisfaction or would you do it differently now? If so, in what way?

CRITIQUE

Evaluate how you go about critiquing your work and the work of others.

19 What were the major stumbling blocks to remaining fair, impartial, or constructive while critiquing your classmates' presentations?

20 In what way did critiquing your classmates help you critique your own performances?

21 Did you find it easier to evaluate a performance that was closer to "outstanding" or more on the order of "needs much improvement"? Why?

EXTENSIONS

- Look at the image to the left. Use your powers of observation, sense memory, and recall to perform a short pantomime of someone eating this sundae.

- Practice standing in positions that show the following feelings, and then choose one to present to the class: impatience, sorrow, hope, delight, concern, contempt, anticipation, support.

Unit Two

Elements of Acting

Chapter

5 Movement

Whether you're the lead or one of the supporting
players, whether you have long monologues or no lines
to speak at all, the one thing you will be doing as an
actor on stage is *moving*. How, when, and where to
move takes some practice, so get moving!

Project Specs

Project Description You and a partner will plan and
present stage movement for a two- to four-minute scene.

Purpose to practice moving naturally onstage

Materials a written scenario that details the movement
needed for the scene or the Movement Activity Sheet
provided by your teacher

Theatre Terms

cheating out
gestures
muscular memory
offstage
onstage
scenario
stage business
upstaging

On Your Feet

With a partner, use only movement to communicate the
situations below. Stand about five feet apart. Depending
on the situation you are enacting, you will move toward
or away from your partner and use body language to add
further texture to the moment.

- a surprise meeting between friends who haven't seen
  each other in a long time

- two strangers pretending not to notice one another

- friends or siblings who have just had a big argument

- friends saying good-bye knowing they will not
  meet again

The Magic of Movement

In some ways, an actor is a magician who must present to the audience a world they can't help but accept and believe. The actor must persuade the audience that the small environment **onstage** is whatever the scene calls for—whether it be a ship, a living room, a faraway galaxy, or a doctor's waiting room—and that he or she is a real person interacting within that environment.

In daily life you probably don't pay all that much attention to the way you move. To be physically believable and natural onstage, however, the instruction that follows should help you.

Actors move together in a scene from *The Mikado* by the English National Opera, September 1994.

Moving on Stage

Entering

Make sure you are in position and ready to enter the stage at the appropriate time. Enter with your head up, unless your character demands otherwise. Know the exact point at which you become visible to the audience. You don't want to be seen by the audience when you think you're hidden **offstage**—it takes away from the magic of the performance.

Walking

Your normal walking movement should be rhythmical and smooth. As you walk, look ahead. To portray certain characters, however, your walk may be slow, labored, jittery, and so on.

Standing

Keep your weight on the balls of your feet. Unless you have a motivated movement to make, stand still. An actor's shuffling feet reveal nervousness and inexperience, and can make the audience uncomfortable.

Turning

When turning on stage, keep the audience in mind and turn toward them. The only exception to this rule is when such a turn would be obviously awkward because you are already in a position facing mostly away from the audience.

Sitting

If the scene calls for you to sit, place yourself in a comfortable position, but make sure you are poised to get up when you need to. Never slouch unless the role specifically calls for it.

If you must back up to the chair to sit down, do so until you touch it with the back of your leg, and then sit.

Rising

When getting up from your seat, anticipate the move by slowly easing forward on the chair. Keep your spine straight and rise with your weight on one foot and then shift it to the other to ensure balance.

Gesturing

The gestures and the expressions of the actors below show their feelings.

Gestures are expressive bodily actions, such as shrugging, pointing, or raising the eyebrows. Gestures should be definite and clear. Halfhearted or extraneous gestures are the mark of an inexperienced or unfocused actor.

Moving forward before rising helps you get up with ease.

Exiting

Be sure you stay in character until you are offstage and invisible to the audience.

As a student actor, you should practice these movement techniques until you can use them so effectively that they appear effortless to the audience. Only through sustained practice will you be able to move naturally onstage without having to think about it constantly. This constant repetition of motion helps you develop **"muscular memory."**

Theatre Journal

Keep notes on what you notice about the way people move when doing various things, such as getting on a bus, walking down stairs, running to catch up with friends, describing something large and impressive, walking into class late, or getting up from a sunken couch.

PREPARE

Working Out the Scene: Beginning, Middle, and End

With a partner, you are to perform a two- to four-minute scene that incorporates basic movement principles and action. You will have to coordinate the onstage movement between you and your partner. You will perform a scene that shows what both characters want (their intentions), a conflict, and a resolution. Your scene will have a beginning, middle, and end.

Create a Scenario

You will not need to create dialogue for this scene. You will accomplish everything through movements, gestures, and facial expressions. However, you and your partner will have to collaborate to write a detailed **scenario**—an outline that includes information about the plot, what each character wants, how their intentions conflict, and what they do about it.

You can use one of the suggestions at the right as a jumping-off point or you can create a scenario of your own. As your scenario takes shape, write down each action and each major shift in the two characters' intentions using as much detail as possible.

Add the Movement

Once you have written the scenario, add detailed notations about movement, gestures, and facial expressions. For example, if one character enters a scene in which the other character is already onstage, from what direction does the entering actor come? Where is the onstage actor standing (or sitting)? How do the actors greet each other? Do they smile or frown? Indicate movement with specific notations such as these:

Character 1 moves from left to right and opens the door. Character 2 enters.

After they exchange pleasantries, Character 1 motions for Character 2 to sit in the chair on the left side of the playing area.

Character 2 sits in the right-hand chair instead.

Character 1 looks displeased and sits opposite Character 2.

Discuss what you want to convey with each action. For example, when Character 2 doesn't sit in the recommended chair, what effect does this have on each character—and on the scene? Make sure you have a specific reason for each new movement. Take the scene as far as you can.

Possible Scenarios

- You wait for a competitive friend to come and play chess. When your friend arrives, you begin to play. Show what happens during and after the game.
- You are typing a research paper when there is a knock at the door. A pushy neighbor who wants to sell you tickets to a school carnival enters. You don't want to buy any tickets. What happens next?
- You enter a shoe store and sit down to be waited on. You tell the tired clerk the type of shoe you want. He brings three pairs. You begin trying on shoes. What does the clerk do? What do you do? Do you buy any shoes?

Each of the actors in this scene has a good sense of his motivation and position onstage.

Rehearse the Scene

Now that you've created a scenario and added the movement, practice your scene with your partner. Watch each other's movements, gestures, and facial expressions. Is everything clear? Does the scene make sense? Does the movement illustrate the characters' relationship and the situation? Make and accept suggestions for improvement. Go through the scene again. This time, make sure you are staying within the two- to four-minute time frame. When you have shaped the scene to the best of your ability, think of a title for it. Then work out the technical details of how you will set up for the scene, which of you will introduce the scene, and what you will do once you've finished performing.

Remember that no move you make will matter if the audience can't see it. Successful actors develop an innate sense of their positioning onstage in relationship to the audience.

Here's How
To Incorporate Stage Business

Any small action that the character performs without major movement is called **stage business.** Sometimes stage business is written into the script as directions, but generally it is added by the director and actor. If your character continually knits or is forever whittling a piece of wood, this reveals something about his or her nature. Stage business may communicate the time of day or the season. If you toast bread at the table, it suggests morning. Fanning yourself with a newspaper indicates a hot day in summer. Business can also create atmosphere or add interest to the play. Whatever specific business is used, it should be planned early in the rehearsals and practiced at each one. Remember, you must have a good reason for performing all stage business.

Spotlight on

The Rules of Stage Movement

Become familiar with these six basic principles of stage movement.

1 Onstage, movement should always be *motivated* by the intentions of the actors in the scene. Make sure that when you move onstage you know exactly *why* you are doing so. React as though experiencing a stimulus to which you respond instinctively.

2 Movement must be *simplified*. There is no point in creating busy traffic patterns onstage. Simpler is best.

3 Movement must be *heightened* from real life. In real life you might wander into a room for no apparent reason and promptly walk back out again. In a scene onstage, however, each action counts.

4 Movement must *delineate* character. Movement tells the audience a great deal about characters and their relationship to one another. Make sure your movement is in keeping with your character.

5 Movement must be *toward the audience*. To create realistic interactions actors must have contact with the other people onstage. However, keeping an "open" position—one that turns you slightly toward the audience—works best. Often this is referred to as **cheating out.**

6 To maintain balanced and pleasing stage pictures an actor must *adjust to the movement of others.* Taking out a handkerchief on stage while another actor is the focus of the scene or angling your body so that your scene partner must turn away from the audience to speak to you is called **upstaging.** It is rude. Never do it.

Actors cheating out.

PRESENT

Perform a Scene Using Stage Movement

When your name is called, hand in your scenario or Activity Sheet and walk to the playing area. Deliver your introduction to the scene as you and your partner rehearsed it. Then perform your two- to four-minute scene for the class.

At the end of the scene, turn to your classmates and ask, "What just happened here?" If you have performed well, they should be able to track the plot of your scene.

Allow only two minutes for the discussion. When you are finished, thank your audience and bow politely before leaving the playing area. Remember to retain a professional demeanor until you have reached your seat.

CRITIQUE

Evaluate Classmates' Scenes

Evaluate one or two of the scenes presented in class. Begin your critique by listing all the positive aspects of the scene. Then move on to the areas that in your view needed improvement, including anything that seemed unclear in the scene. Then, using the following rating scale, give the scene a number score. "Outstanding" = 5; "well done" = 4; "fair" = 3; "needs some improvement" = 2; "needs much improvement" = 1.

To give an accurate, well-supported critique, ask yourself these questions:

- Did the scene have a beginning, middle, and end?

- How did each character make his or her intentions clear?

- Did each performer respond to what the other was doing?

- Were movements motivated by the characters' intentions?

- Did the movement seem appropriate and spontaneous or was there unnecessary business?

- Were you interested in the outcome, or resolution, of the scene?

Write a paragraph explaining why you gave the score or scores you did.

Additional Projects

1 Determine basic movement that you can use to communicate the following characters: a loudmouthed, ignorant person; a nervous, high-strung person; a vigorous athlete; an extremely weak or tired person; a timid, self-conscious person; and one other of your choice. Pay particular attention to mannerisms and gestures, the placement of your weight, and the degree of tension in your movements. If you are up for the challenge, try doing one or two of the above without any facial expression.

2 Visit a zoo, farm, wooded area, or park near your home. Select a bird or animal to observe. Note the individual movements of this creature's paws, head, eyes, tail, wings, and so on. Pay close attention to specific mannerisms. In class, portray the animal's action. Then transfer those characteristics into human action. Your human portrayal should maintain the basic movements, rhythm, and patterns of the animal.

3 Think of a situation that involves waiting—waiting in line, waiting for a bus, or waiting for a friend's arrival.

Choose an age at least ten years older or younger than your current age. Then go to the playing area and portray a person of that age in your chosen situation. Make sure you incorporate the body rhythm, facial expressions, and the basic movements and attitudes of that age group. Keep your movements selective and specific.

4 Read the scene from Paula Vogel's Pulitzer Prize-winning play *How I Learned to Drive* found in Unit Eight. With several partners, work out how the characters Li'l Bit and Peck would move in the scene.

"One onstage movement can convey pages of thought and yet the same movement—overdone—has a hammy meaning all its own."

—Actor Richard Baseheart

Theatre **Then** and **Now**

Ritual Dance Movement

Dance and music have been important parts of human interaction since the beginning of recorded time. Sound, rhythm, and exuberant physical movement are as much a part of theatre today as they were thousands of years ago.

The theatre as we know it is believed to have evolved from shamanism and ritual dance. A shaman was a priest figure common to almost all very early cultures. Part of the shaman's job was to communicate with the gods on behalf of his community. This communication often took the form of physical imitation of animals and symbolic movements depicting weather systems or crop growth. As early as 2500 B.C., rituals merged with traditional dance to form elaborate theatrical ceremonies.

Dancing is an important part of Native American society.

Modern Movement

In the Canadian town of Gaspe, a group of stilt walkers, jugglers, and specialty performers created a new kind of circus—a mesmerizing blend of theatre, circus techniques, street performance, high-tech lighting and sound, and eye-popping costumes. The year was 1984, and they called themselves **Cirque du Soleil** (Circus of the Sun). Their goal was nothing less than to "reinvent the circus." Pure physical movement and music form the common language that allows audiences to journey with Cirque du Soleil to a place of dreams and wonder. Cirque du Soleil has also made films of its shows for television and I-Max theatres. For more information, visit their Web site at www.cirquedusoleil.com.

The Blue Man Group features three bald-headed, blue-faced characters who take their audience through a fast-paced, multi-sensory experience that blends slapstick, music, art, and science into a thrilling new theatrical form. The group's award-winning theatrical productions have been described as "groundbreaking," "visually stunning," and "musically powerful." Their props include Jell-O, marshmallows, rolls and rolls of toilet paper, and cans of

Cirque du Soleil shines on.

paint, among other things. These inventive blue fellows have a unique style of percussion music, which they play primarily on invented instruments—such as large plastic tubing, flexible fiber rods, gigantic gongs, and sheets of aluminum. Visit their entertaining Web site at www.blueman.com.

Blue Men move to the beat of their own drums.

6 Stage Directions

Don't just stand there—do something! Theatre is all about dramatic action. The action and excitement in a play are both supported by—even created by—movement. Effective stage movement is an indispensable part of a gripping production, and the actor must know how to follow stage directions every step of the way.

Project Specs

Project Description You will plot three stage crosses for a classmate to execute and then perform a classmate's three stage crosses in two to three minutes.

Purpose to learn to create and follow stage directions and to assume body positions accurately and with confidence

Materials a drawing showing three stage crosses or the Stage Directions Activity Sheet your teacher gives you

Theatre Terms
backstage
counter-cross
cross
downstage/upstage
full back/full front
profile
quarter turn
raked
sightlines
stage left/stage right
three-quarter turn

On Your Feet

Play "Simon Says Staging!" with a small group. A "director" calls out directions in which the group must move either "stage right" or "stage left" while facing the director. For example, "Hop stage left" or "Kick stage right."

A Look at the Stage

The stage didn't always look the way it does today. Early on in theatre history, players found that people could see them better on a **raked,** or slanted, surface. So they built their playing areas on an incline. The back of the playing area was actually higher than the front. Thus, the back part of the stage became known as "upstage," while the front part of the stage was called "downstage." So back when the audience was on a flat level, the stage was raked. As the audience seating became raked, as it is today, the stage got flatter.

Even today, some stages have a small incline, or rake, to improve visibility, or **sightlines,** for the audience. Whether they do or not, however, the tradition remains, and actors everywhere move away from the audience to be **upstage** and toward the audience to be **downstage.**

Where Am I?

When directors and choreographers sketch an acting area, they generally divide it into nine locations, as seen on page 56.

Generally, the downstage area is considered a "strong" position, or a position of power. That's because it is near the audience and thus has a greater impact than other positions.

Upstaged!

You've heard of upstaging—and you know it's NOT the thing to do, but do you know where the term originated? When actors deliver lines from upstage, they steal the focus by forcing the other actors to turn with their backs to the audience in order to speak to the upstage actors.

It is possible for a play to take place entirely in one spot, with the actor buried up to her neck in sand, as in *Happy Days* by Samuel Beckett, but it happens rarely.

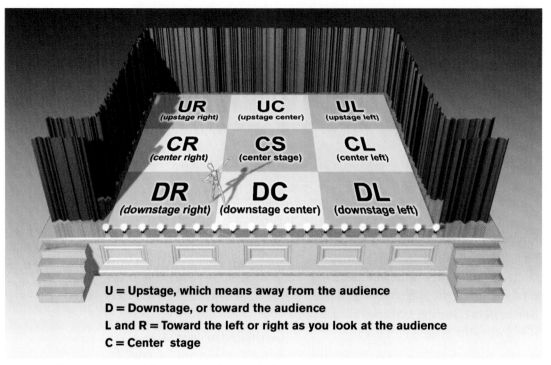

UR (upstage right) **UC** (upstage center) **UL** (upstage left)

CR (center right) **CS** (center stage) **CL** (center left)

DR (downstage right) **DC** (downstage center) **DL** (downstage left)

U = Upstage, which means away from the audience
D = Downstage, or toward the audience
L and R = Toward the left or right as you look at the audience
C = Center stage

The many areas of the stage. **Backstage** is the area behind the stage that the audience cannot see.

Stage right is a stronger position than **stage left** because Western audiences are conditioned by reading to look from left to right. Thus, they tend to look stage right for the flow of action or the drama's movement. Because of the strength of downstage and stage right, important scenes will often be played there, and strong characters will tend to settle there.

The following body positions also affect the strength of one's character onstage:

1 Actors who share a scene equally often use a **quarter turn** toward each other. This places their bodies so that the audience can easily see them.

2 If a scene becomes intense, actors may turn in **profile** to the audience. This tightens their focus on each other and the audience's focus on them.

3 When one character's lines are especially important, other actors might make a **three-quarter turn** toward that actor, in order to "give" that actor focus.

4 For monologues and asides to the audience, actors often stand **full front,** facing the audience.

5 In unusual circumstances, an actor might turn his or her **full back** to the audience.

Getting Your Bearings

A **cross** is a movement from one stage area to another. The director will indicate a stage cross as an "X" on paper. Generally, the actor takes the shortest, most direct route, which is straight across some portion of the stage. Sometimes, however, a director will call for a complicated cross. That's because straight crosses tend to imply strength and decisiveness. A director may want to convey feelings of indecision, casualness, grace, or ease.

Following a complicated cross is not really that hard. How many times have you gone to the refrigerator for a drink, stopping first at the cabinet for a glass and then pausing to look for something to eat? Still, you will want to practice a complicated cross before performing it for an audience so that it looks natural.

The director's notations on this script indicate that Me (Meryl) stays where she is while W (Win) enters from the upper left (the porch). Win then crosses left to Meryl.

> again he is staring at some point in the mid
> know, Boo-Boo," he says. "Your world—th
> *wouldn't* exist without you. It's an excellen
>
> _____ (*Beat. She throws the ashes.*
>
> Enter: *in the backyard at her fathe*
> Me stays *winter coat, a hat, and mitte*
> W. En UL/Porch *notice when* WIN *enters be*
> XL/Me *moment or two.*)
>
> I was wondering what happened to you.
>
> It's stultifying in there.

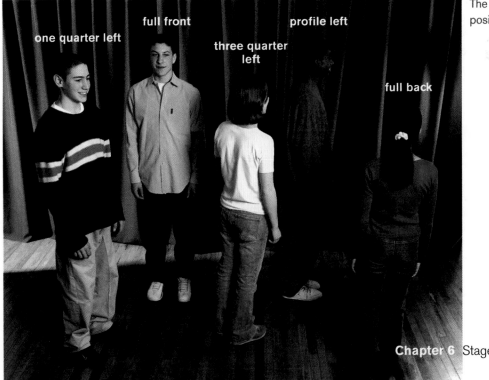

The five body positions.

one quarter left

full front

three quarter left

profile left

full back

Like people in all other walks of life, some actors learn through action. They learn by doing the crosses they need to do. Others learn visually. They are more comfortable seeing the movements on paper first.

In order to keep your body turned to the audience, begin a cross by stepping forward on the foot nearest your destination. For example, if you are standing stage right and making a cross to stage left, you should take your first step with the left foot. (Most people do this naturally.)

If you are speaking while you make your cross, go ahead and walk in front of the other characters. Generally, it's best to avoid moving when another character is talking, as your movement will steal attention away from the speaker. But if you need to cross when others are speaking, cross quietly behind them while staying in character.

Here's How
To Move Without Crashing into Anyone

1 The moving figure dominates! If you are the speaking character and must cross, walk in front of the other characters.

2 If another character is talking, do not move. However, if the script calls for you to move during another character's lines, cross behind that person while staying in character.

3 If two actors cross the stage together, the one with more lines should be downstage, a short step ahead of the other actor.

It is usually necessary for actors to adjust to one another's crosses by using a **counter-cross.** If you find yourself in the direct path of another's cross you may "counter" by giving way a little and then by adjusting your position after the cross, as in the diagram.

Audience

The speaker (green arrow) crosses right in front of the listener. The listener (purple arrow) "counters" by moving in the opposite direction and turning toward the speaker. Both should finish moving at the same time.

PREPARE

Plot Three Stage Crosses

On the Activity Sheet for this chapter, which your teacher will provide, or on a separate piece of paper, list three stage crosses and body positions, and plot them on a stage diagram. You may list any combination of crosses and positions you wish. The following should serve only as an example.

Sample Directions:

a X DR; stand quarter position left; raise right hand

b X UC; stand in a full front position; bow

c X UR; stand in a one-quarter position left; click your heels twice

d X DC; stand in a profile, face left; raise both arms as high as you can

e X DL; stand in a three-quarter position, face right; twist from your waist

f X UL; stand in a full front position; turn right; sit down

Be sure your name appears on both the top and bottom sections of your paper. Divide the page by cutting it in two (or along the dashed lines of the Activity Sheet) and place it in a box along with your classmates' directions for stage crosses.

PRESENT

Read Aloud and Execute Three Stage Crosses

When your teacher calls your name, rise and draw at random a set of directions from the box. Be sure you do not get your own. Hand the directions to the person who wrote them. Then go to the playing area, and as your classmate calls out directions, follow them as though you were on stage. Be sure you begin each cross on the foot nearest your destination and cross to the correct stage area as directed. Finish each cross by assuming the proper body position.

When a classmate selects your set of directions from the class box and hands them to you, read each clearly. Proceed to the next direction only after your classmate has correctly followed your previous order.

Theatre Journal

Next time you're in a public place, such as a sports or cultural event, watch the unconscious movements of people in a group. Do some people in the group upstage others? Who gets the most focus? Who do the group members seem to think is their audience? Write about what you observe.

CRITIQUE

Evaluate a Classmate's Stage Crosses

Choose one of the sets of stage crosses performed by your classmates and evaluate it. Think about the impression your classmate would make if he or she were moving in ordinary life. Rate the crosses on a scale of 1 to 5, with 1 being "needs much improvement" and 5 being "outstanding." Your critique should answer these questions:

- Did the performer move to the correct locations?

- Did the performer end up in the proper body position?

- Did the performer move with confidence?

- Did the performer move with the proper foot first?

- Did the performer's movements seem natural and in character?

Write a paragraph defending your reasons for the rating you gave.

Spotlight on

Taking Your Bows

The curtain closes and the lights go up, but the show isn't over until the actors take their bows. The type of bow they perform depends on the style of the play and the particular production. Most often, actors perform a humble bow, standing straight, then bending the head and back slightly forward.

Sometimes you may be asked to perform a more genteel bow, in which you bend at the hips, keeping your back straight and your head dropped slightly.

Rarely, an actor will be asked to curtsey. To do a bob curtsey, keep your feet close together, swing one foot slightly behind the other, bend your knees quickly, and bob your head. A court curtsey is similar, but deeper and slower.

Remember to take your bows seriously. They are your way of telling the audience you are honored to perform for them and appreciate their attendance and applause.

Additional Projects

1 Go to the stage area and make several crosses, ending with varied body positions. Challenge your classmates to identify each stage area you are in and the body position you are assuming.

2 With two partners, plot a series of crosses that might define a character type, such as a CEO at a successful board meeting, a criminal under indictment, a shy immigrant, a couple quarreling, or a child with something to hide.

3 With a partner, plot crosses for a two-person scene. You can use stage directions from an existing play or plot movements of your own. Once you have mastered the scene, try reversing the staging. What do the different crosses do to the relationship between the characters?

4 With one or more partners, plot the movement, including crosses, for the scene from *A Raisin in the Sun* by Lorraine Hansberry found in Unit Eight. Decide when to walk while speaking a line and when to walk between lines. Make sure to keep the focus on the proper actor in the scene.

The director, on the left, is helping the actor who is playing an apologetic young man cross to the actor who is playing his angry friend.

Theatre Then and Now

The Actor Onstage

With flexibility, creativity, and a good concept, theatre can be performed almost anywhere. In ancient times, outdoor theatre was the norm. Excavations in ancient Crete and the mainland nearby have uncovered evidence of early outdoor performance spaces that consisted of a rectangular area flanked by rows of stone seats.

Ancient Arenas

The Theatre of Dionysus in Athens was the West's first public *theatron,* or seeing-place. It was situated on a hillside below the Acropolis. Originally people simply sat or stood on the hillside to watch choral performances. As time went on and choral performances turned into full-length tragedies, terraces were built into the hillsides. Wooden seats were added, and when those deteriorated, stone seats were built. The stone auditorium completed some time around 330 B.C. could seat 14,000 to 17,000 people. Some historians believe stages were built into the theatres; others do not.

Nevertheless, historians agree that the audience—and the performances—remained outdoors. Music and dancing were an integral part of productions. And as time went on, spectacle became increasingly important. Indeed, some productions after the Romans conquered the Greeks became little more than loud and gory spectacle.

Under these conditions, actors relied heavily on pantomime and large gestures. Roman actors studied great orators and made extensive use of stylized movements, including stock placement of the head, hands, and feet, along with special intonations to signal specific emotions. Tragic acting involved slow, stately movements befitting the dignity of the characters and subject matter. Comic plays always included running, fighting, beatings, and physical humor. These acting conventions persisted through the Elizabethan age and into the 19th century.

This Roman statuette of a comic actor is from around the 1st century. It is from the collection of The Newark Museum.

Today's Intimate Spaces

Today, arenas are reserved for sporting events and large scale entertainment such as rock concerts. Big musicals like *Stomp, Rent,* or *The Lion King* might play to houses that seat 2000 to 3000 people. But most commercial theatre takes place in smaller, indoor houses that seat 200–1200. Off-Broadway and off-off-Broadway shows might take place in storefronts that seat 50 or fewer audience members.

As a result, stages have been scaled back. So have conventions in movement, gesture, and intonation. Actors in most plays today don't seek to impress the audience. Their movements tend to be smaller, realistic, even intimate.

Tragedy might include simple stillness or tears. Comedy might include the broad physical humor of an earlier burlesque, but it might rely instead upon quick, witty wordplay such as that perfected by playwrights David Mamet or Tom Stoppard.

Today it is not uncommon for actors who are entering or exiting to wind their way through the house. And sometimes audience members are invited to become part of the play, as in *Tony 'n Tina's Wedding,* shown below.

The audience joins the conga line during the play *Tony 'n Tina's Wedding.*

Chapter 7 Voice Production and Articulation

It has been said that good stage actors can make a "person in the last row wearing earplugs hear them clearly." In this chapter, you will learn how to train and exercise your voice for just that purpose.

Project Specs

Project Description For this assignment, you will have two minutes to perform a vocal exercise, or exercise for the voice, which will be one part of a foundation for daily vocal practice.

Purpose to build and use proper breathing and articulation and produce quality vocal tone

Materials a written description of your chosen vocal exercise or the Voice Production and Articulation Activity Sheet your teacher provides

Theatre Terms
audible
circumflex
diaphragm
inflection
larynx
pitch
project
rate
resonance
volume

On Your Feet

Use the word "Oh" to communicate each of the following situations:

- sudden understanding
- great shock or horror
- irritation
- happiness or joy
- extreme sadness

Note the differences in the volume and tone of your voice for each.

PREVIEW

Your Voice Is Your Key

As an actor, you know that your voice is a basic element of your craft. In addition to having enough **volume,** or strength, to be **audible** to the audience no matter what size the theatre, your voice must be flexible enough to add subtle layers of character, emotional texture, and meaning to your lines. And it must be strong enough to withstand long rehearsals and intense performances.

Unless you have serious vocal problems that need a specialist's attention, you can do much to build vocal audibility and flexibility by practicing vocal exercises every day. Some professional

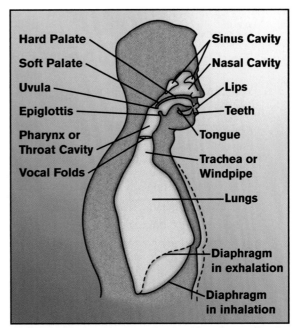

These areas of the body are involved in voice production.

John Hall performs in a 1995 production of Shakespeare's *A Midsummer Night's Dream.*

actors work for years with vocal coaches and teachers to develop the most versatile voice they can. An actor's training is continuous—the learning, practicing, and exercising go on for his or her whole career. Even if you are not intent on becoming a professional actor, your voice will benefit from proper exercise.

Voice Production

Technically, speech sounds are produced by air that has been forced through the lungs by the action of certain rib muscles and the **diaphragm,** a flat muscle that separates the chest from the abdominal cavity. The exhaled air vibrates the vocal cords in the **larynx,** which is found in the pharynx.

Here's How
To Protect Your Voice

Vocal training begins by taking care of the voice you have. After all, you can *improve* your voice, but you can't *exchange* it. Prevent vocal problems by following these simple rules.

- Eat well, get enough sleep, and exercise regularly. This should help you avoid colds and other respiratory illnesses; they present a serious threat to your voice.

- Don't smoke or drink alcohol. While there are many reasons to avoid these substances, the chemicals and toxins in them are exceptionally harmful to the voice.

- Never strain your voice by shouting when you have a cold or by singing in an improper range.

- Never shout yourself hoarse at a ball game. Such strain makes throat membranes sore and invites infection that can lead to permanent damage. When in doubt, don't shout.

The sound produced is modified by the resonators (throat, nose, mouth, and sinuses) and formed into vowels and consonants by the articulators (tongue, jaw, teeth, cheeks, lips, and hard and soft palates).

When exercising your voice you will be working to achieve controlled breathing and **resonance,** or a rich, warm sound quality. In addition, variety in **pitch,** volume, **inflection,** and **rate** is important. Clear articulation, or way of speaking, and proper pronunciation round out the important elements of voice production. The diagram on page 65 shows all the areas of your body that contribute to the sound of your voice.

Proper Breathing

Actors and singers know that to have the necessary air control for a performance they must breathe from the diaphragm. This means that the chest cavity stays relatively still, while the waist expands and contracts, and the lower ribs rise and fall slightly. Once you have mastered diaphragmatic breathing, you will notice that it requires less effort than chest breathing, allows you to breathe more deeply, and provides the control you need to project long passages without running out of breath. That said, breathing from your diaphragm might feel strange at first. To get comfortable with this type of breathing, practice daily.

Richer Tone

Tone depends on many factors, including the shape and size of your vocal mechanism, which you will not be able to change. However, you can learn to make the most of what you've got by keeping your throat open and controlling your breath. If your voice sounds harsh or raspy, it is usually the result of a closed throat. If your voice sounds breathy, you are probably using more breath than you need.

To relax your throat and improve your tone, try this exercise:

Yawn exaggeratedly. Take a deep breath, stretch, and then yawn again. With your throat open and relaxed, quietly, and slowly say the following while prolonging the vowel sounds "Ma-a-ah, blo-o-oh, fla-a-aw, pla-a-ay, be-e-e, t-o-o." Yawn again to relax, then

Karita Mattila performs in a Royal Opera production of *Lohengrin*.

Try This

1 Lie flat on your back with one hand on your abdomen and the other on your chest. Keep your chest still. The abdomen should move up when you inhale and down when you exhale. Now stand up and try the identical action. Gradually speed up your breathing until you are panting like a dog. Remember to use only your abdomen—try to keep your chest still.

2 Using your diaphragm, take a deep breath and see how far you can count as you exhale. Do not force or speed up the count. If you start to get tense, breathe normally, and start again. Practice this until you can exhale to a count of sixty.

continue with other vowel sounds. Read a passage from your literature book, prolonging the vowels.

Tone is the vocal element you use to create different emotional colors when you speak or sing. Try these simple techniques to experiment with tone:

1 Say each of these words—*oh, yes, well, really, possibly*—to convey each of these emotions or states of being: happiness, pride, fatigue, fright, anger, suspicion, innocence, pleading, and sorrow.

2 Reproduce the tone color of these words by making your voice sound like the word's meaning: *bang, crackle, swish, grunt, tinkle, roar, coo, thin, wheeze, bubble, buzzy, splash, clang, gurgle.*

Pitch, Inflection, Volume, and Rate

Pitch is the relative highness or lowness of your voice. You can produce a medium pitch by relaxing your throat. This is the easiest pitch to project and the easiest for an audience to listen to. In acting, high pitch indicates nervousness, excitement, anger, or fear. A low pitch conveys despair or disgust.

Inflection, in combination with pitch, allows you to glide from high to low on a single word, syllable, or phrase. Rising inflection connotes questioning. Falling inflection signifies finality. **Circumflex** is a combination of the two, expressing sarcasm, doubt, and innuendo.

Inflection Marks

Laura:
Oh, Jack! What are you doing?
[rising inflection]

Damon:
Jack always has a reason.
[sustained inflection]

Lateefa:
Stay out of this, Jack.
[falling inflection]

Volume is the relative loudness of your voice. To send, or **project,** their voices to all areas of the theatre, performers often must speak very loudly, yet they must seem to the audience to be speaking at a normal volume. Breathing from the diaphragm is the key to vocal projection.

Rate is the speed at which you speak. Rate of speech can indicate many things about a person or a character. For example, a slow rate usually indicates old age, important ideas, and/or a state of sorrow or exhaustion. A faster rate indicates youth and/or the emotions of excitement, happiness, and anger.

Try This

Test yourself for breathlessness. Light a candle and hold it about five or six inches away from your face. Speak directly toward the flame. If the candle flickers or goes out, you are using too much breath. When you produce a clear tone, you actually use very little breath—the candle flame will move only a tiny bit, if at all.

Articulation and Pronunciation

Proper breathing technique, great tone, and perfect pitch will make no difference at all if you have poor articulation. After all, the audience has to understand what you're saying. Poor articulation is generally the result of carelessness and sluggish speech; it can make you sound as if you're talking through a mouthful of oatmeal. People can get by with this type of speech in real life; but on the stage, where every word counts, it can cause real problems.

Using proper pronunciation means making sure you know how to say each word you speak. If you do not know the meaning of a word you read, or you are unsure of its pronunciation, look it up *before* you say it in front of an audience! There is no excuse for mispronouncing a word in performance.

On pages 4 and 8 of Chapter 1, you tried a few tongue twisters to practice articulation. Repeat those once again and then try the additional phrases below. Remember to open your mouth wide as you say each one. Pick up speed as you gain control.

- Six slim sleek saplings stood silently.
- She sells seashells by the seashore.
- A big black bug bit a big black bear.
- Fill the sieve with thistles; then sift the thistles through the sieve.
- Better buy the bigger rubber baby buggy bumpers.

PREPARE

Choose Your Exercise

Choose one of the exercises suggested below and on the following page to perform in front of the class. Write down your ideas for presenting this exercise or use the Activity Sheet your teacher provides. Practice your selection several times using proper breathing, a medium pitch, sufficient volume, and clear articulation. Remember that your presentation should not exceed two minutes.

Feel free to adapt any of the suggestions in an imaginative way.

- Choose a favorite childhood poem or song lyrics such as "My Shadow" or "She'll Be Comin' 'Round the Mountain" to recite.

Practice articulation and pronunciation so that you are prepared when you go onstage.

Breathe from your diaphragm as you practice saying the lines from memory. Work toward saying the poem or lyric with expression. Try to finish one stanza on a single exhalation. Try to control your breath so that you don't run out of air in the middle of a phrase or sentence.

- Choose a dramatic paragraph from the text of your literature book or from your personal reading. Alternatively, you may write a paragraph of your own. Practice reading the paragraph aloud varying your pitch, volume, and rate to convey meaning and feeling. Remember to use proper breathing technique. Keep your throat relaxed and open to achieve the best tone possible, and read with feeling.

- Select an excerpt from one of Shakespeare's monologues or scenes found in Unit Eight of this book. Read it over, and then read it aloud for the class. You will need a partner for the scene.

- Create a new tongue twister consisting of two to four lines. Use the tongue twisters on pages 4, 8, and 69 as a guide. Share the tongue twister you create with the class.

PRESENT

Perform Your Vocal Exercise

When your name is called, hand your description of your vocal exercise or Activity Sheet to your teacher, and then proceed to the playing area. Perform your exercise for the class. Remember to take your time. Every word and breath counts.

When you have finished your presentation, try not to make faces or shrug your shoulders if you feel you didn't do as well as you would have liked. Remember that your presentation doesn't truly end until you sit down.

Theatre Journal

To some extent, improving your voice is based on listening. So listen to the way others speak. Listen to recordings by famous actors and orators. Listen to yourself on a tape recorder. Then write down an analysis of what you hear. Use the inflection marks on page 68 to help you remember the sounds of people speaking.

CRITIQUE

Evaluate Classmates' Vocal Exercises

Take notes as you watch your classmates' vocal presentations. Use a scale of 1 to 5, with 5 being "outstanding," 4 being "very good," 3 being "good," 2 being "needs some improvement," and 1 being "needs much improvement." Ask yourself the questions below as you evaluate.

- Did the performer use proper breathing?

- How audible was the performer's presentation?

- How clearly did he or she articulate?

- Did the performer speak at the proper rate—neither too fast nor too slow?

- If the performer stumbled over a word, did he or she move on gracefully?

Choose two of the presentations you have already critiqued and write a paragraph explaining why you gave each the score you did. Use the answers you wrote to the questions above to help in your evaluation.

Career Focus

Voice-over Actor

Many stage actors supplement their theatre careers by working as voice-over performers. Though you may never have seen a voice-over actor, you hear them all the time. Typical voice-overs are radio spots, television commercials, corporate training films, documentary and educational film narration, and so on. Some actors make their livings entirely from this type of work. Most live in larger urban areas where talent agents aid them in their search for work.

Agents take ten percent or more of a voice-over actor's pay in exchange for getting the actor auditions with companies who are hiring for voice-over jobs. A career in voice-over requires a strong, supple voice; a personable, professional demeanor; and the ability to do dialects and/or impressions. A musical background can also be very helpful. To showcase their talents, most voice-over actors have a professional CD made. Created in a sound studio, this type of CD features multiple short samples of the actor's voice from commercials, films, or other recordings. A good voice-over CD gives a well-rounded idea of the actor's overall voice and versatility.

Being able to convey a strong personality is an asset to the voice-over actor.

Additional Projects

1 With a partner, select a two- to four-minute scene in which two characters exchange dialogue. In reading the scenes, employ the various vocal techniques you have learned. Try to go further with a particular element than you have gone before.

2 Say the following lines aloud, using the inflection indicated in brackets.

- I'm sorry, but I must decline your invitation. [falling inflection]

- What's the big idea? [rising inflection]

- So you took my new sweater! [rising inflection]

- I think I've solved the problem. [sustained inflection]

3 Read aloud two poems that feature contrasting emotional content. Imagine that you are delivering these poems in a large crowded auditorium. Experiment with your volume, articulation, inflection, tone, and the flexibility of your voice.

4 Practice projecting your voice to the last row in the classroom. Stand up and focus your eyes on the back wall. Say your name, the name of your street, and the name of your favorite song. Repeat all of this information using only vowels; then do the same using only consonants. Finally, repeat your name, street name, and favorite song articulating and projecting to the best of your ability.

5 Rehearse the monologue from *Clear Glass Marbles* by Jane Martin found in Unit Eight. Use all the techniques you have learned in this chapter to give your reading as much emotional color as possible. Experiment with a number of different accents. Time yourself to make sure the monologue will fit within a four-minute time period.

"Speech finely framed delighteth the ears."

—2 Maccabees.II, 39

Master of the Craft

John Leguizamo: Man of Many Voices

"I see the new Latin artist as a pioneer, opening up doors for others to follow. And when they don't open, we crowbar our way in . . . . "

—John Leguizamo

As it turns out, John Leguizamo doesn't need a crowbar. Instead, he has become a major star by way of his talent and ambition. Born in Bogota, Colombia, in 1964 and raised in New York City, he was voted Most Talkative in his high school class. But this charming chatterbox went on to become a respected comedian and serious actor, writer, and director. No matter what the role, he has won fans with his sharply observed takes on the life and times of Latinos; he pokes fun at stereotypes as he merrily shatters them.

Leguizamo studied acting at New York University where he was the only Latino in his class. Opting for further professional training, he enrolled in the Lee Strasberg Institute. Leguizamo only studied with Strasberg for one day, however, before the legendary teacher died. (Leguizamo, never one to ignore the potential for a dark joke, later said of his teacher's unexpected death: "I have that effect on people.") He began his stand-up comedy career in clubs in and around New York City. From there he began getting small roles in movies.

In 1991 his first one-man show, *Mambo Mouth*, premiered off Broadway and became a runaway hit. He received multiple awards for his renditions of seven different Latino characters. He has since premiered several more one-man shows with great success. In each of these shows he has used his stamina, razor-sharp timing, versatile voice, and one-of-kind storytelling to create multifaceted characters that move audiences to both tears and laughter.

In 2001 he played Toulouse-Lautrec in Baz Luhrmann's film *Moulin Rouge* alongside Nicole Kidman.

John Leguizamo in his one-man show.

Theatre Then and Now

Storytellers Across Time

The Griot

The ancient griots were native West African storytellers. They fulfilled a wide variety of roles in African society, serving not only as the keepers of a community's oral tradition, but also as genealogists, teachers, masters of ceremonies, and advisors. Some historians believe that through their efforts to mediate conflicts and take part in ceremonials, griots became a form of social glue, which worked to keep African societies united. Griots were present at births, weddings, sports events, and governmental meetings, and also spread the word to others. In short, they played a vital part in every aspect of society. No other profession in any part of the world comes close to the intricate and intimate ties the griots had to their people.

The griot is not simply a cultural and historical oddity. Modern-day griots have become extremely popular, thanks in part to the 1970s television miniseries "Roots." In it, author Alex Haley authenticated the story of his ancestry by listening to village history told to him by an African griot. Over the past twenty-five years, African griots, weaving a spellbinding collage of spoken word, song, and movement, have played to packed houses in New York, London, and elsewhere around the world.

Gambian griot Dembo Jobarteh tuning his kora. The instrument's body is made from a gourd that is cut in half and partially covered with cow skin. Fishing line is used for the twenty-one strings.

The Moth

Of course, storytelling has played a key part in almost every culture. In the United States, the American Indians had an extensive oral tradition. The immigrants who came to America from all over the world brought their oral traditions with them. And storytelling in the United States today? It's alive and well. In fact, there are a number of organizations that are completely devoted to the fine art of storytelling. One such organization is The Moth.

The brainchild of poet and novelist George Dawes Green, The Moth started small. Green thought back to his Georgia childhood, where some of his fondest memories were of sitting in any one of many backyards in the evening and listening to his friends telling amazing stories. He even told a few of his own. Often these stories focused on a tale of woe about some unlucky character, which drew the listeners in like moths to a flame. Green wanted to recreate these evenings of storytelling in an urban environment. He started in 1997 with just a few friends in his living room. But The Moth, as he called it, quickly developed a following. Soon the event moved to Joe's Pub at New York's Joseph Papp Public Theatre and later to the Brooklyn Academy of Music and the Players Club. The Moth often moves from location to location, drawing a wide audience of approving spectators and storytellers. It is usually presented in a comfortable lounge environment. Each evening features a specific theme, such as "A Savage Mood" or "Gigs Gone Bad." Each event features five to seven storytellers, each of whom has about ten minutes to tell a story.

Because the storytellers at The Moth usually are not professional performers, and because most of them tell stories from their own lives, audiences find the stories exhilarating, fresh, and unique. You can learn more about The Moth by visiting www.themoth.org.

Moth storyteller Jason Kordelos responds to the theme "Love and War."

Chapter
8 Ensemble Work

What if every night of your life were a one-person show? What if every conversation ended in a monologue? Life would be quite dull. Human beings are social creatures. We want to know all about the nooks and crannies of one another's lives. We want to be involved in those lives too—not as helpers or onlookers, but as participants—as part of the ensemble.

Project Specs

Project Description For this assignment, you and several partners will perform a three- to five-minute improvised ensemble scene.

Purpose to develop the concentration, skill, teamwork, and courtesy necessary to work in an ensemble

Materials an annotated list of your character's relationship with other characters in a scene or the Ensemble Work Activity Sheet your teacher provides

Theatre Terms

emoting
ensemble ethic
fall
going up
illusion of the first time
interplay
step on
supporting roles

On Your Feet

With one to three partners, improvise one of the scenes below:

• Four of you are in the family room at home. Two of you want to clean up the clutter; the other two try to find ways out of the job.

• A boy attempts to make a date with a girl he just met. She likes him, but doesn't think she should accept. He is determined, however.

• One of you is packing a suitcase, determined to take a trip. Two friends try to keep you from packing.

PREVIEW

Ensemble Acting

Acting demands **interplay,** or interaction, between all of the characters. To be realistic, characters must play off one another in an interactive way. They must pay attention to everything going on around them. Every time an actor speaks, his or her words should seem new and interesting to the others onstage. The actor must communicate the **illusion of the first time,** which means that the action must seem spontaneous and fresh even after hours and hours of practice. When your character is not speaking, you must react as though you are hearing the other characters for the first time. It takes practice, but it's not hard. Watch carefully as the other actors speak and move. You'll find yourself more engrossed in the nuances of what the other actors are doing than you are in yourself.

When you interact purposefully with your fellow actors, you begin to develop a working relationship based on trust and respect. You become not just an individual, but an important part of the whole. That's what the **ensemble ethic** is all about.

The Ensemble Actor's Safety Net

It is empowering to be part of a mutually supportive group onstage. Interacting wholeheartedly with others offers the ensemble actor the benefits below.

- Your close ties to the other characters won't let you **"fall"** out of character or forget your lines.

- You won't have time for your own private speculations or fears.

- If you have learned your lines well, the reality of your situation won't allow you to forget them.

In the play *Experiment with an Airpump,* each member of the ensemble contributes a unique individual interpretation that impacts on the dynamics of the entire group.

PREPARE

Choose Your Situation

Divide into mixed groups of five. (Your teacher may wish to assign groups, scenes, and roles.) With your partners, choose a group of characters and situations from the following chart, or invent a detailed situation with characters of your own.

Location	Character	Objective/Intention/Need
A spring garage sale in an empty building downtown	Antique dealer	Hopes to find something of value
	Old woman	Has to crochet 50 booties for bazaar
	Theatre prop person	Looking for a cane
	Real estate salesman	Needs a commission
	Young man	Has no place to live
An airport in which a boarding flight has been delayed	Ticket agent	Trying to help customers
	Business executive	Has to keep an important appointment
	Orphan	Going to meet new foster family
	College student	Heading back to school
	Foreign visitor	Anxious to get back home
A living room on prom night	Young man	Just meeting his date's parents
	Young woman	Anxious about her parents' reaction to her date
	Mother	Anxious about her daughter
	Father	Not impressed with his daughter's date
	Younger brother	Getting in the way
A lakeside resort full of vacationers	Older woman	Wealthy, concerned with social position
	Personal assistant	Works for the wealthy woman
	Reporter	Looking for a scoop
	Competitive swimmer	Training for the next Olympics
	Manager of the resort	Trying to keep everyone happy
A drawing room in a Victorian mansion where a murder has just occurred	Detective questioning those assembled	Wants to solve this murder before dinner
	Butler	Named in the will
	Business partner of the deceased	Was being sued by the deceased
	Brother of the deceased	Argued with the deceased recently
	Neighbor	Disliked the deceased

Developing Relationships

In an ensemble, all the parts are **supporting roles,** or roles that support another role. When working on any of your group projects in drama, make a point of encouraging everyone to contribute. Respect everyone's ideas, even if they differ markedly from your own. Strong discussions and disagreements over various points of view are to be expected—this is a healthy and productive way of working within the group. Getting angry in order to convince others you are right or insulting others' opinions is not acceptable.

Working with the Group

With the others in your group, decide on the situation you are going to improvise together. Choose your parts and decide what your various objectives will be. Throughout this project you should each be keeping a list of your own character's relationship to the other characters in the scene (or using the Activity Sheet provided by your teacher). Briefly discuss your characters' relationships, being sure to consider carefully what your partners have to say.

Working Alone

On your own, quickly sketch out in more detail what your character thinks of the other characters in your scene, as well as how your character sees himself or herself. Think about the kind of person your character will be and how your character might move, speak, and gesture.

Back with the Group

When you all think you have a fairly good understanding of your characters, meet again as a group. Decide upon the opening line in your scene. To ensure that all characters play a part in the

Even with such a large cast, everyone's role is equally important.

Theatre Journal

Next time you sit down to a meal, watch and listen to the people around the table. Who starts most of the conversations? Who is the joker at the table? Who's the rebel? Keep an eye on the way body language conveys people's roles and attitudes. You can make use of the same attitudes and habits in your acting roles.

scene, sketch out a sequence of events that includes dialogue for each of the characters. Decide as a group how the scene will develop and what the outcome will be.

If you feel confident with what you have established this far, continue by working on how each of your characters will move throughout the scene. When you have created a scene to your satisfaction, practice it a few times, making sure you do not exceed five minutes. Remember, this project is improvisational. Don't go over it so often that you memorize it. You are now ready to present your ensemble scene.

Dominic West rises to the actor's ultimate challenge: playing a character of the opposite sex (in Caryl Churchill's *Cloud Nine*).

Spotlight on

Stage Etiquette

Understanding and respecting the roles, responsibilities, and efforts of all those you work with on stage is an important part of theatre work. Whether you are a beginner or a seasoned professional, you can go a long way toward winning the respect of your colleagues by simply being courteous and following the rules below.

Actor

- Be on time for rehearsals and performances—don't make others wait for you.
- Know your lines.
- Pick up your cues on time. Don't miss your lines or say them too late.
- Don't **step on** another actor's lines (cut them off) or upstage another actor.
- Avoid stealing focus by moving, gesturing, or **emoting** too much (overacting) while another actor is speaking.
- Find ways to cover for an actor who gets lost in a scene or goes blank, called **"going up."**

Director

- Whenever possible, set the schedule more than one week in advance, and stick to it.
- Listen respectfully to the thoughts and opinions of the actor, as well as the design and tech crews.
- Use positive and encouraging words.

Designer

- Talk to the cast and crew before finalizing your concept.
- Alter your design according to cast and crew feedback.

Technical Professionals

- Always keep tools in their proper location when not in use.
- Maintain respect for the needs of other professionals at work.
- Be very careful with tools while working around others (see Safety Rules on pages 220 and 244).

PRESENT

Perform Your Ensemble Scene

Before your name or the name of someone in your group is called, decide
which member of the group will introduce the scene. Give your lists or
Activity Sheets to your teacher. The
group member who has agreed to do the
introduction should briefly describe the
location of the scene, the characters and
the situation, as well as indicating who
plays which character. Perform your
scene for the class. Remember that trust
is an important part of the ensemble.
When you have finished, bow politely.

Here's How
To Keep Your
Ensemble on Track

If you think a scene is going off track,
remind yourself or the other actors
of your relationship in one of the
following ways:

1 State the relationship outright. Say
something such as, "You may be my
boss, but . . ." or "I know you are angry
about my being five hours late, Dad,
and . . . ."

2 Use a gesture or action that reinforces your relationship to a character.
Hug or strong-arm someone, flirt, or
shoot a glance of withering scorn.

3 Pause. Take a breath. It's better than
rushing headlong out of control.

CRITIQUE

Evaluate Your Classmates' Scene

Choose one of the ensemble scenes
presented in class to critique. As you
watch and take notes, ask yourself the
following questions:

- Could I describe each character's
  objective in the scene and the tactics
  used to get what he or she wanted?

- Could I outline each character's relationship to the other characters in
  the scene?

- Could I describe each character's
  attitude toward the other characters
  in the scene?

- Did any one character stand out
  among the others? Why?

- Did all the characters have some
  action, event, relationship, or motivation in common?

Use a scale of 1 to 5 to rate the scene,
with 5 being "outstanding" and 1 being
"needs much improvement." After you
have rated the scene, write a short
paragraph explaining why you gave
the rating you did.

Additional Projects

1. Choose a partner and wait onstage for your partner to enter the scene. Based on the way in which your partner acts toward you and responds to you, try to determine what your relationship is. When you respond correctly, your partner should let you know and end the scene.

2. Choose a three-person scene and rehearse it with your partners. Then, at the moment of performance, switch characters and perform one another's parts.

3. Work with a group to make a simple task into an ensemble job. For example, make use of six actors to build a birdhouse, make a stew, or get someone a job. Make sure each group member has an equally important role.

4. To enhance your teamwork and listening skills, play the following alphabet game in a large group. Starting with *A*, each player names a person, place, and object—always repeating everything said previously. So, for example, player number four would say, "*Anna* lives in the *attic* with an *apple, Bob* lives in a *boat* with a *bicycle, Carl* lives in a *cabin* with a *cat*," and might add, "*Doris* lives in a *dungeon* with a *duck*." As you continue through the alphabet, try to be dramatic and expressive, and don't forget anything you've heard!

5. Perform a staged reading of the scene from *Blithe Spirit* by Noel Coward found in Unit Eight. Take into account the way the comedy depends upon listening and precise responses between each actor in the scene.

"We were never cute, I think that still holds true. Everyone always liked everyone's work, and that's what also kept it together. There was very much a shared sensibility . . . but also a respect for one another's work."

—John Malkovich, discussing his work as a member of Chicago's Steppenwolf Theatre Company

Theatre Then and Now

Ensembles of Old

Elizabethan Actors

Elizabethan England saw theatre grow from an occasional, itinerant art form to a commercial enterprise complete with permanent playhouses and professional acting companies. These early companies embraced a star system, by which the most celebrated actors won leading, sympathetic roles, while other actors specialized in playing particular types. Leading Elizabethan actors like Richard Burbage learned more than 50 plays and performed about 70 roles in rotation—over and over again—during a typical three-year period. This system encouraged actors to think in terms of generalized types and to play to the audience rather than to each other.

19th-Century Actors

In the 19th century, however, things began to change. New playwrights like George Buchner in Germany and Anton Chekhov in Russia began experimenting with naturalistic and expressionistic plays. Directors like Duke George II of Meiningen and Stanislavski of the Moscow Art Theatre began asking actors to work closely together to create a unified, realistic picture onstage. Companies began working together for weeks, even months on end, to develop a unified approach to a single play. Stars still emerged, but they gave themselves over to each production's social or artistic ideals.

Chekhov's *The Three Sisters*, one of the earliest ensemble productions, has been produced continually since its debut in 1901.

Ensembles of Today

Steppenwolf Theatre Company

There are many theatre companies today who work entirely as ensembles, such as Steppenwolf Theatre in Chicago. At Steppenwolf, plays are chosen that will reflect the artistic vision and theatrical values that the company members hold. Steppenwolf is famous for being an ensemble of very strong, determined actors willing to "look the fool" and take on unusual roles and offbeat characters. The actors have made names for themselves not only as stage actors, but as directors and producers, and in many cases, as movie actors also. The plays that Steppenwolf has become known for are often contemporary and cutting-edge, even raw. This is a company that is not averse to controversy.

Ensemble Theatre of Houston

The Ensemble Theatre of Houston strives to promote collaboration among theatre professionals of all races, genders, and ethnicities. Too often in the past, Black actors, directors, and crew members had trouble finding a place in the theatre. Over the years, however, this ensemble has helped to encourage and preserve African-American artistic expression. The company brings its mission to both classics and contemporary plays, international and local work, and even children's productions. The core troupe is African American, but the ensemble is committed to maintaining a "color-blind" approach to casting, as well as to hiring directors, designers, and playwrights. They are unified in their theatrical values, their social vision, and their artistic mission. They invite visiting stars to join them on occasion, but the ensemble itself is the star of its shows.

Top: The Ensemble Theatre of Houston offers family entertainment. Bottom: The 1994 Steppenwolf Theatre Company's production *Of Mice and Men.*

Unit **Two** Review

PREVIEW

Examine the following key concepts previewed in Unit Two.

1 Where should you put your weight when you stand naturally?

2 Define the terms below.
   a. scenario   b. stage business   c. cheating out   d. upstaging

3 Of the following, which are the stronger positions, and why?
   upstage or downstage   stage right or stage left

4 In what body position is the person below standing?

5 What does X DL mean?

6 Which of the following is NOT essential to voice production
   and articulation?
   pitch   volume   articulation   emoting   inflection

7 Say this sentence using rising inflection, falling inflection, and sustained
   inflection: *You always go for a run in the park before you eat breakfast.*

8 What would you say is the most important thing an ensemble actor
   must learn?

9 Which of these are important qualities for a good actor, and why?
   discipline   trust   good looks   courtesy

PREPARE

Assess your response to the preparation process for projects in this unit.

10 How did you and your partner work together to create the scenario and
   add the movement to your stage movement project?

11 When working on voice and articulation, which aspect of the
   process did you find most difficult and why?

12 What advice would you give to others learning about stage crosses?

13 Were you able to fully trust the people in your ensemble? Why
   or why not?

14 Were you and your partner or partners able to work together
   smoothly and efficiently to prepare your ensemble improvisation?

PRESENT

Analyze the experience of presenting your work to the class.

15 Which project did you find the most rewarding? Why?

16 Did you find it easier to write the three stage crosses or to execute them? Why?

17 Were you happy with the vocal exercise you chose to do, or do you now wish you'd chosen another one? Explain your feelings.

18 Were you able to present your ensemble improvisation in an atmosphere of trust and support?

CRITIQUE

Evaluate how you go about critiquing your work and the work of others.

19 Did you find it easier to critique your classmates in terms of movement, vocal presentation, or ensemble work?

20 Ask a classmate who critiqued one of your presentations to share the critique with you. How balanced and insightful do you find it to be?

21 Evaluate the critiques you wrote in this unit. In what way could they have been more balanced and helpful?

EXTENSIONS

- Read each group of letters below until you understand their meaning. Then play with pitch and inflection as you say them aloud.

  I C U R A Q T   I N V U   G U R O K   P T S N X T C

- Create gestures for the following sentiments:

  I'm really tired and need to get some sleep.
  This is one mighty boring conversation.
  Stop lecturing me, please.
  This guy is definitely not telling the truth.
  The dog needs to go for a walk, and I'm not in the mood to do it.
  These dirty dishes have been sitting on the counter for five days!

Unit
Three

Creating a Character

Chapter
9 Character Analysis

To be a good actor, you must become a student of humanity. Your knowledge of people is one of the most valuable assets you have when it comes to creating a believable character. As you analyze and develop a role, you will draw upon the text of the play, your own experiences, and remembered observations of people you meet, read about, or see on film.

Project Specs

Project Description You and a partner will each create distinct characters with specific goals in a three- to five-minute improvised scene.

Purpose to analyze a character in terms of internal and external traits, motivation, objectives, and stakes

Materials a list of shared information between your own and your partner's character, a list of your character's internal and external traits, or the Character Analysis Activity Sheet provided by your teacher

Theatre Terms
artistic selectivity
conflict
dual role
external traits
internal traits
motivation
objectives
obstacle
outcome
stakes

On Your Feet

Spend two minutes interviewing a partner. Ask questions about his or her background, family, friends, personal preferences, hobbies, accomplishments, and so on. Take notes and try to create a composite of the person. At the end of two minutes, look over your notes and tell your partner about himself or herself. Then switch roles.

PREVIEW

The Actor and the Character

As an actor in a play you have a **dual role.** You are both the actor-as-character and the actor-as-actor. If you are to be convincing onstage, you must use your imagination—and the work you've done analyzing and developing your character—to maintain your belief in what you as the character are doing, feeling, and saying. You should think as the character thinks and concentrate on fulfilling his or her goals, or **objectives.** On the other hand, as an actor you must maintain technical control and a professional attitude at all times. None of your performing will matter if the audience has trouble seeing or hearing you. You the actor and you the character must work as a unit to create the delicate balance of believable characterization.

This may sound like a demanding job—and it is. But characterization shouldn't be a strain. Relax and enjoy the process as you create a believable individual onstage.

Developing the Character

To be an effective onstage presence you will need to know hundreds of things about your character—much more than you will actually be able to portray onstage. Your job then becomes one of **artistic selectivity.** What are the really important aspects of this character? How can you effectively communicate the essentials of the character? At the same time, remember that none of the work you do while developing your character is wasted. The more you know about the character, the more textured your performance will be.

And you must harness your character's emotions and avoid overacting, which offends both the audience and your fellow actors.

Julian Glover and Alan Doble create distinctive characters in the Piccadilly Theatre production of *Waiting for Godot.*

The hundreds of things you understand about your character will reveal themselves through the various layers and colors you are able to bring to the role.

Motivation and Conflict

In real life people often do and say things for no apparent reason. A character in a play, however, needs a specific reason, or **motivation,** for doing or saying anything. Motivation determines your character's objectives. Whatever is standing in the way of your character's objectives is an **obstacle.**

This is the essence of **conflict,** which in turn is the basis of drama. The **outcome** of a conflict is the result of the steps the characters take to overcome their obstacles. What the characters may gain or lose as a result of the outcome are the **stakes.** The higher the stakes are in a play, the greater the character's motivation; the more powerful the conflict, the more important the outcome.

The Character Inside and Out

To find your way into the mind and body of a character, you must know the role inside and out. That means you must understand both the character's internal and external traits.

To determine a character's **internal traits,** challenge yourself to discover what he or she is like inside. Find out the character's background—that is his or her family circumstances, environment, occupation, level of education, hobbies, and so on—and his or her emotional reactions to all of these circumstances. You can break internal traits into three basic categories.

1 **Mental characteristics** Is the character intelligent, clever, dull, slow, or average?

2 **Spiritual qualities** What are the character's ideals, ethical code, and beliefs? What is his or her attitude toward other people and toward life in general?

3 **Emotional characteristics** Is the character confident, outgoing, happy, and poised or sullen, confused, nervous, cynical, and timid? What are his or her likes and dislikes? How does he or she respond to others? (One good technique when analyzing emotional characteristics is to ask yourself how a character's temperament is similar to and different from your own.)

Answering all these questions should give you a good idea of your character's personality. Now it's time to get even more specific. You will have to determine your character's motivating desire within the play or scene. In other words, what does your character *want*? You may have to do the additional work of imagining the circumstances that led to the events of the play or scene.

To play the title role in *Mary Stuart* convincingly, actor Jenny Bacon must convey the motivation and obstacles faced by the Scottish queen.

A character's **external traits** have to do with outward appearance and what that appearance says about him or her. Here are some external traits to think about.

1 Posture Does the way the character sits and stands suggest confidence, timidity, awkwardness, or grace?

2 Movement and gestures Does the character's movement and gait reveal poise, nervousness, weakness, or strength? What does the character's movement reveal about his or her age, health, or general attitude?

3 Mannerism Does the character have any tics or little habits that provide keys to his or her personality? Examples might be nail biting, gum chewing, head scratching, or table tapping.

4 Voice Does the character have a specific regional dialect or any vocal mannerisms?

5 Mode of dress Is the character's appearance neat, casual, prim, or sloppy? Are the clothes clean or dirty? Are they in good taste?

Mannerisms can tell a lot about your character.

When analyzing and developing a character's external qualities, you'll want to avoid stereotypes. For example, you don't necessarily want to choose a cartoonlike drawling "hick" voice simply because your character is supposed to be uneducated. Try to make the more interesting, less obvious choice.

Theatre Journal

Go to a public place such as a museum, a park, or a mall. Sit down on a bench and do a bit of people watching. Take note of the way people walk and the expressions on their faces. Imagine what the lives of these people might be like. Choose one passerby to use as the basis for a character. Write a history for this character. Use what you see and your imagination to create a rich character study.

PREPARE

Create a High-Stakes Scenario

You are now going to work with a partner to improvise a scenario in which the stakes are high for each of your characters. You will need to think of a situation in which two characters come into conflict over a physical object of some kind (perhaps a bag of money, a legal document, or a treasured family heirloom). Decide when and where your scene takes place and what the relationship between your characters should be. Then nail down a bit of their shared history (if any). Write down everything you decide upon. Here's an example:

Scenario for Two Siblings

Characters: Rita and Joe
Relationship: Sister and Brother
Ages: Rita is 15; Joe is 14
Situation: Rita desperately needs to use the telephone; Joe is searching an online Web site and has been tying up the phone line for an hour.
Time of year: Just after Thanksgiving
Time of day: 10 P.M.

Decide which character will ultimately achieve his or her objectives. This will serve as the outcome of the scene. DO NOT determine what your characters will say and do in the scene ahead of time—you are to improvise your actual exchange.

After you have come up with your shared situation and history, take some time to work independently. Both of you should come up with external and internal traits for your character, as well as motivations (Rita: Why does she need to use the phone? Joe: Why does he have to be online?), objectives (Rita: How will she get Joe offline? Joe: How will he distract Rita until he can finish what he is doing?), and stakes (Rita: What will happen if she doesn't make her phone call? Joe: What will happen if he doesn't finish what he is doing?).

At the right are a few other possible scenarios. You can use one of them or create your own. The important thing is to be specific about your shared history and your character's internal and external traits, motivation, and objectives. Rehearse your scene so that you know only the basic shape of the improvisation. Don't write down specific lines you want to say; keep this improvisation spontaneous. Time yourselves to make sure you will come within the three- to five-minute time frame.

Suggestions for Scenarios

- Two students compete for a school award.
- Two siblings both want a particular item that belonged to their dead grandfather.
- Two bank robbers want to be in charge of divvying up the loot.
- Two people at a library want to use the only available computer.
- Two people bid on a price- less object at an auction.

Two characters clash over a high-stakes real estate deal in David Mamet's *Glengarry Glen Ross*.

PRESENT

Perform Your High-Stakes Scene

When your or your partner's name is called, give your lists or Activity Sheets to your teacher. Then take a few moments to set up your scene (arrange chairs if you need them, for example). Do not rush.

Remember to keep the stakes high with the choices your character makes during the scene. If one method doesn't work, try another. Each character must work hard to achieve the goal. When you perform your scene, you will no doubt find out things about the other character that you didn't know. You must respond to these things in the moment. Try to make everything clear within the scene. You will not be using an introduction for this activity.

Remember to keep yourself open to the audience, both physically and emotionally as you perform your scene. When you have finished your scene, turn to the audience and bow politely before returning to your seat.

CRITIQUE

Evaluate Your Classmates' Scene

Choose one of the scenes presented and evaluate it on a scale of 1 to 5, with 5 being "outstanding" and 1 being "needs much improvement." Your critique should answer these questions:

- How old were these two characters?

- What was their relationship to one another?

- What was each character's objective?

- How high were the stakes for each character?

- What did each character do to get what he or she wanted?

- Which character got what he or she wanted—and how was this achieved?

- Did one character appear stronger than the other? If so, in what way?

Write a paragraph detailing the reasons for the score you gave.

Additional Projects

1 Select newspaper human-interest stories to analyze. In groups, supply the necessary characters for the action of the story. Establish the characters' physical, emotional, and social dimensions. Then improvise a scene built around them.

2 In groups, build a scene around a historical event, such as Lewis and Clark's first meeting with Sacajawea, General Lee's surrender to Ulysses S. Grant at Appomattox Courthouse, the Lincoln/ Douglas debates, and so on. Be sure your story has characters in conflict, high stakes, a clear outcome, and is historically correct.

3 Choose a hand prop or costume accessory such as a pair of long white gloves, an oversized umbrella, a colorful silk handkerchief, a pocket watch, or a stuffed bird. Create a brief scene in which you portray a character who is wearing this costume or holding this prop.

4 Work with a partner to create a scene. Character A goes on stage and waits for Character B to enter. A decides upon a definite character relationship with B, but does not tell B what it is. B must discover who he or she is strictly through the way A talks and behaves toward him or her. B responds as sensibly as possible until his or her identity becomes clear.

5 Read the scene from *A Marriage Proposal* by Anton Chekhov found in Unit Eight of this book. With a partner, choose a part and read the scene through together. As you read, be aware of each character's motivation, obstacles, and stakes in this particular scene.

This image might help you build a scene around one of the debates between Abraham Lincoln and Stephen A. Douglas that took place throughout Illinois in 1858. It is possible to find transcripts of these debates at your library or on the Internet.

Theatre Then and Now

Ibsen and Miller— Appointment with Humanity

Henrik Ibsen and Arthur Miller both wrote plays with universal themes about the human condition. They created flesh-and-blood, flawed characters on desperate quests for meaning and fulfillment. A testimony to this universality is the fact that much of Ibsen's work is still produced more than 110 years after it was written, and *Death of a Salesman,* a play that celebrated its fifty-fourth birthday in 2003, remains one of the world's most produced plays.

Henrik Ibsen (1828–1906)

Throughout history, playwrights have struggled to define and illustrate what it means to be human. The Greeks gave the world classical tragedy, a form that depicted a noble-born person who, through a flaw in his own character, brings about his own ruin. William Shakespeare's dramas also focused on highborn individuals whose character flaws brought them down.

In the mid- to late-1800s the Norwegian writer Henrik Ibsen created a series of social dramas about middle-class people. These were plays of such psychological

Amira Casar and Marie Adam in a recent production of *Hedda Gabler.*

depth that Ibsen later became known as the "Freud of the theatre," a reference to the famous psychoanalyst Sigmund Freud. Ibsen wrote about characters who struggled with the often negative forces in their own minds. And he slammed these tortured souls up against conventional society in ways that revealed much about both the characters and the social order of the day.

In his 1890 play *Hedda Gabler,* the formidable but desperately unhappy title character sets about changing and destroying the lives of those around her as a way of fulfilling her own dreams of freedom and independence. Hedda is a strong, intelligent woman who is trapped by the role society has created for her.

Ibsen created characters whose desperate need to live differently drove them to self-destruction while also ruining the lives of others.

Arthur Miller (1915–2005)

Nearly sixty years after *Hedda Gabler* was written, playwright Arthur Miller's 1949 masterpiece, *Death of a Salesman,* took the American theatre by storm. The play focuses on Willy Loman, a salesman long past his prime, who is still waiting in vain for his small corner of the American Dream. Like Ibsen, Miller was interested in how society affects the individual. Willy Loman is a complex blend of desperation and bravado. At his core, he knows he is a failure, but he spends much of the play trying to convince himself and those around him that he is just about to make a comeback as the great salesman he once was.

As the play progresses, it becomes clear that Willy is reinventing his past and that in fact he was never a great salesman. He has always been an average man with unreachable dreams. Toward the end of the play, Willy realizes that his failure as a salesman is mirrored in his failure as a husband and father. The American dream has escaped his grasp, and, like Hedda Gabler, Willy Loman makes a desperate final statement.

The role of Willy Loman has attracted many fine actors over the years, including Dustin Hoffman, above.

Chapter
10 Character Development

An old theatre adage states, "There are no small roles—only small actors." Even roles with very few lines are important to a play. No matter what size your role, you will need to develop your character in detail. This chapter will provide you with some tools to help you through the process.

Project Specs

Project Description For this assignment, you and a group of classmates will perform a seven- to ten-minute scene from a play involving three or more characters.

Purpose to sharpen your analytical skills and develop a vivid characterization

Materials an analysis of your character's attributes or the Character Development Activity Sheet your teacher provides

Theatre Terms
cue
cue pickup
denouement
fourth wall
nonrealistic play
presentational
realistic play
representational
subtext

On Your Feet

Think of a close friend or family member. Try to re-create this person using only your posture, vocal rhythm and tone, facial expression, and a few key phrases.

Rebecca Winsocky creates the character Bananas, the wife in John Guare's *House of Blue Leaves*.

PREVIEW

Using the Right Tools

In Chapter 9 you learned how to analyze a character's internal and external traits, motivation, and objectives. But when you act in a play you must also understand the relationship your character has to the play as a whole. A thorough study of the play's other characters, and its plot, structure, and theme, will give you the tools you need to portray your character in a way that comes close to the playwright's intention.

Staying in Style

As an actor onstage, you must understand the style and tone of the play you're performing. Plays can be realistic or nonrealistic. A **realistic play** imitates real life—it shows recognizable

characters in dramatic situations. Examples of realistic plays include Henrik Ibsen's *A Doll's House,* Cheryl L. West's *Jar the Floor,* and Rebecca Gilman's *Spinning into Butter* (see Unit Eight for scenes from these plays). Typically, realistic plays utilize the convention of the **fourth wall**, meaning the audience looks and listens in on the action through an imaginary wall. The actors in these plays perform in a **representational** style—in other words, as if they are unaware that there is an audience watching.

In a **nonrealistic play**, the characters and/or situations are exaggerated or depart from real life. Nonrealistic plays include fantasies in which plants and animals talk as well as people; symbolic plays where the characters and setting represent ideas; and romantic plays where life is pictured ideally and imaginatively, dreams come true, and the language is often poetic. Examples of nonrealistic plays include Christopher Durang's *The Actor's Nightmare* (fantasy and symbolic), Rostand's *Cyrano de Bergerac* and Shakespeare's *A Midsummer Night's Dream* (romantic), and Caryl Churchill's *Far Away* (fantasy and symbolic). In many nonrealistic plays, actors use a **presentational**, or direct address, approach—meaning that they break the stage illusion by speaking directly to the audience.

Surreal scenic elements and lighting reveal the mood of David Saar's play *The Yellow Boat*, about Saar's real-life son's death from AIDS.

Plot and Structure

To analyze your character effectively, you must analyze the play's plot and structure. Like any good work of literature, a play's plot is made up of a series of incidents linked by a theme. It involves conflict (struggle) that is revealed through action, which leads to the dramatic turning point, or climax, and then to a logical conclusion, or resolution.

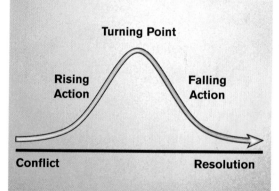

The basic structure of most plays includes these five elements.

The Actor and the Traditional Play Structure

In order to really understand drama, an actor must understand the importance of a play's structure. The structure of a play is what holds together the characters' actions and words. By analyzing the elements of a story's structure, the actor has important insight into the plot, the theme, and his character's motivations. Study the elements that follow as they relate to the actor.

1 **Conflict** As you know, in most plays, the plot is built around a conflict, a problem or struggle of some sort. The conflict may be between characters, between a character and some object or event, or between a character and the character's inner self. It is your job as an actor to assess your character's role in the conflict and to determine how your character should act and react as the conflict intensifies.

2 **Rising Action** (or complications) Any additional events that stem from the conflict are important elements for you to be aware of and to think about in terms of the forward movement of the play and your character's role in it.

3 **Turning Point** This is the highest point of emotional intensity in the drama. It usually occurs near the end of the play. Here, the main character will most likely take an action to end the conflict. All the play's action leads to this point, and again, as an actor, you must be aware of the momentum that has been generated to this point and adjust your performance intensity accordingly.

4 **Falling Action** (also called the **denouement**) These are the events that happen after the turning point. As an actor, you must adjust your performance to the atmosphere of the denouement.

5 **Resolution** Here is where the complications are worked out. And, although the play is at this point winding toward its conclusion, be careful not to lose your energy as an actor or to slide into sluggish line delivery or posture. Stay with the rhythm and flow of the play, but keep your performance energy high.

Keep in mind that some contemporary playwrights do not adhere to this traditional structure and may omit one or more of these elements.

Mood

The mood of a play is its emotional texture. The audience should sense the play's mood early on—during the rising action. Nearly every aspect of the play contributes to the mood—from the characters to the plot to the design elements.

When you have studied the plot, mood, and structure of the play or scene in which you've been cast, you can at last begin to focus on your particular character and how he or she fits into the play.

Light, setting, and the actor's body language all create a mood of defeat in this scene from *Death of a Salesman*.

After you have read the play once to understand all of its elements, read it again to identify with your specific role. Visualize the action through your character's eyes. Understand your character's behavior and dialogue in view of his or her motivation.

Characterization

In previous chapters, you've learned that making observations, drawing upon your own experience, using your imagination, and investigating the character's internal and external traits all help you understand a given character. To concentrate on knowing your character through and through, use the steps below as you memorize your script.

• Concentrate on your character's internal and external traits via the clues the script provides you. (See Chapter 9, pages 92–93 for more on internal and external traits). Think about people you know who remind you of your character. Discover ways in which your character is like you, and determine how the character is unlike you. Research aspects of your character that are unknown to you.

Theatre Journal
When you create a character, you build a whole new world for yourself. And that means you must learn to look at the world from a different point of view. As an exercise, try to re-examine a very familiar person in your life. Try to see this person in a fresh, new way, then write about what you notice.

- Have a clear sense of what happened to your character before the events depicted in the play. Some actors make complete histories of their character's family life, employment, friendships and alliances, and so on as a way of delving as deeply as possible into the person they are playing.

- Ask yourself what your character wants and what he or she does to get it. Does the character want different things from different people?

- Figure out whose side your character is on. Is yours the central character? Or, does your character oppose the central character in some way? Or, does your character assist the central character? Most characters fall into one of these categories.

- In addition to the dialogue (what your character *says*), you should pay close attention to the stage directions to figure out what your character *does*—and why.

- Pay attention to what the other characters say about your character and how they behave toward him or her.

- Think about how your character *changes* over the course of the play. Does the character experience a major shift—a change of attitude or circumstance? How will you convey this?

- Remember that plays, like real life, are mostly about what *isn't* said. The dialogue of a play can be compared to the tip of an iceberg. What's said represents only a part of the whole story. The information that is implied but not stated by a character is called the **subtext.** For example, consider the character who tells another character, "I hate you! I'm leaving!" but proceeds to stay onstage. What the character *does* contradicts what he or she says—so you can be fairly certain the character is experiencing something besides hatred—perhaps even its exact opposite! The subtext a character conveys is often much more important than what the character actually says.

- Pay special attention to your character's rhythms. Does he or she speak in a staccato manner (short, choppy sentences and fragments) or in long fluid sentences? The way the character speaks is likely to reflect the way the character moves.

Love Your Character!

Acting teachers often tell their students they must "love" their characters. By this they mean that you must respect, understand, and empathize with a character in order to bring life to the role. This does not mean that you as a person would make the same choices the character does, nor does it mean you necessarily approve of the character's actions. But you must attempt to live inside the character's skin—and that's impossible to do if you stand outside and judge him or her. Above all, remember that if you're not fascinated by your character, no one else will be either.

Spotlight on

Cues and Cue Pickup

Cues are the last few words of the speech that precedes yours. Sometimes a sound or movement will be your cue, but generally you take your cue from someone else's lines. A **cue pickup** occurs the minute you begin saying your lines. To pick up your cues at the correct time, you should learn to take a breath before the other actor has finished speaking, so that you are ready to come in with your line.

Most plays call for quick cue pickup, a tempo that holds audience interest and simulates real-life conversation. Quick cue pickup does *not* mean you should race through your lines. Vary each line according to the ideas and emotions it expresses.

Never anticipate your cue. Picking up the phone before it rings or bursting into tears before you hear a piece of bad news can render your acting ridiculous.

If the script indicates an interrupted sentence—in other words, one actor cutting off another actor's line—give special attention to this timing. If someone is to cut in on your speech, make sure that you have concocted a completion for the line, just in case your scene partner doesn't come in right on cue!

In this scene from *The Good Doctor*, the actors must pick up their cues even in unusual body positions.

PREPARE

Choose a Play and a Character

Get together with several classmates and choose a ten-minute play, a scene from a one-act play, or a scene from a full-length play (your teacher may wish to assign a scene to you). Try to read the entire play to understand its general structure and approach. With your group, discuss the mood, basic action, and climax of the play. DO NOT concentrate on your specific role at this time. Work to understand the play as a whole. Then analyze the characters together. Decide how the scene you have chosen relates to the play as a whole.

Next, each of you should study your individual role in the scene. Identify your character's actions, feelings, and words. Work hard to create a vivid character.

Rehearse the Scene

The next step is to come together again to rehearse the scene. As a group, create basic movements and stage business for the scene. When you are not speaking your lines, listen in character to your fellow actors.

After you have read the scene together a few times, have someone time it to be sure you are not exceeding the ten-minute limit.

Memorize Your Lines

Finally, you must memorize your dialogue in the scene. It's impossible to achieve complete character concentration when you still have the script in your hand. When you and your partners have memorized the scene to the point where it runs smoothly, you are ready to perform.

Listening closely to others helps actors remain in character while allowing the audience to focus on the speaker.

PRESENT

Perform Your Group Scene

Choose one person to introduce your scene. This person will also set the scene by providing a bit of background about how this section fits into the larger play. This need not be long; just make sure the audience has enough information to know what's going on. Make sure you have all the necessary props. Once the designated person has introduced the play and given the audience a bit of background, play the scene as you rehearsed it. Stay focused and remain in character throughout.

CRITIQUE

Evaluate Your Classmates' Scene

Evaluate a presentation by one group of classmates. Because the scene represents a team effort, you should evaluate the ensemble as well as the individual performances. Your critique should answer these questions about the group:

- Did the actors work together as an ensemble?

- How did they develop and maintain viable characters?

- What did the actors do to make their characters' motivations and intentions clear?

- Did the actors pick up their cues?

- In what way did the actors establish a consistent mood in the scene?

- Were the relationships between the characters clear?

- Did the actors maintain a consistent style and tone?

Then choose one actor from the scene and evaluate his or her performance using a rating of 1 to 5, with 5 representing "outstanding," 4 representing "very good," 3 representing "good," 2 representing "needs some improvement," and 1 representing "needs much improvement." Use the criteria below to help in your evaluation.

Did the actor

- have a specific goal within the scene?

- listen and respond in character?

- embody the character both physically and vocally?

- have clearly established external traits?

- provide information as to the scene's subtext?

Write a short paragraph explaining why you gave this particular actor the score you did.

Additional Projects

1 Write a prose biography of the character you portrayed in the class project. Include as many facets of the character as possible; for example, you might include family background, level of education, leisure activities, employment status, favorite food, favorite color, most memorable experience, greatest disappointment, and so on. Base your writing on your interpretation of your character within the play.

2 Read a full-length play and write a review of its style, mood, characters, plot, and structure.

3 It is sometimes said that a majority of plots are about one of two things: either a stranger coming to town or a character going on a journey. Write a scene in which three distinctive characters take part in one of these basic plots.

4 Attend a full-length play staged by a professional or amateur group. Write a critique of the play answering the following questions:

- Did the play's theme convey an important idea?

- Did the plot consist of related events that rose to an exciting climax and created a logical conclusion?

- Were the characters true to life? Were they interesting?

- Did the dialogue reveal the characters and enhance the story?

- Was the author's style distinctive?

- Did the audience respond to the play the way you think the author intended them to?

- Did you enjoy the play? Why or why not?

5 Read the scene from *Macbeth* by William Shakespeare found in Unit Eight. Get together with two classmates and choose different parts. Discuss the subtext of this short scene and the emotions and motivations of the characters, as well as its realism and romanticism. Work on the scene together.

Theatre Then and Now

Elizabethan Drama to Epic Theatre

William Shakespeare and the Elizabethan Drama

The Elizabethan period began in 1558 with the coronation of Queen Elizabeth I of England. The period ended with her death in 1602. Although many people think of William Shakespeare (1564–1616) as *the* Elizabethan dramatist, there were a number of other fine playwrights creating work during this period, such as Christopher Marlowe and Ben Johnson. Marlowe (1564–1593) was considered by many of his contemporaries to be Shakespeare's equal. Unfortunately, Marlowe died in a barroom knife fight at the age of twenty-nine.

Because there was no artificial lighting, performances were often held outdoors in the afternoon. Performances that took place at night were lit by huge standing torches. No women were allowed to perform in the plays. Young boys often played female roles as it was thought they could better assume the character and movement of a woman. They would speak in lighter voices and use exaggerated feminine gestures.

Many of Shakespeare's plays were first seen in the original Globe Theatre.

Shakespeare's plays featured many highborn or noble characters. The language is rich and layered with images. Low-born characters were often used for comic relief or as the hero's sidekick.

William Shakespeare

The style of acting during Shakespeare's time was much more overblown than actors use today. Actors were not much concerned with rendering subtle emotions. They tended to shout their lines, which in fact was usually necessary given the size of the theatre. The actors concentrated on getting the play's words and ideas across. After all, as Hamlet says, "The play's the thing . . . ."

Bertolt Brecht and the Epic Theatre

Bertolt Brecht (1898–1956) was a German poet and playwright. His plays were openly political and usually addressed issues such as poverty, war, and class struggle. He rejected the principles of classical drama and realism and did not believe a play needed a dramatic climax. He often employed direct address to the audience as well as songs to comment on the play's action. His theory of drama came to be known as epic theatre. It is best illustrated in his plays *Mother Courage, The Good Woman of Setzuan,* and *The Caucasian Chalk Circle.* Above all, Brecht believed that drama should not try to create the illusion of reality, but should exist on its own terms. Rather than attempting to persuade the audience of a play's *reality,* Brecht tried to distance viewers. In this way, he thought that the audience would think for themselves.

Achieving this type of alienation effect, as it came to be called, required a highly stylized performance method. Brecht believed in the idea of argument as opposed to plot. Traditional plots, Brecht believed,

attempted to implicate the viewer in the action as opposed to allowing the viewer to remain an outside spectator. In Brecht's view, the epic theatre's detached methods aroused the viewer to take action—to take a side in the argument. Brecht's views on characterization are perhaps best illustrated by this quote: "The actor has to discard whatever means he has learnt of getting the audience to identify itself with the characters which he plays . . . . At no moment must he go so far as to be wholly transformed into the character played . . . ."

Bertolt Brecht

A classic of epic theatre, Brecht's *Mother Courage* depicts the lengths to which people will go to survive during wartime.

Chapter

11 Dramatic Roles

Many actors believe that dramatic roles are the real "meat" of acting. Plays that treat their subject seriously are placed into three broadly defined categories— tragedy, social drama, and melodrama. While exploring each of these dramatic forms, you will acquire the tools to take on serious dramatic roles yourself.

Project Specs

Project Description For this assignment, you and a classmate will write and perform a three- to five-minute dramatic scene.

Purpose to use strong characterization and controlled emotional intensity

Materials an outline of your scene or the Dramatic Roles Activity Sheet your teacher provides

Theatre Terms

antagonist
catharsis
melodrama
protagonist
regional accent
social drama
tragedy
tragic flaw

On Your Feet

Think about a difficult, sad, or dramatic event that happened to a friend or family member. Capture the emotions that event holds for you in one sentence. Practice saying the sentence out loud, taking on the character of your friend or family member. Create a specific posture and facial expression for the character, and then repeat the line until you can "hear" the person on whom you based the character.

Donald Sinden creates one of the most dramatic roles of all time as the title character in *Othello*.

PREVIEW

The Elements of Drama

Dramatic productions are categorized in three ways: as tragedy, social (or serious) drama, or melodrama. Each type has its own unique characteristics and each requires its own set of acting skills.

Greek Tragedy

Considered to be the highest form of drama, **tragedy** magnifies the intensity of profound human emotions to tell the story of a person who achieves a sense of nobility by means of unswerving sacrifice and/or suffering. In classic Greek tragedy, the **protagonist** (or main character) struggles with a particular problem or an opposing force (the **antagonist**) and eventually goes down in defeat—usually death—but not before achieving an aura of dignity. Because of the depth of a tragedy's emotion, the audience tends to experience horror, pity, and deep sadness, which are typically followed by a **catharsis,** the sense of calm that comes from purging such emotions.

Also typical in Greek tragedies is a tragic hero who comes into conflict with the gods. The audience always knew the plot of these classic myths, but was eager to see how a particular playwright would handle the relationship between the gods and the hero. Violence, as such, was never witnessed by the audience in these tragedies. The chorus or a messenger would report the violent action. The tragedies of Sophocles (c. 495-406 B.C.), such as *Oedipus Rex* and *Antigone,* are perfect examples of classic Greek tragedy.

Shakespeare's Tragedies

The Elizabethan playwrights ignored the classical tragic form, for the most part. The tragedies of William Shakespeare (1564-1616) often focused on a protagonist at odds with himself. This often highborn hero has a **tragic flaw,** a weakness of character, which ultimately brings about his or her own destruction. Shakespeare and his contemporaries often mixed comedy into their tragedies; and music, song,

and dance were sometimes part of a scene as well. Dialogue that was intellectual or meaningful would be presented in iambic pentameter (ten syllables with five stresses to the line); the uneducated or foolish often spoke in prose. The tragic universe of Shakespeare's plays often highlights a disrupted life that seeks to regain order within a spiritual context. *Hamlet, Macbeth,* and *King Lear* are fine examples of Shakespearean tragedy.

Liam Neeson plays the flawed but courageous John Proctor in Arthur Miller's *The Crucible*.

Serious Drama Today

Of course, actors are still taking on the plays of the Greeks and Elizabethans, but there are many contemporary plays that investigate issues similar to those in the tragedies of the past. This serious drama, also called **social drama,** tackles subjects that do not fall strictly into the category of tragedy—the everyday struggles and failures of ordinary folk in the hard-edged landscape of the 20th and 21st centuries. Arthur Miller's heroes, in such plays as *All My Sons* and *Death of a Salesman,* struggle to maintain their dignity and humanity while acting in immoral ways. Lawrence and Lee's *Inherit the Wind* and Rebecca Gilman's *Boy Gets Girl* also explore important contemporary issues. In *Waiting for Godot* and *Endgame,* Samuel Beckett's antiheroes come to realize the modern world is meaningless and chaotic.

All of these dramatists point out the problems people face today, without necessarily suggesting solutions to them.

Building a Dramatic Character

There are four essential elements when it comes to acting in a tragedy or a serious drama.

The actor must convey:

1 strong characterization

2 emotional intensity

3 simplicity of objective

4 motivation

In serious and tragic plays, the characters are usually fully drawn individuals who have one dominant trait that the actor must project. Hamlet is indecisive; Othello is jealous; Anne Sullivan in *The Miracle Worker* is stubborn and determined. The protagonist of just about any tragedy or serious play is in some definable way very impressive. This is the result of not only the character's indomitable spirit but also because he or she has the courage to stand up against a great obstacle. It should go without saying that the antagonist must also be played with strength to provide an adequate conflict for the protagonist. Keep this in mind as you prepare to write your scene.

Using Emotion

The intense emotions called for in dramatic roles must be portrayed with utter conviction and sincerity while maintaining the poise necessary to put the play across. To create these emotions, you may need to use emotional recall. This is the process by which you use the memory of emotional incidents from your own past and transfer them to the similarly emotional situation your character is in. To do this, you must focus on the details of the past event and try to visualize and feel the

Gay Nineties melodramas such as *Lily, the Felon's Daughter* feature stock characters such as Lord Monty, played by Kent Streed, a suitor with slicked-down hair and an offering of roses.

emotion all over again. Then try to create that same emotion in the character. (See Chapter 2 for more on recall.)

Melodrama

Melodrama is a type of play that focuses more on cliff-hanging action and tugs on the heartstrings than on character development or society's real problems. The purpose of a **melodrama** is to create great suspense and excitement in the audience. It was very popular in the United States in the early 1800s and is still performed by small theatre groups and high school drama groups across the country. Most melodramas have a happy ending. Examples of contemporary melodramas include Frederick Knott's *Dial M for Murder,* Agatha Christie's *The Mousetrap,* and Maxwell Anderson's *The Bad Seed.*

A subcategory of melodrama are the Gay Nineties melodramas (meaning they were written and first performed during the 1890s). These plays have exaggerated values of right and wrong. They feature such stock types as the mustachioed villain and the sweet, innocent heroine. Though modern audiences find these plays humorous, in their time such works also aroused tears.

Using Regional Accents

A **regional accent** is the particular sound of speech of a region. Inexperienced actors are not usually cast in roles for which an accent is necessary, but even actors with plenty of experience can be frustrated by tricky speech patterns associated with particular places.

If you are cast in a role that requires you to speak with an accent of a certain region, you can, of course, get a book on the subject, but a better choice would be to listen to a native speaker, either in person or on tape.

To do a credible accent, you will need to develop your ear. For example, imagine that you have been cast as the cockney flower girl, Eliza Doolittle, in *Pygmalion* by George Bernard Shaw (or the musical version of that play, *My Fair Lady*). You might get a videotape of the play, or you might find a tape that includes a lower-class urban English accent. Listen for specific sounds in the accent and think about how they differ from your normal speech. You will need to figure out the phonetic differences so that you can re-create them consistently. In fact, consistency is the most crucial element when it comes to developing a believable accent. When you perform, it's important to give the suggestion of the accent rather than concerning yourself with making every sound recognizable as being from a particular place. The important thing is that you be clearly understood.

Most actors take on the acquisition of an accent privately, not during rehearsal time. However, professional theatres sometimes employ coaches to help the actors in this regard. These experts work with the cast to hone and perfect their speech and create the kind of consistent accents that audiences expect.

Here's How
To Stay in Control

When acting in an intense dramatic play, you may feel the need to drain yourself completely during the climactic scene. Resist this impulse! To present the strongest characterization possible, you need to maintain control. Always hold something in reserve. Some acting teachers suggest that you "give it ninety percent—and hold back ten percent." If you do this, the audience will think you're acting with abandon, when in reality you will be in complete control—able to stay focused and aware.

And don't turn on those water works, either. Many young actors feel that they must work themselves up to tears to get the audience to feel the emotion of a sad scene. But good actors know that succumbing completely to tears can have a distancing effect on the audience. Uncontrolled tears can also lead to inaudibility. The better choice for an actor is almost always to work against breaking into tears. An actor struggling against falling apart creates tension; that tension draws the audience in.

PREPARE

Ready, Set, Write!

What would you consider to be one of the most tragic events that could happen to someone? You will have the chance to dramatize your idea in this presentation.

First you will work with a partner to brainstorm your scene. The suggestions on the following page may help you. Then improvise back and forth, and outline the scene and some of the dialogue for both characters. You may wish to use a tape recorder so that you can remember your best lines. When you have completed the outline of your scene, go over it and reshape it so that each moment is clear and distinct.

Ready, Set, Act!

Now rehearse your scene. Create basic movement, and critique each other's performance as you go through the script. You may find that some of the lines you wrote do not sound quite right as you rehearse. Edit these lines accordingly.

Remember to employ emotional recall and sense memory to help you fully realize the situation. Concentrate on what your character *does,* rather than on the specific emotional content. Stay in character, focus on the objectives, and respond to your partner. Time your scene to be sure it remains within the three- to five-minute time range.

PRESENT

Act in a Dramatic Scene

When either your own or your partner's name is called, give the outline of your scene or the Dramatic Roles Activity Sheet to your teacher before you begin your presentation. Then introduce your scene briefly. You only need to give the audience enough information to allow them to understand the basic situation.

Take a moment before you begin. This "moment before" is a handy tool for actors. It allows you to focus more completely before you launch into a scene, and it allows the audience time to settle down.

Perform your scene. Stay focused and remain in character throughout. When you are finished, take a brief bow and return to your seat.

Suggestions for Dramatic Scenes

- A mother learns that her only child is critically injured.
- A brilliant painter finds that she is going blind.
- A young man about to be married finds out he has a terminal disease.
- A father is sentenced to life in prison for a crime he did not commit.
- A woman with a proud family background discovers that her brother has committed a serious crime.

CRITIQUE

Evaluate Your Classmates' Scene

Evaluate a presentation by one pair of your classmates using a scale of 1 to 5, with 5 being "outstanding" and 1 being "needs much improvement." Your evaluation should be confined to the performance, not the writing. Ask yourself these questions:

- How were the presenters able to convey the drama of the scene?

- How well did the actors convey their characters' objectives?

- In what way did the actors' movements and gestures impact the scene?

- Did the actors stay in character, listen to each other, and respond throughout the scene?

Write a short paragraph explaining why you gave this pair the score you did.

Theatre Journal

Skim through the daily newspaper. Find a story that has serious elements, such as a fire, a car accident, or some other life-or-death incident. In your journal, write a short account of the event from the point of view of someone either directly or peripherally involved. Try to think about the events as they might seem to that person.

Spotlight on

The Worst Romeo Ever

Over the course of history, plenty of actors have made a mess of Shakespeare's lines. But many theatre historians agree that Robert Coates was perhaps the worst offender. Coates (1772–1848) had no talent but plenty of money—enough to finance vanity productions to star in. He produced *Romeo and Juliet* often and, to the utter despair of his various Juliets, he always played Romeo. Audiences loved Coates or, more accurately, they loved to use him for target practice by lobbing rotten fruits and vegetables at him during the show. In the scene in which Romeo discovers that Juliet has killed herself, audiences would jeer at Coates and yell such comments as "Why don't YOU die?" The critics weren't kind to Coates either. Reviews of his performances were often descriptions of the rioting audience and the flying foodstuffs.

Robert Coates

Additional Projects

1 Dramatize a dramatic event from your life or from your family history.

2 Improvise serious group scenes that build to a climax. Your scenes should include classical, contemporary, realistic, and nonrealistic elements. Here are some suggestions for sample scenes:

- A group of miners working underground senses something is wrong. As they prepare to go up, rocks begin to cave in on them.

- A group of striking workers are demonstrating outside an office building. They see that other workers have arrived and are crossing the picket line. Shouting ensues.

- A political speaker is heckled at an outdoor rally until bedlam breaks loose.

- A bus driver picks up various passengers. One woman appears to have wings. A man is able to read the minds of other passengers.

3 Write a short dramatic monologue (a long speech given by one character) and present it to the class.

4 Memorize either the monologue from *Saint Joan* by George Bernard Shaw or the monologue from *The Janitor* by August Wilson found in Unit Eight. Present the monologue to the class. Think about the accent you might use to convey your character.

Master of the Craft

Kenneth Branagh

Born in 1960 in Belfast, Ireland, actor Kenneth Branagh was the second of three children born to a working-class family. When he was still a boy, his family moved to England. At the age of fifteen, a crucial event took place in Branagh's life: He saw English theatre legend Derek Jacobi play Hamlet. From then on, he knew he wanted to be an actor.

At eighteen he was accepted into one of the best theatre schools in the world—the Royal Academy of Dramatic Art. Once out of school he was immediately cast in a play on the West End (London's version of Broadway). The Royal Shakespeare Company subsequently hired him into its repertory company, and at the age of twenty-three, he took on the pivotal role of Prince Hal in Shakespeare's *Henry V.* He became an immediate sensation, winning many awards for his performance.

Kenneth Branagh, as Hamlet, with Kate Winslet.

In 1987, Branagh and a friend started a theatre company of their own, the Renaissance Theatre Company. Branagh's productions of the Shakespeare plays *Twelfth Night* and *Much Ado About Nothing* won rave reviews. Then Branagh fulfilled one of his many ambitions by playing Hamlet. Shortly thereafter, in 1989, he directed and starred in a film version of *Henry V.* The success of the film brought Branagh unexpected international fame.

He was quickly scooped up to make several more films.

Kenneth Branagh has, of course, had some failures along the way, but he is an artist whose ambition is evenly balanced with his great talent. He continues to challenge himself as an artist, acting in and directing film, television, and theatre. In 2001, he directed a West End hit, *The Play What I Wrote,* which won multiple Olivier Awards (the English equivalent of the Tony Award). The play opened on Broadway in 2003.

Branagh as Prince Hal in *Henry V.*

Theatre Then and Now

A Role for All Eras: Hamlet, Prince of Denmark

For more than 300 years, actors have coveted the role of Hamlet, the brilliant, angry, indecisive title character of Shakespeare's tragedy. The role's richness, humor, and emotional depth have challenged generations of actors.

Edmund Kean (1787–1833) was the leading English actor of the early 1800s. He specialized in tragic roles and was best known for his many portrayals of Hamlet. He had many opportunities to sharpen his skills in this role—he first played it when he was only fourteen years old. Extremely charismatic, Kean brought romanticism to every role. His acting was once described by a critic as "quietly imploding before his audience." The great poet Coleridge said of Kean, "Seeing him act was like reading Shakespeare by flashes of lightning." Kean's reputation as a great interpreter of Shakespeare was assured. His excessive drinking and wild lifestyle earned him quite another reputation, however, and eventually it took its toll. He died in his mid-forties.

Edwin Booth (1833–1893) "An actor is a sculptor who carves in snow." So said Edwin Booth with regard to the fleeting nature of the theatre: Once a scene is played, it is gone forever.

Edwin Booth played the role of Hamlet for a remarkable 100 consecutive nights. The melancholy Dane was a role for which Booth's appearance, voice, and bearing were ideally suited. Slender and darkly handsome, Booth possessed a voice that was both musical and tempered with a natural air of reserve. His acting style, quieter than most other actors of his day, became increasingly sensitive and subdued.

His career was tarnished in 1865 when his brother, John Wilkes Booth, assassinated President Lincoln. After that, Edwin did not reappear onstage until January 1866, when he again played Hamlet. The audience's applause after this performance showed their conviction that the glory of one Booth brother had not been eclipsed by the infamy of the other. Edwin Booth's final stage appearance was in Brooklyn, New York, as Hamlet in 1891.

Sir Laurence Olivier (1907–1989).
"If I wasn't an actor, I think I'd have gone mad. You have to have extra voltage, some extra temperament to reach certain heights. Art is a little bit larger than life, and I think you probably need a little touch of madness." These are the words of legendary English actor Laurence Olivier. He began his career in 1926 as a member of the Birmingham Repertory Theatre. He was known for his physical athleticism and his dazzling vocal ability and range—particularly in Shakespearean roles. There is a famous story that shines a light on Olivier's acting technique. While making the 1976 film *Marathon Man,* Olivier found out that his costar, American actor Dustin Hoffman, had been preparing for his role by going without food and sleep. Hoffman wanted to look and feel just like the character he was playing—a torture victim. Olivier, mystified, asked Hoffman, "My dear boy, why don't you just *act?*" Olivier's film version of *Hamlet,* which he starred in and directed, is available on videotape.

Laurence Olivier as Hamlet in 1948.

It won Oscars for Best Picture and Best Actor in 1948. In 1970, Olivier was made a lord, the first member of the theatrical profession to receive such an honor. Olivier's extraordinary ability to illuminate the words and ideas of Shakespeare won him a well-deserved place in theatre and film history.

Edwin Booth as Hamlet, the "Melancholy Dane."

Chapter
12 Comic Roles

It is said that tragedy is when you fall down the stairs and comedy is when someone else does. It's not that we enjoy seeing others suffer—it's that we know how to laugh at ourselves—after it stops hurting. Good comedy requires perspective: The comic actor presents a character's misfortune while providing just enough emotional distance to let us laugh. It's a juggling act, but when it works, it's magic.

Project Specs

Project Description You will write and perform a comic monologue of three to five minutes in length.

Purpose to develop a sense of comic presentation and timing

Materials a list of character traits that describe your character or the Comic Roles Activity Sheet your teacher provides

Theatre Terms
burlesque
comedy of manners
farce
high comedy
hold
low comedy
middlebrow comedy
parody
rule of three
satire
travesty

On Your Feet

Think of a funny story from your childhood. It can be an actual experience or something funny you once read or saw. Practice telling the story, then tell it to a friend and ask for feedback as to what the friend found funny.

The play *A Flea in Her Ear* employs elements of burlesque to create its comic effect.

PREVIEW

What's So Funny?

No two people have funny bones in exactly the same spot. What some people find hilarious, others find painful or sad. What sends you rolling on the floor might only nudge a smile out of the person next to you. In fact, humor varies so greatly that it can be classified in several different genres.

Low comedy, which is physical and sometimes vulgar, includes outlandish, exaggerated forms of humor such as **farce** and **burlesque.** Both genres make use of oddly harmless violence. Farce stretches common plots to the very edge of believability through exaggeration and surprise. Burlesque uses a great deal of exaggeration too—but it's directed at a person, custom, artifact, or event. A burlesque can take the form of a **travesty** and poke fun at respected subjects. It can **parody** a famous work

Arsenic and Old Lace is an example of a middlebrow situation comedy.

by imitating the author's style in a humorous way. The loftier the subject, the more likely it will become a target for burlesque. As you may have guessed, burlesque and farcical characters tend to be fairly extreme in their appearance, movements, and reactions. They often don't think they are being funny, but their circumstance and habits are laughable.

Middlebrow comedy includes more plot-based, sentimental genres, such as romantic comedy, situation comedy, and sentimental comedy. These genres may provoke chuckles and smiles, but they also encourage weeping and other emotional responses. Characters in these comedies are more realistic, though their situations and responses can still be quite broad.

High comedy includes **satire** and **comedy of manners.** Satire makes fun of individual people and their follies in an attempt to change their foolish behavior. A comedy of manners, such as Sheridan's *The School for Scandal*, often makes fun of upper-class pretentiousness and the accepted standards of

The Rule of Three

If there is one thing comic writers and comedians hold sacred, it's the **rule of three.** It goes like this: Pratfalls, accidents, misunderstandings, and similar "schticks" are funny only three times in a row. After that, they tend to fall flat. No one knows why exactly; they just know that fourth time won't get a laugh.

What's the exception to the rule? The rule of three times three. Sometimes, a play offers an opportunity to use the rule of three on three separate occasions. On the third occasion, you might get away with adding a fourth surprise—repetition. After the third set of three, you may actually go for a fourth time. The schtick is funny the fourth time, because it's not expected.

Oscar Wilde's *The Importance of Being Earnest* is a perfect example of a comedy of manners.

the wealthy. Both these genres appeal to the intelligence of their audience. They poke fun at political situations, cultural habits, and entrenched attitudes. The more you know about the subject of a satire and how these comedies approach this subject, the more you can appreciate the characters' sly and subtle sarcasm. Characters in these genres must be fairly realistic and restrained, yet quirky and witty enough to provoke laughter.

What do almost all comic actors have in common? Commitment. No matter how ridiculous their situation. . . they take their acting seriously!

Engaging the Audience

Obviously, drama and comedy have some things in common. However, some necessary techniques are particular to comedy. A comic writer and performer must engage an audience in the comic character, employing at least some of the elements below.

- Be sure that the audience identifies with your character.

- The audience should feel that it knows something your character doesn't.

- Help the audience feel superior to your character.

- Throw in the unexpected just when the audience is least expecting it.

- Invert the logic of a situation by doing what seems illogical. For example, two enemies might hug in the middle of an argument.

- Juxtapose two opposite things to heighten confusion. For example, pair a short, fat person with a tall thin one, or create a character who loves kittens but is full of rage.

- Use rapid-fire dialogue and movement.

- Remember the Rule of Three.

Once an audience starts to respond, the actor must remember to **hold** for laughs. This means you must pause a bit to wait until the laughing dies down. If you speak and act over the laughing, the audience will start to restrain their laughter in order to follow the action, or they may lose an important point in the dialogue. If, however, you freeze—while staying in character and focusing on the situation at hand—you can continue when the laughter subsides. This allows the laughter to build and, perhaps, fill the house.

PREPARE

The Comic Edge

Comic playwrights such as Oscar Wilde and Tom Stoppard have created characters full of wit, charm, and snappy dialogue to comment on the social pretensions of their times. While making fun of his characters in *The Importance of Being Earnest,* Wilde also imbued them with such charm and grace that the audience couldn't help but be fond of them. Stoppard's brilliant use of language in *Rosencrantz and Guildenstern Are Dead* also endears the audience to this pair of rogues.

It is very important that comedy stays on the edge of what is considered safe and polite. Too polite equals boring, and too edgy may offend the audience. The comic character must hold the audience in a tenuous balance between the two. A good comedy makes fun of the foibles and pretensions of the audience while also recognizing that we all share these faults.

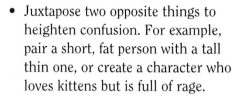

Gary Oldman, Tim Roth, and Richard Dreyfus in *Rosencrantz and Guildenstern Are Dead.*

Find Your Comic Character

You too must try to create in your comic character someone who is flawed in some way—silly, vain, snobbish, gossipy, for example—but someone who also draws the audience in and arouses their interest. At the left are a few suggestions to help you find your character and create your monologue.

Think about yourself as the character in your monologue. How is your character different from the other characters that might be in this situation? How can you emphasize the uniqueness of your character? What surprises can you inject into your character's speech or actions?

Make a list of your character's traits or use the Comic Roles Activity Sheet provided by your teacher. Refer to these notes as you write a rough description of your character's activities in the scene. You can write this first draft more as an outline than a monologue. Then read your first draft aloud to a family member, friend, or even the mirror. Based on what was funny and what was not funny, write a new draft with specific lines and stage directions. Don't give up. It may take several drafts to get the comic monologue you are happy with.

Rehearse your monologue until you are sure of your character, actions, and lines. Your audience will enjoy the scene only if they can relax—confident that you are well prepared. Do not exceed the five-minute time limit.

Suggestions for Comedy Characters

- a prim person visiting a tattoo or piercing parlor
- Beethoven at a rave
- a sedate man buying women's lingerie in an exclusive store
- a parent with four children, arms full of bundles, trying to find change for the bus
- a tourist in Hawaii eager to learn the hula
- a parent teaching a sixteen-year-old to drive the family car
- a person trying to build a bookcase using directions in a foreign language

Theatre Journal

Next time you embarrass yourself, stop as soon as you are able and make a note of the event. Analyze what it was that made the event funny to others. Think about the kinds of characters who might find themselves in such a situation and the circumstances in which it might occur. Consider ways to make the event funnier and then rehearse it as a comic bit!

PRESENT

Perform a Comic Monologue

When your name is called, give your list of character traits or the Activity Sheet to your teacher and walk quietly to the playing area.

Present your comic scene to the class. Remember the importance of engaging your audience. When you have finished your monologue, pause, and then bow politely before leaving the playing area.

Here's How
To Deal with the Giggles

Of course, if you remain focused, you will not get the giggles during a comic performance. But momentary lapses happen to everyone. If it happens to you, bring yourself back into your character using any of the following methods:

1 Tell yourself the situation is laughable. Let your character be overtaken by disbelief.

2 As the character, tell yourself—and communicate by your actions or gestures—that you simply cannot believe the circumstances. If you must, repeat them to yourself, in order to bring your character's situation back to the center of your awareness.

3 Turn your laughter into a character trait. Become a character who laughs, cries, and reacts uncontrollably.

CRITIQUE

Evaluate a Classmate's Monologue

Choose one of the monologues presented in class and evaluate your classmate's comedy performance. Use a rating system based on 5 points in your evaluation, with "outstanding" being a 5; "well done" being a 4; "fair" being a 3; "needs some improvement" being a 2; and "needs much improvement" being a 1. To give an accurate, well-supported critique, ask yourself these questions:

- Was this a performance of a low, middlebrow, or high comedy?

- What genre or genres of comedy could I identify in this performance?

- What elements of humor did the performer use (for example, the rule of three, sarcasm, and so on)?

- Was one moment particularly funny? Which one, and why?

Write an explanation of how you arrived at the score you gave.

Additional Projects

1 Translate the funny story you told at the beginning of this lesson—or some other funny experience—into a humorous scene.

2 With a partner, research an audio library in order to find and learn a classic comedy routine. Rehearse it thoroughly and then perform it for the class.

3 In a group with two or three others, read a classic farce such as *Tartuffe* by Molière or *What the Butler Saw* by Joe Orton and discuss the humorous elements it contains. Work on a scene you find particularly funny, and then present it to the class.

4 Read a comedy of manners. Then memorize and present a humorous two- to three-minute monologue from it. The following plays are possible sources for monologues: *The Women* by Clare Boothe Luce, *Blithe Spirit* by Noel Coward, *The Importance of Being Earnest* by Oscar Wilde, or *The School for Scandal* by Richard Brinsley Sheridan.

5 Read the scene from *The Importance of Being Earnest* by Oscar Wilde or the scene from *The Imaginary Invalid* by Molière found in Unit Eight. Choose a character, and then write a short description of how you would play this character. Include physical details.

"Laughter seems like a trifle, yet it has a power ... that is well-nigh irresistible; it often changes the tendency of the greatest affairs, as it very often dissipates hatred and anger."

–Quintilian, Roman orator

Master of the Craft

Lily Tomlin

"All my life, I always wanted to be somebody. Now I see that I should have been more specific."

–Lily Tomlin

Mary Jean Tomlin didn't know she wanted to be a famous comedian when she was growing up in Detroit, Michigan, but she did enjoy gags. In fact, when she ordered gag items from the back of a comic book and couldn't pay for them, her mother paid for the package and made her do odd jobs until she could pay the money back. Such is the price of comedy.

When she got older, Tomlin didn't try acting until her second year of college at Michigan's Wayne State University. She appeared in student productions, including a variety show, where she presented a character called "The Tasteful Lady," which she still plays today.

Tomlin left Wayne State after her junior year and moved to New York. Beginning in 1960, she worked during the day at temporary jobs and performed in cabarets at night. Tomlin's career caught fire in 1969, when she was cast in the television comedy revue *Laugh-In.* There, she developed some of her classic characters, including Ernestine, the obnoxious telephone operator, and Edith Ann, the precocious child who tells outlandish stories ending with "And that's the truth!"

Tomlin has appeared in comic and dramatic roles in movies and television for more than thirty years. She has a recurring role on TV's *The West Wing*, and she continues to tour and perform onstage. Her most celebrated work is her one-woman show entitled *The Search for Signs of Intelligent Life in the Universe,* which was written for her by Jane Wagner.

If flexibility and creativity are keys to a successful life, then Lily Tomlin has a pocketful of keys. But she is not overly impressed with success. "The trouble with the rat race," says Tomlin, "is that even if you win, you're still a rat!"

Lily Tomlin as Ernestine.

Theatre Then and Now

Great Comic Playwrights

Molière (1622–1673)

Jean-Baptiste Poquelin's father was a well-respected court upholsterer. His mother was aristocratic and devout in her religion. Poquelin was well on his way to a comfortable life at court—except for one thing. He was smitten by theatre.

He was also smitten by Madeleine Bejart, who was an actress. So he changed his name to Molière, probably to avoid embarrassing his family, and founded a theatre troupe called The Illustrious Theatre.

Unfortunately, The Illustrious Theatre was not very good. Fortunately, the troupe decided to do something about it. They left their failures behind in Paris and traveled from town to town for twelve years, honing their skills.

Molière began writing plays for the company, and the plays began to find success. Then, in 1658, Molière and his company were invited to perform for King Louis XIV in Paris. Molière asked if the company might present a play of his own. That play, *The Love-Sick Doctor,* so delighted the king that he gave the company the title of Troupe

Molière at work.

de Monsieur and granted them the use of the Hotel du Petit Bourbon, one of the most important theatres in Paris.

Over the next twenty-four years, Molière's plays included such classics as *The Imaginary Invalid, The Misanthrope, The School for Wives,* and *Tartuffe.* They ridiculed powerful courtiers, clergymen, and tragedians of the time. But as the plays ripened from clever satirical farces into comedies of manners, they came to have a lasting impact on theatre and on society as a whole. Molière's work earned him powerful enemies who tried to destroy his career. But his enemies were unsuccessful, and his controversial plays are still performed today.

"The more we love our friends, the less we flatter them. It is by excusing nothing that pure love shows itself."

—Molière

Neil Simon (1927–)

Neil Simon has always been devoted to comedy. He got his first major childhood injury by laughing so hard he fell off a stone wall. He earned his childhood nickname, Doc, through his accurate imitation of the family doctor. In the 1940s, he co-founded a comedy team with his brother Danny and began writing comedy sketches for radio and television personalities.

In 1961, Simon opened his first play, *Come Blow Your Horn,* on Broadway. He followed up the first play with *Barefoot in the Park* and *The Odd Couple,* both of which became popular hits. In 1966, when Simon's *The Star-Spangled Girl* opened at the Plymouth Theatre, he had four plays running on Broadway at the same time.

Audience members loved Simon's plays from the start, but critics complained that Simon's characters were not as developed as they might be. So, over the years, Neil Simon deepened his work. Once, he says, he tried to figure out what kinds of things were funny. Now he tries to think about serious things he can write about in a humorous way.

Neil Simon

"It was my [low] SAT scores that led me into my present vocation in life, comedy."
—Neil Simon

This approach has been successful. Simon's *Biloxi Blues* won a Tony award for Best Drama in 1985. In 1991, he won both a Pulitzer and a Tony award for *Lost in Yonkers.* Today, Simon enjoys double good fortune: popularity and professional respect. Even so, he won't rest on his laurels. He continues to write at least five days a week, almost every week of the year.

Richard Dreyfus and Marsha Mason in Neil Simon's play *The Prisoner of Second Avenue.*

Unit Three Review

PREVIEW

Examine the following key concepts previewed in Unit Three.

1 Describe an actor's "dual role."

2 Which of the following are a character's external traits?
a. posture   c. mode of dress   e. voice
b. spiritual qualities   d. mental characteristics

3 What is the fourth wall?

4 Name the five elements of plot structure.

5 What do we call information that is implied but not stated by a character?
a. subculture   b. subtext   c. secret script   d. innuendo   e. gossip

6 Explain how a protagonist differs from an antagonist.

7 Compare social drama to melodrama.

8 What is the difference between low and middlebrow comedies?

9 Which of the following is NOT important when engaging an audience
in a comedy?
a. the audience feels superior to your character
b. the character can be easily identified with
c. the character has a tragic flaw
d. something happens when least expected

PREPARE

Assess your response to the preparation process for projects in this unit.

10 In analyzing your character for the high-stakes scenario, was it easier to
determine the character's traits or motivation? Explain why.

11 As you prepared a scene from a play, was it easier to work out the character's
actions, words, or feelings? Why?

12 How did you go about finding your comic character while preparing for
your comic monologue?

13 Was it easier to prepare your dramatic scene or your comic monologue? Why?

14 Did you find it more satisfying to work out a character on paper or onstage?

PRESENT

Analyze the experience of presenting your work to the class.

15 When you performed your high-stakes scenario, could you feel the audience responding to your situation? How were you able to keep the audience interested?

16 Was it difficult to remain in character while presenting a dramatic scene?

17 Which presentation in this unit did you find the most challenging? Why?

18 Which was more satisfying: acting in a scene you wrote yourself or acting in a scene written by another? Explain why.

CRITIQUE

Evaluate how you go about critiquing your work and the work of others.

19 Did you find it easier to evaluate a comedy or a dramatic work? Why?

20 Describe an insightful critique you received from your teacher or classmate and how it helped your performance.

21 What one thing did most performers have trouble with in creating a character, and what could they do to improve their performance?

EXTENSIONS

- Based on what you learned in this unit, write a short paper entitled: "How I Create a Character." It can be as serious or humorous as you would like.

- Look at the photograph at the right. Write a list of all the things you know about this character just from her appearance.

Unit
Four

The Play: From Vision to Reality

13 The Playwright

Theatre requires more collaboration than any other art form. The playwright, director, designers, actors, and crew must combine their talents to create a final production. The script is the blueprint for the work. In this chapter you will take on the role of playwright.

Project Specs

Project Description You will write and present a five- to ten-minute scenario for a play—complete with theme, plot, and characters in conflict.

Purpose to understand basic dramatic concepts and the structural elements of a play

Materials a one- or two-page scenario for an original play or The Playwright Activity Sheet your teacher provides

Theatre Terms
archetype
climax or turning point
crisis
diction
epic
exposition
inciting incident
plot
resolution
spectacle
staged readings
theme
workshop

On Your Feet

Think about a play you have seen or read. Ask yourself what happened in the play. (What was the plot?) Now ask yourself what the play was about. (What was the main idea, or theme?) Discuss the play's plot and theme with your classmates.

Writing a Drama

Theatre is as old as humankind itself. The earliest forms of theatre emerged from religion and ritual. Ancient people used to act out the success of a hunt or a harvest as well as rituals having to do with life events such as birth, coming of age, and death. Many of these accounts were handed down orally and didn't achieve written form until around 500 B.C., the beginning of the classical age of Greek drama.

The Greeks developed a written body of work, including the **epic** (a long narrative poem that told the story of legendary heroes and their travels and exploits), all of which originated with the oral tradition. The Greeks then developed ways of dramatizing some of these stories for performance. The great philosopher Aristotle (384–322 B.C.) was one of the first to analyze these plays. From watching and reading, Aristotle came up with six basic elements of drama, which he defined in a text called the *Poetics*. These elements still serve as guideposts for playwrights today.

Aristotle's Elements of Drama

Thought This is the central idea the playwright is exploring, which embodies a truth about life. Today, this is usually referred to as the **theme.**

Plot The **plot** is the story of the play, or the progression of the main character, called the *protagonist,* which includes his or her conflict with an opposing force. The manner in which the protagonist deals with this force is what illuminates the play's theme.

Action The central action is the pivotal dramatic moment when the issues and progression of the play become clear through a decision made and carried out by the protagonist.

Diction The language, or the **diction** as Aristotle called it, includes the style, dialect, rhythm, and the actual words of the characters.

American playwright Arthur Miller shares his ideas about the theatre.

The spectacle of the play *Camino Reál* is a treat for the eyes.

and why. The play will involve a central character who becomes involved in a conflict. As in other literary genres, a play's conflict and the progress of the central character can include an **archetype** or two—a character who represents a certain type. An archetype can symbolize universal ideas about human behavior.

There are lots of different ways to write a play. But every playwright must discover a plot (characters in conflict); choose a central course of action that illuminates the theme; select diction appropriate to the desired time period and style; and use sound, scenery, and spectacle to bring the play to vibrant life.

Sound Everything the audience hears in the play—from the words to the music to the sound effects—is included in the sound.

Spectacle Everything the audience sees—including scenery, costuming, dance, pantomime, and swordplay—is included in the **spectacle.**

Note that the first four elements are also found in other literary forms, such as novels and short stories. The last two elements, however, are unique to the theatre.

Why Is It Called a Play?

The answer is simple. A play is exactly that—an event carried out with the spontaneity, intense concentration, and commitment of children at play.

But *writing* a play requires planning the entire course of action—what happens

Theatre Journal

As a playwright, you are a student of human nature—and what better human can you practice on than yourself? Spend some time analyzing an incident from your life. Perhaps it was a comment someone made to you that bothered or confused you. Maybe you did something that made you proud or that you regret. In your journal, write about the incident until you feel that you have a handle on why it happened and what it means to you.

PREPARE

Gather Ideas for Your Scenario

Many playwrights claim that they do not choose what to write about—instead, they say, ideas and subject matter choose them! You may find the same thing yourself. However, to jumpstart your process, try the following writing exercises to develop an idea for a play.

1 **Find a Subject.** Think of a starting point for your play—a challenging question, an interesting character, or a problem to solve—and write it at the top of a sheet of paper. You may take your idea from a newspaper article, a person you know, an incident from your own life, a story you heard, and so on. Once you have chosen your starting point, take five to ten minutes to freewrite about everything you can think of that might be included in the play. For example, if your idea has to do with a robbery, ask and answer questions for yourself about the perpetrators, the victims, the bystanders, and so on. Where did the robbery take place? Why? What time of year? What time of day? How might personal circumstances drive a person to commit a robbery? What are the consequences of such an action—both legally and morally? Be specific, and include every detail and question you think you might be able to use later.

2 **Create a Character.** Using the information you've created about the subject, think of a character to represent a part of the idea. In the example of the robbery, you might choose the robber, the victim, a relative of either of these, a bystander, and so on. Take five minutes to write a short monologue from this character's point of view. This should open up other areas of thought. It may lead you in any number of directions. For example, you may decide that your play is about how witnessing a crime affects a bystander's life. Or you might decide that it's about the events that led up to the robbery or made it seem necessary. You can write a play about almost anything, as long as your characters and your situation are specific and meaningful to you.

3 **Develop a Conflict.** This is a simple exercise based on the same principles used in many improvisations. Your job here is to let the audience know the "Ws." *Who* is in the scene? *Where* are they? *What* are they doing? The *What* should be the conflict, which creates a problem to be solved. Remember that conflict results when one character's objective, or goal, bumps into an obstacle.

Sample Scene

(A small, cluttered kitchen [where]. MOLLY [who] sits at the table clipping coupons. RAY [who] enters suddenly from outside. He has a cut on his forehead and is very agitated.)

RAY. Ma, I gotta use the car *[what/objective]*.

MOLLY. Raymond.

RAY. I got no time to talk, Ma. Give me the keys.

MOLLY. What's happened?

RAY. Listen, I gotta get out of town for a couple days *[what/objective]*. I'll call you. Keys?

(A silence. RAY shifts uncomfortably under his mother's steady gaze.)

MOLLY. You're not taking my car. You're not going anywhere till you tell me what's going on here, Raymond Joseph *[what/obstacle]*.

(A siren sounds in the distance.)

RAY. You want me to go to jail?! Is that it?

MOLLY. No.

RAY. Then give me the keys.

(He spies the keys on the table and makes a grab for them. MOLLY snatches them away and puts them in her pocket.) [what/obstacle]

MOLLY. Talk to me, Raymond . . . You know I am trying to help you. Please . . .

Read the sample scene above. Notice how much information the scene provides in a small amount of space. Also notice how the tension between the characters is heightened by Molly's refusal to give up the keys and by the sound of the approaching police siren.

Create a one- to two-page scene of your own using the subject, main character, and conflict you devised in the three steps just discussed. Then add a second or third character. Make sure that your situation is driven by conflict between the characters or between a character and some obstacle.

Think About a Scenario

Where will your play go from here? That depends on the statement you are trying to make and the story you want to tell. Now that you have a basic situation, two or more characters, and the conflict or obstacles they must face, you are ready to think about a whole play that might stem from them.

You and a partner were asked to create a scenario for your project in Chapter 5, Movement. For the project in this unit, you will create a more detailed scenario that applies Aristotle's elements of drama. First, you will need to develop the theme. Based on the example of a robbery given previously, the theme might be that crime doesn't pay. Or it might be that desperate situations call for desperate solutions. It could be both of these—and more. Above all, the theme you choose should contain ideas that you care about and are interested in.

Then you must decide who your characters are and what they are trying to do in the play. No matter what your theme is, you must tell a story in which the characters are believable or interesting enough to draw the audience into the play.

As you write your scenario, think about all of the elements on the following page.

You will need a plot, the beginning of which you have already created while developing the play's conflicts. What happens next? What happens after that?

Your scenario must show that the action arises logically from the conflict and leads to a crisis and climax. You have probably discovered the characters' ways of speaking while exploring the theme, the characters themselves, and their conflicts. Also keep in mind the spectacle and sound of your play— in other words, what it will look and sound like.

Keeping all these principles in mind will help you create a scenario that structures the progression of your idea for a play. In Chapter 10, you learned about play structure from the perspective of an actor working on character development. Now we will add a few more elements and look at the play from the perspective of the playwright creating a new work.

1 **Exposition** This is the setup of the play. You learned about the three Ws of exposition previously (Who, Where, and What), and it is important that as a playwright you have a clear idea what your characters' lives were all about before the events of your play begin. In the sample scene on page 142 the **exposition** informs us that Molly is Ray's mother. The scene takes place in her house. It also allows us to see that Ray has committed a crime. This is not stated, but it is strongly implied by the playwright's dialogue and by the actions created in the stage directions for Ray.

2 **Inciting Incident** The event that sets the action on its course is called the **inciting incident.** In the example, the inciting incident is Molly's refusal to give Ray her car keys. Here is where the conflict begins. The playwright must be sure that this conflict has enough dramatic impetus to carry the scene forward, because the rest of the play will spin out from it.

3 **Rising Action** The playwright must carefully build the dramatic tension as characters encounter obstacles to their goals. It is important for the playwright to keep the drama tight and to give the characters ways to help the audience understand how they rationalize their feelings and actions.

4 **Crisis** As the play continues, the playwright must create an event that occurs just at the moment when it seems things could either resolve or get much worse. This is the **crisis.** The playwright must be sure not to infuse in the crisis too much emotional intensity, as this could make the climax to follow seem anticlimactic.

5 **Climax** In the **climax,** which is the high point of the play, the playwright creates a situation in which the protagonist makes an irrevocable decision. The playwright must strive to convince the audience that this highly emotional event will either result in victory or in some way bring an end to the conflict. The climax is also called the *turning point.*

6 **Falling Action** The events after the climax must seem logical and true to the play. This is where the playwright wraps up any loose ends and moves toward the outcome of the play.

7 **Resolution** The end of the story, in which the conflicts are resolved, is called the **resolution.** It takes a light touch in terms of writing. At this point, the playwright must be sure that the audience can see clearly the result of the choice or action of the protagonist.

Write Your Scenario

You are now ready to write your scenario. Go back to your seed idea, then begin to make choices. There is

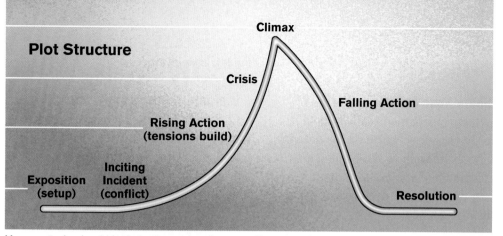

Plot Structure

Climax

Crisis

Falling Action

Rising Action
(tensions build)

Inciting
Incident
(conflict)

Exposition
(setup)

Resolution

Your scenario should include these plot elements. Be aware that not all plays contain all elements.

a benefit to restricting yourself by making strong choices. Each time you make a decision about the play, you rid yourself of other elements that you no longer have to deal with. For example, once you decide that your play takes place in a kitchen, you need no longer worry about other scenic considerations. If your play features only two characters, you know who's going to be doing the talking and when. Once you have boxed in the essential ideas of the play, you have effectively boxed out other nonessential ideas—you've given your play a direction. Your goal is to set the play's structure up so effectively that it will have a logical, effective, and satisfying ending—the seeds of which were planted in the beginning.

You will need to make the following choices:

- **Who is in the play?**
- **Where does it take place?**
- **Who is the protagonist?**
- **Who or what is the antagonistic force?**

- **Where do these two meet?** (the inciting incident)
- **What does the protagonist decide to do** about it?
- **What is the response of the antagonistic force?**
- **What is the critical choice or action of the protagonist** that brings the play to its logical conclusion?
- **What happens after the play ends?** (This should be clear from what happens within the play.)

Your scenario should be a scene-by-scene telling of the story in narrative form. Be sure to come up with a title.

When you have completed your writing, exchange your scenario with a classmate. Discuss each other's work in terms of the progression of the story and the clarity of the theme. Make any necessary changes and create a clean copy.

Practice reading your scenario aloud, and time yourself to be sure it is between five- and ten- minutes long.

PRESENT

Share Your Drama Scenario

When your name is called, hand in a copy of your scenario or the Activity Sheet and walk to the playing area. As always, take a moment to gather yourself by drawing a deep relaxing breath before you begin.

Begin by telling the audience the title of your play. Then read through your scenario. Rhythm and pacing are important when you're reading aloud. Avoid speaking in a monotone! Remember that you are telling a story. Vocally emphasize the most important or interesting parts of that story. It's important to establish a connection with the audience, so make eye contact with your listeners periodically.

When you have finished, thank your audience, and return to your seat.

CRITIQUE

Evaluate a Classmate's Scenario

Choose one of the scenarios presented in class and evaluate it on a scale of 1 to 5, with 5 being "outstanding" and 1 being "needs much improvement." Ask yourself the questions below to help focus your evaluation.

- What details did the playwright use to make the plot clear?

- How would you describe the theme (or themes) of the play?

- What was the conflict, and was it strong enough?

- What changes to the play would you suggest based on this scenario?

- In what way did the speaker's manner of presentation impact your appreciation of the scenario?

Write a paragraph that details your evaluation and explains the rating you gave.

Spotlight on

Collaboration

Unlike the novelist or the poet—who can work alone—playwrights are dependent upon the artistic vision of others to bring their work to life. Collaboration is a vital aspect of a playwright's job. First-time playwrights should seek out directors who enjoy working on new plays and actors who are eager to create a role for the very first time. These collaborators can often help the playwright create more vibrant and believable scenes. Above all, plays are meant to be seen and heard. They can be developed and refined through private and public readings and through productions.

"The Eugene O'Neill Center National Playwrights Conference is dedicated to the development of new work for the theatre . . . ." So begins the mission statement of one of the most prestigious theatre organizations in the United States. Founded in 1964, the Eugene O'Neill Theatre Center has set a high standard for new play development. Named after one of America's greatest playwrights, the O'Neill Center is a haven where playwrights can develop their craft free from the pressures of the marketplace. It offers many different programs, but perhaps the most famous is the annual summer workshop known as the National Playwrights Conference. Each year, playwrights from all over the country compete for a workshop slot there. Located in Waterford, Connecticut, the conference typically receives 650 play submissions annually. Of these, only 12 to 15 are selected for participation. Each selected play is assigned a director and a group of actors. Together with the playwright, these artists **workshop** the play—discussing, analyzing, and reading it aloud many times over the course of one month. The playwright has the opportunity to revise and rewrite the play. The process, culminating in two public **staged readings,** is designed to take a good script and make it stronger and more producible.

Over the years, many of the country's most distinguished writers have developed their plays at the O'Neill—including John Guare, August Wilson (see the Master of the Craft on page 149), Edwin Sanchez, and Kia Corthron.

Three artists collaborate on a play at the Eugene O'Neill Theatre Center.

Additional Projects

1 Write a one-act play from the scenario you created. When you have finished it, collaborate with a small group of classmates to refine and act out the script. You may wish to perform your new play for the entire class.

2 Read a full-length play and then write a two-page scenario for it. Include a statement of the play's theme, a summary of its plot and conflict, and brief sketches of each character.

3 Put on a playreading for your classmates. You can read something you've written or select a published work. Perform the play as a sit-down reading. Cast the reading and make sure you have someone to read the stage directions. Remember that a committed reading can sometimes almost fool the audience into thinking they've watched a full-fledged production.

4 Take a current news story and create a scenario for it. Describe the story's exposition, inciting incident, plot, characters, conflict, and resolution (if any). Try to come up with a theme that pertains to the story.

5 If you have written a play, enter it in a playwriting contest. You can find a wealth of information about writing contests on the Internet. You might start with the Young Playwrights Inc.'s National Playwriting Contest (see Theatre Then and Now on page 151).

6 Read *The Drummer* by Athol Fugard, which can be found in Unit Eight. Re-create this simple pantomime as a two-character scene with dialogue that motivates the action.

Master of the Craft

August Wilson: Master Playwright

Frederick August Kittel was born in Pittsburgh, Pennsylvania, in 1945. At an early age, he knew he wanted to be a poet. He dropped out of school in the tenth grade, but went on to educate himself—at the library and on the street. His father essentially abandoned the family, and in 1965 the young August changed his last name to Wilson—his mother's maiden name.

In 1978, Wilson took a job in St. Paul, writing scripts for the Science Museum of Minnesota. The move put him in close proximity to The Playwrights' Center, a Minneapolis-based play development organization, which granted Wilson a fellowship in 1980. In 1982, Wilson's play *Ma Rainey's Black Bottom* was selected for participation in the O'Neill Theatre Center's National Playwrights Conference. There Wilson met the center's artistic director, Lloyd Richards. It was a fruitful alliance. Richards went on to direct six of Wilson's plays on Broadway.

In an interview with the *New York Times* in 1984, Wilson said, "My generation of blacks knew very little about the past of our parents. They shielded us from the indignities they suffered." Wilson began to throw light on that shadowy past with an ambitious series of plays, each set in a different decade of the 20th century and focused specifically on black issues.

Fences, Joe Turner's Come and Gone, Two Trains Running, and *Seven Guitars* are some of these plays.

His roots as a poet are evident in each of Wilson's dramas. His work is explosive and fiercely beautiful—the language is alive and real, yet lyrical. In a 1990 review of *The Piano Lesson, New York Post* critic Clive Barnes stated, "This is a play in which to lose yourself—to give yourself up . . . to August Wilson's thoughts, humors and thrills, always talking the same language of humanity."

Wilson died in 2005.

Pulitzer Prize-winner August Wilson.

Theatre Then and Now

Sophocles

Playwriting Contests of Old: Greek Goat Songs

Written drama as we know it began in Greece around 500 B.C. A playwriting competition was held at a yearly festival in honor of the patron of Greek theatre, Dionysus, god of wine, agriculture, and fertility. The festival featured choruses of goatskin-clad men who played satyrs (the half-man/half-goat creatures devoted to Dionysus). In fact, the word *tragedy* originated from the idea of these goat costumes, *tragos* ("goat"), and the words and music of the chorus, *ode* ("song"), or "goatsong."

Originally, tragedies were in the form of spoken song performed by a leader and a chorus. But in 534 B.C., at the Athenian festival, Thespis starred in a tragedy he'd written himself. He impersonated a character who engaged the traditional Greek chorus in dialogue. Thespis won first prize and became history's first known actor and its first true playwright. The word *thespian,* which means "actor," is derived from this ancient innovator.

From these ancient contests sprang some of the world's greatest drama. Many of the winning playwrights are thought to have been extremely prolific, yet only a few of their works survive. Euripides (484–406 B.C.) holds the record. Of the 90 plays he wrote, 18 remain, including *Medea.* His plays mine the deep sorrow of the human condition. Aeschylus (525–456 B.C.) is believed to have written 90 tragedies. Of these, only 7 remain, including the Oresteia trilogy. Sophocles (496–406 B.C.) wrote perhaps 125 tragedies, of which only 7 survive, including *Antigone* and *Oedipus Rex.* These great classical tragedies continue to influence generations of playwrights.

Tara Fitzgerald plays the title role in *Antigone* at the Old Vic Theatre in London.

Playwriting Contests Today: Up-and-Coming Playwrights

"If you want to say you knew them when, you have to see them now." That's the philosophy of Young Playwrights Inc.'s annual playwriting contest for young writers. Young Playwrights Inc. began in 1981, the brainchild of composer Stephen Sondheim, who made it his mission to foster new American writers. Today Young Playwrights Inc. has grown to be a major force in American theatre.

Each year the contest receives approximately 1100 submissions from all over the United States. The judges select only seven winners. These young writers attend a nine-day summer workshop of their plays. During that time they work with a professional director and actors, peers, and mentor playwrights. At night they attend Broadway and off-Broadway shows. At the end of the workshop process, each playwright has a public reading. Some of the plays are selected for full off-Broadway production by Young Playwrights Inc. in a festival the following season.

Professional writers who got their start at Young Playwrights Inc.'s annual contest include Rebecca Gilman *(Spinning into Butter, Boy Gets Girl)* and Kenneth Lonergan *(You Can Count on Me, This Is Our Youth, Lobby Hero)*. If you're interested in becoming a playwright, start now! This contest offers amazing opportunities for talented young people— but it's only open to writers under the age of eighteen. For more information, write to Young Playwrights Inc. Dept. WEB, 306 W. 38th Street #300, New York, NY 10018. Or visit the Web site at www.youngplaywrights.org.

World-renowned composer Stephen Sondheim began Young Playwrights Inc. in 1981.

Chapter
14 The Director and Producer

The production of a play represents the talent and commitment of many people. Whether on the stage or in the wings, you should have an understanding of all phases of the production process. This chapter will give you more information about each job—focusing particularly on the work of the director and the producer.

Project Specs

Project Description For this assignment, you will analyze a play as a director would and give a three- to five-minute presentation.

Purpose to hone your skills at play analysis and interpretation and to understand some of the basic elements of directing a play

Materials a written breakdown or a graphic representation of the important elements of a play you would like to direct or the Director and Producer Activity Sheet your teacher provides

Theatre Terms
director
dramaturg
general admission
producer
prompt book
royalties
strike
symbol

On Your Feet

With a classmate, discuss what you think the director and producer do to make a play happen. Who else is necessary for the production of a play? Make a list of who does what on a play. When you finish working on this chapter, compare your list to what you have learned.

Director Jean-Pierre Vincent, right, and actor Daniel Auteuil discuss the leading role in Molière's *That Scoundrel Scapin* for the annual theatre festival in Avignon, France.

PREVIEW

The Director

It is the responsibility of the **director** to create a cohesive group that will work together to accomplish a successful dramatic presentation. In high school, the director is often the drama teacher, but students should also have the opportunity to try out their directing skills. A good director has a keen sense of the play and the playwright's intentions as well as the ability to encourage actors and designers in interpreting the play. The director helps the actors use their skills and intuition to create meaningful characters. A director must also be able to see trouble coming among the cast and/or crew and figure out ways to circumvent it, pinpoint areas that need improvement, and come up with plans

to overcome any weaknesses in the staff—and communicate solutions to all these problems in a diplomatic way. A director must be insightful, dependable, responsible, and able to take on many tasks at once. It is a job that demands a very special individual.

The Producer

Most high school drama groups do not have a **producer,** but they are very common in the legitimate theatre. The producer finds the people who are willing to invest money in the show and creates a budget. The producer also hires the director and the staff who will work on the production. And while the producer will have help from members of the crew in running the advertising campaign, he is responsible for its direction. In many high schools, the producer is also the director.

If you're interested in directing or producing plays, you'll need to familiarize yourself with every aspect of the theatre. Involvement in a production means you will deal with actors, design staff, stage managers, technical crew members, and much more.

A Short List of the Director's Duties

If you choose to be a director, you have a big job ahead of you. On the following pages are just a few responsibilities of the director.

1 Getting Started The director selects the play, sets the dates for auditions, rehearsals, and the performance, and develops the artistic vision for the play. The chosen script should be well written and of high artistic quality, and the director should connect with it strongly. The theme should truthfully reveal some important element of the human experience. The play should feature strong characters, cohesive dialogue, and an interesting plot. It should be suitable to the school and community audience as well as the available talent pool and the school's technical capabilities. The fact is, if you don't have the necessary casting pool and facilities, you can't use the play.

2 Reading and Researching The director studies the play through multiple readings. If the play takes place in a different historical period, the director should also check a number of references to learn more about how people who lived during that time looked, spoke, worked, and so on. Often the director gets help from a **dramaturg** (see the box on page 157).

3 Assembling the Team The director enlists the aid of the production team to establish both continuity of design and a production schedule.

4 Assembling the Tools The director prepares a **prompt book** using a three-ring loose-leaf binder. Each page of the prompt book contains a page of the script, glued onto a piece of paper. The wide margins allow the director to write detailed notations about movement, technical cues, and so on. Think of the prompt book as the entire production written down on paper.

5 Getting Down to It The director conducts auditions, casts the play, and schedules and conducts rehearsals.

A Short List of the Producer's Duties

While the director is analyzing the script, creating the preliminary prompt book, and thinking about all the other onstage aspects of the production, the producer is hard at work on the business end. He or she finds investors, pays bills, oversees the budget, and works closely with a variety of different production crews. Here are some of the production areas for which the producer is ultimately responsible.

1 Getting Permission The producer must figure out a budget that takes into consideration the costs of producing the play, including the payment of **royalties,** money paid to the author for the use of the script. The box office receipts should help to pay the royalties, which can sometimes involve a great deal of money. Be sure to check the royalty fees before committing to any play. (It should go without saying that even schools *must* pay the necessary royalties. Failure to do so is a criminal offense.) To secure the royalties, the producer must contact the play's publisher by mail or fax. Rights cannot be secured by telephone. Information the producer gives to the publisher includes performance dates, number of seats, ticket price, and type of theatre (in the case of a school, nonprofessional/educational).

2 **Getting an Audience** Of course there's no point in producing a play if you don't have an audience. A large part of the producer's job is to bring in a crowd—in other words, to let the school and community know about the production and to get them excited about attending. This involves:

- Creating and distributing posters/flyers advertising the show. Posters should be put up at least two or three weeks before opening night.
- Writing public service announcements (PSAs) for local radio and TV stations. These brief announcements are typically made free of charge.

- Sending press releases to local newspapers. With planning and imagination, a producer can sometimes wrangle a feature story from the newspaper or a public radio station.
- Running an ad in the paper or on the radio (if the school's budget allows for this). The ad must be turned in far enough in advance so that it will do some good. The approved copy should be submitted at least two weeks before opening night. The copy should be edited and proofread to make sure all the information a potential ticket-buyer will need is included.
- Selling program ads. The money from these ads goes to pay for the program printing and to fund other areas of the production.

3 **The Program** The producer is also in charge of creating the program. There should be artistic continuity between the program and the advertising, posters, and flyers. Per the royalties agreement, the program must credit the playwright. Each publisher provides the guidelines for this credit, so check the agreement carefully. The program recognizes each cast and production team member. Programs may include a "Special Thanks To" section in which people

The production team works to prepare for an upcoming play.

The Production Team

It takes a lot of people to put on a play. The director, producer, designers, and actors may have the jobs with the highest profiles, but they wouldn't get far without the production team. Following is a list of backstage and offstage personnel and their duties.

The *assistant director* helps the director in conducting rehearsals, making phone calls, and sometimes doing research or taking on the role of a dramaturg (see the box at the right).

The *stage manager* is in charge of all stage crews. He or she also assists the director. During rehearsals, the stage manager takes notes, informs the production team as to the director's needs, and helps with scheduling. During final rehearsals and performances, the stage manager has complete supervision of the stage. He or she gives warning calls for lights, special effects, and curtains. After the play has closed, the stage manager assists with the **strike** (disassembling) of the set.

The *prompter* must attend every rehearsal to become completely familiar with the script and all its cues and pauses. The prompter is responsible for feeding actors their lines should they forget them. The prompter also makes sure the rehearsal room or theatre is ready, and during rehearsals he or she holds the prompt book, noting all

and organizations that have made contributions to the production are credited. Depending on the budget, the program may be anything from a single sheet of paper folded in half that lists the names and roles of the cast and crew to an elaborate document that includes biographies (and sometimes photographs).

4 Running Interference The duties of the director and the producer overlap at times. The producer's role often expands as the director gets deeper into the rehearsal process. A good producer stays in very close contact with the director—and picks up the slack when needed!

movements assigned by the director. (For more on prompting and the rehearsal process, see Chapter 15.)

Stage crews build, paint, and set up stage scenery. *Running crews* shift scenery during the performance. After each performance, the running crew sets up for Act I of the next night's show. They also help with strike after the final performance. (See Chapter 18 for more on set design and the stage crew.)

The *light crew* uses the lighting charts and cue sheets to properly hang and focus the lights. The crew then runs the lights during the show. The light crew assists with strike. (See Chapter 19 for more about lighting design and the light crew.)

The *sound effects* crew works on the sound cue sheet and provides the necessary sound effects. Under the direction of the sound designer, they may help select music to enhance the scene transitions and the mood of the play. (See Chapter 20 for more about sound design.)

The *costume crew* supplies the costumes and assigns dressing rooms. During the run of the play, the costume crew keeps the costumes clean, organized, mended, and pressed. (See Chapter 21 for more about costuming.)

Spotlight on

The Dramaturg

What is a dramaturg? You may not have heard this word before, but a dramaturg plays a vital part in many production teams. He or she may serve as a script reader in the theatre's literary department, evaluating plays that are under consideration for production. The dramaturg often does research into the historical or societal issues of a play and shares that information with the director and cast. Most dramaturgs know a great deal about playwriting structure, so they are particularly useful during productions of world premiere plays.

Although dramaturgs have been a part of the theatre scene since the 1800s, it has only been relatively recently that their place within the American production process has been clearly defined. Twenty or so years ago, most American theatres did not work with a dramaturg. Now these multifaceted professionals represent a strong creative component in theatre productions large and small.

The *makeup crew* plans makeup for each actor, obtains necessary supplies, and arranges for a separate makeup room if possible. During the final rehearsals and the run of the show, the makeup crew assists the actors in applying their make-up. (See Chapter 22 for more about makeup design and the makeup crew.)

The *properties (props) crew* prepares detailed props lists for each scene and locates all props and furniture, includ-ing those props that will not be used in performance but are used during rehearsal. The head of the props crew assigns each crew member specific props to set and strike for each act. The crew organizes the props, keeping those for each scene in a separate basket or on a separate table. Although actors are expected to check their individual props, the props crew is responsible for making sure the props are in the cor-rect spot for the actor to check. (See Chapter 23 for more about props.)

The *business manager* is in charge of the money. In a school setting, this person is often a faculty member. He or she serves as public relations officer and supervises the publicity, ticket sales, and program issues.

The *publicity crew* advertises the show by giving the school and local papers various news stories concerning performance dates, people involved, and information about the play, the playwright, and so on. This crew remains alert for possible feature stories engendered by the rehearsal process and arranges for photographers or arts and community reporters to have access to the cast. The crew puts up posters in the community and sends out postcards and flyers. The work of the publicity crew is crucial when it comes to attracting an audience.

The *house manager* is responsible for the seating and comfort of the audience during performances. The house man-ager sees to it that the auditorium is cool enough or warm enough, that the doors open on time, and that there are plenty of programs for distribution. He or she also supervises the ushers.

Ushers escort the audience members to their seats. If the performance is **general admission** (meaning that no seats are assigned and audience members can sit where they like), the ushers' main duty is to hand out programs and present an upbeat and courteous attitude. Ushers ask latecomers to wait in the lobby until the next scene change to avoid disturbing others (including the actors who are performing onstage). After the audience has left the auditorium, the ushers are responsible for picking up any trash or programs that may have been left behind.

Symbolic Elements of Drama

In previous chapters, we have looked at characters in conflict and analyzed the elements of plot. But to direct a play, you must also understand its theme (or themes) and the symbols it employs. A **symbol** is a concrete image that is used to represent an abstract concept or principle. In Arthur Miller's *Death of a Salesman,* Willy Loman's vegetable patch represents the old way of life with its opportunities for growth and renewal. In Jane Martin's *Clear Glass Marbles,* a bowl of marbles represents the waning days of a dying mother's life. In August Wilson's *The Piano Lesson,* a piano symbolizes for one character the need to remember the past; for another character, it represents the key to a new future.

A play's setting can often be symbolic as well. Think about what the following settings might convey.

- cemetery
- dining room
- train
- corporate boardroom
- museum
- Las Vegas

Theatre Journal

Think about the jobs in theatre production that do not involve acting, and choose one that interests you. Think about why this position interests you, and write about it in your journal.

PREPARE

Put on Your Director's Hat

In order to fulfill your assignment, you will first have to look at a play the way a director would. Follow the steps below.

1 Select a play you think you will like and read through it carefully. Pay close attention to what the characters say and do.

2 Once you have become familiar with the play's plot and characters, read the play a second time. Look for its themes and symbols. Remember that very often a play's theme is not explicitly stated. Complex plots have a major or central theme and an array of secondary ideas. Ask yourself questions as you go along. If you notice a recurring idea, track that idea all the way through to the end of the play. Take notes. Be sure this is a play you are excited about directing.

3 When you have finished analyzing the play, you should be able to
   - Name the protagonist.
   - Name the antagonistic force.
   - Explain the major plot line. (This should not take more than five sentences.)
   - Specify the conflict.
   - Define the play's theme.
   - List one or more symbols.
   - Explain why this play is the one you want to direct.

Next, you may either write a one- or two-page paper that illuminates all the points on the previous page or create one or more visual aids that illustrate your points graphically. Your teacher may supply a Director and Producer Activity Sheet, which you may also use to work through this assignment. Whichever way you decide to handle your preparation, be sure that you cover each of the elements listed in the previous paragraph.

Rehearse Your Presentation

If you have written a paper, practice reading it aloud a few times, making sure you have covered each of the assignment's points and that you don't go over three minutes. Be sure to include time for about two minutes of questions from the audience. You should be familiar enough with the material that questions about theme, symbolism, plot, character, and your vision of the play will not throw you.

If you choose to present your project by means of visual aids, make sure you can explain each element and how it is linked to the other elements. Cover the same elements you would cover in a written essay. If you need an easel or a small table to show your work, arrange this with your teacher ahead of time. Make sure your presentation does not exceed five minutes, including questions from the audience.

Career Focus

Stage Director

As is the case in so many areas of the theatre, becoming a successful stage director takes more than just talent. Directors must have the drive to succeed. They must educate themselves in all areas of the theatre, read and analyze both new plays and classics, and be comfortable in the rehearsal room.

Many professional directors begin learning their craft in high school and college and go on to obtain master of fine arts degrees in directing. Some directors begin their careers as actors and gradually shift their focus to directing. The time they spent as actors is not wasted, however—in fact, having been an actor can prove very helpful for a director in terms of understanding the collaborative process.

If you are interested in becoming a director, you will need to read as much as you can. Read plays, read books on directing, and read magazines with articles about directors and their process. For that all-important real-world experience, you might apply to apprentice at a local theatre as an assistant director.

The stage director discusses a scene with a lead actor while other actors rehearse.

PRESENT

Share Your Director's Vision

When your name is called, step to the playing area and either arrange your graphics or make certain your written information is in order. Hand in any written material or the Activity Sheet to your teacher. Take a moment before introducing your presentation to breathe and focus. Tell the class the name of the play and its author before you begin. Once you begin, keep up the pace, but make sure you cover each point.

When you have finished, ask the audience if they have questions. Set a limit of three questions. If someone asks you a question for which you simply have no answer, admit that you don't know, but try to suggest ways that one might find the answer. After you have answered the third question, thank your audience and return to your seat.

CRITIQUE

Evaluate a Classmate's Presentation

Choose one of the class presentations to review. Evaluate the presenter using a scale from 1 to 5, with 5 being "outstanding," and 1 being "needs much improvement." To begin, ask yourself the questions below.

For verbal presentations:
- Was the presenter's overall vision of the play clear and insightful?
- Did the presenter cover the play's theme adequately?
- How well did the presenter convey an understanding of the play's symbols?
- Was the statement of the conflict clear?
- How did the presenter handle the plot description?
- In what way did the presenter answer the questions from the audience?

For graphic presentations:
- How did the graphics convey the play's plot and theme?
- In what way did the presenter involve conflict, symbols, and character?
- Were you able to get a good sense of the play?
- How comfortable did the presenter appear while answering questions?

Write a paragraph explaining why you gave the presenter the rating you did.

Additional Projects

1. Coach a classmate in the performance of a mono-logue. Encourage your classmate to read through the monologue silently several times before reading it aloud. Once he or she has delivered the monologue aloud, work together to clarify its theme. Give your classmate notes on charac-ter and physical/vocal presentation. When the two of you have rehearsed the monologue to your satisfac-tion, present it to the class.

2. Use the Internet, interviews, or other resources to research one small element of a play that interests you but you know little about. This element could be the occupation of one of the characters, a pasttime enjoyed by the characters, or some other specific item found in the play. Write a short description based on your research.

3. Write character sketches for each character in the play you worked on for this chapter's project. Analyze the play thoroughly to create the most detailed sketches you can.

4. Select a full-length period play to research. Your research should focus on a wide-ranging issue, such as the politics of the time, the social issues, or some other issue inherent to the play. Write a paper outlining your dramaturgic findings.

5. Select one of the longer excerpts from the mono-logues and scenes in Unit Eight. Discuss the excerpt in terms of how you might direct the scene. Think about the play's theme, plot, symbols, major con-flict, and the classmates you would cast to play the various parts.

Master of the Craft

Peter Brook (1925–)

Peter Brook is an English theatrical producer and director who became known in the 1950s for his experimental productions with London's Royal Shakespeare Company. As a young man, he directed a startling variety of plays—from Shakespeare to musical comedy—with skill and ingenuity.

His early work was inspired by the theories of experimental theatre; these plays and theatrical events defied the notions of realistic and naturalistic acting and pushed the boundaries of the stage. In one memorable Brook production of Shakespeare's *Titus Andronicus,* actress Vivien Leigh spouted a seemingly endless length of bright red ribbon in a scene in which her character's tongue was cut out. Such visual touches would influence a generation of theatre practitioners.

Over the course of his nearly sixty years in the theatre, Brook has acquired a well-deserved reputation as the greatest living inventor of the modern stage. But by his own admission, he has never lost his sense of being an apprentice to his craft. "I think you can't lose this, because a craft has no end. A craft is a ladder. There always has to be another level to everything . . ."

Brook's work is challenging, physical, electrifying, and visually alive. He values the audience's intelligence. "In being aware of what holds an audience and what loses them, you develop more and more the awareness that rhythm, space, all the physical sides of theatre are playing on the audience, and it is in this way you develop your tools."

Peter Brook

A scene from *The Persecution and Assassination of Jean-Paul Marat as Performed by the Inmates of the Asylum of Charenton Under the Direction of the Marquis de Sade.*

Theatre Then and Now

The Evolution of the "Director"

The role of the director as a creative force in the artistic process is a relatively recent phenomenon. Only over the course of the past 120 years has the director become an active, vital component in the production of the play. Prior to that time, the "director" of a theatre troupe was typically either a kind of business manager or an actor or playwright who assumed extra responsibilities. Following are two theatre luminaries: the Japanese playwright Zeami and the Broadway director Hal Prince.

Zeami: The Father of Japanese Noh Drama

Zeami Motokiro (1363–1443) was the son of an itinerant actor. This familial connection naturally led Zeami into the world of the theatre at an early age. When he was eleven, he performed with his father's company at a shrine in Kyoto. His audience that day included Yoshimitsu, the ruler of Japan. Yoshimitsu was so taken with the performance of young Zeami that he set the troupe up in his palace and thereby became their financial protector. Over the course of his life, Zeami's fortunes tended to change with the political climate. But along the way, he became an accomplished playwright, penning more than one hundred plays that would form the basis of Noh drama.

What this 14th-century pioneer created was a dramatic form written in the upper-class language of the time that based its stories on people and situations of an earlier period. The result was a series of plays of poetic richness and universality. Many of these works are regularly performed today. In 1423, Zeami documented the skills and methods of the Noh actor; his teachings are still studied by young actors.

Noh drama is still performed in much the same way it was over six hundred years ago.

Hal Prince: Broadway Innovator

The *New York Times* once said that director/producer Hal Prince "may be one of the most innovative directors on Broadway. He may be the one most obsessed with craft as well . . . ."

According to Prince, he owes his success to theatrical legend George Abbott. Prince was apprenticed to Abbott at the age of twenty-five as a stage manager. But what belies Prince's modesty is the fact that, at the age of twenty-six, he co-directed a new musical called *The Pajama Game.* It became the hottest ticket in town and instantly made Prince one of the top names on Broadway.

Since that time, Hal Prince has directed more than fifty Broadway musicals. Among his hits are *Cabaret, Evita,* and *Phantom of the Opera.* His most artistically daring and groundbreaking productions, however, were the result of collaborations with composer Stephen Sondheim. Beginning in the early 1970s, these two theatre pros brought a new notion to the stage—the "concept musical," a musical play in which theme takes precedence over plot. Prince's productions of the Sondheim musicals *Company, Pacific Overtures, Sweeney Todd,* and others took the American musical into brand-new territory. Each was different from the one before—and each challenged the notions of standard musicals to that point. Along the way, Prince picked up twenty Tony Awards.

Hal Prince approaches his craft from an intensely personal standpoint.

Mrs. Lovett sharpens her knife in a production of *Sweeney Todd.*

Chapter
15 The Cast

The process of selecting actors for various roles, called **casting,** can make or break a show. Some directors consider casting to be ninety percent of their job! It's important to find the best actor for each role so that the performance will be as effective as possible. This chapter will focus on the cast as they audition and rehearse in preparation for opening night.

Project Specs

Project Description For this project, you will create and discuss for no more than six minutes a rehearsal schedule for a production of a two-act play.

Purpose to learn how to create a real-world rehearsal schedule using information from a particular play

Materials a sheet listing various personnel and duties for six weeks of rehearsal or The Cast Activity Sheet provided by your teacher; colored pens or pencils; an overhead projector and the appropriate transparency sheets

Theatre Terms
auditions
callbacks
cameo
casting
casting call
casting director
cold reading
double cast
offbook
rehearsals
spiking
understudy

On Your Feet

With a partner, improvise a very short scene in which you both play actors waiting in line for the opportunity to audition for a play.

The casting director of *Martin Guerre* had to find actors who could look, speak, and move according to the parts played—from farmer to war hero.

PREVIEW

Assembling the Cast

Casting is usually accomplished through a series of tryouts or **auditions.** The audition time, place, and specific procedures for community tryouts are often published in local newspapers. The **casting call** for your school auditions might appear in the school paper, be announced over the PA system, or be posted in the school building. Scripts often may be found in the school or local library, where those who are interested in auditioning may read them and prepare scenes.

Some theatres employ a **casting director** to find actors for particular parts (see page 175). Directors may sometimes prefer a **cold reading** at auditions. This means the performer is probably unfamiliar with the script, and is reading the lines of the scene for the first time.

If you audition, you will usually start by filling out a casting sheet similar to the one on page 168. You will then read a scene or scenes in combination with others. The director will announce the first audition scene and assign two or more actors to perform it.

After the preliminary auditions, the director selects those actors who seem best suited to the parts. Sometimes there are as many as four people chosen

as possible candidates for a particular role. When this happens, the director will hold **callbacks,** a second audition in which only those who are under serious consideration for the roles are called in. At the callbacks, the director may give you suggestions as to how to perform a particular scene. He or she might also direct you in terms of how and where to move. You may be asked to memorize a scene or speech or to improvise a scene.

When casting the play, the director takes into account your physical appearance,

personality, level of acting, and the chemistry between you and other possible cast members. Singing or dancing skills may also be noted. In drama class, performers are cast according to what skills they need to develop. For public presentation, however, the director casts the actors best suited to the roles.

The director will be looking for people with expressive, supple voices; good physical presences; and emotional intensity. In short, the director wants to find a group of actors who can engage

When auditioning for a part, you may be asked to fill out a form similar to this one.

Casting Sheet

Name _____ Height _____ Year in School _____
Address _____ Female _____ Male _____
Phone _____ E-mail _____ Hair Color_____
Special Talents (sing, dance, play musical instrument, etc.) _____
_____

Check what you would like to work on:

_____ Costumes	_____ Makeup	_____ Publicity
_____ Director's Assistant	_____ Prompter	_____ Stage Manager
_____ Lighting & Sound	_____ Props	

On back of page, please list:
1. Previous acting experience (include play, role, place)
2. Hours when you can rehearse
3. Other commitments (orchestra, sports, work, religious schedule, etc.)

Director's comments:

Appearance _____	Ability to take direction _____
Voice _____	Personality _____
Speech _____	Possible for role of _____
Interpretation _____	_____
Movement _____	_____

Spotlight on

The Audition

As a beginning actor, you may not get many chances to perform for a paying audience. But you can perform for theatrical peers or professionals every time you audition.

Most auditions begin with a notice, to which you must respond by calling to make an appointment or by appearing at an open call. The notice will probably indicate whether actors will be expected to read a scene from the play, perform a serious or comic monologue from memory, sing, dance, or do any combination of these things.

In any case, it is a good idea to read the play and make note of the characters it calls for. The better you know the play, the better you will be able to concentrate on acting in the scene, rather than reading or, worse, finding your place!

Once you have read the play or a description of the play, ask yourself:
- Which of these characters would I like to play?
- As which character am I likely to be cast?

Then prepare yourself for the audition by thinking about the character in the context of the play. Get a sense of the character's history and circumstances, hopes and fears, and loves and hates. Incorporate them as best you can into your monologue or scene.

As you wait for your audition, do so quietly. If you are allowed to, listen to the other readers. You may learn something that will help you in a later reading.

When you are called onstage, assume the role of a professional. Focus on the character's objective. Remember to breathe. And remember that the director wants you to do well—he or she is on your side. As you perform, be open to any acting advice the director may have. And have fun—isn't that the point?

Being relaxed and well prepared is important when auditioning.

an audience's attention and imagination, have a variety of physiques and voices, and seem to work well together.

The director will either phone the actors he or she has chosen or post the cast list on a bulletin board. Not getting a part you wanted can be hard, but just remember that no actor—whether famous or not—has ever gotten all the roles he or she wanted. Learning to face disappointment is part of being an actor.

"Leave your dirty shoes at the door!"

Thus states an old rehearsal adage. It means that no matter what your mood or current situation, you must come to each rehearsal fresh and ready to do your best. Leave your worries at home.

To provide acting opportunities for a larger number of students, some schools **double cast.** With a double cast, two groups split the performances. However, this process takes a lot of extra rehearsal time, sometimes at the expense of a polished performance. Another choice is to select a single cast with understudies for the main roles. An **understudy** attends all rehearsals and learns a role thoroughly. If an actor becomes ill or can't perform, the understudy is able to go on in his or her place.

Rehearsals

Once the play is cast, the director must organize **rehearsals,** various run-throughs of the play. A rehearsal schedule makes the best possible use of everyone's time. To this end, the director should group together scenes that feature the same characters. With proper attention to detail, only the necessary actors need be called for each rehearsal. This avoids the long waits that can lead to boredom and inattention. At the beginning of the rehearsal process, the director hands out a rehearsal schedule to the cast and the crew. One copy of the schedule is tacked to a board where the rehearsals take place. Often this schedule cannot be altered, so all the cast involved must meet it! Even if a role is a small **cameo,** a brief one-scene part, the actor is expected to show up to every rehearsal to which he or she is called. Being prompt and maintaining the highest standards of behavior are very important. Rehearsals are hard work, but if everyone cooperates and works as a team, the time spent will be not only fun, but also productive. After all, each member of the cast is working toward the same goal: a great show.

Rehearsal schedules vary according to the difficulty of the play, the experience of the actors, and the time available. Full-length school plays typically require at least a five- or six-week rehearsal period. That means committing five or six days a week of two to three hours each to rehearsal time. One-act plays obviously take less rehearsal time. For these shows, rehearsal generally lasts only three to four weeks with three to four sessions per week. It's important to schedule as many rehearsals as possible to maintain the highest performance standards. Some casts practice after school and some in the evenings. Cast members should count on at least two long Saturday rehearsals at some point in the schedule. The director (or teacher) may ask for a personal pledge that cast members will attend all rehearsals required of them.

The Rehearsal Sequence

The director typically provides specific goals for each rehearsal session. The following illustrates a standard rehearsal sequence.

Reading rehearsals begin right after casting is complete. Actors and designers work as a group to gain an overall understanding of the play. The director discusses his or her concept for the show—including specifics about characters, plot, and theme. The actors read through the script, after which the director may ask them questions about the play or their specific characters. Actors should also take this opportunity to ask questions about motivation and character relationships.

Blocking rehearsals are conducted onstage or in a large room where the floor plan of the set is taped onto the floor. Blocking rehearsals work out the actors' onstage movements. You will read more about blocking in Chapter 16.

Developing rehearsals begin on each act once the blocking is set. When the actors have memorized their lines, which is called being **off book,** they can fully concentrate on projecting emotion and relating to others onstage. During this stage of rehearsal, you will begin to work with rehearsal props and certain costume pieces. These rehearsals may be tailored to specific situations within the script, for example, love scenes, fights, or crowd scenes.

Polishing rehearsals are all about the little touches that make a good production great. In polishing, the director works on the actors' projection and

An Actor's Credo

Never accept a role unless you are also willing to accept the responsibility of attending each rehearsal to which you're called.

Theatre Journal

Think of a character from a play you have read or seen. Looking around the classroom, think about which of your classmates might play the role in a school production. Write a short entry explaining your choice.

emphasis. Murky moments between actors are cleaned up and strengthened. The pacing and rhythm of the play are perfected. Any extraneous movements are eliminated at this point, and group scenes are tightened to allow for stronger ensemble playing. Polishing rehearsals are very important. Rehearsal schedules should be planned to allow

Actors rehearse on a spiked stage in order to practice moving around furniture that will be positioned onstage.

for sufficient polishing before the show opens. Including enough time to polish the production is very important.

Technical rehearsals must be held onstage. The purpose of the technical rehearsal is to synchronize technical and performance aspects of the production. The first technical rehearsal can be long and arduous. It is often referred to as a "dry tech," meaning a rehearsal specifically to set technical cues, without actors. Also at this point, scenery shifts are choreographed and curtains are hung.

The next technical rehearsal is with the whole cast. The director asks only for those scenes requiring scene shifts, light and sound, or major prop changes. Crews now mark the furniture positions on the stage floor with masking tape, a process called **spiking.** If the schedule allows, actors do a dress parade. This means that they put on their costumes and walk across the stage under the proper lighting. This is done so that the costume crew can make any necessary adjustments.

Three dress rehearsals should be conducted in full costume. Prior to the first dress rehearsal, the director gives the cast and crew instructions— usually in writing—about the time, procedure, and requirements of each dress rehearsal and performance. Dress rehearsals begin on time, whether the cast and crew are ready or not! The purpose of dress rehearsal is to get the show to performance level. There is an old saying that "A bad dress rehearsal means a great opening night." Don't fall for this. A bad dress rehearsal usually only creates opening night jitters. Dress rehearsals should go smoothly, however, if everyone works efficiently.

The first dress rehearsal is the most hectic, as it coordinates sound, lights, scenery, and props. The cast wears full costumes. The director sits in the audience and watches the entire show. The prompter times the show and each scene shift. (Scene shifts should be executed within a matter of seconds.) Intermissions should be no longer than ten minutes. The only time a dress rehearsal should be interrupted is if someone is injured or a major technical problem occurs. The director gives notes on the performance at the end of the rehearsal.

The second dress rehearsal adds make-up and other technical requirements. The director also stages the curtain call—or actors' bows—at the end of the show. (See the Spotlight on Taking Your Bows on page 60 for more on this.) After this dress rehearsal, most productions have a photo call. The director usually selects the setups in advance and hands out copies of the sequence of photos. Because the cast will be in costume for the end of the show, the photographer usually shoots the photos in reverse order. Sometimes the director will give notes after the second dress rehearsal, but many directors withhold the critique until just prior to the final dress rehearsal.

The third or final dress rehearsal should run exactly like a performance. There should be absolutely no interruptions, and every detail should be in place. Some directors make this an *invited dress,* meaning that there will be some guests in the audience. This is particularly important when the production is a comedy because the cast will need practice holding for laughs. Before this final rehearsal, there is generally a full cast-and-crew meeting backstage. At this point, the cast gives the crews a round of applause for all their hard work.

The Performance

At last the opening night arrives. Now all the hard work on the part of the cast, crews, director, and producer will pay off in a memorable performance. Here are some final thoughts to help you prepare to create the best show possible.

Before and During the Performance
- Only those with specific jobs are allowed backstage.

- Crews should arrive early enough to have the stage set up two hours before show time.

- The cast should arrive at least one hour before curtain time to warm up, put on makeup and costumes, and check personal props. When these duties are completed, each cast member should remain quietly in the dressing room getting into character.

- The stage manager calls roll about fifteen minutes before curtain time. Then the director talks to the cast and crew. This is generally a pep talk, but most directors also remind the cast not to change anything regardless of what their friends and family members may have to say about the show.

- Remember that when you're onstage, small errors usually go unnoticed by the audience. If you make a mistake, such as calling another character by the wrong name, do not call attention to your error. Go on. If another character fails to enter on time, create inconsequential talk to fill the gap. Do not check your watch and say, "I wonder where [the missing character] is."

- As in dress rehearsal, during the production the stage manager has charge of the performance. The director sits out front and takes notes or observes the audience reaction.

- The show should always begin on time. Prompt curtain times ensure that the audience will arrive on time.

After the Performance

- The actors remove their makeup and costumes and tidy the dressing rooms. Actors should never leave a mess for the crews.

- After the final show, the crews should immediately strike the set and props.

- Borrowed items should be returned on the day following the last performance.

- Return any missing pages to the prompt book.

- Have a cast party. This is a theatre tradition; everyone is invited—cast, crews, and director. It is often held onstage after strike. If the strike is expected to go late, the party sometimes is scheduled for another night.

PREPARE

Create Your Rehearsal Schedule

Imagine that you are a director about to begin rehearsals for a two-act play. You may have a particular play in mind, or you can find one at the library. You may choose from plays listed in Unit Eight or you may be assigned a play by your teacher. Your assignment is to create a complete six-week rehearsal schedule. You may create your own calendar or list or use the Activity Sheet your teacher gives you. You may wish to make a larger copy of the Activity Sheet so that you can include all the relevant information on your rehearsal schedule. If an overhead projector is available for this project, be prepared to transfer the schedule you create to transparency sheets.

On the following page is a sample rehearsal schedule. Note that it does not include which actors are called for each rehearsal or the hours during which the rehearsal will take place.

Career Focus

Casting Director

If you're a "people person," you might consider a career as a casting director. These consultants contact and secure suitable actors to audition for various projects. They are the conduit that connects actors and their agents to the people and organizations that do the hiring.

Many professional theatre companies have full-time casting directors. But casting directors may also work on a freelance basis to cast for film, radio, and television. Some casting directors work for advertising agencies to find the right actors for television and radio spots, print ads, and voice-overs. Through a blend of experience, intuition, and savvy, the casting director brings the best possible group of actors into the audition process.

In general, the casting director prescreens possible actors. He or she secures actors to audition but does not make final casting decisions, which are typically left to the director or producer. Once casting is complete, however, it is often the casting director who negotiates money and scheduling with the actor's agent.

Most professional casting directors are located in large cities such as Los Angeles, New York, and Chicago. They are familiar with a vast number of actors within their home city, but they also create and maintain connections with other casting services and talent agencies to secure the largest possible actor list. In fact, many casting directors began their careers as actors or directors. Some have worked in stage management or as other behind-the-scenes theatre personnel. Others may have begun working as assistants to film or theatre producers. Firsthand theatre, film, or television experience is vital for the successful casting director.

You will create a schedule that includes the date of each rehearsal, the specific actors called for each rehearsal, the hours of the rehearsal, and the location where the rehearsal will take place (auditorium, rehearsal room, and so on). Remember that rehearsals close to opening night, especially technical and dress rehearsals, always take place on the stage where the performance will be.

Remember to schedule only those actors you will need for each rehearsal. For example, if you are only rehearsing the first half of Act I, don't call in actors who appear only in the second half of Act I. Your job is to make the most efficient use of everyone's time. Write schedule information pertaining to cast members in one color. For crew members, use a different color. For scheduling that involves both cast and crew, use a third color.

Remember that Saturday rehearsals can be longer and can take place during the day. Also bear in mind what you have learned about technical rehearsals and performances. Have a specific goal for each rehearsal on your schedule.

You will need a calendar of the current year so you can write accurate dates next to each rehearsal day.

You may decide that your schedule is for the fall or the spring production. Choose your dates accordingly. Note that on the first day of rehearsal all cast and crew members are called. For subsequent rehearsals, you may either schedule by act and scene numbers or (for smaller cast shows) by character names.

Copy the Schedule and Rehearse Your Talk

Make a copy of your schedule for use on an overhead projector or try to make an oversized copy on a copier. Rehearse your presentation. Allow about a minute to address comments or answer questions about the play or your rehearsal schedule after your talk. The talk itself should not exceed five minutes.

This schedule calls for five rehearsals a week, two Saturday rehearsals, and three performances. Adjust your schedule to fit the needs of the play you chose.

Sample Rehearsal Schedule for a Two-Act Play

1st week:

Monday	Read complete play with all cast and crew.
Tuesday	Read first half; discussion and analysis.
Wednesday	Read second half; discussion and analysis.
Thursday	Act I: block first half; repeat to set.
Friday	Act I; block remainder; repeat to set.

Sample Rehearsal Schedule for a Two-Act Play (Continued)

2nd week:
Monday	Act I; characterization and motivation.
Tuesday	Act II; block first half; repeat to set.
Wednesday	Act II; block remainder; repeat to set.
Thursday	Run through Acts I and II; adjust groupings if necessary.
Friday	Act II; characterization and motivation.
Saturday	Special private rehearsals for love scenes, fight scenes, etc.

3rd week:
Monday	Act I memorized; no books; work on detailed business.
Tuesday	Run through Act I (no books).
Wednesday	Act II; work on belief and response; actors should look at each other and listen to each other.
Thursday	Act II memorized; no books; work on business detail.
Friday	Run through Act II memorized; clarify business detail; use hand props.

4th week:
Monday	Run through Acts I and II memorized; work on detailed business.
Tuesday	Run through Acts I and II; work on audibility, groupings, characterization.
Wednesday	Polish Act I; business, lines, tempo, climax, props.
Thursday	Polish Act II; business, lines, tempo, climax, props.
Friday	Run through Acts I and II; concentrate on minor roles.
Saturday	Polish Acts I and II.

5th week:
Monday	Run through Acts I and II; work on audibility, unity, tempo, climax, line pickup, transitions, ensemble playing. Check for spontaneity. Actors must not anticipate lines or mouth the lines of others.
Tuesday	Polish difficult scenes, climaxes, etc.
Wednesday	Technical rehearsal without actors. Set up scenery, furniture, lights, etc. Practice shifts. Actors may run a line rehearsal with the prompter. No movement; just say lines and pick up cues readily.
Thursday	Technical rehearsal with actors. Repeat scenes needed for technical changes. Do costume review.
Friday	Run through complete show with set, lights, props.

6th week:
Monday	First dress; full costume, lights, sound, props, scenery, and shifts.
Tuesday	Second dress; as Monday, plus makeup. Plan curtain calls; take pictures.
Wednesday	Invitational dress; performance level.
Thursday	Opening night performance.
Friday	Performance.
Saturday	Performance, strike, and cast party.

PRESENT

Display and Explain Your Rehearsal Schedule

When your name is called, bring your rehearsal schedule or Activity Sheet to the front of the classroom. If your teacher has arranged for the use of an overhead projector, place the transparency containing your schedule on the projector and display it.

Your presentation will include a very brief description of the play you chose. Then take about five minutes to talk about your schedule. Be sure to mention any special rehearsal considerations the play warranted. You may wish to discuss why you broke the schedule down the way you did. Your entire presentation (with comments and questions) should not exceed six minutes. When you are finished, remove the schedule and hand it to your teacher. Then return to your seat.

CRITIQUE

Evaluate a Schedule

Select one classmate's rehearsal schedule to evaluate. Imagine that you are an actor in the play. Listen carefully to what your classmate says about the schedule. Look carefully at the way the schedule is set up and organized. You will not have time to do an in-depth analysis. You will mainly be judging this schedule on legibility, clarity of organization, color coding, and consistency. Rate the schedule on a scale of 1 to 5, with 5 being "outstanding," and 1 being "needs much improvement."

After you have rated the schedule based on the qualities suggested above, write a short paragraph explaining your evaluation.

Additional Projects

1 Read one of the following plays, and create a list of suitable actors you might cast. You can use well-known theatre, television, or film actors.

- *Medea* by Euripides

- *The Seagull* by Anton Chekhov

- *The Crucible* by Arthur Miller

- *The Heidi Chronicles* by Wendy Wasserstein

- *Arcadia* by Tom Stoppard

- *Cloud Nine* by Caryl Churchill

2 Watch a video of a play and write a review of the performance based on the casting of three characters.

3 Create two or three pages for the playbill that will accompany a play of your choice. Include interesting biographies of all the cast members.

4 Read the excerpt found in Unit Eight of *A Jamaican Airman Foresees His Death* by Fred D'Aguiar. Write a short rehearsal schedule for this scene, along with the names of classmates and the roles they would play. Try to cast both males and females.

Scene from *Arcadia* by Tom Stoppard.

Theatre **Then** and **Now**

A Leading Lady of His Time: Edward Kynaston

Edward Kynaston

Some of the greatest women's roles of all time were first played by . . . men. That's right, toward the middle of the 17th century, the most beautiful woman on the London stage was not a woman at all. And that didn't bother audiences one bit. The "leading lady" in question was actor Edward Kynaston (1619–1687), and he would go on to play an interesting role in theatre history.

At that time in England, women weren't allowed to set foot on the stage for any reason—and that included playing female characters in the plays of William Shakespeare and others. These roles were instead taken by smooth-faced, fair-skinned young men. And Kynaston was one of the best of these—he was much admired for the naturalness of his delivery, not to mention his physical beauty, in roles such as Desdemona in Shakespeare's tragedy *Othello*.

In 1660, Charles II took the throne as king of England, and with him came a new era of tolerance and religious and social reforms. In 1662, he decreed that from then on women would be allowed to play female roles in the theatre. But

King Charles wasn't content to leave it at that. He also enacted a law forbidding men to play women.

And so it was that poor Edward Kynaston became the last of the great male players of women. He went from being a popular leading player to an often out-of-work actor unable to make a successful transition to male roles. In building his celebrity by playing only female roles, Kynaston effectively shut himself out of his own profession.

Contemporary playwright Jeffrey Hatcher chronicles and re-envisions the life and times of Edward Kynaston in a play called *Compleat Female Stage Beauty*.

A Leading Lady of Our Time: Cherry Jones

In his review of the 1995 Broadway revival of *The Heiress, New York Times* critic Vincent Canby called Cherry Jones "a splendid young actress who's new to me." This is a somewhat ironic quote in view of the fact that at the time Jones had more than fifty productions under her belt, a Tony nomination for *Our Country's Good* (1991), and a 1992 OBIE Award for her performance in Paula Vogel's play *The Baltimore Waltz.*

Before landing the lead role in the Lincoln Center's production of *The Heiress,* Jones had played characters both far younger and far older than her actual age. In fact, when she was called in to audition for *The Heiress,* she believed it was for the role of the play's older character, Aunt Penniman. Jones did not realize she'd been called in for the lead role of Catherine Sloper until she came to the audition and informed the director that she was unwilling to play the aunt.

Cherry Jones has a unique ability to disappear into a role by completely changing her voice and physical bearing. She's had plenty of opportunity to perfect this versatility. She trained at Carnegie-Mellon University and spent a year at the Brooklyn Academy of Music (BAM) before joining the American Repertory

Company (Cambridge, MA) in 1980. There she performed in twenty-five plays in six seasons. She developed a reputation as a risk-taker, playing roles in everything from Shakespeare to Brecht.

Over the years, Cherry Jones has gone from a nearly anonymous actor to a major theatrical star. Her celebrity is easy to explain: She is completely dedicated to the craft of acting.

Cherry Jones

Chapter
16 Blocking

The actor is here . . . and then there . . . and then here again—all the while speaking, gesturing, and doing odd bits of stage business. What helps the actor keep all this together? Blocking!

Project Specs

Project Description For this assignment, you will block a scene of from four to six minutes long involving more than one actor.

Purpose to understand blocking and to apply techniques for handling complex movement onstage

Materials pencil and paper; a ground plan or the Blocking Activity Sheet your teacher provides

Theatre Terms
aesthetic balance
asymmetrical balance
blocking
counter-focus
direct focus
floor plan or
    ground plan
open stance
symmetrical balance
unity

On Your Feet

With a partner, discuss how you might break down the elements of playing a particular sport. One of you should slowly pantomime the action "frame by frame," while the other draws each step in the sequence. Then change roles. You don't have to draw well; creating stick figures will do.

Blocking: Skills in Action

Theatre is a composite art. As you have begun to learn, it is not a particular skill, but a combination of technical, verbal, and visual skills. One very important element is the **blocking,** or planning of the movement and arrangement of the actors within scenes and from one scene to the next. Blocking tells the actor how to get his character from one place to another on the stage. It also supports communication between the characters within the play. And it creates a visual picture that affects the experience of performing and watching the play. Thus, effective blocking creates meaningful, functional, and artistic movement.

Meaningful Movement

Of course, movement in a play must carry out the plot. Juliet must swallow the sleeping potion and Hamlet must stab Polonius if their stories are to follow the playwright's intent. But movement can also be engineered to carry information about the characters' motivations, emotional states, and relationships. What a character does is often more important than what he or she says!

The way in which a character places a prop can telegraph his or her feelings. The way a character primps in a mirror, thumbs through a magazine, or buttons a coat may suggest details about his or her emotional life. An arrangement of characters on a sofa can reveal a wealth of details about their relationships.

The Flying Karamazov Brothers must carefully plan the blocking of their action-packed stage productions.

Functional Movement

In order to fully communicate a play's meaning to the audience, you must be sure that the blocking emphasizes important characters, moments, and even objects in the play. In order to facilitate the blocking, a **ground plan,** or **floor plan,** must be created. This plan is a diagram on paper that shows the walls, doors, windows, furniture, and other important architectural details of the stage drawn to scale. The director should create a blocking plan well in advance. This saves rehearsal time and helps to keep the movement organized and unified. Even with this plan, however, changes will always be made during the evolution of the play.

A ground plan of a very symmetrical set. The ground plan is drawn as though looking down from a place high above the stage.

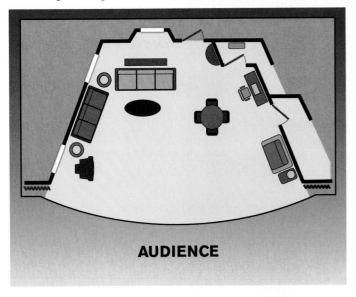

AUDIENCE

Creating a center of interest that catches and holds the audience's attention is important onstage. Usually the actor who is speaking important lines receives the emphasis. Sometimes audience attention is drawn to an inanimate object, an important line of dialogue, or significant movements that show feelings or desires. A center of interest is achieved in subtle ways so that the audience members give their attention effortlessly. The following are the director's tools for creating emphasis.

The Actor As you learned in Chapter 6, an actor will face the audience, full front, to convey important dialogue. This is called an **open stance,** and it draws attention to the character. When blocking a scene, remember that standing full front is the most emphatic stance, followed by one-quarter, profile, three-quarter, and full back stances. (See page 57 for a photograph of these.) A standing position is usually more dominant than a sitting position; sitting is more emphatic than lying down. An erect posture generally commands more attention than a slouched posture.

Stage Areas The diagram on page 185 shows the relative strength of stage areas, with number 1 being the strongest and 6 the weakest. The exception to area strength occurs when a downstage character assumes a three-quarter position in order to face an upstage character who is then emphasized.

The director must choose the playing area according to the scene's importance. If it is a climactic scene, a strong area may be chosen. Or to weaken a strong action, such as a gory stabbing, the scene can be softened by playing it in a weaker stage area.

Some directors subscribe to the theory that each stage area has an emotional value that lends itself to certain types of scenes. You can see these connections in the following list:

Area 1 Climactic scenes
Area 2 Dignified scenes
Area 3 Love scenes
Area 4 Scenes that build tension
Area 5 Eavesdropping or
        foreshadowing events
Area 6 Horror and unrealistic scenes

While the link between acting area and scene can be helpful when working out a blocking plan, remember that these connections are only suggestions, not hard and fast rules.

Stage Levels The higher the level, the more attention a character receives. Not only is this because the audience can readily see raised figures, but there is also a psychological aspect of height dominating a scene. For example, the tall person dominates the short person. Elevation can be varied by using platforms and stairs, as well as by having some figures stand, sit, and kneel.

AUDIENCE

A stage mapped out with areas of strength.

Eye Focus People look where others look, so if characters A and B are looking directly at C, the audience will look at C also. This is called **direct focus.** To add variety, a director sometimes employs **counter-focus,** where A focuses on B who looks at C who looks at the speaking figure D. The audience will follow the pattern from A to B to C and finally to D. The most effective stage arrangement is the triangle, because the eyes of the audience travel along either side and focus on the figure in the middle. Generally the middle person is upstage with the downstage characters turned in three-quarter positions.

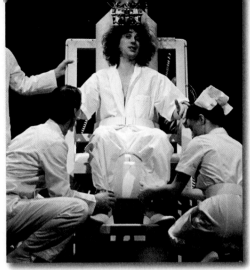

In the triangle arrangement seen here in *A Clockwork Orange*, we focus on the character in the center. While effective, avoid overusing the triangle.

Space and Contrast A character surrounded by space draws attention because of being easily seen, and the audience wonders about the isolation from the group. The more space between the character and the group, the more emphasis on the character. In the diagram below, character A receives

Because she is set apart spatially from the group, character A receives the attention of the audience.

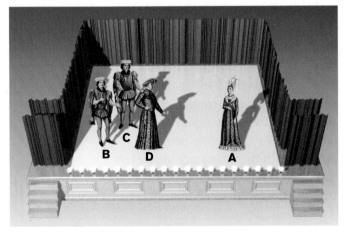

emphasis. If one actor is different from all the rest, dominance is achieved through contrast. A person who sits while others stand, who is in a full back position while others are full front, or who is dressed in one color while others are all dressed in another color will be accented through contrast.

Light and Color A character in a strong pool of light dominates those in a dim light.

The more brilliant the costume color, the more emphasis on the actor. Depending on the costume design for the play as a whole, of course, it is generally assumed that only principal characters should wear red or white, and these colors should be used with care, since they easily attract audience attention.

Speech and Movement The speaker dominates unless there is movement on stage. The moving figure always achieves emphasis. Remember that forward movement is strong; retreating movement is weak.

"Talky" scenes can be made more interesting if you add movement. To accent certain words in the dialogue, move before the line or phrase. Movement after the line stresses the action, not the words. Movement during the line weakens the words, and so is often used when the lines are to be subordinated or "thrown away."

Reinforcement Any major figure who is reinforced or backed up by minor figures achieves attention. A business executive with three secretaries hovering behind is more emphatic than one without any secretaries. The queen with her attendants or the gang leader with thugs behind him are impressive because of the reinforcement. Also, a character can be emphasized with scenery, such as being framed by an arch, a column, or a tree; or a person can be emphasized with furniture such as a high-backed chair.

Artistic Movement
Artistry in blocking means that the stage picture you create with your actors' movement is pleasing to the mind and senses. For stage movement to become satisfying, it must employ the three qualities below.

Variety By presenting various levels of emphasis and changes of mood, a play maintains variety and avoids monotony. Variety helps the audience stay focused on the elements of the plot and follow the progression of the story.

Unity There must be **unity** in the variety and kind of movement the play requires. Unity provides continuity so that a play's disparate elements come together as a whole.

Balance The elements on either side of the playing area should seem to be equal.

The aim is to move from one balanced picture to another during most scenes.

The Balanced Stage Picture
Of course, it's impossible to keep the stage balanced constantly, but the ideal is to attempt to do so. Following are three balance formats to keep in mind:

Symmetrical balance is achieved when there is an equal number of figures on each side of the stage, and all are placed

This scene from *Twelfth Night* creates an artistic picture.

equidistant from the center. This composition is usually artificial and stylized, and it is extremely formal. It is sometimes used to indicate church, state, or courtroom scenes or with certain period plays that demand stylized acting such as Oscar Wilde's *The Importance of Being Earnest.*

Asymmetrical balance is informal. It employs the teeter-totter principle. A lighter figure on one side balances a heavier figure on the other side if the lighter figure is farther from the center. Or a character on one side can balance a group on the other side.

Aesthetic balance is sometimes called psychological balance. It gives the impression of equal weight on both sides of the center, even though the actual weight is not equal. For instance, one major character in the play gives the impression of outweighing several less important characters. A standing figure can balance several seated people. A speaker has more weight than a listener, and a character reinforced by scenery can balance a large group. Strong movement and bright colors also balance large masses.

No matter how you balance your stage area, one curiosity remains: If only one stage area is used for a scene and that area is balanced, the audience will be oblivious to the empty portion of the stage.

These two symmetrically balanced groups present a stylized, formal picture.

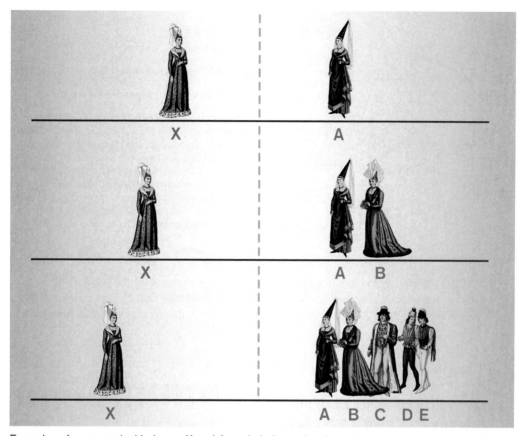

Examples of asymmetrical balance. X and A are in balance, but in order to remain in balance with A and B, X must take one step toward the side. To balance A, B, C, D, E, or more, X must take two steps to the side.

The Director Plots the Blocking

Using the ground or floor plan of the set, the director will place the furniture, being sure to keep important entrances and exits free. Furniture grouping should provide a variety of playing areas. While there should be ample space on stage for movement, there should be enough furniture to prevent the stage from looking bare, unless that is the desired effect.

Next, the director will go through each scene, recording the basic crosses of each character in the margins of the prompt book. He or she will usually block the climactic scenes first to prevent repetition of the climax pictures in earlier, less important scenes. To work out the blocking, some directors use chess pieces, buttons, or inverted golf tees for characters, moving them in various positions on the floor plan.

Alice (A) is standing by the round table. Bob (B) is sitting in a chair. Carl (C) is UR. For the first move ①, Carl exits UC. For the second move ②, Alice crosses to Bob. For the third move ③, Alice moves to the desk. All three movements are indicated at the appropriate place in the script.

When a movement seems effective, the director notes it in the prompt book by drawing in the margin a small rough draft of the stage floor with its furniture placement. Using a different colored pencil for each character, the character's position is labeled, and an arrow is drawn to indicate new movement. Each move is numbered using a corresponding number notated in the script at the exact place in the dialogue where the movement is to be made. Dots or crosses may be used to indicate characters. Sometimes stick figures are used to better visualize the picture and to show characters standing, sitting, and facing in certain directions.

Theatre Journal

When you next find yourself at a large dinner or the school lunchroom, sketch the seating arrangement at a table that holds your interest. Then answer these questions: Who appears to be drawing the most attention at the table? Who appears to be drawing the least attention? What effect does closeness to the center of attention have upon the dynamics of the conversations and behaviors at the table?

PREPARE

Plot the Blocking of Your Scene

You are to assume the director's duties by choosing and analyzing a scene and then blocking it on paper. Your teacher may provide a Blocking Activity Sheet to help you in this. After you have planned the blocking of the scene, you will direct classmates in the scene until the movement is believable, appropriate to the dialogue, and well executed. Follow the steps below as you work on this project:

1. Select a favorite one-act play that has literary merit and that has meaning for you.

2. Consider the theme, style, mood, and structure of the play as well as the motivations and relationships of the characters.

3. Choose a four- to six-minute scene from the play, preferably one with only two or three characters in it. Copy the scene in such a way that you have wide margins for your blocking notations. Make as many copies as there are characters so that each of your actors will have a script from which to read. On a piece of paper or the Activity Sheet, complete a master floor plan using your classroom playing area as the stage size. Draw the necessary furniture, doors, and windows as near to scale as you can approximate.

4. Visualize the scene. Then, on your copy of the script, pencil in blocking notes in the margins by drawing a small, rough floor plan, labeling the characters, and indicating with arrows and lines each cross you want them to make. If the scene you have chosen is "talky," break up the speeches with motivated movement. Remember to consider the meaning, function, and artistic effect of the movements you employ.

5. Set up makeshift furniture, and provide your actors with their scene copies. As they read the scene aloud, direct them according to the blocking you have plotted on your script. As you direct, call each actor by the character's name. Ask the actors to write down their crosses on their scripts. This will enable them to remember the blocking accurately. If necessary, explain your reasons for wanting certain movements. While your directions should be concrete, your aim is to guide, not dictate. Be pleasant, patient, and willing to listen and make changes based on the actors' ideas.

6. Work out your planned movements with the cast. Change and refine them until they work smoothly onstage. Rehearse several times until the actors feel sure of the movement. Time them to be certain the scene does not exceed six minutes.

PRESENT

Introduce and Enjoy Your Blocked Scene

In order for you to present your scene and act in someone else's, this project will probably take several class periods to complete. When your teacher calls for your scene, hand in a copy of your script and ground plan or the Activity Sheet. Set up any furniture that will be needed in the playing area.

Briefly discuss which of the principles provided in the Preview section you used to block this scene. Then introduce your cast and announce the play's title. Finally, join the audience, watching your scene objectively.

Your instructor may offer to show more effective movement for your scene. Accept any suggestions cheerfully.

CRITIQUE

Evaluate Your Classmate's Blocked Scene

Choose one of the scenes presented in class, and evaluate the blocking. Your evaluation should be based on a scale of 1 to 5, in which 1 is equal to "needs much improvement" and 5 is equal to "outstanding." Your evaluation should answer these questions:

- Which character was made to seem most important to the action of the scene, and why?

- How did the blocking help focus attention on the character emphasized in the scene?

- Did you feel that this emphasis was true to the script?

- In what way was the stage picture balanced?

- What did the blocking tell you about the emotional states and relationships of the characters?

Write a short explanation for the rating you gave this scene.

Stage Combat

Actors in a play that involves violence must perform realistic movements safely. Through the use of stage combat, they can make it appear that they are dueling, hitting, punching, pulling hair, or even throwing each other around a room. What they are actually doing is more like dancing than fighting, however. Because it makes use of quick, sharp movements and near misses, stage combat can be dangerous. *Do not attempt stage combat without special training and careful preparation.*

Stage combat is choreographed much like a dance. Like dance, it requires a good deal of rehearsal to get the moves just right.

Hair Pulling One actor grasps the other actor's hair. The second actor hangs on to the wrists of the first and shouts as if hair is being pulled.

Slaps and Punches One actor aims a slap or punch near the victim. The other performs a hidden clap to simulate contact, then reels backward as if hit.

Stabbing An actor shows a knife, dagger, or sword, then turns so that it is hidden to the audience. He or she then plunges forward, thrusting the weapon under the armpit or in some other spot near, not on, the victim. The victim recoils as if stabbed. The weapon is withdrawn with more force than it took to plunge it in and is then disposed of so the audience won't notice the lack of blood.

Falling The secret of falling is to stay relaxed. To lessen the shock, actors break their falls a little at a time–knees, torso, arms, and then head. Whenever possible, they land on soft furniture!

Dying A person who's been shot, stabbed, or beaten tenses immediately, inhales, and doubles toward the wound. The dying person who speaks is generally short of breath, speaking in broken lines with a voice that suggests weakness.

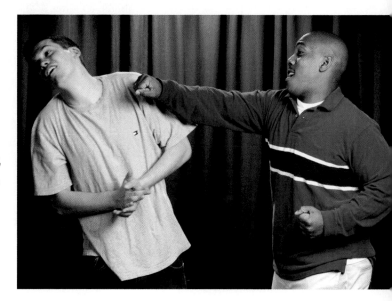

Additional Projects

1 Using one big sofa or over-stuffed armchair, see how many varied groupings you can achieve with two characters.

2 Block scenes which reveal the following situations:

- three people whispering
- two people quarreling
- four people looking for something
- a messenger bringing good news to a group
- three people shopping
- five people showing surprise
- three people telling a story to four others

3 Study famous paintings, and identify the artist's use of balance and emphasis. Write a short essay relating this technique to the theatre. Suggested paintings for study:

- Cézanne's *Card Players*
- De Hooch's *A Dutch Courtyard*
- da Vinci's *The Last Supper*
- Hopper's *Nighthawks*

4 Ask your teacher for help in performing an element of stage combat. Practice the technique, under supervision, until you can execute it well. Then demonstrate your technique for the class.

5 Block a scene from a period play such as *MacBeth* by William Shakespeare or a stylized play such as *A Waitress in Yellowstone* by David Mamet. You can find scenes from these plays in Unit Eight of this book.

Cézanne's *Card Players*

Master of the Craft

Anne Bogart

Method actors are generally directed to first find meaning in a script and let that meaning direct their movements. "Viewpoints," a technique developed by Mary Overlie and made famous by director Anne Bogart, begins with actions and gestures, using them to stimulate emotion and meaning. In intensely physical, expressive stage productions such as "Bob" and "Going, Going, Gone," Bogart has created a radical and influential new way of putting together a play.

Drawing on Overlie's influences as well as Martha Graham, the pioneer of modern dance, and Japanese director Tadashi Suzuki, Bogart has created a distinctive body of work. She once told *American Theatre* magazine that "Viewpoints is a way to practice creating fiction using time and space." It allows actors to create as they rehearse. Thus, they collaborate rather than simply follow directions.

In her actor training workshops, Bogart has actors use Viewpoints to develop a common language of movement. The technique calls for actors to relate to time and space in nine different ways. The four time elements are: tempo, duration, kinesthetic response, and repetition of a movement.

The five elements of space are shape, gesture, architecture, topography, and spatial relationships. The technique unifies the actors and the production. The movements that emerge become part of the play's choreography, so that the physical, mental, and emotional components develop at the same time.

Bogart declares that Viewpoints is not THE way to produce a play, it is ONE way. She is committed to letting every actor—and every production—develop in its own unique way.

"Depending on the point of view, Anne Bogart is either an innovator or a provocateur assaulting a script."

–Mel Gussow, *New York Times*

Anne Bogart

A scene from Bogart's *Dispute*

Theatre **Then** and **Now**

The Ancient Greek Chorus

In ancient Greece, being a member of the chorus was an important role. Early Greek tragedies featured only one actor, who often exited to change costumes, leaving the chorus to continue the story until he returned. The chorus learned about half the lines in the play, all the songs, and all the dances. And every play included dances.

Most often, the Greek chorus made its entrance on stage in a stately march. Chorus members sang and danced in unison and recited their lines together. Occasionally, the chorus would be split into groups. The groups would enter separately and take turns performing.

This Greek chorus in the National Theatre of London's production of the Oresteia trilogy was made up entirely of men.

Once in a while, a second chorus stood mute onstage, except for a few lines. Rarely did individual chorus members have more than a line of their own.

The reason for all this togetherness? The lines, the songs, and the movement of the chorus represented the voice, the sentiment, and the action of society. Greek theatre was about the common good.

A Chorus Line

While the common good in Greek drama was represented by a group that acted as one person, most contemporary work emphasizes the individual who represents one aspect of society. At least, that's the message that comes through in Michael Bennett's *A Chorus Line,* a musical production that opened on Broadway in 1975 and ran continuously for fifteen years.

A Chorus Line celebrates the individual talents and dreams that converge whenever dancers audition for parts in a Broadway chorus line. It allowed the members of a chorus line to present their individual stories before being subsumed into the collective of the Broadway chorus. By the last scene, when the light fades on a kick-line that shows no sign of ending, the audience has come to appreciate the individuals in the chorus line as much as the line itself.

A Chorus Line opened the way to a new sub-genre of musical plays that celebrate creative interchange between the individual and the community. *Rent,* for example, celebrates the power of community to help individuals survive a crisis. In *Stomp,* group members use sticks, brooms, pipes, and trash can lids to create a percussive orchestra celebrating the power of individuals to come together in a collaborative effort. Each of these productions endeavors to portray a community respectful of all its contributors.

Watching *A Chorus Line,* the audience is entertained by the group's precision dancing, but is also touched by the life stories of its individual members.

Chapter
17 Attend a Play

"All the world's a stage," says Jacques in Shakespeare's *As You Like It.* Today that statement may seem particularly appropriate in view of the global world in which we live. While you probably feel very comfortable with television and movies, your experience with live theatre may be limited. This is about to change!

Project Specs

Project Description For this chapter's project, you and a group of friends will attend a local theatre production and then present a ten-minute improvised talk show based on the performance.

Purpose to analyze and better understand the experience of seeing a live performance of a play

Materials the program from a local theatre production; a two-page written description of your experience or the Attend a Play Activity Sheet provided by your teacher

Theatre Terms
active listening
audience participation
ephemeral
metaphoric

On Your Feet

With your classmates, demonstrate several things you should and should not do as an audience member. When you are finished, you may want to look back to Audience Etiquette on page 36.

The Audience and the Theatre

It is often said that theatre requires three things: a story, someone to tell it, and someone to listen and respond. Think about it. As an audience member you are one-third of the theatre experience.

You are part of an audience every day in school. Being an audience member requires participation. Sometimes the participation is active, as when you answer a question asked by a teacher. At other times your participation is limited to **active listening.** When you listen actively, you use what you hear to build meaning and to answer questions you have asked yourself or that have been asked by someone else.

As an audience member at most plays, you will participate by concentrating on the story, asking yourself questions about what you're watching, making connections between what the actors say and what they do, and so on. If you are caught up in the play, you will likely be unaware of the part you are playing in the proceedings. But remember that the audience's concentration and participation is vital to the actors onstage. The actors' energy is reflected back to them in the audience's engagement.

What We Feel in the Theatre

Certainly the aim of all types of theatre should be to help us understand ourselves better as we learn about other people and the world in which we live. There are all kinds of ways theatre can

Audience members enjoy an open-air performance in Oberammergau, Bavaria.

accomplish this goal; even the silliest comedies can make us feel more human by making us laugh at our weaknesses and follies.

Movies, videos, and television may seem similar to live theatre in that each of these media uses a script, actors, directors, and crew members. Each form has plot and characters. However, the experience of seeing a movie is very different from that of seeing a play.

When you watch a movie, you are seeing a series of images arranged into scenes. The scenes are often shot out of sequence. They are then put through an editing process, which controls what audiences end up seeing. The final version of the film is permanent—you can watch a movie over and over again and always see the exact same production. The show is frozen in time.

By contrast, live theatre is **ephemeral.** It is always in the now. Each moment as it passes is gone forever—as is true in life. Even if the play is performed night after night, each performance is a unique experience, because each night there is a different audience dynamic, and various degrees of energy pass among the actors and out to the audience. Unlike other art forms, such as paintings, which remain forever constant, or novels, which present the past reported in the present, theatre lets us experience that which is happening right now. Actors speak as

if for the first time. There is immediacy as theatre gives us a **metaphoric** statement of life, that is, what is happening in that moment onstage represents the events of real life. When we attend the theatre, we have a sense of occasion, of sharing with others the essence of the human condition.

What We See in the Theatre

As playgoers, we can look anywhere on the stage at any time. We change focus depending on what draws our attention. It may be a costume, the look on an actor's face, a particular bit of business, or a painted backdrop upstage. We are free to create the environment in our minds rather than having it focused for us by the camera's lens and the editing process.

Theatre Journal

The next time you are in an audience situation, pay close attention to your fellow audience members. Are they listening attentively? How can you tell? Write a definition of an active audience member.

Spotlight on

Audience Participation

Some shows, particularly those with an improvisatory component, use the audience as part of the act. Many improv troupes, for example, ask audience members to shout out ideas for the improvisers to use as the basis for sketches.

Audience participation is a big part of the fun at the Chicago-based performance phenomenon known as *Too Much Light Makes the Baby Go Blind.* For this show, a small group of improvisers, the Neofuturists, performs "thirty plays in sixty minutes." The material changes from week to week; the performers spend the days in between performances writing batches of new, extremely short plays. During the show the company performs the plays at breakneck speed. The numbers 1 through 30 are pinned onto a clothesline. The audience shouts out a number and the actors rip it down and perform the sketch to which that number was assigned. The Neofuturists also ask questions of the audience, sometimes demanding feedback, sometimes bringing members of the audience onto the stage to participate.

As a special audience-participation bonus, after every sold-out performance, the cast members order pizza for the audience.

By means of a unique blend of performance velocity, improvisation, and sharp writing, the Neofuturists and their ever-changing show *Too Much Light Makes the Baby Go Blind* have become an international phenomenon.

PREPARE

Attend the Play of Your Choice

When we attend a play, we are offered a look into our lives. Sometimes we feel an affirmation as we laugh at situations and characters that encourage us to loosen up. Other times we are pulled into life's serious issues that demand deep thinking and genuine emotional investment. For example, Henrik Ibsen's *An Enemy of the People* addresses environmental issues; Edward Albee's *Three Tall Women* reveals female generational relationships; and Tony Kushner's *Angels in America* focuses on the social, political, and personal ramifications of the AIDS crisis. While many plays do not carry the heavy messages of those named above, most plays give us the opportunity to examine ourselves and our values.

Sometimes as audience members we are not aware of a play's theme until we analyze the play later. At other times the theme is clear throughout the performance.

With a group of friends, you will attend a play. As part of the experience, you will monitor your own, your companions', and the rest of the audience's experience.

Before You Go

To prepare for your theatre-going experience, you and your companions should:

- Buy your tickets in advance.
- Dress appropriately.

- Arrive at the theatre at least fifteen minutes prior to curtain time.
- Consider and discuss your responsibilities as thoughtful and responsive audience members.

While You're There

Before the play begins, observe the audience as they take their seats and settle in. Do they seem excited and happy to be there? Take notes on their behavior before and after the play and during the intermission. You can generally tell by body language, facial expressions, and the amount of shifting or coughing going on whether the audience as a whole is engaged. During the intermission you might even ask your companions and a few of the other audience members what they think about the performance so far. Be aware of your own response as well.

Try to track the play's theme or guiding statement. Remember that the theme is usually found in the way the protagonist handles the play's central conflict. Check in with yourself periodically as you watch the play. When you believe you have become aware of the play's theme, jot it down using as few words as possible. You can always adjust your analysis later on.

When You Leave the Theatre

After the play, make sure you still have your program. Look through it for any director's notes or playwright's notes that might give you further insights into the play. Keep the program. Later, you will turn it in to your teacher.

Sometimes the most enjoyable part of a theatre outing is talking about the play afterward, so try to discuss the play for at least a few minutes with your companions.

When you get home, take some private time to think about your experience at the theatre. Then, with the aid of your notes, write a two-page paper describing that experience. Include the following:

- a summary of the play's theme
- any particularly intriguing perform-ances or memorable lines
- your emotional reaction to the play or to a particular character
- a description in your own words of how attending a play differs from attending a movie or watching television
- at least one paragraph in which you describe the audience response

You will not be reading from your paper. Instead, you will use it as the basis for a panel discussion in which you and the people with whom you attended the play will talk about the experience. You should be familiar enough with the points discussed in your paper that you can easily chat about each.

The Talk Show Format

You will be presenting a live talk show based on your experience of attending the play. Choose a discussion leader (the talk show host) to help focus your group's discussion. This person will introduce each of you and tell the name of the play you attended together. He or she will then ask questions and give each participant a chance to respond. The talk show host must take part in the discussion as well, giving his or her point of view for each question. Questions should be loosely based on the notes each of you took before, during, and after the play. Panel members must answer the ques-tions informally without reading from their notes.

As a group, decide in advance the order of the questions and which topics you will deal with. The talk show host will keep track of the time and make sure your group doesn't go on longer than the ten-minute limit.

Try This

To practice answering questions and giving opin-ions spontaneously, ask a friend or relative to write down four or five questions for you. The questions can range from serious to silly, but they should require some thought on your part. Sit in a chair, read the questions aloud, and prac-tice answering them. This should help prepare you for your talk show participation.

PRESENT

Put on Your Talk Show

When your name or another group member's name is called, give all of your papers or Activity Sheets to your teacher, along with the program for the play. Step into the performance area and set up your chairs in a talk show arrangement, side by side in a straight line or a semicircle.

The talk show host will introduce each of you and begin the discussion by asking a question. When it is your turn to answer, try to present as clear a picture of your experience as you can. For example, if you felt excitement during the performance convey that to the class. Make sure you discuss both your own reaction and your perception of the audience's reaction to the play.

When nine minutes have passed, the host should start to wrap things up by asking the group for any final thoughts. At the end of the ten minutes, stop the discussion, shake hands with your fellow participants, and return to your seat.

Students present a talk show.

CRITIQUE

Evaluate a Panelist's Performance

There is a difference between playing a part and playing yourself. Some people have a much more difficult time being themselves in front of an audience than they do playing a character.

Remaining relaxed and comfortable in front of an audience without notes or a script can be nerve-wracking. You will see that some of your classmates are better at it than others. Select one classmate from a talk show panel who struck you as the most effective speaker in the group, the student you would rate as "outstanding." Write a paper explaining why. Ask yourself the questions below as you evaluate the outstanding individual in the talk show panel.

- What did the panelist do to appear physically comfortable?

- What elements (humor, enthusiasm, storytelling, etc.) did this person use to engage the audience?

- What aspects of the panelist's behavior particularly engaged you?

- How did the other participants in the presentation react to this panelist?

- What insights into the theatre-going experience impressed you in the panelist's remarks?

- What insights brought you to a higher level of understanding?

Additional Projects

1 Attend a play, or watch a filmed version of a play of your choice. Choose a particular actor to focus on throughout the play. Keep a list of questions you would ask this actor about the performance.

2 Imagine that you are the house manager and you have been asked to deliver a curtain speech before the beginning of the current play. Your goal is to make the audience feel welcome and to give them a few pre-show instructions. Confine your speech to ninety seconds but make sure you include the following elements.

- Greet the audience and thank them for coming.
- Warn them not to take photographs during the show.
- Tell them to turn off their beepers and cell phones.
- Tell them to unwrap their candy before the show begins.
- Thank them again, and tell them to enjoy the show.

3 A good audience is often a knowledgeable audience. Write an outline with as much detail as you can find about the theatre of a particular country or era.

4 Read the scene from *The Actor's Nightmare* by Christopher Durang, found in Unit Eight of this book, and think about the nightmare aspect of this scene. Write a short scene of your own entitled *The Student's Nightmare*.

Think of a few questions you might ask the actor playing Charlotte in *Charlotte's Web*.

Theatre **Then** and **Now**

The Roman Audience in 200 A.D.

Imagine that you are attending a play at the imposing Roman theatre at Sabratha, around 200 A.D. You are one of thousands of people lucky enough to get a seat in the largest theatre in North Africa. By this time Roman theatres have been constructed all over Italy, Spain, and France, as well as North Africa.

Imagine the noise all these people are making. Then consider the fact that the performance is held outdoors and the performers onstage have no microphones or other artificial amplification.

In such a large performance space, subtlety won't be the first order of business. In fact, most of the actors wear masks painted with characteristic facial expressions that can be seen by audience members seated great distances away.

If you picture yourself sitting high in the stands at a football stadium watching a play going on down there on the 50-yard line, you'll have some idea of the dimensions. You should also consider that your seat is made of stone. There are no artificial lights of course, so the play is performed using that most natural of lighting systems—the sun.

For your theatre comfort, there are awnings, fruit vendors, and if it gets particularly hot, showers of perfumed water. More likely than not, you are watching a bawdy farce full of greed, horseplay, infidelities, and women in scanty costumes. Here you are, centuries in the past, watching a performance not unlike the TV situation comedies of today!

In the theatre at Sabratha, the audience sat on the tiered stone seats at the left while the actors performed on the dark street-like area to the right.

An Off-Broadway Audience Today

Flash forward to a typical off-Broadway theatre in the early 21st century. There are anywhere from 150 to 300 seats in a performance space that seems almost intimate. You sit down on a soft cushioned seat in a room that, no matter what the weather outdoors, is temperature-controlled for maximum comfort. You and your fellow audience members are cautioned via a high-tech sound system to turn off your cell phones, beepers, and other noisemakers for the duration of the performance.

The lights go to black. Then they rise again, and the actors begin to perform. They could be in your living room—that's how well you can hear them, thanks to that same high-tech sound system, which has tiny powerful microphones placed on, around, or above the stage. You have no problem seeing the actors, partly because they're not all that far away from you and partly because of an offstage light board, which is run by computer. The lights create subtle effects that allow you to enjoy a very realistic setting.

The acting is very natural, and the play's subject speaks to the issues of our day and the concerns of our hearts. When the play ends, the actors take their bows. You can see the pride in each of their faces.

This off-Broadway experience bears little resemblance to watching a sitcom—it is much more real and immediate. And while we may sometimes choose the farce and fantasy of TV, there's so much more being offered in live theatre.

The Culture Project on Bleecker Street in New York City performs *Rev. Billy and the Church of Stop Shopping.*

Unit Four Review

PREVIEW

Examine the following key concepts previewed in Unit Four.

1 What are Aristotle's six basic elements of drama?

2 Put the following plot elements in the order they should occur.

Climax	Falling Action	Exposition	Inciting Incident
Crisis	Resolution	Rising Action	

3 Who selects the play, the producer or the director?

4 What are royalties?

5 What is the difference between an audition and a callback?

6 The most important thing a casting director looks for in an actor is:
   a. enthusiasm   b. intensity   c. best suited to role   d. a supple voice

7 If you agree to perform in a full-length play, how long can you expect to be in rehearsal?

8 How does a ground plan help block a play?

9 Match the scenes described below to the area where they would most likely be presented onstage.

a scene in which two lovers kiss	Area 1
a fantasy scene	Area 2
a scene in which two nobles meet	Area 3
a scene that is the play's dramatic high point	Area 4
a scene where someone listens in	Area 5
	Area 6

10 Compare watching a movie to attending live theatre.

PREPARE

Assess your response to the preparation process for projects in this unit.

11 Explain which of the following was the most difficult for you in preparing your drama scenario: finding the subject, creating the characters, or developing a conflict.

12 What was the most difficult aspect of creating a rehearsal schedule?

13 Which of the steps in blocking your scene did you find most challenging?

14 Which do you find most satisfying: writing scenes, blocking scenes, discussing scenes, or acting in scenes? Explain why.

PRESENT

Analyze the experience of presenting your work to the class.

15 In sharing your drama scenario, did you feel that you were connecting with the audience?

16 Do you find question-and-answer sessions after giving a presentation interesting and informative or nerve-wracking and embarrassing? Explain.

17 In your talk show discussion, did all members have an equal chance to describe their theatre-going experience?

CRITIQUE

Evaluate how you go about critiquing your work and the work of others.

18 Did you find it easier to assess a classmate's drama scenario, play analysis, blocking, or talk show contribution? Why?

19 Did you feel that the presenters were asked meaningful questions during question-and-answer periods? Give two examples.

20 How did evaluating the work of others help you approach your own?

EXTENSIONS

- With a partner, block a short scene in which you play a game of imaginary darts and discuss the wonders (and flaws) of the opposite sex.

- Research and discuss additional elements of stage combat.

Unit Five

Technical Theatre

211

Chapter
18 Set Design and Construction

The magic of theatre, like the genius of invention, is as much a matter of sweat as inspiration. Set designers and construction experts use hard work and imagination in order to help realize a play's vision.

Project Specs

Project Description You will create a set design for a one-act play or a scene from a longer work. Then you will present your work in a five- to ten-minute talk.

Purpose to understand the basics of set design and the connection between stage design and the effectiveness of a production

Materials a hand-drawn, computer-generated, or three-dimensional design for a stage plan and/or the Set Design and Construction Activity Sheet provided by your teacher

Theatre Terms

arena stage
box set
curtain set
cyclorama (stage
  curtain)
drops
elevation sketch
flats
minimal set
permanent set
prism set
proscenium stage
scrim
set pieces
teaser
thrust stage
unit set

On Your Feet

Using the materials available in the room, design a space that is especially suited to one of the following functions: a business meeting, a friendly lunch, a therapy session, a flea market. Test your design by inviting two or more students to improvise a short scene in the space you have created.

The set design for *Phantom of the Opera* is suitably atmospheric and elaborate.

PREVIEW

Principles of Design

The same skills that help you match your wardrobe, decorate your room, and fulfill art projects can be put into play for stage design. Learning set design and construction principles can take you a long way toward understanding the play's meaning. Scenery is often the first thing that shows the audience something about the time, the setting, and the even the purpose of the play.

Some sets tell you immediately about the people who live in these surroundings. Others tell you more about their environment, their psychological states, or conditions under which they live. For example, *Our Town* is a very powerful play about human emotion that uses very little scenery. Instead, the imagination of the audience, and the strong interpretations of the actors set the scene.

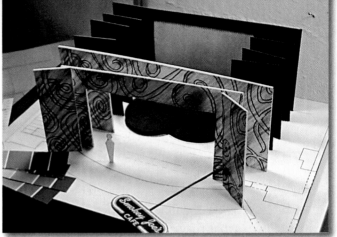

Some designers create a model of the proposed set, such as this one for *Smokey Joe's Cafe.*

When designing scenery, the director, set designer, and technical director study the play to determine the style, atmosphere, and color they want to create. In Chapter 16, you learned how important a ground plan (or floor plan) is to blocking the play. This bird's-eye view of the set—showing doors, windows, walls, stairs, platforms, ramps, and furniture placement—is also important to the people working on the design and construction of the set. The ground plan should be as detailed as possible so that that the stage crew can build the set to the necessary specifications.

The designer also does an **elevation sketch,** which shows how the stage will look from the audience, and a color rendering of the set. These sketches and the ground plan will go into the prompt book. Some scene designers also construct a three-dimensional model that is an accurate miniature reproduction of the set, showing construction, furniture, and so on.

Types of Stages

The kind of stage available for your production influences the kind of set design you can create. You must know your performance space very well— its challenges and its potential. Get to know the different types of stages and what they can offer a production.

The Proscenium Stage The **proscenium stage** is like a picture frame. The audience sits looking into the frame to see the play. It is separated from the audience by three stage walls and an invisible "fourth wall," which the audience looks through. Proscenium productions generally require the most elaborate set designs since they cover three sides of the performance space.

The Thrust Stage A low platform stage that juts (or "thrusts") out into the audience, with seating on three sides, is called a **thrust stage.** This kind of stage offers opportunities to create several distinct acting areas. Set designs are usually minimal.

The Arena Stage Arena staging, sometimes called "theatre-in-the-round," seats the audience entirely around the playing area. An **arena stage** encourages actor-audience interaction, but it requires a set that allows for continuous movement onstage and one that does not block audience viewing from any side of the house. Due to the closeness of the audience, props and scenery must look authentic.

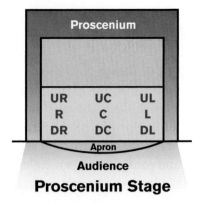

Proscenium Stage

The proscenium stage, with its grand frame, is the most common of all types of stages.

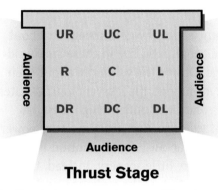

Thrust Stage

The thrust stage comes in many different shapes, but always juts out into the audience. The Globe Theatre is a thrust stage.

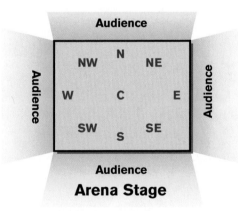

Arena Stage

The arena stage, in which only the center of the stage corresponds to traditional stage positions. Here the points of the compass are often used instead.

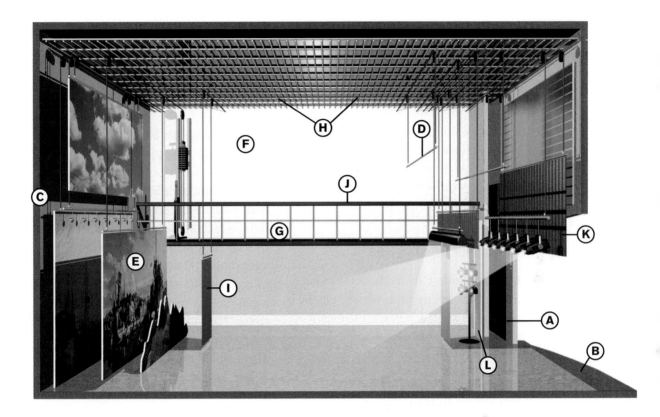

Stage Elements

Knowing, understanding, and using the terms that follow will help you as you learn about designing and constructing stage sets. Take time to read the definitions. Some of their counterparts can be seen on the accompanying diagram.

Act Curtain (A) Curtain that masks the acting area from the audience. Sometimes called the front or grand curtain, it is opened at the beginning of the play and closed between acts or scenes. It usually parts in the middle.

Apron (B) Acting area between the front edge of the stage and the front curtain.

Back Wall (C) Opposite the proscenium opening; it can be used as a background for exterior sets.

Battens (D) Long pipes or poles from which curtains, lights, or flats are hung.

Cyclorama or **Cyc** Background curtain covering stage back and sides.

Drop or **backdrop (E)** A canvas or muslin curtain, usually painted, that forms part of the scenery.

Flies (F) Area above the stage where scenery is hung out of view.

Fly Gallery (G) Narrow platform about halfway up the backstage side wall from which the lines for flying scenery are worked. Without a fly gallery, you may work fly lines from the backstage floor. For a close-up of the rigging for flying flats, see page 219.

Gridiron or **Grid (H)** Framework of beams above the stage that supports riggings for flying scenery.

Ground Cloth Canvas that covers the floor of the acting area, which may be painted to resemble bricks, stones, carpet, and so forth.

Leg (I) One of a pair of drapes hung stage right and left behind the tormentors to mask the backstage.

Pin Rail (J) Rail on the fly gallery or backstage wall to which lines are pulled and tied off. (See page 219.)

Proscenium Arch Frame or opening of a proscenium stage through which the audience views the play.

Teaser (K) Heavy curtain or canvas-covered wooden frame hung above the proscenium opening to adjust the height of the opening. Shorter curtains hung at intervals to mask lights and unused scenery are called *borders*.

Tormentors (L) Curtain or flat at each side of the proscenium opening used to regulate the width of the opening.

Trap Opening in the stage floor.

Wings The offstage area to the left and right of the stage.

Constructing the Sets

When the ground plan, sketch, and model are complete, the scene construction and painting crews begin their work. Most sets are built using **flats,** which are wooden frames covered by canvas, muslin, or lightweight wood and painted. Flats can be lashed together to create walls and doorways. They can be painted in realistic or symbolic styles. They can become the backdrop for the furniture or **set pieces** (three-dimensional objects such as rocks, trees, or ramps).

Building Flats
Basic Construction

With adequate equipment and knowledge, and with assistance from the school's shop director, technical director, or other knowledgeable adult, you can create flats—wooden frames made from 1-inch x 4-inch white pine. Most flats are 12 feet high and no wider than 5 feet, 9 inches. Wider flats won't fit through doors and are hard to handle. Most flats are covered with eight-ounce flameproof canvas or six-ounce muslin, but some use a hard lightweight sheet of wood (often lauan) that is glued and stapled to the frame. Hard-cover flats are more expensive but easier to make. Muslin is cheaper, but it is not as durable as canvas and must be made flameproof. All flats must be made ready for painting. Follow the instructions that follow and refer to the illustrations to build a canvas-covered flat.

1 Cut the frame

- To use a butt joint, which is the most common way to join pieces of the frame, cut the two horizontal pieces, the rails, the width you want the finished flat to be. Measure carefully: Lumber sizes are not exact. Lumber marked 1 x 4 inches will actually measure 3/4 x 3 1/2 inches.
- Cut the two vertical pieces, the stiles, the required height less the width of the two rails.
- Cut the toggle rails the width of the flat minus the width of the two stiles. Use one toggle rail about every 5 feet.
- Cut the keystones and corner blocks out of 1/4-inch plywood. Keystones are 6 inches long; corner blocks have 8-inch legs.

2 Assemble the frame

- Place the ends of the stiles against the edges of the rails. Using a framing square to ensure square corners, nail the corner blocks over the butt joints, setting them 3/4 inch inside all outer edges. (This border allows two flats to be placed tightly together at right angles.)

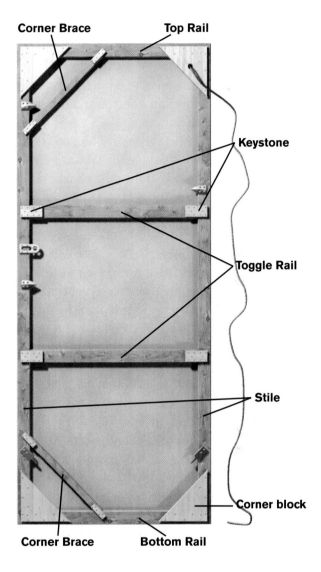

Corner Brace   Top Rail

Keystone

Toggle Rail

Stile

Corner block

Corner Brace   Bottom Rail

- Set in the toggle rails and nail them between the stiles with keystone blocks.
- Attach the two corner braces (cut approximately the length of the rail) on the same side to prevent the flat from twisting.

3 Cover the flat

- Turn the frame over so that it rests on the corner blocks.
- Cut a piece of flameproof canvas or muslin 4 inches wider than the frame.
- Starting at the center of a stile, tack or staple the fabric along the side of the stile closest to the opening of the frame every 4 or 5 inches.
- Lift the fabric and spread glue along the top of the stiles and rails. Then bring the muslin over the glued surface, smoothing it with a wooden block. The muslin should sag a bit because it will shrink when painted.
- Tack or staple the fabric to the outer edges of the stiles, spacing tacks to fall between the staples already placed.
- Paint the flat with sizing (a mixture that seals and provides a good painting surface).
- When the fabric has dried, use a utility knife to trim the fabric 1/8 inch from the edge.

4 Join the flats

- Screw in both the lash-line cleats for connecting flats as a wall and the tie-off cleat about two feet from the floor.
- Attach the lash-line cord.
- Drill a hole in the upper right corner block.

Staple the fabric to the inner edge of the stile.

Be careful not to glue the braces or the toggle rail.

Cutting 1/8" from the edge avoids having loose threads hanging over the edge.

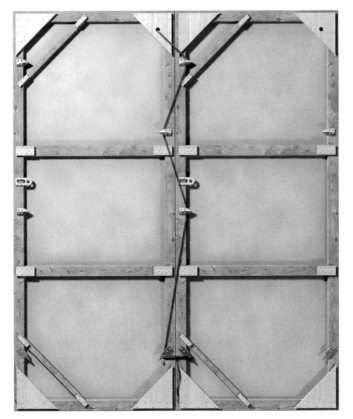

Lashed flats

- Thread a 1/4-inch cotton sash cord through the hole and knot it. Pull the cord tight, and cut it off 6 inches longer than the flat.
- Apply dutchman, 4-inch strips of muslin, to cover the cracks between the flats.

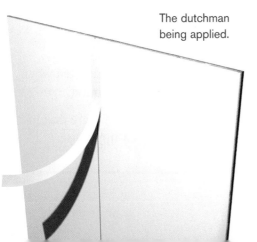

The dutchman being applied.

Drops and Set Pieces

Drops can be painted on muslin or **scrim** (theatrical gauze). You hang these above the **teaser,** a curtain or other flat piece hung behind the act curtain, so that the audience cannot see them until they are dropped. Many theatres use a counterweight system to make drops easy to raise and lower. Set pieces are usually rolled in from the wings. Sets should be finished at least one week before production, to allow technicians and actors to have several "tech rehearsals," in which all technical elements are polished before opening night.

Close-up of a drop with a counterweight. Lines or cables run through pulleys and are tied off at the pin rail.

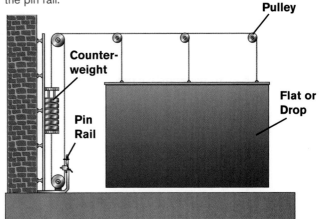

Construction Safety Tips

Scene shops and stages abound with potential hazards. People are working simultaneously at different jobs—sawing, nailing, painting, and moving sets. Ropes and cables are hung overhead to suspend heavy instruments that, if accidentally dropped, could cause severe injury. Often actors need to walk backstage in the dark amid furniture, properties, and lighting cable. To prevent people from getting hurt, observe these safety rules—and make up more if the situation demands!

General Safety Tips

- Keep all working areas clean and organized.

- Be alert to what others are doing. As in driving, construction safety requires a defensive approach.

- Know the location of fire extinguishers on the stage, in the shop, and in the control booth, and know how to use them.

- Know the location of a well-equipped first-aid kit.

- Report all injuries or potential hazards to your instructor.

- Before raising or lowering a batten yell "Heads up!" and wait for everyone to respond before continuing.

Shop Safety Tips

- Wear protective clothing, including long pants, long sleeves, and hard-toed, rubber-soled shoes. Avoid loose clothing or jewelry that could get caught in power tools.

- Tie back long hair to prevent its being caught in power tools.

- Wear protective gear when necessary. Depending on the job, you might need goggles, earplugs, a dust mask, or a mask that filters out fumes.

- Know how to use your tools. Obey any warnings on tools. If you don't know what you are doing, don't do it!

- Pay attention. Don't talk and become distracted.

- Unplug all power tools immediately after using them.

- Look for and correct any potential hazard, such as nails sticking out of boards.

- Watch where you are going. Look up if people are working above you. Also, don't work on the floor when someone is overhead on a ladder, as tools can fall.

- Keep the shop well ventilated when dust and fumes are around.

- Use tools only as they were designed to be used. Do not improvise.

Basic Supplies for Scene Construction

Tools
box cutter
drill, electric and hand
hammers
hot glue gun
level
pliers
saws, hand and electric
screwdrivers, cordless and hand
staple gun
wood clamps
wrenches

Hardware
cleats
   lash-line
    stage brace
    tie-off
hinge
nails
screws

Painting
brushes
brush cleaner
drop cloths
masking tape
paint
rollers
sizing

Measuring
framing square
miter box
tape measure

Miscellaneous
canvas/unbleached muslin
dust masks
ear plugs
gaffers tape, black and white
goggles
ladder
nails, screws, tacks
rope
white glue
wire
wood
   1/4" plywood
   1" x 2" boards
   1" x 4" boards

Working with the Space

Like the actor, the set must help tell the story that is being presented on stage. Sets must be effective, easy to move, and solidly built. Most importantly, the set must create a space in which the actor can easily move and feel in character.

The **box set,** consisting of two or three walls and, perhaps, a ceiling, is the most common theatrical set. Its simplicity makes it very flexible. On one hand, it can be made to look incredibly realistic. On the other, it can provide a bland backdrop for experimental or surreal productions.

To change this unit set, the balcony may be removed and a small porch added to the house, while apples or fall leaves may be attached to the tree.

The **unit set** is made of several pieces, or units, which can be rearranged to produce more than one setting. Unit sets are useful in plays requiring many scene changes. One kind of unit set is made of many individual flats that can be moved or struck completely to form a different setting. Another kind of unit set uses generic openings that can be dressed to represent doors, windows, or other elements.

The **permanent set** remains in place throughout a production. Additional elements may be added to the set to imply a change in scene, but the basic structure always remains. Some permanent sets have many playing areas, and so they are sometimes known as *multiple sets*.

This box set contains a number of windows and a door. Using *backing*, flats that mask the backstage area from view, makes the set seem more realistic.

Changes to the permanent set will probably involve lighting and props.

A dramatic statement can be made in a minimal set with the use of bold pattern and color.

The **minimal set,** which is sometimes called the profile set, is usually made of two-fold or three-fold flats that can be used to represent walls or hide and reveal furniture.

The **prism set** uses prisms, or *periaktoi,* three-sided flats mounted on a wheeled carriage. They can be moved or pivoted, and individual flats can be inserted between prisms to create scenic elements.

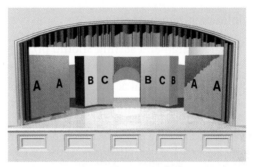

A prism set showing one possible arrangement.

The **curtain set** makes use of the **cyclorama,** or **stage curtain,** at the back of the stage, as part of the background. A few additional flats can highlight doors, fireplaces, or architectural elements, and set pieces can be arranged as if the curtains were walls and drapes.

The same prism set with the flats rearranged.

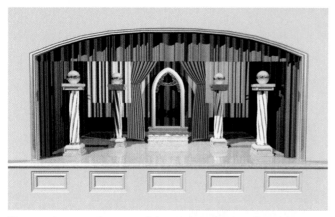

The curtain set makes use of the cyclorama as well as other curtains to create a formal setting.

Design Requirements

Though your play's scenery will depend upon the stage facilities, available crew, and your budgeted time and money, your design should meet the following requirements.

- The design and setting should provide adequate space for movement, including several acting areas or levels to provide variety and interest and to motivate the actors into using the whole stage in the course of the play.

- The design and setting should communicate the time and place in which the action occurs and the cultural, social, and economic status of the characters.

- From observing the scenery with its particular color and design, the audience should immediately be able to judge the mood and style of the play.

- The design and setting must be technically usable and safe. Doors and windows must open if they are to be used. Stairs, platforms, and ramps must be built firmly if they are to bear the actor's weight. If there are set changes, scenery must be planned for quick shifts carried out safely.

What mood does this set, used in the play *Broken Sleep*, create?

- The design and setting should be pleasing to the eye. It should be unified, balanced, and varied, and it should allow for the actors' faces to be readily seen. Most of all, it should be unobtrusive—except in the rare case when the characters are in conflict with their environment.

- The design should include set pieces that are functional and that contribute to the overall design of the set.

Setting the Mood

Your set can help establish the mood of your production by its angularity or softness, its luxury or sparseness, its complexity or simplicity. None of these elements will have as immediate an effect, however, as the colors you use in your design. Scientists who have studied color have learned that various colors have specific emotional effects. Reds, oranges, and yellows, for example, are considered warm tones. They tend to be stimulating and exciting. Blues, greens, and violets are cool colors that tend to be relaxing or sobering. Of course, too much of any one tone or set of tones can be simply annoying. But careful use of color can help establish the character and overall mood in a play and influence the audience's response.

Certain colors arouse specific emotions. The set designer is always aware of this.

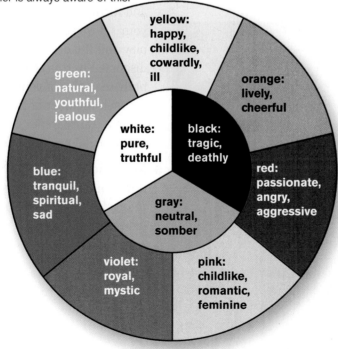

yellow: happy, childlike, cowardly, ill

orange: lively, cheerful

green: natural, youthful, jealous

white: pure, truthful

black: tragic, deathly

red: passionate, angry, aggressive

blue: tranquil, spiritual, sad

gray: neutral, somber

violet: royal, mystic

pink: childlike, romantic, feminine

PREPARE

Work on Your Set Design

In order to create a set design, you will first have to determine the type and size of stage you will be working on (or perhaps the size and layout of your classroom playing area). Measure the stage or acting space and draw a ground plan using either the Activity Sheet your teacher provides, a computer program, or pencil and paper. A good scale of measure might be 1 foot equals 1/4 inch. If you have access to graph paper, this might be very helpful in drawing your ground plan. Follow the step-by-step instructions at right to continue working on your set design.

1 **Read a play.** (Your instructor may wish to assign you one.) Determine the kind of design, style, and color you think will best communicate the play's intent.

2 **Make a list of your ground plan needs,** such as all necessary doors, windows, furniture, set pieces, and stairs.

3 **Fill in the Activity Sheet** or create your drawn or computer-generated ground plan, always keeping in mind your understanding of the play's theme, mood, period, and locale.

4 **Prepare a five- to ten-minute talk** explaining your set design in terms of its colors, style, sets, and scenery and furniture placement. Tell how your set meets both the intent of the play and the design requirements discussed in this chapter. If possible, prepare copies of your ground plan for each member of the class or make a transparency to be used on an overhead projector as a visual aid.

5 **Rehearse and time your report** until you can give it in a smooth and interesting manner in no more than ten minutes.

A very minimal set can make a strong statement.

PRESENT

Unveil Your Design

When your name is called, hand in your Activity Sheet or ground plan and walk to the playing area. Be sure to hand out copies of your ground plan to the class before you begin your talk. If you have prepared a transparency, place it on the overhead projector before you begin. Remember, if you show interest and enthusiasm in what you are saying, your listeners will be interested and alert also.

Theatre Journal

Write a description of one or more of the spaces you frequent. Examine the design elements of the space. See if you can figure out how the designers achieved or failed to achieve a desired mood. Try to determine how the appealing elements would be translated to the stage.

CRITIQUE

Evaluate Your Classmate's Set Design and Presentation

Choose one of the designs presented in class and evaluate it using a scale from 1 to 5. A rating of 5 equals "outstanding," while a rating of 1 equals "needs much improvement." As you prepare your critique, think about the following questions.

- How easy to read and understand was the set design?

- What elements necessary for a production of the play were incorporated in the ground plan?

- In what ways did the set design plan fulfill the needs of the play's theme?

- Did the set design cover all the important design requirements?

- How did the speaker go about convincing you that this design would enhance the play?

- What were the strengths and weaknesses of the speaker's presentation style?

Write a paragraph explaining why you gave this presentation the score you did.

Additional Projects

1 Construct a model of a set you have designed.

2 Research one of the following subjects and give a report or demonstration on it:

   a Painting special effects

   b Constructing a practical rock, tree, and/or column

   c Using materials to make masks and/or props

3 Choose a musical such as *Stomp* or *Rent* and design on paper or computer a backdrop for the set.

4 Indicate the kinds of color, design approach, kind of set, and kind of stage you would ideally use for two of the books listed below if they were brought to the stage. Explain your choices in a few sentences.

   Lord of the Rings
   Catcher in the Rye
   The Joy Luck Club
   Hatchet
   Native Son

5 On paper or a computer, create a set design for *The School for Scandal* by Richard Brinsley Sheridan based on the scene found in Unit Eight of this book. Keep in mind the time period and tone of the scene, as well as set elements such as screens, curtains, set pieces, furniture, and a background.

Master of the Craft

G. W. "Skip" Mercier

One day, when he was an English major at the University of California at Berkeley, G. W. "Skip" Mercier walked into Henry May's office. May was a set designer who took great joy in his work and who won awards no set designer had ever won before. May's office was covered with photos and drawings, and Mercier studied them for more than an hour. He fell in love with the "visual magic" he saw on May's walls, and from that moment, his career was decided.

Mercier went on to design numerous plays on and off Broadway. Over the years, he's been nominated for a Tony Award and several Drama Desk Awards for his set design. And he's in constant demand, working on Broadway and for major regional theatres throughout the country, including Arena Stage, Alliance Theatre, and Lincoln Center. He has also taught design at the National Theatre Institute for the past 18 years.

Mercier says that his mentor, May, "showed me that being a good designer was in direct proportion to being a good man." If that's true, Mercier must be an impressive person. His set designs are creative, effective, and true to the productions they support.

G.W. Mercier

A 1" scale model set was created by Mercier for Shakespeare's *The Taming of the Shrew*, directed by Julie Taymor.

Mercier created this elegant set for *Dead Guilty*, presented at Studio Arena Theatre and directed by Jane Page.

Theatre **Then** and **Now**

Staging Through the Ages

Early Mechanics

Although staging in ancient Greece was simple, it did include the use of a large crane, which could lower and raise characters above the playing area. Since these "flying" characters were often gods who arrived in time to resolve a problem, the apparatus was named *deus ex machina,* or "god in the machine." The Greeks also used the three-sided *periaktoi,* discussed previously on page 223.

The Romans, whose appetite for spectacle knew no bounds, developed more elaborate special effects. In their productions, forests filled with exotic animals appeared from nowhere, and fountains spouting wine rose up from under the stage or arena floor.

Theatre died out during Europe's Dark Ages, but plays based on biblical themes began to be performed in churches during the second half of the 11th century. Large audiences and increasingly bawdy subject matter forced drama out of the churches and into the streets.

In the Middle Ages, plays were mounted on pageant wagons that traveled throughout Europe. Each scene of the play might be set on a separate wagon,

The pageant wagon rolls into town.

with machinery and costumes stored below and the playing area above. Guilds, or groups of tradesmen, sponsored these wagons and competed with each other to create elaborate effects. One device, called Hell's Mouth, resembled the jaws of a fire-breathing dragon, complete with smoke and flames.

The Renaissance, which began in Italy in the 14th century, brought a rebirth of interest in art, including theatre, and spectacular effects continued to play an important part. In England, where the Renaissance was slower to take hold, dramas were performed on simple stages with little or no scenery, but by the 17th century, England too began to experiment with trapdoors, "flying" characters, raked stages, and movable scenery.

Current Technology

The Industrial Age that spread through Europe and the United States in the late 18th and 19th centuries brought new technology to the theatre. Crews needed technical help to move heavy furniture, roll flats on and off the stage, and handle more complex scenery and theatrical effects.

Today, it is not uncommon for entire stages to rotate and for scenery to move by an unseen hand. Many professionally staged musicals include spectacular technical effects. *The Phantom of the Opera,* for example, features a computerized chandelier that swings out over the audience as well as a gondola that floats through misty, candlelit waters. (See pages 212–213.) *Les Misérables* uses massive wooden barricades that pivot in from each side of the stage and connect to become a "practical" unit onto which the actors can climb. (See page 211.) The staging for *Starlight Express* includes multiple tracks on which actors skate around the audience area and uses a double-decker railroad trestle bridge on stage that moves into place as the audience watches.

Technology is still a handmaiden to the play, but it is an increasingly capable servant, providing ever more impressive effects.

Wiring helps the descending angel in Tony Kushner's play *Angels in America*.

Chapter
19 Lighting

You are sitting in a theatre as the house lights slowly dim. There is a hush as the audience waits in anticipation. The curtain opens and the lights rise on the scene. It's a different world up there on the stage—both magical and recognizable. The lighting is a key factor in its creation.

Project Specs

Project Description You will create a lighting plot for one scene in a play and present it to the class in a five- to ten-minute talk.

Purpose to understand the basics of stage lighting and to implement principles of visibility, mood, and color

Materials a lighting plot on paper (showing color, type, intensity, and beam of lighting) for a scene from a play or the Lighting Activity Sheet your teacher provides

On Your Feet

Think back to a play or television show you saw recently. Discuss with a partner anything you can remember about the lighting. Your discussion might consist of statements such as, "The kitchen was lighted with warm lights, including a lamp the actors could turn on and off" or "There was dim light outside the windows of the office building, which made it look like a winter afternoon."

Theatre Terms
barn doors
batten or teaser batten
border lights or
  strip lights
cross light
dimmers
ERS (ellipsoidal
  reflector spotlight)
floodlights
followspots
Fresnel
gelatins (gels)
gobo
roundels
scoops
spill
spotlights
tableau

PREVIEW

The Functions of Lighting

Among other things, effective stage lighting provides visibility, establishes emphasis and mood, and provides logical light sources.

1 First, the audience has to be able to see the onstage action. Visibility is the number one requirement of stage lighting. If there is too much light, the result will be a glare. If there is too little, the audience must strain to see. The goal for a lighting designer is to create a balance of intensity that allows the audience to see without being overly aware of the lights. Even if a scene is to be played "in darkness," it should start with extremely dim lighting that rises very gradually as the scene progresses.

2 Lighting also creates emphasis and mood. Bright lights tend to dominate while dim lights subordinate, so stage areas that carry the most important action usually need brighter and more dramatic lighting. The mood of the play serves as a guide for how the lights will be blended. Comedies generally require a mix of bright lights in mostly warm colors. A tragedy or serious drama usually calls for a blend of medium to low tones, shadows, and cool colors.

3 Finally, lighting should be "logical." It should accurately reproduce obvious light sources such as the sun, moon, a fireplace, lamps, and so on. By suggesting the light source, you can often imply the time of day and the weather. A cool blue apparently coming in through a window can suggest early morning. A bright, warm amber light may indicate late afternoon on a warm, sunny day.

The Williamstown Theatre Festival's production of Arthur Miller's *All My Sons* uses evocative lighting.

Equipment and Accessories for Lighting

Piece of Equipment	Description	
ERS (ellipsoidal reflector spotlight), sometimes called a Leko	throws strong, focused light from long distance	
Fresnel spotlight	throws softer light on larger area from shorter distance	
scoop floodlight	lights large areas in strong light	
followspot	throws bright focused light on a moving actor	
border lights/strip lights	washes light over a large area	
lighting control board	the unit that controls the operation of lights and dimmer board	

Accessory Piece	Description	
batten	metal pipe that holds lights	
gelatins or gels	color filters for creating colored light	
twist-lock connectors	connect lights to source of power	
pin connectors	connect lights to source of power	
gobos	metal disks with cutouts for creating patterns of light, sometimes called cookies	
roundels	colored glass disks used in strip lights to create color onstage	

The Types and Elements of Lighting Instruments

There are four main types of stage lights. **Spotlights** produce focused illumination, while **floodlights** illuminate, or flood, broad areas of the stage. **Strip,** or **border, lights** provide a wide, uniform wash of light; **followspots** produce a strong beam of light that follows an actor while he or she moves about the stage. These instruments and their accessories are pictured on pages 234–235.

The main elements of these lighting instruments are:

1 a bulb, referred to as a *lamp,* which produces the light

2 a *reflector,* which reflects the light and throws it forward onto the area to be lighted

3 the *lens,* which focuses and shapes the light

4 the *housing,* or metal framework, which encloses the unit and holds the gels

5 shutters, used in the housing of some lights to shape the beam of light.

Spotlights One very efficient spotlight is the **Fresnel,** which has a ridged lens, tubular lamp, and a parabolic mirror reflector. Beams from the Fresnel cast diffused or soft-edged light pools, which blend easily with other lighted areas. **Barn doors** are usually used with Fresnels to control the beam of light with their movable flaps.

Another type of spotlight is the **ERS (ellipsoidal reflector spot).** It features a plano-convex lens, a tubular lamp, and an oval-shaped reflector. Spots such as these are excellent for situations in which the light must be thrown a great distance, as the beam is strong and can be focused with extreme precision. This instrument is ideal for lighting an area without **spill,** or unwanted light leakage. The beam can be narrowed or widened to provide either a harsh or

The logical light in this scene comes from the fire pit.

The starlight pattern for this scene from *Space* by Tina Landau was created using a gobo.

a soft edge. As a rule, ellipsoidals are hung out in the house, while Fresnels are used onstage. A **gobo,** which is a metal sheet with a punched out design, can be placed inside the ERS to produce a patterned or textured effect.

Border lights or **strip lights** are long narrow metal enclosures that house a row of lamps and reflectors. These lights provide general illumination; they tone the lighted areas without changing the contrast or emphasis provided by the specific spotlighting.

Floodlights, known as **scoops,** are large lamps—500 to 1000 watts—that are mounted in an open-faced housing. Floodlights differ from spots in that they have no lens. They provide soft, widely diffused light, which is perfect for backdrops and the background behind doors and windows. These instruments are equipped with yokes for hanging the units.

Colored Light: Glass, Gels, and Plastics

Three media are used to provide colored light on stage: gelatins, plastics, and glass.

Gelatins (or **gels**) are transparent color sheets inserted into a frame that mounts in front of spotlights and floods. Gelatin is popular because it comes in a wide variety of colors and it is inexpensive. However, it must be replaced often because it becomes brittle and fades with use. Plastic costs more than gelatin but it also lasts longer. Both gelatin and plastic sheets are available in a variety of colors from most theatrical or lighting supply houses.

Strip lights usually have a standard color combination of red, blue, and amber or green lights. When amber and blue are mixed, they produce a nearly white light that illuminates without drastically changing costume and makeup colors. Colored glass disks called **roundels** are used in some strip lights instead of gels or plastic. However, because of their intense color, they tend to lower the illumination and make blending more difficult.

In preparing your lighting plot, your choice of lighting colors will depend on the mood of the play and its setting (location, time of day, season). Experiment with colors until you obtain the effect you're looking for. As you experiment you may wish to try the following combinations of gel colors to see how they look with the scenery and costumes. Your teacher may have sets of color samples for you to use. The popular colors seen below can create many different effects.

Be aware that these colors may appear slightly different in this textbook than they do in real life.

This scene from Eugene O'Neill's *Moon for the Misbegotten* suggests late afternoon by using blue lighting.

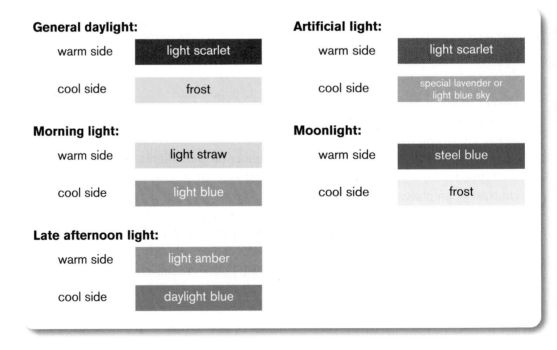

General daylight:

warm side	light scarlet
cool side	frost

Morning light:

warm side	light straw
cool side	light blue

Late afternoon light:

warm side	light amber
cool side	daylight blue

Artificial light:

warm side	light scarlet
cool side	special lavender or light blue sky

Moonlight:

warm side	steel blue
cool side	frost

Here's How
To Create Special Lighting Effects

Special effects usually require a bit of experimentation if they are to be convincing. Try the following techniques, and refer to a specialized lighting text for additional ideas.

- *Burning logs.* Well-positioned lights can make the audience think they're seeing logs burning in a fireplace. Place an amber or orange light at the back of the logs. Attach a small tin pinwheel in front of the light. The hot air rising from the lamp will turn the pinwheel and provide the necessary flicker. You can also achieve this effect by screwing different colored lamps into flicker sockets (often used for holiday lights) that are attached to a board and placed behind the logs. A small orange or amber flood will provide a warm glow while the other lights give off a flicker.

- *Burning coals.* To simulate burning coals, place small pieces of broken amber-colored glass or crumpled orange and red gelatins over an amber lamp placed in the bottom of the grate.

- *Lighted floor lamps and table lamps.* On the stage, all floor and table lamps should only use low-wattage globes. The actual light should come from stage spots focused on the area. If floor lighting is used, be sure it is clear of all flammable materials, such as curtains.

Connections and Controls

Lighting instruments are connected to the electric current by special stage connectors and cables. Some schools use twist-lock connectors, which provide a safe connection without the worry of accidentally pulling the connectors apart. Others prefer the more expensive pin connectors. While pin connectors must be tied with an overhand knot to ensure the connection, they are much more durable than twist locks. In many states, electrical codes require that schools use a grounded plug for all connections.

Use heavy three-conductor grade cable for theatre lighting; it can carry a larger load than ordinary household cord. For school use, you should have #140-gauge cable that carries 15 amperes or #12-gauge that carries 20 amperes. Be careful not to overload the circuit. Wires can safely handle only the stated wattage.

The control board contains switches for the various lights. It also houses the **dimmers** that change the level of lighting intensity. If possible, all instruments should be connected to dimmers. Dimmers can be controlled manually or electronically. Electronic systems are operated by remote control with preset scene devices. School lighting control boards vary greatly. In some, each dimmer is wired to a specific light or group of lights. In others, a special panel gangs lights together according to certain areas of the stage. Every board has a master dimmer that can turn off all the stage lights for a blackout.

Lighting Plots, Charts, and Cue Sheets

A lighting designer must be familiar with the script so that he or she knows the play's mood, setting, time of day, season, weather, and any necessary special effects. The lighting designer consults with the director and views the floor plan to figure out the number and location of doors and windows, the light sources, such as a fireplace or table lamps, and the color of scenery and costumes. The lighting designer also works closely with the set and costume designers to create an overall effect.

The lighting designer determines the light plot by tracing over the ground plan of the set and applying to this copy the position of each light that will be used for each scene. He or she then numbers each light and indicates its

This partial lighting plot shows which spotlights light which areas of the stage.

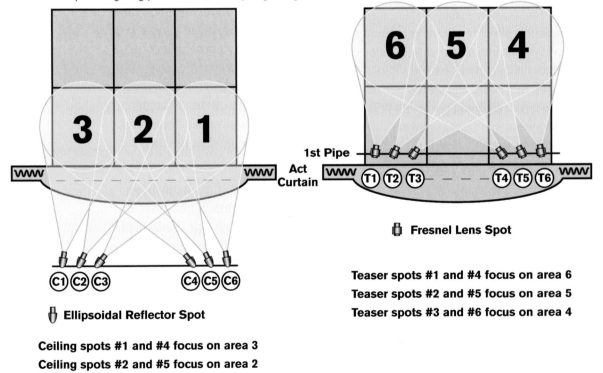

Ellipsoidal Reflector Spot

Ceiling spots #1 and #4 focus on area 3
Ceiling spots #2 and #5 focus on area 2
Ceiling spots #3 and #6 focus on area 1

Fresnel Lens Spot

Teaser spots #1 and #4 focus on area 6
Teaser spots #2 and #5 focus on area 5
Teaser spots #3 and #6 focus on area 4

color. The light plot shows all the light units, including foots, strips, spots, backing lights, and special lighting effects, as well as the throw of the spot beams.

Finally, the lighting designer makes a light chart or instrument schedule, listing each light, its number, type, watt, color, and dimmer connection. A light cue sheet is also prepared that tells the light level and the changes needed at exact places in the script.

With the cue sheet, the light crew can see at a glance when to use which lights.

INSTRUMENT SCHEDULE

Number	Instrument Type	Wattage	Color	Dimmer
T1	Fresnel	500	#4 Pink	A4
T2	"	"	"	A7
T3	"	"	"	A5
T4	"	"	#17 Lau	A3
T5	"	"	"	A2
T6	"	"	"	A1
C1	ERS	1000	Frost	B1
C2	"	"	"	B2
C3	"	"	"	

An instrument schedule lets the light crew know which lights are being used in the production.

CUE SHEET   Act 1 Scene 1

CUE 1	House Lights Full
CUE 2	Stage Lights – On
	C1 & C2 – full
	C2 & C5 – full
	C3 & C6 – up 2/3
	Teaser Spots – full
	Border – up 2/3
CUE 3	Slowly dim house
CUE 4	Foots – up 2/3
CUE 5	Harry "I'm Tired"
	teasers on dimmers 4 & 6 – dim 1/2
CUE 6	

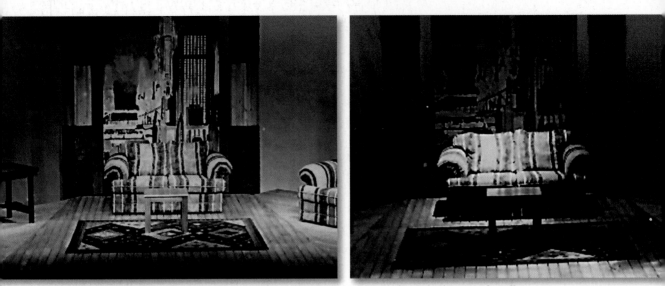
This set is identical in each photo above, but the different lighting used in each changes the effect.

Positioning Lighting Instruments

To provide adequate visibility, emphasis, and mood, lights must be properly positioned. To some extent the lighting will depend on the size of the performance space, but here are some general rules.

ERS lights, with their capacity to throw light over long distances, should be hung from beams in the auditorium ceiling or on stands in the balcony. Large stages generally require 1000-watt ERS's, but smaller stages can use 500-watt lamps. ERS's should be carefully focused to light the downstage area while avoiding spill onto either the audience or the proscenium arch. To light the upstage area, hang Fresnels by clamping them to the teaser batten. **Battens** are metal pipes hung above the stage. The batten directly behind the teaser curtain is called the **teaser batten.**

Strip, or border, lights are also attached to the overhead battens. While some school stages have the luxury of many border strips, two are essential. There should be a teaser unit of six or more compartments hung just upstage of the teaser curtain. It is best placed in the center of the batten, with spots filling out the rest of the batten on either side. The second border strip should be placed upstage to light the top of the backdrop. Each color in the border should be wired to a separate circuit so that they can be adjusted individually.

To prevent the actors' faces from being in shadow, **cross light** each stage area with two spots placed on opposite sides of the stage at a 45-degree angle. To focus these spots, position an actor in each lighting area and aim the center of the light pool at his or her face. Do not aim at the floor or the scenery. The set will be adequately lit by the spill. Cross lighting can also be used to enhance natural shadows and highlights. For this type of effect, the spots on one side of the stage should have a warmer color than those on the other side. For example, if the spots on stage right are warm light pink, those on stage left may be cool, pale lavender. The actor's face will then have a very natural, three-dimensional appearance, as this arrangement of colors provides subtle highlights on the warm side and shadows on the cool side. To create an interesting visual effect called a **tableau,** in which a group of characters form a silent frozen picture, light the actors from overhead.

A Basic Lighting System

Few schools have what a professional theatre would consider an adequate lighting system. But by making smart choices, your drama department can create a system that fulfills at least the most basic lighting needs. What equipment will you need to effectively light a play? Ideally you should have at least

- ten Fresnels for the lights on the teaser batten
- six ellipsoidals for auditorium spots
- two floods
- two strip lights (one teaser strip and one for lighting the backdrop)
- an adequate dimmer system

If money is available for lighting supplies, instead of buying small spotlights, you are better off putting it toward the eventual purchase of ellipsoidal reflective spotlights and Fresnels.

Hanging Lighting Instruments

The lighting crew mounts and connects the lights for the play at least 10 days before performance, working when the stage is not in use. At least a week before production, the director will call a special lighting session during which the lights are focused and set. Each light cue will be rehearsed at this time. The lighting crew must make sure that all connections are securely fastened, that circuits are not overloaded, and that there is no glare from the stage into the audience. If there are unwanted shadows on the back wall, the crew will lower the intensity of the border strips a bit.

During the week of dress rehearsal, complete stage lighting is used, and all the cues are carefully rehearsed so that the action and the lights are perfectly synchronized. The cue sheet should always be close at hand. (See page 241 for a sample cue sheet.)

At the right are a few safety tips to keep in mind when working with lighting components.

Lighting Crew Safety Tips

- Wear cotton gloves to protect your hands from heat. With tungsten-halogen lamps, grease or fingerprints on the lamp could cause it to explode when it reaches a high temperature.

- Mark the handle of each instrument with its wattage and the type of light it is to ensure proper connections.

- Make sure that you have your tools safely pocketed or attached by clips to your clothing or tool belt. When you are working above the stage, a dropped tool could injure someone down below.

- Using a piece of tape, mark each cable to show the number of the instrument and its circuit. That way, even if the cables are ganged together, you will be able to see where each must go. It's also handy to write down the cable's length.

- Check cables periodically and replace any that are worn.

- Disconnect a plug by pulling the connector body—not the cord.

- Always wear closed-toe shoes—steel-tipped, if possible.

Career Focus

Lighting Designer

A lighting designer can work in a variety of media, including theatre, dance, opera, television, and film. He or she might also be hired to light museum exhibits or public spaces. No matter what the media, the designer's first task is to meet with the director, or whoever is in charge of the project, to discuss the mood and action of each scene or event. The designer then develops a lighting plan that charts changes in tone and mood.

Lighting designers often do double duty as technicians—they design the lights placement, then hang and operate the lights. This naturally requires quite a bit of technical skill. A designer/ technician must be comfortable working the rigging—in other words he or she must be unafraid to work at great heights.

Some designers thrive on the excitement of a career in the theatre, film, or television. Others prefer to work in the architectural realm, lighting building exteriors as well as residential and commercial interiors. A lighting designer who works architecturally may design task lighting for a modern kitchen, accent lighting for the art in an office building, as well as landscape lighting for gardens of all kinds.

Until recently, most theatrical lighting designers received their training on the job. Beginning as an apprentice and then as an assistant technician, the budding professional gradually moved up through the ranks to become a chief electrician and then a full-fledged designer. However, with more and more universities offering degrees in lighting design, a new breed of designer has emerged. When these designers hit the marketplace in their early twenties, they often have had a great deal of training and experience not only in university theatres, but also in associated professional theatres.

No matter which path a person takes into the business, he or she must be organized and work well with others. Designers who work in the theatre must read and analyze scripts, perform research if necessary, and often work long and inconsistent hours. An architectural lighting designer must know how to please the client.

If you are beginning to tackle lighting design, be sure to start a portfolio showing your work.

PREPARE

Work Out Your Lighting Plan

In this project, you are going to assume the initial duties of a lighting designer by planning a light plot for a designated scene or play. Employ your school's lighting equipment and any additional homemade spots that you wish to indicate.

1 Choose a play appropriate to your school's lighting capabilities. As you read the play, picture the scenes and imagine the lighting you would use. You may want to draw upon the lighting in a play you have seen. Try to remember the lighting used and decide if you want to create a similar effect.

2 Keeping your school's lighting equipment in mind, plan your light plot. Decide the position of each light, its identifying number, its color, and the type of beam. Indicate all the lighting instruments you plan to use. Remember that your cross beams should be placed at approximately 45-degree angles. Be sure the important acting areas are well lighted. Choose colors that will establish the proper mood, light source, weather, time of day, and visibility (refer to the color chart on page 238). Provide highlighting and shadows with warm colors on one side and cool colors on the other.

3 Trace the ground plan of the set and overlay the lighting plot you planned in step two. Be sure you show each light and its number and color. For example, you may number your lights by the abbreviation C1—standing for ceiling spot number one; T1—for teaser spot number one; and so on. Be sure the lights overlap for proper light blending. Provide lighting for the complete scene, including any special effects lighting.

4 When your plan is finished, ask your teacher to either help you make enough copies for everyone in your class or create a copy on a transparency to be used on an overhead projector.

5 Practice your presentation so that you are comfortable talking about the choices you made in devising this plan. Be sure you do not exceed ten minutes.

Theatre Journal

Think about a room in your house—a bedroom, a family room, or a kitchen. Describe how the lighting changes in this room over the course of a day—in the morning, at noon, and at night. Write some notes about what kinds of theatrical lighting you might use to represent this room onstage.

PRESENT

Explain Your Lighting Plan

When your name is called, step to the front of the room and pass out copies of your plan or use the overhead to project it. Give the name of the play and tell something about the scene your plan reflects. Discuss your lighting plan in terms of how it relates to the plot, the theme, and the characters. Explain the effects you want to create in this scene. Invite your classmates to ask questions and make comments on your work. Answer any questions they might have about the decisions you made, taking care not to exceed the allotted ten minute time limit.

CRITIQUE

Evaluate a Classmate's Lighting Plan Presentation

Evaluate the work of a classmate. Rate the work on a scale of 1 to 5, with 1 being "needs much improvement" and 5 being "outstanding." Ask yourself the following questions:

- Was the presentation well organized and easy to understand?

- Did the speaker display a good understanding of lighting?

- How well did the speaker answer questions?

- How well did the speaker's lighting plan successfully reflect the play's intent?

- How clear and easy would it be to use the lighting plot?

Then write a few sentences to explain why you gave this rating. Include in your paragraph suggestions for any alternative creative choices.

Additional Projects

1 Make an instrument chart and cue sheet for the same play or scene you selected for this chapter's project.

2 On a computer, design a lighting plot for a contemporary play. Discuss your design with the class.

3 Demonstrate the effect of colored lights on costumes made of different fabrics, colors, and textures or on a made-up face. Refer to pages 238 and 294 for color information.

4 Research and report on the principles of electricity, explaining such terms as *watt, ampere, volt, circuit, direct current,* and *alternating current.* Create a graphic organizer to help explain your research.

5 Interview a local lighting designer or technician about his or her early career. What did this person do to break into the field? Tape-record your interview and play it for the class.

6 Read the excerpt from *Icarus* by Edwin Sánchez found in Unit Eight, and create a cue sheet for it.

"Theater is magical and evanescent; examine it closely and it turns into tricks of lighting . . ."

Robertson Davies, Canadian novelist

Theatre Then and Now

Let There Be Light: From Candles to Computers

Theatre by Candlelight

Lighting has come a long way since the ancient Greeks first took to the stage. They performed only in daylight; the plays were designed to take full advantage of the sun, and performance spaces were chosen to gain the best possible natural light.

Most historians believe that the ancient Romans were the first to use torches in theatrical presentations. This allowed them to present evening performances. Medieval lighting consisted primarily of stationary torches, but there were also some that could be moved by torchbearers. Although these illumination sources created a fair amount of smoke and odor, they also produced some exciting lighting effects.

In the 18th century, stage lighting was problematic for theatres located in enclosed buildings since the smoke, odor, and flammability of open-flame light sources presented both discomfort and danger. Theatre fires were not uncommon. Later in the century, chandeliers and huge candelabras came into fashion. It was also common to use

Up until the late 1700s, theatres such as the old Covent Garden in London were lit by candles.

carefully placed reflectors to bounce the available light onto the stage. Toward the end of the century, theatres began to use scrims, gauze drops that become transparent when a light is shined from behind but that appear opaque when lit from the front.

It wasn't until the middle of the 19th century that a new invention, the gaslight, effectively snuffed out the lamps, candles, and torches that had served as standard lighting elements for hundreds of years. Gaslight was first developed in England in 1817. By 1849 it could be centrally controlled— although it also caused some major fires over the years. The first spotlight, called a limelight because a flame was directed on a cylinder of lime, was introduced in 1816.

Lights Up on the 20th Century

It was the invention of the incandescent bulb in 1879 and its rapid-fire use in the 20th century that brought lighting into the modern age. Perhaps the person most directly credited for creating modern stage lighting was a Swiss designer named Adolphe Appia (1862–1928). Hired to create the sets for Richard Wagner's operas, Appia rejected the tradition of the painted backdrop and instead opted for a three-dimensional set. According to his theory, shadow was as important as light as a way of creating a link between the actor and the setting. Appia's use of lighting with varying degrees of intensity, color, and mobility created a revolution in lighting and stage design.

Today, stage lighting effects are typically run by a computerized dimmer board that can transform a stage from sunlight to moonlight to a lightning storm in seconds. Lighting has become not simply a tool but a high-tech art form all its own. With a small arsenal of scoops, ERS's, and Fresnels, a trained lighting designer can add layers of visual and atmospheric magic to any production. And although the basic principles of lighting have not changed much in recent years, the technology of illumination continues to evolve, and design trends come and go. It's impossible to know just what the stage lighting of tomorrow will bring.

This scene from the play *Corners* uses computerized lighting effects to create a dramatic mood.

Adolphe Appia is considered the father of modern stage lighting.

Chapter
20 Sound

Somewhere up there in the back of the house, maybe behind the last distant row of balcony seats, there's a small booth from which all the sound effects and music for a play are controlled. Inside this booth, a sound operator manipulates all the electronic equipment that will ensure the audience's listening pleasure.

Project Specs

Project Description With a partner, you will make and present a detailed cue sheet and sound effects tape for a scene that is no longer than fifteen minutes.

Purpose to understand the role and production of sound for theatrical presentations

Materials paper or the Sound Activity Sheet your teacher provides; a tape recorder with a seconds counter and a sensitive microphone

Theatre Terms

amplifier
body mic or lavalier mic
CD-R (compact disk, recordable)
crash box
DAT (digital audiotape)
digital audio software
equalizer
minidisks
public domain
sound board, console, or mixer
transmitter

On Your Feet

Sit quietly for a few moments and listen to the sounds going on all around you. As your teacher points to individuals, each person will name a sound that he or she can hear, such as a ticking clock or people talking in the hall. List the sounds as they are named. This would be an excellent starting point for the sound design of a play set in a classroom.

PREVIEW

Sound and the Play

Sound design has become an increasingly important element in the theatre. Advances in audio technology and computerized electronic mixing of sounds and music greatly enhance the quality of productions.

In theatrical performances, the main purpose of sound design is to support the mood and purpose of each scene. To achieve this end, sound is used:

1 To amplify the actors' voices.

2 To supply incidental or dramatic music and underscoring.

Stomp uses sound, rhythm, and movement to create an exciting evening of theatre.

3 To provide special, realistic sound effects (crickets chirping, dogs barking, car doors slamming, children playing, and so on).

The sounds that are generally used in a play are prerecorded music and sound effects from special CDs, **minidisks,** or cassette tapes; sounds using compiled live music and/or sound effects; and environmental sounds recorded by the stage crew in locations such as beaches, shopping malls, or city streets. A show's sound design, like its other technical elements, should not be intrusive in any way. If the sound designer does the job right, what the audience hears will be experienced as an integral part of the world of the play.

The Sound Production Process

The sound designer's first job is to become familiar with the script. To effectively analyze a script, the designer must read it more than once. The first reading should be for understanding; the second should be dedicated to finding the obvious places where sound effects, voice-overs, or music will be required. A third reading will typically show the designer even more areas of sound possibility and should lead to a preliminary plan for the show. After researching the music of the play's time period and consulting with the director and other technical designers about the mood and purpose of the play, the sound design is created.

The sound crew has a variety of responsibilities both before and after the show opens. Before the production goes into final rehearsals, the sound crew must put together a detailed list of cues and then find or create the necessary sounds. If recorded music is used in the show, the sound crew must either obtain the rights to the music or ascertain that the music can be used without payment of royalties because it is in the **public domain,** in other words, it belongs to the public.

During tech crew sessions, technical rehearsals, and performances, the sound crew is responsible for setting up, checking, and maintaining the microphones, speakers, recorders, and all other sound equipment used in the show.

During performances, the sound crew sees and hears everything the audience does because, for the most part, the crew must take their real-time cues from the performance in progress.

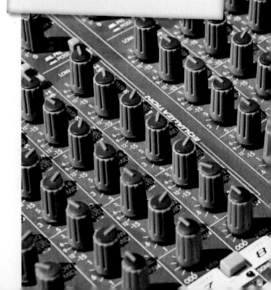

Theatre Journal

Go to a shopping mall or supermarket. Stop and listen for three minutes. Write an entry on what you heard. What sound effects might you record if you were the sound designer for a play set in one of these environments?

A Basic Sound System

A workable sound system consists of equipment to produce and control sound elements. A well-equipped sound crew will need:

The **sound board,** also referred to as a **mixer** or **console,** is the heart of the sound system. It controls input from mics, tape recorders, DAT and CD players; allows levels and equalization to be set; adds effects such as reverberation, and sends all this to the amplifier.

Equalizers balance the high, medium, and low frequencies from each sound source (e.g. the microphones) to achieve the desired blending of the sounds.

The **amplifier** provides the power supply for the speakers.

Speakers project the sound. They are typically hung at the front of the house near the proscenium arch, facing toward the audience.

Headphones allow the crew to establish levels, check the quality of the sound, and cue up sounds.

CD-R player/recorder, cassette deck, digital audiotape (DAT) can be used for recording and playing back sound.

Microphones are used for recording and amplifying sound. Hardwired mics are directly connected to the sound board. A **body,** or **lavaliere,** mic is small enough to be hidden on the performer and has a small battery-powered **transmitter** that sends a signal to a receiver unit attached to the sound board. Handheld mics and body mics provide excellent mobility for the performer.

A **crew intercom system** allows the sound operators and other crew members to communicate with each other. It is totally separate from the main sound system.

Also used, but not usually tied into the sound system, is the computer-driven **digital audio software** that allows for the mixing of a wide variety of sound sources and effects on a personal computer. Once the desired mix is obtained, it can be downloaded from the PC to a CD-R for playback on the sound board's CD or minidisk player.

You will also need a variety of smaller supplies including cassettes, CDs or minidisks, and batteries.

PREPARE

Think About Your Sound Design

You are now ready to create a simple sound design. As a sound designer you would ordinarily work closely with the director when making decisions about the show's music, voice-overs, and sound effects. For this project, you will work with a partner to analyze a one-act play or a scene from a full-length play for sound possibilities.

With your partner, choose a script that offers a number of opportunities to use sound. Examples from Unit Eight of this book might include Paula Vogel's *How I Learned to Drive* or Christopher Durang's *The Actor's Nightmare.* Other possibilities might include something from David Ives's collection *All in the Timing* or one of the plays from the collection *Plays in One Act* edited by Daniel Halpern. If you prefer, you can use a short scene of your own that incorporates a number of sound effects and music. Make sure your scene or play will take no longer than 15 minutes to perform.

As you read your selected scene, think about the mood it creates. You will want to select music to reflect and enhance that mood. Almost all contemporary music is subject to copyright laws, which means you must get

permission from the music publisher to use it for a theatre performance. For classroom use, however, you can feel free to use any music you like. If your selected scene does not take place in the present, try to find music that is reflective of the time period of the setting.

The Sounds of the Scene

Next, you and your partner should analyze the script. What information must be conveyed by sound? Think about where the play is set, and the sounds you would hear in this location. For example, let's say your scene takes place

In this scene from *Sky Girls,* the only sound accompanying the dialogue is the lonely drone of an antique airplane engine.

at night on the porch of a house out in the country. First look for any sounds that are specifically called for in the script. Make a list, complete with page numbers. Then try to imagine yourself in the scene. What do you hear? Crickets? The wind? A distant train whistle? The television from inside the house? Remember that your goal is to enhance the scene with sound, not to turn it into a scene *about* sound. Add the new sounds to your list. Also include ideas for music, either as background for some part of the scene and/or as introductory music that plays before the scene begins and that fades out as the house lights dim.

Create the Sound Effects

You are now ready to create sound effects for each cue in the scene or play. Although most common sounds are available on CD, you may wish to create "live" sound effects. Many schools have a doorbell unit—a board with a button that can be pushed to activate a buzzer or other ringer. A ringing telephone can be handled the same way.

You will probably have to experiment a bit to create your sound effects. Slamming or creaking doors, falling rain, and other effects can have a variety of "tones," and you will need to figure out how best to achieve the one that works best for your scene.

You may wish to listen to some sound tapes or CDs to decide whether you want to use any prerecorded effects.

Record Your Scene

The CD, cassette, or minidisk contains all the music and sound you will use in the scene in the order they will be used. Record all your sounds and set up any manual cues (such as a handheld doorbell that will be rung by a technician, and so on). Although your recording equipment will not be as sophisticated as a theatre system, try to record as pure a sound as possible. Record only the sound and not yourself breathing, moving the microphone, or rattling papers, all of which break the mood of the scene. Allow a bit of silence in between each cue so that you will have some space to set up for the next one.

Remember, you must record the sounds and the music in the order they are presented in the script. You cannot change the order of cues or add new ones once they are recorded. Note also that if you plan on using two sounds at the same time or a series of sounds that occur one right after the other, you will probably need two separate recordings and two players.

Make a Sound Cue Sheet

To guide you in operating the sound, create a cue sheet like the one below on a piece of paper or on the Sound Activity Sheet that your teacher provides. For each sound cue, you will fill in a cue number, the number of the page of the script on which it appears, the sound cue, the tape recorder's counter number or the CD or minidisk player's track number, the spoken line or when the sound cue begins, the volume level, and the line when the sound cue ends. If you use a cassette recorder, cue up the sound using headphones because counters aren't exact. Tape can stretch, and you may have to back up to find the exact spot.

It's easy to create your own sound if you have the right equipment and an imagination.

Be sure to write a cue for every sound in your scene.

Sound Cue Sheet

Name of Play   *Wonder of Wonders*

Crew Members   *Darlene and Calvin*

Cue No.	Script Pg.	Sound	Counter or Track No.	Cue	Level	Cue to End
1	1	doorbell	005	He's 15 minutes late.	7	Finally!
2	3	crash	78	Oh, my gosh!	9	Are you OK?
3	5	music	94	Let's have some fun.	8	I'm not in the mood!
4	8	dog bark	208	Something strange is going on.	8	But we don't have a dog!

Cast and Rehearse the Scene

Choose members of the class to perform in your scene, and ask them to read it through aloud. Stop the actors from speaking every time you come to a sound cue. Then, play the sound for them. You will need to go over each cue several times to get the timing right.

If you have music or sound cues that are to play underneath the scene, make sure the actors are projecting enough to be heard over the sound.

Time your presentation to make sure you remain under the fifteen-minute time limit. Rehearse the scene at least three or four times with the sounds in place. If you need to rehearse the scene more than this to be sure that everything goes smoothly, by all means do so.

Here's How
To Create a Crash Box

Have you ever seen a play that featured a loud offstage crashing sound—perhaps to sound as if a person is falling down the stairs or tripping over a pile of junk? This sound effect is most often created by a **crash box,** a wooden or metal box weighted at the bottom and filled with broken dishes or glass. The box is securely taped or fastened at the top. When the box is dropped on the floor it makes a loud crashing sound that can be very convincing!

PRESENT
Play the Scene with Sound Effects

When your name is called, gather your tape recorder, CD player, or minidisk player and other materials, and walk with your partner and actors to the playing area. Place chairs so that the actors can sit down to read. Set your own chair off to the side near a desk or table to hold your equipment. Introduce your presentation by announcing the title and author of your play. You may wish to say a few words about why you selected this particular scene and the sound challenges it presented.

Make sure your equipment is properly cued up and that your other sound tools are close at hand.

Go through your presentation exactly as you rehearsed it. If you miss a cue, do not try to go back. Instead, check your cue sheet and move ahead to the next cue. When you have finished your presentation, allow the actors to take a bow. Then hand your paper or Activity Sheet to your teacher and return to your seat.

CRITIQUE

Evaluate the Sound Effects in the Presentation

You will be evaluating how well your classmates integrated their sound effects into the scenes they presented. The presentations will be rated on a scale of 1 to 5, with 5 being "outstanding" and 1 being "needs much improvement." As you listen to the presentations, ask yourself the following questions:

- How could the technical execution (volume, recording, etc.) be improved?

- In what way did the music and other effects fit the theme and mood of the scene?

- How good was the quality of the sound effects?

- Was the timing of sound cues appropriate to the scene?

- How original was the presentation?

Choose one of the presentations and give it a rating from 1 to 5, explaining in a few sentences your reasons for giving this score.

Career Focus

Sound Technician

A good sound technician should
- have a "good ear" for subtle sound differences.
- enjoy working with electronic equipment.
- be detail oriented.
- work well under pressure.
- be able to make split-second decisions.

There are plenty of options for a person with these qualities who chooses a career as a sound technician, or sound operator. These professionals can work in a variety of settings where live performances are staged, either as an employee of the facility or production team or as part of an entertainer's road crew. They may also find work in radio, television, in a recording studio, or in businesses that specialize in the sale and rental of sound equipment.

Sound techs must be able to determine sound requirements, build and install sound systems, set up and test equipment, service and maintain audio and recording equipment, and dub and edit tapes. In addition, they must be able to operate the controls to maintain proper sound levels.

For the right individual, the job of sound technician can be rewarding. But because many of the available jobs are oriented toward live performances, sound technicians must be willing to travel and work long hours—including evenings and weekends. They often work under difficult conditions with tight deadlines.

Additional Projects

1 Create a radio play using two or more tape recorders or other recording equipment.

2 Create a movement-based performance that uses sound rather than dialogue to tell a story.

3 Interview a sound technician or sound designer at a local theatre. Ask about the various pros and cons of the job. Tape your interview, and play it for the class.

4 Make an audio documentary of your class. Pick a theme— for example, first love, family relationships, or money— and create a brief series of questions. Tape-record the members of your class as they answer one or more of these questions. Then compile their remarks and your own into the documentary.

5 Read the "Dead Parrot" excerpt from *Monty Python's Flying Circus* found in Unit Eight, and create a sound cue sheet for the scene.

John Cleese in the "Dead Parrot" episode from *Monty Python's Flying Circus.*

Theatre Then and Now

Sound Effects Through Time

Early Thunder

Theatre has been using sound effects for hundreds of years. In ancient times, when a play called for thunder, for example, the sound was created by bouncing balls of lead onto stretched leather. During Shakespeare's time, the same sound came from the practice of rolling a cannon ball down a wooden chute and allowing it to hit a large drum.

In later years, another popular source of theatrical thunder was the rumble cart. This contraption consisted of a large wooden box mounted on irregularly shaped wheels and filled with heavy objects. When pulled along the floor or ground, the cart lurched along, displacing the objects inside and causing them to rumble and crash into one another.

In 1708, a playwright named John Dennis came up with yet another way to produce a thunderous sound for the stage. For one of his plays, he strung a copper sheet from wires and put a handle at one end. When the time came for the thunder effect, a stagehand would shake the copper sheet, which produced a very natural thunder effect. Soon, other theatre practitioners began using this technique themselves. It is said that Dennis, upset by the callous appropriation of his invention, routinely chided his imitators that they were "stealing his thunder." Today that phrase is used to describe situations in which someone who should be getting credit is eclipsed by the actions of another.

The rumble cart and the thunder sheet were very effective ways of producing thunderous sound.

The Sound of Curly's Knuckles

Musical instruments have been a popular source of sound effects through the ages. From the 1930s through the 1940s, the Three Stooges perfected the use of the musical sound effect. Perhaps you've seen old films of the Stooges gouging and poking one another, and, when knocked unconscious, sliding down walls. Among the sound effects these film buffoons used were:

- cracking the shells of nuts to simulate crunched knuckles
- the plucking of a violin string for eye pokes
- a bang on a bass drum for a belly thump
- ratchets for twisting limbs, ears, or noses
- a slide whistle for a slide down the wall after an injury

Sound designer Rob Milburn recorded multiple thunderstorms and the felling of twenty trees to create just the right sound for this scene from Frank Galati's production of *The Grapes of Wrath*.

The Three Stooges crack a nut.

The Sounds of Today

Today, theatrical sound designers have access to a wide variety of prerecorded sound effects—or the means of producing their own. If a designer wants to simulate the sound of a waterfall, for example, he or she will have to decide just how much rushing water the effect calls for. Is it water trickling over rocks or Niagara Falls? Is the play's rainstorm a summer shower or a typhoon? Many libraries and larger professional theatres have collections of recorded sound effects that can be rerecorded onto a CD-R and so on. If you have a minidisk system, you can find and record sound effects from the Internet, usually for a fee.

Sound effects have always played an important part in our theatre enjoyment—and theatres today have more sophisticated sound effects than ever before—whether we notice them or not.

Chapter
21 Costumes

Do clothes really make the man or woman? Probably not. But in the theatre, they add a visual element that enhances the audience's understanding of the character, the period, and even the theme.

Project Specs

Project Description You will prepare a set of three to five costume designs for one character from an existing play, then in a five- to ten-minute presentation, you will show your designs to the class.

Purpose to learn the basics of costume design

Materials hand-drawn or computer-based costume designs or the Costumes Activity Sheet provided by your teacher; fabric swatches, colored pencils, and appropriate paper

Theatre Terms
building
costume parade
costume plot
crinolines
modified authenticity
notions
pinking shears
silhouette
swatches
trim

On Your Feet

What do you already know about historical styles? Four classmates should go to the chalkboard and write one of these years: 1776, 1850, 1920, 1950. The rest of the class brainstorms design features from each period, which are recorded under the appropriate heading. Consider clothing, hairstyles, and footwear for both men and women.

Paul Freeman and Joanne Pierce wear costumes that reflect their characters' personalities in the Royal Shakespeare Company's production of *Cymbeline*.

Costume Design Meets Stage Design

Costume designers are an important part of the design team. Their work, like that of set, lighting, and sound designers, supports the mood, the style, and the message of a play. This requires more than a flair for fashion; it requires careful study and planning. Before you design costumes for a play, you must first research the time period, the setting, and any relevant social situations. When you understand why the fashions of a certain period developed as they did, you will also begin to understand the manners and beliefs of the time. Research can take many forms, but good sources include paintings, books, photos, and illustrations from the period, as well as costume design books.

After a few careful readings of the play and researching the period, the costume designer meets with the director and other technical designers. Together, they discuss the theme and style of the production and decide on an approach to color, scenery, and lighting. Then, with this and the production budget in mind, the costume designer begins to develop design concepts and sketches.

Pull, Rent, Borrow, Buy, or Build?

Once the designer has a concept in mind, he or she must decide how the costuming will be achieved. There are generally five ways to get the costumes needed, and all of the methods will probably have to be used at some point.

Pull Some schools and theatres are fortunate enough to have their own wardrobe of costumes from previous productions. This is the first place the designer looks—not only for appropriate costumes, but also for any items that could be modified to meet current needs.

Rent Renting can be both expensive and disappointing. Rented costumes are often ill-fitting, not available in the size and color required, or in poor condition. In addition, since rented costumes are usually available for only dress rehearsal and production, actors have little time to become used to wearing them. Still, there are times when renting is the only option. If a costume must be rented, it is best to deal with a large company with a good reputation, or better still, a local company with costumes on display.

Borrow While it is tempting to borrow costume items from friends, relatives, and neighbors, it is a risky idea. No matter how careful the costume crew and the actors are, costumes take a beating onstage. Actors perspire under the lights, and it is almost impossible to avoid getting makeup on clothing. Plus, borrowed items are often fragile and easily snagged or torn. If a costume is borrowed, it must be returned promptly and in good, clean condition.

A Roman gladiator's attire from around 500 B.C.

An Egyptian costume from about 3000 B.C.

What an upper-class lady might have worn in the 1300s.

This Elizabethan costume could be that of a pirate or a nobleman.

Medieval servant presents the meal.

Buy It is rare to actually buy a complete costume, however, parts of costumes such as shoes, boots, shawls, and hats can often be found at secondhand stores, flea markets, and garage sales—places haunted by savvy designers. These locations, plus discount stores, are also good sources for costume jewelry, clothing that can be modified, and draperies and bed linens that can be used as fabric for making costumes.

Build Making a costume, or **building** one as it is referred to in the theatre, is the most difficult, but probably the most satisfying method of costuming. When costumes are built from scratch,

the designer can get the exact look he or she has envisioned and has more creative control over color and harmony among all costumes. Costumes should not war with each other or with the scenery—unless their disharmony is part of the director's message.

After the director has approved the costume design, but before costumes are actually built, a wise costume designer gathers **swatches,** or samples, of fabric for various costumes and tries them under the lighting in which they will be seen. Colors and patterns are also checked to make sure they work together—and with the scenic elements onstage.

An elegant lady of the 1800s would have worn a gown like this to a formal gathering.

What a typical beggar might wear to plead for "alms."

Ben Franklin himself might have worn this American outfit from the 1700s.

This costume suits a Victorian chap of the 1890s.

A simple homespun dress suits this American prairie girl.

Modified Authenticity

No matter how you acquire them, note that period costumes require only **"modified authenticity."** That is, the fashions do not have to be replicated stitch by stitch, as long as prominent design elements and the basic **silhouette,** or line of the garment, that identifies the era are in place. Lines can be simplified, and elements such as hats and collars can be modified so that the audience can see the stage and the actors' faces clearly. Most accessories can be eliminated—just a few important, symbolic pieces such as a cane or fan may be necessary.

Oddly, underwear often becomes important to a period costume. Greek robes require long slips to prevent "see-through" under the lights. The skirts of the Elizabethan era need special frames underneath to produce the proper shape and fullness. A dress from the Civil War period needs a hoop and plenty of **crinolines,** full stiff underskirts. A "Gay Nineties" dress must have a corseted form for the smooth, snug waist and midriff.

Elements of Style

As designers build or gather costumes, these are the elements they keep in mind.

What the typical flapper wore in the 1920s.

A zoot suit of the 1940s.

The poodle skirt was popular with teenagers in the 1950s.

This fellow from the 1970s is ready for the disco.

A typical tribal costume of Nigeria, Africa.

Fabric Textures and types of fabric communicate a great deal about characters. Unfortunately, most theatres are on a limited budget. Fortunately, substitutes can often stand in well for expensive fabrics. For example, instead of brocade, you can stencil designs on muslin. Unbleached muslin has another advantage too—it looks like linen at a distance. Burlap, monk's cloth, and terry cloth can substitute for wool. Instead of velvet, use heavy cotton flannel or corduroy. Silks can be made from cheesecloth and nylon chiffon. For lace collars and cuffs, use paper or plastic doilies.

Color Colors can help identify and define characters and also establish a tone for the play as a whole. Costume colors must harmonize or contrast with the set; if the costume is the same color as the background, the audience "loses" the actor. Costumes and sets must also play off each other. Especially in plays with large casts, costuming characters in different tones helps audience members identify and remember relationships between the characters.

Proper choice of color will help establish the play's mood. For example, blues and greens are restful; red conveys danger, power, or anger; black denotes tragedy or elegance; purple suggests royalty; and white is associated with purity and innocence. Principal characters should wear the more dominant

In *Romeo and Juliet,* the Montagues often wear gradations of one color, while the Capulets wear another.

colors in a show—either the brightest or the darkest on stage. Sometimes groups of characters are dressed in the same color with varying shades. If the right color is unavailable in the right fabric, choose the fabric in a light color and dye it.

Decoration Decoration includes all the **trim**—buttons, rickrack, lace, and so on—and accessories such as hats, shoes, fans, canes, and jewelry.

Each of these can be used to produce a psychological effect on the observer. As long as decorative items are used sparingly, they serve to emphasize and project details about the character in the play.

Note that essential decorations must be slightly oversized to remain visible. To keep one element from overtaking others, remember that white or light-colored tights are eye-catching, that glitter steals focus, and that personal jewelry destroys the illusion of the character, not to mention the time and place of the entire play! Be sure that all actors leave their personal jewelry at home. Before they go onstage, give the actors any jewelry that will serve to enhance their characters.

Here's How
To Make the Actor Fit the Part

Sometimes the actor is built differently than the character he or she is to play. Costumes can help create the right illusion. You can use fabric, color, and line to make people appear taller, shorter, heavier, or thinner than they actually are.

Use fabric with long, vertical lines to make a person appear taller and thinner. Also use dark colors to create a slim silhouette. Velvet, which absorbs light, tends to make people appear smaller and thinner as well. Long skirts, high hats, and v-necks add height.

Satin and other glossy fabrics add bulk to a figure, as do glaring colors, loud patterns, and horizontal lines. Placing the waistline of an outfit a bit high can obscure a small waist—and layering fabric adds actual inches.

Of course, these principles are only the most basic elements of design. But they will help you make sure your costumes complement and support the mood, the style, and the message of a play.

The Question of Comfort

Fashion often cares little for the comfort or ease of movement of the wearer. Onstage, however, in order to perform convincingly, actors must be able to move nimbly and perform comfortably onstage. Their costumes should not get in the way. This means that the costume designer should collaborate with the actors, listening to what they have to say about their characters' clothes. The actors should try on the costumes before the designer completes them. If an actor feels awkward in a costume, it will show onstage. No matter the play's time period, the goal is to have the actor look like a person inhabiting his or her own clothes.

For this reason, it is helpful to have costumes ready as early as possible so that actors can rehearse in the armor, hoopskirts, tights, and corsets they will wear during the show. If this is not possible, the costume crew should try to provide rehearsal garments that simulate the costumes. Rehearsal shoes are imperative for both men and women.

Keeping Track of It All

Costume designers work at the intersection of the big picture and the tiny details. They need to keep track of each costume piece for each character in every scene of a play. That's not easy under any circumstances. Following are the tools that designers use to stay organized.

Costume Plot A costume designer's most valuable tool is a **costume plot.** It lists every character and costume for each scene. It also offers a way to record the stage of development for each costume. To use a costume plot effectively, make a separate page for each scene of the play. For each scene, list every character who appears in the scene, and describe his or her costume and accessories. It can be helpful to list each accessory separately, in order to track the progress of each character's costume. Some designers make a separate costume list for this purpose.

Acquisitions List This is a chart headed "Pull/Rent/Borrow/Buy/Build." Some theatre companies can pull items from their own stock or borrow them from other theatres. Sometimes, they build costumes from scratch. Often, however, at least some costumes and accessories must be bought, borrowed, or even rented from costume shops. In order to keep track of what you have, what you

Costume Plot

Name of Play   _The Crucible by Arthur Miller_

The Time _1692_   **The Place**   _Salem, MASS_

Act _One_

Reverend Parris (45 years old–a righteous man):
• _Black sleeveless gown with tabs and skullcap_
• _Black Pilgrim suit with collar, hat_

Thomas Putnam (40 years old–a wealthy man):
• _Pilgrim suit of fine cloth, white collar and pilgrim hat_

John Proctor (35 years old–a farmer):
• _Leather sleeveless jerkin, rough shirt and homespun Pilgrim suit (wears coat only for Trial scene)_

Abigail Williams (17 years old–niece of Reverend Parris):
• _Typical Pilgrim dress with white collar, cap_

Betty Parris (a young girl–daughter of Reverend Parris):
• _Nightclothes_

need, and where things will come from, you keep a Pull/Rent/Borrow/Buy/Build list, entering each item in the appropriate slot. Some costume designers attach this list to their costume plot. Others keep that list separate so they can lend it to members of the costume crew. However you decide to use it, use it faithfully. It will help you keep the details in your grasp.

Measurement Cards For costuming purposes, it might not be enough to know that Martha is a size 10. You might need to know the circumference of her head, the length of her inseam, and so on. The sensible thing to do is to take detailed measurements of each actor, and write them on measurement cards. Even if you're not building a costume, measurements are still important. They can help you pull, rent, borrow, or buy costumes that fit.

Costume Spaces To encourage continued organization, assign a hanger or piece of shelf space for each costume piece. Label the space so that anyone in the production can find any piece at any time. This will not only prevent losses, it will allow the costume crew to check costumes periodically for possible repair or cleaning.

Costume Parade When the costumes are almost finished, have each actor move onstage in costume. Ask for comments about the comfort, utility, and movement of the clothes and accessories. Be aware of how the lights play on the costumes. Take notes during the costume parade, and make final alterations so that there are no surprises on opening night.

Basic Equipment for Costume Design

If you plan to build or modify costumes, these are supplies you will need to have on hand.

- sewing machine
- hot glue gun and refills for gluing on trims
- tape measure
- scissors
- **pinking shears** (the zig-zag pattern keeps the fabric from unraveling)
- adjustable dressmaker's dummy

- iron and ironing board
- basic costume patterns
- lace, rick-rack, costume jewelry, feathers, and other types of trimmings
- Velcro™, two-part hook and eye closure material
- Miscellaneous sewing **notions:** needles, thread, pins, elastic, hooks and eyes, snaps, buttons, and so on

PREPARE

Costume a Character and Prepare a Talk

For this assignment, you will read a play and do research about the time and place it portrays. Your research will allow you to accurately develop a set of wardrobe designs for a particular character in the play.

1 Read a one-act or full-length play that has been approved by your teacher. After you have read the play once, choose a character to costume. Go through the script again and take notes from passages that provide clues to your character.

2 Research the time period of the play.

3 Using your research and notes from the script, make a list of colors, fabric, and decorations that will help define the time, place, and character.

4 Fill in the costume chart on the Activity Sheet for this chapter, which your teacher will provide.

5 Create from three to five drawings of costumes suitable for one character in the play. Draw each costumed figure as large as you can, then complete your sketches with colored pencils, pens, watercolor, or acrylic paint. Be sure your drawings are neat and detailed. For each costume, try to include a swatch of the material you would use.

6 If you feel your completed costume drawings will be too small for your classmates to see easily, reproduce them in color on a transparency for use with an overhead projector. Your teacher can help you with this.

7 Prepare a five- to ten-minute presentation on the costumes you have sketched. This report should begin with a short summary of the play and a description of the character's personality, age, and social status, as well as the mood and period of the play. The body of your talk should refer to the costumes you have created. Support your presentation of the costumes by describing the styles of the period and explaining why you chose the fabric, color, line, and decoration elements you did. Conclude with a summary.

8 Rehearse your talk before class so that you can give it in an interesting, fluid way. Stay within the ten-minute time limit.

Theatre Journal

What are the style elements of your generation? Describe, and if possible, sketch, the shape or basic silhouette of the clothes you and your friends wear. Why do you think these styles are popular?

PRESENT

Show and Discuss Your Costume Designs

When your name is called, hand your costume designs or Activity Sheet to your teacher and go to the front of the class. Pause and look at the class before you begin to speak. With poise and with a pleasant, audible voice, present your costume designs. If your drawings are large enough, or if you have reproduced them as handouts or on a transparency for use in an overhead projector, point to elements in each design and discuss their significance. If you complete your talk before the ten-minute time limit, ask the audience for questions. Answer any questions as thoroughly as you can.

Sketch and actual costume from a production of Shakespeare's *Twelfth Night*.

CRITIQUE

Evaluate a Classmate's Designs and Presentation

Choose a design presentation by one of your classmates and evaluate it on a scale of 1 to 5, with 5 being "outstanding" and 1 being "needs much improvement." Think about the appropriateness of the costumes and the thoroughness of the presentation. Ask yourself these questions as you prepare your critique:

- In what way are the costumes appropriate to the time and place of the play?

- What was memorable about any of the costumes in terms of the theme of the play?

- What mood did the costumes evoke?

- What did the costume communicate about the personality and status of the character?

- How did the presenter use fabric, color, and decoration to support conclusions about the character in the play?

- How well did the speaker understand this character based on the costumes?

- How did the speaker present the important elements of the costumes?

Write a paragraph defending the number grade you gave this presenter.

Career Focus

Costume Designer

Are you
(a) visionary   (b) creative
(c) hands-on   (d) practical
(e) all of the above?
If your answer is (e), the art of costume design might be for you. Costume designers need to understand or imagine the general style of people in various times, places, social positions, and occupations. They need to harmonize the differing styles in one production. They need to develop skill at drawing or using computer programs to draw silhouettes and costumes.

They need to learn enough about sewing to understand which designs are simple and which are complex. They also need to be able to beg, borrow, and shop for the cloth, costumes, and accessories they need—usually on a budget that is too small.

Luckily, you can develop each of these skills before you get a job in the theatre. You can read history or fantasy, study costume books and historical photos and paintings. Learn to sew. Hold a period costume party and provide the clothes.

Then volunteer to help out in a community theatre or school production in the costume or wardrobe department.

Additional Projects

1 Report on a specific costume period, such as ancient Rome or China, medieval or Renaissance Europe, feudal Japan, or the 17th, 18th, or 19th century in Europe or the United States. From your research, explain the reason for the style, its basic characteristics, and its accessories. Show pictures.

2 Using sheets, demonstrate correct draping of a Greek or Roman costume.

3 Report on the influence that men's fashions have had on women's fashions throughout the ages or on the impact women's fashions have had on men's fashions.

4 Prepare a chart showing the silhouettes of basic costume periods in America.

5 Report on women's shoes or another decorative element from Greek to modern times.

6 Design and create a period costume that you might wear in a favorite play.

7 Read the scene found in Unit Eight from either *Cyrano de Bergerac* by Edmond Rostand or "Baucis and Philemon" by Mary Zimmerman, and design a costume for one of the characters.

Master of the Craft

Julie Taymor

Director, designer, puppet master, and writer, Julie Taymor is involved in every creative aspect of making plays. Her work has been informed by her studies at Oberlin and at Bread and Puppet Theatre, and it has been deeply influenced by her travels in such locales as Sri Lanka, Paris, Indonesia, and Japan. Pulling together all these influences, Taymor has developed her creative vision.

Taymor launched her first major production, *Way of Snow,* which was based on Inuit legend, using both puppets and masks. Later she designed the set, costumes, puppets, and masks for *The Odyssey* at Baltimore's Center Stage. This successful production led to work with the New York Shakespeare Festival,

"Imagination is much better than reality."
—Julie Taymor

The American Repertory Theatre, and the La Jolla Playhouse, among others.

To date, Taymor has worked on theatrical productions as diverse as Wagner's *The Flying Dutchman,* Shakespeare's *Titus Andronicus,* and Disney's *The Lion King.* In film, she is most famous for directing *Frida,* about the artist Frida Kahlo.

Taymor has been called "one of the most imaginative and provocative directors in theatre arts today." Her work is effective because she knows what is important. In *The Lion King,* for example, she recalls an argument over whether to use real glass

or fake plastic beads. Taymor explains, "I knew they had to be real even if the audience couldn't tell the difference. I knew that the people wearing the beads would know, and that the spirit . . . of craftsmen would be in the fabric and materials."

That spirit infuses Taymor's entire body of work, so that in her hands, theatre regains the magic of ritual and the wonder of make-believe.

Julie Taymor and her replica of the head of Titus Andronicus.

Theatre **Then** and **Now**

The Art of Costuming

Costumes in the Middle Ages

Spectacle has always been part of the theatrical experience; in the late Middle Ages, it was sometimes the whole thing. Costumes were very elaborate—often intricately embroidered or bejeweled. Leather was used to clothe many a character—from the devil's body suit (equipped with tails and scales) to a young man's breeches—and angels often wore halos of gold. As the Middle Ages progressed in Europe, miracle plays, in which actors were costumed in elaborate Oriental or Byzantine costumes, evolved into morality plays, based on stories from the Bible.

In secular drama, the May Day games and Mumming plays, a kind of pantomime, of rural England drew crowds of folks to watch the antics. Tournaments in which royals and nobles could challenge each other to contests were also held in elaborate and rich costumes. Performers were often colorfully costumed as they sang and danced during the course of these tournaments.

Interludes, short and simple plays performed between longer and more serious

Mythic characters wore striking and amazing costumes in English masques, such as the costume Inigo Jones designed to represent a "Fiery Spirit."

presentations, grew ever more elaborate—and more popular. In England, they came to be called masques, and they were often sponsored by the court. Beginning in the early 1600s, English court masques were lavish and spectacular events held once or twice a year at court. Some of the costumes were designed by Inigo Jones, one of the most famous theatrical designers of all time.

Costumes Today

Today, authentic-looking costumes are the norm, but flights of fancy are common in large-scale productions, especially on Broadway. Productions with simple fairy tale themes, such as *Cats, Beauty and the Beast,* and *The Lion King,* fill theaters with adults who marvel at the effects. Scenery and lighting in these shows are spectacular, but so are the costumes. They include capes that look like wings, patterns that express character traits, and striking masks and headpieces. Some of these incorporate both realistic and fantastic elements by allowing the actor's face to be seen beneath or below the character mask.

Performance art and experimental theatre groups such as Mummenschanz expand the costume repertoire even further by creating costumes made of unusual materials such as brightly colored tubes and other shapes. The group has even utilized rolls of toilet paper to create witty and expressive costuming.

The performers in such dance-based productions as *Rent* and *Stomp,* which are relatively gritty and raw, wear outfits that make extravagant use of color to define their characters.

By embracing fantasy and inventiveness, the costumes of today offer not only a feast for the eyes but for the intellect also.

Mummenschanz exhibits a creative approach to costuming.

Beth Fowler is cleverly costumed as Mrs. Potts in *Beauty and the Beast.*

22 Makeup

Women used to speak jokingly about "putting on their face." This is not a joke in the theatre, where skillfully applied makeup can enhance—even greatly alter—the image the actor projects.

Project Specs

Project Description You will apply character makeup and give a five- to ten-minute talk about the process.

Purpose to learn and use the principles of effective stage makeup

Materials hand-drawn makeup plan or the Makeup Activity Sheet provided by your teacher; standard makeup kit; character makeup items

On Your Feet

Using the chalkboard or large pad of paper, draw a face with a distinctive facial feature such as a raised eyebrow or pursed lips. Ask classmates to identify the personality characteristics they associate with the feature as you have drawn it.

Actress Kathryn Harries performs the role of the sorceress Kundry in Richard Wagner's *Parsifal.*

Theatre Terms

acetone
cake makeup
character makeup
collodion
complementary colors
creme foundation
crepe hair
makeup morgue
putty wax
spirit gum
stippling
straight makeup
water-soluble
  foundation

Makeup: An Overview

In real life, people wear makeup to cover perceived flaws in their appearance. In the theatre, the purpose of **straight makeup,** that is, makeup that enhances natural features and coloring, is to make actors more visible and distinctive on stage. If it is applied well, makeup can both communicate a character's personality as well as enhance the actor's own features. Stage makeup can reflect the character's age, health, occupation, physical characteristics, and even attitudes. For example, a young character who plays tennis every day would probably have a ruddy or tanned face. An ancient scribe might look shriveled and wise.

The style of the play and the size of the theatre space must be considered when

Cory Claussen wears straight makeup in this scene from the Des Moines Playhouse production of *Damn Yankees.*

determining how makeup is applied. If the play is realistic, the makeup should look natural to the audience. If the play is a fantasy or has many symbolic elements, then elaborate, imaginative makeup can be used to obtain special effects. If the actors are performing in a large space with strong lighting, makeup must be bold, even slightly exaggerated. Otherwise, their features may be "washed out" or made pale by the bright lights. In an intimate space, makeup should be subtle. As a rule of thumb, the objective is to create an acceptable effect for the first few rows of the audience while also making sure that the actor's face can be seen in the back rows.

Ron Perlman in character make-up as the Beast in the television show *Beauty and the Beast.*

While straight makeup is the norm, there are times when an actor must wear **character makeup,** additional makeup that changes his or her appearance drastically. A young person playing someone who is bald, bearded, or elderly will need character makeup, as will an actor portraying an animal, a gnome, or anyone with unusual features.

Most stage actors are closely involved in designing and applying their own makeup. They have developed a sense of facial bone structure and skin texture. They know faces. You too should try to be aware of faces—and how age, emotion, and other factors affect them. Most important of all, get to know your own face from crown to chin.

Applying Straight Makeup

Following are general instructions for applying straight makeup.

1 **Clean your face.** Remove all street makeup with either soap and water or cold cream and tissues. If you use cold cream, make sure it is completely removed before applying stage makeup. Also use a toning astringent to obtain a clean, dry face.

2 **Apply your foundation.** Use either **creme** or **water-soluble foundation** in a color that is close to your own natural skin tone. Creme, which comes in round plastic containers, blends well, holds up well when the actor sweats, and can be reworked until finally set with powder. Water-soluble foundation, also called **cake makeup,** is applied with a damp sponge, but washes off easily when sweating, and is harder to blend. Most students usually find cremes easier to manage. Whichever you use, just be sure that the makeup you apply has a formula similar to your foundation. Apply creme with your fingers or a dry sponge wedge and cake with a damp sponge. Then blend smoothly and evenly. Cover all visible areas of your face, including the chin, neck, and ears. Fade out at least two inches down the neck to avoid a line at the jaw. Make sure there are no streaks.

3 **Add shadows.** Shadows of a darker color than the foundation are added to help emphasize the features of the face. This will help audience members sitting at a distance see the actor's facial features clearly. You can easily see the areas of the face that need shading:

• The cheek hollows are shaded to give them dimension.

- Shadow below the jaw line to make it stand out from the face and neck.
- Add shadow to the crease above the eye to give the eye socket more dimension.
- Shadow the sides of the nose so it doesn't flatten.

4 **Add highlights.** Highlights of a lighter shade than the foundation are added next to further define the features of the face. Here too you can see the areas that need highlighting by following the contours of the face:

- Highlight directly under the brow to counteract the effects of overhead lights that tend to create hollows in the socket.
- Add highlights to the cheekbone to balance the shadows you added to the hollow of the cheek.
- Create subtle highlights down the ridge of the nose.
- Add subtle highlights to the chin area.

5 **Accent the eyes.** We've already shadowed the crease and highlighted the brow bone; now using an eyeliner pencil (which has a thicker form of creme), we will continue to define the eyes. Starting at the outside of the eye, draw a fine line along the roots of the lower lashes with a dark brown pencil or cake liner. Do not use black, as it looks hard and artificial. On the upper lid, start at the inside corner

With foundation and cake makeup already applied, shadows are added.

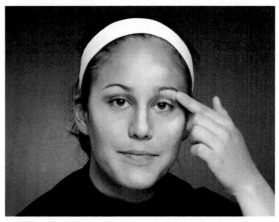

Highlights are now added to further accentuate bone structure.

Eyeliner and mascara are added to bring out the eyes.

(by the nose) and follow close to the lashes, extending the line about 1/4 inch beyond the outside corner. The bottom is the most important. On the lower lids, start the line at the outside and fade the line off at the middle of the eye. Do not go all around the edge. Apply one or two coats of brown mascara to all the upper lashes and to the outer portion of the lower lashes.

6 **Accent the eyebrows.** If necessary, darken your eyebrows to make them more visible. Using a medium or dark brown pencil, apply short, feathery lines drawn in the normal direction eyebrow hairs grow. Eyebrows should extend 1/4 to 1/2 of an inch beyond the eye to frame it properly. The heaviest color should be near the center, with the brows tapering at the outer end. Keep the effect soft and natural looking.

7 **Apply rouge.** Use rouge sparingly; a little goes a long way. Using your finger, dot the rouge in a crescent shape just below the cheekbone. Blend to soften all edges. The color should be strongest just below the cheekbone and should grow weaker as it moves away until it blends unnoticed into the base. There should not be a sharp delineation. For a healthy glow, males should carry rouge farther into the temples than females do, and farther down the jaw.

8 **Accent the lips.** Females should use lipstick made for stage use in a shade that matches their rouge. For a clean line, apply lipstick with a personal lipstick brush. To make lips smaller, draw the new shape using red lip-liner pencil. Then apply foundation and powder over the part of the lip you are eliminating. Men can either softly outline their lips with a brown pencil or apply a brownish-red moist rouge that they then gently wipe off, leaving only a suggestion of color.

9 **Apply the finish.** Use a powder puff to apply a thin dusting of translucent powder over the face. Remove excess powder with a powder brush. If necessary, touch up your cheeks and eyelashes.

Only amateurs appear outside the theatre in stage makeup. As soon as the play is over and curtain calls are complete, remove creme makeup with cold cream and facial tissue followed by soap and water.

Applying Character Makeup

The techniques for applying character makeup are more complex and time-consuming that those for straight make-up. Following are suggestions for the most common character makeup effects.

The Eyes and Brows With the use of shadows and liners, you can make the eyes appear larger, often indicating eagerness, innocence, or exuberance. You can make eyes appear sunken for an evil or threatening look. Eyebrows, as a natural frame to the eye, can do a lot to establish character. Changing the position or size of the eyebrows will create a character. To change the shape, you must first mask out all or part of your own brow. Block out and highlight your natural brows with foundation, or rub them with a cake of very wet soap. When they are dry, apply foundation over them and draw new brows in the desired position and shape. **Crepe hair,** artificial hair made of wool, can be added to make the brows bushier. The sketches at the right indicate a few of the eyebrows you can create.

Common Character Eyebrows

Normal

Sad/Pathetic

Evil

Surprised/Innocent

Mischievous

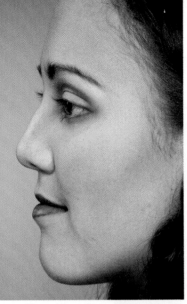

The actor with her natural nose.

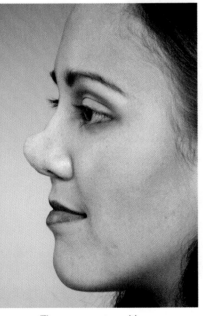

The same actor with an upturned, puckish nose.

The Nose and Mouth

You can vary nose proportions with shadow and highlighting, or you can create a three-dimensional change such as a large, upturned, or misshapen nose with **putty wax** (also called derma wax or nose putty). Prepare the putty by gently kneading it with your fingers until it is soft and pliable. Next apply **spirit gum** adhesive to a clean area of the nose. Embed a few fibers from a cotton ball into the spirit gum to create a "rug" to hold the wax onto your nose. Form the wax into the desired shape using the back of your thumb and place it over the dried spirit gum rug, molding it to the shape of your nose. Smooth out the edges until they blend into the face, and cover the wax with makeup as needed. This may take a bit of practice. Use hair gel to smooth the overall surface. To remove the nose, pull a thread tight and run it along the area under the wax.

You can alter the size of the mouth and change its expression by painting the corners up to suggest happiness or painting them down to indicate sadness, pain, or meanness.

Hair Hair can be slickly combed, messy, or elaborately coiffed as an indication of the character's personality. Women can make their hair look longer by using hairpieces or extensions. Men should get an appropriate haircut three to four weeks before performance and then let their hair grow until after the show. Sprays, gels, and pastes can be used to "mold" the hair into the desired style. To change hair color, use temporary tints found in drugstores. For gray, use a liquid hair whitener. A bald head is achieved with the use of a rubber skullcap. Since wigs are expensive to rent and difficult to fit, avoid them if possible.

Beards and Mustaches Before you apply a beard, observe men who have them. You will notice that facial hair has certain boundaries and that it grows forward under the chin and downward at the sides. It is thinner where the growth starts and becomes thicker farther down on the face. If your character hasn't shaved in a few days, create a stubble effect by **stippling,** or dabbing the face with gray-blue makeup.

Here's How
To "Grow" Beards and Mustaches

To prepare crepe hair for your beard, unbraid the amount and colors you'll need. To straighten the kinks, dampen the hair, put it between two pieces of muslin or other light cloth, and press it with an iron. Since beards are rarely one solid color, combine the colors needed and then comb the pressed hair.

When applying beards:

1 Be sure the face is shaved and the part to be covered is free of foundation.

2 Define the bearded area by applying spirit gum. If you want to use the beard again, apply 2 layers of liquid latex as a base.

3 Hold a small piece of crepe hair in your hand and cut the ends on an angle. Do not use too thick a piece of hair, but have it longer than the desired finished length.

4 Paint a second coat of adhesive just above the larynx and apply a layer of hair, sticking it out toward the front. Hold until it is dry.

5 In this same manner, cut the hair, apply the adhesive, and work up in layers—like shingles on a roof—until the front of the chin is covered with hair pointing down. Continue until you reach the desired shape.

6 When completed, let spirit gum get completely dry, then gently comb out any loose hairs. Shape it into the desired style, and do a final trim. A light coat of hairspray will help it hold its shape.

7 At the top of each beard, you may need to pencil in hairs to blend the beard's edge so that it looks natural.

To create a mustache, complete steps 1–3 above. Then apply the hair at the outer corner of the lip. Work in several layers toward the center. Follow the lip line. Hold each layer in place until dry. Comb and trim.

1. Cover under the chin, pointing the hair out.

2. Add more crepe hair and cover the chin, pointing the hair down.

3. Cover the sides, pointing hair down, and trim to shape the beard.

Scars To make a fresh scar, build up the center of the scar in an irregular shape with putty wax or tissue and liquid latex. If a healed scar is desired, apply three to four coats of nonflexible, or rigid, **collodion,** a clear, thick liquid, directly to the skin, drying between each coat. Collodion will give a drawn, indented look. Collodion can irritate the skin, so be very careful and try a small test patch first. Remove collodion with **acetone,** which can be found in common nail polish remover. Follow the cleaning by applying skin moisturizer.

Missing Teeth To make teeth look like they are missing or broken, use black tooth enamel or black wax directly over the teeth.

Stage Blood Below is the standard recipe for stage blood:

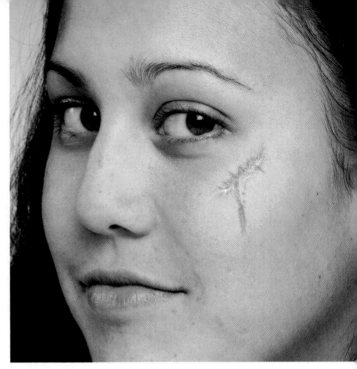

This scar was created using nonflexible collodion.

Recipe for Gore

One 16-oz. bottle of corn syrup
One tablespoon red food coloring
1/4 cup liquid laundry detergent
Blue food coloring

- Mix first three ingredients in a jar.
- Add blue food coloring, one drop at a time, to achieve the desired color.
- Shake well before using.
- Keep jar shut tightly between uses.

Aging a Face

As people age, the flesh sags around the bone structure. Wrinkles form, the texture of the skin changes, and the contours of the face shift and sag. All of these features can be reproduced on young actors through sculpting in the contours that begin to form using highlights and shadows.

Remember that age occurs gradually. When applying makeup, you must guard against making yourself look older than your character actually is. If you are playing someone who is forty or so, you will need different makeup than playing someone who is over sixty. To look in your forties, apply darker rouge lower down on the cheeks to indicate the beginning of sagging facial muscles.

Shadow softly in the eyebag area. Begin a soft shadow in the crease that runs from your nostrils toward your mouth (the smile line). Use less lipstick if you are a female and brown liner if you are a male.

To appear in your fifties or sixties, increase the darkness of the sculpted shadows under the eyes and smile lines, follow this by adding wrinkles, which should accent the natural lines on your face. Frown and then smile, or make a characteristic expression, and then outline the natural wrinkles that appear with liner. Break up the texture of your skin by stippling the surface slightly by using a sponge and a darker base color.

Eye pouches should be more pronounced the older the character. Indicate facial hollows and sags with brown shading, and subtly highlight them with white.

Emphasize wrinkles in the forehead, around the eyes, and from the nose to the mouth. Gray the hair at the temples, and add a few gray streaks elsewhere for more aging. Apply gray to eyebrows also.

Spotlight on

The Makeup Morgue

A **makeup morgue** is a visual reference tool for creating special makeups. To create one for yourself, page through magazines and cut out any interesting faces you find. Glue each picture to a blank page, and label it with a designation that tells how you might use it, i.e. as an example of age, gender, race, skin texture, eyebrows, mouth, and so forth.

After you have gathered enough images, organize them by category and put them in a binder or accordion file. As it continues to grow, your makeup morgue will become a rich resource for future makeups.

Foundation and sculpting shadow is first applied to the face.

Highlights are added and blended.

Create a Very Old Face

1 Apply a pale creme foundation—lighter for a frail character and darker for a healthy character.

2 With the fingertips and a brown liner, add soft shadows to
   a eye sockets
   b indentations below the cheek bones
   c hollows at each temple
   d the sides of the nose
   e the corners of the mouth
   f under the jaw and chin
   g the depressions on both sides of the throat

3 Using off-white liner for highlights above each shadow, apply soft highlights to the bone
   a over each eyebrow
   b in each cheek
   c at the point of the chin
   d along the line of the lower jaw
   e at the throat

4 To further define wrinkles, use brown liner to create them where they naturally form
   a on the forehead
   b between the eyebrows and outer eye corners (worry lines and crow's feet)
   c in the smile lines from the nose to the corners of the mouth

5 With off-white liner on a brush, highlight below all the wrinkles.

6 With the fingertips, blend the edges of the highlight, shadow, and base.

7 Thin the lips using a dark reddish color. Stipple rouge, and apply texture

Lips are made thinner and hard edges are added around the eyes.

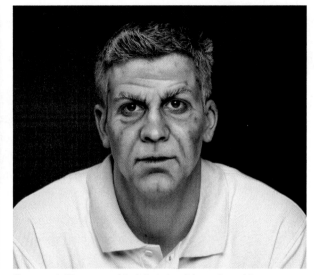

Deep wrinkles are added, hair is whitened, and liver spots can be added.

(i.e. liver spots) if desired. Allow a thin portion of the natural lip to show.

8 Whiten hair and eyebrows. Make eyebrows bushy by brushing them the wrong way. Apply whitener at temples as desired.

9 Powder creme makeup.

Makeup Essentials

Every student of acting should have his or her own makeup kit. This is not only more convenient but hygienic. Many actors outfit a fishing tackle box or tool-box. You should purchase a small makeup kit made for students. Theatrical makeup companies sell them inexpensively. Makeup can get expensive, however, so use only what is necessary, and always replace lids tightly.

On the following page are lists of the essential materials you will need for straight and character makeup.

Theatre Journal

Observe the facial characteristics and hairstyles of the people in a public place, such as a park, mall, or supermarket. Capture a few of these people in your journal by drawing their faces and writing short descriptions of their features.

The Essentials for Straight Makeup

1 **Foundation** in creme or cake. Include white, light, and medium shades.

2 **Liners** (**highlight** and **shading colors**) give the face a three-dimensional effect by providing shadows and highlights. Basic liners are black, brown, maroon, yellow, off-white, and blue.

3 **Lipsticks** in shades of red for women and a brownish shade for men.

4 **Rouge** in red or medium-red for women; reddish-brown for men.

5 **Powder (and puffs)** sets creme so it won't smudge or create a glare under the lights. Choose a shade lighter than the foundation, or use a translucent powder you can apply over any foundation.

6 **Eyebrow pencils** to darken eyebrows and line eyes. Use either medium or dark brown.

7 **Fluff brushes** to apply dry rouge, powder, and eye shadow and to remove excess powder.

8 **Lining brushes** made of sable to line the eyes and to give the appearance of wrinkles and to paint the lips. A common size is 3/16-inch or 1/4-inch.

9 **Mascara** in dark brown.

10 **Cold cream** for removing makeup.

11 **Miscellaneous** sponges, hand mirror, thread, scissors, soap, comb, tissue, brush cleaner, cotton balls, and a pencil sharpener.

The Essentials for Character Makeup

1 **Putty wax** for making false noses, warts, scars, and so forth.

2 **Liquid latex** liquid rubber that can be used for building up facial features such as chins, jowls, noses, eye pouches, and scars and for attaching crepe hair.

3 **Nonflexible collodion** a clear, thick solution used on the skin to make scars.

4 **Crepe hair** for fashioning beards and mustaches. Choose several colors including gray and one that is close to your own color.

5 **Spirit gum** an adhesive for attaching hair, false noses, scars, and so on.

6 **Rubbing alcohol** to remove spirit gum and **acetone** to remove collodion.

7 **Hair whitener** liquid or spray.

Makeup Hygiene

For the sake of safe hygiene it is strongly recommended that you have your own makeup kit and use only your own makeup. Be sure to have a good supply of:

- sponges
- powder puffs (or cotton balls)
- tissue
- soap or cleanser

Sponges should be thrown away after each use. Take a tissue and clean the surface of all makeup before using it. Although a liquid brush cleaner is available and is certainly effective, you may also clean your brushes in hot, soapy water. Clean them after every use. You may be tempted to borrow someone else's lipstick. This is not recommended, but if you are careful, you can use a cotton swab to remove a small amount of lipstick from another's tube (after wiping the area with a tissue first). Apply a small dab of the lipstick from the swab to your own lip brush.

Also be aware that you should never take makeup directly from containers with your fingers. Instead, squeeze a bit of makeup onto a paper towel or use a small spatula to remove a bit of makeup from jars, pots, sticks, or tubes. Always keep the lids securely closed. Wash your hands well with soap and water before applying your makeup.

The illustration above shows the effect of various colored lights on a color wheel.

Always Adjust Makeup to Lighting

Colored lights dim similar colors on stage and completely darken **complementary colors** (those colors opposite each other on the color wheel). Use these techniques to adjust makeup to the existing lighting.

- A red light subdues red makeup and makes green look black. Consequently, if you have red lights on stage, you'll need to apply heavy pink base and a rouge with a blue tint.

- If you have strong amber stage lights, apply rouge heavily and use a pink base, since amber "eats up" red.
- With blue lights, the reds look purple or black, so for a blue moonlight scene use a light foundation and very little rouge.
- Since green light makes the face look ghastly, it is rarely used unless that effect is needed.

PREPARE

Apply Your Makeup

For your project, you will apply character makeup to yourself to achieve the look of an older or unusual character. You may prefer a character who is more animal than human, such as the creatures in Edward Albee's *Seascape*. Whichever character you choose, be sure to think about this character seriously before you begin experimenting with makeup. You will want to do a bit of research into the time period of the play and read closely any descriptions of the character in the script. Keep notes, and use this information as you create your character. Follow these steps to complete the project.

1 Create a character makeup sheet like the one below or use the Activity Sheet for this chapter, which your teacher will provide. Consider what colors you should use based on your own face, the play's time period and setting, the character you are portraying, the size of the performance space, and the lighting conditions.

2 Secure a makeup kit.

3 Prepare a desk or table at home by spreading papers over it and placing it near a light source. Lay out your makeup, including cold cream, facial tissues, and a large mirror. Wear a smock or old shirt to protect your clothes. Tie your hair back if necessary.

4 Use the step-by-step procedure for applying your makeup found on the previous pages. As you proceed, keep notes as to what you are doing and why. Then practice explaining your choices to the class within the five- to ten-minute framework.

Character Makeup Sheet

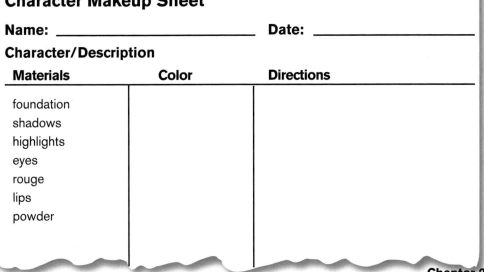

Name: _____ **Date:** _____

Character/Description

Materials	Color	Directions
foundation		
shadows		
highlights		
eyes		
rouge		
lips		
powder		

PRESENT

Discuss Your Makeup Choices

When your name is called, walk throughout the classroom in such a way that all your classmates and your teacher can get a good look at your makeup. Continue to the front of the class. Describe the character you are representing. If you prefer not to come to class in makeup, videotape and edit the process of applying character makeup and show it to the class with live narration. Or you could bring in "before" and "after" photographs showing your makeup process. Be prepared to explain to the class how you achieved your character's look.

Whichever way you choose to present your final character makeup, be sure to use your notes and makeup worksheet or the Activity Sheet to talk about the considerations that went in to the makeup choices you made. Be sure your talk does not exceed ten minutes.

CRITIQUE

Evaluate a Classmate's Makeup and Presentation

Evaluate a classmate's makeup as well as the reasons behind the makeup, on a scale from 1 to 5, with 5 being "outstanding," and 1 being "needs much improvement." Ask yourself these questions:

- How effective is the actor's makeup when viewed fairly closely?
- Is the effect of the actor's makeup visible from a distance?
- In what ways does the makeup represent the character?
- What other choices could have been made to better bring out the character?
- How well did the presenter explain the reasons for applying the makeup in this way?

Write a paragraph that tells why you gave this classmate the rating you did.

Career Focus

Makeup Artist

Makeup artists are employed in professional theatres and for film and video productions, as well as in photo studios that do actors' headshots and commercial photo shoots. Many makeup artists begin as photographers' assistants. Others begin as cosmetologists or hair stylists, and then apply their skills in theatrical venues.

You can develop your own skills as a makeup artist with practice. Check out makeup books and videos and practice the techniques they offer. When you have gained some skill, try to replicate effects you see in still photos. Invite friends to come over in costumes, and apply makeup that matches their attire.

Jot down the steps you use to apply makeup and take photographs for reference. Attach the photos to the notes to create a personal makeup handbook.

Additional Projects

1 Demonstrate the application of putty wax to alter facial features such as the nose, ears, chin, or cheeks.

2 Report on special makeup techniques used in the movies and in television.

3 Create an "available materials" makeup. Choose any character you wish from fiction or real life. For makeup, use only the materials you have available at home other than actual makeup. Avoid anything that will stain the face, such as some food dyes. An example of available materials makeup is to create old age using white liquid glue as a base and potting soil as a beard. Or, an owl might be created with wheat paste and raw oatmeal on your face. Use your imagination.

4 Start your makeup morgue by collecting magazine pictures of various faces. Share your morgue with others in your class and discuss the ideas for makeup that you find there.

5 Research and explain how science and technological advances have impacted set, light, sound, makeup, and costume design and implementation for the theatre.

6 Working with a partner, create one of the following on each other:

a A forty-year-old woman

b An eighty-year-old man with a beard

c a young rabbit

7 Choose a specialized character from Unit Eight, such as the old woman in *Driving Miss Daisy* or Sam in *The Janitor,* and describe how you would create the makeup for this person.

Theatre **Then** and Now

The Actor's Face

The Face of Ancient Asia

Sanskrit drama as performed in India is probably the oldest existing classical theatre form in the world, having originated close to 2000 years ago. It is said to have come from the ancient custom of reciting poetry at social and religious gatherings. The *Natyasastra* by Bharatha Muni is the oldest text on theatre performance.

Acting in ancient India was an art that made great use of both costume and makeup. Actors were rigorously trained, adhering to strict dietary and exercise regimens. The characters they depicted included gods, kings, heroes, jesters, courtiers, and common folks. Everyone involved in the drama—actors, dancers, and musicians alike—were committed to presenting the audience with a luscious feast for the eyes and ears.

Kalidasa is generally agreed to be the greatest of Indian playwrights. He is thought to have lived between about 375 A.D. and 450 A.D. Three of his plays exist today, including *Sakuntala,* the story of a humble girl loved by King Dushanta. The couple must overcome the curse of a sage to find happiness in the final act.

Throughout India and Southeast Asia, the influence of the great Indian epics *Ramayan* and *Mahabharata,* whose stories appear in the form of dance and drama as well as puppet theatre, are still performed. In these dramatic dances, gods such as Shiva and Krishna are often integrated into the stories. The dances are very stylized and exuberant, with each dancer made up and dressed as befits the character.

The ancient theatre of India and Southeast Asia is still alive and well, and its face is as beautiful and colorful as ever.

Arunja, one of the characters in the *Mahabharata*, wears the green makeup typical of the heroes of Sanskrit drama. This performance was given in Kerela, India.

Actors in straight makeup in Rebecca Gilman's *Spinning into Butter.*

Contemporary Dramatic Faces

Of course, worldwide contemporary drama uses makeup in any number of ways. Makeup must reflect the intention and style of the play. In plays such as *Spinning into Butter* or *Proof,* the actors use straight makeup that reflects their characters' contemporary, day-to day situations.

Other plays, however, must approach the actor's face as a way to tell more of the story. In *A Streetcar Named Desire,* for example, while other characters in the play may wear straight makeup, Blanche often requires heavy applications of lipstick, mascara, and rouge to indicate a woman trying desperately to remain youthful and attractive. And Nobel Prize winner Wole Solinka's blend of Western experimental theatre and Nigerian folk tradition often requires special makeup. The Yoruba pageantry— "masks" and dances—must be depicted in an authentic, yet symbolic way.

Then there are the plays that pull out all the stops. The face becomes a canvas, a playground for the makeup designer, a way for the actor to reflect the theme of the play itself. In *Starlight Express* the actors become trains. In *Cats,* each actor is a very specific breed of cat, and each cat has his or her own personality as reflected in the costume and makeup. And, of course, the faces and bodies of the actors in *The Lion King* are converted not only into lions, but also into jackals, antelopes, and giraffes.

Using just some paint and putty, a bit of crepe hair, a few feathers, and perhaps a new hairdo and some glitter, an actor is transformed. In turn, the actor transforms the world on the stage.

In Wole Solinka's *The Road*, the masked character represents the spiritual level of the play.

Chapter
23 Props

One of the final pieces of the production puzzle is the addition of properties—or props. The right props can provide the set with crucial details that help to bring the audience into the world of the play.

Project Specs

Project Description For this assignment, you will create a prop plot (a detailed list of props) for a full-length play and describe it in a three- to eight-minute presentation.

Purpose to understand the different kinds of props, how to acquire them, and their function in the play

Materials a prop plot for a play or the Props Activity Sheet your teacher provides

Theatre Terms
decorative props
hand props
prop plot
props master
pull
set dressing
set props

On Your Feet

Look around the room and imagine that you are making a prop list for a play about this class. As your instructor calls on various people, each should name a prop that would be important to include, such as books, desks, or a chalkboard.

The Balcony, a play by Jean Genet, abounds in characters, costumes, and props.

PREVIEW

Props and What They Do

Imagine the set for a play that takes place in a dining room. On the set there are shelves of china and knickknacks, potted plants, thick brocade drapes, a mirror, paintings, and a huge table set with silverware, dishes, and goblets. There are piles of food on the plates. There are place mats, a tablecloth, and napkins. Which of these items are considered props?

The answer is: all of them. A show's props include anything the actors handle onstage as well as any furniture, draperies, carpets, or paintings on the set. To obtain suitable props, a **props master** may borrow, build, buy, rent, or **pull** them. Pulled props are those you already own—you pull them from storage.

Furniture, carpets, and lighting fixtures—known as **set props**—work along with the other technical elements of the play to establish time period, place, income level of the characters, and so on. Details such as paintings, newspapers, and curtains, which make up the **decorative props** or **set dressing,** can tell an audience a lot about the characters that inhabit this environment. Then there are the **hand props**—items used directly by the actors during the show. These might include a letter, a manuscript, a gun, a telephone, and so on. Hand props can help establish a specific character—think of the elegant heroine gazing demurely out from behind her fan or the poverty-stricken young man who, despite hardship, can't bring himself to part with his father's gold watch.

The props used in this production of Noel Coward's *Private Lives* reflect the early 1930s.

Analyzing a Script for Props

You wouldn't use a boom box as a radio prop for a play set in 1930. If your play is set in 1970, the magazines on the coffee table, if they are visible to the audience, must be from 1970 (or at least appear to be so). Even if they are not visible, some props masters insist that the authenticity of the prop is mandatory if the actors are to believe in the setting. When it comes to props, even small oversights can take the audience (and the actors) right out of the play. So it's important that the props crew analyzes the script very carefully. If necessary, the props master must do research into the time period to make sure

that once the props crew begins to build, borrow, buy, rent, or pull existing props, they have all the information they need to get just the right articles.

Some published scripts feature a prop list that offers a breakdown of all the props needed for each scene. But if the play your school is producing doesn't have one, you will need to create your own **prop plot.** This will require that you go through each scene line by line, paying particular attention to the stage directions, and write a list of the props needed. You should code the items in terms of those already available at your school—those items you will pull. Your list should be specific. Rather than simply saying, "clock," describe the ideal clock ("contemporary clock radio with large digital numbers" or "metal alarm clock from the 1950s"). Once you have completed your prop plot, you can begin the gathering process. Note that the props crew must work closely with the set and lighting crews to make sure that furniture, rugs, and draperies don't clash with the walls, flooring, or lighting effects.

Gathering Props

If you don't have a necessary prop in storage, the easiest way to obtain it is to buy it. However, for reasons of budget and/or practicality, this is not always possible.

Large set pieces such as beds can be constructed by the set crew. Your

Be a Good Borrower!

Remember that props are used in each performance, and they can take a real beating. Check with the director and producer before borrowing anything to use onstage. Don't borrow any prop your school would be unwilling to pay to replace. Above all else, be sure to return items promptly and in good, clean condition.

school may already have some smaller furniture, such as tables and chairs, in stock. Assess the school's inventory carefully. Sometimes you can make an old lamp or piece of furniture look new or different with a new shade, a coat of paint, or other decoration.

Remember, it's the illusion that counts. The audience will be sitting out in the house, not onstage. From that distance, an inexpensive, shiny-finished fabric can simulate silk, a papier-mâché vase can become a priceless marble urn, and chunks of foam covered with painted canvas can look exactly like boulders.

Prop Plot

Name of Play   *What the World Needs Now*

Characters Who Handle Props:

Lisa (Sally Klein)

Kent (Damon Warner)

	Scene Description	Properties Needed
ACT I	Living Room 1950s	TV, sofa, 2 chairs, book, coffee table, 2 water glasses, newspaper, an orange
Scene No. 1		TV—wooden floor model small screen Sofa—clean lines, wood trim 2 Chairs—wood, no arms Coffee table—glass top, metal legs with book on top
Scene No. 2		Same as No. 1 / Add orange, 2 water glasses (remove at end of scene)
Scene No. 3		Same as No. 2 / Add newspaper (remove at end of scene)
ACT II	Porch of same house 1950s	Porch swing wooden, old Shrubs
Scene No. 1		

Here's How
To Search for Props

A true props person is an imaginative scavenger who can see prop potential in things other people throw away. Here are some ideas for locating items on your prop list.

- Scour secondhand stores like the Salvation Army and Goodwill.

- Become a garage sale fanatic.

- Shop at outlets and discount stores.

- Borrow from family and friends.

- Check with other theatre groups in your area, such as other high schools, colleges, and community theatres.

- Skim through books on stagecraft to see what the stage crew could build.

- Send out a list of needed items to classmates and teachers.

- Broadcast your "most wanted" list over the school PA system.

- Get yourself an interview on school or local access radio or television shows.

- Post your list on bulletin boards in school, at supermarkets, and other public locations.

- Research prices at rental stores.

- Ask local shops if you can borrow their window dressing props.

Perishable Props

Plants and food are often found on prop lists. If possible, invest in plastic or silk plants that can be reused for other shows. Real plants tend to wilt under stage lights and need constant watering and tending.

Food can be faked if the actors aren't going to be eating it onstage. For example, the Christmas roast goose on the set's dining table may be built out of papier-mâché—as long as no one has to carve or eat it. But if the play calls for the actors to actually consume the food, then it must be prepared, stored, and disposed of properly so that it doesn't spoil or attract pests. The important thing to remember about stage food is that it only needs to *appear* to be real.

Imagine that your production calls for a character to come in eating French fries. Instead of cooking up a batch of fries for each performance, you might bring in a few pieces of toast cut into the long thin shape of fries. The audience will believe these are French fries if they are told that's what they are. And cut-up dry toast won't get the actor's fingers greasy!

Mashed potatoes are used to simulate ice cream on stage. It doesn't melt, so it can be stored backstage and brought on at the appropriate time.

The fruit looks tasty in this scene from *Reflections*, but it is actually colorful plastic.

Avoid using salty foods as they may cause dry mouth or even choking. In a play that requires a character to drink alcohol, the liquid in the bottle may be tea to simulate whiskey and grape or cranberry juice to be red wine. The props crew should always check with the actors who will be eating the food to see if they are allergic to anything.

During Rehearsal and Production

The props crew's work is not complete when all props have been acquired. They are also responsible for managing the props during rehearsals and the show itself. Hand props, in particular, should be obtained as quickly as possible so that actors can become used to working with them. However, an actor should never be allowed to walk away backstage with these props in hand. They need to be available and accounted for at all times. Most props masters set up a prop table on both sides of the stage. The table is covered with plain paper and all props needed on that side of the stage are placed on the table. Outlining and labeling the items with black marker will help both actors and crew keep track of the items.

The props crew also has a job to do during the run of the show. These are the people that remove and replace props between scenes and acts. They must choreograph their work with that of the stage crew so scene changes can occur quickly and quietly.

PREPARE

Work on a Prop Plot and a Talk

Choose a play to use as the basis for a detailed prop plot. Read the complete play. Make a note of each prop you will need, scene by scene. For example, consider a stage direction such as this one:

(The morning sun streams in through the window. A breeze ruffles the curtains. Iris is asleep in the easy chair by the door. Clutched in her hand is a letter. Agnes enters with a can of aerosol room deodorizer. She sprays it all around the room. The noise wakes Iris, who quickly slips the letter into her pocket. Agnes snaps off the lamp on the small table next to Iris without speaking. She then moves to the portrait of their mother on the wall and straightens it ever so slightly.)

In just one stage direction, there are:
- four set props—the curtains, the easy chair, the lamp, and the small table
- two hand props—the letter and the can of aerosol room deodorizer prop
- one decorative prop—the portrait

These would all be listed on your prop plot. Try to be as specific as possible by providing a description of the props you see in your mind's eye. For example, is the lamp a reading lamp, a fancy glass lamp, or a fringed silk-shaded lamp? Decide and then write down that description.

When you have made your way through the play once, read it again and look for anything you may have missed. When you are sure you have recorded every prop, complete your prop plot.

Beginning with the first scene, list each prop. Use three different pens to color code your list. Use a black pen for set props, a red pen for hand props, and a blue pen for decorative props. When you get to scene two, make a new scene heading, and continue listing the props.

Set props need only be listed once as long as they are not removed from the stage at any time. The same is true for decorative props. But hand props should be listed each time they appear in a new scene. So you might have to list the same letter, book, or gun in every scene of the play.

Once you have completed your prop list, write a synopsis of the play. Then imagine that you are the props master for a production of this play. Think about what you would say in a meeting about the play's props. What special prop challenges does the play present? What will the props add to the play's mood and tone? Where will you begin your prop search process? Can you make some of the props? What will you need to buy? Prepare a three- to eight-minute talk about these elements. Rehearse your talk a few times, being sure that you do not go over the time limit.

Career Focus

Properties Master

If you have an eye for detail and you've always enjoyed a good treasure hunt, a career as a props master might be a good fit for you. Many who work in props say that the thrill of the hunt is an integral part of the job. Let's say you need a 19th-century grandfather clock . . . and you have to get it for twenty dollars or less. Maybe your show needs an ancient samurai sword . . . one that collapses. Where will you find such things? Can you rent or borrow them? Or will you have to make them? A props master looks at these dilemmas as a challenge.

As in other technical theatre fields, props masters and their crews are responsible for hundreds of small and large tasks before, during, and after every single performance. A good memory is one prerequisite. The ability to take detailed notes is another. A props master also needs good communication skills. After all, he or she must build strong relationships with prop rental houses, other theatres, and the rest of the production crew.

A career as a props master can begin with a theatre degree or with practical experience in community or professional theatre. To see if this work appeals, try working as a props assistant on a play at your school or in your community.

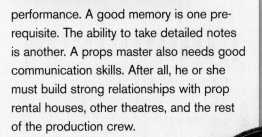

PRESENT

Talk About Your Prop Plot

When your name is called, hand your prop plot or Activity Sheet to your teacher and walk to the playing area.

Introduce the play and give a short synopsis. Then discuss the props you plan to use, how they relate to the play's mood, and how you plan to obtain them. (Which you will make, which you can pull or borrow, and which you will have to rent or buy.) When you have finished, thank your listeners, and return to your seat. Your instructor may wish to pass the prop plot around to your classmates.

Theatre Journal

Think of a recent conversation you had with a friend. If your conversation were a scene in a play, what props would be needed? To answer this, you need to think about where your conversation took place. Write down everything you can remember about the setting of your conversation. Then make a list of what props and set pieces the staging of your conversation would require.

CRITIQUE

Evaluate a Classmate's Prop Plot and Talk

Choose one classmate's presentation to evaluate. You will rate the presentation taking into consideration several aspects of the talk. Use a scale of 1 to 5, with 5 being "outstanding," 4 being "very good," 3 being "good," 2 being "needs some improvement," and 1 being "needs much improvement." Ask yourself the following questions as you critique your classmate's presentation.

- How informative was the synopsis of the play?
- To what degree did the presenter understand the prop needs of this play?
- Was the speaker's prop plot sufficiently thorough or did it need work?
- How realistic were the speaker's plans for making, renting, borrowing, or purchasing the items?
- In what ways might the speaker make or fabricate props that he or she intends to buy or rent?
- How well did the speaker impart the information?

Remember that to do the job well, a props person must be detail-oriented. Although the presentation's time limit is short, evaluate your classmate in terms of how efficiently he or she used the allotted time. Write a paragraph explaining why you gave the rating you did.

Additional Projects

1 Create a short pantomime on a specific theme using a few symbolic props.

2 Bring to class an object that you feel symbolizes your life. Share your feelings and perceptions of this "prop" with your classmates.

3 Create a prop portrait. You can do this by copying a photograph, enlarging it, and painting over it to make it appear completely painted. Build and decorate a frame for the portrait.

4 Experiment to create edible and inexpensive prop foods that look like the real thing. Share your results with your classmates.

5 Read the scene from *The Glass Menagerie* by Tennessee Williams found in Unit Eight. Create a prop list based on this scene. Which of these props might be symbolic or emblematic?

Theatre **Then** and **Now**

Symbolic Props Across Time

14th Century Noh Drama

In the Japanese Noh drama of the 14th century, stage props were few—but those that were used were highly symbolic and crucial to the performance. Among these props, the fan was the most important. Because the drama was presented in a formal, aristocratic language that the average viewer could not understand, the actors used fans to accentuate or illustrate almost every gesture throughout the performance.

The fan was manipulated to illustrate anything from the rising sun to a long journey. A character might open a fan to simulate a vast mountain range when mountains were described on the stage. Shortly thereafter, a character might use a closed fan to simulate a boat's oar in water—thereby symbolizing the emotions of someone who feels emotionally adrift.

The scenery in Noh plays consisted entirely of impressionistic props that formed the outlines of buildings, coaches, boats, and just about any other important object in the play. The result was a spare staging with an emphasis on precision movements and the symbolism of important props.

A Noh actor uses a fan to convey meaning.

A Japanese fan

A 20th-Century Reinterpretation

Hundreds of years later, in the 1940s and '50s, German playwright and director Bertolt Brecht became intrigued with Japanese theatrical forms. He also worked with the idea of sparse but symbolic props. His plays *The Caucasian Chalk Circle* and *The Good Woman of Setzuan* reflect his great interest in Asian theatre. Like practitioners of Noh and Kabuki, Brecht was not interested in presenting a "realistic" depiction of life.

In his study of Asian theatre, Brecht saw a way to use non-realistic sets and props to keep the audience in an intellectual state of mind. His goal was to keep the audience thinking about the characters' situations and the themes of the play. He accomplished this goal through a variety of means, among them masks and other symbolic items.

One of his favorite Asian-influenced prop tricks was to have the actors sling a board across two chairs to simulate a bridge. Brecht also favored having stage personnel bring on and take off props in full view of the audience. This technique comes from the Kabuki theatre practice of using a *kurogo* (man in black), who shifted props, costumes, and scenery, and even served occasionally as a prompter. Because the *kurogo* was not a character in the play, the audience was able to disregard him.

The chair simulates a speaker's platform in this scene from *The Caucasian Chalk Circle.*

Unit
Five

PREVIEW

Examine the following key concepts previewed in Unit Five.

1 Draw a simple diagram of the three common stages.

2 Identify the following stage elements:

fly gallery	teaser	back wall	drop
batten	wings	trap	

3 The illustration at the right is a common set piece. What is it called, and how is it used?

4 Discuss the functions of stage lighting.

5 What are the important safety issues in lighting design?

6 List a few of the duties of the sound crew.

7 What does it mean to pull, rent, borrow, buy, or build?

8 Match the color below to the mood it evokes

danger	purple
restfulness	white
tragedy	green or blue
royalty	red
purity	black

9 What makeup product is used to create the appearance of a scar?

10 Why is a prop plot important?

PREPARE

Assess your response to the preparation process for projects in this unit.

11 In preparing your set design according to the ground plan, how did you keep all the elements in scale?

12 What difficulties did you encounter in working on your lighting plan?

13 What was the most inventive thing you did when preparing your sound effects for a scene?

14 In designing your costume for a character in a play, how did you determine the amout of detail to include?

15 Did you make your presentation in full makeup or did you take photos or videotape the process? Why did you decide to do it this way?

PRESENT

Analyze the experience of presenting your work to the class.

16 Did your audience understand your intentions in creating the set design the way you did? Why or why not?

17 How did your lighting plot reflect the theme of the play?

18 Is there anything you would change about the costume designs that you presented?

19 Were you able to convince your audience that the makeup you created for your character captured his or her spirit?

CRITIQUE

Evaluate how you go about critiquing your work and the work of others.

20 How heavily do you stress originality when evaluating someone's creative efforts? Why?

21 Which do you feel is more important in a costume, that it conveys the time and place of the play or the personality of the character? Explain.

22 Do you think the audience responded better to makeup presented in person, on videotape, or in photographs? Why?

EXTENSIONS

- Gather together scraps of fabric and other items that you feel represent a character in a play of your choice. Discuss how you might use these elements to create a costume for the character.

- Think of ways you might create props for such perishable items as fruit, vegetables, bread, and a chocolate soda.

Unit
Six

Theatre and Its Counterparts

Chapter
24 Musical Theatre

When people say the word *Broadway* these days, they are usually referring to musical theatre. In the mid-20th century, **straight plays** (nonmusical comedies and dramas) were a major component of Broadway theatre, but today the big musical productions are the ones that typically bring the crowds.

Project Specs

Project Description For this assignment, you will create and present a five-minute proposal for a new musical.

Purpose to understand the elements of musical theatre

Materials written notes on the proposal or the Musical Theatre Activity Sheet provided by your teacher

Theatre Terms

choreographer
chorus
musical
musical comedy
music director
onstage director
pitch
principals
production numbers
straight plays

On Your Feet

With a classmate, create lyrics for a short song. Alternate lines so that each of you creates some of the lyrics. Then work together to come up with a simple tune that fits the rhythm, emotions, and style of the lyrics you co-wrote.

A scene from the popular musical *Camelot*.

The American Musical

The modern **musical** is a uniquely American art form. While other kinds of musical theatre, such as opera, have existed for centuries, plays set to music began in the 1920s, with the compositions of George Gershwin, Irving Berlin, and others. These musical craftsmen wrote popular songs that became the perfect accompaniment for the light plots of the comedies of the day. They were called **musical comedies,** appropriately enough. The shows typically featured a slight—even silly—story, plenty of tuneful melodies, and a chorus of leggy dancers.

In 1927, musicals took a dramatic turn. Jerome Kern's *Showboat* changed

The gals sing and dance in a 1998 Lyceum Theatre production of *Oklahoma.*

everything. First, it dealt with serious subject matter: racism, spousal abuse, and abandonment. Second, it did something that was revolutionary: It tied the songs into the plot of the play. Suddenly, songs were being used not just as background and distraction, but also as a way of actually *telling* the story. Another innovation occurred in 1943, when *Oklahoma,* the Richard Rogers and Oscar Hammerstein musical, opened to rave reviews. Some consider this the true beginning of the modern musical because every element—music, dialogue, dance, and plot—were seamlessly woven together to create a totally integrated production.

Since then, musicals and musical comedies have been a favorite American theatre form. And the musical has gotten richer, more complex, and more dramatic than ever. Such award-winners as *Bye-Bye Birdie,* which incorporated rock and roll into the plot; *West Side Story*, a dramatic retelling of *Romeo and Juliet* set in New York with powerful songs and dances; *Hair*, all exuberance and counter-culture; the rollicking *Jesus Christ Superstar*, and others, reflected not only the musical interests but the social issues of America.

Today's musicals often feature complex staging with multiple sets, elaborate costumes, and huge casts. It takes a lot of money and a large team of professionals to produce the kind of full-scale musical you might see on Broadway. Many communities just can't afford to produce these kinds of shows and don't have the seating capacity to draw the large-scale traveling productions. Luckily there has also been a recent movement toward smaller-cast, simpler musicals such as the popular *I Love You, You're Perfect, Now Change.* These small-cast musicals are produced on a much lower budget, and consequently can charge a much lower admission price, thus helping the musical gain an even wider audience.

The acclaimed musical *Rent* combines catchy music and lyrics with a powerful statement about urban gentrification and homelessness.

The stage musical *Fosse* is constructed around the choreography of the late Bob Fosse.

More and more musicals are full of singing but feature almost no dancing, for example, *Les Misérables* and *The Spitfire Grill*. Others, such as *A Chorus Line* and *Chicago,* feature an abundance of singing and dancing. And at least two major musicals, *Contact* and *Movin' Out,* choreographed by Twyla Tharp, are told entirely in dance. *Contact* features only a prerecorded tape of pop songs, and *Movin' Out* has a live singer at the side of the stage singing the hits of pop star Billy Joel. There are those who may not consider these two pieces musical theatre; however, *Contact* won the Tony Award for Best Musical of 2000.

Another recent group of musicals are actually modern operas—all singing and no spoken dialogue. These include *Joseph and the Amazing Technicolor Dreamcoat, Tommy, Jesus Christ Superstar,* and *Les Misérables.*

If you're going to be auditioning for a musical, it's a good idea to have some vocal training and to be able to execute at least a few basic dance steps.

Musical Personnel

As is the case in the professional theatre, high school musicals are much more complicated to produce than straight dramas. This is because musicals feature orchestral music, multiple elaborate sets, larger casts requiring huge numbers of costumes and, often, special effects. This complexity demands a larger production staff than is typically needed for a play.

Performers who can sing, dance, and act are in high demand on Broadway and in films based on Broadway productions. Pictured here is Catherine Zeta-Jones, who sang and danced along with Richard Gere and Renee Zellweger in the movie version of *Chicago*.

The Actors The songs performed in musicals are typically used to heighten the emotions of the audience. Musical theatre actors must be able to bring their characters to life through song—in other words, they must have the confidence to "sell it." Of course a trained voice is also essential, but many successful musical theatre actors have interesting as opposed to traditionally beautiful voices.

Good actors who can sing are in great demand in the world of today's professional musical theatre. But most **principals** (actors in major roles) begin their careers as members of the **chorus.** This is the group of singers that provides the backup for the principals. Sometimes chorus members have short solos, but most often they are asked to harmonize and to serve in crowd scenes and production numbers.

The Two Directors Most musicals have two directors—one who directs the actors onstage and another who directs the musicians (both onstage and off). The **onstage director** functions much as a director would in a straight play. He or she blocks the actors (except for dance numbers), coaches the actors in their non-singing scenes, and sees to the overall style and flow of the show. The onstage director is also in charge of casting the show, although most directors collaborate with the music director

on this part of the process. The director may be a teacher with a theatre background or a hired theatre professional.

The **music director** works with the actors, singers, and dancers throughout the rehearsal process to ensure that they are on key, up to speed, and creating the best sound possible. He or she guides the performers through the musical part of the rehearsal process and often serves as conductor during performances. The music director's job is very important to the overall effect of the show because so many of a musical's dramatic moments are conveyed through song. He or she must be able to collaborate effectively with the director and choreographer.

The music director is usually responsible for selecting the show's instrumentation. Depending on the performance space, the play, and the budget, the instrumentation might include a single piano, a small band with just a few instruments, or a full-scale orchestra. The music director usually holds special rehearsals with individual principals and periodic rehearsals for just the chorus members. He or she is typically a teacher who works with musicians in the school's band and/or orchestra programs, or is the school's music teacher (however, some schools hire outside music professionals).

The Choreographer The person responsible for designing a show's dance numbers is the **choreographer.** Many musicals feature **production numbers,** elaborate song-and-dance sequences in which almost the entire cast takes part. The choreographer must be knowledgeable about music and movement and must have a facility for working with large groups of performers all at once. At the high school level the choreographer will typically be working with individuals at a variety of experience levels and abilities. It takes both talent and patience to create a unified choreographic vision.

Career Focus

Choreographer

Choreographers are among the most multifaceted of all theater professionals. Ask them how they define themselves, and they'll tell you they are dancers, actors, directors, scene designers, mediators, and more.

Like directors, choreographers do their most important work during the rehearsal period. They begin by reading the script. They think about the mood and style of the play and look for important moments in the plot. Then they develop movements to express the emotions in those moments. When they work on musicals, choreographers develop dances and train dancers. But they also direct other movements in other kinds of productions. They design the movements for pratfalls and fight scenes. They make sure entrances and exits flow smoothly. In short, they make sure the movements in every scene are effective.

If you think you might want to become a choreographer, you can begin by studying dance. You don't need to become a great dancer, but you will need to know a lot about movement. When you think you have learned enough to help others, you can volunteer your time and talent on a school or community play or teach dance classes. Through these experiences, you will learn what works and what doesn't work in actual practice.

Once you have gained both education and experience, you can collaborate with directors you admire or you can create dance pieces of your own. You might want to test your abilities in some of the competitions that take place all over the world.

Designers Just as in straight plays, the set, lighting, and costume designers must contribute their creative expertise to the overall vision of the production. (See Unit Five for chapters devoted to these theatre personnel.)

The Producer No matter what the production level, a large-scale musical is an expensive proposition. The number of actors, sets, and production staff needed for a musical is very large compared to a straight dramatic work. A high school musical can cost anywhere from $2000 to $15,000. (A professional-level musical may cost up to $10 million.) At the front end, this means that a good producer must be very savvy about recognizing a potential show's marketability. The question is often not so much "Is it good?" as "Will it sell?"—the point being that if it won't sell, it won't matter if it's good. So although a high school production has a built-in audience of friends, classmates, and family members, most producers try to market the show to a larger cross-section of the community in order to ensure sufficient ticket sales to meet the budget.

Often several producers—a teacher and selected students or a group of affiliated teachers—may work together to secure funding for the production and to manage the show's marketing. The musical producer's job is made up of the same general tasks as that of a straight play producer (see Chapter 14).

The Technical Crews The crews for musicals are usually larger than those for smaller-cast straight plays. But they are similar in terms of the types of tasks they fulfill. (For more on technical crews and their functions, see Chapter 14.)

The Business Manager Like any business manager, the business manager for a musical production is in charge of the budget. Musicals, however, can present special challenges because they are often extremely expensive to produce, due to the additional cost of hiring musicians, a conductor, dancers, a choreographer, special technicians, creating lavish costumes and sets, and so on. The business manager may decide that ticket prices have to be higher or that the advertising budget must be doubled—all in the hopes of bringing in money to finance the production.

PREPARE

Create a Proposal for a New Musical

These days, the subject of a musical can be just about anything. There are musicals about war, politics, race, immigration, parenting—even taxes! What would *your* musical be about?

You're now going to create a proposal for an original musical that will appeal to your fellow students. Everyone in your class is a potential backer. Your musical can be comic or dramatic. You are not restricted by subject matter. Your musical can tackle any issue you would like. Of course it's always best if the subject has a special meaning for you and will interest an audience. All the proposals will be rated by the entire class, and your teacher will tabulate the votes to see who will get to "produce" his or her show.

Possible Musical Subjects

Begin by writing down some broad ideas for the subject of your musical. Possibilities might include:

- professional sports
- dating
- family relationships
- friendship
- crime and punishment
- working

Four Steps to Creating Your Proposal

1 **Decide on a Subject, Size, and Setting.** Once you have decided on the subject of your musical (something you find interesting or meaningful), you must think about its size. Will it have a small cast or be a large-scale musical? Some musicals feature only two characters; others require a cast of thirty or more.

The size of the musical will strongly affect the way you tell your story. Then, decide on a setting. It might be a beach, a party, a museum, or anywhere else your imagination takes you.

2 **Develop the Characters.** Think about the people who will give your musical personality. Remember that, just as in a straight play, the characters in a musical must have objectives (goals or needs). Ask yourself these questions:

- Who is the main character?

- What does he or she want?

- Who or what stands in the way of the character accomplishing the goal?

- Who are the other characters?

- What do they want?

Write a brief sketch of each character. Include his or her age, personality type, physical appearance, and anything else you feel will allow a reader to understand the character's basic qualities. If you envision a large chorus for your musical, you don't have to write sketches for the choral roles. Just include sketches of the characters that will be crucial to the advancement of the play's main plot.

3 Write a Plot Synopsis. In order to plot your musical, ask yourself the questions below and jot down your ideas.

- Where does the story begin?

- What is its theme?

- What happens first?

- What happens next?

- What happens after that point?

- How does the story end?

- Does the main character attain his or her goal?

- Does the main character learn an important lesson?

Now write a plot synopsis. You do not need to tell every moment in the story—just chart the main course of the action. Include indications of where songs might be placed and what those songs might be about. Try to come up with titles for each song. For example: "Adrian sings 'What Next?' which expresses her shock and excitement at the incredible turn her life has taken."

4 Write a Theme Statement. Now review your character sketch and your plot synopsis. What is the dominant idea expressed? Write one sentence that sums up the play's theme.

Once you have completed your character sketches, plot synopsis, and theme statement, give your musical a tentative title. Now think about how you would use all the elements of your musical to gain interest and support for its creation. In other words, think about how you might try to sell, or **pitch,** your idea for the musical to your class-mates—your potential backers. What will they find intriguing about your theme, characters, and plot? Jot down a few specifics. You can use your notes in your presentation.

Rehearse Your Proposal
You will not be required to memorize your proposal, but you should be familiar enough with it that you can cover all the necessary information in the time allotted. Use expressive language and convey your ideas in an enthusiastic manner. Your job is to excite your class-mates' interest, so make every moment count. You may refer to your notes, but it's important that you don't read them aloud. Time your presentation to make sure it does not exceed the five-minute time limit.

Here's How
To Choose a Musical for Your School

You should always try to stage a musical that you find exciting and interesting, but there are a number of things to consider before you make a commitment. Below are a few things you should think about.

- **Money** How much will things cost (consider all the elements)? How much do you have to spend? How many tickets need to be sold to break even?

- **Space** Do you rent a space or use school facilities? Musicals require large spaces for the dance numbers. How much room will the production need both onstage and off?

- **Cast** Are there good singers, dancers, and musicians available who can handle the requirements of the show?

- **Production staff** Are a music director and choreographer available? What about a knowledgeable designer and the large, experienced tech crew you will need?

- **Audience** Will it be large enough to support the cost of the show and the efforts of everyone involved? Will the audience be receptive to the theme, style, and message of the play?

PRESENT

Pitch Your Idea for a New Musical

When your teacher calls your name, gather your notes and head to the front of the room. Take a moment to prepare. Breathe deeply and relax your muscles while maintaining good posture.

Present your proposal as you rehearsed it. Remember to stay positive, enthusiastic, and upbeat. If you lose focus for a moment, use your notes to get back on track. Remember that your class will be voting on which proposal will actually become a new musical.

When you have finished your presentation, thank your audience, give your notes or your Activity Sheet to your teacher, and return to your seat.

CRITIQUE

Evaluate a Classmate's Pitch

The critique for this presentation will be a little different from others you have done in this drama class. This time, you will listen carefully to all the proposals your classmates present, taking notes based on the four points below—plot, characters, theme, and audience appeal. You are not evaluating the presenter's speaking ability; you are evaluating his or her ideas for a new musical. Use the scores you give for each of the four points to determine the overall rating for the proposal.

Plot

1   2   3   4   5

Characters

1   2   3   4   5

Theme

1   2   3   4   5

Audience appeal

1   2   3   4   5

Overall proposal

1   2   3   4   5

Write specific comments describing what you believe was or was not successful in each category. Keep your comments constructive and realistic. Then cast your vote for the musical you would produce and explain why you voted as you did. Base your vote on the descriptions below.

5 = Sold!

4 = I'm interested, but I would need to hear more.

3 = Has potential, but it needs work.

2 = Risky business.

1 = This one has less than a slim chance.

> **Theatre Journal**
>
> What does it take to "sell" a song to an audience? Think about a musical performer whose work you have admired either in a musical play or in a non-theatrical medium. What is it about this person's style that attracts and intrigues you? Write your thoughts and impressions.

Additional Projects

1 Write the lyrics for the opening number of a musical about an aspect of your school.

2 Prepare a musical audition piece, and perform it for the class.

3 Collaborate with a classmate to perform a duet from a musical.

4 Rent a videotape of *The Music Man* or *West Side Story* and write a review of the play, the music, and the overall production.

5 Rent a video of the film version of the musical *Chicago*. Discuss the changes that might have been made to transform this stage piece into a movie. How would the film differ from the stage version?

6 Design a promotional plan for the new musical one of your classmate's proposed.

7 Read the scene from *Promenade* by Maria Irene Fornes or *The Dining Room* by A. R. Gurney, Jr. found in Unit Eight, and create an original song that might appear in a musical based on your chosen scene.

Master of the Craft
Andrew Lloyd Webber

Ask most people to name a modern musical, and the chances are good that they will answer with a work crafted by the English composer Sir Andrew Lloyd Webber.

Born into a musical family in 1948, young Andrew began playing the violin at age three. By the age of six he was writing his own songs, and by nine, one of his pieces was published in a magazine for music teachers. An aunt introduced him to the theatre, and he was thrilled by such musicals as *My Fair Lady* and *South Pacific.*

When he was 17, Webber met the lyricist Tim Rice. A short time later, they were hired to co-write a musical for a London prep school. They chose a story from the Bible about Joseph and his coat of many colors. The resulting rock opera was *Joseph and the Amazing Technicolor Dreamcoat.* Although the music was strong, the lyrics catchy, and the story entertaining, *Joseph* didn't get much notice. Webber and Rice's next collaboration was the successful international hit *Jesus Christ Superstar.* This was followed by *Evita* in 1976, a full-scale blockbuster.

In 1981, writing the music entirely on his own, Webber wrote *Cats,* based on T. S. Eliot's *Old Possum's Book of Practical Cats.* The year 1984 brought *Starlight Express,* and two years later came the musical many consider his masterpiece, *The Phantom of the Opera.* Throughout the following decades, Webber's success continued.

From an early and profound fascination with music, Andrew Lloyd Webber has become one of the world's most popular composers.

Sir Andrew Lloyd Webber

Theatre Then and Now

The Common Language of Music

Peking Opera

Peking Opera, China's most famous and popular theatrical form, isn't an opera at all. Westerners began calling it this because of the music and singing that often accompany it. The Peking Opera originated in 1790 when, at the order of the imperial court, four performance companies from Anhui Province came to Peking (Beijing) on a tour. The tour was successful, and the troupes stayed on in Beijing. Over time, the artists absorbed the music and techniques of the local opera companies. The result was a new kind of theatre—formed from the talents of many.

The Peking Opera performances were full of spectacle and included actors in brightly colored face paint. The colors of the faces signified different characters and personalities.

The music of the Peking Opera was typically graceful and pleasing to the ear. The musicians played wind, percussion, and a variety of stringed instruments including *jinghu,* which has two strings and a very high register, and *yueqin,* which has four strings and is played by plucking.

Today, as in the old days, the repertoire of Peking Opera is drawn from tales of previous ages, notable historical events, and legends of emperors, geniuses, and other important people. Having thrived for more than two centuries, Peking Opera is considered the quintessential Chinese art form.

A Peking Opera performer displays his martial arts prowess.

High-Tech Spectacle and Small-Scale Wonders of Today

Today's musical theatre is bigger, glitzier, and more expensive to produce—and to attend—than ever before. Part of this is due to the audience's increased expectations regarding the level of a show's spectacle. After all, when one is used to seeing incoming helicopters landing onstage (as in Claude-Michel Schönberg and Alain Boublil's *Miss Saigon*) or action played out on a roller rink featuring a 5.5-ton steel suspension bridge and a set built from 6 miles of timber, 2.5 acres of plywood, and 60 tons of steel (as in Andrew Lloyd Webber's *Starlight Express*), it's hard to imagine a musical on a smaller scale being truly exciting.

Yet smaller-scale musicals continue to draw crowds as well. *Pump Boys and Dinettes* is one example of a simple yet lively musical that still holds audience interest, and only recently did the simple, but ever-popular *The Fantasticks* close in New York after 17,162 performances. Today's musicals tackle almost any subject. Adam Guettel and Tina Landau's musical *Floyd Collins* is based on the true story of a Kentucky man who became trapped while exploring a cave in 1925. People continue to be drawn to and moved by musicals of all sizes and subjects. Perhaps that is at

The famous helicopter hovers over the actors on the stage of *Miss Saigon*.

least in part because music offers a common language that everyone can understand and enjoy.

Chapter

25 Other Theatre Forms

Although we typically associate theatre with the production of plays, there are a number of other forms that fall into the basic category of theatre.

Project Specs

Project Description You will create a performance poem and take part in a classroom poetry slam. Your performance must last no longer than three minutes.

Purpose to combine writing and performance skills, and to explore forms outside the realm of traditional theatre

Materials the text of a performance poem or the Poetry Slam Worksheet your teacher will provide

Theatre Terms

Bunraku
multimedia
nonlinear
performance art
poetry slam
Readers Theatre

On Your Feet

Work with three other classmates to represent a common emotion or concept (loneliness, joy, curiosity, fear, political struggle, and so on) using only three words, your voice, gestures, and movement.

Suheir Hammad, Beau Sia, and Georgia Me perform in *Russell Simmons Def Poetry Jam on Broadway* at Longacre Theatre in New York.

The "Other" Theatre

Theatre began as ritual performance, and over the centuries the art form has taken many different paths and transformed itself many times over. As you read through this section, notice the similarities as well as the differences among these various forms.

Performance Art

With its roots in music, dance, and storytelling, theatre has given rise to **performance art,** which has in turn become its own popular form. Performance art came from the "happenings" of the 1960s. Often politically charged, happenings were a spontaneous combination of movement, music, improvisation, and sometimes even theatre games. They were, for the most part, unstructured events, usually held in a venue that was not typically associated with theatre or performance—

Artist Laurie Anderson creates performance pieces that are visually and musically exciting.

public parks were often the best place to see happenings. Performance artists often experimented with the conventions of traditional theatre. Performance art is often seen in nontraditional performance spaces—parking garages, churches, parks, galleries, and so on.

Performance art tends to be **nonlinear** in its structure—in other words, it does not attempt to tell a chronological story. It typically focuses on neither character nor plot, but instead concerns itself with putting across a statement that is political or in some way controversial. Many politically charged performers use humor to express their ideas. Danny Hoch, Margaret Cho, and John Leguizamo all use comedy in performing works of social, political, and artistic relevance.

Multimedia

The advent of film and video has had a lasting impact on the theatre. Early in the 20th century, innovative stage directors began using film projections

Despite the fact that shadow puppets are seen only as shadows by the audience, they are colorfully decorated and detailed.

as a design element in their plays. And as time went on, using more than one medium to achieve a desired effect became increasingly popular and elaborate. In addition to using film and video, **multimedia** might incorporate live painting, dance, music, puppetry, animation, and computer and laser technology on stage. More and more plays are being written in cyber collaborations—multiple playwrights working via the Internet—and some theatre groups are using the Internet as the very latest in high-tech performance space.

Puppet Theatre

Puppetry is a very old art form—some claim it is nearly as old as humankind itself. The **Bunraku** puppetry of Japan, the water puppets of Vietnam (which shoot up from underwater via long rods), and the shadow puppets of Java (which are viewed through a backlit screen), are but a few of many puppetry forms that are centuries old. (Read more about Bunraku on page 342.)

In ancient times, puppetry was closely linked to feats of magic and conjuring. Throughout history, magicians and other entertainers have used puppets in street performances and later on the stage. The puppets Punch and Judy, who battle with one another throughout their show, are famous icons throughout Europe. Puppetry has enjoyed a popular resurgence in contemporary theatre. It has moved from being primarily a children's theatre form to one that charms and mesmerizes adults as well.

With the emergence of the Bread & Puppet Theatre in the early 1960s, American puppetry became politicized. The shows Bread & Puppet produced were both visually stunning and ideologically compelling. (See Theatre Then and Now on page 343.) Since then, similar puppet theatres have sprung up around the globe. Some of these puppet theatres focus on adaptations of literary works as well as commissioning original works. The puppets they use comprise everything from finger puppets to gigantic, incredibly complex and detailed figures that can simulate intricate human movements and expressions.

Readers Theatre

Readers Theatre is a form in which two or more actors read aloud from a script. The basis of the performance is usually a standard play script, but it can also involve anything from poetry to letters

The Bread & Puppet Theatre—humans in a puppet mode.

to journals to fiction. The actors usually sit on stools and read from scripts set on music stands. Sometimes all the performers dress in similar attire.

Readers Theatre uses a stage convention that allows the actors to deliver their lines out front while reacting as if they were speaking directly to their scene partners. Many larger cities have theatres that produce Readers Theatre exclusively. A. R. Gurney, Jr.'s popular *Love Letters* is a play that is performed in Readers Theatre style. Because this play requires only two actors and no memorization, it is a popular vehicle not only for theatres but also for arts fund-raising events.

Young performers enjoy the relaxed atmosphere of Readers Theatre.

Poetry Slams

A **poetry slam** is a form of competitive performance poetry that was born in Chicago in 1987. Since that time, slams have become enormously popular and there are national and international competitions administered through an organization called Poetry Slam Inc. The Nuyorican Café, founded by Reg E. Gaines, Bob Holman, and others, in New York City is famous for its poetry slams.

At these rousing celebrations of the spoken word, poets are judged on both the writing and the performance aspects of their work by a panel of judges who use a 0–10 rating system.

Career Focus

Stage Manager

One of the hardest working people in any production is the stage manager. This is a job that requires organizational skills, a sharp sense of timing, the ability to work with many different kinds of creative people, a cool head in a crisis, and the confidence to oversee all elements of a production. It is also a job that most people learn by doing. Most stage managers get their start as members of other technical crews or as assistant stage managers.

During rehearsals, the stage manager writes down all the blocking and sometimes writes down and hands out the director's notes to the cast between rehearsals. During the actual performances, the stage manager takes over where the director leaves off. He or she is responsible for seeing that each performance runs smoothly. A small sample of the stage manager's duties include:

- cueing the performers before and during the show
- cueing the technical crews before and during the show
- supervising the stage crew
- making sure performers and crew know their call times for all rehearsals and performances
- relaying notes to the performers or technical team from the director
- scheduling and overseeing meetings and rehearsal times for the technical personnel

In the professional theatre, stage managers are typically members of Actors' Equity Association (AEA), the professional union for actors and stage managers. Qualified stage managers are typically very much in demand.

Following are the basic rules for a poetry slam:

- Each poem must be an original work by the poet.

- Each poet gets three minutes of performance time. If the poet goes over that period of time, points will be deducted.

- Poets may not use costumes, props, or musical instruments.

- Of the scores from five judges, the highest and lowest are subtracted and the three middle scores are added together to give the poet a total score of anywhere from 0 to 30.

- The judges are selected from among the audience members.

Poetry slams are designed to be audience interactive. In other words, the audience members are free to react to the performances in any way they see fit.

Theatre Journal

What if someone asked you to create a performance piece about your day so far? Would you create performance art, a poem, a dance, or a monologue? Write a short description of the kind of project you would like to work on.

PREPARE

Work on Your Poem

You are going to write an original poem and use it to compete with your classmates in a modified version of a poetry slam.

As you prepare to write your poem, keep in mind that it need not rhyme, and there is no limitation in terms of style. Here's an excerpt from the performance poem "After Cages" by well-known performance poet Cin Salach:

But you are feeling the wind in your hair, finally

After all these years

And the answer is almost too easy:

Send history packing,

But keep the future panting.

Claim this sky for yourself.

Make it sacred.

Declare it off limits to anyone

Who isn't madly in love with you.

Understand that not everyone will be.

Recite the excerpt aloud a few times. Experiment with its rhythm and sound. Choose specific words to emphasize. Think about what the poem is saying but also how it sounds as you speak it. Think about movements that might enhance the poem.

Now you're ready to try your hand at writing your own poem.

Writing a Performance Poem

Follow the steps below to write a poem of your own.

1 Relax your mind and body, and let images and words come to you. Spend five minutes writing down the images as they pass through your mind. Don't judge them; just let them in. At the end of five minutes, stop writing. Read through what you've written, and decide which image or line appeals to you most. Use that as a jumping-off point for creating your poem.

2 Make sure what you're writing is something you care about. Your poem might be about anything: a favorite photograph, a deep fear, a lonely feeling, or a great day. Whatever you choose to write about, try to come up with images that paint verbal pictures and/or make strong statements.

3 Once you've written a few lines, begin to speak them out loud. This should lead you to other images and lines.

4 Get your body into it. Performance poets tend to use their bodies expressively, so don't feel as if your feet are nailed to the floor. You can use your voice, body, and expressions to enhance the meaning of your poem.

5 Pay attention to the rhythm of your poem, and think about where you might pause or extend a moment for effect.

6 Rework your poem based on the movement you can add to it. When choosing words, think in terms of how they will help you perform the poem. Think about how the words sound as you say them aloud.

When you feel that you've created a poem that fulfills your intentions, rehearse it a few times to make sure it comes in under the three-minute time limit. You don't have to memorize your poem; you may prefer to read it. However, if you can memorize it, do so. This will add to your freedom of movement and help you better "feel" the language. However, whether you choose to memorize your poem or not, you should be familiar enough with it to be able to move and create a relationship with your audience as you perform.

PRESENT

Perform Your Poem

When your name is called, take your poem and/or your Activity Sheet with you to the front of the room. Wait as your teacher randomly chooses five judges from among your classmates. The teacher will also choose a timekeeper.

When the judges have been selected, take a moment to center yourself. A few deep breaths will help you. When you are ready, nod to the timekeeper, who will then begin timing your presentation. Introduce the title of your poem. Then begin to perform. Remember that this is a poetry slam—the way you perform your poem will greatly affect your score. Keep your performance fresh and exuberant.

When you have finished, take a brief bow, hand in your poem and/or Activity Sheet to your teacher, and return to your seat. The judges' results regarding your performance will be tabulated at the end of the class.

CRITIQUE

Evaluate a Classmate's Poetry Performance

As a judge for the class poetry slam, listen carefully and then take a moment to create a Poetry Slam Rating Sheet similar to the one below. You will be giving an overall rating from 0 to 10, with 10 being the best possible score. Here are some pointers from the official Poetry Slam Inc. Web site:

- "We use the word poem to include text and performance. Some say you should assign a certain number of points for a poem's literary merit and a certain number of points for the poet's performance. Others feel that you are experiencing the poem only through the performance, and it may be impossible to separate the two. You will give each poem only one score."

- "Trust your gut; and give the better poem the better score."

- "Be fair. We all have our personal prejudices, but try to suspend yours for the duration of the slam. On the other hand, it's okay to have a prejudice that favors the true and the beautiful over the mundane and superficial, the fascinating over the boring and pedestrian."

Poetry Slam Rating Sheet

Judge:

Poet:

Title of Poem:

Score from 0 to 10

Under three minutes?
(If NO, subtract 1 point.)

Final score:

Additional Projects

1 Make your own puppet. It can take any form you like: finger puppet, marionette, sock puppet, or a design of your own.

2 Work with a small group of classmates to create a multimedia performance using the spoken word, live and recorded music, and movement.

3 Choose a literary selection or a collage of shorter pieces from newspapers, magazines, or letters from which to create a Readers Theatre performance. Direct the performance piece for the class, and then explain and justify your artistic choices and interpretation.

4 Make a videotape of the performance poem you created for this chapter's project. Use it to further refine your poem and your performance.

5 Research and write a report on a theatre counterpart such as Bunraku, shadow puppets, Punch and Judy, and so on, or other popular poetry forms such as the television program *Def Poetry*. Be prepared to present your report to the class. Include two visual aids.

6 Choose a monologue or scene from those found in Unit Eight and create a performance piece based on that play—change the play in any way you see fit in order to make a statement.

Master of the Craft

Marc Smith: The "Slampapi"

"Smith's almost visionary on the need to rescue poetry from its lowly status in the nation's cultural life."

—*Smithsonian* magazine

Not many people can lay claim to single-handedly creating a brand-new art form. But in 1987, poet Marc Smith had a big idea. It was spawned from his feeling that poetry needed a public forum beyond the sometimes academic readings at colleges and bookstores. He wanted a forum for competitive performance poetry. The big idea began to take shape in 1987 when he persuaded the owner of Chicago's Green Mill Tavern to open its doors to the first ever poetry slam. And from that point on, the poetry slam phenomenon has just kept growing. Today more than 150 American cities host their own slams. And now there are even versions of the slam going on in England, Germany, Israel, and Sweden.

The man who made it all happen—the father of the poetry slam, or "Slampapi," as he is called in the performance community—is a terrific poet in his own right. Smith's innate sense of rhythm and his grittily realistic, urban poems tend to break poetic boundaries. His performances, both as a soloist and with his ensemble of performance poets and jazz musicians, blend the eloquence and beauty of poetry with the drama of theatre. His work has gained an international following—and Smith has become one of the most influential performance poets in the world.

In addition to a heavy touring schedule, Smith writes, performs, and continues to host and perform for the Uptown Poetry Slam's avid standing-room-only houses.

Marc Smith, aka the Slampapi

Kiss It

If you need to kiss it,
Kiss it.
If you need to kick it,
Kick it.
If you need to scream it,
Scream it.
But kiss it, kick it, scream it
Now.

–Marc Smith

Theatre Then and Now

Puppetry for All Time

Bunraku: An Ancient Puppetry Form
Many consider Japanese Bunraku the most highly evolved form of puppetry in the world. Offering a unique combination of puppet manipulation, recitation, and music, Bunraku takes many years to master. Its name, loosely translated, means "puppets and storytelling."

Bunraku developed from an ancient Japanese tradition of traveling storytellers. At the same time there were also traveling puppeteers. It is not clear when these two art forms came together, but Bunraku is thought to have come about in 1684. That is when the first known Bunraku theatre opened in Osaka.

Bunraku puppets were about half the size of human beings. They had many moveable parts: Their eyes (and eyebrows) moved, their mouths opened and shut, and their arms and hands moved in very human-looking ways.

The puppeteers in Bunraku were always visible to the audience. They brought the puppets onstage in full view of the audience. Three puppeteers were needed to operate each main character puppet.

The narrator, meanwhile, told the entire story—also in full view of the audience—using a variety of vocal techniques. In addition to telling the story, he or she whispered, chanted, sang, or wept the dialogue for each puppet in the play. A musical accompanist provided music and sound effects to simulate rain, wind, and so on.

Today Bunraku is enjoying a revival. In 1985, The National Bunraku Theatre was granted a permanent home in the place of its origin, Osaka, where it produces four shows a year. Bunraku masters and puppet-makers are aging, however, and there is some question as to whether there will be sufficient interest from the younger generation to continue the Bunraku tradition.

A Bunraku puppetry performance.

Bread & Puppet Theatre: Today's Political Puppetry

Peter Schumann founded the Bread & Puppet Theatre in 1962. During the Vietnam War era, Schumann and his collaborators staged outdoor performances on New York City's Lower East Side. These were often in the form of block-long processions of papier-mâché puppets depicting anti-war themes. Bread & Puppet's figures moved hypnotically. They also varied greatly in scale: The smallest puppets fit on one finger. The largest were more than eight feet tall and were designed to be held high above the audience by means of long poles draped with fabric and manipulated by several puppeteers.

The Bread & Puppet Theatre became widely known for its unique brand of puppet-and-mask political theatre, and its work has inspired and influenced a generation of artists. In 1974, the group moved to Vermont and settled on a farm just outside the tiny village of Glover. One of the outbuildings became a museum for the retired puppets, masks, and paintings once used by the company. The museum is open to the public from May through October, and admission is free, in keeping with Bread & Puppet's egalitarian philosophy.

Members of Bread & Puppet Theatre display their creations.

One of the oldest nonprofit, self-supporting theatre companies in the United States, Bread & Puppet Theatre tours its shows all over the world. But during the summer months, visitors can often catch a performance at the farm.

A typical puppet from the Bread & Puppet Theatre collection.

Chapter
26 Stage to Film

The inspiration for a film can come from many different sources. Autobiographies, news stories, historical events, and novels are just a few of the possibilities. Live theatre plays are another rich resource for film plots.

Project Specs

Project Description For this assignment, you will turn a scene from a play into a screenplay of no more than ten minutes and then direct it.

Purpose to understand how the elements of theatre and film differ

Materials an outline or the Stage to Film Activity Sheet your teacher provides

Theatre Terms
adapt
screenplay
storyboard
takes

On Your Feet

In a group with three or four classmates, improvise a scene from an important moment in history. Have members of the "audience" try to be the first to guess what historical event you are portraying.

Donald Sutherland, Stockard Channing, and Will Smith appear in the film adaptation of John Guare's *Six Degrees of Separation*.

PREVIEW

Theatre and Early Film

In the very early days of film, moviemakers borrowed heavily from the theatre—a dramatic art form that could easily be translated to this new medium. Films made in the early 1900s were essentially nothing more than plays captured on film. The camera took the place of the audience—sitting in a fixed position, taking in all the action in its limited range of view. The camera looked straight ahead, to the left a bit, and to the right a little. And just as on the stage, the actors played to their audience—the camera.

By the 1920s, innovations had been made that revolutionized film. Editing became an art, so that scenes on film could now be shifted, shortened, rearranged, or cut out completely. The camera could move in many directions: up and down and in close enough to allow the audience to see the actor's face alight with joy or stained with tears. New types of lights were being created for the sole purpose of lighting movies. Indeed, a brand-new industry was born to supply filmmakers with all the technical equipment they needed.

Theatre was also changing during this period. The stage and sets were being used in new ways, and innovative approaches to conveying the themes and plot of the play were introduced. But never again would the stage and the screen be so closely aligned as they were in those early days of movies.

The Theatre Script and the Screenplay

The script is the basic tool of both theatre and film. Producers, directors, actors, and technical professionals working on the stage and in the movies rely on the script for its plot, characters, and language—then they apply their own creative inspiration and expertise. The kinds of scripts used in these two mediums are very different.

Although theatrical scripts provide varying amounts of information about characters' attitudes and technical elements such as lighting and scenery, the main emphasis is on what characters say—the dialogue. Technical professionals are often left to their own devices and directors to their own concepts in communicating the details of time, place, movement, and mood of a play.

A film script, or **screenplay,** on the other hand, is much more of a technical document. It includes all the characters' dialogue, but it also provides audio and visual information. Settings, camera shots and angles, and other effects are all described. A page of a film script usually equals one minute of film time. If a character appears on film for ten seconds, his or her part must take up no more than an inch or so of space on a page. If a scene goes on for five minutes, the writer must describe elements of the action for five pages.

Writers who **adapt,** or modify, theatrical work for film must consider all the audio and visual elements of their scenes. Each element must appear in the script at the time it will appear in the film. Thus, screenplay writers must think in audio, visual, and verbal terms throughout each scene they write.
In order to describe camera angles and shots, visual effects, scene descriptions and so forth, screenwriters use special terminology. You will use these terms as you adapt a scene.

The Film Script Up Close
The common film script terms below should be indicated in all caps.

Technical Terms for the Screenplay
INT. interior shot

EXT. exterior shot

CLOSE SHOT a shot that shows only the head and shoulders of a person

CLOSEUP (CU) a shot that shows only a person's head

DISSOLVE a gradual fading out of the picture

DOLLY when the entire camera is moved toward or away from the subject

FREEZE FRAME when the image is momentarily stopped, or "frozen"

INTERCUT camera shots that go back and forth between scenes or people

INSERT a momentary closeup shot of an important person, place, or thing that cuts into another shot

LONG SHOT (LS) a long-distance shot that shows people from head to toe along with considerable background

MATCH CUT shot that cuts from highlighting something in one situation to highlighting the same thing in a different situation

MEDIUM SHOT (MS) a shot of people or a person from the waist up

MONTAGE two or more related scenes blended onscreen at the same time (label "MONTAGE" and "END OF MONTAGE")

O.C. off-camera sounds or dialogue

MOVING SHOT indicates that the camera moves with the characters

PAN a shot that moves slowly from left to right or right to left

P.O.V. point of view, a shot seen from the point of view of the character

SERIES OF SHOTS shots showing different aspects of a scene

SFX special effects, either audio or visual

SPLIT SCREEN one or more subjects shown on screen at the same time, as from two different films

SUPER superimpose one object over another, such as title over a setting

TWO SHOT a camera shot of two people

V.O. voiceover; a voice is heard, but the speaker is not seen in the shot

ZOOM the camera lens is used to create a rapid closeup

Requirements for Stage vs. Film

Following are different ways of approaching movie and theatre presentations.

Acting Smaller gestures and more nuanced expressions are needed by the film actor because the camera is so close. Theatre calls for broad gestures.

Makeup Age can't be camouflaged on film—even with makeup. Makeup needs to pass the "closeup" test. Makeup can take off or add years onstage.

Voice and Sound Unlike stage actors, film actors don't have to worry about projecting to "the last row of the theatre."

Costumes and **Scenery** must look real on film even in closeups.

Takes When working in film, actors get as many **takes,** or filmed scenes, as is necessary to get it right. Stage actors can't go back and repeat misspoken lines.

Continuity Hair, costumes, sets, and so on, need to match from shot to shot in film (the actor holding a glass in the right hand for one shot, can't be holding it in the left for the next).

Sequence A play is done from beginning to end. With film, scenes are done in any order that makes sense financially—usually organized by setting. All the scenes for one location are done at the same time.

Cast of thousands Film can use hundreds of extras; even with a small cast, film needs many people.

EDDIE
Where are they?

Angie stares back defiantly.

EDDIE (cont'd)
I don't have time for this.
(to Ushers)
Take her back the theatre. Call Luther
and tell him we got her.

Two ushers advance on Angie. She plants her heavy boot in one of their guts. He goes down. Two others grab her from behind and drag her fighting all the way to the van.

Formatting for a screenplay includes a margin of about 1.25 inches for scenes and 1.75 inches for directions and scene headings. Dialogue margins are deeper—about 2.25 inches. Technical directions are set on a line length of 58 characters.

PREPARE

Work on Your Screenplay

Create an outline or use the Stage to Film Activity Sheet your teacher has given you. Use the sample screenplay, the abbreviations found in Technical Terms for the Screenplay on pages 346–347, and the formatting suggestions discussed previously to help you.

First, choose a scene to adapt. Try to choose a play that you are very familiar with and that you find interesting. Remember that you are adapting only a small portion of this play into a screenplay, so choose a scene with a good deal of impact.

Second, plan your camera shots. Visualize how you will shoot the action. Where will each character be relative to the camera? How will the camera follow each character? How much of the setting will be included? Will you start with a long shot or a closeup? Will one scene dissolve into the next? To help answer these questions, you should create a **storyboard.** A storyboard is a series of drawings showing the sequential shots needed in a scene. A simple drawing of each important camera shot will give you a concrete idea as to the angle and distance of the shot, as well as showing how each shot relates to the next. You can also use a small box with a square cut out at each end to look through in order to "frame" the shot and get an idea of how it would look on camera. Also,

ask yourself what can be shown visually in each scene rather than being talked about in the dialogue?

Next, work on the script. Indicate audio and visual elements on the script in the appropriate places, as well as the camera shots needed based on your storyboard. Have fun with the flexibility film offers. Remember that cameras allow quick changes in time and place that are much more difficult in theatre. Then, think about the dialogue. Will you use all the dialogue that appears in the play, leave some out, or condense it?

Then, do an informal reading. When you have a rough draft of your screenplay, ask classmates to help you with a reading. In addition to assigning each role, assign one person the job of reading the audio and visual elements you have incorporated into the screenplay. Time the reading to make sure it does not exceed ten minutes. Make notes indicating any necessary changes.

Last, have a final reading and rehearsal. When you have written a draft with which you are completely satisfied, call for a final reading and a rehearsal.

PRESENT

Hold a Reading of Your Screenplay

When your name is called, give a copy of your screenplay and the original play script to your teacher. With the actors who will be helping you present the screenplay, walk to the playing area. Be sure chairs are arranged facing the audience with the actors arranged in a line across the playing area.

Stand to the side and announce the title of your screenplay. Then identify the play on which it is based and the scene your actors will read. As in your rehearsals, one of the actors will read any camera, lighting, or sound directions aloud. Take your seat and enjoy the performance.

When the actors have finished reading your screenplay, initiate a short round of applause. The actors should then stand, bow, and return to their seats.

Answer any questions your classmates may have about your screenplay.

CRITIQUE

Evaluate Your Classmate's Adaptation

Choose one of the screenplay readings presented in class and evaluate it. Think of yourself as a producer being pitched a plan for a film. Ask yourself the questions below.

- Were you able to visualize the film from the presenter's description?

- Did the technical directions add to the drama or effectiveness of the script?

- How effective were the writer's choice of camera shots and special effects?

- Did the screenplay's plot incorporate enough action to be suitable for filming?

Based on your evaluation of the screenplay, give it a rating between 5 and 1, with 5 being "outstanding " and 1 being "needs much improvement." Write a paragraph explaining the reasons for scoring the screenplay the way you did.

Theatre Journal

Realistic scenic elements are more important in film than they are in theatre. To practice thinking in terms of film, highlight or list the set directions from a play you enjoy. Then jot down possible film settings that might communicate the same mood or stand in for the settings indicated in the play.

What the Stage Does That Film and Video Can't

When talking movies first appeared on the scene, there were many who thought theatre was dead. When television developed, people thought film had seen its last days. Neither of these predictions came true, of course, because each medium has something special to offer. Theatre is unique in the following ways:

Theatre is active. While film and television audiences are largely passive viewers of events, theatre audiences are active participants in the shows they attend. Their responses to the action affect the performances onstage. And in some cases, their active participation is requested or even required for a full performance.

Theatre is multidimensional. When they attend a theatrical production, audiences have to look around. Even proscenium arch theatres have characters that enter and exit from various locations. Sometimes, actors use the house for exits and entrances, and sometimes they even play scenes with or among audience members.

Theatre is a multimedia event. Many stage productions make use of visual arts in the production of a set and costumes. Some make use of video, film, and dance. There can be a lot going on up on the stage, with lots of different places for audience members to cast their eyes.

Every performance is unique. Because theatrical events are live, they are different every time they are performed. Each performance is open to new understanding and therefore, new opportunities for improvisation. You can see or perform in a theatrical performance a hundred times, and each time it will be different in some way.

Additional Projects

1 Videotape the screenplay you created using the actors who worked with you. Be aware of safety issues as you work. Share it with the class.

2 Research the differences between one-camera and three-camera scripts. Write a scene for a screenplay with each of the two formats in mind.

3 Film an improvised skit, and then write a screenplay taking into consideration what worked and what didn't work in your film.

4 Write a screenplay based on a scene that you thought was particularly effective in a play you've seen within the last year.

5 Do a reverse adaptation: Acquire a film script for a film you admire, and then adapt it for the stage.

6 Create and implement a production schedule for a scene from a film script of your choice.

7 Adapt the scene from *Copenhagen* by Michael Frayn or *The Prisoner of Second Avenue* by Neil Simon found in Unit Eight for use as a screenplay.

Theatre Then and Now

Homer to Home Viewing

Homer's *The Odyssey*

The Odyssey is an epic poem attributed to an author we call Homer. The story is probably 3000 years old, and the written version is about 1000 years old. *The Odyssey* was written to be recited—and perhaps read. Though not written as a play, it has nevertheless inspired many a poet, playwright, and filmmaker to adapt and expand its themes and plot.

The Odyssey tells the story of Ulysses, a hero of the Trojan War, who attempts to return to his home in Ithaca after the war. Unfortunately, he has angered the gods, who present him with a series of obstacles. During his ten-year journey, Ulysses encounters a land with a flower that causes deep sleep; a one-eyed monster called the Cyclops; Circe, the enchantress who turns men into beasts, and many others. All the while, his wife, Penelope, waits patiently for his return.

Homer's epic is exciting and beautifully written, and should certainly be read for its own sake as well as for an understanding of all the poems, paintings, plays, and films that allude to it.

"Every day in rehearsal there are moments that I feel . . . the presence and the weight of this text and its history and its long life, and how we're the part of this telling that has gone on for twenty-seven hundred years."

–Mary Zimmerman

Ulysses and Penelope

Mary Zimmerman's *The Odyssey*

Mary Zimmerman's adaptation of *The Odyssey* tells a tale much like the original poem. While Ulysses battles monsters and escapes the deadly sirens' call, his wife is being heavily pressured by suitors to forget him.

Like the poem, Zimmerman's play uses flashback and interesting details to tell the story. It also takes advantage of

Hermes and his men march onstage in Mary Zimmerman's 2000 production of **The Odyssey.**

contemporary technology. For example, gigantic video projections help create the setting for the underworld. And the lighting designed by Daniel Ostling represents settings ranging from "rosy-fingered dawn" to stormy seas.

The production draws on traditions in dancing and music, and the lyrical poetry of the original to communicate the breadth of Homer's epic tale.

O Brother, Where Art Thou?

Joel and Ethan Coen also owe much of their film *O Brother, Where Art Thou?* to Homer. They don't try to hide the fact—their references to the ancient epic are fairly easy to spot. But someone who didn't know a thing about Homer would think it was a modern tale.

The movie is a quirky comedy set in 1930s Mississippi. It tells the story of a chain-gang escapee, appropriately named Ulysses, who endures a series of trials as he makes his way home. It comes complete with sirens, a cyclops, and suitors for his estranged wife. In the end, Ulysses is restored to his family.

In the Coen brothers' adaptation, Homer is not only retold in a new medium—it is given a new translation, and a new audience.

John Turturro, Tim Blake Nelson, and George Clooney star in *O Brother, Where Art Thou?*, the contemporary film based on *The Odyssey.*

Chapter
27 Movies

Film and theatre share many common characteristics. They are both based on story and character, and they both have a lot to tell us about the human condition. Movies, however, approach storytelling in their own, unique way.

Project Specs

Project Description You will develop an idea for an original screenplay, follow it through all phases of development and production, and present your plan in five to ten minutes.

Purpose to understand the filmmaking process and to develop the art of conceptualizing a script and presenting it to others

Materials paper or the Movies Activity Sheet your teacher provides

Theatre Terms
backlot
continuity
development
final cut
postproduction
preproduction
production
rough cut
shooting script
soundstage
trailer
working script

On Your Feet

Think about the many jobs associated with making movies. There are actors and a director, of course. But many more people are needed to make even a small, low-budget movie. As a group, brainstorm and list as many of these as you can.

James Cameron's 1997 film *Titanic,* with Leonardo DeCaprio and Kate Winslet, used spectacular special effects.

PREVIEW

If you've ever sat through all the credits at the end of a movie, you have some idea of just how many people are involved in making a typical film. From the producer to the screenwriter to the cameraperson to the caterer, the making of most films requires the skills and talents of hundreds of professionals.

The Four Phases of the Filmmaking Process

Phase One: Development

The first phase of the production process is called **development.** This term refers to the actual creation of a script as well as the plan by which the film will be produced. The producer generally handles much of a film's early development work, which includes

- hiring or approving the director

- hiring or approving screenwriters or the script

- securing the financial resources needed to make the film

Once the director, screenwriter(s), and financial backing have been secured, the director puts together a plan for getting the best writing, acting, and technical

crew for the project. A part of the director's job is creating the production schedule, a detailed plan that maps out all the film's stages of production.

To attract investors, the producer puts together a marketing packet containing the **working script** (a script-in-progress that is subject to change during the development, preproduction, and production phases). The packet also includes a list of the artists who will most likely be working on the film and a preliminary budget. Depending on the presentation, the script, and the artists involved, investors may opt to back the film financially. To do so, they usually must have a strong sense of the film's marketability or its potential for winning an audience. The investors make a percentage of the film's profits, so they naturally want the largest audience possible. Put simply, the investors pay advertising and production costs before the film is made in the hope that they can make money when the film is shown in theatres.

Phase Two: Preproduction

The next phase of the process is called **preproduction.** There are many tasks that must be completed during this phase before the director and the staff can move on to the actual shooting of the film. The production manager has key duties having to do with finalizing the shooting schedule and developing a workable budget.

An artist looks over the storyboard.

Next, actors must be auditioned for the various roles. Typically, the producer and the director work with a casting director (see the Career Focus on page 175) to find just the right actor for each role.

Once the casting is complete, there may be time in the schedule to have a brief rehearsal period before actual production begins. However, rehearsals are not necessarily a part of every preproduction phase—the film process differs from theatre in this crucial way. Without rehearsal, it's very difficult to put on a play. However, many film actors are used to doing films with little or no rehearsal. The director may work with the writers to create a storyboard— the series of images roughly depicting the chronological sequence of the film. From the storyboard process comes the **shooting script.** In a shooting script, each shot in the film is tracked by a specific number and type of shot. (See Technical Terms for the Screenplay on pages 346–347 of Chapter 26.) The shooting script usually goes through quite a few changes as preproduction and production move along.

Phase Three: Production

When a film moves into **production,** the work most people associate with moviemaking begins. The director works closely with the actors and crew and begins to shoot the film. Shooting may take place at a variety of locations—

Theatre Journal

Have you ever seen a movie that seemed to speak directly to you? Maybe it was about a family situation, a friendship, or an incident that reminded you of your own life. Maybe it spurred your imagination. Write about how the film affected you, and identify the reasons why you think it made such a strong impression.

some films are shot on location in the actual place where the story is set; this might be anywhere from the Iowa countryside to a mountaintop in Nepal. Other films may be shot on a **backlot,** an outdoor lot where sets are created to simulate the location specified in the script. Indoor scenes can be shot on a **soundstage,** where a set has been built, or at an actual indoor location that has been rented for the shoot.

Films are hardly ever shot in the chronological sequence of the script. There are many factors that dictate what the shooting sequence will be. One major factor is location. Filmmakers typically shoot all the scenes that take place in a given location at the same time, rather than in the sequence in which they will appear in the film. For example, if several scenes take place at a restaurant over the course of the film, all the restaurant scenes will likely be shot at the same time. This saves setup time and money.

There are also situations in which the actors' makeup must be taken into account. For example in the 1970 film *Little Big Man,* Dustin Hoffman begins as a hundred-year-old man, and most of the film is shown in flashbacks as

Dustin Hoffman as the ancient Jack Crabb telling his story in *Little Big Man.*

Hoffman's character remembers his life as a much younger man. At the end of the film, he is an old man again. The scenes of Hoffman in his hundred-year-old-man makeup were all shot at the same time, even though they actually appear at the beginning and at the end of the film. The makeup took several hours to apply, and it was more efficient in terms of both time and money to shoot those scenes all at once.

The director's job is split between coaching the actors in terms of performance and position, and collaborating with the camera crew. Most scenes are usually done in more than one take. To be sure that the shot will be workable later in the process, it may be filmed from a variety of angles, using different film techniques and performance perspectives. In other words, multiple takes allow the film crew to make sure the job is done right.

As the shots are completed, they are sent on to a special lab for processing and printing. The unused takes are not thrown away—they may be needed later during the editing process.

After shooting has been completed each day, the director, production manager, and cinematographer (shot designer) discuss the shooting that will take place on the following day. Each day, the shooting script is likely to change a bit

place to that point. The actors must keep themselves up to speed on the most current version of the script. At the end of a typical day's shoot, the actors study the script for the following day, and the film editor makes a copy of the best takes.

While the production phase is going on, the producer is taking care of the business aspects of the film. The producer usually becomes involved with the day-to-day artistic aspects only if there is a problem involving personnel changes, budget concerns, or scheduling questions. Otherwise the producer is generally taken up with issues of how to market the film. To that end, he or she (or they) will create a **trailer.** A trailer is a special preview advertisement that provides publicity for the film's upcoming release. Timing is important when it comes to advertising the film. The trailer is usually released six months before the film itself begins playing in theatres. Other advertising, such as that in newspapers, magazines, or outdoor signage, precedes the film's release by about a month.

Phase Four: Postproduction

After production of the film is complete, the crucial **postproduction** phase of the filmmaking process begins. At this stage, the editor steps into the spotlight. It is the editor who mixes the sound tape—including the music and sound effects needed—with the film images, matching them up for maximum effect. The editor performs one of

America in Film

The American film industry has reinforced cultural values since cameras began rolling. Silent films often featured the strong, handsome hero saving the beautiful and innocent girl from the grips of danger. During the Great Depression, movie audiences wanted to see idealistic and hopeful images. *Gone with the Wind,* even though it dealt with the devastation of the Civil War, portrayed the beautiful and genteel plantation South with strong characters who could solve their own problems. Shirley Temple made people sing, the Marx Brothers made people laugh, and that classic Depression-era film *The Wizard of Oz* encouraged audiences to forget their troubles and travel down that "yellow brick road" to a better future.

In the 1940s and 50s, Westerns gave life to the American belief in rugged individualism and self-reliance. Films about World War II reinforced the patriotism of the American public, in stark contrast to he darker films of the Vietnam War era.

This is why America loves the movies—to see who they are and what they can become.

the most important functions in the production process. The editor's assistant keeps a careful log with notations about every single shot. Often, the editor makes a **rough cut** first. This is similar to a writer's first draft. And like a writer, the film editor will probably continue to rework the raw material for some time. Others then view the rough cut and make suggestions for adding, rearranging, and cutting scenes. After again rearranging and cutting the film based on this input, the editor presents the **final cut,** or finished film, similar to a writer's final draft. At this stage, it is agreed that the film is as good as it is going to get. The final cut can make the difference between a good film and a great one.

A Little Thing Called Continuity ...

If you see a lot of movies, you may have occasionally noticed a problem having to do with **continuity.** Continuity is the cohesion of visual elements from take to take and from scene to scene. For example, if the top button of an actor's shirt is unbuttoned in one take and it is buttoned in another take there is an error in continuity. Continuity problems are common—and some go unnoticed all the way through to final film. To avoid this embarrassing situation, most film sets designate a particular member of the crew to watch for continuity in every scene.

PREPARE

Develop a Concept for a Screenplay and Work on Its Production

To help you gather your ideas and to understand the art of the screenplay, you might first want to read a classic screenplay, such as one of those listed below. You can find plays in your local library and also on the Internet.

- *Ordinary People*
- *Adaptation*
- *The Hours*
- *The Effect of Gamma Rays on Man-in-the-Moon Marigolds*
- *In the Bedroom*
- *The Grapes of Wrath*

After reading the screenplay, obtain a videotape or DVD of the film. As you watch the movie, pay attention to the plot, characters, theme, and dialogue. Notice how camera angles and lighting affect the mood of the film, how the actors interpret their characters, and how the director goes about presenting the story. Ask yourself whether the film met or exceeded your expectations based on your reading of the screenplay.

Use your understanding of the screenplay and the film as a springboard to help you develop a concept of your own. What story would you like to tell? How would this story translate to film? Remember, it is always best to tell a story that has meaning for you personally— a story that you think is important and worthwhile. Then, follow the steps below or use the Movies Activity Sheet to create your presentation.

1 **Describe Your Story** Write a short description of the story you would like to film. Give it a title, describe the characters, and give a brief plot description.

2 **Pitch Your Idea** Next, assume you have completed your screenplay. What happens next? How will you get the script made into a film? How will you convince investors that this is an idea worth backing? What kind of audience will it appeal to and why? Why will your idea draw an audience?

3 **Hire the Development Team** List the various personnel who will be needed to bring your script to the screen. Some people, such as the camera crew and other technicians, may be listed by title. Others, such as the director and actors, should be listed by personal name, with reasons given for these particular selections.

4 **Develop the Preproduction Storyboard** Create four to six important scenes that show the sequence of the plot on a storyboard. You needn't be an artist to accomplish this task, just sketch the progress of the scene as it would appear on the screen.

5 **Plan the Production Location and Sequencing** Decide where the film should be shot. Make a list of the various locations, keeping in mind that the budget to produce your first film will probably be very small. As you think about the locations, consider which scenes will need to be shot at the same time (and perhaps out of chronological order), and make a list of these also.

6 **Include Postproduction Considerations** Imagine that most of the film based on your screenplay has been shot. What sound effects will be needed to add to the reality of the film? What kind of music would best set the tone for the movie? Write a short description of the music and special sound effects needed, or make a tape or CD of these sounds, and discuss how they will enhance the film.

Next, gather all your material, and use it to practice convincing your audience that your screenplay and the film produced from it will be a worthwhile undertaking. You might want to use a computerized presentation program such as Power Point™ to help in your presentation. Be straightforward and sincere, and be sure that you do not exceed the ten-minute time limit.

PRESENT

Share Your Concept

When your instructor calls your name, bring all of your material or the Activity Sheet with you to the playing area. You may wish to use a bulletin board or easel to display your storyboards or you may want to use your computer and a monitor to present your work. Talk about each phase of your concept point by point, from 1 through 6.

Invite classmates to ask questions and offer comments as you present your ideas.

When you are finished discussing your concept, exhibiting your storyboards, and perhaps playing the music and sound effects, thank everyone and give your materials to your teacher.

CRITIQUE

Evaluate a Classmate's Presentation

Select one classmate's presentation to evaluate. Ask yourself the following questions as you think about the speaker's proposal:

Was the presentation well organized and clearly presented?

Did the speaker cover all the important points, or was something missing?

Were the speaker's ideas imaginative and interesting as well as feasible?

Did the speaker engage the audience?

Was the speaker articulate in his or her presentation?

Would you invest in this proposed new film? Why or why not?

Use a scale of 1 to 5 to evaluate the presentation, with 1 being "needs much improvement" and 5 being "outstanding." Write a one-sentence evaluation of each of these elements, and then write a paragraph explaining why you rated the presentation in this way on each point.

What Film Does That Theatre Can't

Although film and theatre share some common elements, there are stark differences between the two in terms of performance techniques, production elements, and audience experience.

The Intimacy Factor Stage actors are taught to project their voices to fill the auditorium. In a film, an actor can speak softly and make slight gestures. The camera picks up incremental but telling changes in facial expression. To be a good actor in either medium requires hard work, dedication, and emotional honesty.

Playing the Angles Stage directors must block the actors in such a way that they can be seen by the audience at all times. In film, the camera can be angled first one way and then the other to show exactly the movement the director intends. The audience's vision is focused by the camera's lens. As film audience members, we see *only* what the director and cinematographer intend us to see.

A Picture Is Worth a Thousand Words The expression on an actor's face can convey his or her innermost feelings more clearly than a monologue would. In general, a film accomplishes as much with its visual world as a play does with its verbal world. Screenplays typically have much less dialogue than plays, yet a screenplay has more pages than a play because of its formatting and its detailed scenic directions.

Transcending Time and Space Film can jump time and place in a matter of seconds. In the 2001 film *Traffic,* for example, the central action takes place in southern California; Mexico; and Washington, D.C. The filmmaker, Steven Soderbergh, created three highly specific worlds. One of the techniques he used involved subtle changes in light at each separate location; the scenes in Mexico had a sepia tone; the scenes in Washington, D.C., were cool blue. As a result, the viewer was aware on several levels each time there was a change of location.

Additional Projects

1 Use the storyboards you created while studying this chapter to videotape at least a portion of your screenplay. Try to incorporate several different kinds of camera angles.

2 With two other classmates, develop an idea for a screenplay about the life of a high school student. Brainstorm scenarios and create a detailed outline.

3 Research and report on your favorite film. Tell who wrote it, who produced it, who directed it, and any interesting details about how it came to be made.

4 Choose two classmates as actors to work with you on a scene from a screenplay. Rehearse the actors briefly. Then, using a handheld video camera, have them do several takes of the scene. Play the scene back on the monitor, and see if the three of you agree on which take is the best.

5 Create a poster or graphic that advertises the film based on the screenplay you planned for this project.

6 Using the scene from *A Jamaican Airman Foresees His Death* by Fred D'Aguiar found in Unit Eight, decide how you would recreate this scene on film. Write a detailed description of your concept for the scene.

Master of the Craft

Spike Lee: On the Scene with a Wake-up Call

When Spike Lee first came to the attention of the film world in 1986, young African-American filmmakers were a rarity. But Lee quickly made a name for himself, not only because of his impressive skills, but also because of his reputation as an independent, outspoken black artist.

Lee's New York University thesis film, *Joe's Bed-Stuy Barbershop: We Cut Heads,* won a Student Academy Award in 1984 (Bed Stuy is short for Bedford Stuyvesant, a neighborhood in Brooklyn, New York). Lee later said: "I thought that now that I had this plaque on top of my television that Columbia, Warner Brothers . . . Spielberg, Lucas, would call me. So I just sat by the phone. Then the phone got turned off.

That's when I decided to try to do it more independently."

Lee's stylish and ably directed independent feature debut, *She's Gotta Have It,* used what he later described as "guerrilla filmmaking." He focused on controversial social issues in a unique, unorthodox, and even combative way. Lee's second feature, *School Daze,* released in 1988, secured backing from Columbia Pictures, who offered him a third of what they typically paid filmmakers. Despite lukewarm reviews, *School Daze* earned more than twice what it had cost to make. It satirized issues of class and race differentiation at an all-black college in the form of a musical comedy, establishing Lee as a director who would not compromise his vision.

Lee's 1989 film *Do the Right Thing* scored him an artistic and commercial success. Many films followed, including *Mo' Better Blues* (1990), *Malcolm X* (1992), *He Got Game* (1998), *Bamboozled* (2001), and *25th Hour* (2002). In all his films Lee focuses on the divisions within American society as well as in the black community.

He continues to make films with his production company, 40 Acres and a Mule, in which he asks viewers to wake up and open up their minds.

Spike Lee

Spike Lee appears in his own film *Do the Right Thing.*

Theatre Then and Now

Chicago to California . . . and on to Toronto

Film in the Early 1900s: Essanay

When it comes to American movies, many people think it all began in Hollywood, California. But in fact, the early days of filmmaking were ruled by Essanay Studios in Chicago, Illinois.

Essanay was founded in 1907 by George K. Spoor and Gilbert "Bronco Billy" Anderson. (The name comes from a combination of the two men's initials, S and A.) The company they built produced hundreds of early silent films, many of them featuring such movie stars as Charlie Chaplin and Gloria Swanson. Anderson himself was a silent film star who became the world's first western movie hero. Bronco Billy cranked out action-packed tales featuring himself as a brave and noble cowboy. Essanay's films were short, which was common in those early days.

But Chicago was well known for something else besides moviemaking: bad weather. Spoor and Anderson realized that it would be more cost effective if they could film outdoors year-round, so they built themselves a new studio in Niles, California. They continued to maintain their Chicago studios, but the big stars—Chaplin, in particular—preferred California.

By 1915, audience tastes were changing. Longer (feature-length) films were becoming popular. After ruling the industry in its early days, Essanay began to decline and went out of business in 1916.

Charlie Chaplin and Jackie Coogan in the silent film *The Kid.*

Film in the Early 2000s: Toronto Film and Television Office

Established in 1979 in Toronto, Ontario, The Toronto Film and Television Office has built the city a reputation as one of the top locations for making movies and television shows. The original purpose of the company was to coordinate location filming by means of supplying easily attainable film permits. This would bring international business to Canada, which would in turn create jobs for Canadian citizens.

Today, Toronto is an international hotspot for filmmakers. It ranks number three in film and TV production in North America (after Los Angeles and New York), and it is the second largest exporter of TV programming. The streets of Toronto are typically teeming with crews from feature films, made-for-television movies, and television series. Particularly for those projects on a tight budget, the producers are drawn to the lower costs, the experienced Canadian technical crews who are willing to work long hours to get the job done, and the state-of-the-art technical services Toronto offers—from preproduction all the way through postproduction. Combine those factors with a

The popular independent film *My Big Fat Greek Wedding* was filmed in Canada.

favorable exchange rate on the Canadian dollar—and recently introduced tax credits for shooting in Toronto—and the cost of making a film or TV show in Toronto can be about half that of shooting the same film in the United States.

The film industry has changed its physical location to fit its goals over the years. As the international film world continues to reinvent itself, the primary locations for shooting are apt to continue to shift as well.

28 Television

When we watch TV, we often see the same personalities or characters one or more times a week. Eventually, we come to know and care about the people we see on our household screens.

Project Specs

Project Description You will write an outline for an episode of a well-known television drama or situation comedy, then present your outline in five to ten minutes.

Purpose to explore the unique aspects of television and to understand the demands of writing for this medium

Materials paper or the Television Activity Sheet provided by your teacher

Theatre Terms

demographic
PBS
pilot
reality TV
sitcoms
syndication
target audience

On Your Feet

How influential is television? Does it really have an effect on people's thoughts? Take turns with your classmates humming a theme song or saying a signature line from a popular television show from the past or present. Challenge your classmates to identify the show from the song or line you've provided.

Courtney Cox, Jennifer Aniston, and Matthew Perry in what has become a television classic—*Friends*.

PREVIEW

Early Television and Beyond

Television, when it emerged, did not compete with theatre so much as other recorded media. Movies had established themselves as a strong competitor to theatre with their first silent films. Television, in turn, threatened radio and film. TV offered an alternative home for the drama, comedy, and documentary. And its flexibility made it useful for news and other live programming as well.

TV is an intimate medium, so it is perfect for presenting the continuing dramas and situational humor of everyday life. It is also ideal for acts with a more subtle approach to entertainment.

George Burns and Gracie Allen

Aside from news programs, the first things shown on television were entertainment shows such as wrestling and variety shows, full of dancing, singing, sketches, and so on. The most popular and memorable of these were Milton Berle's *Comedy Hour* and *The Ed Sullivan Show.*

Situation comedies, or **sitcoms,** became popular too. Among the most-watched early shows were programs such as *The George Burns and Gracie Allen Show, The Jack Benny Show* (both of which had their roots in radio), and *I Love Lucy.* Each of these programs was supported by corporate sponsors who paid to have their products advertised during the shows.

Vanna White spins the big letters on *Wheel of Fortune.*

Daytime TV

In television's infancy the daytime viewer had little to choose from. Viewers watched fifteen-minute programs, which ranged from talk shows to recitals and continuing dramas. These came to be known as soap operas because in the days of radio soap companies had sponsored similar shows, and the name stuck. Over time, these shows became longer, more dramatic and complex, with convoluted plots and characters of all ages and socioeconomic levels.

Next, producers added game shows and children's programming to the daytime mix. Shows such as *The Price Is Right* became popular, and soon offerings such as *The $64,000 Question, Jeopardy, Wheel of Fortune,* and *Family Feud* became popular nighttime fare as well. Programming in each of these areas expanded until around-the-clock television was no longer a novelty, but the norm.

Television and Controversy

Because it depends on a wide audience base, television tends to avoid taking programming risks. Nevertheless, innovative television writers throughout the years have used comic and dramatic forms in new ways. The 1971 sitcom *All in the Family* brought contemporary social issues to television by presenting in a humorous way the conflicts between a bigoted middle-aged man and his liberal son-in-law. The *Mary Tyler Moore Show* presented positive images of professional women when the idea was still novel. *The Jeffersons, Sanford and Son,* and *Chico and the Man* brought minority issues to the mainstream. Politically inspired shows such as *The Great American Dream Machine* and even *The Smothers Brothers Comedy Hour* were often in trouble with their sponsors over the issues they raised and the stances they took.

More recently, makers of dramas such as *Hill Street Blues* and *West Wing* have developed new standards regarding subject matter and character development. Experimental dramas such as *Twin Peaks* included alternative approaches to plot, character, lighting, and sound. Comedies such as *Seinfeld* and *Friends* brought a contemporary sensibility to the airwaves that sometimes caused critics to assert that they were going a bit too far. The network known as MTV is often credited as

The Bunkers of *All in the Family* were played by, from left to right, Rob Reiner, Sally Struthers, Carroll O'Connor, and Jean Stapleton.

being the first to expand on conventional ideas of programming. It turned single songs into miniature movies, with the songs as soundtracks. In the process, it drew in thousands of young people to watch its innovative visual style and creative programs.

Producers of cable television shows such as *The Osbournes* and *Sex and the City* have stretched public perceptions of who—and what—are worthy of dramatic treatment, and of what is considered suitable for home viewing.

Despite the controversy surrounding some of these programs, the fact is that over time, we often come to care about the characters we watch each week on the small screen.

Sarah Jessica Parker, Cynthia Nixon, Kristin Davis, and Kim Cattrall appear in the controversial cable program *Sex and the City*.

Television for the Public Good

Educational programming made its debut in 1953, when station KNXT in Los Angeles set aside an hour of "public service time" on Saturdays. Like commercial

Big Bird and friends continue to instruct and entertain children on the PBS program *Sesame Street.*

television, it owed a debt to theatre. A professor named Frank Baxter agreed to appear during that hour to present a show about Shakespeare. To everyone's surprise—including Baxter's—Shakespeare was a hit! Over the years, Baxter won six Emmy awards and numerous other honors.

Eventually, through government and corporate sponsorship and the dedication of various producers, educational programming expanded into public television. The community of stations that produce public programming came to be known as the Public Broadcasting Service, or **PBS.**

In 1961, public television unveiled its first hit dramatic series—which was also based on Shakespeare. *An Age of Kings* presented Shakespeare's history plays. Until this series aired, public television had been more plainly instructional. But *An Age of Kings* signaled the onset of more vivid and varied programming. It was followed over the years with the kinds of series that public television is known for. They included *Hollywood Television Theatre, American Playhouse,* and Britain's *Masterpiece Theatre.*

These offerings were balanced by college courses, news programs, and children's educational programming. Charming and innovative children's shows such as *Mister Rogers' Neighborhood* and *Sesame Street* set the standard for children's programming in both public and commercial television.

Eventually that spirit of experimentation reached adult educational programming, and stations began running cooking shows, home building shows, and episodic historical programs in addition to their traditional offerings. The documentary also gained a strong foothold and hit its stride with fine programs such as *Eyes on the Prize,* a history of the civil rights movement; *The Atomic Café,* which documents how the atomic bomb changed our world; and Ken Burns' *Lewis and Clark: The Journey of the Corps of Discovery.*

Until recently, all of this programming was free of commercial interruption, though corporate sponsors were listed and thanked for their involvement in various programs.

Beyond the Networks

Today, cable and satellite television, offered by subscription, are the place to go for more varied programming. For the most part, both satellite and cable offer the same kind of fare as network television, but cable offerings often seem more varied and innovative and more willing to explore controversial subjects than network TV, and satellite television broadcasts programs from around the world.

More conventional programs have reached into experimentation, as well. Young adult shows like *Lizzie McGuire,* for example, mix cartoons with live actors while allowing for a running commentary on the action, as *The George*

Burns and Gracie Allen Show once did. Continuing hour-long dramas like *The Sopranos* and *Six Feet Under* explore little-known subsets of American culture and are able to foster strong viewer emotions—from repulsion to empathy and from laughter to tears.

Reality programming, such as *Road Rules* and *The Real World,* incorporates elements of the sitcom and drama, as real people encounter various challenges followed by (and playing to) the camera lens. **Reality TV** breaks boundaries between entertainment and real life. Many of the programs are criticized for their poor aesthetic quality, but because they have gained audiences, they are having an overwhelming effect on mainstream television.

Kelly Clarkson was voted the winner on the first *American Idol.*

Here's How
Television Differs from Film

Whether you're an actor, director, producer, or crew member, you'll find that working in television is different from working in film. Here are some of the ways they differ:

	Television	Film
Performance	• Programming can be presented live. • It lends itself to intimate, confessional styles. • It requires hooks and cliff-hangers to grab audiences. • Audiences are casual and expectations are low. • Many shows have a laugh track; the soundtrack is minimal.	• Film is not presented live. • It lends itself to dramatic, heroic styles. • It can build slowly toward a climactic event. • Audiences buy tickets, therefore expectations are higher. • There is no laugh track; the soundtrack is important.
Structure	• Programs vary in length—most are about 30 minutes; some are three hours. • Programs are interrupted by commercials. • Many programs are weekly or daily serials.	• Programs vary in length from about 1 1/2 to 3 1/2 hours. • Programs usually run uninterrupted. • Though sequels exist, each movie must stand on its own.
Technical Elements	• Close-ups can be extremely effective. • Mid-range shots are also effective. • Panoramic shots are rarely effective. • Characters tend to seem approachable and real.	• Close-ups are less effective. • Mid-range shots are effective. • Panoramic shots can be extremely effective. • Characters and topics sometimes seem larger than life.

If you are a sports enthusiast, particularly a fan of athletic events not covered in the United States, satellite television offers a wide range of programs from all over the globe. If you love soccer, steeple chasing, sumo wrestling, or kick boxing, satellite offers all that and more.

Cable television broadcasts athletic events not carried by networks, such as the semifinals of the French Open, in which Venus Williams participates.

Producing a Pilot Program

Producing a television program is a complex process, requiring the cooperation of people with many different talents. A single program that introduces a potential new series is called a **pilot.** It airs initially as a single program with the expectation that if it is popular, it will become the introduction to a new series. Like any other large and risky project, the making of a pilot program is achieved step by step.

1 **Acquire the Script and Director.**
It is the job of the producer to obtain or commission the writing of a pilot script and also to find the right director for the project.

2 **Hire Production Specialists.**
This step is often delegated to the art director, who hires the technical crew, a costume designer (who obtains costume elements), a property manager (who obtains props, furniture, and equipment), and a production manager (who coordinates the production specialists). The producer must, however, oversee the day-to-day operations of these elements.

3 **Audition and Hire Talent.** Actors, composers, musicians, and other talented individuals must be auditioned for their suitability for the tasks at hand. Contracts must be negotiated, and everything must be in place before production begins.

4 Hold Rehearsals. Actors will need off-camera rehearsals. When they are ready to perform, a camera rehearsal is held in which everyone runs through the script together.

5 Tape the Show. Some producers present a show live and simply keep the tape as an archive. Most, however, tape a show one scene at a time.

6 Edit the Tape. Some producers simply edit out extraneous elements, leaving a show mostly intact. Most, however, edit each segment they tape, and then join them together to create the final product.

Career Focus

Cameraperson

Camera crew members in television and movies straddle the line between technical theatre and art. They must know about lighting, camera shots, and angles, but they must also understand creative composition and visual styles.

You can gain an introduction to all these things through classes in photography, television, and film, but the way to master them is through experience. As in theatre and film, you become a cameraperson by working as a cameraperson. That is, try it out on your own time.

Cameraperson Sidney Lubbitch explains, "The most important thing is to learn the language of the viewfinder." By that, he means that you must learn how the camera frames images and action.

You can start out small. Video cameras are expensive, so you can begin working with still cameras. From them, you can learn about light and speed. You can learn how to focus a lens and experiment with camera angles and composition. After you feel comfortable with the basics, you can begin experimenting with stylistic shots.

If you're still in love with the work, progress to video. You may be able to find used equipment that is inexpensive. Then you can be in charge of filming family occasions, producing your own documentaries, or collaborating with someone who has a story to tell. If you feel confident enough to work with a production team, you might find that a cable access show in your area needs your help.

Make sure you keep a record of your work by holding onto still shots and videotapes; you can review them in order to learn from them. You can also use the successful pieces as samples of your work for a video portfolio.

PREPARE

Outline Your Proposed Episode for a TV Show

For this project, you will develop an outline for an episode of a television show with which you are very familiar—a drama or a comedy.

Television writers often write concepts, outlines, and pilots or other scripts "on spec." That is, they work without any up-front payment, in the hopes that a producer will either buy the work or hire them as staff writers. Before you begin your outline, try to obtain a copy of the program's writer's guidelines. These can help you understand what producers are looking for in scripts for their particular show. If this is not possible, use a writer's handbook with guidelines for writing scripts and screenplays. Be sure you consider the following points as you write your outline.

Your Outline Should Reflect:

- **The TV Category** Your proposal will be easier to sell if you can identify it as part of a specific kind of programming, such as a sitcom, an adult cartoon, a family drama, a medical drama, a crime drama, an action series, or a law and justice series.

- **The Correct Tone** Each TV series has its own distinctive tone. *Friends,* for example, is breezy, but *The X-Files* is dark science fiction. Producers are apt to buy scripts in keeping with the usual tone of the show.

- **The Right Plot Elements** Some shows feature a continuing plot thread, while others are self-contained. As an outside writer, you must show an understanding of plot developments that have happened so far without imposing any new plot line.

- **Familiar Character Types** Characters in most television programs have specific roles. Many characters feature one or two defining characteristics, such as bossy, fun-loving, goofy, predatory, spacey, suspicious, innocent, sweet, malicious, and so on.

- **A Target Audience** Most shows are aimed at a specific **demographic,** or group of people (for advertising purposes), such as white males who are 18–35 years old. This would be called your **target audience.** If you know a particular show's demographic, you can include references and topics that appeal to this group.

- **Commercial Breaks** Think about the time slot your particular episode is likely to fill. Then find out where commercials are inserted into programming for that time slot. Structure your script so that suspenseful moments fall just before commercials. This will reel your audience in—and hold them during the commercial break.

PRESENT

Share Your Outline for a Proposed TV Episode

When your name is called, step to the front of the room and share your outline with the class. First, give the name of the television program to which your episode pertains. Then read your outline. Be sure to stay within the ten-minute time limit.

When your presentation is complete, hand your outline or your Activity Sheet to your teacher and return to your seat.

CRITIQUE

Evaluate a Classmate's Outline

You will choose one outline and rate it on a scale of 1 to 5, with 1 being "needs much improvement" and 5 being "outstanding." Ask yourself the following questions as you evaluate your classmate's presentation.

- In what ways did the outlined episode seem suitable (or unsuitable) for this particular TV series?

- Did the plot and characters seem to fit in smoothly with the TV program as you have experienced it?

- In what way would the episode outlined in this presentation draw in the target audience of this show?

- Did the presentation seem well researched and well thought out in terms of the time slot, demographics, and style of the show?

Write a short paragraph explaining why you gave this outline the rating you did.

Spotlight on

Reality TV

Based on how they feel about it, people tend to think of reality TV as either a new innovation or a new low in television. Actually, neither one is true. CBS unveiled the first show in this format more than thirty years ago. It was called *Wanted,* and it focused on alleged criminals in much the same way that *America's Most Wanted* and *Cops* do today. Allen Funt's *Candid Camera* revealed long ago how people act under stressful circumstances—and this same premise is found today in an updated *Candid Camera,* as well as in *The Jamie Kennedy Experiment* and *America's Funniest Home Videos.*

Continuing reality stories have a history, as well. PBS aired the first reality show, called *An American Family,* in 1973. It featured the Louds, a seemingly typical family, who opened up their home to video cameras for a period of seven months. This footage was heavily edited, but the resulting twelve-hour program included the breakup of the Louds' marriage and the coming out of their son Lance. Viewers found it riveting. Thirty years later, a new Loud family program was aired—this time following the death of Lance due to AIDS.

An American Family was the inspiration for MTV's *The Real World,* in which people video their lives together for a period of weeks. The action-oriented *Survivor,* which challenges people to live and compete under difficult conditions, is a variation on this same theme, as is *Get Me Out of Here! I'm a Celebrity!* Similar in nature are the romance-inspired shows *The Bachelor, Blind Date,* and *The Bachelorette.*

Many reality shows lack aesthetic value, but they are popular with networks because they cost very little to produce. They are popular with audiences because they are novel and unpredictable. And they are popular with sponsors because they are popular with audiences. The down side of these types of programs is that they will probably never make any money in **syndication.** That is, the network will never be able to resell these reality programs (as they have such stalwarts as *Star Trek, The Dick Van Dyke Show,* and *M*A*S*H*) for millions of dollars because the reality won't be there and neither will the audience.

Nevertheless, PBS is experimenting with the reality format. In 2002, it aired *Pioneer House,* which challenged people to attempt to live in the manner of the American pioneers. It also featured *1900 House,* a program produced in England, in which the Bowler family moved into a home from the year 1900. These programs have been reasonably successful.

Reality TV is in its infancy, and it is clearly ready to become more of an art form.

Candid Camera actually has its roots in radio! Allen Funt began his career by taping the complaints of his fellow servicemen and airing them for a broadcast audience.

Additional Projects

1 Write a satire on or a tribute to an early television program.

2 Produce a live television program featuring a school play or talent show.

3 Experiment! Develop a plan for a mixed-genre program, such as a news/game show or a reality/sitcom.

4 Read a teleplay by a playwright such as Paddy Chayevfsky or Arthur Miller, and write a plan for a sequel.

5 Research the career and life of an early television pioneer such as Lucille Ball, Ernie Kovacks, Ed Sullivan, or Sid Caesar. Share your findings with the class.

6 Research and write about the history of public television, focusing on popular programs such as *Sesame Street* and *Mister Rogers' Neighborhood*. Create a timeline to accompany your report.

7 Choose an existing television series, and write a short script for this program based on one of the scenes found in Unit Eight of this book. You must adapt the scene so that it will appeal to the people who typically watch this TV show.

Master of the Craft

Larry Gelbart

"One doesn't have a sense of humor. It has you."

—Larry Gelbart

Writer Larry Gelbart's professional career began at the age of 16. His father, a barber in Los Angeles, had been bragging about him while cutting the hair of early radio and television star Danny Thomas. To his surprise, Thomas gave Larry a job as a staff writer for a popular radio show called *The Maxwell House Coffee Hour.*

With this credit under his belt, Gelbart won writing jobs with other major stars, including comedian Bob Hope. Gelbart has high regard for the demands of radio, especially the show *Duffy's Tavern,* which he says required that he demonstrate his verbal skill and dexterity on a weekly basis.

After serving a one-year tour in the military at eighteen, Gelbart began a civilian career with Bob Hope as a member of Hope's comedy writing team. He toured much of the world with Hope and then made the transition to television. Here he worked with writers Carl Reiner, Mel Brooks, and Neil Simon on shows starring comic greats such as Sid Caesar and Danny Kaye.

Gelbart lived for a time in London, where he wrote the pilot for *M*A*S*H,* a sitcom that satirized the Korean War and lasted for ninety-seven episodes. After *M*A*S*H,* Gelbart worked on the pilot for *Three's Company,* as well as the feature-length television movie *Barbarians at the Gate.*

Over the past sixty years, Larry Gelbart has won Emmy and Peabody Awards for *M*A*S*H;* Tony Awards for the theatrical plays *A Funny Thing Happened on the Way to the Forum* (recently revived on Broadway) and *City of Angels;* and Academy Award nominations for *Tootsie* and *Oh, God.*

Larry Gelbart has been honored for a lifetime of excellence by the Writers Guild of America and its Freelance Writers Committee. But it is not the awards that people remember. It's the warm and incisive humor that has informed all of his work.

Larry Gelbart

Theatre Then and Now

Theatre and Television: The Odd Couple

Theatre and television have had a love-hate relationship from the start, but, when they share their expertise with each other, both are enriched.

Theatre on the Small Screen

Theatre's early influence on television came in the form of the anthology series—plays written for television and performed live by both rising theatrical stars and hopeful unknowns.

Early television series such as *Philco Television Playhouse, Goodyear Television Playhouse, Kraft Television Theatre,* and *Revlon Theatre* opened a new door for writers, and they responded with timeless TV dramas such as Paddy Chayefsky's *Marty,* Horton Foote's *A Young Lady of Property,* and Reginald Rose's *Twelve Angry Men.* Each of these teleplays dealt with what Chayefsky called "the marvelous world of the ordinary."

During the 1950s, sponsors became increasingly uncomfortable with the controversy some of the early teleplays aroused. These theatrically-based shows were then replaced with an era of shorter action shows and a myriad of sitcoms. Most of these new programs catered to sponsors who preferred to underwrite light entertainment.

New programs featured dashing, unsullied heroes like the eligible young Dr. Kildare or the dedicated detective Ellery Queen. Situation comedies such as *Ozzie and Harriet* presented a sweet, comforting view of family life as television settled into an entertainment routine, with the occasional game show, news show, or mini-drama thrown in. For a time, authentic drama was all but forgotten.

David, Ricky, and their mom, Harriet Nelson, in *Ozzie and Harriet.*

Small Screens Onstage

These days, playwrights creating television drama is not as common as it once was. Theatre's influence on television is perhaps more subtle, while film techniques have become more obvious.

It should not come as a surprise to learn that over the years television has influenced theatre to some degree. Recently, theatrical professionals have begun using television as a dramatic tool.

At their most ordinary, televisions are just set pieces with characters watching them onstage. But TV sets have also been used as a technical element of theatre. They are sometimes featured as alternative narrators or as symbolic characters. American directors have begun to incorporate television technology into their dramatic images. The Wooster Group in New York used television monitors in its staging of *Our Town* by Thornton Wilder. The group feels it plays "a pivotal role in bringing technically sophisticated and evocative uses of sound, film, and video into the realm of contemporary theater."

Television also has fostered audience participation by moving theatrical professionals to offer what television

Tony Hernandez of the Actors Gymnasium's Flying Griffin Circus in Evanston, Illinois.

cannot. It has spurred theatrical productions to be daring, in order to woo audiences away from their TV sets, and it has inspired productions based on television, from tributes to *Gilligan's Island* and *The Brady Bunch,* to Green Mamba's satirical take on *Big Brother.*

29 Critique a Performance

"Everybody's a critic." While this statement is often made in jest, it contains a nugget of truth. The fact is, we all have opinions and make judgments about nearly everything, including dramatic performances.

Project Specs

Project Description As part of a group, you will write a review of a performance of your choice in theatre, film, or television. Then the group will give an eight- to ten-minute presentation.

Purpose to understand and explore the elements of criticism

Materials an outline of your presentation or the Critique a Performance Activity Sheet your teacher provides

Theatre Terms
American Theatre Critics
  Association (ATCA)
dramatic criticism
Goethe's principles
pan
rave review
suspend disbelief

On Your Feet

Name a currently popular film or television show and take about a minute or so to tell the class your opinion of it. Call on one of your classmates to explain what he or she thinks of the same show. Compare the two opinions and discuss any differences.

An interior view of
the Avalon Theatre on
Catalina Island in California.

PREVIEW

You Be the Critic

Dramatic criticism is an area in which nearly everyone takes part now and then. Viewers of plays, movies, and television are quick to evaluate and judge. In so doing, they are stating their opinions about an artistic product. But opinions vary, and often people have conflicting views concerning the same subject. One of your classmates may praise a play and give it a **rave review;** another may **pan** it, that is, give it an extremely negative review.

How, then, are you to know which opinion to respect? You might begin with the question "Why?" "Why did you think the play was good (or weak)?" The viewer who answers with a shrug, or with a statement such as "I don't know—it just was," will probably not be taken seriously. But the viewer who can back up his or her opinion with intelligent reasons and insights deserves your attention.

Of course, the best way to decide the worth of a play, film, or television drama is to see it yourself. But your evaluation will depend to a large extent on what you bring to it as an audience member. If you understand the various aspects of dramatic criticism, you might very well become an intelligent, discerning critic. You will know why a production succeeds or fails.

Here's How
To Practice Critical Ethics

There are ethical considerations to being a good critic. Read each point below before you begin your project.

- Back up your opinions with valid reasons based on appropriate standards. Your critical opinion is only worthwhile if you can soundly substantiate it.

- Be objective and fair. Recognize your own biases and tastes and make allowances for them. Keep an open mind.

- Evaluate the whole production. Although in this exercise you will focus on one aspect of the production, you must be aware of the production as a whole to know whether the aspect you are reviewing is working within its context.

- Be constructive. Indicate good points along with those that need improvement. No matter what your criticism is, be diplomatic.

- Be sincere. Believe in what you say. The opinion must be your own. Although in many cases you will be guided by professional critics, you must learn to develop and stand behind your own beliefs—provided they are grounded in knowledge and understanding.

- Don't be overly negative.

- Don't try to be clever at the expense of the artist. Your job is to evaluate, not to ridicule.

- Don't sweat the small stuff. Always approach a performance with an idea that you'll enjoy it. If you constantly look for something to go wrong, you won't be able to give a fair review. You will dwell on minutiae—fluffed lines or poorly executed light cues—and miss the possible wonders of the production.

- Don't be arrogant. As a critic, you need humility, understanding, and kindness.

Unfortunately, the word *criticism* often has a negative connotation. Many drama critics have a reputation for being derogatory or overly harsh. However, if you begin to pay attention and read drama reviews regularly, you will find that many critics also have many positive things to say. In fact, theatre producers often use quotes from the reviews to advertise a show.

A Critical Foundation
The performance arts should be emotionally and intellectually involving. They should challenge, thrill, or inspire us; make us laugh one moment and cry

the next. But if a production bores us, it has failed. While we watch a play, film, or other dramatic presentation, we should be suspended in an intensified illusion of reality. We see more of life on stage or screen over the course of two or three hours than we could live in the same amount of time in the real world. We don't turn to the dramatic arts to see smaller interpretations of our lives; we come to see larger ones. Yet what we see must appear truthful and believable in the moment. The characters, events, and dialogue must remain consistent and true. The viewers must accept what they see and hear. This is often called the ability to **"suspend disbelief,"** and good critics must be able to do this to give the dramatic work a proper understanding.

When a play receives raves, it often uses them in advertisements.

PREPARE

Work on Your Review of a Dramatic Performance

Divide into groups of four. As a group, choose the play, film, or television show you would like to evaluate. You will all review the entire production, but each of you will also be required to give special attention and consideration to one particular aspect of the show. Decide which of you will be responsible for reviewing the production's

- writing
- acting
- directing
- staging (set, lights, costumes, make-up, technical execution)

Once you have decided who is responsible for each element, use the Critique the Performance Activity Sheet or create an outline to help you focus on your assignment. Then follow these four steps to work on the first part of this project.

PART ONE: Preparing Your Portion of the Review

1 **Appoint a chairperson for your group.** This person will make all the necessary arrangements for obtaining reservations for the play, coordinating the starting times of the film, play, or television show, and deciding where the group should meet in order to see the performance together.

2 Follow audience etiquette at all times. Get to the theatre early, and stay on your best behavior. (See page 36 for more on Audience Etiquette.) Good behavior should also hold true if you are watching television at the home of one of your friends.

3 Enjoy the show. Leave yourself open to the possibility of both tears and laughter. Use your imagination. Suspend disbelief. Take notes throughout the performance about what you see and how you feel. Pay close attention to the particular production aspect to which you have been assigned.

4 Write your review. The best time to do this is immediately after the show. Don't wait too long—you want your impressions fresh. First, judge the overall quality of the production—script, performance, direction, and technical elements—according to **Goethe's principles** of criticism. Then write several paragraphs analyzing the production aspect to

Goethe's Principles of Criticism

Critics in many fields tend to agree that the principles of Goethe (1749–1832), a German philosopher, critic, and playwright, provide a sound basis for criticism. Goethe's critical methodology always used three questions:

1 **What was the artist (author, actor, director, designer) trying to do?** Did the author mean to write a tragedy? A fantasy? A farce? What was the author trying to tell us? What world was the director trying to illuminate? Was the actor showing off his or her own personality or attempting to embody a character? What was the aim of the designer?

2 **How well did the artist accomplish it?** Was the artist successful? Does the author's tragedy/fantasy/farce contain the necessary elements of that genre? Were the actor's technique and the director's methods effective?

3 **Was it worth doing?** Here you must form your own opinion as to whether or not the time and effort were worthwhile for both artists and audience. Even if the artist succeeds in achieving his or her aim, the efforts may not be of value to everyone. After considering the entire production, you must decide its worth.

These three questions provide a valuable foundation for criticism because they allow you to judge the work of an artist only after you have considered the purpose, use of technique, and intrinsic value of the individual efforts.

which you were specifically assigned. Back up your opinions with reasons and examples. This written report will be used later when your group creates its full presentation.

The following questions should help you as you evaluate specific elements of a dramatic presentation. Be sure to give concrete, detailed examples in support of your opinions.

Playwriting

Consider these questions when you critique a script. Did the work have:

- the necessary elements of its genre?

- a general appeal wide enough to interest most audience members?

- individuality and freshness of style?

- subtle suggestion (subtext)?

- clear organization, so that events rise to a strong climax?

- clearly drawn, believable characters who are able to arouse audience empathy?

- clear and expressive dialogue that draws the audience into the plot?

- a unified effect that builds interest through variety and contrast?

- A good balance of emotional climax and release?

Acting

Evaluate the following elements when considering the actor's performance:

Theatre Journal

Pay attention to the way your friends speak about films they have seen or television shows they've watched. Are there certain people whose opinions you trust more than others? Write your thoughts on the subject.

- Was each character believable? Was each true to the intent of the production?

- Was the acting spontaneous (did it have the illusion of the first time)?

- How did the actors project visually and verbally? Did they communicate with economy, clarity, control, and conviction?

- Were the quality, interpretation, and projection of the voice suitable for the character? Did the actors use proper tempo and rhythm in their line delivery and cue pickup?

- Were gestures and movement motivated, clear, varied, and appropriate?

- Was there a good balance between emotion and control? Were reactions true? Was the mood sustained? Were the climaxes of scenes achieved?

- Did the actors establish the proper relationships among the characters? Was there teamwork? Ensemble playing?

Directing

When assessing the work of the director, think about the following issues:

- Were all aspects unified and faithful to the author's purpose?

- Was scene composition handled effectively and smoothly with proper emphasis on balance, variety, and contrast?

- Did rhythm and tempo provide the right mood, with appropriate climax and release in each scene and act?

- Was there a good balance of aesthetic distance and empathy?

- Did each actor suit the part he or she was playing?

Set and Costume Design

Consider these technical aspects of the production when evaluating the staging:

- Did the set design provide appropriate background and mood?

- Were the costumes and makeup in harmony with the character, period, mood, and style of the work?

- Were the lights, sound effects, special effects, etc., handled effectively?

Collaborate with Your Fellow Critics

At this point, you and each of your three fellow critics have created a portion of a review of a dramatic presentation. Now you will put your various responses together into a unified whole.

PART TWO: Putting It All Together

1 **Have a group discussion.** Discuss your impressions of the entire performance, focusing on the plot, theme, staging, acting, directing. What do you all agree on? What are some issues you disagree about? Make note of these.

2 **Read your individual paragraphs.** Read aloud the review you each wrote about your specific aspect of the production. Discuss how your opinions connect and how they vary. Keep notes on these.

3 **Listen for overlap.** For example, if the person reviewing the script brings up a point about the acting, there may be a way to use this area as a transition into the portion of the review dedicated to the actors' performances.

4 **Write and edit your presentation.** Work together to write and edit your presentation. Use the transitions that have come up in your discussions to help present a smooth, seamless flow from one aspect of the production to the next. This will help you to decide the order of the presentation

5 **Rehearse your presentation once.** Be aware that your individual parts of the review don't have to agree with one another. One person may think the acting is wonderful, while another thinks it needs a lot of work.

Practice presenting your review together. Make sure the transitions are clear and that each of you knows exactly when to begin reading. Be sure that it can be given in between eight to ten minutes. If it is too long, decide where to cut text. If it is too short, go over your notes and add pertinent information.

6 Rehearse your presentation again. Practice your presentation from start to finish without interruption. Whoever begins the presentation will also introduce the group and tell the name of the production and a little bit about it. Each of you will pick up where the previous person leaves off, introduce the element on which you will focus, and read through your presentation.

Career Focus

Theatre Critic

Becoming a critic at a major newspaper, magazine, or radio or television station today typically requires a college education in theatre, dramaturgy, and/or criticism—or considerable direct experience working in the professional worlds of theatre and journalism.

Many smaller or alternative newspapers do not have a full-time critic but instead deal with writers who review on a show-by-show or freelance basis. Some of these freelancers are highly trained and educated professionals; others are basically enlightened audience members with an interest in theatre but little or no direct education or training.

Most professional American critics are members of the **American Theatre Critics Association** (ATCA). The purpose of this organization, according to its bylaws is, "To make possible greater communication among United States theatre critics; to encourage absolute freedom of expression in theatre and in theatre criticism; to increase public awareness of the theatre as an important national resource; and to reaffirm the individual critic's right to disagree with his colleagues on all matters including the above."

The organization also gives awards for outstanding achievement in the theatre at its annual conference. The members vote on the Theatre Hall of Fame awards, give recommendations for the annual Tony Award for Regional Theatre, honor an emerging playwright with the M. Elizabeth Osborn Award, and present the annual American Theatre Critics/Steinberg New Play Awards and Citations at the Humana Festival of New American Plays at the Actors Theatre of Louisville.

PRESENT

Read Your Group Review of a Dramatic Performance

When your names are called, go with your group to the playing area. Don't forget to bring your reviews or the Critique a Performance Activity Sheets with you, as you will be reading from them.

When your turn comes, read your portion of the review with expression, just the way you rehearsed it. Try to leave as few gaps as possible between the sections. Remember that this is a performance. The idea is to try to present the collaborative review as a unified whole.

When your group has finished presenting your review, take a short pause before leaving the playing area. Hand your materials to your teacher on your way back to your seat.

CRITIQUE

Review the Reviewers

Choose one of the group presentations to evaluate. Remember that it is best to begin with the positives. Rate the presentation on a scale of 1 to 5, with 1 being "needs much improvement," and 5 being "outstanding." Ask yourself the following questions as you listen to each group:

- Were the group members able to present their material in a well-organized and well-structured way?

- How well was the group able to articulate ideas and concepts?

- Did the individuals in the group have clear and pleasant vocal projection and expression?

- How were the group members able to convince you that their opinions were well-supported?

- Did members of the group seem poised and comfortable in their presentations?

- How unified was the group's presentation?

Write a paragraph explaining why you gave this group the rating you did.

Additional Projects

1 Compare the criticisms of two different professional critics concerning the same dramatic production—a play, a film, or a television show. Suggested sources: the *New York Times, The Washington Post, The New Yorker,* and *Time.* Notice the difference between the two points of view—and the similarities. Do both reviews appear to use the criteria presented in this chapter?

2 Write a review of a current film. Read your review to the class and discuss other interpretations.

3 After attending a stage production, survey several audience members about their reactions. Compare the results to your own evaluation. Think about what might account for the discrepancies.

4 Choose a small group to review a current television show. Each of you will write a complete review. Then get together to present and discuss your impressions.

5 Read the scene from *A Star Ain't Nothin' but a Hole in Heaven* by Judi Ann Mason found in Unit Eight, and write a short critique of the dialogue and the general appeal.

"A good drama critic is one who perceives what is happening in the theatre of his time. A great drama critic also perceives what is not happening."

—Kenneth Tynan, British theatre critic

Theatre **Then** and **Now**

Strong Views and Famous Feuds

Alexander Pope: Brilliant Early English Critic

Critic, poet, essayist, and playwright Alexander Pope was born in England in 1688, the son of a Roman Catholic merchant. During those days, Catholics suffered from repressive legislation, which denied young Pope access to both a university education and public employment. He would have had very little education had it not been for an aunt who taught him to read. He went on to learn Latin and Greek from a local priest. Sometimes he attended secret Catholic schools, but for the most part, he steadily consumed his father's large library. According to one relative, he "did nothing but write and read." In 1711 he contracted Potts disease, a form of spinal tuberculosis, which resulted in a severe curvature of the spine. As a grown man he was only four feet six inches tall. His deformity made him the object of ridicule, but as time went on, no one could dispute his brilliance. At the age of twenty-three he published a monumental work called *An Essay on Criticism*. In it he penned an ironic line that is still used today: "A little learning is a dangerous thing."

Alexander Pope

Pope was famous not only for his witty satires and his brilliant, quotable essays, but also for his bitter feuds with other writers. When one of his literary works was attacked by his peers, he shot back with a raucously savage poetic send-up entitled *The Dunciad*. In it he ridiculed bad writers, scientists, and critics. A representative line reads: "While pensive poets painful vigils keep, / Sleepless themselves to give their readers sleep."

He was a man of small worldly experience but wide learning. There wasn't much that didn't interest him, including, late in his life, the study of horticulture and landscape gardening. He scored huge successes with excellent translations of Homer's *Iliad* and *Odyssey*. In 1717, with the publication of his collected writings, cantankerous Alexander Pope became one of the leading literary figures of his day. He died in 1744.

Robert Brustein: Feisty Critic for Our Time

Born in 1927, Robert Brustein has developed many talents throughout his life. He is a respected critic, teacher, director, playwright, and one of America's leading thinkers on the subject of, among other things, the theatre. He does not shy away from thorny issues, as you might be able to tell from a quick scan of the titles of some of his books of theatre criticism and commentary: *The Theatre of Revolt* (1964), *Who Needs Theatre?* (1986), and *Dumbocracy in America* (1994).

Brustein is credited with bringing dramaturgy (see Spotlight on the Dramaturg on page 157) into America by way of academia, which then brought it into the theatre community at large. As a professor at Yale University, he lobbied to move the study of theatre criticism from the English Department to the Drama Department.

He believed that theatre critics must be something more than just enlightened audience members. To that end, his students learned the basics of acting, directing, and the technical side of theatre. In addition to learning the ins and outs of journalism, they studied plays and playwrights. This caused some turmoil within the program and brought about a split that divided future theatre critics/journalists from future theatre professionals/dramaturgs. The American theatre community suddenly had a corps of highly educated dramaturgs. And over time, it found a way to make use of them.

In recent years, Brustein grabbed the spotlight by locking horns with celebrated playwright August Wilson (see Master of the Craft on page 149) in a very public and emotional debate over the politics and racial implications of contemporary theatre funding. The debate, complete with name-calling, developed into a full-scale feud between two great men of the theatre.

Robert Brustein

PREVIEW

Examine the following key concepts previewed in Unit Six.

1 Most musicals have two directors. Who are they and what do they do?

2 Which of the following are important considerations when choosing a musical for your school?
   a. length   b. humor   c. money
   d. space   e. cast   f. audience

3 What is Bunraku?

4 Is it important to write poetry about things you care about? Why or why not?

5 Compare the dramatic structure of a movie to that of live theatre.

6 What do the abbreviations INT., EXT., O.C., P.O.V., and V.O. stand for?

7 Explain how film, TV, electronic media, and the theatre may be interdependent.

8 What are the four phases of filmmaking, and what do they entail?

9 What is a demographic, and why is it important to a television writer?

PREPARE

Assess your response to the preparation process for projects in this unit.

10 Did you find it more difficult to write character sketches or the plot synopsis for your musical? Why?

11 As you prepared your performance poem, did the ideas and images flow freely or was it a struggle to find the right words? Give details.

12 Do you think it is easier to write an original screenplay or a screenplay adapted from a play? Explain your answer.

13 Compare the challenges in writing a proposal for a TV episode to those of writing a proposal for a new musical.

PRESENT

Analyze the experience of presenting your work to the class.

14 In creating your presentations, which medium did you find the most interesting—musical theatre, film, television, or other theatre forms? Why?

15 Were you able to remember all the important points you wanted to make in presenting your proposal for a new musical? Explain.

16 What were your impressions of sharing your poetry in a slam format? Would you like to do it again? Why or why not?

17 How did you present your screenplay concept? Would you do it differently next time? Explain.

18 Were you able to use any unusual or inventive ways to make any of your presentations? Discuss them.

CRITIQUE

Evaluate how you go about critiquing your work and the work of others.

19 Did the comments, questions, and other feedback after presenting your outline for a TV episode encourage you to write the episode?

20 What did you learn about your own work while critiquing the work of others?

21 Do you feel that most students are sensitive and fair in their evaluations of classmates' work? Explain.

EXTENSIONS

- Choose any art form that interests you and create a short performance piece based upon it.

- Create a ten-minute video using only inanimate objects as your characters.

- Write and perform a theme song for a new television show about a ten-year-old who finds a tiny universe of aliens dressed in formal attire in her bedroom closet.

Unit
Seven

Exploring Theatre History

To know the development and historical underpinnings of theatre is to understand the development of the human race. As the theatre grows, civilization grows; when theatre flourishes, human culture flourishes; when theatre is suppressed, people live in darkness. Study the theatre of a particular era and you will learn the religious, social, political, and economic influences of that time. You will learn the people's desires, their ideals, and their needs. Perhaps more importantly, looking into the past helps give you insight into the present. A comparison of past eras not only emphasizes the evolution of drama, but also furthers your understanding of the theatre of today, and it points the way to the theatre of tomorrow.

Part One The Dawn of Theatre

Primitive Peoples

Drama, a Greek word, means "to do" or "to act." But drama itself is much older than the Greek civilization. It was born out of the dance ceremonies of primitive people, when instinctive rhythmic movements and the desire to imitate evolved into pantomimes that told of various tribal traditions or rites of passage.

> **Theatre Terms**
> pacify
> ritual
> shaman

There were initiation dances to teach the tribe's customs to boys approaching manhood, war dances to kindle bravery in young warriors, story dances to enact events of a hunt or a great battle, and religious dances to **pacify** or try to satisfy the numerous unseen spirits that these tribes believed controlled the world.

From these religious dances evolved a **ritual.** The chief representative of the gods—the medicine man, **shaman,** witch doctor, or priest—donned a mask believed to have powerful magic and prayed, chanted, and danced in an attempt to drive away evil spirits while the tribe assisted or watched. Out of this religious ritual, performed in a circle in front of the temple, drama began to emerge.

Today, we can still see some of these dramatic forms in the dances of South African and Australian tribes. Remnants of ancient ritual are equally evident in Hawaiian hula and American Indian dances, such as the snake dance, the corn dance, and the sun dance.

Egyptian Theatre

As far as we know, the Egyptians were the first people whose ritualistic rites took a form very similar to our idea of a play, performing them as early as 3000 B.C. The Egyptian people were very concerned with life after death. The rulers of Egypt,

> **Theatre Terms**
> hieroglyphics
> pharaohs

called **pharaohs,** and other wealthy citizens built huge pyramids and furnished them with great splendor, for they intended to dwell there in the afterworld. This philosophy of life and death is illustrated in their dramas, which were sometimes written in **hieroglyphics** on the walls of tombs.

Plays were often written for important events, such as the coronation of a new pharaoh or an important year in the pharaoh's rule. Some plays revolved around magical healing, and some were religious dramas written on tomb walls and enacted by priests.

The hieroglyphics adorning the hallowed walls of this Egyptian tomb display one of the first forms of theatre.

Hebrew Theatre

Although dance and ritual are mentioned in the **Old Testament,** there is no reference to a definite theatre in Judea. However, two books of the Bible read as dramatic literature. *The Song of Solomon,* which was probably chanted at wedding festivals, contains beautiful poetic dialogue spoken by a bride and groom.

> **Theatre Terms**
> Book of Job
> Old Testament

The play *J.B.,* by Archibald MacLeish, is based on the Book of Job.

The **Book of Job** has many of the elements of a five-act drama with a prologue and epilogue. There is no record, though, of its having ever been performed in ancient times. Today it is usually classified as dramatic poetry rather than drama. However, there have been several modern versions of the story that have been successfully adapted for the stage.

Greek Theatre

The legacy of the ancient Greek theatre has never been surpassed. Only the Elizabethans came close to achieving such a wealth of plays. The Classic, or Golden Age, of Greece (500–400 B.C.) brought human civilization the greatest tragedies of all time, as well as outstanding creativity in such fields as architecture and government.

> ## Theatre Terms
> City Dionysia
> *deus ex machina*
> dithyrambs
> mantle
> *periaktois*
> rhetorical
> skene
> thespian

A Festival of Theatre

Greek theatre had its beginnings in the religious rites that paid homage to Dionysus, the god of wine and fertility. These public celebrations were held around stone altars at the foot of hilly vineyards. There was much dancing and singing of hymns, called **dithyrambs,** to honor Dionysus, and as these religious celebrations gained popularity, choral groups were organized with vocal contests among them.

Out of these dithyrambic rituals developed tragedy, which literally means "goat song" (*tragos* in Greek). There is disagreement among scholars as to why it was called this. There are several possibilities. Perhaps the chorus wore goatskins, or they draped the altar with one. Another theory is that a goat was sacrificed at the end of the festival as an offering to the gods. It is possible that all of these were true.

Of the four Dionysian festivals, the one held in March, the **City Dionysia,** developed into a festival of tragedies, where a coveted prize was awarded to the best series of plays. The festival, which took place in Athens, was both a national and religious ceremony. Since business was suspended for a week, everyone participated. Crowds came from the surrounding villages, and if someone could not afford the nominal ticket price, the state would pay their entrance fee. Both men and women attended, although theatre production and acting were restricted to males (as was the case worldwide for many centuries).

The annual festival lasted five or six days. The first day included a procession that carried the image of Dionysus to the city limits where people spent their time performing religious rites, drinking wine, singing, and making merry. At night the image was returned to the theatre (*theatron* in Greek, or "seeing place") by candlelight.

The final three days were reserved for the play contests. Each day a different dramatist was featured, offering four plays: a trilogy of tragedies and a satire that provided comic relief after the three heavier plays. At the end of the festival, the winning author and his financial backer (*choregus*) were allowed to wear the coveted ivy garland on their heads.

Dug out of the slope under the south side of the Acropolis in the late 16th century B.C., the Theatre of Dionysus was the center for presenting the works of the great Greek playwrights Euripides, Aeschylus, and Sophocles. It was rebuilt many times, so its original shape is difficult to determine.

Comedies (from *komos,* meaning "a band of revelers") were sometimes performed in the afternoon during the City Dionysia. However, most comedies were performed at the Lenaea Festival (in early February), where prizes were awarded for the best comic writer.

Greek Plays in Performance

Plays were performed outdoors. At first, the theatre consisted of crude benches placed on a sloping hill and looking down on a circle of hard-packed ground where the chorus performed around an altar. Later, the side of the mountain was scooped out into a bowl shape, something like our amphitheatres today, and tiers of stone seats in concentric semicircles were built on the hill. These theatres provided seating for up to 20,000, with a special first row reserved for dignitaries. The acting area, called the orchestra, was the circular space marked out on the ground at the foot of the hill. It varied from 65 feet to 85 feet in diameter.

The actors changed costumes in the **skene,** a small building first situated at the side of the orchestra and later permanently placed behind it. The skene, from which we derive the word *scene,* had three doors through which actors would enter. To the right and left between the skene and the orchestra was a wide passageway, called the *parodos,* which was used for the chorus to enter and exit. Eventually, a platform called a *proskenion* (from which we get the term *proscenium*) was placed in front of the skene for the actors. On each side, two wings called the *paraskenia* were introduced.

Since the theatre was large and the distance between audience and playing area was great, the drama was **rhetorical,** containing more speech than action. The actors used broad gestures and a declamatory vocal style. To be seen by the audience, the actor made himself taller by wearing thick-soled shoes, called *cothurnus,* and a high headpiece, called an *onkus.* In addition, he wore a wooden, cork, or linen mask that fit over his entire head. These masks not only denoted character, station in life, and emotion, they also projected the actor's voice through a type of inside megaphone.

Actors perform a Greek drama in traditional masks.

From left to right, the *chiton*, *himation*, and *chlamys* of the ancient Greek attire.

Costumes of both the actor and the chorus consisted of standard Greek attire: the sleeveless *chiton,* or tunic, belted below the breast; the *himation,* or long **mantle,** draped around the right shoulder; and the *chlamys,* or short cloak. These costumes were very colorful and often featured elaborately embroidered patterns.

Staging was accomplished simply with the use of *pinakes,* or scenery painted on boards and placed against the skene, and *periaktois,* triangular prisms that could be revolved for scenery changes. A few properties were also used. Drums were sounded for thunder, and the *eccyclema,* a small wagon platform, was wheeled on to show a corpse to the audience (all killing had to occur off-stage and be reported to the audience by the chorus or a messenger). The *deus ex machina,* or "god in the machine," was a unique mechanical crane used for lowering and raising gods. The term is still used today for any plot device, such as the death of a rich uncle, that unexpectedly occurs to assist the main character in the convenient solution of a major problem.

The Great Greek Playwrights

The Greek tragedies were based on ancient myths, which were well known to the audience. Most of the plays encompassed certain elements that Aristotle (384–322 B.C.) later identified in his *Poetics.* (See pages 139–140 for more about Aristotle's *Poetics.*)

The first tragedian to win the City Dionysia playwriting prize was Thespis.

In his plays that year (534 B.C.), he introduced a leader for the chorus. The leader spoke, and the chorus responded in chants. Thus, the leader became the first Greek actor. Thespis also instigated another first in his drama: the use of masks. It is from his name that the word *thespian* comes—another way of saying *actor*.

Three great writers of tragedy developed during the Golden Age. Some of their plays have survived and are still performed today.

Aeschylus (525–456 B.C.) has been called the Father of Tragedy. He is considered by many scholars to be the greatest tragic poet of all time. Aeschylus frequently participated in the City Dionysia, winning first prize thirteen times. He is credited with inventing the trilogy and adding a second actor to the plays. He reduced the chorus from fifty to twelve, but that honored group still handled most of the play, relating the events and setting the mood. Aeschylus loved spectacle, and his plays abounded with it. He had one character, Prometheus

The Colosseum, Rome's ancient arena of death and slaughter, reopened its gates for the first time in 1500 years for this performance of *Oedipus Rex*.

(who steals fire and gives it to humans), fall from a cliff. He dressed the Furies (spirits of revenge who chase down those who do not atone for their sins) in such frightful masks that women and children fainted at the sight of them. Of Aeschylus's ninety plays, only seven survive, of which the Oresteia trilogy may be the most enduring.

Sophocles (496–406 B.C.) is the second great writer of tragedies. He was a handsome, well-educated man of many talents: musician, singer, and athlete. He was also interested in civic affairs, becoming the treasurer of Athens. Sophocles, like Aeschylus, had a brilliant career in theatre. He wrote more than a hundred scripts and won eighteen Dionysia festivals. In his plays, he introduced a third actor and changed the number of chorus members to fifteen. Sophocles was a polished literary craftsman who had keen theatrical sense. His plays feature beautiful language, a well-balanced plot, and excellent character development. Today his work is considered the essence of great Greek drama. The best known of his seven surviving plays are *Electra, Oedipus Rex,* and *Antigone.*

Euripides (480–406 B.C.), although apparently good at boxing and painting, confined himself to a literary life. He would often retire to a cave overlooking the sea, and there he would meditate and write. Euripides was an unorthodox thinker who questioned traditional religious ideas. His plays emphasize psychological motivations and social consciousness, particularly accentuating the plight of women and the problem of the outsider. He was the first to humanize drama with little household details and events that appealed to the emotions. His *Medea* is a potent tragedy that shows the mental anguish of Medea, a woman driven mad by jealousy. In *Alcestis,* Euripides created a play that combined both the serious and the humorous.

Besides these three great tragedians, two writers of comedy gained note.

Aristophanes (circa 448–380 B.C.) is considered the finest comic writer of ancient Greece. His biting, bawdy satires, such as *The Birds, The Frogs,* and *The Clouds* abound with humorous ideas and bold attacks.

Menander (circa 342–291 B.C.) was also a celebrated writer of comedy. Unlike Aristophanes, who wrote about aspects of public life, Menander lampooned domestic or private life. His plays are filled with cunning servants, parasitic relatives, protective fathers, and young lovers. Until the 20th century, only fragments of Menander's plays were known; our knowledge of his work was understood mainly from ancient Roman writers who copied him extensively. But in 1957, the complete work of Menander's *The Curmudgeon,* a farce full of physical and slapstick humor, was discovered.

Greek drama began to deteriorate as Caesar's armies marched over the land. From the seeds of Greek drama, the victorious Romans established their theatre.

Roman Theatre

As the Romans invaded, they began to take special interest in Greek literature and art. Soon, Rome's crude native drama was replaced by translations and adaptations of Greek plays.

The Roman aristocracy frowned upon theatre, so audiences consisted mainly of the lower classes. They wanted entertainment. Scoffing at the art-loving and intellectual, they demanded spectacle and vulgarity. Thus, the imitated Greek theatre became decadent and hollow. Tragedies gradually degenerated and comedies slipped into common slapstick.

The Circus Maximus, where charioteers raced around the track.

The Stage and the Playwrights

Because the Roman senate was hostile to theatre, the Roman playhouses were merely portable wooden platforms around which the audience stood. But in 61 B.C., the Roman leader Pompey had a huge outdoor auditorium built. In order to make it legal, he erected a small statue of Venus at the top and called it a temple of worship. The steps of this temple, of course, served as seats for the theatre.

Not to be outdone, the next Roman emperor, Caesar, ordered a playhouse built that was in the shape of two wooden theatres, back to back, each of which could be revolved to face the other. After a play presentation, the seats could be swung around into an amphitheatre for chariot races and gladiatorial contests.

The Romans were the first to use a front curtain. It rolled up and down from a trough in the downstage floor. Roman theatre also instigated the **claque,** a person or persons paid to arouse the audience into clapping and shouting. (For more on Roman theatres, see page 206.)

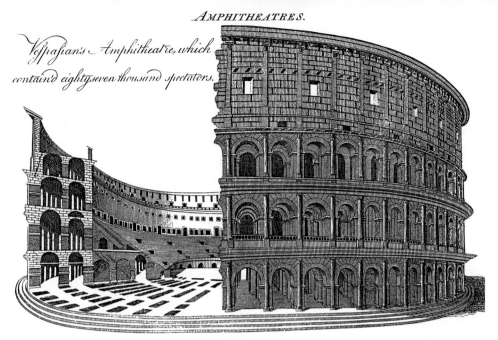

Vespasian's Amphitheatre, which contain'd eightyseven thousand spectators.

This ancient amphitheatre seated 80,000 spectators.

Seneca (circa 4 B.C.–65 A.D.) was a major Roman dramatist. His plays are so bombastic and full of gory details, however, that they are more effective as **closet drama** (plays to be read rather than performed).

The comic writer **Plautus** (254–184 B.C.) is important mainly because his plays served as a pattern for later writers. His *Menaechmi* influenced Shakespeare's *Comedy of Errors,* and his *Pot of Gold* served as Molière's pattern for *The Miser.*

The Fall of Roman Theatre
Soon Roman theatrical activity gained impetus, with plays and other entertainment being presented for every holiday—and there were many Roman holidays—up to 175 at one point, which would have occupied about six months' time.

The production of plays was eventually overshadowed by sensational spectacles. In the coliseums, gladiatorial contests were interspersed with Christians being fed to lions. Special arenas called *naumachiaes* were filled with water, and slaves on ships fought until all hands were killed.

Finally, theatre entertainment became so base that when Rome fell in 475 A.D., the Christian church banned all theatrical activity. For hundreds of years afterward, theatre lay dormant throughout the continent. The East, however, did not suffer the darkness of Europe. Instead, theatrical forms that had been nurtured from years past, gained momentum throughout India and the Orient.

Chinese Theatre

The beginning of Chinese drama dates back to 2000 B.C., when **interpretative dance,** that is, dance that tells a story, became more dramatic in form as ancestor worship and military celebrations were staged. These early performances, however, were not presented as entertainment. The Chinese revered their ancestors; dramatic ritual was solely religious with only the emperor, the priests, and the court as participants and audience.

The Blossoming of Chinese Drama

Later, the religious rituals developed into definite plays, but it was not until the 8th and 9th centuries A.D. that Chinese drama blossomed, led by Emperor Ming Huang (713–756 A.D.), who founded a school for actors in his garden. The school was so successful that Chinese actors are traditionally called "Children of the Pear Tree Garden." Ming Huang continues as the patron saint of Chinese theatre, and actors traditionally burn incense to his statue before they begin a performance.

The drama of Ming Huang's time was highly formal. It dealt primarily with three themes: ancestor worship, military glory, and faithfulness to a husband. It was written in classical Chinese that only the exceptionally well educated could understand. This classical tradition changed, however, when the Mongols invaded in 1280 A.D. Lacking

A Peking Opera production being performed in present-day Beijing.

in cultural background, the Mongols demanded action, acrobatic stunts, songs, and dances. It was in this period that such plays as *The Chalk Circle* and *The Lute Song* were written.

The dramas associated with the Mongolian influence became traditional theatre, and throughout the centuries, they were enacted in their original form until the Communists took over China after World War II. After 1949, the Communist government rewrote many of the classical plays using them to preach government policy.

The Peking Opera

Because Chinese drama features chanting, singing, and musical accompaniment, Westerners began calling it **Peking Opera**. Traditional Peking Opera can still be seen today, along with new trends that reveal the influences of the West. Although Chinese drama may seem unusual and exotic to the Western world, its symbolic quality has influenced the writing of many plays, including Thornton Wilder's *Our Town*. (See page 330 for more on the Peking Opera.)

Most of the acting is done by men, who also take women's parts. Acting is regarded as a life study. It uses movements and poses that are highly symbolic. The stylized traditional movements are graceful, and every gesture means something specific. For example, a sleeve passed over the eye denotes weeping; a shaking of the shoulders signifies grief.

Props also have symbolic meaning. White paper falling from a red umbrella means snow; a man with a whip indicates that he is on horseback; an actor carrying a flag indicates an army; a flag with wavy lines symbolizes a river. An onstage prop man, dressed in black, hands properties to the actor. The actors wear dazzling costumes and thick makeup in which color signifies character: red means faithfulness; blue, cruelty; white, evil; and so on. The greatest influence of Chinese drama has been on the theatre of Japan.

Japanese Theatre

Early drama in Japan was probably based on the ritualistic dance of the Shinto religion, but in the 14th century the Japanese **Noh** plays appeared. Similar in form and content to Chinese drama, these pieces were written in a formal, classical language meant only for the aristocrats. They remain remarkably unchanged and are still performed in Japan today. They are short, serious, philosophical studies that combine poetry with dance and music. The dance is completely unlike Western dance, which tends to feature vigorous movements. Instead, Japanese Noh movements

> **Theatre Terms**
> **Bunraku**
> **flowerway**
> **Kabuki**
> **Kyogen**
> **Noh**

A Japanese woodcut by Okumura Masanobu of a Kyogen play being performed before a large audience in the 1700s.

comprise a series of sedate postures in which a specific attitude is expressed.

Noh Drama

Noh stages are always built to specific measurements. They are wooden 18-foot squares, with the audience sitting on three sides. The stage's pointed roof, a carryover from the early days when Noh plays were performed outside, is similar to that of a Shinto shrine and is supported by four pillars. The floor is of highly polished Japanese cypress, specially constructed with large empty jars underneath to provide a unique resonant sound when the actor thumps his feet at a climactic moment.

The characters enter from the green-room off stage right by means of a narrow upstage corridor. As each character enters, he bows to the audience, announces his name, where he has come from, and what he will do. The

chorus, which consists of six to eight men, sits on stage left and provides chanting background music.

Scenery consists of a pine tree tapestry hung on the back wall. Only essential properties are used, and they are often a suggestion rather than an actual representation of the object. For example, a folding fan the actor uses for his various acting poses may at times suggest a dagger, a tray, or a letter, depending on what is needed.

Costumes are ornate silks, worn by all characters whether they are rich or poor. The cut of the costume and the makeup differentiate social class. Major actors wear carved wooden masks that have stereotyped expressions from one of the fifteen standard masks allowed in Noh plays. To offset the often depressing, foreboding quality of the Noh plot, the **Kyogen** was developed to serve as a comic interlude. Kyogens are farcical comedies performed without music and without masks. Usually five Nohs are presented at one performance, interspersed with three Kyogens. (For more on Noh drama, see page 310.)

Bunraku

In the 17th century another form of Japanese theatre became popular. **Bunraku,** or doll theatre, features four-foot-tall, full-body wooden marionettes, carved in such realistic detail that eyelids, eyebrows, mouth, and fingers can all be moved. Each doll is elaborately costumed. While narrators read the dialogue and a musician plays, three attendants dressed in black and wearing gauze masks (a convention that tells the audience to regard them as invisible) manipulate the dolls. (See page 342 for more on Bunraku.)

Kabuki Theatre

The Japanese drama of the common man is called **Kabuki,** which incorporates song and dance, and is thought to be more melodramatic and sensational than Noh drama. Kabukis have a wide range of subject matter. There are heavy, tension-filled historical tragedies that realistically portray scenes of suicide, murder, and torture; there are domestic love triangles; and there are unspoken dance dramas that often feature grotesque demons.

The Kabuki playhouse uses a wide extended platform, but it dispenses with the roof, pillars, and bridge of the Noh theatre. Actors enter from a **flowerway,** a ramp that extends through the audience from the back of the auditorium up to the stage. The stage floor contains trapdoors where actors may also make spectacular entrances and exits.

Kabuki utilizes colorful, extravagant scenery. Since 1793, most Kabuki theatres have been equipped with a revolving stage, which allows quick and impressive scene shifting. In recent years, theatrical devices such as the ramp, trapdoor, and revolving stage have been borrowed from Japan by the Western world.

Kabuki is noted for its lavish use of elaborate and colorful silk costumes. Although Kabuki actors do not use masks, they apply stylized masklike makeup. The actors wear wigs that denote their character's station, personality, and age; these wigs can weigh as much as twenty-five pounds. (For more about Kabuki, see page 30.)

In both Kabuki and Noh, acting skill is all-important. Actors are traditionally men who are versatile at impersonating women. Today, it is legal for women to act in Kabuki, although few do. For centuries the torch of the acting profession in Japan has been passed along family lines, with children as young as five sometimes appearing onstage as they begin their lifelong profession.

Acting follows the Chinese tradition. It is highly symbolic, presentational, and rhythmic, moving slowly from one studied pose to another. Even the tilt of the finger or the flutter of an eyelash has meaning and can evoke a certain mood in the audience.

Hindu Theatre

Dramatic form in India is ancient, dating back to 1500 B.C., when dialogue was used in religious hymns. According to Hindu mythology, Brahma invented theatre and commanded the first playhouse be built; but real theatre did not emerge until the 5th century B.C. Plays were composed in **Sanskrit,** the literary language used and understood only by the aristocrats. In fact, most Hindu drama was for the upper classes, being performed in either the gardens or courtyards of the palaces or in specially built palace playhouses.

The stage was situated at one end of the room with the audience sitting around. The only scenery was a decorated wall with doors leading to the **greenroom,** a place where the actors changed and relaxed before and after performances.

Lord Shiva, disguised as a hunter, in the Sanskrit drama *Mahabharata*.

The tradition continues, and today almost every theatre and TV studio has a greenroom.

Theatre patrons had a great love of beauty, and Hindu theatre is very intimate, delicate, and restrained. It is performed strictly for pleasant entertainment, with the plays always ending happily. As far as we know, Hindu theatre was the first to permit women to act onstage. (For more on Sanskrit drama, see page 298.)

> **Theatre Terms**
> greenroom
> Sanskrit

Suggested Projects

1 From current articles, such as those in *National Geographic* magazine, report on the drama of another culture. Show pictures if possible.

2 Draw an idea for a mask that might symbolize a great warrior, an elder leader, a shaman, or a clown.

3 Research and report on some aspect of ancient Egyptian civilization. Use visual aids in your report.

4 Read and report on one of the plays below. Analyze the physical, emotional, and social dimensions of the characters.

> *Agamemnon, Libation Bearers, The Furies,* or *Prometheus Bound* by Aeschylus
> *Oedipus Rex, Antigone,* or *Electra* by Sophocles
> *Medea* or *Alcestis* by Euripides
> *The Curmudgeon* by Menander

5 Read several Japanese haiku, then choose one to read to the class. Discuss how this literary form relates to Japanese acting.

6 Study the puppets of the Far East, including the Japanese doll theatre, Bunraku. Make a puppet in the tradition of the Far East, and share it with the class. (See Haar's *Japanese Theatre,* pages 43–87, for excellent pictures and information on Bunraku.)

7 Report on contemporary theatre trends in China, including recent developments in Peking Opera.

8 Use an Internet site, such as didaskalia.berkeley.edu to learn all you can about ancient Greek theatres. Based on your findings, create a model or drawing of one of them.

9 With two or three classmates, work on a scene from a famous Sanskrit drama, such as *The Fatal Ring* or *Little Clay Cart.* Act out the scene for the class.

The Middle Ages to 1800

Medieval Theatre

The Middle Ages in Europe was a period often called the Dark Ages because there was little or no cultural activity. The Middle Ages began with the fall of Rome in 476 A.D. and continued until the 15th century. **Feudalism,** in which peasants worked land and paid rent to land-owning lords, was the political system of the time. Poverty and illiteracy among the masses was common. Travel and the exchange of ideas all but vanished. For approximately 400 years there was no theatre, except for sparse folk festivals and a few wandering jugglers and minstrels, who managed to stir the theatrical coals that were routinely extinguished by the church.

Theatre Terms

cycles
feudalism
guilds
mansions
miracle play
morality play
mystery play
passion play
trope

Theatre Born of the Church

Strange as it may seem, the church that buried drama in the 5th century resurrected that same art sometime during the 9th century when it introduced the **trope,** short drama-tized scenes, into the mass. The trope began in France, but the idea soon spread throughout the European subcontinent. At first, brief Easter and Nativity tableaus (representa-tions of a scene performed by motion-less people in costume) were given to help the illiterate congregation under-stand the service. Pantomimes devel-oped, which soon gave way to dialogue, first in Latin and then in the common language. Priests and choirboys enacted this religious drama. The scenes became so popular that whole stories began to be enacted. Small platforms called **man-sions,** or stations, were placed within the cathedral. Separate scenes were per-formed on these with the crowd moving from one mansion to another until they had seen the whole story.

Three types of plays were presented in the Middle Ages.

1 **Mystery plays** Bible stories re-enacted

2 **Miracle plays** Enacting the lives of the saints

3 **Morality plays** Stories teaching right from wrong in which characters personified abstract qualities.

An excellent example of a morality play is *Everyman,* which is still performed today. As Everyman journeys to Death, his Friends, Worldly Goods, and so on, all leave him. Only Good Deeds accompanies him to the grave.

In the 10th century, a nun, Hrosvitha, wrote religious comedy that was performed on the cathedral mansions.

An early artist's interpretation of a scene from a miracle play.

Drama in the church became boisterous when comedy was added, and the crowds became so large that in the 13th or 14th century, the mansions were moved outside to the marketplace. The comedy vein persisted: Herod became a devil and the audience laughed at his antics; Noah's wife stubbornly refused to enter the ark and had to be carried inside kicking and screaming; devils with pitchforks prodded the wicked.

Staging the Plays

Elaborate staging devices were contrived, such as Hell's Mouth, which would open and close amid smoke and flames, as well as a rack that exhibited tortured souls, complete with realistic screams. Eventually, the trade **guilds** (unions) sponsored the plays, with each guild presenting an applicable episode. The shipbuilders staged Noah's Ark;

A recent European passion play is presented just as it was in the Middle Ages.

the cooks handled Hell's Mouth, since they were used to smoke and flames. Each scene was prepared in great detail and was carefully rehearsed. The productions, which were often quite spectacular, were presented to throngs of people on festival days in an atmosphere of gaiety and fun.

In England, France, and the Netherlands, pageant wagons were often used instead of stationary mansions. These were double-decker wagons. The lower story was curtained off and served as a changing room. The play's action was staged on the upper level and sometimes on the street around the wagon. Audience members would find vantage points and remain there as the wagons were brought to them, episode by episode— something like our parade floats today. In England the plays performed on pageant wagons were called **cycles,** and they were given in the spring on Corpus Christi day. Four of these cycles still exist: those of York, Chester, Wakefield, and Coventry. These old plays are periodically performed today in England during special summer festivals. (For more about medieval staging and pageant wagons, see page 230.)

The **passion play** evolved during the late Middle Ages. It depicted scenes from Christ's life, particularly the last days of his suffering and his resurrection. Of these, the passion play at Oberammergau, Germany, is still performed. More than 300 years ago, residents of that small village prayed that if they were spared the black plague that was laying waste to the continent, they would periodically dramatize a passion play. Their village was spared, and they kept their vow. In 1633 they presented their first play. Since then, the Oberammergau Passion Play has been performed every ten years, at the turn of the decade. Only in 1940, during WWII, were the townspeople unable to give a show. Today thousands throng to see this intriguing play from the past. Similar passion plays, though on a smaller scale, are enacted in the United States in Spearfish, South Dakota; Lake Wales, Florida; and Eureka Springs, Arkansas.

The effects of medieval theatre would be felt in later drama. Because audience members were brought close to the performers, and because the playing area provided increased freedom, the art of acting became as important as the dialogue. Medieval drama also brought in a mixture of the comic and the serious, a combination that would be imitated by both the improvisational players in Italy and the Elizabethan writers in England.

Renaissance Theatre

The Renaissance, which means "rebirth" in French, took place largely in the 15th and 16th centuries, and was an exciting time for theatre. As the ancient classic

A scene from a recent American production of a *commedia dell'arte* play by Molière.

writers were rediscovered, a rebirth of learning occurred throughout Europe, with vigorous activity in all of the arts and sciences. The Renaissance started in Italy, and men such as Petrarch, Leonardo da Vinci, Michelangelo, and Machiavelli contributed to a great flowering of knowledge and ideas.

Italian Theatre of the Renaissance

An important form of theatre that originated in Italy at this time was the *commedia dell'arte.* Developed years before from mimes and pantomimes that may have been remnants of ancient Roman comedy, this art was flourishing by 1550. *Commedia dell'arte* was professional improvised comedy performed in the streets for the masses. A company, consisting usually of seven men and three women, would ad lib action, dialogue, song, and dance around a scenario that usually involved love and intrigue. To improvise effectively,

actors had to be inventive, clever, and witty, with agile bodies for the many acrobatic stunts, fights, and dances.

Stock characters developed: Harlequin, who wore patches that later evolved into the stylized diamond costume still used today, was the clever, witty servant; Pierrot was love-lorn and moody; Columbine was flirtatious and pretty; Pantalone, who wore baggy trousers (and from whom we derive the word *pantaloons*), was the gullible father. The cast of a *commedia dell'arte,* which included the first women on the stage since Indian drama, wore half masks. The popularity of this art form spread throughout Europe and was particularly well received in France, where it would later influence the writings of Molière. (For more on *commedia dell'arte,* see page 38.)

> **Theatre Terms**
> *commedia dell'arte*
> **neoclassicism**

Spanish Theatre of the Renaissance

While Italy was developing its *commedia* and opera, Spain became interested in drama. From about 1550 to 1680, Spanish theatre flourished. It was influenced by both *commedia dell'arte* and Italian court staging. Three major playwrights evolved at this time: Miguel de Cervantes (1547–1616), who is better known today for the novel *Don Quixote* than for his 30 plays; Lope de Vega (1562–1635), who wrote a phenomenal 2000 plays, many of them full of beautiful poetry, vigorous action, and dashing romance; and Calderon (1600–1681), who created 200 plays, which were distinguished by their spiritual emphasis and elevated poetry.

These dramatists were all successful in establishing an original art form, free from the classical rules that fettered so many Italian and French writers. Spanish dramatists, ignoring the unities of time and place, wrote beautiful flowing dialogue and centered their action around adventure, romance, and chivalry.

French Renaissance Theatre

Because of France's many wars, and because one theatre group had exclusive rights to the public playhouse, the Renaissance came late to French theatre, reaching its height during the 17th century. At that time the increased theatre activity gave rise to **neoclassicism,** a form in which dramatists were supposed to observe the classic unities and write in a restricted verse form. This French drama developed into entertainment mainly for royalty. Playhouses were ornate, with carvings

This open-air production of *Entremeses* by Miguel de Cervantes was performed in Guanajuato, Mexico.

washed in gold, velvet-covered seats, and lavish drapes, following the Italian tradition of luxurious surroundings for the nobles.

Molière (1622–1673) represents the high point of French Renaissance drama. He wrote such witty satire that his plays continue to entertain audiences around the world. Molière's real name was Jean-Baptiste Poquelin, but when he chose the theatre as his life's work, he also chose another name so that his parents would not be disgraced by having an actor in the family.

Molière toured for twelve years as an actor in a *commedia dell'arte* company. As he began to write comedies, he drew from the *commedia's* farcical style. His many plays, performed both for the public and for the court of Louis XIV, are masterpieces of satire, a perfect blend of the humorous and the caustic. In *The Doctor in Spite of Himself,* Molière lampoons the field of medicine; in *Tartuffe* he satirizes hypocrisy; in *The Imaginary Invalid* he spoofs hypochondria. Throughout his writing career, Molière continued to act. In his last years he was ill from tuberculosis, and, ironically, he died onstage just after completing a performance of *The Imaginary Invalid.* (For more about Molière, see page 132.)

Although the theatrical activity in Italy and Spain (and later, in France) advanced Renaissance drama, it was not in these countries where drama realized its greatest potential. Instead, we look to England for a unique form that reached staggering heights.

Elizabethan Theatre

Elizabeth and the Playwrights

There was great vitality, zest, and intellectual curiosity throughout England during Queen Elizabeth I's reign (1558–1603). Her country swelled with national pride over its voyages of discovery, its defeat of the Spanish armada, its expanding trade markets, and its increased literary vistas—the result of the introduction of printed books in 1475.

When Elizabeth became queen of England, the theatre gained a friend, for even though the Lord Mayor and other civil authorities were hostile to drama (because of the fear that the crowds would spread disease and start fights), Elizabeth loved the theatre. She commanded many court performances, protected groups of players through court sponsorship, and looked upon London's feverish dramatic activity with approval.

The Elizabethan period was an age of literary enlightenment. There were many brilliant playwrights, and most of them wrote with great freedom, disregarding the classic unities of time and

> **Theatre Terms**
> discovery space
> groundlings
> masques
> soliloquies
> tiring house
> Wooden O's

place, and the rule—left over from the ancient Greeks—that violence should not be seen on stage. Moreover, they mixed poetry with prose and interspersed comedy with tragedy. Competent though they were, Thomas Kyd, John Lyly, Robert Greene, George Peele, John Webster, Thomas Dekker, Thomas Heywood, and Beaumont and Fletcher were overshadowed by the three giants of Elizabethan theatre: Christopher Marlowe, Ben Jonson, and William Shakespeare.

Christopher Marlowe (1564–1593)
Next to Shakespeare, Marlowe is considered the greatest dramatist of tragedy in England, even though he lived only to the age of twenty-nine. Marlowe's blank verse is often termed "Marlowe's Mighty Line." In his short life, he wrote seven plays. *Tamburlaine, Edward II, The Jew of Malta,* and *Dr. Faustus* became his best known.

Ben Jonson (1572–1637)
Like Marlowe, Jonson scorned Shakespeare at first because Shakespeare knew "small Latin and less Greek." Jonson was a classic writer, always correct, always abiding by the Aristotelian unities. Much of his work is biting, humorous satire. *Everyman in His Humour, Volpone,* and *The Alchemist* are but a few of his plays. When James I inherited the throne, Jonson entertained the court with **masques,** great extravaganzas of song,

dance, and recitation. It is said that on one Jonson production alone, James spent the equivalent of $500,000 on lavish costumes and sets designed by Inigo Jones, who had studied perspective scenery in Italy.

William Shakespeare (1564–1616)
Considered the greatest of all English dramatists, it is strange and unfortunate that we know so little about Shakespeare's life. Born in Stratford-upon-Avon, where his father was a glover and, for a time, a respected town official, Shakespeare attended grammar school, his only formal education. At eighteen, he married Ann Hathaway, eight years his senior. Although the exact reason is not known, he left his wife and three children and went to London, where he began working in the theatre world as an actor, manager, and writer. By 1596, he was well established and in royal favor, for Queen Elizabeth granted him a coat of arms.

In the thirty-eight plays attributed to him, Shakespeare created histories, comedies, tragedies, and fantasies. His plays combined skillful plot and character development with majestic use of language. Among his masterful creations are the melancholy Hamlet, Prince of Denmark; the fat, braggart Falstaff; the impish Puck; the boyish Rosalind; the impetuous Hotspur; the youthfully passionate Juliet; and the jealous Othello.

Shakespeare's luminous **soliloquies** (speeches where actors talk alone to reveal their thoughts aloud) encompass great breadth of emotion and intellect and are beloved throughout the world. But his less grand phrases are a part of our world as well. We quote Shakespeare without even knowing it. Phrases such as "grim necessity," "as luck would have it," "Greek to me," "the short and long of it," "a rose by any other name," "haven't slept a wink," "all the world's a stage," "the unkindest cut of all" and "eating out of house and home," are straight out of Shakespeare's playful, compelling, and inventive language.

The Theatres

The first public playhouse to be erected during this time was The Theatre, constructed by James Burbage in 1576, accommodating about 1,500 people.

Shakespeare is as popular today as he was over 400 years ago, as can be seen in this lively and imaginative scene from a recent production of his *Twelfth Night.*

It was placed outside of London to escape the city's jurisdiction. Other theatres, including The Rose, The Fortune, The Swan, Blackfriars, and The Globe, were soon built. Although we do not know the exact nature of Elizabethan theatre structure, we know that the playhouses were modeled upon the inn yards where earlier plays had been presented. Called **Wooden O's,** the theatres were usually round or octagonal with two or three tiers of thatched roof galleries surrounding an open court on three sides. One end served as a multiple acting area with a large platform (equipped with trap-doors), which was elevated by four to six feet and extended into the open court. Each theatre also had a **discovery space** located between two doors at the back of the stage and used for small interior settings, such as Juliet's burial vault. The two doors at the back of the stage led to the **tiring house,** or back-stage area, where the actors would go to change costumes.

On the second level of the stage facade, there was another acting space (an "inner above"), as well as balcony windows and a terrace. A third level could also provide a playing area but was used mainly for the musicians as they accompanied songs and dances and played musical interludes. A fourth level was a structure called the hut,

Stage in an inn yard, around 1565. Portable platforms upon which plays were performed were set up in the inn yards. This image is based upon a sketch from the 16th century by Pieter Breughel the Younger.

which housed stage machinery for the special effects.

Plays were held in the afternoon (with the daylight serving as lighting system), and to announce performances, a flag—white for comedy, black for tragedy—was raised at the top of the theatre. All classes of people attended, for the theatre was to Elizabethans not only their drama, but also their movies, novels, radio, television, and newspapers rolled into one. The **groundlings**—usually tradespeople, soldiers, apprentices, and servants—paid a penny and stood in the pit around the acting platform. Lords and ladies paid more and had seats in the gallery. A few rich, young gallants might even occupy a portion of the stage. The whole atmosphere was joyful and at times boisterous. Peddlers sold oranges and nuts that were noisily eaten—and sometimes thrown—by the audience.

There was no scenery. The spectators used their imaginations as they listened to the playwright's descriptions and the characters' dialogue. Some properties were used, and so were certain sound effects. In fact, the burning of The Globe Theatre in 1613 was the result of the thatch roof catching a spark from the cannon shots that announced the king's entrance in Shakespeare's *Henry VIII*. By June of 1614 it was rebuilt and in use again.

Since costumes were usually handsome styles of the day donated by patrons, there was little attempt made toward historical accuracy. Julius Caesar, along with Dr. Faustus, wore Renaissance clothes on the Elizabethan stage.

The modern Globe, an open-air theatre reconstructed through the efforts of many, including American actor Sam Wanamaker. The original Globe was destroyed in 1644.

Only a few stylized costumes, those for fairies, witches, lawyers, and churchmen, were used.

The Players

Actors were all men, with the women's parts being taken by boys whose voices had not yet changed to masculine lowness or by men with higher-than-usual voices. Acting was a strenuous life, for often roles required singing, dancing, fighting, and fencing. Three great actors emerged during this period:

Richard Burbage

(1567–1619, son of the man who built The Theatre in 1576) Born, like Shakespeare, in Stratford-upon-Avon, Burbage played many of Shakespeare's tragic figures, including Hamlet, Othello, Richard III, and King Lear. He and his brother Cuthbert built The Globe Theatre in London.

Richard Burbage

Edward Alleyn (1566–1626)

Alleyn played the title roles in *Tamburlaine* and *Dr. Faustus* as well as Barabas in *The Jew of Malta,* all written by Christopher Marlowe. In 1600, Alleyn and his partner Philip Henslowe constructed

Edward Alleyn

The Fortune Theatre north of London to compete with the Globe.

William Kemp or Will Kempe

(circa 1560–about 1603)
Kemp's greatest success came from the role of Nick Bottom in *A Midsummer Night's Dream.* Shakespeare created this character with the supposed intention of ridiculing the scene-stealing actor, but Kemp made the character his own, even down to Bottom's donkey ears. In early manuscripts Shakespeare inadvertently identifies Bottom as "Kempe."

James I (1603–1625) reigned after the death of Elizabeth I. The political unrest that had been brewing throughout his reign continued after Charles I was crowned in 1625. Eventually, civil war broke out, and Oliver Cromwell, the Puritan leader, gained control. Charles was beheaded, and the rest of the Stuart line fled to France. The Puritans, always against the theatre, closed what they considered "dens of iniquity" in 1642. Public theatre died in England until Charles II regained control of England in 1660. During Cromwell's time, however, plays were performed surreptitiously, as the historical record of arrests of actors and audience members shows.

Restoration and 18th-Century Theatre

The Restoration came about with the reestablishing of the monarchy in England in 1660 under Charles II. When Charles returned from France and was restored to the English throne, he started a new era of drama that was fashioned after the theatre he had seen in Paris.

Since the Elizabethan playhouses had been torn down by the Puritans, new indoor theatres were built with a deep apron on which to act and with a proscenium arch, behind which a series of flats were painted in perspective and were set parallel to the curtain. These flats were spaced upstage of each other to give the

Theatre design in the 18th century featured box seats, a pit, a wide apron in front of the curtain, and a gallery for the audience. The scene depicted here is the wrestling match in Shakespeare's *As You Like It* at the Drury Lane Theatre, London, 1841.

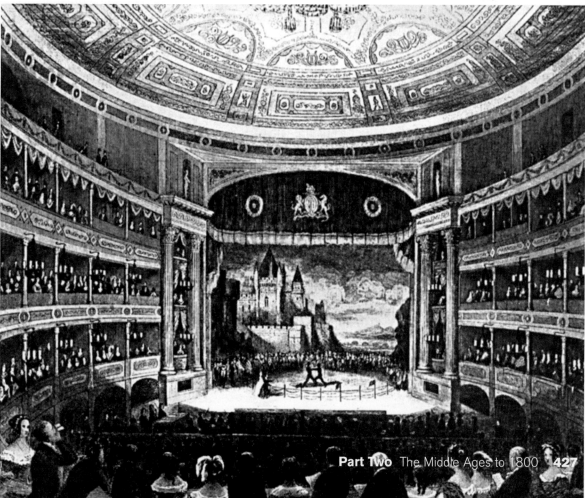

illusion of distance. Candles and oil lamps provided lighting in these indoor theatres, and women were allowed to perform.

The audience was the sophisticated aristocracy. Broadly generalized, this crowd was witty, insincere, and apt to indulge in foolish pleasures. The plays staged at this time were comedies of manners that satirized the artificiality of the day, and so they, too, were witty and concerned with foolish pleasures.

Plays of the Restoration include John Dryden's *All for Love,* George Etherage's *Love in a Tub,* William Wycherly's *The Country Wife,* George Farquhar's *The Beaux' Stratagem,* and William Congreve's *The Way of the World.*

The Restoration ended in 1737, when Parliament passed the Licensing Act, which limited London's public playhouses to two: Covent Garden and Drury Lane. All others were illegal. Thus, evolved the term **legitimate theatre,** which today has changed meaning and refers to all live play performances (as opposed to film).

The Comedy of Manners

Later in the century and roughly corresponding to the period of the American Revolution, two other English dramatists carried on the comedy of manners tradition with a brilliance and inoffensiveness that must have pleased the licensing board. Oliver Goldsmith (1728–1774) unveiled his witty, upbeat *She Stoops to Conquer,* and Richard Brinsley Sheridan (1751–1816) fashioned the best English comedies since those of Shakespeare.

During this period, some great actors made their names on the English stage. David Garrick (1717–1779), both actor and director, is credited with establishing a less **bombastic** style of acting, that is, one that didn't appear pompous or overdone. He did many Shakespearean revivals, often rewriting, deleting, or adding scenes. The tragic actress Sarah Kemble Siddons (1755–1831) and her brother John Phillip Kemble (1757–1823) were also famous stage personalities. Later, Edmund Kean (1787–1833) achieved great acclaim, particularly for his role as Shylock in Shakespeare's *The Merchant of Venice.*

Suggested Projects

1 Read one of the following plays, and discuss the elements in it that depict life and philosophy in the Middle Ages:

The Second Shepherd's Play
Master Pierre Patelin
Everyman
Gammer Gurton's Needle

2 Do Internet research to find out more about the Oberammergau Passion Play today. Write a report on the production preparation, playing procedures, and so on.

3 Read Simonson's description of medieval staging in his book *The Stage Is Set* and use the information to stage a scene from *Everyman.*

4 Write a plot outline for a morality play. List the sequence of events and describe each character.

5 Research *commedia dell'arte* characters and draw costumes for each. Select a few fabric samples for each costume also.

6 Pretend that you are an Italian manager of a *commedia dell'arte* troupe, and write an original scenario from which your actors will improvise.

7 Rehearse and present a scene or soliloquy from a Shakespeare play. Read the complete play from which the scene is taken so you will better understand your character's motivation.

8 Compare Elizabethan theatres with those of Renaissance Spain. (See *The Living Stage* by Macgowan and Melnitz.)

9 Read and act out scenes from one of Molière's comedies, such as *The Doctor in Spite of Himself, The Would-Be Gentleman, The Miser, The Affected Young Ladies, The Imaginary Invalid,* or *Tartuffe.*

10 Learn more about The Globe and take a virtual tour by visiting www.shakespeare.palomar.edu/ theatre.htm#Globe. Discuss your impressions with your classmates.

Three 1800 to the Present

Continental Theatre in the 19th Century

Romance and Realism

The dramatic style that firmly established itself in the early 19th century was **romanticism,** an emotional escape into adventure, beauty, and sentimental idealism. Started by Goethe (1749–1832) and Schiller (1759–1805) in Germany, the movement blossomed in France with the works of Victor Hugo (1802–1885) and Alexander Dumas (1802–1870), who adapted for the stage his well-loved adventure stories, such as *The Three Musketeers.*

Theatre Terms
realism
romanticism

In the mid-19th century, however, drama radically changed direction. **Realism,** which depicts a selected view of real life, emerged. The dominant figure in this theatre movement was Henrik Ibsen (1828–1906), a Norwegian who is often called the father of realism. His work was well written and constructed, and it had keen insight into characterization. Although his plays seem mild to today's audiences, his themes completely revolutionized the theatre of his day, shocking the spectators and bringing on a storm of criticism about the way his plays dealt with social problems. In *A Doll's House,* Nora leaves her husband and children; this single action presented to the world a new position of women in society. Ibsen's other plays, among them *Hedda Gabler, The Master Builder, An Enemy of the People,* and *Ghosts,* have equally provocative themes that realistically revealed the problems of Ibsen's time and place. His work influenced other dramatists, such as August Strindberg of Sweden, who wrote expressionistic drama that became the forerunner of today's avant-garde theatre. (For more about Henrik Ibsen, see page 98.) Anton Chekhov's *The Cherry Orchard* and Maxim Gorki's *Lower Depths* continued the movement away from romanticism. Konstantin Stanislavski (1863–1938), the great Russian director, also contributed to the movement with his experimental Moscow Art Theatre, where he trained actors in a technique of realistic acting. (For more on Stanislavski, see page 18.)

In England, George Bernard Shaw (1856–1950) introduced Ibsen to the larger theatre world by producing *Ghosts.* Shaw then continued his own realistic bent by writing comic satire in which he attacked all cherished beliefs, leaving little untouched by his caustic yet delightful wit. Considered the finest English playwright since Shakespeare, Shaw was also very prolific. *Androcles and the Lion, Pygmalion, Major Barbara, The Devil's Disciple, Arms and the Man, The Doctor's Dilemma,* and *Candida* are but a few of his successes. Shaw hoped that his comic writings would reform the world. That they failed to do so, he felt, was no fault of his own.

Although realism grew to great heights, many authors around the world continued to write noteworthy romantic, symbolic, or mystical plays. In England, Oscar Wilde (1854–1900) produced witty farces. *The Importance of Being Earnest* is in the best 18th-century comedy of manners style. Sir William Gilbert (1836–1911) and Sir Arthur Sullivan (1842–1900) wrote hugely popular operettas such as *The Mikado, HMS Pinafore,* and many others. In France, Edmond Rostand (1868–1918)

Ian McKellen performs with a young actor in Ibsen's *An Enemy of the People,* at the Royal National Theatre.

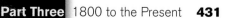

wrote *Cyrano de Bergerac* in 1897; and in Russia in 1836, Nikolai Gogol (1809–1852) wrote *The Inspector General.*

Among the famous continental actors of the 19th century were France's Sarah Bernhardt and Coquelin; Italy's Eleanora Duse; and England's Sir Henry Irving and his leading lady, Ellen Terry, who together were largely responsible for returning the acting profession once again to respectability.

American Theatre in the 19th Century

Early American Theatre

The theatre of the American colonies had been sparse, as most people regarded the entire art form as sinful. In fact, in the New York colony the governor's council passed an act in 1709 forbidding "playacting and prizefighting." Theatre fared better in the Virginia colony, where students at the College of William and Mary performed a play in 1702, and where the first playhouse in America was built in Williamsburg in 1716.

> **Theatre Terms**
> minstrel shows
> vaudeville

The first American play worthy of consideration was written by Royal Tyler in 1787. Called *The Contrast,* it was a pleasing comedy dealing with American problems. Apparently, the play was most successful, for when it was published, President George Washington's name was first on the subscription list. In fact, Washington was a theatre lover and periodically attended plays where he saw Shakespearean and other classic revivals.

American Theatre Comes into Its Own

It was not until the 19th century, however, that theatre blossomed in America. By then, most of the moralist opposition had disappeared. Numerous showboats entertained up and down the Mississippi. Playhouses were built in major American cities. These buildings followed the new trend of smaller auditoriums, narrow aprons, box settings (instead of wings and backdrops), and after 1880, incandescent lighting.

Powerful managers formed stock companies where groups of actors received excellent training in repertory theatre. This was the age of the actor, and many outstanding stars found fame. Edwin Booth (1833–1893) was considered to be America's greatest actor; appearing as Hamlet, he played one hundred nights, a record broken by few other Hamlets. Joseph Jefferson (1829–1905) made a name for himself with his many performances as Rip Van Winkle; the brilliant Richard Mansfield (1857–1907) starred in many productions; Maude Adams delighted audiences in such plays as *Peter Pan;* and Mrs. John Drew, whose daughter married a Barrymore and started that famous acting family, found success in Sheridan's *The Rivals.*

Many of these beloved actors toured America with their shows playing frequent one-night stands. During this time, touring shows did great business. For more than fifty years, road companies traversed the country until the competition of radio and movies and the increased railroad rates brought about a decline in business. With the disappearance of road shows and repertory companies, the long-run performances on Broadway began, and New York City became the theatrical center of the United States. There, the theatre again burgeoned into big business.

Three major types of native theatrical activity developed in 19th-century America. The **minstrel shows,** performed in black face and featuring African-American songs and jokes, were exceptionally popular throughout America and England. **Vaudeville** was even more popular. It was a variety show featuring everything: trained seals, singers, acrobats, jugglers, dancers, comedians, and animal acts. Shows were relatively inoffensive so the whole family could enjoy the entertainment. Vaudeville was an important part of the American entertainment scene for many years until movie and radio competition made it obsolete. Now it is almost a lost art, except for a few nightclub variety shows. **Melodrama** that dripped with sentimentality also thrived during this time, as audiences throughout the country wept at the plight of poverty-stricken heroines in the clutches of evil villains.

Theatre in the 20th Century and Beyond

At the beginning of the 20th century, new stagecraft methods revolutionized the theatre. Through the creativity of such innovative designers as Switzerland's Adolphe Appia and England's Gordon Craig, the theatre was introduced to **impressionistic** settings that used color and line to evoke the mood of a place rather than realistic painting. Also implemented were revolving stages, projected scenery, and a variety of amazing lighting effects.

> **Theatre Terms**
> absurdism
> epic theatre
> impressionistic
> regional theatres

Theatre on the Continent
Continental playwrights made numerous contributions. In Germany, Bertolt Brecht (1898–1956) developed his **epic theatre,** where he hoped to encourage audience members to think critically and to promote social reform through political action. To do so, Brecht purposely broke the realistic illusion and stressed theatricality. He deliberately inserted narration and songs between episodic scenes; he made stage light units visible to the audience; he used placards, projections, and any other effect to get the spectator to think and

ask questions that would encourage societal changes. His most popular plays include *Mother Courage, The Caucasian Chalk Circle, The Good Woman of Setzuan,* and *The Three Penny Opera.* (For more on Bertolt Brecht, see pages 111 and 311.)

In France, Jean Giraudoux (1882–1944) wrote the popular *Tiger at the Gates, Ondine,* and *The Madwoman of Chaillot.* Jean Anouilh (1910–1987) wrote a modern version of *Antigone* and a play about Joan of Arc called *The Lark.* In each, he showed an uncompromising protagonist maintaining integrity by choosing death.

In Spain, Federico García Lorca (1898–1936) achieved acclaim with themes of love and honor in *Blood Wedding* and *The House of Bernarda Alba.* In Italy, Luigi Pirandello (1867–1936) wrote about appearance versus reality in *Six Characters in Search of an Author.*

Ireland's John M. Synge (1871–1909) wrote in poetic prose about the Irish people and the conflict between a desire for freedom and an oppressive way of life in his play *The Playboy of the Western World* and in *In the Shadow of the Glenn.* Sean O'Casey (1880–1964) dealt with the effects of the Irish rebellion on ordinary people in *The Shadow of a Gunman, Juno and the Paycock,* and *The Plough and the Stars.*

Popular English dramatists in the first half of the century include: T. S. Eliot (1888–1965), who wrote poetic drama in *The Cocktail Party and Murder in the Cathedral;* Christopher Fry (1907–), who created intellectual comic verse plays with *The Lady's Not for Burning* and *Venus Observed;* and J. B. Priestly (1894–1984), who wrote mysteries such as *An Inspector Calls.* James M. Barrie (1860–1937) wrote *Peter Pan,* and Noel Coward (1899–1973) developed witty, sophisticated comedies including *Blithe Spirit* and *Private Lives.*

Post-War Drama and the Absurdists

Opening up a new post-World War II era of English drama, John Osborne's *Look Back in Anger* became a rallying cry for a group of playwrights who became known collectively as the "angry young men." In the 1950s and '60s innovative playwrights such as Peter Shaffer (*Black Comedy, Five Finger Exercises, Equus,* and *Amadeus*) and Tom Stoppard (*Rosencrantz and Guildenstern Are Dead, Travesties, Hapgood,* and *Arcadia*) came to prominence. Many of the playwrights of this period have become even more prolific in recent years. Tom Stoppard, in particular, has created a phenomenal series of plays covering everything from love to astrophysics to mathematics to world history.

One school of playwrights are often combined together, not because of nationality, but because they are

Italian playwrights Dario Fo and Franca Rame

exponents of the avant-garde theatre called **absurdism.** In their plays, the absurdists argue that all life is meaningless. Characters speak and act at random with no societal (or theatrical) rules. Proponents of the Theatre of the Absurd include Samuel Beckett (1906–1989), whose plays *Endgame, Happy Days,* and *Waiting for Godot* concern the sense of loneliness and alienation that results when people face the task of establishing real communication with one another. Eugene Ionesco (1912-1994) in *Rhinoceros, The Chairs,* and *The Bald Soprano,* rejected traditional plot lines and consistent characters and instead wrote comic plays about the meaninglessness of a life ruled by chance. Other examples are Jean Genet's *The Balcony,* Harold Pinter's *The Dumb Waiter,* Dario Fo and Franca Rame's *Accidental Death of an Anarchist* and *We Won't Pay! We Won't Pay!,* and Edward Albee's *The Sandbox.*

The American Scene
The United States began developing its own unique theatre, largely through the efforts of Professor George Pierce Baker and his playwriting course at Harvard. This remarkable teacher nurtured many of the century's most notable American dramatists, including Phillip Barry, Robert Sherwood, Sidney Howard, S. H. Behrman, and Eugene O'Neill. These playwrights were aided by Baker and two major theatre companies willing to stage their work, the Washington Square Players and the Provincetown Players.

Eugene O'Neill
Of these new writers, Eugene O'Neill (1888–1953) became the leading

American dramatist in the first part of the 20th century. His plays were both realistic and expressionistic, often dealing with difficult psychological truths. After mastering the one-act form, O'Neill turned to writing longer scripts. *The Emperor Jones, The Hairy Ape, Strange Interlude, A Long Day's Journey into Night, Mourning Becomes Electra,* and many other plays made him—and the American theatre scene—famous throughout the world.

Other U.S. playwrights who came to prominence were George S. Kaufman and his comedies *You Can't Take It with You* and *The Man Who Came to Dinner;* Lillian Hellman with *The Little Foxes* and *The Children's Hour;* Robert Sherwood with *Idiot's Delight* and *Abe Lincoln in Illinois;* Maxwell Anderson, who penned the poetic dramas *Winterset* and *Elizabeth the Queen;* and Clifford Odets with *Waiting for Lefty* and *Golden Boy.*

Special attention should be given to the following four American dramatists:

Thornton Wilder (1897–1975)
Wilder contributed to dramatic literature one of the world's best-loved and most frequently produced plays—*Our Town.* This play depicts American small-town life in the early 1900s and shows the eternal patterns of human existence. In *The Skin of Our Teeth* Wilder exhibits zany humor and great passion in portraying humanity's ability to overcome disaster.

Tennessee Williams (1911–1983)
Southern characters that were often neurotic and nearly always desperate were his specialty, but Williams's unique form of poetic realism got inside the hearts and minds of these characters, telling universal truths. This has continued to make an indelible impression on audiences. His best-known works include *The Glass Menagerie, A Streetcar Named Desire,* and *Cat On a Hot Tin Roof.*

Tennessee Williams

Arthur Miller (1915–2005)
Miller wrote of the dilemma of American families and the tragedy of common citizens in such plays as the classic *Death of a Salesman* and the WWII morality play *All My Sons.* In *The Crucible* Miller used the historical setting of the Salem Witch Trials to criticize the methods of Senator Joe McCarthy and the House Un-American Activities Committee. (To read more about Arthur Miller, see page 99.)

Neil Simon (1927–)
Simon remains one of the world's most popular and prolific writers of comedy. He combines wisecracks and barbed wit with family realism and serious themes.

Some of his best-known works are *The Odd Couple, Lost in Yonkers, Brighton Beach Memoirs,* and *Biloxi Blues.* (For more information on Neil Simon, see page 133.)

Other Playwrights

Other notable living American playwrights include Sam Shepard (*Buried Child, Fool for Love*), David Mamet (*American Buffalo, Glengarry Glen Ross*), Marsha Norman (*'Night, Mother*), Beth Henley (*Crimes of the Heart*), Lanford Wilson (*Tally's Folly, The Fifth of July*), Tony Kushner (*Angels in America*), Christopher Durang (*Sister Mary Ignatius Explains It All for You*), Arthur Kopit (*Wings, Y2K*), A. R. Gurney, Jr. (*The Dining Room*), Wendy Wasserstein (*An American Daughter*), Rebecca Gilman (*Spinning into Butter*), Kia Corthron (*Breath, Boom*), and Julie Jenson (*Two-Headed*).

African-American theatre has been enriched by the work of Lorraine Hansberry (1930–1965), who wrote *A Raisin in the Sun,* and by August Wilson (1945–2005), who wrote a history of black America with a cycle of plays set in different decades

Lorraine Hansberry

of the 20th century. Known as the "Pittsburgh Cycle," these plays include *Ma Rainey's Black Bottom, Fences, The Piano Lesson, King Hedley II,* and *Radio Golf.* (To read more about August Wilson, see page 149.) Charles Fuller (1939–) won success with *A Soldier's Play.* He is writing a series of plays about African Americans since the freeing of the slaves. Suzan-Lori Parks, with her vibrant language and overtly political themes, won the 2002 Pulitzer Prize for her play *Topdog/Underdog.*

Beyond Broadway

Today, the theatre is alive with activity. Broadway is still considered the hub of professional theatre in the United States, but rising costs have kept producers away from many newer, more risky ventures. Most Broadway shows are comedies or musicals with mass appeal to ensure their status as commercial hits. Consequently, new plays have had to find homes elsewhere. Off-Broadway theatre (New York theatres seating fewer than 299 people) welcomes new names and plays because shows can be produced less expensively—and therefore at less risk to investors. Not being tied so tightly to the box office allows for the staging of experimental productions. Some of these shows become hits and occasionally move to Broadway.

Laura Esping and Judson Pearce Morgan in *Comedy of Errors* at the Guthrie Theatre in Minneapolis.

Professional productions also thrive outside of New York City. In the 1960s, **regional theatres** were established in many major cities across the United States. The first began under the direction of Tyrone Guthrie in 1963 in Minneapolis, Minnesota. The Guthrie Theatre remains among the top regional theatres in the country. Later, other companies opened in San Francisco, Chicago, Louisville, Seattle, Dallas, Los Angeles, and Denver, to mention a few.

These resident companies encourage new talent and playwrights, including those who represent various ethnic groups and social minorities. For example, David Henry Hwang writes about the Chinese and Chinese-American culture, as do Frank Chin and James Yoshimura. José Rivera, Migdalia Cruz, Maria Irene Fornes, and Edwin Sanchez concern themselves with Hispanic issues and culture. John Belluso and others focus on disability issues. Still other playwrights concentrate on plays for children.

Nonprofessional community theatre is strong almost everywhere. Community theatres usually perform New York successes several years after the original run. Most also produce musicals and sometimes classical plays. They attempt to involve townspeople, and their enthusiasm and imagination help them to overcome the barriers of insufficient funding and/or facilities.

In recent years, voices have sporadically cried that the theatre is becoming decadent, a wasteland filled with plays of questionable merit. Theatre, of course, depends to a great extent upon the tastes of the audience. If an audience demands good theatre—that which not only entertains but stimulates worthwhile thinking and feeling—and insists that its wishes be satisfied, then the theatre must respond accordingly. You who are today's dedicated student of drama will be tomorrow's talented practitioner and/or audience member. Your desires and expectations will help to shape the future of theatre.

Suggested Projects

1 Read and report on one of the following plays, briefly giving its plot and telling how it realistically shows life at the time it was written.

A Doll's House or *An Enemy of the People* by Henrik Ibsen
The Cherry Orchard or *The Seagull* by Anton Chekhov
Arms and the Man or *Pygmalion* by George Bernard Shaw

2 Read and report on one of the following plays, highlighting its contribution to the dramatic world.

The Importance of Being Earnest by Oscar Wilde
Cyrano de Bergerac by Edmond Rostand
The Inspector General by Nikolai Gogol
Six Characters in Search of an Author by Luigi Pirandello

3 Write and present a biographical sketch on a great American actor or actress of the 19th century.

4 Create and stage a class vaudeville show.

5 Hold a panel discussion on "Television and Its Contribution to the Theatre World."

6 Read a play by a 20th-century author. Cast the play and present a fully rehearsed scene to the class.

7 With a group of classmates, attend a community or university theatre production. Arrange to visit backstage. Find out about the theatre's use of advanced technology in set, light, costume, and sound design. Take notes and discuss these implementations in class.

8 Report on how the Elizabethan stages have influenced the style of our modern thrust stages. You might find help at www.bartleby.com/216/1017.html.

9 Report on the style and success of famous actors in the 20th century. The book *Famous Actors and Actresses on the American Stage* by William C. Young might prove helpful.

10 Select a current playwright from a culture other than your own and, after research, give an oral report on the contribution of that person's dramatic work to modern theatre.

Unit
Eight

Monologues and Scenes

Monologues

Monologues for a Woman

Monologues for a Man

*Indicates annotated monologue

Romeo and Juliet

by William Shakespeare

Attending a dance, Juliet meets Romeo, and they fall in love. Later, Romeo hides in her garden. When she walks onto her balcony and romantically speaks aloud to herself about Romeo, he discloses his presence. Embarrassed, Juliet addresses him.

JULIET.   Thou know'st the mask of night is on my face,
Else would a maiden blush bepaint my cheek
For that which thou hast heard me speak tonight.
Fain would I dwell on form, fain, fain deny
What I have spoke; but farewell compliment!

Dost thou love me? I know thou wilt say "Ay,"
And I will take thy word; yet, if thou swear'st,
Thou mayst prove false: at lovers' perjuries
They say, Jove laughs. O gentle Romeo,
If thou dost love, pronounce it faithfully;
Or if thou think'st I am too quickly won,
I'll frown and be perverse and say thee nay,
So thou wilt woo; but else, not for the world.
In truth, fair Montague, I am too fond,
And therefore thou mayst think my 'haviour light;
But trust me, gentleman, I'll prove more true
Than those that have more cunning to be strange.
I should have been more strange, I must confess,
But that thou overheard'st, ere I was ware,
My true love's passion; therefore pardon me,
And not impute this yielding to light love,
Which the dark night hath so discovered.

Charlotte Randle as Juliet in the National Theatre production of *Romeo and Juliet*

Saint Joan by George Bernard Shaw

Joan of Arc has been sentenced to life in prison, instead of burning at the stake, for leading soldiers into battle based on voices she has heard from Heaven. When she realizes that she is to be continually confined, she recants her confession and boldly addresses her inquisitors.

JOAN.   Yes: they told me you were fools *[the word gives great offence]*, and that I was not to listen to your fine words nor trust to your charity. You promised me my life; but you lied *[indignant exclamations]*. You think that life is nothing but not being stone dead. It is not the bread and water I fear: I can live on bread; when have I asked for more? It is no hardship to drink water if the water be clean. Bread has no sorrow for me, and water no affliction. But to shut me from the light of the sky and the sight of the fields and flowers; to chain my feet so that I can never again ride with the soldiers nor climb the hills; to make me breathe foul damp darkness, and keep from me everything that brings me back to the love of God when your wickedness and foolishness tempt me to hate Him: all this is worse than the furnace in the Bible that was heated seven times. I could do without my warhorse; I could drag about in a skirt; I could let the banners and the trumpets and the knights and soldiers pass me and leave me behind as they leave the other women, if only I could still hear the wind in the trees, the larks in the sunshine, the young lambs crying through the healthy frost, and the blessed, blessed church bells that send my angel voices floating to me on the wind. But without these things I cannot live; and by your wanting to take them away from me, or from any human creature, I know that your counsel is of the devil, and that mine is of God.

The Prisoner of Second Avenue by Neil Simon

When Edna's husband Mel is laid off, she takes a job to tide them over. Although the playwright deals with a serious subject, he adds a good deal of humor to the situation. Here, Edna has rushed home during her lunch break.

EDNA.   Mel?. . . Mel, I'm home. *(She closes door and crosses to living room, turns off radio, then into kitchen.)* You must be starved. I'll have your lunch in a second . . . *(Takes things out of package.)* . . . I couldn't get out of the office until a quarter to one and then I had to wait fifteen minutes for a bus . . . God, the traffic on Third Avenue during lunch hour . . . I got cheese soufflé in Schrafft's, is that alright? I just don't have time to fix anything today, Mr. Cooperman wants me back before two o'clock, we're suddenly swamped with work this week. . . He asked if I would come in on Saturdays from now until Christmas but I told him I didn't think I could . . . *(She is crossing into kitchen and getting out pots.)* . . . I mean we could use the extra money but I don't think I want to spend Saturdays in that office too. We see each other little enough as it is . . . Come in and talk to me while I'm cooking, Mel, I've only got about thirty-five minutes today . . . *(Edna has put the casserole on the stove and is now crossing into kitchen, setting up two places with dishes and silverware.)* My feet are absolutely killing me. I don't know why they gave me a desk because I haven't had a chance to sit at it in a month . . . Hi, love. I bought you *Sports Illustrated* . . . Mr. Cooperman told me there's a terrific story in there about the Knicks, he thought you might be interested in it . . . *(Mel tosses the magazine aside with some contempt . . .)* You just can't move up Third Avenue because there's one of those protest parades up Fifth Avenue, or down Fifth Avenue, whichever way they protest . . . Fifteen thousand women screaming "Save the Environment" and they're all wearing leopard coats . . . God, the hypocrisy . . . Come on, sit down, I've got some tomato juice first. . . *(She pours tomato juice* into two glasses. Mel listlessly moves to table and sits.)* Isn't that terrible about the Commissioner of Police? . . . I mean kidnapping the New York Commissioner of Police? . . . Isn't that insane? I mean if the cops can't find him, they can't find anybody . . . *(She sits, picks up her glass of juice and sips.)* . . .

"Trudy" from The Search for Signs of Intelligent Life in the Universe
by Jane Wagner

In this one-woman show written for Lily Tomlin, the playwright investigates the lives of many characters, including Trudy, a bag woman with a mind of her own.

TRUDY.   Here we are, standing on the corner of "Walk, Don't Walk." You look away from me, tryin' not to catch my eye, but you didn't turn fast enough, *did* you?

You don't like my *ras*py voice, do you? I got this raspy voice 'cause I have to yell all the time 'cause nobody around here ever LISTENS to me.

You don't like that I scratch so much; yes, and excuse me, I scratch so much 'cause my neurons are on *fire*.

And I admit my smile is not at its
Pepsodent best
'cause I think my
caps must've somehow got
osteo*porosis.*

And if my eyes seem to be twirling
around like fruit flies—
the better to see you with, my dears!

Look at me,
you mammalian-brained LUNKHEADS!
I'm not just talking to myself.
I'm talking to you, too.
And to you
and you
and you
and you and you and you!

I know what you're thinkin'; you're
thinkin' I'm crazy.
You think I give a hoot? You people
look at my shopping bags,
call me crazy 'cause I save this junk.
What should we call the
ones who
buy it?

It's my belief we all, at one time
or another, secretly ask ourselves
the question,
"Am *I* crazy?"
In my case, the answer came back:
A resounding
YES!

You're thinkin': How does a person
know if they're crazy or not?
Well, sometimes you don't know.

Sometimes you can go through
life suspecting you *are*
but never really knowing for sure.
Sometimes you know for sure
'cause you got so many people tellin'
you you're crazy
that it's your word against
everyone else's.

Another sign is when you see life so
clear sometimes
you black out.
This is your typical visionary variety
who has flashes of insight
but can't get anyone to listen to 'em
'cause their insights make 'em sound
so *crazy*!

In my case,
the symptoms are subtle
but unmistakable to the trained eye.
For instance, here I am,
standing at the corner of
"Walk, Don't Walk,"
waiting for these aliens from outer
space to show up.
I call that crazy, don't you?
If I were sane,
I should be waiting for the light like
everybody else.

They're late
as usual.

You'd think,
as much as they know about time travel,
they could be on time *once* in a while.

I could kick myself.
I told 'em I'd meet 'em on the corner of
"Walk, Don't Walk"
'round lunchtime.
Do they even know what
"lunch" means?
I doubt it.

And "'round." Why did I say "'round?"
Why wasn't I more specific? This is so
typical of what I do.

Now they're probably stuck somewhere
in time, wondering what I meant by
"'round lunchtime." And when they get
here, they'll be dying to know what
"lunchtime" means. And when they
find out it means going to Howard
Johnson's for fried clams, I wonder,
will they be just a bit let down?

I dread having to explain
tartar sauce.

This problem of time just points out
how far apart we really are.
See, our ideas about time and space are
different from theirs.
When we think of time, we tend to
think of clock radios, coffee breaks,
afternoon naps, leisure time,
halftime activities, parole time,
doing time, Minute Rice, instant tea,
mid-life crises, that time of the month,
cocktail hour.
And if I should suddenly

mention *space*—aha! I bet most of
you thought of your closets.
But when they think of time and space,
they really think
of
Time and Space.

They asked me once my thoughts on
infinity and I told 'em
with all I had to think about,
infinity was not on my list
of things to think about.
It could be time on an ego trip,
for all I know. After all, when you're
pressed for time,
infinity may as well
not be there.
They said, to them, infinity is
time-released time.

Frankly, infinity doesn't affect
me personally one way or the other.

You think too long about infinity,
you could go stark raving mad.
But I don't ever want to sound
negative about going crazy.
I don't want to overromanticize
it either, but frankly,
goin' crazy was the *best* thing ever
happened to me.
I don't say it's for everybody;
some people couldn't cope. . . . .

A young woman is standing next to an end table with a lamp on it, holding a crystal bowl filled with ninety clear glass marbles.

LAURIE. ① The day my mother found out she was dying she asked me to go out and buy her these clear glass marbles. Dad and I hadn't even known she was ill which was nothing new. ② Whenever you asked my mother if she was ill she would throw things at you, sesame buns, the editorial page, a handful of hair ribbons. "Do not," she would say, "suggest things to suggestible people." ③ Anyway, I brought her the marbles and she counted ninety of them out and put them in this old cut-glass bowl which had been the sum total of great Aunt Helena's estate. Apparently, the doctor had given her three months and she set great store by doctors. She said she always believed them because they were the nearest thing to the Old Testament we had. "I wouldn't give you two bits for these young smiley guys," she'd say, "I go for a good, stern-furrowed physician." ④ She wouldn't even have her teeth cleaned by a dentist under fifty. So she counted out ninety clear glass marbles and set them in the bowl on her bedside table. Then she went out and spent twelve hundred dollars on nightgowns. She said, "In my family you are only dying when you take to your bed, and that, my darlings, is where I am going." And she did. Oh we hashed it around. Dad said she couldn't possibly be dying but the doctors convinced him. I told her it seemed a little medieval to lie in state up there but she said she didn't want to be distracted from what she loved, us, and what she wanted to mull. . . ⑤ And she said there was nothing outside except drugstores and supermarkets and drycleaners and that given her situation they were beneath her dignity. I asked her what she intended to do up there and she said study French, visit with us, generally mull and maybe call a few pals. Study French. ⑥ She said she had made a pledge to herself years ago that she would die bilingual. Dad and I cried a lot, but she didn't. He was fun to cry with. From then on the doctors had to come see *her* because, as she put it, she *came in* with a house call and she was *going out* with a house call. ⑦ And all day, every day, she would hold one of these marbles in her hand. Why? She said it made the day longer. ⑧ Mother had her own bedroom. That was the way it always was, for as long as I can remember. She called my father "The Thrasher." Dad could really get into a nightmare. Apparently early on in the marriage he had flipped over and broken her nose and that was it. Separate beds. Her room was very spare really. Wooden floors, an old steel-and-brass bed, oak dresser, bedside table, and don't ask me why, a hat rack. No

① In this first sentence, what are the two most important ideas that the actor must emphasize?

② What does this tell you about the family?

③ Besides her mother's words, what attitude of her mother's must Laurie mimic?

④ In your mind, picture the wrinkled brow of the old physician.

⑤ What does *mull* mean in this context?

⑥ How do you think the actor should say "Study French"?

⑦ What does this indicate about the mother's birth?

⑧ Why does the mother want the day to be longer?

pictures on the walls. She never understood how people could look at the same darn thing day after day. She said it was bound to "deflate the imagination." We'd sit with her after dinner and talk about "issues." She told us she was too far gone for gossip or what we ate for lunch. Then we'd all turn in and in a little while, just before I'd drift off I'd hear this. . .* *(She rolls one of the marbles across the stage floor.)* Happened every night. After the third or fourth day I saw one on the floor and started to pick it up but she said "leave it." She said it very sharply. ⑨ I asked, "How come?" She said she was "learning to let go of them." *(From now on the actress frequently rolls marbles across the stage, indicated hereafter by an asterisk, ending up at last with only one.)* Oh, she passed the time. There were things she wanted. She made out a list of children's books from her own childhood and we got as many of them as we could find from the library. She said they were still the only good books she'd ever read.* ⑩

She wrote notes to, I don't know, maybe sixty or seventy people, and they told us later on that they were sort of little formal goodbyes, each of them recalling some incident or shared something, not very significant, but the odd thing was that in each one she included a recipe. A recipe in every one of them.

We got out the big cookie tin full of snapshots that somehow never became a scrapbook. She liked that. She showed my father how to do the medical insurance and how she handled the accounts. We went through her jewelry.* She wrote down the names of the roofers and plumbers and air-conditioning people. She called it "wrapping it up." "Well, this is good," she'd say, "I'm wrapping it up."*

She had the television moved up in her room and she called me aside to say that it was entirely possible that she might reach a stage where she really wouldn't know what she was watching but that I must promise her that I'd keep it on P.B.S. ⑪

Later on, when it started getting hard,* she told Dad and me that she would like to spend more time alone. "I'm afraid," she said, "that I'm going to have to do this more or less by myself." She said that she was glad, and she hoped we would be, that this was arranged so that you got less attached to the people you loved at the end. The next period isn't worth going into, it was just. . . hard. *(She picks up the bowl of marbles.)* Do you know that from the very beginning down to the very last she never admitted to any pain. Never. She called it "the chills." The last thing she asked for was a picture we had in the front entrance hall of a Labrador retriever she and Dad had

⑨ Try to mimic the sharpness in the mother's voice.

⑩ What do the marbles symbolize? Why did she want only clear ones?

⑪ Use clues in the monologue (Study French, watching P.B.S., etc.) to describe the mother's personality or tastes.

12 Why were there a lot of marbles left to roll on the floor at this point in the monologue?

13 How should these last three lines be spoken: in sadness, regret, hope, or courage? Are there other alternatives?

owned when they were first married. He was, she said, a perfectly dreadful dog. "When you are young," she said, "you believe in the perfectibility of dogs."

I was in bed two weeks ago Wednesday toward dawn, then this. . . *(She pours the rest of the marbles on the floor. When they have stopped rolling, she speaks.)* **12** Dad and I ran in there. The bedside table was turned over and she was gone. Dead. When the emergency medical people got there they found this. . . *(She opens her hand to disclose one more marble.)* The rest spilled when the table fell, but this one was still in her hand.

13 I keep it.

I keep it in my hand all day.

It makes the day longer.

Real Women Have Curves
by Josefina López

Ana is a top-notch student who wants to attend college, but her mother insists that she help in her sister Stela's struggling dress factory. Ana sees that the factory employees work very hard for their pay and that dresses that cost little to make are sold in stores for hundreds and hundreds of dollars. Ana awakens her mother, sister, and coworkers to the idea that they shouldn't be misled by the body image promoted by these stores. In the end, Ana too learns a lesson.

ANA.   I always took their work for granted, to be simple and unimportant. I was not proud to be working there at the beginning. I was only glad to know that because I was educated, I wasn't going to end up like them. I was going to be better than them. And I wanted to show them how much smarter and liberated I was. I was going to teach them about the women's liberation movement, about sexual liberation and all the things a so-called educated American woman knows. But in their subtle ways they taught me about resistance. About a battle no one was fighting for them except themselves. About the loneliness of being women in a country that looks down on us for being mothers and submissive wives. With their work that seems simple and unimportant, they are fighting. . . Perhaps the greatest thing I learned from them is that women are powerful, especially when working together. . . As for me, well, I settled for a secondhand typewriter and I wrote an essay on my experience and I was awarded a fellowship. So I went to New York and was a starving writer for some time before I went to New York University. When I came back, the plans for making the boutique were no longer a dream, but a reality. *(Ana picks up a beautiful designer jacket and puts it on.)*

Because I now wear original designs from Estela Garcia's boutique, "Real Women Have Curves."

(The lights come on and all the women enter the door wearing new evening gowns and accessories designed by Estela. The women parade down the theatre aisles voguing in a fashion-show style. They take their bows, continue voguing, and slowly exit. Lights slowly fade out.)

Hamlet by William Shakespeare

Polonius, who is the Danish court's Lord Chamberlain, bids good-bye to his son Laertes, who is returning to a French university. Polonius gives some fatherly advice.

POLONIUS.   Yet here, Laertes? Aboard, aboard, for shame!
The wind sits in the shoulder of your sail,
And you are stayed for. There—my blessing with thee,
And these few precepts in thy memory
Look thou character. Give thy thoughts no tongue,
Nor any unproportioned thought his act.
Be thou familiar, but by no means vulgar.
Those friends thou hast, and their adoption tried,
Grapple them unto thy soul with hoops of steel;
But do not dull thy palm with entertainment

Of each new-hatched, unfledged courage. Beware
Of entrance to a quarrel, but being in,
Bear't that th' opposed may beware of thee.
Give every man thy ear, but few thy voice;
Take each man's censure, but reserve thy judgment.
Costly thy habit as thy purse can buy,
But not expressed in fancy; rich not gaudy,
For the apparel oft proclaims the man,
And they in France of the best rank and station
Are of a most select and generous chief in that.
Neither a borrower nor a lender be,
For loan oft loses both itself and friend,
And borrowing dulls th' edge of husbandry.
This above all, to thine own self be true,
And it must follow as the night the day
Thou canst not then be false to any man.
Farewell. My blessing season this in thee!

Cyrano de Bergerac
by Edmond Rostand

Although charming and witty, Cyrano de Bergerac, a 17th-century poet, has an exceptionally large nose that brings him excessive ridicule. Tiring of mundane comments about his nose, he imaginatively describes various remarks that could be made about it by a clever person.

CYRANO.   I'm afraid your speech was a little short, young man. You could have said . . . oh, all sorts of things, varying your tone to fit your words. Let me give you a few examples.

In an aggressive tone. "If I had a nose like that, I'd have it amputated!"

Friendly. "The end of it must get wet when you drink from a cup. Why don't you use a tankard?"

Descriptive. "It's a rock, a peak, a cape! No, more than a cape: a peninsula!"

Curious. "What do you use that long container for? Do you keep your pens and scissors in it?"

Gracious. "What a kind man you are! You love birds so much that you've given them a perch to roost on."

Truculent. "When you light your pipe and the smoke comes out your nose, the neighbors must think a chimney has caught fire!"

Solicitous. "Be careful when you walk; with all that weight on your head, you could easily lose your balance and fall."

Thoughtful. "You ought to put an awning over it, to keep its color from fading in the sun."

Pedantic. "Sir, only the animal that Aristophanes calls the hippocampelephantocamelos could have had so much flesh and bone below its forehead."

Flippant. "That tusk must be convenient to hang your hat on."

Grandiloquent. "No wind but the mighty Arctic blast, majestic nose, could ever give you a cold from one end to the other!"

Dramatic. "When it bleeds, it must be like the Red Sea!"

Admiring. "What a sign for a perfume shop!"

Lyrical. "Is that a conch, and are you Triton risen from the sea?"

Naïve. "Is that monument open to the public?"

Respectful. "One look at your face, sir, is enough to tell me that you are indeed a man of substance."

Rustic. "That don't look like no nose to me. It's either a big cucumber or a little watermelon."

Military. "The enemy is charging! Aim your cannon!"

Practical. "A nose like that has one advantage: it keeps your feet dry in the rain". . . .

There, now you have an inkling of what you might have said to me if you were witty and a man of letters.

Death of a Salesman by Arthur Miller

Biff has returned home for a short time. With his brother, Happy, as a sounding board, Biff confesses that he has wasted his life and still does not know what to do. He is torn between the demands of his father and his own self-desires. [If Happy's speech is omitted, the speech becomes a monologue.]

BIFF.   Well, I spent six or seven years after high school trying to work myself up. Shipping clerk, salesman, business of one kind or another. And it's a measly manner of existence. To get on that subway on the hot mornings in summer. To devote your whole life to keeping stock, or making phone calls, or selling or buying. To suffer fifty weeks of the year for the sake of a two-week vacation, when all you really desire is to be outdoors, with your shirt off. And always to have to get ahead of the next fella. And still—that's how you build a future.

[HAPPY.   Well, you really enjoy it on a farm? Are you content out there?]

BIFF.   Hap, I've had twenty or thirty different kinds of jobs since I left home before the war, and it always turns out the same. I just realized it lately. In Nebraska when I herded cattle, and the Dakotas, and Arizona, and now in Texas. It's why I came home now, I guess, because I realized it. This farm I work on, it's spring there now, see? And they've got about fifteen new colts. There's nothing more inspiring or— beautiful than the sight of a mare and a new colt. Add it's cool there now, see? Texas is cool now, and it's spring. And whenever spring comes to where I am, I suddenly get the feeling, my God, I'm not gettin' anywhere! What the hell am I doing, playing around with horses, twenty-eight dollars a week! I'm thirty-four years old, I ought to be makin' my future. That's when I come running home. And now, I get here, and I don't know what to do with myself. *(After a pause)* I've always made a point of not wasting my life, and every time I come back here I know that all I've done is to waste my life.

The Drummer by Athol Fugard

A pile of rubbish is seen on the pavement, waiting to be cleared away. This consists of an over-filled trash can and a battered old chair with torn upholstery on which is piled cardboard boxes and plastic bags full of junk. Distant and intermittent city noises are heard.

At RISE: A BUM enters. He walks over to the pile of rubbish and starts to work his way through it . . . looking for something useful in terms of that day's survival. He has obviously just woken up and yawns from time to time. After a few seconds he clears the chair, sits down, makes himself comfortable, and continues his search. One of the boxes produces a drumstick. He examines it and then abandons it. A little later he finds a second drumstick. He examines it. Remembers! He scratches around in the pile of rubbish at his feet and retrieves the first. Two drumsticks! His find intrigues him. Another dip into the rubbish but it produces nothing further of interest. Two drumsticks! He settles back in his chair and surveys the world.

An ambulance siren approaches and recedes stage right. He observes indifferently. A fire engine approaches and recedes stage left. He observes. While this is going on, he taps idly on the lid of the trash can with one of the drumsticks. He becomes aware of this little action. Two drumsticks and a trash can! It takes him a few seconds to realize the potential. He straightens up in his chair and with a measure of caution, attempts a little tattoo on the lid of the can. The result is not very impressive. He makes a second attempt, with the same result. Problem. Solution! He gets up and empties the trashcan of its contents, replaces the lid, and makes a third attempt. The combination of a serious intention and the now resonant bin produces a decided effect. He develops it and in doing so starts to enjoy himself. His excitement gets him onto his feet. He has one last flash of inspiration. He removes the lid from the can, up-ends it, and with great bravura

drums out a final tattoo . . . virtually an accompaniment to the now very loud and urgent city noises all around him. Embellishing his appearance with some item from the rubbish . . . a cape? . . . and holding his drumsticks ready, he chooses a direction and sets off to take on the city. He has discovered it is full of drums . . . and he has got drumsticks.

The Beginning

The Janitor by August Wilson

Sam, a janitor, enters an empty ballroom. He is pushing a broom near the lectern. He stops and reads the sign hanging across the ballroom.

SAM.   NATIONAL . . . CONFERENCE . . . ON . . . YOUTH. *(He nods his approval and continues sweeping. He gets an idea, stops, and approaches the lectern. He clears his throat and begins to speak. His speech is delivered with the literacy of a janitor. He chooses his ideas carefully. He is a man who has approached life honestly, with both eyes open.)* I want to thank you all for inviting me here to speak about youth. See . . . I's fifty-six years old and I knows something about youth. The first thing I knows . . . is that youth is sweet before flight . . . its odor is rife with speculation, and its resilience—that means bounce back—is remarkable. But it's that sweetness that we victims of. All of us. Its sweetness ... and its flight. One of them fellows in that Shakespeare stuff said, "I'm not what I am." See. He wasn't like Popeye. This fellow had a different understanding. "I am not what I am." Well, neither are you. You are just what you have been ... whatever you are now. But what you are now ain't what you gonna become... even though it is with you now... it's inside you now this instant. Time... see, this is how you get to this... Time ain't changed. It's just moved. Or maybe it ain't moved ... maybe it just changed. It don't matter. We are all victims of the sweetness of youth and the time of its flight.

See... just like you I forgot who I am. I forgot what happened first. But I know the river I step into now... is not the same river I stepped into twenty years ago. See, I know that much. But I have forgotten the name of the river... I have forgotten the name of the gods... and like everybody else I have tried to fool them with my dancing ... and guess at their faces. It's the same with everybody. We don't have to mention no names. Ain't nobody innocent. We are all victims of ourselves. We have all had our hand in the soup ... and made the music play just so.

See now... this is what I call wrestling with Jacob's angel. You lay down at night and that angel come to wrestle with you. When you wrestling with that angel, you bargaining for your future. See. And what you need to bargain with is that sweetness of youth. So... to the youth of the United States I says... don't spend that sweetness too fast! 'Cause you gonna need it. See. I's fifty-six years old and I done found that out. But it's all the same. It all comes back on you... just like sowing and reaping. Down and out ain't nothing but being caught up in the balance of what you put down. If you down and out and things ain't going right for you... you can bet you done put down a payment on your troubles. Now you got to pay up on the balance. That's as true as I'm standing here. Sometimes you can't see it like that. The last note on Gabriel's horn always gets lost when you get to realizing you done heard the first. So, it's just like—

[MR. COLLINS *(entering).* Come on, Sam... let's quit wasting time and get this floor swept. There's going to be a big important meeting here this afternoon.]

SAM. Yessuh, Mr. Collins. Yessuh. *(He goes back to sweeping, as the lights go down to black.)*

① Where is Copenhagen?

② Check an encyclopedia to see what role German scientists played in the development of the atomic bomb.

③ What would "quantum ethics" suggest? Check a dictionary. Why was the study of energy so intense during this period in history?

④ Why do you think Heisenberg feels there is a place for the SS man in heaven? Keep reading to find out.

⑤ Who were the Allied troops? It might help you to research the history of World War II.

⑥ What does this sentence suggest about the situation then in Germany?

Copenhagen by Michael Frayn ①

In 1941, the German physicist Werner Heisenberg made a visit to Copenhagen to see his Danish mentor, Niels Bohr. The two had worked together in the 1920s to revolutionize atomic physics. WWII was raging and they were on opposite sides of the conflict. No one really knows what they said to one another, but the play imagines them meeting after their deaths to discuss that mysterious meeting in 1941. Near the end of the play, Heisenberg speaks of the destruction of Germany. ②

HEISENBERG.   Then we should need a strange new quantum ethics. There'd be a place in heaven for me. ③ And another one for the SS man I met on my way home from Haigerloch. ④ That was the end of my war. The Allied troops were closing in; there was nothing more we could do. ⑤ Elisabeth and the children had taken refuge in a village in Bavaria, so I went to see them before I was captured. I had to go by bicycle—there were no trains or road transport by that time—and I had to travel by night and sleep under a hedge by day, because all through the daylight hours the skies were full of Allied planes, scouring the roads for anything that moved. ⑥ A man on a bicycle would have been the biggest target left in Germany. Three days and three nights I traveled. Out of Württemberg, down through the Swabian Jura and the first foothills of the Alps. Across my ruined homeland. Was this what I'd chosen for it? This endless rubble? This perpetual smoke in the sky? These hungry faces? Was this my doing? And all the desperate people on the roads. ⑦ The most desperate of all were the SS. Bands of fanatics with nothing left to lose, roaming around shooting deserters out of hand, hanging them from roadside trees. The second night, and suddenly there it is—the terrible familiar black tunic emerging from the twilight in front of me. On his lips as I stop—the one terrible familiar word. 'Deserter,' he says. He sounds as exhausted as I am. ⑧ I give him the travel order I've written for myself. But there's hardly enough light in the sky to read by, and he's too weary to bother. He begins to open his holster instead. He's going to shoot me because it's simply less labour. And suddenly I'm thinking very quickly and clearly—it's like skiing, or that night on Heligoland, or the one in Faelled Park. What comes into my mind this time is the pack of American cigarettes I've got in my pocket. And already it's in my hand—I'm holding it out to him. The most desperate solution to a problem yet. I wait while he stands there looking at it, trying to make it out, trying to think, his left hand holding my useless piece of paper, his right on the fastening of the holster. There are two simple words in large print on the pack: Lucky

Strike. He closes the holster, and takes the cigarettes instead. . . It had worked, it had worked! ⑨ Like all the other solutions to all the other problems. For twenty cigarettes he let me live. ⑩ And on I went. Three days and three nights. Past the weeping children, the lost and hungry children, drafted to fight, then abandoned by their commanders. Past the starving slave-labourers walking home to France, to Poland, to Estonia. ⑪ Through Gammertingen and Biberach and Memmingen. Mindelheim, Kaufbeuren, and Schöngau. Across my beloved homeland. My ruined and dishonoured and beloved homeland. ⑫

⑦ How would Heisenberg say these six sentences?

⑧ Why is Heisenberg exhausted?

⑨ Why do the American cigarettes yield such power, and why does Heisenberg offer them?

⑩ Explain the irony of this situation.

⑪ Who were these people? Why were they on the road?

⑫ From this monologue what have you learned about Heisenberg? Try to read the complete play.

Scenes

Scenes for One Man and One Woman

Scenes for Two or More Men

Scenes for Two or More Women

*Indicates annotated scene

Scenes for Mixed Groups

The Imaginary Invalid

by Molière, adapted by Fran Tanner

In this 17th-century French satire, the young girl Louison is teasing her father, Argan, by refusing at first to disclose that her older sister, Angelique, is seeing a gentleman. When forced to speak, she enjoys embellishing her story.

(Louison, a girl of twelve or thirteen, enters.)

LOUISON.   Did you call me, papa?

ARGAN.   Yes, little one. Come here. *(She advances part way.)*

ARGAN.   *(Beckoning slyly.)* A little closer.

Manuel Denis in *The Imaginary Invalid* at the Theatre du Châtelet, 1990.

(*Louison comes closer.*)

ARGAN.   Now then. Look at me.

LOUISON.   (*With seeming innocence.*) Yes, papa?

ARGAN.   Don't you have something to tell me?

LOUISON.   (*Sweetly.*) Well, I can tell you a story. Would you like to hear the Donkey's Skin or the fable of the Raven and the Fox?

ARGAN.   (*Angrily.*) That's not what I had in mind.

LOUISON.   My apologies, papa.

ARGAN.   Don't you obey your father?

LOUISON.   Of course, papa.

ARGAN.   And didn't I ask you to report all that you see?

LOUISON.   Yes, papa.

ARGAN.   Have you told me everything?

LOUISON.   (*With some doubt.*) Yes, papa.

ARGAN.   Haven't you seen something today?

LOUISON.   No, papa.

ARGAN.   No?

LOUISON.   (*Quite doubtful.*) No . . .

ARGAN.   Aha. Then I shall have to renew your memory.

(*Picks up his cane and starts toward LOUISON.*)

LOUISON.   (*Frightened.*) Oh, papa.

ARGAN.   Is it not true that you saw a man with your sister Angelique?

LOUISON.   (*Crying.*) Oh, dear.

ARGAN.   (*Raising his cane to hit her.*) I shall teach you to lie.

LOUISON.   Oh, forgive me, papa. Angelique made me promise not to tell. But I'll tell you now.

ARGAN.   Very well. You shall tell me, but only after I have punished you for telling a lie.

LOUISON.   Don't whip me, dear papa. Please don't whip me.

ARGAN.   I shall! (*Raises his cane and strikes once.*)

LOUISON.   (*LOUISON backs against the couch, crying loudly, pretending to be hurt.*) Oh, I'm hurt. Papa, stop. I'm hurt. Oh, I'm dying, I'm dead. (*She falls on couch, pretending to be dead, but keeping one eye open to see what her father will do.*)

ARGAN.   What's this? Louison, my little one. Louison, what have I done to you? Oh, dear. My poor Louison. Oh, my poor child.

LOUISON. *(No longer able to hide her laughter, sits up suddenly.)* Come, come, papa. It's all right. I'm not quite dead.

ARGAN. *(Surprised, but relieved.)* Oh, you imp, you. What a rascal I have. Well, I'll overlook it this once, but you must tell me everything.

LOUISON. Yes, papa. But don't tell Angelique I told.

ARGAN. Of course not.

LOUISON. *(Looks to be sure no one is listening.)* Well, while I was in Angelique's sitting room, a handsome man came, looking for her.

ARGAN. *(Eagerly.)* Yes?

LOUISON. When I asked what he wanted, he said he was her new music teacher.

ARGAN. Aha. So that is their little plan. Continue.

LOUISON. Then Angelique came and when she saw him she said *(over dramatically.)* "Oh, go away, for my sake, leave."

ARGAN. *(Disappointed.)* Oh.

LOUISON. But he didn't leave. He stayed and talked to her.

ARGAN. *(Eagerly.)* What did he say?

LOUISON. He told her . . . *(Teasing her father.)* many things.

ARGAN. Yes?

LOUISON. That he loved her passionately, and that she was the most glorious creature in the world.

ARGAN. And then?

LOUISON. And then he fell on his knees before her—

ARGAN. *(Excitedly.)* Yes, yes.

LOUISON. *(Dramatically.)* And kissed her hand— *(Giggles.)*

ARGAN. *(Eagerly.)* And then?

LOUISON. And then—*(Pause full of suspense, followed by a matter of fact.)* Mama came and he ran away.

ARGAN. *(Disappointed)* That's all? Nothing more?

LOUISON. No, papa. There was nothing more. *(She giggles and runs out. Argan groans and sinks into a chair.)*

The School for Scandal
by Richard Brinsley Sheridan

Sir Peter is scolding his young wife for her extravagance. She humorously confronts him with her determination to do as she pleases, in this 18th-century comedy of manners.

SIR PETER. Lady Teazle, Lady Teazle, I'll not bear it!

LADY TEAZLE. Sir Peter, Sir Peter, you may bear it or not, as you please;

but I ought to have my own way in everything, and what's more, I will, too. What! Though I was educated in the country, I know very well that women of fashion in London are accountable to nobody after they are married.

SIR PETER.   Very well, ma'am, very well; so a husband is to have no influence, no authority?

LADY TEAZLE.   Authority! No, to be sure, if you wanted authority over me, you should have adopted me, and not married me. I am sure you were old enough.

SIR PETER.   Old enough! Ay, there it is. Well, well, Lady Teazle, though my life may be made unhappy by your temper, I'll not be ruined by your extravagance.

LADY TEAZLE.   My extravagance! I'm sure I'm not more extravagant than a woman of fashion ought to be.

SIR PETER.   No, no, madam, you shall throw away no more sums on such unmeaning luxury. 'Slife! To spend as much to furnish your dressing-room with flowers in winter as would suffice to turn the Pantheon into a greenhouse and give a *fête champêtre* at Christmas.

LADY TEAZLE.   And am I to blame, Sir Peter, because flowers are dear in cold weather? You should find fault with the climate, and not with me. For my part, I'm sure, I wish it was spring all year round, and that roses grew under our feet.

SIR PETER.   Oons! Madam, if you had been born to this, I shouldn't wonder at your talking thus; but you forget what your situation was when I married you.

LADY TEAZLE.   No, no, I don't; 'twas a very disagreeable one, or I should never have married you.

SIR PETER.   Yes, yes, madam; you were then in somewhat a humbler style, the daughter of a plain country squire. Recollect, Lady Teazle, when I saw you first sitting at your tambor, in a pretty figured linen gown, with a bunch of keys at your side; your hair combed smooth over a roll, and your apartment hung round with fruits in worsted, of your own working.

LADY TEAZLE.   Oh, yes! I remember it well, and a curious life I led—my daily occupation to inspect the dairy, superintend the poultry, make extracts from the family receipt book, and comb my aunt Deborah's lap-dog.

SIR PETER.   Yes, yes, ma'am, 'twas so indeed.

LADY TEAZLE.   And then, you know, my evening amusements! To draw patterns for ruffles, which I had not materials to make up; to play Pope Joan with the curate; to read a sermon to my aunt; or to be stuck down to an old spinet to strum my father to sleep after a fox-chase.

SIR PETER.   I am glad you have so good a memory. Yes, madam, these were the recreations I took you from; but now you must have your coach—*viz-à-viz*—and three powdered footmen before your chair; and in the summer, a pair of white cats to draw you to Kensington Gardens. No recollection, I suppose, when you were content to ride double, behind the butler, on a docked coach-horse?

LADY TEAZLE.   No; I swear I never did that. I deny the butler and the coach-horse.

SIR PETER.   This, madam, was your situation; and what have I done for you? I have made you a woman of fashion, of fortune, of rank; in short, I have made you my wife.

LADY TEAZLE.   Well, then, and there is but one thing more you can make me to add to the obligation, and that is—

SIR PETER.   My widow, I suppose?

LADY TEAZLE.   Hem! Hem!

SIR PETER.   I thank you, madam; but don't flatter yourself for though your ill conduct may disturb my peace, it shall never break my heart, I promise you; however, I am equally obliged to you for the hint.

LADY TEAZLE.   Then why will you endeavor to make yourself so disagreeable to me, and thwart me in every little elegant expense?

SIR PETER.   'Slife, madam, I say, had you any of these little elegant expenses when you married me?

LADY TEAZLE.   Lud, Sir Peter! Would you have me be out of the fashion?

SIR PETER.   The fashion, indeed. What had you to do with the fashion before you married me?

LADY TEAZLE.   For my part, I should think you would like to have your wife thought a woman of taste.

SIR PETER.   Ay, there again: taste! Zounds! Madam, you had no taste when you married me!

LADY TEAZLE.   That's very true indeed, Sir Peter; and after having married you, I should never pretend to taste again, I allow. But now, Sir Peter, if we have finished our daily jangle, I presume I may go to my engagement at Lady Sneerwell's.

SIR PETER.   Ah, there's another precious circumstance; a charming set of acquaintances you have made there!

LADY TEAZLE.   Nay, Sir Peter, they are all people of rank and fortune, and remarkably tenacious of reputation.

SIR PETER.   Yes, egad, they are tenacious of reputation with a vengeance; for they don't choose anybody should have a character but themselves! Such a crew! Ah! Many a wretch has rid on a hurdle who has done less mischief than these utterers of forged tales, coiners of scandal, and clippers of reputation.

LADY TEAZLE.   What! Would you restrain the freedom of speech?

SIR PETER.   Ah! They have made you just as bad as any one of the society.

LADY TEAZLE.   Why, I believe I do bear a part with a tolerable grace. But I vow I bear no malice against the people I abuse. When I say an ill-natured thing, 'tis out of pure good humor; and I take it for granted they deal exactly in the same manner with me. But, Sir Peter, you know you promised to come to Lady Sneerwell's too.

SIR PETER.   Well, well, I'll call in just to look after my own character.

LADY TEAZLE.   Then indeed you must make haste after me, or you'll be too late. So, good-bye to ye. *(Exit)*

SIR PETER.   So, I have gained much by my intended expostulation; yet, with what a charming air she contradicts everything I say, and how pleasingly she shows her contempt for my authority! Well, though I can't make her love me, there is great satisfaction in quarreling

with her; and I think she never appears to such advantage as when she is doing everything in her power to plague me. *(Exit)*

A Marriage Proposal
by Anton Chekhov,
adapted by Fran Tanner

In this Russian comedy, Ivan Vassiliyitch Lomov's proposal of marriage to his neighbor's daughter, Natalia, is thwarted as they quarrel about ownership of the meadows separating their land.

NATALIA.   Oh, hello. Father said there was someone here to see me with an important question. How are you Ivan Vassiliyitch? **①**

LOMOV.   I am fine my dear Natalia Stepanovna.

NATALIA.   You must excuse me for wearing my apron and looking like this, but I've been working. Do sit down. Goodness, you haven't visited us for ages. You should come more frequently. *(They sit.)* May I offer you something to eat? **②**

LOMOV.   No, thank you. I've just had lunch.

NATALIA.   Well, do smoke if you wish. There are some matches. It's hard to believe that the weather is so wonderful today, when yesterday it rained so much

① Russian names may seem difficult to pronounce. Repeat the names of both characters until you are comfortable with them.

② What are Natalia's feelings here? Is she matter-of-fact? Embarrassed? Flustered? Uneasy?

we couldn't work outside. How many bricks have you made? Wouldn't you know it. I had the workmen mow all of the hay, and now I'm worried for fear it will rot. I suppose I should have waited longer. ③ *(Notices his suit.)* Oh, but what have we here. Why, you are all dressed up. Are you going to a party? You certainly look nice. What is the occasion?

LOMOV.   *(Excitedly)* It's—well—my dear Natalia Stepanovna—I have something to ask you—something that will be a surprise, I know, but you must not be angry—for—I—well—*(Aside.)* ④ How cold it is in here!

NATALIA.   What are you talking about? *(Pause.)* Well?

LOMOV.   Briefly—we have been friends for a long time—since childhood. My aunt and uncle, who gave me their estate—as you know—greatly admired your parents. Indeed your family and my family have been on good terms with each other for generations. In fact, as you know, my property is adjacent to yours. My meadows touch your woods.

NATALIA.   Excuse me, Ivan Vassiliyitch, but those meadows. Did you call them yours?

LOMOV.   Yes, they are mine.

NATALIA.   Well, I'm sorry to differ with you, but the meadows belong to us, not to you. ⑤

LOMOV.   Not mine? Now my dear—

NATALIA.   Why, I've never heard the like of this. What makes you think they belong to you?

LOMOV.   Because I'm speaking of the meadows that run between your woods and my brick ground.

NATALIA.   Precisely. They belong to us.

LOMOV.   No, they belong to me. You are quite mistaken. As far back as I can remember they have belonged to my family.

NATALIA.   Not so.

LOMOV.   But it is on record, my dear. True, at one time the ownership was disputed, but now it is common knowledge that the meadows are mine, without argument. In fact, my aunt's grandmother permitted your great grandfather's servants to use the land rent-free while they made bricks for my grandmother. They used the meadows for over forty years, with my family's permission. However, when— ⑥

NATALIA.   But you are mistaken. My great grandfather's land touched the swamp, so the meadows of course are ours. There is nothing more to say. I can't understand your reasoning.

LOMOV.   I'll be glad to show you the records, Natalia Stepanovna. ⑦

③ Should Natalia be pausing before each sentence or running all of her sentences together in this speech? Which would seem more in character to you?

④ What is the question going to be? Notice the play's title.

⑤ Natalia should stress "us." From here on, the polite, courteous courtship behavior begins to shift.

⑥ Lomov must let the audience sense that he is trying to control his temper as he gives Natalia this explanation.

⑦ Would Lomov say these words sweetly, sarcastically, calmly, or angrily?

⑧ Natalia's sarcasm here reflects back to her earlier comment about Lomov's nice suit.

⑨ What gesture might Lomov use as he says these words?

⑩ Both characters have become gradually more intense. As you build to the end, use quick cue pickups, topping one another's line. Both voices and bodies should communicate anger.

NATALIA.   That is not necessary. Either you are joking or you are trying to make me angry. Whichever the case, you ought to be ashamed of yourself. It is most unpleasant to hear all of a sudden that the property we have owned for almost 300 years is not ours. I will be the first to admit that the meadows are not worth much. They cover less than five acres and would probably sell for only a few hundred rubles, but the principle of the thing is what interests me. I cannot stand peacefully by while you take my land.

LOMOV.   Please, let me finish speaking. Your great grandfather's peasants, as I have already stated, made bricks for my aunt's grandmother. She wanted to be nice to them, so she—

NATALIA.   Grandmother! Grandfather! Aunt! I don't know a thing about your ancestors but I do know the meadows are mine. And that's that!

LOMOV.   No, the meadows belong to me!

NATALIA.   You can talk until you're blue in the face, and put on full evening dress for all I care, ⑧ but the meadows are, and always will be, mine—mine—mine. I have no intention of taking your land, but neither will I relinquish that which rightfully belongs to my family!

LOMOV.   Well, the meadows mean nothing to me. I don't need them. Please, let us stop this. I present the meadows to you as a gift. ⑨

NATALIA.   How can you give them to me when they belong to me? Ridiculous. Here we have always considered you to be our good friend. Why only last year we loaned you our threshing machine when we needed it ourselves—and now you are stealing our property. How dare you give me my own land. I call that a very dirty trick. In fact, to give you a piece of my mind, I'd say—

LOMOV.   You are calling me a thief? My dear lady, I'll have you know that I have never taken anyone's land and I will not be accused of doing so now. The meadows belong to me! ⑩

NATALIA.   Liar. They are mine!

LOMOV.   Mine!

NATALIA.   So. We'll see who they belong to. This afternoon I'll order my reapers into my meadows.

LOMOV.   You'll what?

NATALIA.   My reapers will go into my meadows—today.

LOMOV.   Then I'll have the pleasure of kicking them out.

NATALIA.   How dare you.

LOMOV.   The meadows belong to me. Can't you understand. They are mine!

NATALIA. It's not necessary to shout. If you want to rant and rave, please leave. In my house you must conduct yourself like a gentleman. ⑪

LOMOV. Oh. If my head wasn't throbbing and my heart beating wildly, I would handle you the way you should be handled. *(Loudly.)* The meadows are mine!

NATALIA. Mine!

LOMOV. Mine! ⑫

A Doll's House

by Henrik Ibsen,
translated by Michael Meyer

In this Norwegian play written in 1879, the question of women's rights is addressed. Nora is a wife who is treated as a child by Torvald Helmer, her husband. In this scene, Nora realizes what she must do to achieve her own identity.

NORA. *(Looks at her watch.)* It isn't that late. Sit down here, Torvald. You and I have a lot to talk about. *(She sits down on one side of the table.)*

HELMER. Nora, what does this mean? You look quite drawn—

NORA. Sit down. It's going to take a long time. I've a lot to say to you.

HELMER. *(Sits down on the other side of the table.)* You alarm me, Nora. I don't understand you.

NORA. No, that's just it. You don't understand me. And I've never understood you—until this evening. No, don't interrupt me. Just listen to what I have to say. You and I have got to face facts, Torvald.

HELMER. What do you mean by that?

NORA. *(After a short silence.)* Doesn't anything strike you about the way we're sitting here?

HELMER. What?

NORA. We've been married for eight years. Does it occur to you that this is the first time that we two, you and I, man and wife, have ever had a serious talk together?

HELMER. Serious? What do you mean, serious?

NORA. In eight whole years—no, longer—ever since we first met—we have never exchanged a serious word on a serious subject.

HELMER. Did you expect me to drag you into all my worries—worries you couldn't possibly have helped me with?

NORA. I'm not talking about worries. I'm simply saying that we have never sat down seriously to try to get to the bottom of anything.

HELMER. But, my dear Nora, what on earth has that got to do with you?

⑪ A lower volume and pitch might be more effective at this point. The audience should feel that Natalia could explode again at any moment.

⑫ As the last "Mine!" is spoken, how should each character move?

NORA. That's just the point. You have never understood me. A great wrong has been done to me, Torvald. First by Papa, and then by you.

HELMER. What? But we two have loved you more than anyone in the world!

NORA. *(Shakes her head.)* You have never loved me. You just thought it was fun to be in love with me.

HELMER. Nora, what kind of a way is this to talk?

NORA. It's the truth, Torvald. When I lived with Papa, he used to tell me what he thought about everything, so that I never had any opinions but his. And if I did have any of my own, I kept them quiet, because he wouldn't have liked them. He called me his little doll, and he played with me just the way I played with my dolls. Then I came here to live in your house—

HELMER. What kind of a way is that to describe our marriage?

NORA. *(Undisturbed.)* I mean, then I passed from Papa's hands into yours. You arranged everything the way you wanted it, so that I simply took over your taste in everything—or pretended I did—I don't really know—I think it was a little of both—first one and then the other. Now I look back on it, it's as if I've been living here like a pauper, from hand to mouth. I performed tricks for you, and you gave me food and drink. But that was how you wanted it. You and Papa have done me a great wrong. It's your fault that I have done nothing with my life.

HELMER. Nora, how can you be so unreasonable and ungrateful? Haven't you been happy here?

NORA. No; never. I used to think I was; but I haven't ever been happy.

HELMER. Not—not happy?

NORA. No. I've just had fun. You've always been very kind to me. But our home has never been anything but a playroom. I've been your doll-wife, just as I used to be Papa's doll-child. And the children have been my dolls. I used to think it was fun when you came in and played with me, just as they think it's fun when I go in and play games with them. That's all our marriage has been, Torvald.

HELMER. There may be a little truth in what you say, though you exaggerate and romanticize. But from now on it'll be different. Playtime is over. Now the time has come for education.

NORA. Whose education? Mine or the children's?

HELMER. Both yours and the children's, my dearest Nora.

NORA. Oh, Torvald, you're not the man to educate me into being the right wife for you.

HELMER. How can you say that?

NORA. And what about me? Am I fit to educate the children?

HELMER. Nora!

NORA. Didn't you say yourself a few minutes ago that you dare not leave them in my charge?

HELMER. In a moment of excitement. Surely you don't think I meant it seriously?

NORA. Yes. You were perfectly right. I'm not fitted to educate them. There's something else I must do first. I must educate myself. And you can't help me with that. It's something I must do by myself. That's why I'm leaving you.

HELMER. *(Jumps up.)* What did you say?

NORA. I must stand on my own feet if I am to find out the truth about myself and about life. So I can't go on living here with you any longer.

HELMER. Nora, Nora!

NORA. I'm leaving you now, at once. Christine will put me up for tonight—

HELMER. You're out of your mind! You can't do this! I forbid you!

NORA. It's no use your trying to forbid me any more. I shall take with me nothing but what is mine. I don't want anything from you, now or ever.

HELMER. What kind of madness is this?

NORA. Tomorrow I shall go home— I mean, to where I was born. It'll be easiest for me to find some kind of a job there.

HELMER. But you're blind! You've no experience of the world—

NORA. I must try to get some, Torvald.

HELMER. But to leave your home, your husband, your children! Have you thought what people will say?

NORA. I can't help that. I only know that I must do this.

HELMER. But this is monstrous! Can you neglect your most sacred duties?

NORA. What do you call my most sacred duties?

HELMER. Do I have to tell you? Your duties towards your husband, and your children.

NORA. I have another duty which is equally sacred.

HELMER. You have not. What on earth could that be?

NORA. My duty towards myself.

Blood Wedding

by Federico García Lorca

This opening scene, set in Spain in the early 1900s, suggests the lyrical gloom that envelopes the bridegroom's family and his upcoming wedding to a woman who loves another.

BRIDEGROOM. *(entering)* Mother.

MOTHER. What?

BRIDEGROOM. I'm going.

MOTHER. Where?

BRIDEGROOM. To the vineyard. *(He starts to go.)*

MOTHER. Wait.

BRIDEGROOM. You want something?

MOTHER. Your breakfast, son.

BRIDEGROOM. Forget it. I'll eat grapes. Give me the knife.

MOTHER. What for?

BRIDEGROOM. *(laughing)* To cut the grapes with.

MOTHER. *(muttering as she looks for the knife)* Knives, knives. Cursed be all knives, and the scoundrel who invented them.

BRIDEGROOM. Let's talk about something else.

MOTHER. And guns and pistols and the smallest little knife—and even hoes and pitchforks.

BRIDEGROOM. All right.

MOTHER. Everything that can slice a man's body. A handsome man, full of young life, who goes out to the vineyards or to his own olive groves—his own because he's inherited them . . .

BRIDEGROOM. *(lowering his head)* Be quiet.

MOTHER. . . . and then that man doesn't come back. Or if he does come back it's only for someone to cover him over with a palm leaf or a plate of rock salt so he won't bloat. I don't know how you dare carry a knife on your body—or how I let this serpent *(She takes a knife from a kitchen chest.)* stay in the chest.

BRIDEGROOM. Have you had your say?

MOTHER. If I live to be a hundred I'd talk of nothing else. First your father; to me he smelled like a carnation and I had him for barely three years. Then your brother. Oh, is it right—how can it be—that a small thing like a knife or a pistol can finish off a man—a bull of a man? No, I'll never be quiet. The months pass and the hopelessness of it stings in my eyes and even to the roots of my hair.

BRIDEGROOM. *(forcefully)* Let's quit this talk!

MOTHER. No. No. Let's not quit this talk. Can anyone bring me your father back? Or your brother? Then there's the jail. What do they mean, jail? They eat there, smoke there, play music there! My dead men choking with weeds, silent, turning to dust. Two men like two beautiful flowers. The killers in jail, carefree, looking at the mountains.

BRIDEGROOM. Do you want me to go kill them?

MOTHER. No . . . If I talk about it it's because . . . Oh, how can I help talking about it, seeing you go out that door? It's . . . I don't like you to carry a knife. It's just that . . . that I wish you wouldn't go out to the fields.

BRIDEGROOM. *(laughing)* Oh, come now!

MOTHER. I'd like it if you were a woman. Then you wouldn't be going out to the arroyo now and we'd both of us embroider flounces and little woolly dogs.

BRIDEGROOM. *(He puts his arm around his mother and laughs.)* Mother, what if I should take you with me to the vineyards?

MOTHER. What would an old lady do in the vineyards? Were you going to put me down under the young vines?

BRIDEGROOM. *(lifting her in his arms)* Old lady, old lady—you little old, little old lady!

MOTHER. Your father, he used to take me. That's the way with men of good stock; good blood. Your grandfather left a son on every corner. That's what I like. Men, men; wheat, wheat.

BRIDEGROOM. And I, Mother?

MOTHER. You, what?

BRIDEGROOM. Do I need to tell you again?

MOTHER. *(seriously)* Oh!

BRIDEGROOM. Do you think it's bad?

MOTHER. No.

BRIDEGROOM. Well, then?

MOTHER. I don't really know. Like this, suddenly, it always surprises me. I know the girl is good. Isn't she? Well behaved. Hard working. Kneads her bread, sews her skirts, but even so when I say her name I feel as though someone had hit me on the forehead with a rock.

BRIDEGROOM. Foolishness.

MOTHER. More than foolishness. I'll be left alone. Now only you are left me—I hate to see you go.

BRIDEGROOM. But you'll come with us.

MOTHER. No. I can't leave your father and brother here alone. I have to go to them every morning and if I go away it's possible one of the Felix family, one of the killers, might die—and they'd bury him next to ours. And that'll never happen! Oh, no! That'll never happen! Because I'd dig them out with my nails and, all by myself, crush them against the wall.

BRIDEGROOM. *(sternly)* There you go again.

MOTHER. Forgive me. *(pause)* How long have you known her?

BRIDEGROOM. Three years. I've been able to buy the vineyard.

MOTHER. Three years. She used to have another sweetheart, didn't she?

BRIDEGROOM. I don't know. I don't think so. Girls have to look at what they'll marry.

MOTHER. Yes. I looked at nobody. I looked at your father, and when they killed him I looked at the wall in front of me. One woman with one man, and that's all.

BRIDEGROOM. You know my girl's good.

MOTHER. I don't doubt it. All the same, I'm sorry not to have known what her mother was like.

BRIDEGROOM. What difference does it make now?

MOTHER. *(looking at him)* Son.

BRIDEGROOM. What is it?

MOTHER. That's true! You're right! When do you want me to ask for her?

BRIDEGROOM. Does Sunday seem all right to you?

MOTHER. *(seriously)* I'll take her the bronze earrings, they're very old—and you buy her. . .

BRIDEGROOM. You know more about that. . .

MOTHER. . . . you buy her some open-work stockings—and for you, two suits—three! I have no one but you now!

BRIDEGROOM. I'm going. Tomorrow I'll go see her.

MOTHER. Yes, yes—and see if you can make me happy with six grand-children—or as many as you want, since your father didn't live to give them to me.

BRIDEGROOM. The first-born for you!

MOTHER. Yes, but have some girls. I want to embroider and make lace, and be at peace.

Driving Miss Daisy

by Alfred Uhry

Miss Daisy's son has hired Hoke to drive the elderly Miss Daisy wherever she needs to go. Miss Daisy is a proud, opinionated white woman, and the idea does not sit right with her. In Hoke, an equally determined black man, she has met her match.

DAISY.   Good morning.

HOKE.   Right cool in the night, wadn't it?

DAISY.   I wouldn't know. I was asleep.

HOKE.   Yassum. What yo plans today?

DAISY.   That's my business.

HOKE.   You right about dat. Idella say we runnin' outa coffee and Dutch Cleanser.

DAISY.   We?

HOKE.   She say we low on silver polish too.

DAISY.   Thank you. I will go to the Piggly Wiggly on the trolley this afternoon.

HOKE.   Now, Miz Daisy, how come you doan' let me carry you?

DAISY.   No thank you.

HOKE.   Ain't that what Mist' Werthan hire me for?

DAISY.   That's his problem.

HOKE.   All right den. I find something to do. I tend yo zinnias.

DAISY.   Leave my flower bed alone.

HOKE.   Yassum. You got a nice place back beyond the garage ain' doin' nothin' but sittin' there. I could put you in some butterbeans and some tomatoes and even some Irish potatoes could we get some ones with good eyes.

DAISY.   If I want a vegetable garden, I'll plant it for myself.

HOKE.   Well, I go out and set in the kitchen, then, like I been doin' all week.

DAISY.   Don't talk to Idella. She has work to do.

HOKE.   Nome. I jes sit there till five o'clock.

DAISY.   That's your affair.

HOKE.   Seem a shame, do. That fine Oldsmobile sittin' out there in the garage. Ain't move a inch from when Mist' Werthan rode it over here from Mitchell Motors. Only got nineteen miles on it. Seem like that insurance company give you a whole new car for nothin'.

DAISY.   That's your opinion.

HOKE.   Yassum. And my other opinion is a fine rich Jewish lady like you doan b'long draggin' up the steps of no bus, luggin' no grocery store bags. I come along and carry them fo' you.

DAISY.   I don't need you. I don't want you. And I don't like you saying I'm rich.

HOKE.   I won' say it, then.

DAISY.   Is that what you and Idella talk about in the kitchen? Oh, I hate this! I hate being discussed behind my back in my own house! I was born on Forsyth Street and, believe you me, I knew the value of a penny. My brother Manny brought home a white cat one day and Papa said we couldn't keep it because we couldn't afford to feed it. My sisters saved up money so I could go to school and be a teacher. We didn't have anything!

HOKE.   Yassum, but look like you doin' all right now.

DAISY.   And I've ridden the trolley with groceries plenty of times!

HOKE.   Yassum, but I feel bad takin' Mist' Werthan's money for doin' nothin'. You understand?
(She cuts him off in the speech.)

DAISY.   How much does he pay you?

HOKE.   That between me and him, Miz Daisy.

DAISY.   Anything over seven dollars a week is robbery. Highway robbery!

HOKE.   Specially when I doan do nothin' but set on a stool in the kitchen all day long. Tell you what, while you goin on the trolley to the Piggly Wiggly, I hose down yo' front steps. *(Daisy is putting on her hat.)*

DAISY.   All right.

HOKE.   All right I hose yo' steps?

DAISY.   All right the Piggly Wiggly. And then home. Nowhere else.

HOKE.   Yassum.

DAISY.   Wait. You don't know how to run the Oldsmobile!

HOKE.   Miz Daisy, a gear shift like a third arm to me. Anyway, thissun automatic. Any fool can run it.

DAISY.   Any fool but me, apparently.

HOKE.   Ain' no need to be so hard on yoseff now. You cain' drive but you probably do alota things I cain' do. It all work out.

DAISY.   *(Calling offstage.)* I'm gone to the market, Idella.

HOKE.   *(Also calling.)* And I right behind her! *(Hoke puts on his cap and helps Daisy into the car. He sits at the wheel and backs the car down the driveway. Daisy, in the rear, is in full bristle.)* I love a new car smell. Doan' you? *(Daisy slides over to the other side of the seat.)*

DAISY. I'm nobody's fool, Hoke.

HOKE. Nome.

DAISY. I can see the speedometer as well as you can.

HOKE. I see dat.

DAISY. My husband taught me how to run a car.

HOKE. Yassum.

DAISY. I still remember everything he said. So don't you even think for a second that you can—Wait! You're speeding! I see it!

HOKE. We ain' goin' but nineteen miles an hour.

DAISY. I like to go under the speed limit.

HOKE. Speed limit thirty five here.

DAISY. The slower you go, the more you save on gas. My husband told me that.

HOKE. We barely movin'. Might as well walk to the Piggly Wiggly.

DAISY. Is this your car?

HOKE. Nome.

DAISY. Do you pay for the gas?

HOKE. Nome.

DAISY. All right then. My fine son may think I'm losing my abilities, but

I am still in control of what goes on in my car. Where are you going?

HOKE. To the grocery store.

DAISY. Then why didn't you turn on Highland Avenue?

HOKE. Piggly Wiggly ain' on Highland Avenue. It on Euclid, down there near—

DAISY. I know where it is and I want to go to it the way I always go. On Highland Avenue.

HOKE. That three blocks out of the way, Miz Daisy.

DAISY. Go back! Go back this minute!

HOKE. We in the wrong lane!
I cain' jes—

DAISY. Go back I said! If you don't, I'll get out of this car and walk!

HOKE. We movin'! You cain' open the do'!

DAISY. This is wrong! Where are you taking me?

HOKE. The sto'.

DAISY. This is wrong. You have to go back to Highland Avenue!

HOKE. Mmmm Hmmmm.

DAISY. I've been driving to the Piggly Wiggly since the day they put it up and opened it for business. This isn't the way! Go back! Go back this minute!

HOKE. Yonder the Piggly Wiggly.

DAISY. Get ready to turn now.

HOKE. Yassum.

DAISY. Look out! There's a little boy behind that shopping cart!

HOKE. I see dat.

DAISY. Pull in next to the blue car.

HOKE. We closer to the do' right here.

DAISY. Next to the blue car! I don't park in the sun! It fades the upholstery.

HOKE. Yassum. *(He pulls in, and gets out as Daisy springs out of the back seat.)*

DAISY. Wait a minute. Give me the car keys.

HOKE. Yassum.

DAISY. Stay right here by the car. And you don't have to tell everybody my business.

HOKE. Nome. Don' forget the Dutch Cleanser now. *(She fixes him with a look meant to kill and exits. Hoke waits by the car for a minute, then hurries to the phone booth at the corner.)* Hello? Miz McClatchey? Hoke Coleburn here. Can I speak to him? *(Pause.)* Mornin sir, Mist' Werthan. Guess where I'm at? I'm at dishere

phone booth on Euclid Avenue right next to the Piggly Wiggly. I jes drove yo' Mama to the market. *(Pause.)* She flap a little on the way. But she all right. She in the store. Uh oh. Miz Daisy look out the store window and doan' see me, she liable to throw a fit right there by the checkout. *(Pause.)* Yassuh, only took six days. Same time it take the Lawd to make the worl'. *(Lights out on him.)*

Weebjob

by Diane Glancy

Thou hast fenced me with bones . . .

—Job 10:11

Gerald Long Chalk, or Weebjob (wēb jōb), age 48, is the main character. His name is a play on the Biblical Job because he is beset with problems. Weebjob is a holy man, a Mescalero Apache, and he always seems to be at a crossroads in his life. He lets rich land lie fallow. He paints signs and hangs them on his fence. Signs that say: "He hangs the earth on nothing, Job 26:7," etc.)

Weebjob's friend, Pick Up, age 43, is in love with Weebjob's daughter. He is also a Mescalero Apache.

Suzanne Long Chalk, or Sweet Potato, Weebjob's daughter, is 21. She has a mind of her own. She is unhappy with her life because she doesn't know where she belongs.

The setting is the Salazar Canyon in Lincoln County, New Mexico.

Scene 2

The stage is dark except for a spotlight in the corner which falls on Sweet Potato and Pick Up in the truck.

SWEET POTATO.   Why are we stopping? I need to get back to feed Weebjob.

PICK UP.   Let him wait.

SWEET POTATO.   I'll hear him bellering in the valley if we don't get back soon . . . He'll be painting another sign for the fence by the road . . . *(Pick Up touches her face.)*

PICK UP.   Where were you for a week?

SWEET POTATO.   You already asked me, and I told you I was on the road. *(Folds her arms.)* Why did you bring me back to him? You know I didn't want to come.

PICK UP.   You can't run away, Sweet Potato.

SWEET POTATO.   My name is Suzanne Long Chalk.

PICK UP.   I'll call you what I please. I can't have you hitch-hiking on the road for anyone to pick up. You shouldn't be out on the road alone. It's not good.

What would you do in Gallup?

SWEET POTATO.   Get a job. I can cook, wait tables. I worked there last summer, if you remember.

PICK UP.   Yes, it's the first time I came to see you . . . I don't want you to go back there.

SWEET POTATO.   You sound like my father.

PICK UP.   It's not as your father that I'm speaking. Work at the Civil War in Old Lincoln if you must have a job. Let the men gawk at you. Wait tables. *(He pauses and looks at her.)* I care for you, Suzanne. You know that. *(Pause.)* More than as a father. I didn't come to Socorro to see James.

SWEET POTATO.   I told you I didn't want to speak of these things.

PICK UP.   I didn't for many years. But now I can't wait any longer. You're more than Weebjob's daughter to me.

SWEET POTATO.   Maybe we could be like cousins.

PICK UP.   I want you as a close friend.

SWEET POTATO.   We are close friends, Pick Up, my father's friend.

PICK UP.   Yes, I'm his friend.

SWEET POTATO.   You wouldn't be if he heard you speak to me like that.

PICK UP.   I know. *(He touches her face again.)*

SWEET POTATO.   I remember you, Pick Up, when you used to have a brown Volkswagen, and looked like a prune driving it down the road.

PICK UP.   I remember you, Sweet Potato, in a round purple coat, like a plum on narrow legs, with skinny braids sticking out from beneath your cap.

SWEET POTATO.   I remember the night you got drunk in the Civil War Bar in Old Lincoln and came to our house and quoted poetry to the weed-clumps.

PICK UP.   I remember when the faintest bit of snow blew into the valley and you ran into my truck on William's bicycle and sprang the tire.

SWEET POTATO.   I remember—*(Pick Up puts his hands over her mouth.)*

PICK UP.   I remember when you fell into the stream. I should have let you drown. *(He kisses her.)*

SWEET POTATO.   Would you call him father?

PICK UP.   *(He rolls his head back.)* I would rather have a buffalo for a father-in-law.

SWEET POTATO.   *(She takes up for Weebjob.)* He's a better man than any I've known.

PICK UP.   I know.

SWEET POTATO.   Wise and good-hearted. Quick tempered. A little harsh with words and his head too much in the Bible, but a good man.

PICK UP.   I don't know what to do, Suzanne. I want you, and I wonder why. I'm almost as old as your father. How could I think of you as a wife? How could you think of me—

SWEET POTATO.   Don't talk about it.

PICK UP.   Marry me, Suzanne.

SWEET POTATO.   I can hear Weebjob roaring about it now.

PICK UP.   He will be all right. Think about me, Sweet Potato. *(He kisses her again.)* Marry me.

SWEET POTATO.   Maybe it's what you deserve.

FOB

by David Henry Hwang

In this play, Steve has entered the back room of a Chinese restaurant in Torrance, California, and asked Grace, who sits at a table, if they have a certain dish. She tells him they are not yet open, and he proceeds to tell her that he is the legendary Chinese hero Gwan Gung.

STEVE. Tell me, how do people think of Gwan Gung in America? Do they shout my name while rushing into battle, or is it too sacred to be used in such ostentatious display?

GRACE. Uh—no.

STEVE. No—what? I didn't ask a "no" question.

GRACE. What I mean is, neither. They don't do either of those.

STEVE. Not good. The name of Gwan Gung has been restricted for the use of leaders only?

GRACE. Uh—no. I think you better sit down.

STEVE. This is very scandalous. How are the people to take my strength? Gwan Gung might as well not exist, for all they know.

GRACE. You got it.

STEVE. I got what? You seem to be having trouble making your answers fit my questions.

GRACE. No, I think you're having trouble making your questions fit my answers.

STEVE. What is this nonsense? Speak clearly, or don't speak at all.

GRACE. Speak clearly?

STEVE. Yes. Like a warrior.

GRACE. Well, you see, Gwan Gung, no one gives a wipe about you 'round here. You're dead.

(Pause.)

STEVE. You . . . you make me laugh.

GRACE. You died way back . . . hell, no one even noticed when you died—that's how bad off your PR was. You died and no one even missed a burp.

STEVE. You lie! The name of Gwan Gung must be feared around the world—you jeopardize your health with such remarks. *(Pause.)* You—you have heard of me, I see. How can you say—?

GRACE. Oh, I just study it a lot—Chinese-American history, I mean.

STEVE. Ah. In the schools, in the universities, where new leaders are born, they study my ways.

GRACE. Well, fifteen of us do.

STEVE. Fifteen. Fifteen of the brightest, of the most promising?

GRACE. One wants to be a dental technician.

STEVE. A man studies Gwan Gung in order to clean teeth?

GRACE. There's also a middle-aged woman that's kinda bored with her kids.

STEVE. I refuse—I don't believe you—your stories. You're just angry at me for treating you like a servant. You're trying to sap my faith. The people—the people outside—they know me—they know the deeds of Gwan Gung.

GRACE. Check it out yourself.

STEVE. Very well. You will learn—learn not to test the spirit of Gwan Gung.

(Steve exits. Grace picks up the box. She studies it.)

GRACE. Fa Mu Lan sits and waits. She learns to be still while the emperors, the dynasties, the foreign lands flow past, unaware of her slender form, thinking it a tree in the woods, a statue to a goddess long abandoned by her people. But Fa Mu Lan, the Woman Warrior, is not ashamed. She knows that the one who can exist without movement while the ages pass is the one to whom no victory can be denied. It is training, to wait. And Fa Mu Lan, the Woman Warrior, must train, for she is no goddess, but girl—girl who takes her father's place in battle. No goddess, but woman—warrior-woman *(She breaks through the wrapping, reaches in, and pulls out another box, beautifully wrapped and ribboned.)*—and ghost. *(She puts the new box on the shelf, goes to the phone, dials.)* Hi, Dale? Hi, this is Grace . . . Pretty good.

How 'bout you? . . . Good, good. Hey, listen, I'm sorry to ask you at the last minute and everything, but are you doing anything tonight? . . . Are you sure? . . . Oh, good. Would you like to go out with me and some of my friends? . . . Just out to dinner, then maybe we were thinking of going to a movie or something . . . Oh, good . . . Are you sure? . . . Yeah, okay. Um, we're all going to meet at the restaurant . . . No, *our* restaurant . . . right—as soon as possible. Okay, good . . . I'm really glad that you're coming. Sorry it's such short notice. Okay. Bye, now . . . Huh? Frank? Oh, okay. *(Pause.)* Hi, Frank . . . Pretty good . . . Yeah? . . . No, I don't think so . . . Yeah . . . No, I'm sorry, I'd still rather not . . . I don't want to, okay? Do I have to be any clearer than that? . . . You are not! . . . You don't even know when they come—you'd have to lie on those tracks for hours . . . Forget it, okay? . . . Look, I'll get you a schedule so you can time it properly . . . It's not a favor, damn it. Now goodbye! *(She hangs up.)* Jesus!

(Steve enters.)

STEVE. Buncha weak boys, what do they know? One man—ChinaMan—wearing a leisure suit—green! I ask him, "You know Gwan Gung?" He says, "Hong Kong?" I say, "No, no. Gwan Gung." He says, "Yeah. They got sixty thousand people living on four acres. Went there last year." I say, "No, no.

Gwan Gung." He says, "Ooooh! Gwan Gung?" I say, "Yes, yes, Gwan Gung." He says, "I never been there before."

GRACE.   See? Even if you didn't die—who cares?

STEVE.   Another kid—blue jeans and a T-shirt—I ask him, does he know Gwan Gung? He says, he doesn't need it, he knows Jesus Christ. What city is this now?

GRACE.   Los Angeles.

STEVE.   This isn't the only place where a new ChinaMan can land, is it?

GRACE.   I guess a lot go to San Francisco.

STEVE.   Good. This place got a bunch of weirdos around here.

GRACE.   Yeah.

STEVE.   They could never be followers of Gwan Gung. All who follow me must be loyal and righteous.

GRACE.   Maybe you should try some other state.

STEVE.   Huh? What you say?

GRACE.   Never mind. You'll get used to it—like the rest of us.

(Pause. Steve begins laughing.)

STEVE.   You are a very clever woman.

GRACE.   Just average.

STEVE.   No. You do a good job to make it seem like Gwan Gung has no followers here. At the university, what do you study?

GRACE.   Journalism.

STEVE.   Journalism—you are a writer, then?

GRACE.   Of a sort.

STEVE.   Very good. You are close to Gwan Gung's heart.

GRACE.   As close as I'm gonna get.

STEVE.   I would like to go out tonight with you.

GRACE.   I knew it. Look, I've heard a lot of lines before, and yours is very creative, but . . .

STEVE.   I will take you out.

GRACE.   You will, huh?

STEVE.   I do so because I find you worthy to be favored.

GRACE.   You're starting to sound like any other guy now.

Spinning into Butter
by Rebecca Gilman

We see a dean's office at Belmont College, a small liberal arts college in Belmont, Vermont. It is a large office, with built-in bookshelves full of books and nice white trim and a large warm rug on the floor. The desk is cluttered with papers and more books, and there are several very comfortable-looking chairs. There may even be a fireplace. Large windows provide a lot of light.

Sitting at the desk is Sarah Daniels, who is the college's Dean of Students. She is earnest in her desire to do right by her students.

There is a knock at the door.

SARAH.   Come in.

(Patrick Chibas enters. He is self-assured, dressed in running shorts and a T-shirt.)

PATRICK.   Dean Daniels? I think I was next. I got a note in my box that said you wanted to see me?

SARAH.   *(Smiles.)* I left notes for a lot of students. *(Patrick stares at her.)* I need you to tell me your name.

PATRICK.   Oh. Sorry. Patrick Chibas.

SARAH.   Patrick. Great. Have a seat. *(Patrick takes a seat and looks around while she fishes out a file from a pile on her desk. While she looks)* Welcome back. How's moving going?

PATRICK.   Fine.

SARAH.   *(Finds his file but doesn't open it yet.)* What dorm are you in this year?

PATRICK.   Grange Hall.

SARAH.   Was that your first choice?

PATRICK.   Last.

SARAH.   I guess sophomores always get the short straw, don't they?

PATRICK.   Yeah.

SARAH.   Did you go home for the summer?

PATRICK.   For the first part, and then I went to Florida.

SARAH.   Did you have an internship?

PATRICK.   No. I just bummed around. I waited tables at the Fish Shack.

SARAH.   Just relaxed, huh?

PATRICK.   Yeah. *(Small beat.)* Am I in trouble?

SARAH.   No! No. I'm sorry, Patrick. I actually wanted to talk to you about a scholarship. *(Opens his file.)*

PATRICK.   Oh yeah?

SARAH.   Yeah. You declared an environmental sciences major last spring.

PATRICK.   Yeah.

SARAH.   Well, we have a scholarship that's designated for. . . well, it's designated for an outstanding minority student in environmental sciences, and I just. . . Well. . . I wondered if you might be interested.

PATRICK.   Sure.

SARAH.   Good. There's just one thing, then. I need to ask you, Patrick, on your Belmont application, you . . . Under the voluntary disclosure of your racial/ethnic background you marked "Other."

PATRICK.   Yeah.

SARAH.   Okay. I guess I need to know, so I can make a recommendation to the board, just what "other" is. If you don't mind.

PATRICK.   I don't mind. I'm Nuyorican.

SARAH.   Nuyorican?

PATRICK.   Yeah.

SARAH.   Huh. Would it be fair for me to say, then, that you're, um, Hispanic?

PATRICK.   I prefer Nuyorican.

SARAH.   Of course. I just . . . Well, to simplify things, when I make my recommendation to the board, do you think I could just mention that you're Hispanic?

PATRICK.   What's wrong with Nuyorican?

SARAH.   Nothing, of course.

PATRICK.   Then why don't you just say that?

SARAH.   I will. (Beat.) And then, I think, I'll probably be asked to explain, and I wondered, could I just explain by saying that you're Hispanic?

PATRICK.   Why would you be asked to explain?

SARAH.   Because the members of our scholarship advisory board are . . . well . . . to be honest, Patrick, they're not culturally sensitive. (Patrick stares at her.) If you know what I mean.

PATRICK.   I guess I don't.

SARAH.   I think they tend to see the world in very . . . limited terms, as black or white or re . . . (She stops herself.) . . . racially divided along solid, clearly delineated lines.

PATRICK.   So you're saying they're old?

SARAH.   Yes. They're old. And they're just . . . They're not going to know what Nuyorican is.

PATRICK.   (Sighs.) Look, you understand why I don't want to be called Hispanic, don't you?

SARAH.   As I understand it, and correct me, please, if I'm wrong, it's because it really only applies to imperialists of European descent who colonized Puerto Rico.

PATRICK.   Yeah. I mean, if you understand, then . . .

SARAH.   Why am I suggesting it?

Good question. *(Beat.)* And you're right. I shouldn't compromise your feelings for the sake of expediency. I'm sorry.

PATRICK.   That's okay.

SARAH.   *(Thinking.)* What about Latino?

PATRICK.   *(Irritated.)* No.

SARAH.   How 'bout just plain Puerto Rican?

PATRICK.   No.

(Beat.)

SARAH.   It's a twelve-thousand-dollar scholarship, Patrick.

PATRICK.   It is?

SARAH.   I want you to get it. It just seems like a shame to me to leave money sitting around in a bank when it could be doing you some good. You're a remarkably talented student and I think you should be rewarded in a meaningful way.

(Long pause.)

PATRICK.   You can put Puerto Rican.

SARAH.   *(Smiles.)* Thank you. *(She makes a note.)* I'll let you know as soon as I hear.

PATRICK.   *(Taking his cue, standing.)* Okay. Sure. Thanks, Dean Daniels.

SARAH.   You're welcome. Will you send in whoever's next?

PATRICK.   Sure.

The Importance of Being Earnest
by Oscar Wilde

In this 19th-century English comedy, Algernon is quizzing Jack about the latter's proposal of marriage to Gwendolen. The two men spar with clever remarks, for which author Oscar Wilde is famous. ①

ALGERNON.   Didn't it go off all right, old boy? ② You don't mean to say Gwendolen refused you? I know it is a way she has. She is always refusing people. I think it is most ill-natured of her.

JACK.   Oh, Gwendolen is as right as a trivet. ③ As far as she is concerned, we are engaged. Her mother is perfectly unbearable. Never met such a gorgon . . . I don't really know what a gorgon is like, but I am quite sure that Lady Bracknell is one. ④ In any case, she is a monster, without being a myth, which is rather unfair . . . I beg your pardon, Algy, I suppose I shouldn't talk about your own aunt in that way before you.

ALGERNON.   My dear boy, I love hearing my relations abused. It is the only thing that makes me put up with them at all. Relations are simply a tedious pack of people who haven't got the

① This play pokes fun at the social mores of its time. The cleverness of the dialogue should be maintained with lightness and enthusiasm.

② In what part of this speech do you realize to what Algernon is referring?

③ This is a 19th-century English expression. What does *trivet* suggest about Gwendolen's personality?

④ In mythology what was a "gorgon"? Realize the humor in this line so you can say it to get chuckles from the audience.

remotest knowledge of how to live, nor the smallest instinct about when to die. ⑤

JACK.   Oh, that is nonsense!

ALGERNON.   It isn't.

JACK.   Well, I won't argue about the matter. You always want to argue about things.

ALGERNON.   That is exactly what things were originally made for.

JACK.   Upon my word, if I thought that, I'd shoot myself. (A pause.) You don't think there is any chance of Gwendolen becoming like her mother in about a hundred and fifty years, do you Algy?

ALGERNON.   All women become like their mothers. That is their tragedy. No man does. That's his. ⑥

JACK.   Is that clever?

ALGERNON.   It is perfectly phrased! And quite as true as any observation in civilized life should be.

JACK.   I am sick to death of cleverness. Everybody is clever nowadays. You can't go anywhere without meeting clever people. The thing has become an absolute public nuisance. I wish to goodness we had a few fools left.

ALGERNON.   We have.

JACK.   I should extremely like to meet them. What do they talk about?

ALGERNON.   The fools? Oh, about the clever people, of course.

JACK.   What fools!

ALGERNON.   By the way, did you tell Gwendolen the truth about your being Ernest in town, and Jack in the country? ⑦

JACK.   (In a very patronizing manner.) My dear fellow, the truth isn't quite the sort of thing one tells to a nice sweet refined girl. What extraordinary ideas you have about the way to behave to a woman!

ALGERNON.   The only way to behave to a woman is to make love to her, if she is pretty, and to someone else if she is plain.

JACK.   Oh, that is nonsense.

ALGERNON.   What about your brother? What about the profligate Ernest?

JACK.   Oh, before the end of the week I shall have got rid of him. I'll say he died in Paris of apoplexy. Lots of people die of apoplexy, quite suddenly, don't they? ⑧

ALGERNON.   Yes, but it's hereditary, my dear fellow. It's a sort of thing that runs in families. You had much better say a severe chill.

JACK.   You are sure a severe chill isn't hereditary, or anything of that kind?

⑤ Emphasize the contrast of "how to live" and "when to die" to obtain the humor here.

⑥ Again, emphasize the contrasting ideas. Wilde uses contrasts throughout this scene to create humor.

⑦ This is a very important line on which the whole plot of the play rests.

⑧ Apoplexy is a condition in which the blood supply to the brain is obstructed, causing paralysis or brain damage, now called a stroke.

⑨ This is forecasting of a later scene when the two women do meet.

⑩ Make the following exchange of dialogue quick and adroit.

ALGERNON.   Of course it isn't.

JACK.   Very well, then. My poor brother Ernest is carried off suddenly in Paris, by a severe chill. That gets rid of him.

ALGERNON.   But I thought you said that . . . Miss Cardew was a little too much interested in your poor brother Ernest? Won't she feel his loss a good deal?

JACK.   Oh, that is all right. Cecily is not a silly romantic girl, I am glad to say. She has got a capital appetite, goes for long walks, and pays no attention at all to her lessons.

ALGERNON.   I would rather like to see Cecily.

JACK.   I will take very good care you never do. She is excessively pretty, and she is only just eighteen.

ALGERNON.   Have you told Gwendolen yet that you have an excessively pretty ward who is only just eighteen?

JACK.   Oh! One doesn't blurt these things out to people. Cecily and Gwendolen are perfectly certain to be extremely great friends. I'll bet you anything you like that half an hour after they have met, they will be calling each other sister.

ALGERNON.   Women only do that when they have called each other a lot of other things first. **⑨** Now, my dear boy, if we want to get a good table at Willis's, we really must go and dress. Do you know it is nearly seven?

JACK.   *(Irritably.)* Oh! It always is nearly seven.

ALGERNON.   Well, I'm hungry.

JACK.   I never knew you when you weren't . . .

ALGERNON.   What shall we do after dinner? Go to the theatre? **⑩**

JACK.   Oh, no! I loathe listening.

ALGERNON.   Well, let us go to the Club.

JACK.   Oh, no! I hate talking.

ALGERNON.   Well, we might trot round to the Empire at ten?

JACK.   Oh, no! I can't bear looking at things. It is so silly.

ALGERNON.   Well, what shall we do?

JACK.   Nothing!

ALGERNON.   It is awfully hard work doing nothing. However, I don't mind hard work where there is no definite object of any kind.

The Inspector General

by Nikolai Gogol, adapted
by Fran Tanner

Arriving penniless in a Russian village, Khlestakov is treated shabbily. But when he poses as a government official, the villagers grant his every wish. In this early scene in the play, Khlestakov orders supper from a servant who has been told to refuse this beggar.

SERVANT.   The manager sent me to see what you want.

KHLESTAKOV.   Ah, good to see you, old man. How are things going?

SERVANT.   All right, thank you.

KHLESTAKOV.   Is business booming here at the hotel?

SERVANT.   Yes, sir. Thank you, sir.

KHLESTAKOV.   Lots of guests?

SERVANT.   Adequate, sir.

KHLESTAKOV.   Well fine! You know, it's almost past dinner time and I haven't eaten yet. Do a good turn and bring me a tray immediately, or I shall be late for my appointment.

SERVANT.   Sorry, sir, but the manager will charge no more dinners to you. In fact, today he almost sent a complaint about you to the police.

KHLESTAKOV.   A complaint? That's ridiculous. After all, I've got to eat or I shall starve. The truth of the matter is, I'm quite famished!

SERVANT.   Be that as it may. He said he wasn't going to give you anything else until you had cleared up your bill.

KHLESTAKOV.   Well, can't you talk to him? Put in a good word for me!

SERVANT.   But what can I say?

KHLESTAKOV.   Talk to him seriously and tell him I've got to have something to eat. The money—well—tell him just because his kind can go all day without food, doesn't mean that other people can. Preposterous idea!

SERVANT.   Yes, sir, I'll tell him. *(Exit Servant.)*

KHLESTAKOV.   How disgusting if he refuses to send up dinner. I've never been so hungry. I wonder if I could pawn my clothes? My trousers? No, I'd rather not eat than go home without my Petersburg suit. Too bad that Yokhim wouldn't let me rent a carriage. It would have been great to drive up in style to a landlord's house with my carriage lanterns on and Osip behind in uniform. How impressed they would be. "Who is it? Who has come?" Then my footman would announce *(He imitates footman.)* "Ivan Alexandrovich Khlestakov of Petersburg. Will you receive him?" Those country dunces, though, wouldn't even know what that meant. If any farmer visits them, he stumbles right into the living room like a bear. Hmmm. I'd go up to a pretty young girl and say "Mademoiselle, I am so happy—" Huh! *(He spits.)* I'm so hungry I feel nauseated.

(Enter the Servant.)

KHLESTAKOV.   Yes, what do you want?

SERVANT.   I'm bringing dinner.

KHLESTAKOV.   *(Claps his hands and jumps into his chair.)* Ah, dinner. At last, dinner.

SERVANT.   The manager says this is the last dinner he will send you.

KHLESTAKOV.   Oh, the manager. Who cares about the manager. What's there to eat?

SERVANT.   Soup and roast beef.

KHLESTAKOV.   You mean that is all?

SERVANT.   That's all, sir.

KHLESTAKOV.   Nonsense. I won't hear of it. That's not enough.

SERVANT.   On the contrary, sir, the manager says it's far too much!

KHLESTAKOV.   But what about the gravy?

SERVANT.   There isn't any.

KHLESTAKOV.   Why not? When I

passed the kitchen I saw them making a lot, and earlier in the dining room, I saw two short-looking men eating salmon and other good things.

SERVANT.   Well, there is some and then there isn't.

KHLESTAKOV.   What do you mean?

SERVANT.   I mean, there isn't any, sir.

KHLESTAKOV.   No salmon? No gravy? No chops?

SERVANT.   No, sir. Well, yes, sir. But only for those who pay, sir.

KHLESTAKOV.   Oh, you knucklehead. Why should I go hungry while they eat. Aren't I as good as they?

SERVANT.   No, sir. Well, yes, sir, but the difference is, they have money.

KHLESTAKOV.   Oh, it's a waste of time to argue with you. *(Tastes soup.)* What awful soup. Why, it's only hot water you've poured into the bowl. There's no taste at all, only a dreadful smell. I'll not eat it! You must bring me some other.

SERVANT.   Sorry, sir. The manager said if you didn't like this, you could go without.

KHLESTAKOV.   *(Holding his bowl and plate.)* Well, then leave it. Only, don't talk like that to me. I'll not have it. *(Tastes soup again.)* Heavens, what soup. *(Continues to eat it.)* I'm proba-bly the first to ever eat soup like this. Why, there's even a feather floating on top. *(Spoons a piece of chicken in the soup.)* Ah, even the fowl is foul. Pass me the roast beef. Here, Osip, there's some soup left for you. *(Cuts meat.)* You call this roast beef? It most certainly is not!

SERVANT.   Then what is it?

KHLESTAKOV.   Only the devil knows, but it is not beef. It tastes more like leather. Cheaters! What they won't give a person. Why, my jaw aches from chewing just one bite. *(Picks teeth with finger.)* It's even worse than tree bark. I can't get it out. Such food is enough to ruin one's teeth. *(Wipes mouth with napkin.)* Isn't there anything else?

SERVANT.   No, sir.

KHLESTAKOV.   What cheaters they are. Not even dessert. It's terrible the way they always take advantage of travelers!

You Can't Take It With You

by Moss Hart and George S. Kaufman

In this American comedy, the Sycamore family is considered eccen-tric because of their unusual philoso-phy. Grandpa Sycamore explains to the stalwart Mr. Kirby that people should not work at jobs they dislike.

KIRBY.   *(Outraged.)* I beg your pardon, Mr. Vanderhof. I am a very happy man.

GRANDPA.   Are you?

KIRBY.   Certainly I am.

GRANDPA.   *(Sits.)* I don't think so. What do you think you get your indi-gestion from? Happiness? No, sir. You get it because most of your time is spent in doing things you don't want to do.

KIRBY.   I don't do anything I don't want to do.

GRANDPA.   Yes, you do. You said last night that at the end of a week in Wall Street you're pretty near crazy. Why do you keep on doing it?

KIRBY.   Why do I keep on—why, that's my business. A man can't give up his business.

GRANDPA.   Why not? You've got all the money you need. You can't take it with you.

KIRBY.   That's a very easy thing to say, Mr. Vanderhof. But I have spent my entire life building up my business.

GRANDPA.   And what's it got you? Same kind of mail every morning, same kind of deals, same kind of meetings, same dinners at night, same indiges-tion. Where does the fun come in? Don't you think there ought to be something more, Mr. Kirby? You must have wanted more than that when you started out. We haven't got too much time, you know—any of us.

KIRBY.   What do you expect me to do? Live the way you do? Do nothing?

GRANDPA.   Well, I have a lot of fun. Time enough for everything—read, talk, visit the zoo now and then, practice my darts, even have time to notice when spring comes around. Don't see anybody I don't want to, don't have six hours of things I have to do every day before I get one hour to do what I like in—and I haven't taken bicarbonate of soda in thirty-five years. What's the matter with that?

KIRBY.   The matter with that? Suppose we all did it? A fine world we'd have, everybody going to zoos. Don't be ridiculous, Mr. Vanderhof. Who would do the work?

GRANDPA.   There's always people that like to work—you can't stop them. Inventions, and they fly the ocean. There're always people to go down to Wall Street, too—because they like it. But from what I've seen of you I don't think you're one of them. I think you're missing something.

KIRBY.   I am not aware of missing anything.

GRANDPA.   I wasn't either, till I quit. I used to get down to that office nine o'clock sharp no matter how I felt. Lay awake nights for fear I wouldn't get that contract. Used to worry about the world, too. Got all worked up about whether Cleveland or Blaine was going to be elected President—seemed awful important at the time, but who cares now? What I'm trying to say, Mr. Kirby, is that I've had thirty-five years that nobody can take away from me, no matter what they do to the world. See?

KIRBY.   *(Crossing to table.)* Yes, I do see. And it's a very dangerous philosophy, Mr. Vanderhof. It's—it's un-American.

"Dead Parrot" from *The Complete Monty Python's Flying Circus*
by Graham Chapman, John Cleese, Terry Gilliam, Eric Idle, Terry Jones, and Michael Palin

Mr. Praline walks into the pet shop carrying a dead parrot in a cage. He walks to counter where shopkeeper tries to hide below cash register.

PRALINE.   Hello, I wish to register a complaint. . . Hello? Miss?

SHOPKEEPER.   What do you mean, miss?

PRALINE.   Oh, I'm sorry, I have a cold. I wish to make a complaint.

SHOPKEEPER.   Sorry, we're closing for lunch.

PRALINE.   Never mind that my lad, I wish to complain about this parrot what I purchased not half an hour ago from this very boutique.

SHOPKEEPER.   Oh yes, the Norwegian Blue. What's wrong with it?

PRALINE.   I'll tell you what's wrong with it. It's dead, that's what's wrong with it.

SHOPKEEPER.   No, no it's resting, look!

PRALINE.   Look my lad, I know a dead parrot when I see one and I'm looking at one right now.

SHOPKEEPER.   No, no sir, it's not dead. It's resting.

PRALINE.   Resting?

SHOPKEEPER.   Yeah, remarkable bird the Norwegian Blue, beautiful plumage, innit?

PRALINE.   The plumage don't enter into it—it's stone dead.

SHOPKEEPER.   No, no—it's just resting.

PRALINE.   All right then, if it's resting I'll wake it up. (Shouts into cage.) Hello Polly! I've got a nice cuttlefish for you when you wake up, Polly Parrot!

SHOPKEEPER.   (Jogging cage.) There it moved.

PRALINE.   No he didn't. That was you pushing the cage.

SHOPKEEPER.   I did not.

PRALINE.   Yes, you did. (Takes parrot out of cage, shouts.) Hello Polly, Polly. (Bangs it against counter.) Polly Parrot, wake up. Polly. (Throws it in the air and lets it fall to the floor.) Now that's what I call a dead parrot.

SHOPKEEPER.   No, no it's stunned.

PRALINE.   Look my lad, I've had just about enough of this. That parrot is definitely deceased. And when I bought it not half an hour ago, you assured me that its lack of movement was due to it being tired and shagged out after a long squawk.

SHOPKEEPER.   It's probably pining for the fiords.

PRALINE.   Pining for the fiords, what kind of talk is that? Look, why did it fall flat on its back the moment I got it home?

SHOPKEEPER.   The Norwegian Blue prefers kipping on its back. Beautiful bird, lovely plumage.

PRALINE.   Look, I took the liberty of examining that parrot, and I discovered that the only reason that it had been sitting on its perch in the first place was that it had been nailed there.

SHOPKEEPER.   Well of course it was nailed there. Otherwise it would muscle up to those bars and voom.

PRALINE.   Look matey *(Picks up parrot.),* this parrot wouldn't voom if I put four thousand volts through it. It's bleeding demised.

SHOPKEEPER.   It's not, it's pining.

PRALINE.   It's not pining, it's passed on. This parrot is no more. It has ceased to be. It's expired and gone to meet its maker. This is a late parrot. It's a stiff. Bereft of life, it rests in peace. If you hadn't nailed it to the perch, it would be pushing up the daisies. It's rung down the curtain and joined the choir invisible. This is an ex-parrot.

SHOPKEEPER.   Well, I'd better replace it then.

PRALINE.   *(To camera.)* If you want to get anything done in this country you've got to complain till you're blue in the mouth.

SHOPKEEPER.   Sorry guv, we're right out of parrots.

PRALINE.   I see. I see. I get the picture.

SHOPKEEPER.   I've got a slug.

PRALINE.   Does it talk?

SHOPKEEPER.   Not really, no.

PRALINE.   Well, it's scarcely a replacement, then is it?

SHOPKEEPER.   Listen, I'll tell you what, *(Handing over a card.)* tell you what, if you go to my brother's pet shop in Bolton he'll replace your parrot for you.

PRALINE.   Bolton eh?

SHOPKEEPER.   Yeah.

PRALINE.   All right.

(He leaves, holding the parrot.)

(CAPTION: 'A SIMILAR PET SHOP in BOLTON, LANCS'

(Close-up of sign on door reading: 'Similar Pet Shops Ltd.' Pull back from sign to see same pet shop. Shopkeeper now has moustache. Praline walks into shop. He looks around with interest, noticing the empty parrot cage still on the floor.)

PRALINE.   Er, excuse me. This is Bolton, is it?

SHOPKEEPER.   No, no it's, er, Ipswich.

PRALINE.   *(To camera.)* That's Inter-City Rail for you. *(Leaves.)*

(Man in porter's outfit standing at complaints desk for railways. Praline approaches.)

PRALINE.   I wish to make a complaint.

PORTER.   I don't have to do this, you know.

PRALINE.   I beg your pardon?

PORTER.   I'm a qualified brain surgeon. I only do this because I like being my own boss.

PRALINE.   Er, excuse me, this is irrelevant, isn't it?

PORTER.   Oh yeah, it's not easy to pad these out to thirty minutes.

PRALINE.   Well I wish to make a complaint. I got on the Bolton train and found myself deposited here in Ipswich.

PORTER.   No, this is Bolton.

PRALINE.   *(To camera.)* The pet shop owner's brother was lying.

PORTER.   Well you can't blame British Rail for that.

PRALINE.   If this is Bolton, I shall return to the pet shop.

(CAPTION: 'A LITTLE LATER LTD')

(Praline walks into the shop again.)

PRALINE.   I understand that this is Bolton.

SHOPKEEPER.   Yes.

PRALINE.   Well, you told me it was Ipswich.

SHOPKEEPER.   It was a pun.

PRALINE.   A pun?

SHOPKEEPER.   No, no, not a pun, no. What's the other thing which reads the same backwards as forwards?

PRALINE.   A palindrome?

SHOPKEEPER.   Yes, yes.

PRALINE.   It's not a palindrome. The palindrome of Bolton would be Notlob. It don't work.

SHOPKEEPER.   Look, what do you want?

PRALINE.   No I'm sorry, I'm not prepared to pursue my line of enquiry any further as I think this is getting too silly.

A Jamaican Airman Foresees His Death
by Fred D'Aguiar

Three young Jamaican men are eager to join Britain's Royal Air Force during World War II to fight for a mother country they have yet to see. In the following scene, Alvin Williams, the main character, has his enlistment interview with a civilian, an Air Force man, an Army man and Kojo, in place of the absent Navy representative.

CIVILIAN.   You wish to volunteer?

ALVIN.   Yes sir!

ARMY.   Patriotic.

AIR-FORCE.   Very like a patriot.

ARMY.   And honourable.

AIR-FORCE.   That too.

ARMY.   Patriotic and honourable.

AIR-FORCE.   Honourable and patriotic.

ARMY.   Same difference.

AIR-FORCE.   One must first have honour; with honour one is in a position to be a patriot. Therefore, honourable and patriotic.

CIVILIAN.   There will be neither honour nor patriotism or vice versa unless we can recruit men.

ARMY.   A man with your muscles would do well in a regiment.

AIR-FORCE.   A man of your intelligence would do well in a squadron.

ARMY.   I don't see how you could possibly have assessed the man's intelligence when he hasn't said two words.

AIR-FORCE.   By the same token, I fail to see how you can talk about his muscles when he is fully clothed.

ARMY.   I made a quick assessment as he entered the room and took six steps to his seat. I could tell from the briskness in his opening and closing the door, by the lightness of his step and from his firm handshake, that he is at least a boxer.

AIR-FORCE.   All right, let's test your hypothesis. Now, Mr. Williams, if you will kindly enter the room again.

(Alvin goes out of the room, knocks as before, enters, closes the door behind him and waits.)

ARMY.   See! I am vindicated. There's the briskness of an athlete.

AIR-FORCE.   Nonsense. It doesn't take much to open and close a door.

CIVILIAN.   Gentlemen . . .

ARMY.   These are military matters. We are assessing Mr. Williams as we see fit. Will you walk over to this desk as before.

AIR-FORCE.   Light-footed?! I counted seven steps.

ARMY.   The last one was a pigeon-step.

AIR-FORCE.   I don't care if it belonged to a caterpillar. You are wrong.

ARMY.   Don't jump the gun, he has yet to shake our hands.

(Alvin offers a limp hand.)

ARMY.   You are not the man who walked in that door a moment ago.

KOJO.   More like an Englishman's, that handshake.

AIR-FORCE.   We are all Englishmen, Englishmen abroad, but Englishmen all the same.

CIVILIAN.   Wrong. We are Jamaicans under British rule.

ARMY.   Separate Jamaica from Britain and what are you left with? A poor, small island without a voice or guardian.

CIVILIAN.   Hardly.

ARMY.   Everything we have, and I mean everything, is given to us by Great Britain. A constitution that is British. Think what that means . . .

KOJO.   But at what price?

ARMY.   You don't get anything in this world for nothing.

AIR-FORCE.   Great Britain does not owe Jamaica a living!

KOJO.   Great Britain does not own the lives of our young men.

ARMY.   It's the least we can do.

KOJO.   Ditch the Brits.

ARMY.   We must obey the rule of law.

KOJO.   Who in this room had a hand in making that law?

AIR-FORCE.   The law doesn't apply any less because we're further from Westminster.

ARMY.   Here here.

AIR-FORCE.   A principle's a principle.

KOJO.   But it has to mean something to the people to whom it applies.

CIVILIAN.   Where is all this going?

KOJO.   We're Jamaicans.

CIVILIAN.   So?

KOJO.   And the wonderful constitution you defend is now being contested, right?

AIR-FORCE.   The Fascists want to put theirs in its place.

ARMY.   We are not here to question the Government. We are here to carry out its orders.

KOJO.   Sometimes the Government is wrong.

AIR-FORCE and ARMY.   Anarchist!

KOJO.   As Jamaicans we can act as conciliators; as a British Dominion we are forced to take sides.

ARMY.   As a British Dominion? We are a British Dominion!

AIR-FORCE.   We have the monarchy!

KOJO.   We have plenty monkeys of we own.

AIR-FORCE.   This conversation is stupid.

KOJO.   Stupid/he, stupid/she, stupid-all-a-we!

ALVIN.   It seems to me, sir, unless we have this kind of conversation things will never change.

ARMY and AIR-FORCE.   You too!

ALVIN. Don't get me wrong. I am here to enlist. But I am only here because you and you and you told me again and again that was the honourable and patriotic thing to do for the mother country. I haven't been able to see Jamaica and what it is to be Jamaican without seeing an Englishman and the Union Jack. When I do, I'm condemned for being a follower of Marcus Garvey. He's the only one who has held up an alternative. He's shown me it's possible to be something other than British.

ARMY. What do you think of the Army, Mr. Williams?

ALVIN. It's a good force, sir, but my special interest is in the Air Force.

AIR-FORCE. Bravo! But you know, young man, everyone wants to fly.

ALVIN. I've always wanted to fly.

KOJO. Don't be so concrete.

AIR-FORCE. You've got to do better than that.

ALVIN. It's my dream, sir.

KOJO. (Mocking.) It's my dream, sir.

AIR-FORCE. What can you contribute to the Air Force?

ALVIN. My youth, my strength, and my intelligence.

KOJO. (Mocking.) My youth, my strength, and my intelligence.

AIR-FORCE. I mean what can you contribute to the Air Force? You, Mr. Williams.

ALVIN. When I was a boy, my uncle made me a kite, nearly as tall as me. But when I raised it I was too small to control it. A grown-up had to hold my arms to stop it dragging me away. One day I decided to fly the kite on my own. I was sure if I got the right grip and a sure foothold I could steer it—have fingertip control, like I did with smaller kites. I raised it all right. There was a good breeze and the principle is the same whatever the kite-size. I thought I was on top of it—on top if it and on top of the world. I began to jump up and down. I even called out for everyone to come and see me, Alvin, behind that kite they all thought I'd have to give away. Just then a strong breeze hit the kite. Something pulled me so hard I had to look up. All I saw way up in the sky was this tadpole waving. I thought that small thing can't tug with so much force, it must be the hand of God. I thought, if I could hold on long enough, I'd be hauled up to heaven. And heaven to me was all the things I ever wanted but could never have: shoes, long trousers, black pudding, pepper-pot and souse every day, a new slate for school. Things I dreamed about. Things I knew I would have when I got to heaven. We used to make long lists. We talked to God, but he never replied. When he did answer some people in church we could never understand what they were saying. I tried running along with the pull, but my legs weren't fast enough. I heard the shouts of let go, let go, but I couldn't let go of heaven. I held on for dear life. When I came round they told me I was dragged into a fence. It took me a long time to believe the preacher preaching on Sundays and even longer to get round to praying. But I never doubted for a moment that I had to fly. Not to God. But because in my head that kite is still up there, waiting for me to pilot it to the ground.

AIR-FORCE.   Welcome to the Air Force, Mr. Williams.

(They take turns to shake his hand.)

ARMY.   I knew you had a firm grip, must've been nerves, eh? Box?

ALVIN.   No, sir.

KOJO.   You want to fly? We all want
to fly.
God's up there in the sky, not down
here.
He's up there 'cause he's a bird;
if he's in man's image he'd be down
here
getting his hands dirty with the rest
of us.
We want to be birds so badly,

we cage them. We teach them
our language,
parrot-fashion, in the hope they'll
divulge
how it is you grow hollow bones and
feathers,
instead of hairs and skin. We consume
their
flesh and bones hoping we can digest
their wisdom.
But all we get is the stench of our own
earthboundness.
We call our women after them 'cause
we believe
they were told the secret, but were
sworn to silence,
or deliberately withhold it from us
for spite.
We spend our lives making paper
airplanes,
kites, balloons, airships, real planes,
you name it,
even our wishes when we see a
star shoot.
We send them all up there to find out
where the birds hide their bird-making
formula.
We cry when we're born 'cause the first
thing
we notice is that we've got no wings.
So we bawl. We spent the rest of our
lives
trying to get back to that comforting,
watery,
blub-blub, blub-blub, brilliant dark, in
the hope

that a second journey will somehow, anyhow,
sprout wings.
Remember and deliver us, O lord,
  O John Crow,
O sparrow, O Pterodactyl; deliver us
  this day
from our daily dread of being land-
  locked,
sea-locked, from our gravity straitjacket.
Deliver us to birddom, till birddom
  come,
thy quill be done, on earth as it is
  in heaven,
a-bird.

Othello
by William Shakespeare

Othello believes that his wife, Desdemona, has been unfaithful. Jealous with rage, he sends her to her room with the intent of killing her. Desdemona is blameless and cannot understand Othello's anger. As she prepares for bed, she discusses the situation with Emilia, her maid.

EMILIA.   How goes it now? He looks gentler than he did. ①

DESDEMONA.   He says he will return incontinent; ②
And hath commanded me to go to bed,
And bade me to dismiss you. ③

① Why does Emilia say this? What has happened in the previous scene?

② In Shakespeare's time *incontinent* meant "at once."

③ Why does Othello want Emilia gone?

④ In this scene notice that Desdemona obeys her husband in all that he asks.

⑤ Desdemona breaks into her speech of love for Othello to direct Emilia in helping her undress. Shakespeare is adding little domestic details.

⑥ Desdemona seems to have a premonition of death. Find additional clues to her uneasiness.

EMILIA.   Dismiss me?

DESDEMONA.   It was his bidding; therefore, good Emilia,
Give me my nightly wearing, and adieu.
We must not now displease him. ④

EMILIA.   I would you had never seen him!

DESDEMONA.   So would not I: my love doth so approve him,
That even his stubbornness, his checks, his frowns—
Prithee, unpin me—have grace and favor in them. ⑤

EMILIA.   I have laid those sheets you bade me on the bed.

DESDEMONA.   All's one.
Good faith, how foolish are our minds!
If I do die before thee, prithee, shroud me
In one of those same sheets. ⑥

EMILIA.   Come, come, you talk.

DESDEMONA.   My mother had a maid call'd Barbara:
She was in love, and he she lov'd prov'd mad
And did forsake her.
She had a song of "willow";
An old thing 't was but it express'd her fortune,
And she died singing it. That song tonight
Will not go from my mind; I have much to do

But to go hang my head all at one side
And sing it like poor Barbara.
Prithee, dispatch. ⑦

EMILIA.   Shall I go fetch your nightgown?

DESDEMONA.   No, unpin me here.
This Lodovico is a proper man. ⑧

EMILIA.   A very handsome man.

DESDEMONA.   He speaks well.

EMILIA.   I know a lady in Venice would have walked barefoot to Palestine for a touch of his nether lip. ⑨

DESDEMONA.   *(Singing.)*
"The poor soul sat sighing by a
    sycamore tree,
Sing all a green willow; ⑩
Her hand on her bosom, her head on
    her knee
Sing willow, willow, willow.
The fresh streams ran by her, and
    murmur'd her moans;
Sing willow, willow, willow;
Her salt tears fell from her, and soften'd
    the stones;
Sing willow, willow, willow."
    Lay by these—
(Singing.) ⑪
"Willow"—
    Prithee, hie thee; he'll come anon —
    (Singing.)
"Sing all a green willow must be my
    garland.

Let nobody blame him, his scorn I
    approve—"
Nay, that's not next—
Hark! Who is 't that knocks?

EMILIA.   It's the wind.

DESDEMONA.   *(Singing.)*
"I call'd my love false love; but what
    said he then?
Sing willow, willow, willow.
If I court moe women, you'll couch
    with moe men—"
So, get thee gone; good-night.
Mine eyes do itch;
Doth that bode weeping?

EMILIA.   'T is neither here nor there.

DESDEMONA.   I have heard it said so.
    O, these men, these men!
Dost thou in conscience think—tell me,
    Emilia—
That there be women do abuse their
    husbands
In such gross kind?

EMILIA.   There be some such, no question.

DESDEMONA.   Wouldst thou do such a deed for all the world?

EMILIA.   Why, would not you?

DESDEMONA.   No, by this heavenly light! ⑫

EMILIA.   Nor I neither by this heavenly light; I might do't as well i' th' dark. ⑬

⑦ What does *dispatch* mean?

⑧ Lodovico had just been entertained in Othello's home.

⑨ The *nether* lip is the lower lip.

⑩ Find the melody of this plaintive piece in a book of Shakespearian songs.

⑪ As Desdemona sings this song, Emilia should be doing appropriate business, such as brushing her mistress's hair or hanging up her dress.

⑫ Here we realize that Desdemona is innocent of any unfaithfulness.

⑬ Emilia is joking. Emphasize the contrast between *light* and *dark*.

14 A cheap ring made in separate halves.

15 In the following speech, Emilia suggests that women can (and should) get revenge on husbands who go astray.

16 What does Desdemona think about Emilia's philosophy? Does Desdemona believe that a husband's ill conduct is an excuse for a wife's behaving badly?

DESDEMONA.   Wouldst thou do such a deed for all the world?

EMILIA.   The world's a huge thing; it is a great price
For a small vice.

DESDEMONA.   In troth, I think thou wouldst not.

EMILIA.   In troth, I think I should; and undo't when I had done.
Marry, I would not do such a thing for a joint-ring, **14** nor for measures of lawn, nor for gowns, petticoats, nor caps, nor any petty exhibition; but, for all the whole world—'ud's pity, who would not make her husband a cuckold to make him a monarch? I should venture purgatory for it.

DESDEMONA.   Beshrew me, if I would do such a wrong
For the whole world.

EMILIA.   Why, the wrong is but a wrong i' th' world; and having the world for your labour, 't is a wrong in your own world, and you might quickly make it right.

DESDEMONA.   I do not think there is any such woman.

EMILIA.   Yes, a dozen; and as many to th' vantage as would store the world they play'd for.

But I do think it is their husbands' faults **15**
If wives do fall. Say that they slack their duties
And pour our treasures into foreign laps,
'Or else break out in peevish jealousies.
Throwing restraint upon us; or say they strike us.
Or scant our former having in despite;
Why, we have galls, and though we have some grace,
Yet have we some revenge. Let husbands know
Their wives have sense like them; they see and smell
And have their palates both for sweet and sour
As husbands have. What is it that they do
When they change us for others? Is it sport?
I think it is. And doth affection breed it?
I think it doth. Is 't frailty that thus errs?
It is so too. And have not we affections,
Desires for sport, and frailty, as men have?
Then let them use us well; else let them know,
That ills we do, their ills instruct us so.

DESDEMONA.   Good-night, good-night. Heaven me such uses send,
Not to pick bad from bad, but by bad amend. **16**

The Glass Menagerie

by Tennessee Williams

In an attempt to help her daughter, Laura, gain skills for the job market, Amanda scrapes up the money to send Laura to typing school. But in her shyness, Laura quits the school without telling her mother. In the following scene, Amanda confronts her daughter about her deceit.

LAURA.   Mother, I was just . . .

AMANDA.   I know. You were just practicing your typing, I suppose. *(Behind chair R.)*

LAURA.   Yes.

AMANDA.   Deception, deception, deception!

LAURA.   *(Shakily.)* How was the D.A.R. meeting, Mother?

AMANDA.   *(Crosses to Laura.)* D.A.R. meeting!

LAURA.   Didn't you go to the D.A.R. meeting, Mother?

AMANDA.   *(Faintly, almost inaudibly.)* No, I didn't go to any D.A.R. meeting. *(Then more forcibly.)* I didn't have the strength—I didn't have the courage. I just wanted to find a hole in the ground and crawl in it and stay there the rest of my entire life. *(Tears type charts, throws them on floor.)*

LAURA.   *(Faintly.)* Why did you do that, Mother?

AMANDA.   *(Sits on R. end of day-bed.)* Why? Why? How old are you, Laura?

LAURA.   Mother, you know my age.

AMANDA.   I was under the impression that you were an adult, but evidently I was very much mistaken. *(She stares at Laura.)*

LAURA.   Please don't stare at me, Mother! *(Amanda closes her eyes and lowers her head. Pause.)*

AMANDA.   What are we going to do? What is going to become of us? What is the future? *(Pause.)*

LAURA.   Has something happened, Mother? Mother, has something happened?

AMANDA.   I'll be all right in a minute. I'm just bewildered—by life . . .

LAURA.   Mother, I wish that you would tell me what's happened!

AMANDA.   I went to the D.A.R. this afternoon, as you know; I was to be inducted as an officer. I stopped off at Rubicam's Business College to tell them about your cold and to ask how you were progressing down there.

LAURA.   Oh . . .

AMANDA.   Yes, oh-oh-oh. I went straight to your typing instructor and introduced myself as your mother. She didn't even know who you were. "Wingfield," she said? "We don't have any such scholar enrolled in this school." I assured her she did. I said my daughter Laura's been coming to classes since early January. "Well, I don't know," she said, "unless you mean that terribly shy little girl who dropped out of school after a few days' attendance?" No, I said, I don't mean that one. I mean my daughter, Laura, who's been coming here every single day for the past six weeks! "Excuse me," she said. And she took down the attendance book and there was your name, unmistakable, printed, and all the dates you'd been absent. I still told her she was wrong. I still said, "No there must have been some mistake! There must have been some mix-up in the records!" "No," she said, "I remember her perfectly now. She was so shy and her hands trembled so that her fingers couldn't touch the right keys! When we gave a speed-test—she just broke down completely—was sick at the stomach and had to be carried to the washroom! After that she never came back. We telephoned the house every single day and never got any answer." *(Rises from day-bed, crosses R.C.)* That was while I was working all day long down at that department store, I suppose, demonstrating those—*(With hands indicates brassiere.)* Oh! I felt so weak I couldn't stand up! *(Sits in armchair.)* I had to sit down while they got me a glass of water! *(Laura crosses up to phonograph.)* Fifty dollars' tuition. I don't care about the money so much, but all my hopes for any kind of future for you—gone up the spout, just gone up the spout like that. *(Laura winds phonograph up.)* Oh, don't do that, Laura!—Don't play that victrola!

LAURA.   Oh! *(Stops phonograph, crosses to typing table, sits.)*

AMANDA.   What have you been doing every day when you've gone out of the house pretending that you were going to business college?

LAURA.   I've just been going out walking.

AMANDA.   That's not true!

LAURA.   Yes, it is, Mother, I just went walking.

AMANDA.   Walking? Walking? In winter? Deliberately courting pneumonia in that light coat? Where did you walk to, Laura?

LAURA.   All sorts of places—mostly in the park.

AMANDA.   Even after you'd started catching that cold?

LAURA.   It was the lesser of two evils, Mother. I couldn't go back. I threw up on the floor!

AMANDA. From half-past seven till after five every day you mean to tell me you walked around in the park, because you wanted to make me think that you were still going to Rubicam's Business College?

LAURA. Oh, Mother, it wasn't as bad as it sounds. I went inside places to get warmed up.

AMANDA. Inside where?

LAURA. I went in the art museum and at the birdhouses at the Zoo. I visited the penguins every day! Sometimes I did without lunch and went to the movies. Lately I've been spending most of my afternoons in the Jewel-box, that big glass house where they raise the tropical flowers.

AMANDA. You did all that to deceive me, just for deception! Why? Why? Why? Why?

LAURA. Mother, when you're disappointed, you get that awful suffering look on your face, like the picture of Jesus' mother in the Museum!

(Rises.)

AMANDA. Hush!

LAURA. *(Crosses R. to menagerie.)* I couldn't face it. I couldn't.

AMANDA. *(Rising from day-bed.)* So what are we going to do now, honey, the rest of our lives? Just sit down in this house and watch the parades go by? Amuse ourselves with the glass menagerie? Eternally play those worn-out records your father left us as a painful reminder of him? *(Slams phonograph lid.)* We can't have a business career. No, we can't do that—that just gives us indigestion. *(Around R. day-bed.)* What is there left for us now but dependency all our lives? I tell you, Laura, I know so well what happens to unmarried women who aren't prepared to occupy a position in life. *(Crosses L, sits on day-bed.)* I've seen such pitiful cases in the South—barely tolerated spinsters living on some brother's wife or a sister's husband—tucked away in some mousetrap of a room—encouraged by one in-law to go on and visit the next in-law—little birdlike women— without any nest—eating the crust of humility all their lives! Is that the future that we've mapped out for ourselves? I swear I don't see any other alternative. And I don't think that's a very pleasant alternative. Of course— some girls do marry. My goodness, Laura, haven't you ever liked some boy?

LAURA. Yes, Mother, I liked one once.

AMANDA. You did?

LAURA. I came across his picture a while ago.

AMANDA. He gave you his picture, too? *(Rises from day-bed, crosses to chair R.)*

LAURA.   No, it's in the yearbook.

AMANDA.   *(Sits in armchair.)*
Oh—a high-school boy.

LAURA.   Yes. His name was Jim.

The Effect of Gamma Rays on Man-in-the-Moon Marigolds
by Paul Zindel

Act I

Scene 1

(As the house lights fade, a music theme fades in. A light picks up Tillie sitting on the floor R. of the sofa, she is holding a small white rabbit).

TILLIE'S VOICE.   *(Recorded.)* He told me to look at my hand for a part of it came from a star that exploded too long ago to imagine. This part of me was formed from a tongue of fire that screamed through the heavens until there was our sun. And this part of me—this tiny part of me—was on the sun when it itself exploded and whirled in a great storm until the planets came to be. *(The lights in the room begin to fade up slowly.)* And this small part of me was then a whisper of the earth. When there was life perhaps this part of me got lost in a fern that was crushed and covered until it was coal. And then it was a diamond millions of years later—it must have been a diamond as

beautiful as the star from which it had first come. *(The tape begins to fade and Tillie continues the speech.)* Or perhaps this part of me got lost in a terrible beast, or became part of a huge bird that flew above the primeval swamps. And he said this thing was so small— this part of me was so small it couldn't be seen—but it was there from the beginning of the world. And he called this bit of me an atom. And when he wrote the word, I fell in love with it. Atom. Atom. What a beautiful word. *(Pause. Telephone rings. The lights in the room fade up.)*

BEATRICE.   *(Off upstairs.)* Will somebody get that please? *(Phone continues to ring.)* Aaaaa! *(She enters, crosses downstairs.)* No help! Never any help! *(She answers the phone.)* Hello? Yes it is. Who's this? *(Pause.)* I hope there hasn't been any trouble at school? Oh, she's always been like that. She hardly says a word around here either. I always say some people were born to speak and others just to listen. *(Pause.)* You know I've been meaning to call you to thank *you* for that lovely rabbit you gave Matilda. She and I just adore it and it's gotten so big. *(Pause.)* Well, it certainly was thoughtful. Mr. Goodman, I don't mean to change the subject but aren't you that delightful young man Tillie said hello to a couple of months back at the A & P? You were by the lobster tank and I was by the frozen foods? That delightful and handsome young man? *(Pause.)* Why, I would very much indeed use the expression handsome. Yes, and . . . *(Pause.)* Well, I encourage her at every opportunity at home. Did she say I didn't? Both my daughters have their own desks and I put 75 watt bulbs right near them. *(She crosses to the D. end of the counter, turns her back to the audience and puts instant coffee into a cup.)* Yes. . . yes. . . *(She turns front.)* I think those tests are very much overrated, anyway, Mr. Goodman. Well believe me she's nothing like that around this house. *(She crosses to the L. of the table, pulls the chair out, and sits. Pause.)* Now I don't want you to think I don't appreciate what you're trying to do, Mr. Goodman, but I'm afraid it's simply useless. I'd say as long as she's doing well in your class that's all you should be concerned about. I'm sure with all those modern techniques you must have, you can bring her out— that is the phrase, isn't it?—just as well as anyone. *(Pause.)* I've tried just everything, but she isn't a pretty girl—I mean, let's be frank about it—she's going to have her problems. But with all your charm and patience I'm sure she'll respond and improve to your satisfaction. Are you married, Mr. Goodman? Oh, that's too bad. I don't know what's the matter with women today letting a handsome young man like you get away. *(Long pause.)* Well, some days she just doesn't feel like going to school. You just said how bright she is, and I'm really afraid to put too much of a strain on her after what happened to her sister. You know, too much strain is the worst thing in this modern world, Mr. Goodman, and I can't afford to have another convulsive on my hands, now can I? *(She rises, and crosses to the bottom of the stairs.)* I can't tell you how happy I am that you called. Why, believe it or not you're the first teacher that's ever taken the trouble to call me as a preventative measure. And I truly appreciate that, Mr. Goodman. Oh, the others call you when the damage has been done, but I doubt that Ruth would have had that breakdown, if those teachers down there had taken the trouble to call me. . . Well, she never acted strange at home. But don't you worry about Matilda. There will be some place for her in this world. And, like I said, some were born to speak and others just to listen. . . and do call again, Mr. Goodman, it's been a true pleasure speaking with you. Goodbye. *(She hangs up the phone, and crosses D. C. Tillie puts the rabbit in its cage.)* Matilda, that wasn't very nice of you to tell them I was forcibly detaining you from school. Why the way that Mr. Goodman spoke he must think I'm running a concentration camp. Do you have any idea how embarrassing it is to be accused of running a concentration camp for your own children? Well, it isn't embarrassing at all. *(She crosses*

U. of the kitchen table, to the counter, pours water into the cup with instant coffee, turns the hotplate off, and turns to Tillie.) That school of yours is forty years behind the times anyway, and believe me you learn more around here than that ugly Mr. Goodman can teach you! You know, I really feel sorry for him. Of course, he's not as bad as Miss Hanley. The idea of having her teach girl's gym is staggering. And you have to place me in the embarrassing position of giving them a reason to call me at eight-thirty in the morning, no less.

TILLIE. *(Rising.)* I didn't say anything...

BEATRICE. What do you tell them when they want to know why you stay home once in a while?

TILLIE. I tell them I'm sick.

BEATRICE. *(Crosses U. C., gets the pillow from the window ledge, crosses to U. of the L. sofa unit, puts the pillow on the sofa, and pushes the sofa next to the other section. She sits and drinks her coffee. Tillie picks up her school book from the sofa.)* Oh, you're sick all right, the exact nature of the illness is not fully realized, but you're sick all right. Any daughter that would turn her mother in as the administrator of a concentration camp has got to be suffering from something very peculiar.

TILLIE. *(Pause, as she crosses U. of the sofa, to the kitchen table.)* Can I go in today, mother? *(She picks up a second book, and crosses to the L. of Beatrice.)*

BEATRICE. You'll go in, all right...

TILLIE. Mr. Goodman said he was going to do an experiment...

BEATRICE. Why, he looks like the kind that would do his experimenting after sundown...

TILLIE. On radioactivity...

BEATRICE. On radioactivity? That's all that high school needs!

TILLIE. He's going to bring in the cloud chamber...

BEATRICE. Why, what an outstanding event. If you would've warned me I would've gotten dressed to kill and gone with you today. I just love seeing cloud chambers being brought in...

TILLIE. You can actually see...

BEATRICE. You're giving me a headache.

TILLIE. *(Pause as she crosses to U. of the end table.)* Please?

BEATRICE. No, my dear, the fortress of knowledge is not going to be blessed by your presence today. I have a good number of exciting duties for you to take care of, not the least of which is rabbit droppings.

TILLIE.   Oh, mother, please. . . I'll do it after school.

BEATRICE.   If we wait one minute longer this house is going to ferment. I found rabbit droppings in my bedroom even this time and if you don't start moving you're going to smell hasenpfeffer.

TILLIE.   (Crosses to the small table U. of Nanny's door, puts her books on the table, picks up the rabbit cage, crosses to the R. of the sofa, holding the cage between herself and Beatrice.) I could do it after Mr. Goodman's class. I'll say I'm ill and ask for a sick pass.

BEATRICE.   Do you want me to chloroform that thing right this minute?

TILLIE.   No!

BEATRICE.   Then shut up.

A Shayna Maidel
by Barbara Lebow

Set in New York City in 1946, this play portrays a family separated by the Holocaust. Although born in Poland, Rose, now in her twenties, came with her father to the United States when she was four. Her mother and sister could not follow and were put in concentration camps. In this scene, her sister Lusia, now grown, has just arrived in New York. Her old world ways are a sharp contrast to Rose's "Americanization." Lusia's intent is to find and be united with her husband Duvid. The two sisters discuss their early memories.

(Rose is heard softly humming a popular song. The morning light slowly comes up on her. She is wearing a robe and slippers, but looks dressed up. She is setting the table, trying to be quiet so as not to wake Lusia, although Lusia is not in sight and her bed is made. Rose enjoys arranging the small feast. The doorbell rings, startling her. She goes to the front door.)

ROSE.   Lusia! *(Rose follows Lusia as she puts down her handbag. Lusia is wearing the same clothes as when she arrived.)* I thought you were still sleeping. I've been tiptoeing around. What were you doing? Where could you go?

LUSIA.   To place I come to first. Where you come to get me.

ROSE.   Whatever for? Did you forget something? I'm surprised they're even open today. You went all by yourself?

LUSIA.   *(Struggling with language.)* I go read list. In books they got. And new names every day. People they find yet from the camps. Some coming yet from out woods where they been hiding.

ROSE.   I know. I know, Lusia. But surely by now—

LUSIA. New names every day. And so I make mine list. You see? And sometimes maybe I find a person some place alive, some family, some friend. And this how I find Duvid, or he finding me, too.

ROSE. But that would take a miracle.

LUSIA. Is no miracle. Duvid is a . . . a mensch. Is only knowing Duvid is alive.

ROSE. *(Covering her discomfort.)* I see. Come, you'll tell me more. We'll eat. *(Rose proudly leads Lusia to the laden dinette table. Lusia shrinks back, overwhelmed.)*

LUSIA. Too much food! So much. No, too much, I think.

ROSE. You must eat, Lusia. You've got to eat enough. And there's plenty, really, *(Piling food on Lusia's plate.)* I know you're the big sister, but you've got to let me take care of you, for now. Then, when everything's normal again, you'll be the big sister. *(Rose pours a glass of milk. Lusia sips at it, picks at the food. As they continue talking, they remain contrasted in manner. Lusia is still, Rose animated, using her hands a lot.)*

LUSIA. Funny, big sister, baby sister. I have baby sister one time, long time. . .

ROSE. Ago.

LUSIA. Long time ago. So beautiful I think, and I take for walk in. . .

ROSE. Carriage?

LUSIA. Carriage, yes, I take for walk and show to friends mine baby shvester. Make me feel good. Happy. Then gone. And many years no sister but picture from America and letter from Papa and lady who takes care of.

ROSE. Mrs. Greenspan. Tanta Perla.

LUSIA. Yes. And then no more letter. No more sister. *(Voice.)* And carriage stays empty for too much years . . . And baby shvester woman now who want take care me.

ROSE. I don't remember at all. I wish I did.

LUSIA. You don't remember even Mama? *(Rose shakes her head.)* Nothing?

ROSE. I was only four when we left. It's so strange that you have memories of me, that I was part of your life. That I was born in another world. I don't remember any of it. Just a feeling, maybe. Sometimes there's a particular smell when something's cooking or a song comes on the radio and all of a sudden I feel different, like I'm in another place.

LUSIA. How you feel then?

ROSE. Warm. Safe. Sad.

LUSIA. Mama, that is. The feeling from Mama. *(Rose and Lusia look at one another silently across the table, each mirror to the other for a moment.)*

ROSE.   Eat some more, Lusia. You're not eating enough. *(Pause while Lusia picks at food.)* Lusia, have you wondered about it, thought why you got sick and not me?

LUSIA.   Mama says was plan from God. But she keeps hold our passage, our tickets, till could not read no more. Till thin like old leaf. Till long time after no good, no one . . . they no loz no one . . . no one . . . *(She is frustrated, trying to find the English word.)*

ROSE.   Allowed.

LUSIA.   Allowed leave Poland no more.

ROSE.   And I was playing stickball and going to the movies and eating Mello-Rolls!

LUSIA.   What means this?

ROSE.   Oh, it doesn't matter. *(She pushes away from the table, gets up.)* He should have gotten you out!

LUSIA.   Mama told how whole America changes mind, wants no new Jewish, no new people no more. All fast like this *(Snaps her fingers.)* something happens no one got money. From streets with gold to nothing. And everyone, not just mine father.

ROSE.   That was the Depression. It kept you away, but it didn't make any difference in my life. I remember having bad dreams when I was little, but I don't know what about. Everything else stayed the same; the food, the stories on the radio and Tanta Perla, like a bird chirping around me trying to give comfort after the bad dreams. But she never could.

LUSIA.   De varemsteh bet iz de mamas. Farshtaist?

ROSE.   Yeah, but how could I tell? Mama wasn't real to me. They'd never say her name, or yours. They called you "Them," talking in whispers or in certain looks so I could just pick up little bits of what was going on. And when I was older and could have understood, I knew it was forbidden, Papa wouldn't talk. Not about you, not about Mama. He would just say he was working it out or, later, that Roosevelt would take care of everyone over there. I tried to make myself a family out of the photographs and letters, but they were in Yiddish and I only learned to read English. Tanta Perla used to read them to me and translate. Papa never would. Then, when there were no more letters, I began to forget completely. By the time the war came, it was as if there had been no one there at all. . . until Papa found you. I still don't know exactly how to feel. I mean, I've had it pretty easy and you—

LUSIA.   Mine father don't know I'm here yet?

ROSE.   He'll be in shul all day. We can call him tonight or even go out there.

LUSIA.   No. Tuesday I suppose to come on boat.

ROSE.   Papa was going to come with me to meet you. He'll be mad if we don't let him know you're here.

LUSIA.   This I remember good about Papa. He gets so mad. He makes a big voice, everybody is . . . *(She shakes.)*

ROSE.   Nervous.

LUSIA.   Nervous.

ROSE.   In that way, he hasn't changed.

LUSIA.   I remember him. Papa was a man very . . . pretty?

ROSE.   Handsome? Papa?

LUSIA.   Handsome. And I know from pictures, too. But everything must be certain way or he is so mad. And very . . . *(She gestures.)*

ROSE.   Strict.

LUSIA.   Strict. But very proud when we all dress up. You, too. And Mama. Family all go out together. I see his face and I'm thinking how happy he is, how proud. He don't say nothing, but I can see. You know this face?

ROSE.   I've never seen that look. *(Pause.)* We'll have to call him tomorrow.

Jar the Floor
by Cheryl L. West

Vennie and her friend Raisa have come to visit Vennie's mother MayDee and her grandmother MaDear, although the mother and daughter have long been at odds. Vennie and Maydee can't seem to avoid arguing.

MAYDEE.   I find it so astounding that you never fail to make sure everything careens out of control every time you come home.

VENNIE.   So this is all my fault?

MAYDEE.   Who said anything about fault? Let's just table this. I want MaDear to have a good day. We have plenty of time to discuss this later. How long are you two planning to stay?

VENNIE.   You started it.

MAYDEE.   Started what? What did I start this time? All I asked you was how long you plan to stay. How is that an invitation for conflict?

VENNIE.   Mother please! It's what you start every time I come home . . .

MAYDEE.   I have not started one thing today . . . all I asked . . .

VENNIE.   You and your little ice pick . . . soon's you see me, you go to town. Pick, pick, pick. My clothes ain't right, pick, my hair ain't right, pick,

pick, my grammar ain't right. . .triple pick. . . sum it up, I ain't right. . .

MAYDEE. Whine . . . whine . . . whine . . . grow up, Vennie.

VENNIE. I would if you'd let me.

MAYDEE. That's not true.

VENNIE. *(Sarcastically, but delivered calmly with a smile.)* Oh, let's get real. Y'all have performed for the company so let's take it on down to Front Street. See Raisa, I'm something to be bought for, organized and then laid out so others can marvel at how wonderful MayDee Lakeland is . . . how she overcame every obstacle to get her three degrees in one hand and raise me single-handedly in the other. . . and what's that commercial. . . never let 'em see you sweat. Well that's MayDee Lakeland . . . you'll never see her sweat, queen of control . . . that's what we all love about her . . . *(Feigned innocence, as if the thought just occurred to her.)* Um, do we have an itinerary this week-end, Mother? I was telling Raisa that you always made sure I participated in every activity: karate, dance, art, gymnastics. So did the secretary remember to outline Vennie's activities, you know in those fifteen minute increments. . . what Mother-dear is going to do with daughter-dear this weekend. *(MayDee quietly disposes of the itinerary.)* Oh come on now, you didn't leave our time

together to chance. 'Cause then maybe you would have to enjoy me. And that would be too much like right, wouldn't it Mother? S'pecially given that you don't even like me.

MAYDEE. *(Pausing, embarrassed to have this conversation in front of Raisa, MayDee laughs.)* You're just like your grandmother, such a wicked sense of humor. I love you, Vennie. All I ever wanted was to protect you. Don't you know how much I love you, whatever you do?

VENNIE. What I know is being your daughter hurts . . . bad, or should I say badly. . .

MAYDEE. You can't mean that. *(Exits with hair stuff.)*

Macbeth
by William Shakespeare

After helping her husband kill King Duncan, Lady Macbeth is obsessed with her terrible deed. In this sleepwalking scene, her gentlewoman asks the doctor to observe and diagnose the problem.

GENTLEWOMAN. Lo you, here she comes! This is her very guise, and upon my life, fast asleep. Observe her. Stand close.

DOCTOR. How came she by that light?

GENTLEWOMAN. Why, it stood by her. She has light by her continually, 'tis her command.

DOCTOR. You see, her eyes are open.

GENTLEWOMAN. Aye, but their sense is shut.

DOCTOR. What is it she does now? Look how she rubs her hands.

GENTLEWOMAN. It is an accustomed action with her to seem thus washing her hands. I have known her continue in this a quarter of an hour.

LADY MACBETH. Yet, here's a spot.

DOCTOR. Hark! She speaks. I will set down what comes from her, to satisfy my remembrance the more strongly.

LADY MACBETH. Out, damned spot! Out I say! One, two—why, then 'tis time to do 't. Hell is murky. Fie, my lord, fie! A soldier, and afeard? What need we fear who knows it, when none can call our power to account? Yet who would have thought the old man to have had so much blood in him?

DOCTOR. Do you mark that?

LADY MACBETH. The Thane of Fife had a wife. Where is she now? What, will these hands ne'er be clean? No more o' that, my lord, no more o' that. You mar all with this starting.

DOCTOR. Go to, go to. You have known what you should not.

GENTLEWOMAN. She has spoke what she should not, I am sure of that. Heaven knows what she has known.

LADY MACBETH. Here's the smell of the blood still. All the perfumes of Arabia will not sweeten this little hand. Oh, oh, oh!

DOCTOR. What a sigh is there! The heart is sorely charged.

GENTLEWOMAN. I would not have such a heart in my bosom for the dignity of the whole body.

DOCTOR. Well, well, well—

GENTLEWOMAN. Pray God it be, sir.

DOCTOR. This disease is beyond my practice. Yet I have known those which have walked in their sleep who have died holily in their beds.

LADY MACBETH. Wash your hands, put on your nightgown, look not so pale. I tell you yet again, Banquo's buried, he cannot come out on's grave.

DOCTOR. Even so?

LADY MACBETH. To bed, to bed, there's knocking at the gate. Come, come, come, come, give me your hand. What's done cannot be undone. To bed, to bed, to bed. *(Exit.)*

Blithe Spirit
by Noel Coward

After holding a seance for research on his book, Charles finds that the spirit of his dead wife, Elvira, has appeared. Since only Charles (and the audience) can see her, his present wife, Ruth, thinks he is crazy. In trying to convince Ruth that the spirit of Elvira is indeed present, the following humorous scene ensues.

(Elvira enters by the windows, carrying a bunch of grey roses. She crosses to the writing-table up stage R., and throws the zinnias into the wastepaper basket and puts her roses into the vase. The roses are as grey as the rest of her.)

ELVIRA.   You've absolutely ruined that border by the sundial. It looks like a mixed salad.

CHARLES.   Oh, my God!

RUTH.   What's the matter now?

CHARLES.   She's here again!

RUTH.   What do you mean? Who's here again?

CHARLES.   Elvira.

RUTH.   Pull yourself together and don't be absurd.

ELVIRA.   It's all those nasturtiums; they're so vulgar.

CHARLES.   I like nasturtiums.

RUTH.   You like what?

ELVIRA.   *(Putting her grey roses into the vase.)* They're all right in moderation, but in a mass like that they look beastly.

RUTH.   *(Crosses over to R. of Charles, C.)* What did you mean about nasturtiums?

CHARLES.   *(Takes Ruth's hands and comes round to the L. of her.)* Never mind about that now. I tell you she's here again.

ELVIRA.   *(Comes to above the sofa.)* You have been having a nice scene, haven't you? I could hear you right down the garden.

CHARLES.   Please mind your own business.

RUTH.   If you behaving like a lunatic isn't my business, nothing is.

ELVIRA.   I expect it was about me, wasn't it? I know I ought to feel sorry, but I'm not. I'm delighted.

CHARLES.   Ruth—darling—please . . .

RUTH.   I've done everything I can to help. I've controlled myself admirably. And I should like to say here and now that I don't believe a word about your damned hallucination. You're up to something, Charles—there's been a certain furtiveness in your manner for weeks. Why don't you be honest and tell me what it is?

CHARLES. You're wrong—you're dead wrong! I haven't been in the least furtive—I—

RUTH. You're trying to upset me. *(She moves away from Charles.)* For some obscure reason you're trying to goad me into doing something that I might regret. *(She bursts into tears.)* I won't stand for it any more. You're making me utterly miserable! *(She crosses to the sofa and falls into the R. end of it.)*

CHARLES. *(Crosses to Ruth.)* Ruth—please—

RUTH. Don't come near me!

ELVIRA. Let her have a nice cry. It'll do her good. *(She saunters round to down stage L.)*

CHARLES. You're utterly heartless!

RUTH. Heartless!

CHARLES. *(Wildly.)* I was not talking to you! I was talking to Elvira.

RUTH. Go on talking to her then, talk to her until you're blue in the face, but don't talk to me.

CHARLES. *(Crosses to Elvira.)* Help me, Elvira—

ELVIRA. How?

CHARLES. Make her see you or something.

ELVIRA. I'm afraid I couldn't manage that. It's technically the most difficult business—frightfully complicated, you know—it takes years of study—

CHARLES. You are here, aren't you? You're not an illusion?

ELVIRA. I may be an illusion, but I'm most definitely here.

CHARLES. How did you get here?

ELVIRA. I told you last night—I don't exactly know—

CHARLES. Well, you must make me a promise that in future you only come and talk to me when I'm alone.

ELVIRA. *(Pouting.)* How unkind you are, making me feel so unwanted. I've never been treated so rudely.

CHARLES. I don't mean to be rude, but you must see—

ELVIRA. It's all your own fault for having married a woman who is incapable of seeing beyond the nose on her face. If she had a grain of real sympathy or affection for you she'd believe what you tell her.

CHARLES. How could you expect anybody to believe this?

ELVIRA. You'd be surprised how gullible people are; we often laugh about it on the Other Side.

(Ruth, who has stopped crying and been staring at Charles in horror, suddenly rises.)

RUTH.   *(Gently.)* Charles!

CHARLES.   *(Surprised at her tone.)* Yes, dear—*(Charles crosses to her, R.)*

RUTH.   I'm awfully sorry I was cross.

CHARLES.   But, my dear—

RUTH.   I understand everything now. I do really.

CHARLES.   You do?

RUTH.   *(Patting his arm reassuringly.)* Of course I do.

ELVIRA.   Look out—she's up to something.

CHARLES.   Will you please be quiet?

RUTH.   Of course, darling. We'll all be quiet, won't we? We'll be as quiet as little mice.

CHARLES.   Ruth dear, listen—

RUTH.   I want you to come upstairs with me and go to bed.

ELVIRA.   The way that woman harps on bed is nothing short of erotic.

CHARLES.   I'll deal with you later.

RUTH.   Very well, darling—come along.

CHARLES.   What are you up to?

RUTH.   I'm not up to anything. I just want you to go quietly to bed and wait there until Doctor Bradman comes.

CHARLES.   No, Ruth, you're wrong—

RUTH.   *(Firmly.)* Come, dear—

ELVIRA.   She'll have you in a straitjacket before you know where you are.

CHARLES.   *(Comes to Elvira—frantically.)* Help me—you must help me—

ELVIRA.   *(Enjoying herself.)* My dear, I would with pleasure, but I can't think how.

CHARLES.   I can. *(Back to Ruth.)* Listen, Ruth—

RUTH.   Yes, dear?

CHARLES.   If I promise to go to bed, will you let me stay here for five minutes longer?

RUTH.   I really think it would be better—

CHARLES.   Bear with me, however mad it may seem, bear with me for just five minutes longer.

RUTH.   *(Leaving go of him.)* Very well. What is it?

CHARLES.   Sit down.

RUTH.   *(Sitting down.)* All right. There!

CHARLES. Now listen, listen carefully—

ELVIRA. Have a cigarette; it will soothe your nerves.

CHARLES. I don't want a cigarette.

RUTH. *(Indulgently.)* Then you shan't have one, darling.

CHARLES. Ruth, I want to explain to you clearly and without emotion that beyond any shadow of doubt, the ghost or shade or whatever you like to call it of my first wife Elvira is in this room now.

RUTH. Yes, dear.

CHARLES. I know you don't believe it and are trying valiantly to humor me, but I intend to prove it to you.

RUTH. Why not lie down and have a nice rest and you can prove anything you want to later on?

CHARLES. She may not be here later on.

ELVIRA. Don't worry—she will!

CHARLES. Oh God!

RUTH. Hush, dear.

CHARLES. *(To Elvira.)* Promise you'll do what I ask?

ELVIRA. That all depends what it is.

CHARLES. *(Between them both, facing upstage.)* Ruth—you see that bowl of flowers on the piano?

RUTH. Yes, dear, I did it myself this morning.

ELVIRA. Very untidily, if I may say so.

CHARLES. You may not.

RUTH. Very well—I never will again. I promise.

CHARLES. Elvira will now carry that bowl of flowers to the mantelpiece and back again. You will, Elvira, won't you? Just to please me.

ELVIRA. I don't really see why I should. You've been quite insufferable to me ever since I materialized.

CHARLES. Please!

ELVIRA. *(Goes over to the piano.)* All right, I will just this once. Not that I approve of all these Maskelyne and Devant carryings-on.

CHARLES. *(Crosses to the mantel-piece.)* Now, Ruth—watch carefully!

RUTH. *(Patiently.)* Very well, dear.

CHARLES. Go on, Elvira—take it to the mantelpiece and back again.

(Elvira takes a bowl of pansies off the piano and brings it slowly down stage, below the armchair to the fire; then suddenly pushes towards Ruth's face, who jumps up and faces Charles, who is at the mantel piece.)

RUTH. *(Furiously.)* How dare you, Charles! You ought to be ashamed of yourself.

CHARLES. What on earth for?

RUTH. *(Hysterically.)* It's a trick. I know perfectly well it's a trick. You've been working up to this. It's all part of some horrible plan. . .

CHARLES. It isn't—I swear it isn't. Elvira—do something else, for God's sake!

ELVIRA. Certainly—anything to oblige.

RUTH. *(Becoming really frightened.)* You want to get rid of me—you're trying to drive me out of my mind—

CHARLES. Don't be so silly.

RUTH. You're cruel and sadistic and I'll never forgive you.

(Elvira picks up the chair from down stage L., holds it in midair as if to hit Ruth, Ruth flinches, then Elvira puts it back, and stands above the windows. Ruth makes a dive for the door, moving between the armchair and sofa. Charles follows and catches her.)

I'm not going to put up with this any more.

CHARLES. *(Holding her.)* You must believe it—you must—

RUTH. Let me go immediately.

CHARLES. That was Elvira—I swear it was.

RUTH. *(Struggling.)* Let me go.

CHARLES. Ruth—please—

(Ruth breaks away to the windows. Elvira shuts them in her face and crosses quickly to the mantelpiece. Ruth turns at the windows to face Charles.)

RUTH. *(Looking at Charles with eyes of horror.)* Charles—this is madness—sheer madness—it's some sort of auto-suggestion, isn't it?—Some form of hypnotism, swear to me it's only that— *(She rushes to Charles, C.)* Swear to me it's only that.

ELVIRA. *(Taking an expensive vase from the mantelpiece and crashing it into the grate.)* Hypnotism my foot!

The Dining Room
by A.R. Gurney, Jr.

This scene is of a family celebrating a holiday at their homestead. They are confronted by the fact that their elderly mother is living in the past.

NANCY. I've got the plates, Mrs. Driscoll. You've got your hands full with that turkey. *(She sets the plates and carving utensils at the head of the table and calls toward the hall.)* ① We're ready, everybody! Come on in! *(The singing continues as the family*

① What holiday is this family celebrating? Where has the family gathered?

(2) Why is Stuart escorting his mother to the dining room and not her other sons?

(3) Why is the Old Lady confused? How old do you think she is? How can you physically show old age without using cliché movements?

(4) What words give clues about how the Old Lady was raised and the economic condition of her family?

(5) How does the Old Lady sound? Is she teasing, or does she really not know her children?

(6) Who are Beth and Nancy? Are they children or daughters-in-law? Which one do you think is married to Stuart?

begins to come into the dining room to celebrate Thanksgiving dinner. The oldest son, Stuart, has his mother on his arm. She is a very vague, very old Old Lady.) **(2)**

STUART.   . . .Now, Mother, I want you to sit next to me, and Fred, you sit on Mother's left, and Ben, you sit opposite her where she can see you, and Nancy and Beth hold up that end of the table, and there we are. *(Genial chatter as everyone sits down. The two sons push in their mother's chair. After a moment the Old Lady stands up again, looks around distractedly.)* **(3)** What's the matter, Mother?

OLD LADY.   I'm not quite sure where I am.

STUART.   *(Expansively; arm around her; seating her again.)* You're here, Mother. In your own dining room. This is your table, and here are your chairs, and here is the china you got on your trip to England, and here's the silver-handled carving knife which Father used to use. **(4)**

OLD LADY.   Oh yes. . . *(Genial laughter, ad-libbing: "She's a little tired. . . It's been a long day..." The Old Lady gets up again.)* But who are these people? I'm not quite sure who these people are. *(She begins to wander around the room.)* **(5)**

STUART.   *(Following her around.)* It's me, Mother: Stuart. Your son. And

here's Fred, and Ben, and Nancy, and Beth. We're all here, Mother. **(6)**

NANCY.   *(Going into the kitchen.)* I'll get the turkey. That might help her focus.

STUART.   Yes. *(To Old Lady.)* Mrs. Driscoll is here, Mother. Right in the kitchen, where she's always been. And your grandchildren. All your grandchildren were here. Don't you remember? They ate first, at the children's table, and now they're out in back playing touch football. You watched them, Mother. *(He indicates the French doors.)*

OLD LADY.   Oh yes. . . *(She sits down again at the other end of the table. Nancy comes out from the kitchen carrying a large platter. Appropriate Oh's and Ah's from Group.)*

STUART.   And look, Mother. Here's Nancy with the turkey. . . Put it right over there, Nancy. . . See, Mother? Isn't it a beautiful bird? And I'm going to carve it just the way Father did, and give you a small piece of the breast and a dab of dressing, just as always, Mother. *(He sharpens the carving knife officiously.)* **(7)**

OLD LADY.   *(Still staring out into the garden.)* Just as always. . .

STUART.   *(As he sharpens.)* And Fred will have the drumstick—am I right, Fred?—And Beth gets the wishbone, and Ben ends up with the Pope's nose, am I right, Ben? *(Genial in-group laughter.)*

NANCY. Save some for Mrs. Driscoll.

STUART. I always do, Nancy. Mrs. Driscoll likes the second joint.

OLD LADY. This is all very nice, but I think I'd like to go home.

STUART. *(Patiently, as he carves.)* You are home, Mother. You've lived here fifty-two years.

BEN. Fifty-four.

BETH. Forever.

STUART. Ben, pass this plate down to Mother . . .

OLD LADY. *(Getting up.)* Thank you very much, but I really do think it's time to go.

NANCY. Uh-oh.

STUART. *(Going to her.)* Mother . . .

BETH. Oh dear.

OLD LADY. Will someone drive me home, please? I live at eighteen Summer Street with my mother and sisters.

BETH. What will we do?

STUART. *(Going to Old Lady.)* It's not there now, Mother. Don't you remember? We drove down. There's a big building there now.

OLD LADY. *(Holding out her hand.)* Thank you very much for asking me . . . Thank you for having me to your house. *(She begins to go around the table, thanking people.)*

FRED. Mother! I'm Fred! Your son!

OLD LADY. Isn't that nice? Thank you. I've had a perfectly lovely time . . . Thank you . . . Thank you so much. *(She shakes hands with Nancy.)* It's been absolutely lovely . . . Thank you, thank you. ⑧

STUART. Quickly. Let's sing to her.

BETH. Sing?

STUART. She likes singing. We ⑨ used to sing to her whenever she'd get upset . . . Fred, Ben. Quickly. Over here.

OLD LADY. *(Wandering distractedly around.)* Now I can't find my gloves. Where would my gloves be? I can't go out without my gloves.

BEN. What song? I can't remember any of the songs.

STUART. Sure you can. Come on. Hmmmmmmmmm. *(He sounds a note. The others try to find their parts.)*

BEN & FRED. Hmmmmm.

OLD LADY. I need my gloves, I need my hat . . .

STUART. *(Singing.)* "As the blackbird in the spring . . .

OTHERS. *(Joining in.)* 'Neath the willow tree . . .

⑦ What does his sharpening the knife "officiously" tell you about Stuart's personality? How do you physically show being officious while carving the turkey?

⑧ How would the Old Lady speak and gesture while saying these words?

⑨ To try to distract their mother, the children are eager to start singing. A sense of urgency (and a faster pace) must be accomplished.

10 Look up the music to "Aura Lee." It was once a popular song, and it is easy to sing and fun to harmonize. You can find the song in a book that features songs from the past.

11 Notice how the words *carriage* and *tea* (a special meal) place the Old Lady in the past. When would that be?

12 Both Fred and Ben must communicate their willingness to help their older brother appease their mother. What do you think will happen when they show her that her old house is no longer there?

Sat and piped, I hear him sing,
Sing of Aura Lee . . ." **10**
(They sing in pleasant, amateurish, corny harmony. The Old Lady stops fussing, turns her head, and listens. The other women remain at the table.)

MEN. *(Singing.)* "Aura Lee, Aura Lee, Maid of Golden Hair . . .
Sunshine came along with thee, and swallows in the air."

OLD LADY. I love music. Every person in our family could play a different instrument. *(She sits in a chair along the wall, Down Right.)*

STUART. *(To his brothers.)* She's coming around. Quickly. Second verse.

MEN. *(Singing with more confidence now; more daring harmony.)*
"In thy blush the rose was born,
Music, when you spake,
Through thine azure eye the morn
Sparkling seemed to break.
Aura Lee, Aura Lee, Maid of Golden Hair,
Sunshine came along with thee, and swallows in the air."
(They hold a long note at the end. The Old Lady claps. Everyone claps.)

OLD LADY. That was absolutely lovely.

STUART. Thank you, Mother.

OLD LADY. But now I've simply got to go home. Would you call my carriage, please? And someone find my hat and gloves. It's very late, and my mother gets very nervous if I'm not home in time for tea. *(She heads for the hall.)* **11**

STUART. *(To no one in particular.)* Look, Fred, Ben, we'll drive her down, and show her everything. The new office complex where her house was. The entrance to the Thruway. The new Howard Johnson's motel. Everything! And she'll see that nothing's there at all.

FRED. I'll bring the car around.

STUART. I'll get her coat.

BEN. I'm coming, too. **12**

STUART. We'll just have to go through the motions.

A Raisin in the Sun
by Lorraine Hansberry

Walter and his wife Ruth and sister Beneatha all live with Walter and Beneatha's mother in a cramped apartment in a black neighborhood in a large city. Because some money has come into the family, their mother has put a down payment on a house in a white section of town. Mr. Lindner comes to talk to them about "problems" he foresees in their move.

LINDNER. How do you do.

WALTER. *(Amiably, as he sits himself easily on a chair, leaning with interest forward on his knees and looking expectantly into the newcomer's face.)* What can we do for you, Mr. Lindner!

LINDNER. *(Some minor shuffling of the hat and briefcase on his knees.)* Well—I am a representative of the Clybourne Park Improvement Association—

WALTER. *(Pointing.)* Why don't you sit your things on the floor?

LINDNER. Oh—yes. Thank you. *(He slides the briefcase and hat under the chair.)* And as I was saying—I am from the Clybourne Park Improvement Association and we have had it brought to our attention at the last meeting that you people—or at least your mother—has bought a piece of residential property at—*(He digs for the slip of paper again.)*—four o six Clybourne Street.

WALTER. That's right. Care for something to drink? Ruth, get Mr. Lindner a beer.

LINDNER. *(Upset for some reason.)* Oh—no, really. I mean thank you very much, but no thank you.

RUTH. *(Innocently.)* Some coffee?

LINDNER. Thank you, nothing at all.

(Beneatha is watching the man carefully.)

LINDNER. Well, I don't know how much you folks know about our organization. *(He is a gentle man; thoughtful and somewhat labored in his manner.)* It is one of these community organizations set up to look after—oh, you know, things like block upkeep and special projects and we also have what we call our New Neighbors Orientation Committee...

BENEATHA. *(Drily.)* Yes—and what do they do?

LINDNER. *(Turning a little to her and then returning the main force to Walter.)* Well—it's what you might call a sort of welcoming committee, I guess. I mean they, we, I'm the chairman of the committee—go around and see the new people who move into the neighborhood and sort of give them the lowdown on the way we do things out in Clybourne Park.

BENEATHA. *(With appreciation of the two meanings, which escape Ruth and Walter.)* Un-huh.

LINDNER. And we also have the category of what the association calls—*(He looks elsewhere.)*—uh—special community problems...

BENEATHA. Yes—and what are some of those?

WALTER. Girl, let the man talk.

LINDNER. *(With understated relief.)* Thank you. I would sort of like to explain this thing in my own way. I mean I want to explain to you in a certain way.

WALTER. Go ahead.

LINDNER. Yes. Well. I'm going to try to get right to the point. I'm sure we'll all appreciate that in the long run.

BENEATHA. Yes.

WALTER. Be still now!

LINDNER. Well—

RUTH. *(Still innocently.)* Would you like another chair—you don't look comfortable.

LINDNER. *(More frustrated than annoyed.)* No, thank you very much. Please. Well—to get right to the point I—*(A great breath, and he is off at last.)* I am sure you people must be aware of some of the incidents which have happened in various parts of the city when colored people have moved into certain areas—*(Beneatha exhales heavily and starts tossing a piece of fruit up and down in the air.)* Well— because we have what I think is going to be a unique type of organization in American community life—not only do we deplore that kind of thing—but we are trying to do something about it. *(Beneatha stops tossing and turns with a new and quizzical interest to the*

man.) We feel—*(Gaining confidence in his mission because of the interest in the faces of the people he is talking to.)*—we feel that most of the trouble in this world, when you come right down to it—*(He hits his knee for emphasis.)*— most of the trouble exists because people just don't sit down and talk to each other.

RUTH. *(Nodding as she might in church, pleased with the remark.)* You can say that again, mister.

LINDNER. *(More encouraged by such affirmation.)* That we don't try hard enough in this world to understand the other fellow's problem. The other guy's point of view.

RUTH. Now that's right.

(Beneatha and Walter merely watch and listen with genuine interest.)

LINDNER. Yes—that's the way we feel out in Clybourne Park. And that's why I was elected to come here this afternoon and talk to you people. Friendly like, you know, the way people should talk to each other and see if we couldn't find some way to work this thing out. As I say, the whole business is a matter of *caring* about the other fellow. Anybody can see that you are a nice family of folks, hardworking and honest I'm sure. *(Beneatha frowns slightly, quizzically, her head tilted regarding him.)* Today everybody knows what it means to be on the outside of *something*. And of course, there is always somebody who is out to take advantage of people who don't always understand.

WALTER.   What do you mean?

LINDNER.   Well—you see our community is made up of people who've worked hard as the dickens for years to build up that little community. They're not rich and fancy people; just hard-working, honest people who don't really have much but those little homes and a dream of the kind of community they want to raise their children in. Now, I don't say we are perfect and there is a lot wrong in some of the things they want. But you've got to admit that a man, right or wrong, has the right to want to have the neighborhood he lives in a certain kind of way. And at the moment the overwhelming majority of our people out there feel that people get along better, take more of a common interest in the life of the community, when they share a common background. I want you to believe me when I tell you that race prejudice simply doesn't enter into it. It is a matter of the people of Clybourne Park believing, rightly or wrongly, as I say, that for the happiness of all concerned that our Negro families are happier when they live in their *own* communities.

BENEATHA.   *(With a grand and bitter gesture.)* This, friends, is the Welcoming Committee!

WALTER.   *(Dumbfounded, looking at Lindner.)* Is this what you came marching all the way over here to tell us?

LINDNER.   Well, now we've been having a fine conversation. I hope you'll hear me all the way through.

WALTER.   *(Tightly.)* Go ahead, man.

LINDNER.   You see—in the face of all things I have said, we are prepared to make your family a very generous offer. . .

BENEATHA.   Thirty pieces and not a coin less!

WALTER.   Yeah?

LINDNER.   *(Putting on his glasses and drawing a form out of the briefcase.)* Our association is prepared, through the collective effort of our people, to buy the house from you at a financial gain to your family.

RUTH.   Lord have mercy, ain't this the living gall!

WALTER.   All right, you through?

LINDNER.   Well, I want to give you the exact terms of the financial arrangement—

WALTER.   We don't want to hear no exact terms of no arrangements. I want to know if you got any more to tell us 'bout getting together?

LINDNER.   *(Taking off his glasses.)* Well—I don't suppose that you feel. . .

WALTER. Never mind how I feel—you got any more to say 'bout how people ought to sit down and talk to each other?... Get out of my house, man.

(He turns his back and walks to the door.)

LINDNER. *(Looking around at the hostile faces and reaching and assembling his hat and briefcase.)* Well—I don't understand why you people are reacting this way. What do you think you are going to gain by moving into a neighborhood where you just aren't wanted and where some elements—well—people can get awful worked up when they feel that their whole way of life and everything they've ever worked for is threatened.

WALTER. Get out.

LINDNER. *(At the door, holding a small card.)* Well—I'm sorry it went like this.

WALTER. Get out.

LINDNER. *(Almost sadly regarding Walter.)* You just can't force people to change their hearts, son.

(He turns and puts his card on a table and exits. Walter pushes the door to with stinging hatred, and stands looking at it. Ruth just sits and Beneatha just stands. They say nothing. Mama and Travis enter.)

MAMA. Well—this all the packing got done since I left out of here this morning. I testify before God that my children got all the energy of the dead. What time the moving men due?

BENEATHA. Four o'clock. You had a caller, Mama.

(She is smiling, teasingly.)

MAMA. Sure enough—who?

BENEATHA. *(Her arms folded saucily.)* The Welcoming Committee.

(Walter and Ruth giggle.)

MAMA. *(Innocently.)* Who?

BENEATHA. The Welcoming Committee. They said they're sure going to be glad to see you when you get there.

WALTER. *(Devilishly.)* Yeah, they said they can't hardly wait to see your face.

(Laughter.)

MAMA. *(Sensing their facetiousness.)* What's the matter with you all?

WALTER. Ain't nothing the matter with us. We just telling you 'bout the gentleman who came to see you this afternoon. From the Clybourne Park Improvement Association.

MAMA. What he want?

RUTH. *(In the same mood as Beneatha and Walter.)* To welcome you, honey.

WALTER.   He said they can't hardly wait. He said the one thing they don't have, that they just dying to have out there is a fine family of colored people! *(To Ruth and Beneatha.)* Ain't that right!

RUTH and BENEATHA.   *(Mockingly.)* Yeah! He left his card in case—

(They indicate the card, and Mama picks it up and throws it on the floor— understanding and looking off as she draws her chair up to the table on which she has put her plant and some sticks and some cord.)

MAMA.   Father, give us strength. *(Knowingly—and without fun.)* Did he threaten us?

BENEATHA.   Oh—Mama—they don't do it like that any more. He talked Brotherhood. He said everybody ought learn how to sit down and hate each other with good Christian fellowship.

(She and Walter shake hands to ridicule the remark.)

MAMA.   *(Sadly.)* Lord, protect us . . .

The Actor's Nightmare

by Christopher Durang

To his utter dismay, George finds himself onstage with a role in a play he does not know. In this scene, the famous actress Sarah Siddons is playing the female lead in a play very much like one by Noel Coward. She is in a glamorous evening gown, and she is holding a cocktail glass. After a moment, George arrives onstage, fairly pushed on. He is dressed as Hamlet— black leotard and large gold medallion around his neck. As soon as he enters, several flash photos are taken, which disorient him greatly. When he can, he looks out and sees the audience and is very taken aback. We hear music.)

SARAH.   Extraordinary how potent cheap music is.

GEORGE.   What?

SARAH.   Extraordinary how potent cheap music is.

GEORGE.   Yes, that's true. Am I supposed to be Hamlet?

SARAH.   *(alarmed; then going on).* Whose yacht do you think that is?

GEORGE.   Where?

SARAH.   The Duke of Westminster, I expect. It always is.

GEORGE.   Ah, well, perhaps. To be or not to be. I don't know any more of it. *(She looks irritated at him; then she coughs three times. He remembers and unzips her dress; she slaps him.)*

SARAH.   Elyot, please. We are on our honeymoons.

GEORGE.   Are we?

SARAH.   Yes. *(Irritated, being over-explicit)* Me with Victor, and you with Sibyl.

GEORGE.   Ah.

SARAH.   Tell me about Sibyl.

GEORGE.   I've never met her.

SARAH. Ah, Elyot, you're so amusing. You're married to Sibyl. Tell me about her.

GEORGE.   Nothing much to tell really. She's sort of nondescript, I'd say.

SARAH.   I bet you were going to say that she's just like Lady Bundle, and that she has several chins, and one blue eye and one brown eye, and a third eye in the center of her forehead. Weren't you?

GEORGE.   Yes. I think so.

SARAH.   Victor's like that too. *(Long pause)* I bet you were just about to tell me that you travelled around the world.

GEORGE.   Yes I was. I travelled around the world.

SARAH.   How was it?

GEORGE.   The world?

SARAH.   Yes.

GEORGE.   Oh, very nice.

SARAH.   I always feared the Taj Mahal would look like a biscuit box. Did it?

GEORGE.   Not really.

SARAH. *(She's going to give him the cue again.)*   I always feared the Taj Mahal would look like a biscuit box. Did it?

GEORGE.   I guess it did.

SARAH. *(Again).*   I always feared the Taj Mahal would look like a biscuit box. Did it?

GEORGE.   Hard to say. What brand biscuit box?

SARAH.   I always feared the Taj Mahal would look like a biscuit box. Did it? *(Pause)* Did it? Did it?

GEORGE.   I wonder whose yacht that is out there.

SARAH.   Did it? Did it? Did it? Did it? *(Enter Meg. She's put on an apron and maid's hat and carries a duster, but is otherwise still in her stage manager's garb.)*

MEG.   My, this balcony looks dusty. I think I'll just clean it up a little. *(Dusts and goes to George and whispers in his ear; exits)*

GEORGE.   Not only did the Taj Mahal look like a biscuit box, but women should be struck regularly like gongs. *(Applause)*

SARAH.   Extraordinary how potent cheap music is.

GEORGE.   Yes. Quite extraordinary.

SARAH. How was China?

GEORGE. China?

SARAH. You travelled around the world. How was China?

GEORGE. I liked it, but I felt homesick.

SARAH. *(Again this is happening; gives him cue again.)* How was China?

GEORGE. Lots of rice. The women bind their feet.

SARAH. How was China?

GEORGE. I hated it. I missed you.

SARAH. How was China?

GEORGE. I hated it. I missed. . . Sibyl.

SARAH. How was China?

GEORGE. I. . . miss the maid. Oh, maid!

SARAH. How was China?

GEORGE. Just wait a moment please. Oh, maid! *(Enter Meg)* Ah, there you are. I think you missed a spot here. *(She crosses, dusts, and whispers in his ear; exits.)*

SARAH. How was China?

GEORGE. *(With authority.)* Very large, China.

SARAH. And Japan?

GEORGE. *(Doesn't know, but makes a guess.)* Very. . . small, Japan.

SARAH. And Ireland?

GEORGE. Very. . . green.

SARAH. And Iceland?

GEORGE. Very white.

SARAH. And Italy?

GEORGE. Very. . . Neapolitan.

SARAH. And Copenhagen?

GEORGE. Very. . . cosmopolitan.

SARAH. And Florida?

GEORGE. Very. . . condominium.

SARAH. And Perth Amboy?

GEORGE. Very. . . mobile home, I don't know.

SARAH. And Sibyl?

GEORGE. What?

SARAH. Do you love Sibyl?

GEORGE. Who's Sibyl?

SARAH. Your new wife, who you married after you and I got our divorce.

GEORGE. Oh, were we married? Oh yes, I forgot that part.

SARAH. Elyot, you're so amusing. You make me laugh all the time. *(Laughs)* So, do you love Sibyl?

GEORGE. Probably. I married her. *(Pause. She coughs three times, he unzips her dress, she slaps him.)*

SARAH. Oh, Elyot, darling, I'm sorry. We were mad to have left each other. Kiss me. *(They kiss. Enter Dame Ellen Terry as Sibyl, in an evening gown.)*

ELLEN. Oh, how ghastly.

SARAH. Oh dear. And this must be Sibyl.

ELLEN. Oh how ghastly. What shall we do?

SARAH. We must all speak in very low voices and attempt to be civilized.

ELLEN. Is this Amanda? Oh, Elyot, I think she's simply obnoxious.

SARAH. How very rude.

ELLEN. Oh, Elyot, how can you treat me like this?

GEORGE. Hello, Sibyl.

ELLEN. Well, since you ask, I'm very upset. I was inside writing a letter to your mother and wanted to know how to spell apothecary.

SARAH. A-P-O-T-H-E-C-A-R-Y.

ELLEN. *(Icy.)* Thank you. *(Writes it down; Sarah looks over her shoulder.)*

SARAH. Don't scribble, Sibyl.

ELLEN. Did my eyes deceive me, or were you kissing my husband a moment ago?

SARAH. We must all speak in very low voices and attempt to be civilized.

ELLEN. I was speaking in a low voice.

SARAH. Yes, but I could still hear you.

ELLEN. Oh. Sorry. *(Speaks too low to be heard)*

SARAH. *(Speaks inaudibly also.)*

ELLEN. *(Speaks inaudibly.)*

SARAH. *(Speaks inaudibly.)*

ELLEN. *(Speaks inaudibly.)*

SARAH. I can't hear a bloody word she's saying. The woman's a nincompoop. Say something, Elyot.

GEORGE. I couldn't hear her either.

ELLEN. Elyot, you have to choose between us immediately—do you love this creature, or do you love me?

GEORGE. I wonder where the maid is.

ELLEN & SARAH. *(Together, furious.)* Forget about the maid, Elyot! *(They look embarrassed.)* You could never have a lasting relationship with a maid. Choose between the two of us.

GEORGE. I choose... oh God, I don't know my lines. I don't know how I got here. I wish I *weren't* here. I wish I had joined the monastery like I almost did right after high school. I almost joined, but then I didn't.

A Waitress in Yellowstone or Always Tell the Truth

by David Mamet

Following is the beginning of the play. A narrator takes the stage. He is dressed as a park ranger.

RANGER.   Winnie was a waitress. She worked for tips. Here is a tip: a bad situation generally grows worse.

Things which can get no worse improve. There are exceptions: here is not one. Winnie caught a guy lifting a tip off of her table. Told him "who do you think you are?" and she read him out to the onlooking crowd, what sort of a you-fill-in-the-blank that he *was*... which he was.

It turns out this man was a congressman. In an election year. He had to keep a shining image in the public eye, which is exactly where he kept it.

Would have been better off to be what he wished to seem, but barring that he took the secondary course, lived like a thief and made the Public Pay.

Winnie and her son Doug. Had planned a trip to Yellowstone. To celebrate his Tenth Birthday. He'd, as you might imagine, looked forward to that trip all year. And it was the object of much of their talk and much of their joint happiness.

At the restaurant.

WAITRESS.   Hey, Winnie, quit dreaming, table number three wants the check!

(Old Couple)

OLD MAN.   Could I have the check, please.

WINNIE.   Here you are.

OLD MAN.   Thank you. See you tomorrow, Winnie...

WINNIE.   No you won't, sir. Tomorrow my boy and I leave for our vacation. I'll see you in two weeks.

OLD MAN.   Where are you going?

WINNIE.   Yellowstone Park.

OLD MAN.   That's right, you told me. Here's a little extra, you have a fine trip.

(The Old Couple starts up to leave.)

WINNIE.   That's *very* generous of you, sir... thank you... *(Before she can gather the money, etc., she is called to another table.)*

CONGRESSMAN.   Miss!

WINNIE *(to Old Man)*.   Thank you very much.

CONGRESSMAN.   Miss!

WINNIE.   I'm coming. *(to Congressman)* Yes, sir?

CONGRESSMAN *(of check)*.   What is the meaning of this?

WINNIE *(checking bill).* Ninety-five cents, for a substitution. You had beans instead of the creamed spinach.

CONGRESSMAN. You never told me that.

WINNIE. Yes, sir, I did.

CONGRESSMAN. You certainly did *not.* You did *not* tell me that.

WINNIE. Yes, sir, I am certain, you said "I'll have the Special." Look: It's not important. If you take the check to the boss, I'm sure that he'll. . .

CONGRESSMAN. Well, that's not the point, is it? The point is that you never *told* me. . .

WINNIE. Well, if that's true, I'm sorry, sir.

CONGRESSMAN. No: *say* you never told me. . .

WINNIE. Excuse me. . .

CONGRESSMAN. You owe me an apology.

WINNIE. I think that I apologized, excuse me. . . *(She walks away. To another waitress.)* Some people have too much salt in their diet. . . *(to Congressman)* WAIT A SECOND WAIT A SECOND WAIT A SECOND: *WAIT* A SECOND THERE!

(She walks back to his table, which he has gotten up from. He is standing near the table vacated by the Old Couple. To Congressman.)

You wanna put something back? *(Pause)* You wanna put something back, or you want me to call the police.

CONGRESSMAN. I don't know what you're talking about.

WINNIE. I'm talking about you just lifted my tip off of that table. Now: you put it back or I call the cops.

CONGRESSMAN. You're saying. . . *(Pause)* You're saying I did whhh. . . ? Get out of my way. *(Tries to push past her)*

WINNIE. In a pig's *eye* I will. Somebody call the cops! Somebody call the cops, this guy took my tip off the. . . *(To Congressman)* You aren't going anywhere!

BOSS. What's the trouble?

WINNIE. This guy took my tip off the table.

CONGRESSMAN. Lady, you're in a world of trouble here.

WINNIE. Well, we're just going to see. . .

COP. What seems to be the trouble?

WINNIE. This guy lifted my tip off the table.

CONGRESSMAN. Not only is it not

true, but I want to tell you you've just caused yourself a lot of pain. What's your name, Officer? I'm John Larue, I am the congressman for this district, and this deranged and sick individual has just slandered me. Pick her *tip* off the table? You know WHO I *AM*???

(The Congressman sings about the exalted position he enjoys. He finishes singing.)

CONGRESSMAN.   Now: I'll give you one last chance to retract what you said and take back your vicious lie, or you're going to wish you never were born.

WINNIE.   Well, to wish you never were born you have to be born. Which gives you the option, and I think I'll stick with the truth. You should be ashamed of yourself. Good-bye.

(The Cop takes the Congressman away.)

WINNIE.   What kind of a world is it? That guy should be setting an example. . .

(Winnie and the assembled customers sing "What Kind of a World Is It?" peppering the song with examples from their own lives. The second verse is: "On the Other Hand," where Winnie sings about some of the good things which may be had simply in life, in her case, the trip with her son to Yellowstone Park.

As the clock strikes twelve she sings

"My Day Is Done, and I'm Going on Vacation," and leaves the restaurant. She walks home.)

WINNIE.   Look at the stars, what a beautiful night it is. Always various. *(She walks into her house.)* Look at my son, isn't he gorgeous. And now we have all this vacation time to be alone together. All the rest is basically illusion.

RANGER.   And so she fell asleep, and she and her son dreamed the same dream. In which they were in Yellowstone Park, high upon a ridge, upon a summit, looking down, and they saw mountain sheep, and they saw deer, and when the rain came unexpectedly they made a shelter from a fallen tree. And as in the wild of sleep and as in the wild of the forest their cares fell away. And when Winnie awoke, she saw her son, already dressed, sitting at the breakfast table, and he had made her a cup of tea.

(N.B. They are both dressed in full camp regalia.)

WINNIE.   Good morning. What are you doing up so early?

DOUG.   Oh, I couldn't sleep.

WINNIE.   Why? You worried about school, shouldn't you be off to school?

DOUG.   Well, I thought I wouldn't go to school today.

WINNIE. Wouldn't go to school? Why, of course, you have to go to school today, why wouldn't you?

DOUG. 'CAUSE WE'RE GOING TO YELLOWSTONE PARK!!!!!

(They jump up and down and sing a song about how they must make sure they've taken the right things. They sing about the contents of a rucksack, and emergency gear, which they inspect on each other's person. This gear includes: waxed matches in a waterproof container [several containers secreted in various parts of the clothing and generally high up to keep them dry should one fall into waist-high water], a compass, a spare compass, a topographic map of the area to be camped in. A candle for helping to light fires, needle and thread, steel wool which, though it is not generally known, is, in its superfine variety, great tinder and can just be wrung out when wet, extra clothing, rain gear, pencil and paper, fishing line and hook, bandages, whistle, etc. They finish the song, and, having checked each other out, decide that they are ready to proceed to the bus, which they have ten minutes to catch. In deciding which coat to wear, they turn on the radio to catch a weather report.)

DOUG. I can't believe we're really going.

WINNIE. Have I ever lied to you?

DOUG. No!

WINNIE. Well, then, there you are.

RADIO ANNOUNCER (voice over). In other news, Congressman John Larue, up for reelection, yesterday was accosted for the misdemeanor of Attempting to Defraud of Services or, to put it simply, a waitress at a restaurant he frequents accused the Congressman of lifting her tip off her table.

WINNIE. . . .come on, let's get out of here. . .

CONGRESSMAN (voice over). You know, it's easy to accuse, and I think by far the simplest thing would be to let this sick accusation pass, and go my way, but there comes a time. . .

WINNIE. Turn that creep off, let's go to the *country*. . .

DOUG (turns off radio). What'd he do?

WINNIE. The creep. Lifted a tip off of a waitress's table. Can you believe that?

DOUG (opening door). What a life.

WINNIE. On to the Wilds!

(In the door are two burly plainclothes policemen.)

POLICEMAN. Winnie Magee?

WINNIE. I. . . uh, what is it?

POLICEMAN.   Are you Ms. Winnie Magee?

WINNIE.   I can't talk to you now, we have to catch a bus.

POLICEMAN.   ARE YOU WIN...?

WINNIE.   Yes, but I can't talk...

POLICEMAN *(simultaneously with "talk")*.   You're under arrest. Would you come with us, please?

WINNIE.   I...

DOUG.   Wait, you can't, what's this all...?

POLICEMAN.   Slander, Malicious Mischief, Defamation of Character, would you please...?

WINNIE.   Who, what...?

DOUG.   What are you doing to my mother?

SECOND POLICEMAN.   She insulted a congressman, kid.

WINNIE.   But we... we just have ten minutes to catch the bus...

(They are in a court of law.)

And we're going to Yellowstone P... what is this, what's going on here...?

JUDGE.   You are accused of wantonly, maliciously, and with malice afore-thought having verbally assaulted,

insulted, and impugned the character of one John Larue, Congressman for the Seventh District of...

WINNIE.   HOLD ON A SECOND. I insulted wh...?

JUDGE.   You have no voice in this court, would you please, who is your counsel?

WINNIE.   Say that again?

BAILIFF.   Who's your lawyer?

WINNIE.   I don't have a lawyer, why should... What's going on here? *(Pause)* Come on, I have to catch a bus. *(Pause)*

JUDGE.   You are accused by the congressman here *(Congressman stands.)* of, in simple terms, of lying about him in such a way as to damage his reputation.

WINNIE.   Ah.

JUDGE.   When you said that he stole your tip.

WINNIE.   He *did* steal my tip.

JUDGE.   The court will now appoint you a lawyer.

WINNIE.   I don't need a lawyer, I don't *want* one. Let's settle this here and now, 'cause I'm on my vacation time, alright? You tell me how you want to do this, and let's get this done.

JUDGE. You wish to act as your own lawyer?

WINNIE. That's . . . okay. *(Pause)* Okay.

JUDGE. You're making a mistake.

WINNIE. I've made them before. Nothing to be scared of. Now, what is the thing?

DOUG. Mom, what's going on . . . ?

(Winnie and Doug hold a whispered consultation while the Bailiff and the Judge sing about the charge and the procedure in this case. They are joined by the Lawyer for the Congressman and the Congressman, who sing about her heinous behavior and the grave damage that has been done. They stop. Pause.)

WINNIE. Now what?

JUDGE. You may present your case.

A Star Ain't Nothin' but a Hole in Heaven

by Judi Ann Mason

The Lorraine Hansberry award, of which this play is a recipient, is established for the best plays on the black experience in America. The following scene is set in Louisiana, 1969. Pokie, a high school senior who lives with her senile, dying aunt Mamie and her aged, blind uncle Lemuel, struggles to overcome tradition and her family's disapproval to go north to get a good college education.

MAMIE. Lemuel, Lemuel. That man is a great man, Pokie. Good man.

POKIE. I know.

MAMIE. Sometimes you don't understand him. He is hard to understand sometimes.

POKIE. He treats me like I'm a little baby.

MAMIE. He tryin' to protect you.

POKIE. From what?

MAMIE. What he had to go through.

POKIE. Things ain't like that no more. There's a lotta things I have to do and he won't let me. I think he don't want me to graduate.

MAMIE. Aw, Pokie . . .

POKIE. Every time I ask him for something I need, he tells me that I don't need it.

MAMIE. You got to try real hard to make him see.

POKIE. I told him I needed a white dress—

MAMIE. He's always been like that. Like the time I told him I needed some new shoes for my sister's wedding.

POKIE. I wouldn't ask him for the dress if I didn't have to have it. . .

MAMIE. All the time before that, all the money had to be spent on things for his pappy.

POKIE. Do you think he'll let me buy it?

MAMIE. "Lemuel, the shoes don't cost but $2. And I'll take good care of them. You won't have to buy me no more. . ."

POKIE. I saw a dress that cost only $12 up at the Woolworth.

MAMIE. He told me that we didn't have the money. But I knew we had the money cause I had worked five days straight down to Miss Blema's store that week and I gived him all the money. . .

POKIE. Aint Mamie, will you listen to me?

MAMIE. So I tells him I had the money and he gets mad at me. "You ain't grateful for all I done for you. Who else gon marry a woman like you? You be thankful for me marrying you . . ."

POKIE. Will you listen to me?

MAMIE. I told him that he didn't have to marry me. If he had to wipe my brow with it, he didn't have to marry me.

POKIE. I got problems, too! But nobody around here never listens to me talk. . .

MAMIE. It was just like talkin' to myself. "You told me you didn't make no mind about children. You told me I was just as much a woman cause I couldn't make babies. Lotsa women can't make babies. I ain't the only one, Lemuel."

POKIE. *(Unable to control her moment of disgust.)* For once can't you hear me? Come back and talk to me!

MAMIE. "I love you, Lemuel. I love Jesus, too. Jesus is the Savior! Save me, Lord! Take this curse from my womb!"

POKIE. Come back and talk Aint Mamie!

MAMIE. Too old now. Life done creeped up on me. It done snatched my breath from my lungs. I'm still a woman.

POKIE. Listen to me! *(Mamie bursts into a fit of tears. Pokie goes to her and starts to shake her.)* Listen! You come back here and listen!

MAMIE. Turn me loose! Jesus gonna remember me! Turn Jesus loose! Take the cross from his back! He's the Son of God! Turn the Lord aloose!

LEMUEL. *(At door.)* Mamie, what's the matter? *(Seeing Pokie.)* Pokie, let her be! You trying to kill her? What you doing? Stop hollin' at her! Turn her loose!

POKIE. *(She releases Mamie and stands back staring at Lemuel.)* You saw that?

LEMUEL. It's alright Mamie. All right.

POKIE. How did you see what I was doing to her?

LEMUEL. She was hollin'.

POKIE. No, you saw it. Joretta was right. You can see.

LEMUEL. Girl, stop that barking and help me get her to bed.

POKIE. Do it yourself.

LEMUEL. What you say?

POKIE. Do it yourself. You saw well enough a minute ago...

LEMUEL. Go get the alum so you can rub her down.

POKIE. I ain't gonna do it!

LEMUEL. Is this the thank-you we get after all we done for you? You musta forgot we didn't have to take you in...

POKIE. I'm leaving, Uncle Lemuel.

LEMUEL. Pokie, shut up that noise.

POKIE. Me and Joretta going up north to college.

LEMUEL. Help me get Mamie to bed.

POKIE. I ain't coming back here. You done all this to keep me here, but I'm going to college. And I'm gonna be an artist!

LEMUEL. Then what we suppose to do?

POKIE. You can move to town.

LEMUEL. This is my land.

POKIE. You can sell it and buy somewhere in town.

LEMUEL. Who gon take care of Mamie? She's your ainnie and you talking about leaving her. A decent girl would stay as close to her kin as she could—

POKIE. I ain't willing to sacrifice my life.

LEMUEL. You know we can't take care of ourselves. We subject to die in this house.

POKIE. I can't stay here. I won't.

LEMUEL. If you think I'll let you leave—

POKIE. How you gon stop me? You can't see, remember? All I got to do is walk out of here.

LEMUEL. You shut up! *(He comes toward her.)*

POKIE. I'm leaving. I don't owe nobody nothing but me.

(Lemuel tries to grab her. Pokie dashes out of the way. Lemuel stumbles on the

chair. Pokie rushes to the door and exits.)

LEMUEL.   Pokie! Come back here! Pokie!

(Pokie runs toward the tree, lays her head against it and cries. Lemuel looks after the door.)

MAMIE.   Lemuel, we need to get Pokie a white dress to graduate in. A nice white dress, with ruffles and a big collar. Lemuel, Pokie needs a white dress...

(lights dim)

"Baucis and Philemon" from Metamorphoses
by Mary Zimmerman

Following is the entire segment of "Baucis and Philemon" *from Mary Zimmerman's play,* Metamorphoses, *which is based on the writings of Ovid. Be aware that much of the play takes place in a pool of water.*

(Music. Transition. The raft and candelabra are struck.)

NARRATOR ONE.   It happened that one night, Zeus, the lord of the heavens, and Hermes, his son, came down to earth to see what people were really like. They disguised themselves as two old beggars, stinking and poor, ragged and filthy. They knocked on a thousand doors.

(Zeus knocks on the surface of the deck. Both adopt supplicating poses.)

ZEUS.   Hello, do you have any spare—?

OFFSTAGE VOICE.   Get out of here! Get the hell out of here! I work hard for my money!

NARRATOR ONE.   And a thousand doors were slammed on them.

(They knock on the deck, and a woman opens the door.)

HERMES.   Hello, we're tired, we live on the street, and we hoped that you might—

WOMAN AT THE DOOR.   I'm sorry, I'm... um... soooo sorry. Sorry. (She slams the door shut.)

NARRATOR ONE.   At last they came to a little hut on the outskirts of town.

HERMES.   Why bother knocking here? We've knocked on houses of all kinds, the homes of people with plenty to spare. Whoever lives here obviously has nothing.

ZEUS.   Let's give it a try all the same. We've come all this way.

(He knocks.)

HERMES.   This is hopeless. Let's just go ho—

BAUCIS.   (Entering.) Poor strangers! Philemon, there are guests at our door!

ZEUS.   Hello. We are strangers to these parts. We've lost our way and—

PHILEMON. *(Entering.)* Baucis, why are you standing there! We must bring our guests inside.

ZEUS. Do you know us?

PHILEMON. Of course.

HERMES. You do?

PHILEMON. Yes—

HERMES. Then who are we?

PHILEMON. Why, you are children of God. Come in, come in.

(At this point, the narrative divides among several members of the company. They enter and exit variously, carrying illuminated candles in wooden bowls, which stand in for all the items they will mention. They hand these bowls to Baucis and Philemon, or place them in the water themselves. The scene is active: The entire surface of the water becomes the "table" being set with illuminated candles.)

NARRATOR TWO. The two immortals, satisfied that their disguises had not been seen through, entered the house, lowering their heads to fit through the door.

BAUCIS. No, don't sit on the floor! Sit on chairs, as quality people do.

NARRATOR THREE. Philemon ran to get another chair.

NARRATOR FOUR. And Baucis

fetched two pieces of cloth to pad them so the strangers might rest easy.

NARRATOR FIVE. She stirred the coals in the hearth and fanned the fire to cook them a meal.

NARRATOR ONE. Philemon set out the embroidered cloth that they saved for feast days.

NARRATOR TWO. Baucis saw that one of the legs of the chair was short and she propped it up with a shard of a pot.

NARRATOR THREE. Philemon set out a plate of olives, green ones and black, and a saucer of cherry plums.

NARRATOR FOUR. Then there was cabbage and some roasted eggs . . .

NARRATOR FIVE. For dessert there were nuts, figs, dates, and plums.

NARRATOR ONE. And a basket of ripe apples.

NARRATOR TWO. Remember how apples smell?

(A pause. Everyone inhales and remembers. Then they continue.)

NARRATOR ONE. At last, with a show of modest pride, they brought out a bit of honeycomb for sweetness.

NARRATOR TWO. Philemon poured wine from a bottle, but as he filled the glasses of the guests, he saw that the bottle remained full.

ALL NARRATORS.   And then they knew.

(Narrators exit.)

BAUCIS.   Oh, mercy! Mercy!

(She runs with her husband to kneel in front of the gods.)

PHILEMON.   You are divine and we've served you such a simple meal. Baucis, go and kill the goose!

ZEUS.   Let it live. We are gods and we thank you. You've done enough, more than your nasty neighbors thought to do.

(The original narrator of the scene enters with three other members of the company, all carrying bowls of candles. As she speaks, they come forward, kneel in the water, and set the bowls floating. There is music under the next line of Narrator One.)

NARRATOR ONE.   Suddenly, everything was changing. The poor little house, their simple cottage, was becoming grander and grander, a glittering marble-columned temple. The straw and reeds of the thatched roof metamorphosed into gold, and gates with elaborate carvings sprang up, as ground gave way to marble paving stones.

HERMES.   Old man, old woman, ask of us what you will. We shall grant whatever request you make of us.

(Baucis and Philemon whisper to each other.)

BAUCIS.   Having spent all our lives together, we ask that you allow us to die at the same moment.

PHILEMON.   I'd hate to see my wife's grave, or have her weep at mine.

NARRATOR TWO.   The gods granted their wish. Arrived at a very old age together, the two stood at what had been their modest doorway and now was a grandiose facade.

ZEUS.   And Baucis noticed her husband was beginning to put forth leaves, and he saw that she, too, was producing leaves and bark. They were turning into trees. They stood there, held each other, and called, before the bark closed over their mouths:

PHILEMON AND BAUCIS.   Farewell.

NARRATOR ONE.   Walking down the street at night, when you're all alone, you can still hear, stirring in the intermingled branches of the trees above, the ardent prayer of Baucis and Philemon. They whisper:

ALL.   Let me die the moment my love dies.

NARRATOR ONE.   They whisper:

ALL.   Let me not outlive my own capacity to love.

NARRATOR ONE.   They whisper:

ALL.   Let me die still loving, and so, never die.

Promenade

by Maria Irene Fornes

In this excerpt from her offbeat, bright-spirited play, Maria Irene Fornes's every word is a new surprise. With characters named 106, 105, Miss U and Mr. R, you are instantly aware that this play is a bit out of the ordinary. And don't expect linear plot lines and obvious themes. Do expect intelligence and philosophical insight wrapped in zaniness.

Scene 2

The Banquet. There are ladies and gentlemen in evening clothes around the table. The servant sweeps. The waiter serves the guests. 105 and 106 enter. They put on top hats and tails. They sit at the table and eat.

MR. R.   Speech . . . speech . . .

MR. S.   Let's play croquet . . .

MR. R.   Speeches and music . . .

MR. T.   Let's call Mr. Lipschitz . . .

MR. S.   No speeches . . . No speeches . . .

MR. R.   Let's have a song . . .

(105 and 106 clear their throats.)

MISS O.   Mr. T, was that you I saw on the corner of Fifth and Tenth?

MR. T.   Perhaps.

MISS O.   With Mrs. Schumann and her newly clipped poodle?

MR. T.   Oh, no, it wasn't I. Friday night I was out of town.

MISS O.   Ah! And how did you know it was Friday night I saw you on the corner of Fifth?

(They all laugh.)

MR. T.   Well, I must confess. The lady loves me.

(They all laugh.)

MISS U.   She shows good taste.

MR. R.   Then, introduce us. She'll surely fall for me.

(The ladies giggle.)

(Mr. R writes in a notebook.) Mrs. Schumann . . . lady of taste . . . Bring dog biscuit. *(To Mr. T.)* What is her address?

MR. T.   Tch-Tch.

MISS I.   Oh, Mr. R, what perspicacity.

MISS O.   Are you sure that's what you mean?

(Miss I looks a little embarrassed.)

MR. S.   Let's have a song.

(105 and 106 stand and get ready to sing.)

MISS O.   And who are these? Dear me.

(105 and 106 realize they have been indiscreet. They sit back at the table

and pretend not to hear the others.)

MISS I.   They must be friends of Mr. S.

MISS U.   My dear. You go right to the point . . .

MISS I.   Mr. S. does frequent rather unearthly places, doesn't he?

MR. T.   What do you mean?

MISS I.   I mean the lower depths.

MR. T.   Oh, yes.

MR. S.   If I am sometimes in the company of this and that, my dear, it's only because I like to study life . . . I am what you might call a student of life . . . This . . . and that.

MISS U.   Oh, how incredibly personal you are, Mr. S. Have I not always said you have the artist in you?

MR. S.   I am neither more than I seem to be, nor more than I am, and no less, also.

SERVANT.   *(Mimicking in a low voice.)* And no less . . . also.

MR. R.   Miss I . . .

MISS I.   Yes?

MR. R.   Last Saturday I waited for a certain lady who never arrived.

MISS I.   You did?

MR. R.   Yes.

MISS I.   Oh, she couldn't come. She spent all afternoon walking up and down a certain street where a gentleman *(Referring to Mr. T.)* who shall remain nameless lives. She was hoping to have an accidental meeting. . . a sort of unexpected encounter with him. But he never left his house . . . nor did he enter it.

(Miss O and Miss U giggle. The servant is bored by the ladies' and gentlemen's repartee. Through the following speeches she pantomimes their gestures.)

MR. T.   He didn't, Madam . . . he didn't. He saw the lady from his window and she did indeed walk up and down his street. But he couldn't receive her . . . his heart was torn. You see, he received a letter from the one he loves *(Referring to Miss U)* telling him his love was unrequited. He spent all afternoon sitting by his window plucking petals from flowers, and the answer always was . . . she loves me not.

MISS O.   And who is this he speaks of?

MISS U.   She is not free to love. Her heart belongs to he *(Referring to Mr. S.)* whose glance drives her to a frenzy, and whose mere presence brings color to her cheeks.

MR. S.   The man who puts you in such a state has eyes only for O. Oh, Miss O.

MISS I.   Oh! What tension! A name has been mentioned.

MISS U.   And what have you to say to that, O?

MISS O.   I regret I cannot speak since Mr. S has mentioned me by name. But do you wonder why O shuns you when you are so indiscreet? *(Taking a step toward R.)* And besides, she loves R.
(R takes a step toward I.)
(I takes a step toward T.)
(T takes a step toward U.)
(U takes a step toward S.)
(S takes a step toward O.)
(O takes a step toward R.)

MISS U.   You were there when
   I was not.
I was there when you were not.
Don't love me, sweetheart,
Or I might stop loving you.
Unrequited love,
Unrequited love.

MISS O.   Passionate lips are sweet.
But oh, how much sweeter
Are lips that refuse.
Don't love me, sweetheart,
Or I might stop loving you.

MISS I.   Inviting lips,
Alluring lips
Which shape the word no
No no no no no no.
Don't love me, sweetheart,
Or I might stop loving you.

MR. R.   You know nothing of life,

You know nothing of love
Till you have tasted
Of unrequited love.
Don't love me, sweetheart,
Or I might stop loving you.

ALL.   Unrequited love,
Unrequited love.
There is no love
Like unrequited love.

MISS I.   Oh! We sang that well.

MR. R.   He who scrubs the pot finds it most shiny.

MR. S.   *(To Mr. R.)* And he who soils it, turns up his nose. Mr. R, you were flat.

MISS I.   Touché!

MISS U.   What a marvelous mind.

MR. S.   Just frank.

SERVANT.   *(Mimicking.)* Just frank.

(They all look at the servant, shocked.)

MISS I.   Mr. S, it's up to you to think of a rejoinder.

MR. S.   Dear me, I'm speechless. Wait! Listen to my answer. *(He improvises the following:)*

My frankness, my dear,
My wit, my veneer,
Are something you should revere.

LADIES.   A rhyme! A rhyme!

MR. S.   Instead, you just think
   it queer.

Your unprosperous status
Produces a dubious,
Fallacious, and tedious
Outlook on life.
(The servant makes a face at him.)
You do not know what we're about
We do not know what you're about
Or care to know.
(The servant lowers her head.)
It's sad your career
Depends on our whim.
On with your work, my dear,
Or you'll get thin.
You see, even if you're here,
And we're also here,
You are not near.
Isn't that clear?

MISS U.   Oh, Mr. S, how well
you rhyme.

MR. S.   Not difficult, dear. Just keep
the ending of the word in mind . . . it
will come.

MISS U.   *Incendo, incendis, incendit,
incendimos, incenditis, incendunt.*

MR. S.   No, dear, the ending, not
the beginning.

How I Learned to Drive
by Paula Vogel
Throughout this play, the main character, Li'l Bit, a 40-something-year-old woman, goes back in time to her early years with her family and her uncle

Peck. Three separate Greek Choruses
*(whose members, the author instructs,
"should be able to sing three-part harmony") comment on the action and
move it forward. The year is 1969 and
the family is having dinner.*

MALE GREEK CHORUS.
(As Grandfather.) What kind of things
do you want to read?

LI'L BIT.   There's a whole semester
course, for example, on Shakespeare—

*(Greek Chorus, as Grandfather, laughs
until he weeps.)*

MALE GREEK CHORUS.
(As Grandfather.) Shakespeare. That's a
good one. Shakespeare is really going to
help you in life.

PECK.   I think it's wonderful. And on
scholarship!

MALE GREEK CHORUS.
(As Grandfather.) How is Shakespeare
going to help her lie on her back in
the dark?

(Li'l Bit is on her feet.)

LI'L BIT.   You're getting old, Big Papa.
You are going to die—very very soon.
Maybe even tonight. And when you get
to heaven, God's going to be a beautiful
black woman in a long white robe.
She's gonna look at your chart and say:
Uh-oh. Dog-ugly mean with blood relatives. Oh. Uh-oh. Voted for George

Wallace. Well, one last chance: If you can name the play, all will be forgiven. And then she'll quote: "The quality of mercy is not strained." Your answer? Oh, too bad—*Merchant of Venice:* Act IV, Scene iii. And then she'll send you to fry in hell with all the other crackers. Excuse me, please. *(To the audience.)* And as I left the house, I would always hear Big Papa say:

MALE GREEK CHORUS. *(As Grandfather.)* Lucy, your daughter's got a mouth on her. Well, no sense in wasting good gumbo. Pass me her plate, Mama.

LI'L BIT. And Aunt Mary would come up to Uncle Peck:

FEMALE GREEK CHORUS. *(As Aunt Mary.)* Peck, go after her, will you? You're the only one she'll listen to when she gets like this.

PECK. She just needs to cool off.

FEMALE GREEK CHORUS. *(As Aunt Mary.)* Please, honey—Grandma's been on her feet cooking all day.

PECK. All right.

LI'L BIT. And as he left the room, Aunt Mary would say:

FEMALE GREEK CHORUS. *(As Aunt Mary.)* Peck's so good with them when they get to be this age.

(Li'l Bit has stormed to another part of the stage, her back turned, weeping

with a teenage fury. Peck, cautiously, as if stalking a deer, comes to her. She turns away even more. He waits a bit.)

PECK. I don't suppose you're talking to family. *(No response.)* Does it help that I'm an in-law?

LI'L BIT. Don't you dare make fun of this.

PECK. I'm not. There's nothing funny about this. *(Beat.)* Although I'll bet when Big Papa is about to meet his maker, he'll remember *The Merchant of Venice.*

LI'L BIT. I've got to get away from here.

PECK. You're going away. Soon. Here, take this.

(Peck hands her his folded handkerchief. Li'l Bit uses it, noisily. Hands it back. Without her seeing, he reverently puts it back.)

LI'L BIT. I hate this family.

Icarus
by Edwin Sánchez

A brother and sister, Primitivo and Altagracia, are living in a remote beachside cabin. Each day Primitivo swims farther and farther out to sea and back again. His sister his helping him train to become a celebrity. Soon the two are joined by Mr. Ellis, his dog Betty, Miss the Gloria, and Beau. Beau challenges Primitivo to a race. Following is a conversation among the members of the small community.

PRIMITIVO.   I was kind of afraid of you before but not anymore. You're going to become exhausted out there. Your lungs will collapse, and they'll fill with water, and the only person who can save you will be me, but I'll be too busy touching the sun. *(Pointing to the ocean.)* She's all yours. I'm sure you'll want to practice. I should warn you, she's a little choppy and watch out for her undertow, she doesn't let go easily.

(Primitivo and Altagracia exit. Beau goes to the Gloria. Lights up on the Gloria. She is wearing a facial masque and has a strapped-on ice pack around her eyes.)

the GLORIA.   Halt, who goes there?

BEAU.   It's just me, Miss the Gloria.

the GLORIA.   Ah, my fan. But you shouldn't see me like this. I'm a work in progress. Turn away.

BEAU.   You look fine.

the GLORIA.   Turn away! Have you?

BEAU.   Yes. *(He hasn't.)*

the GLORIA.   I'll have to take your word as a gentleman that indeed you have.

(Beau turns around.)

the GLORIA.   You're here much too early. The Gloria is best seen under man-made illumination. Nonetheless, I'm so glad you're here. I have so much to tell you.

BEAU.   Has it ever occurred to you that every time I see you we only talk about you?

the GLORIA.   You say that as if it were a bad thing.

BEAU.   Do you ever wonder what I look like?

the GLORIA.   You're going to give me frown lines. I won't like you anymore if I get frown lines.

BEAU.   Do you ever ask yourself, "Why you?" "Why are you so beautiful?"

the GLORIA.   Massage my feet, please.

(Beau does.)

the GLORIA.   Because I can handle the stress. Not everyone could, you know. The weight, the burden, the responsibility that comes from being everybody's fantasy.

BEAU.   I have my mask off. Do you wanna see me?

the GLORIA.   Of course not. I already have my image of you. Whatever you do, whatever it takes, maintain the illusion. It's hard work, it's a full-time job, but it's worth it.

BEAU.   And what will you do when your beauty is gone?

(Panic-stricken, the Gloria stops him.)

the GLORIA.   I haven't faded, have I? This is the only currency I have.

BEAU.   No, you're still perfect.

the GLORIA.   You frightened me. I mean, who would ever want me without my face?

BEAU.   Goodbye now.

the GLORIA.   Bye-bye.

(Beau exits. Mr Ellis sits on the beach, a pair of baby shoes by his side. He is too tired to dig.)

MR ELLIS.   I'm not staring, I'm not staring, I'm not staring, I'm not staring, am I staring? I'm not staring, I'm not staring, I'm not staring, I'm not staring, I'm. . . not. . . I don't like to remember. I don't.

(Beau stops. He sits by Mr Ellis and takes his shovel and begins to dig for him. Mr Ellis grabs his wrists and stops him.)

MR ELLIS.   You weren't invited to help. If you have something you don't want to remember, go find your own beach.

(Altagracia brings Primitivo downstairs to the beach.)

PRIMITIVO.   We should be sending out press releases.

ALTAGRACIA.   I'm on it.

PRIMITIVO.   And we'll need V I P seating.

ALTAGRACIA.   Uh-huh.

PRIMITIVO.   And maybe baton twirlers.

MR ELLIS.   What do you think his losing will do to her?

BEAU.   Are you so sure I'm gonna win?

MR ELLIS.   You're not gonna win. You're just gonna beat him.

ALTAGRACIA.   I need to talk to you. We need to discuss the terms of the race.

PRIMITIVO.   The rules.

ALTAGRACIA.   Yeah, the rules.

BEAU.   We get in the water and swim. One of us wins—

PRIMITIVO.   Me.

BEAU.   —and one of us loses.

PRIMITIVO.   You.

ALTAGRACIA.   Primi, let management manage, okay? That's why I'm getting the big bucks. Why don't you practice your victory speech?

PRIMITIVO.   Okay, but don't give away the foreign distribution rights.

Remember, I'm right here.

(Altagracia sits on a step.)

ALTAGRACIA. Step into my office.

(Beau sits next to Altagracia, who finds herself too close to him so she moves up a step.)

BEAU. Well, it's almost race time. Primitivo seems really excited.

ALTAGRACIA. Yeah.

BEAU. How's that?

ALTAGRACIA. I said, "Yeah."

BEAU. Are you talking to me or to your feet?

ALTAGRACIA. Why are you doing this?

BEAU. I thought this is what you wanted.

ALTAGRACIA. I wanted Primitivo to swim.

BEAU. He's not swimming?

ALTAGRACIA. Farther and better than ever. No complaining, either.

BEAU. Then what's the problem? You still believe he can touch the sun, right?

ALTAGRACIA. Sure I do.

BEAU. Then you should be grateful I'm staying. I'll give him a chance to prove it.

ALTAGRACIA. You're right.

BEAU. If anybody can, he can. You just lost your faith for a second, that's all.

ALTAGRACIA. Yeah.

BEAU. I guess I should go practice.

(Altagracia grabs his arm.)

ALTAGRACIA. Are you really gonna go through with this?

(Beau nods his head and strips down to his bathing trunks as he goes into the water. Primitivo does his sun touch, stretched arm with splayed fingers as he watches Beau swimming. Altagracia sits next to Mr Ellis, who opens his suitcase and retrieves a brooch from it. He holds it up.)

ALTAGRACIA. Pretty.

MR ELLIS. Cheap. My wife's one piece of Christmas jewelry. She'd wear it exactly from December first to January seventh. I didn't even know I had it.

(Mr Ellis drops the brooch in the hole and buries it.)

ALTAGRACIA. You know, in the summer, some little kid with a sand shovel is gonna find it.

MR ELLIS. It might be her. Reincarnated.

ALTAGRACIA. Oh, please.

MR ELLIS. She'll have a feeling of déjà vu.

ALTAGRACIA. I can barely survive going through this once. Let alone over and over again.

MR ELLIS. Next time it would be different.

ALTAGRACIA. I'd want it in writing, notarized, and blessed by the Pope.

(She picks up Betty and holds her close.)

MR ELLIS. I don't want you to get hurt, little girl. Dreams can protect you so no one can hurt you.

(He slowly opens his suitcase slightly.)

MR ELLIS. I can help you. 'Cause dreams are my business. Reach in, I'll let you have one on account. Go on. A dream to stand between you and reality.

(Altagracia is unsure. Mr Ellis points to Beau in the water.)

MR ELLIS. The beautiful boy is pretty good out there, isn't he?

ALTAGRACIA. I hadn't noticed.

MR ELLIS. One dream. Any dream at all. 'Cause you mean so much to me.

(Altagracia is about to reach in when Mr Ellis suddenly snaps the suitcase shut, barely missing her hand. She hits him and storms upstairs.)

ALTAGRACIA. I hate you! *(She exits.)*

MR ELLIS. Better I should squash your dreams than someone who doesn't love you.

(the Gloria enters her porch, wearing sunglasses, and sees Primitivo laying in the sun. Mr Ellis, upon seeing her, runs under the porch.)

the GLORIA. You were quite the athlete out there.

PRIMITIVO. Miss the Gloria.

the GLORIA. I've never seen anyone swim quite the way you do, with so much passion. Such a handsome boy. Am I making you blush?

PRIMITIVO. Uh, no.

the GLORIA. Yes, I am. That's so sweet. Hardly anybody blushes any-more. Come on up for that drink I promised you; I have tons of good news. I got invited to the party of the year!

PRIMITIVO. That's great.

the GLORIA. Very last minute, you understand, but what do I care. And I can bring a guest. I'd love to show up with someone as handsome as you on my arm. How about it? It's tomorrow night.

PRIMITIVO. I'm. . . booked for another party.

the GLORIA. Well, that's a shame.

I would have made it a very special evening for you. Maybe I will afterwards.

PRIMITIVO.   Yeah, maybe.

the GLORIA.   And there's more. I got a part!

PRIMITIVO.   You got another feature?

the GLORIA.   Yes! Well, actually I'm just doing it as a favor for a friend, it's sort of a, uh subcameo. I'm in the background, but really the entire scene hinges around me. I'm the center of attention. I've decided I'm going to do it all with my eyes. *(She removes her sunglasses.)*

PRIMITIVO.   Congratulations.

the GLORIA.   In lesser hands this would just be a glorified extra, in my hands it's a lock on a best supporting actress nod.

PRIMITIVO.   I'm sure you'll be wonderful.

the GLORIA.   And beautiful.

PRIMITIVO.   Very, very beautiful.

the GLORIA.   Come on up and give me a little good luck kiss. Don't be so shy.

PRIMITIVO.   I can't.

the GLORIA.   *(Not hearing him. Looking out at the ocean.)* Who's that walking this way?

PRIMITIVO.   Nobody.

the GLORIA.   He's beautiful.

PRIMITIVO.   Yeah.

the GLORIA.   Don't be jealous. You're both very, very attractive.

PRIMITIVO.   Yeah, we're equals.

the GLORIA.   I'll see you after the party then?

PRIMITIVO.   It's a date.

(the Gloria disappears into her bedroom.)

Student Handbook

Part One Acting

Acting Styles

There are two main approaches to acting.

Method Acting Actors who have worked or prefer to work by "becoming" the character are influenced by the tradition of Method acting, originated by Konstantin Stanislavski (1863–1938) and currently taught by schools such as the Actors Studio in New York and Los Angeles. This approach asks actors to fully immerse themselves in the general world of the play and the specific world of their characters. Method work is also called internal or subjective work because actors build the character from within, tapping into the parts of themselves that relate to the character.

Technical Acting Actors who work technically tend to approach a role from a much more objective viewpoint. The technical actor uses powerful vocal and physical work to bring a character to life. The interpretation of the character is often more intellectual or stylized than emotional. Technical work is sometimes called external or objective work, because the actor builds the character through pacing, projection, vocalization, movement, and emotion. These are intellectualized from the script, but not necessarily "felt" by the actor. Technical acting is an important part of contemporary theatre because it emphasizes the disciplined training of the voice and body.

Are you a method or a technical actor? Your style will be determined partly by type and temperament and partly by the teachers, directors, training methods, and acting companies with which you work. You will also be influenced by the styles of plays in which you are cast. Both approaches will be useful to you as an actor in certain roles and productions.

To prepare for work in either style of acting, the actor must still employ a combination of research and imagination. Actors research the given circumstances of the play, and imagination fills in the gaps. Given circumstances include:

- What the playwright says about the character.
- What other characters say about the character.
- What the character says about him or herself.
- What the character does.

This research should be attuned to both the obvious and direct statements, such as one character saying, "You're so selfish," or the more subtle, "What do you expect from her?" The first example is direct text and the second is subtext, or what may lie beneath the surface meaning of the dialogue.

Acting Types

In the theatre, and particularly in movies and television, appearance and stage presence have much to do with an actor's ability to be cast and to work. A role can be, and often is, a combination of the following types:

Antagonist The character who opposes the objectives of the protagonist, or main character.

Bit Part A smaller role, such as GUARD #1 or a chorus member.

Character Part Usually a parental, comic, threatening, or eccentric figure. This person often has odd characteristics or personality quirks that serve as a foil, or contrast, to the protagonist. Character parts provide comic relief, dramatic tension, and/or color to a play. They are often challenging "stretch" roles for younger actors.

Foil A character that serves as either an antagonist or as a significant character to whom the protagonist may be compared.

Ingenue [AHN•juh•nu] A young female love interest, sometimes the protagonist, and in older plays, an example of idealized womanhood.

Juvenile A young male love interest, sometimes a protagonist or hero. In older plays he is often an example of perfect manhood.

Principal A main or leading role, usually the protagonist, antagonist, or love interest in a play.

Protagonist The main character with whom the audience sympathizes. Usually the character that changes the most during the course of the play.

Supporting Role A smaller role, often a sidekick or secondary love interest.

Straight Part A role that can fulfill some of the same functions as a character part but without the eccentricity. A straight part will not be played as broadly as a character part but may still provide comic relief, dramatic tension, and/or color. Straight roles demand less of a stretch for young actors.

Characterization

There are five basic areas to explore when preparing for a role. They are based on the journalistic questions Who? What? When? Where? and Why? Try to find the answers by analyzing the script. If the answers are not in the script, create the answers from your imagination.

Who is your character? To understand the world of the play and, therefore, the world of a character, an actor must explore the character's personality. This understanding is formed by a variety of influences: genetics, environment, and social influences, among others. Here are some questions to ask and answer about a character:

- Where were you born?
- Does this location affect your behavior? The way you speak?
- How important are social institutions such as school, government, and church in your world?
- What are your prejudices, if any?
- What is your attitude toward the opposite sex?
- In what way do you have professional power? Personal power? How well do you use what power you have?
- How would you describe your home life? What was your family life like when

you were growing up? How has it affected your present life?

- How do you want to appear to other characters in the play?

What is going on in the script? First, read the entire play. Then read it again, focusing on your character. Take notes on the following questions:

- What does the playwright say about your character?
- What do other characters say about your character?
- What does your character say about him/herself?
- What does your character do? (Remember that actions speak louder than words.) Does your character say one thing and do another?
- What does your character want and need as written in the script?
- What changes does your character go through over the course of the play?
- What is the playwright trying to communicate? What is the play about?

When? What's going on before, during, and after you are onstage? For every scene you are involved in, you need to be able to answer the following questions:

- Where have I just come from?
- What am I thinking about as I walk into the room?
- How much of my history do I bring into the room with me?
- As I walk into this room, what are my immediate expectations and goals?
- What are my long-range expectations and goals?

- What do I need to accomplish before I leave this room?
- As I leave, where am I going? How do I feel about what just happened? What will I do next?

Where? How do surroundings affect your behavior? If there is more than one setting, ask these questions about each location. People behave differently in different places.

- Where am I and what time is it?
- What kind of room or area is it?
- How does the space I am in impact my behavior?

Why do you do what you do? Every play has a main idea or "spine." In addition to independent character study, you will analyze the play with your director. Once you have a clear concept of the main idea, ask yourself these questions, first for the play as a whole, and then for each scene in which you appear.

- What do I want?
- What am I willing to do to get what I want?
- What is in my way?

Scoring a Role

The term scoring has various definitions depending on your instructor. For some teachers, the scoring of a role relates to the character analysis detailed above. For others, scoring is the literal marking in the script of notes and reminders about line delivery and blocking. Each actor develops his or her own personal shorthand for marking a script. The following elements are usually noted:
- Pauses
- Pitch
- Emphasis

- Speed or Tempo
- Movement
- Character Revelation or Discovery
- Stage Business

Another important aspect to scoring is to break scenes into sections and give them names using concrete noun titles for specific actions. Examples of names for scenes might include:

- The Courtship
- The Denial
- The Rejection
- The Request
- The Secret
- The Illusion
- The Trick

Next, define how your character will fit into the scene using the infinitive verb form. What does your character want at this moment, and how will he or she go about getting it? Examples of infinitives to use within scenes are:

- To Romance
- To Seduce
- To Deny
- To Conquer
- To Conceal
- To Beg
- To Criticize
- To Excuse
- To Supplicate
- To Hide

Auditions

There are two main types of auditions:

- **The audition for a specific role or play.** If possible, read the full play before the audition. This will give you a clear advantage when you approach the role for which you are reading. The director may request a specific type of audition piece, such as one of the types of monologues listed on page 554, or he or she may simply ask you to read from the play itself (see **Cold Reading** on page 555). The more you know about the play, the easier it will be for you to make meaning from even the smallest section or scene.

- **The prepared professional audition.** Most audition situations allow you to prepare beforehand. You are expected to keep the audition material short, usually one to two minutes, and you are often called upon to provide two contrasting monologues—one comic or character and the other dramatic or period—all within the allotted time period. Directors know what they are looking for and are used to assessing actors quickly. An experienced director will immediately spot the qualities needed for the role—which means that the professionalism of your approach in that very short amount of time may make the difference between being cast or forever waiting in the wings.

At most auditions, you will be asked to fill out a form with information about yourself. Take the time to fill in the information clearly and completely; you don't want anything to stand in the way of your success. You will then be given a number or a time, or told to wait until your name is called.

When you are called, make a strong cross to center stage or the center of the audition room and smile. When it is clear that the auditors are ready, state your name clearly. Some auditors will expect you to state the name of your audition piece and its source; however, many auditors only need to hear your name (and talent agency if you have representation) and then will expect you to proceed. At the end of your audition, pause in case the director wishes to ask you any questions, give direction, or invite you to do more. Then say, "Thank you," and leave.

The Audition Resume The resume gives the director a thumbnail sketch of who you are and what sort of work you have done. Your resume reflects how much you care about your acting career, so be sure it looks clean and professional.

The resume begins with your name, contact information, and any personal information you wish to share. This is followed by a listing of your educational background, then your professional credits, and finally any special abilities that might help you in your work. There are a variety of formats, many of which are detailed in library books, textbooks, and even such handbooks as *Resumes for Dummies.* Here are some basic rules:

- Don't leave anything out you want the director to know.
- Don't exaggerate or fabricate experiences.
- Don't list anything more than ten years old.

Audition Selections Every actor should have between four and ten monologues memorized at all times, including contemporary and classical pieces. Try to find selections that are not overused, but avoid monologues that do not originate from published plays. Talk to teachers, directors, and other actors about which monologues might be right for you. Following are the general categories:

- **Dramatic Monologue** Preferably a recent work featuring a character close to your age and range of experience.
- **Comic Monologue** Again, try to choose something from contemporary literature that relates to your own experience and your "type." Comedy and drama will both work if you enjoy and feel comfortable with the piece.

- **Shakespearean Monologue** Choose something that you enjoy and understand. Analyze the scene carefully so that the language makes sense, and don't allow yourself to be trapped in the iambic pentameter (poetry) of the piece. Read for content and meaning. Many thoughts and sentences expand beyond one line and bridge several poetic phrases. Read the entire play, and be sure the character is within your range.
- **Classical Monologue** Choose a selection from classical literature, ranging from ancient Greek to Restoration comedy to Ibsen and Chekov. Having this material in your repertory will show that you are well versed in theatre styles and history.

Callbacks During the audition process, the director will begin to sort out combinations of people who will make the production the best and most cohesive possible. These actors will be called back to read again, usually for specific roles in the play.

Educational institutions and community theatres will post callbacks. If you are not called back by an educational institution, it is acceptable to wait until the casting process is over and then approach the director for feedback. Be sure to check both the callback sheet *and* the final cast list. Even though you are not called back, you may still be cast.

In a professional situation, most callbacks and casting are done via phone calls or E-mail. Be sure to check your messages. Producers rarely make any contact if you are not cast, and it is considered unprofessional to ask the producer for feedback on your audition. Just keep trying.

The best way to handle a callback audition is to treat the event as if it were a rehearsal. Behave as though you already had the part. Watch for clues about how the director sees the character. If the audition or callback involves a group of people and you are able to stay in the room, listen carefully to what the director is asking from each actor.

Cold Reading Some auditions are *cold,* or unprepared, readings. Many callbacks operate in this manner. You will usually have only a few moments to prepare, sometimes with a partner or two. Use whatever time you have to become as familiar as possible with the material. The best preparation for such an audition is to read plays out loud as often as possible— alone, in class, or with friends.

Musical Audition For musical theatre, you will be required to prepare either sixteen bars of music, or a song of a specific type, such as "Broadway belt," "standard musical comedy," ballad, or even contemporary rock. Avoid using operatic-type material unless the audition specifically calls for it. Bring the music for your audition piece(s) with you and be sure it:

- Is in the key that best fits your voice.
- Has a clearly marked introduction.
- Shows what *tempo* (speed) you want.
- Indicates where you wish to start and stop.

Be prepared to sing more than sixteen bars if you are asked and have at least one additional song ready in case the director or musical director wants an "on the spot" callback. Most musical theatre actors keep a notebook of ten to twenty contrasting songs that are well-rehearsed and memorized.

Preparation

- **Memorize your audition pieces.** Nothing will kill an actor's chance of being cast more quickly than "going up" or "blanking" (forgetting your lines). The director will immediately wonder whether or not you have the discipline to memorize an entire script.

- **Rehearse your material.** Have your material in a notebook. Work with a teacher, director, or your peers to make sure your audition plays as strongly as possible.

- **Read the directions.** Auditions are almost always announced with a simple set of expectations. One of the easiest ways to impress a director is to prove that you can follow directions. If the audition calls for one sixty-second monologue, give exactly that and no more. Find out something about the play or company for which you are auditioning. Don't audition with a David Ives comic monologue for a production of *Macbeth.* If the company does only contemporary dramas, audition with pieces that show your ability to tackle David Mamet or Tom Stoppard. Make sure you know your audition time and location and never, ever arrive late.

- **Dress professionally and appropriately.** You will be dressing for both the character and the audition. You do not need to audition in costume, but what you wear should be compatible with the character you are portraying. How you dress also reflects how much respect you have for the director and the audition process. If you show up in sloppy, wrinkled clothes, the assumption may be made that your life is in similar shape.

Difficult Acting Scenes

"I have to cry?"

"I have to kiss him?"

If you are a method actor, you solve these problems with substitution—imagine who you'd really like to kiss, or find something from your life to cry about. If you're a technical actor, you address these situations by showing that you know how to kiss or how to cry because you've practiced the technique and it's something actors are called upon to do.

Crying In order to cry on stage, you can practice the principal of substitution by thinking of something sad in your life that will bring up strong enough emotions to generate tears. A more technical approach is to use eye drops just prior to a scene—as long as it's possible to establish that the crying began offstage. Entering with "tears" in your eyes will appear realistic. Technically, crying shows in the voice and body as much as in the eyes. People who are crying often have to catch their breath and fight to keep their voice from wavering or their shoulders from shaking.

Kissing First, check with your director to see if a real kiss is necessary or if an illusion will do. Once this is decided, there are techniques to make a stage kiss simple and believable. The taller partner, usually the man, should stand in front of the woman with his back slightly to the audience. He can then lean in and either actually kiss or place his cheek against her cheek. His head will keep the audience from actually seeing whether a real kiss takes place. The kiss should last at least three to five seconds, depending on the amount of passion that is to be shown. Getting into and out of the kiss is as important as the event itself. The buildup and response show the level of emotion and nature of the relationship.

Film

Acting Much of what you learn about theatrical acting technique has to be re-learned for film and television. Many of the skills are the same, and a good actor can be accomplished at both, but the small screen (television) and the big screen (movies) can look at the actor so closely that every acting moment must become smaller and more subtle. Actors who excel in a large theatre can easily be "too big" for the screen. In order to learn to act for television and film, every actor should study with teachers who understand the style. There are classes in all the major regional and national theatre centers. Check the credentials of whomever you study under. Make sure that former students really do get work.

The best piece of advice for an actor who wants to work in television and film is to start doing so on any level. Be an extra, work on the production team, get a job as a driver—just stay close to where films are being made.

The Business of Film

Most actors rely on their agents, managers, and/or entertainment lawyers to serve as buffers and negotiators for their work in motion pictures. While the major studios provide the biggest budgets and the best and most lucrative work for actors, independent films are the wave of the late 20th and early 21st centuries. Many independent films are made "on spec." The actors work at the SAG (Screen Actors Guild) minimum wage and donate the remainder of their normal salary to the production budget in the hopes that once the film makes the round of independent film festivals, it will be picked up for distribution. If this happens, everyone involved in the film stands to make a great deal of money. The success of an independent film can also make a sudden star out of a relatively unknown actor or generate "heat" for the screenwriter or director. Independent films account for much of the new talent in the industry.

Improvisation

Improvisation is the spontaneous exploration of the journalistic W's—the same ones that appear in the section under Characterization on page 551–552. The three principal W's that govern an improv are Who? Where? and What?

Who? An improvisation can be character-centered. The who can provide the most important imaginative content. Who might be an old lady, a skunk, a preacher, and so forth.

Where? An improvisation can be location-centered. The where can be the basis for much of the comedy or drama of the scene. Where could be in a zoo, in an elevator, by the shore of a farm pond, or at a funeral parlor.

What? An improvisation can be situation-centered. The what can be an event that provides the imaginative content that drives the direction of the improv. What might be a wedding, a robbery, a funeral, or a game show.

An improv based on these examples could end up being the "wedding of an old lady and a skunk in an elevator."

Improvisations will be too short or die out quickly unless there is conflict involved. If there is a situation where one of the characters wants something and the other will not let him or her have it (motivation and obstacle), then these characters are in conflict and the conversation can become quite heated and animated. The basis of energy in improvisation is conflict, either provided in the setup or created by the characters themselves.

Do's and Don'ts of Improvisation

- **Do accept every offer.** Whatever someone else says is an offer to move forward. If an improv partner says, "You wrecked the car," your response might be, "You wanted a new one anyway, and now you have the insurance money to get it."

- **Do accept what is said as fact.** Again, when a partner says, "You wrecked the car," you did! There are a million explanations, or "yes, . . . ands" available to you, such as, "Yeah it's wrecked, but it's not my fault. Your mother was talking on her cell phone, and she rear-ended me!"

- **Do stay in the world you create.** If you establish the roles of a parent and teenager, stay in that world. "You were out awfully late last night," says the parent, to which you might respond, "Oh, I was with Brian, and his parents were downstairs. Didn't they call you?"

- **Do keep focused on your motivation.** (Work to achieve your objective in the improv.)

- **Do listen, observe, and respond as the character you've created.**

- **Don't dead-end an improv with the word "No."**

- **Don't reject offers.** When your partner says, "You wrecked the car," the response, "No, I didn't," leaves little room to maneuver.

- **Don't reject what is said as fact.**
Again, when a partner says, "You wrecked the car," the response, "Huh-uh, you did it. You were driving," creates an almost insurmountable obstacle for your partner.

- **Don't stray from the world you create.**
If you are a parent and teenager arguing, remember your world. If your response to "You were out awfully late last night," is "You said I could stay out as late as I wanted, and you didn't come home on time either," we lose the sense of the balance of power in the relationships.

- **Don't spend time explaining.** Theatre is action. Use action statements whenever possible.

Motivation

Finding and using motivation is an extension of character development. It is the most important key to how a character responds to a situation in both improvisations and in written dramatic text. Why does your character act the way he or she does? What does your character truly want? How can you figure these things out and apply them to your acting scenes?

Finding motivation comes from analysis of the script, or in the case of improvised scenes, from creating wants and needs for a character. When you break a script into acting units, even the smallest unit will involve the motivation of your character. When you are perfectly clear as to what your character wants, that clarity drives your actions, inflection, and even movement.

Motivation also creates *subtext,* that which is not said or is hidden between the lines. A good playwright will generally not state a character's motivation directly but will cloak it, just as people do in actual conversation. For example, at the crises of Arthur Miller's *The Crucible,* there is a moment when the characters are virtually screaming out between and beneath the lines. John Proctor wants to prove his abiding love for Elizabeth and to seek her forgiveness by being honest, but Elizabeth wants John to lie just this one time in order to save his life. They are completely trapped by the situation and cannot say what they truly wish to have happen when the other onstage characters are listening. The audience knows the motivation that drives each one, empathizes with both, and is drawn into the tragedy of the moment.

Whether you are preparing for an audition, doing scene work, or rehearsing for a play, be sure you know and play your character's motivation. If you are having trouble, discuss it with your director or teacher. Once you have found your motivation, it will be easier to memorize lines and develop stage business, because you will know the reasons behind your words, thoughts, and actions.

Movement

Physical work is extremely important in theatre. Actors spend a great deal of time warming up and looking for ways to fine-tune working with their bodies. In addition to basic stage crosses and knowledge of stage directions, there are several important terms to remember:

- **Counter** This is the term for a move that allows another actor to take the stage or make a clear and forceful movement. Because that actor is moving, the stage picture might become unbalanced, and another actor may need to counter the move by stepping back or out of the way.

- **Dress** This term refers to the idea of an actor as a set piece or decoration. The director "dresses" the set with actors as he moves them about. For this reason, the director will sometimes tell an actor to "dress right" or "dress left" (move stage right or stage left) to balance the position of another actor.

- **Gesture** "What do I do with my hands?" Beginning actors tend to work with their minds first. They understand a character intellectually but cannot make physical the traits of the character. Observe people and other good actors, then imitate what they are doing. The skill of observation is very important when seeking to find the right stance or gesture.

- **Leading Center** Each character has an essential "center" to her or his physical being. An overbearing Henry VIII might feel his center in his belly and lead from that center. An intellectual Thomas More from *A Man for All Seasons* might lead with his forehead. Snoopy in *You're a Good Man, Charlie Brown* might lead with his fast-moving feet or lapping and yapping mouth. Whatever your character's center, leading with that in your mind will help your character take on a look and movement that is individual and unique.

- **Master Gesture** Technical actors may plan and method actors discover a master gesture for their characters. This gesture is a distinctive movement that helps separate the character from the actor playing the character. The gesture might be a walk, a twitch, a stance, or the pulling of a strand of hair—some significant act that reflects the inner life

and nature of the character. The master gesture also separates one character from another as the audience watches each come to life in the same play. The more stylized the play, the larger the master gesture. In an intense realistic drama, the gesture might be as simple as tapping a pencil nervously. In a broad comedy, the gesture might be a funny walk or an exaggerated expression.

- **Stage Picture** The director looks at each moment on stage and sees a picture made up of characters and set pieces. Each actor not only creates an individual role, but also becomes part of this picture.

Creating Believable Action

- **Use all of your senses and your sense memory.** Where are you in the play? When were you in a similar situation in real life? How did you move? What did you do?

- **Register the environment in your brain.** Let it sink in. This may take a split second or several seconds, depending on the situation, but don't react like you already know how you're supposed to act. The reaction must be in real time. Acting is active rather than reactive. The audience needs to sense you making a discovery rather than simply following what's said in the script or reacting to the other actors on stage.

- **Respond physically to the stimulus.** If your scene takes place in a pizzeria, think about what it smells like and how it makes you feel. Whatever the environment, you should have a physical reaction that the audience can perceive.

- **Respond orally.** How you move and speak will be different depending on whether you are hungry, angry, lonely, hot, cold, or tired. Your posture, your physical and verbal reactions, including tone of voice, will be affected by the environment, just as it is in real life. Physical and vocal response to the environment creates belief and represents an opportunity to use your sense of observation in order to be a stronger actor.

Fighting, Slapping, and Physical Force

The principal rule in stage combat is that the victim does all the work. If you are flung to the floor, you are actually flinging yourself. The aggressor in any physical stage work or stage combat starts the blow or attack and then "pulls the punch" in a manner imperceptible to the audience. The reaction of the audience is based on the reaction from the actor receiving the blow or attack.

When an abusive husband character grabs his wife by the arm and flings her down, he simply takes hold of her arm and she makes a rapid movement back and forth, then falls to the ground. If the actor then reaches down to slap her, she may hold up a hand which receives a "slap" from the husband, but at the same time snaps her head to one side to create the illusion that he has slapped her face. The audience will watch and believe the victim.

In another example, when the monster in a production of *Frankenstein* picks the doctor up by the throat, the actor playing the doctor simply grabs the arm of the monster with both hands and does a pull up while moving his head back and forth and gasping for air. Virtually no work is done by the monster, but the audience perceives him as having great strength.

Swordplay and Stage Combat

Rule one is "Be safe." Stage combat is very technical and requires much discipline and practice from both the method and technical actor. Any combat involving props should be choreographed. The director, more experienced actors, or a stage combat or martial arts professional should work with the actors to plot out every beat and every stroke of any swordplay, fistfight, violent chase sequence, or other form of elaborate fight. There is no room for improvisation in stage combat. Both combatants must have a clear idea of where the fight is going.

Training

Many actors attend physical theatre schools such as those mentioned in the following section on mime and pantomime. They also study aerobics, dance, Pilates, and/or yoga. All actors should take some basic dance courses including beginning ballet, tap, and modern dance. This training is good for coordination, and most actors at some time or another are required to do some dancing in connection with a role.

Mime and Pantomime

These terms are often used interchangeably and both imply essentially the same thing—the art of telling a story through body movement and facial gestures alone.

Mime is an art form that involves creating moments of drama and theatricality through movement without vocalization. It is more formal than pantomime. Mimes do not speak, though they may sometimes vocalize. They usually wear simple clown white makeup, often with a touch of personalization such as a tear, a smile, or a frown. Classical mimes usually have extensive physical training and can create tricks and complete environments with their bodies. Some classical mime movements or illusions include creating a wall, ascending and descending stairs, climbing a rope, blowing up a balloon, as well as entire scenes and stories.

Pantomime, strictly speaking, is simply creating a situation or movement that represents something, such as going fishing or sweeping the floor, usually without props and often without sound. Pantomime is very useful in many theatre situations. In much of what is known as "transformational" theatre, the actors create much of the set and the props with their bodies or they use representational objects such as a hanger, piece of fabric, or small box, that can become anything because of the way the actor works with it. For example, a stick can become a fishing pole, a bat, a fly swatter, a cane, an antenna, or anything else the actor imagines.

Some plays have a combination of pantomimed and realistic props. There might be a real bowl for cooking, but the egg that goes into the bowl is pantomimed. Each play will have its own set of rules for the use of realistic versus pantomime props and situations. A simple example of this is the standard children's theatre production of *Peter Pan* in which the main character may actually "fly" using wire rigging or simply pantomime flying. Again, depending on the rules for the given production, all flying may be pantomimed, but all sword fights might use "real" prop swords.

Training Mimes are well grounded in physical theatre. Mime training is related to clown and new vaudeville training, which is taught in specialized schools. Three of the principal schools of physical theatre training are Le Coq in Paris, started by Jacques Le Coq; Decroux in Paris, founded by Etienne Decroux; and in America, the Dell'Arte school in Blue Lake, California, founded by Carlo Mazzone-Clementi.

Musical Theatre

Musical theatre in its present form—a play driven by songs and music—is one of the most uniquely American theatrical institutions. From early works such as *Babes in Toyland,* to Rodgers and Hammerstein's epic *The Sound of Music,* and from classically derived *West Side Story* through Bob Fosse's *A Chorus Line* to *The Lion King, Rent,* and *Hairspray,* the world of theatre is enriched by plays with memorable music.

An actor in musical theatre needs to be a "triple threat"—one part actor, one part singer, and one part dancer. Many theatre programs offer specialty degrees in each area, but an actor who intends to be successful in musical theatre should have a working knowledge of all three.

Acting Everything in the previous sections on acting applies to musical theatre. However, the actor must be prepared to convey a role with a minimal amount of dialogue, some of which is sung rather than spoken.

Choreography Every musical has a choreographer. The choreographer's vision is sometimes of equal importance to that of the director. Occasionally, they will be the same person. *Chicago* is as much a product of the genius of choreographer Bob Fosse as it is of all the stage directors (and even film directors) who have since interpreted the show. Choreography is the art of creating and directing not only the specific dance combinations of any given piece, but also of bringing to life the "look" of the entire production. Some musicals are jazz-based, some modern, and some, like *The King and I,* owe much to the beauty of the waltz and ballroom dancing. In order to learn dance numbers, the actor needs a dance vocabulary. This is achieved through taking basic dance classes and fearlessly trying everything suggested by the choreographer.

Music Voice lessons are important for most actors who seek a professional career but are absolutely necessary for actors who wish to participate in musical theatre. Most colleges will offer voice as part of their curriculum, but there are also excellent private vocal coaches and voice teachers. In addition, you should learn to play a musical instrument, one that requires you to read music. Piano helps you learn the structure and theory of music. Guitar is excellent because it gives you an instrument with which to accompany yourself when you sing. If you don't read music, be prepared to keep a small tape recorder with you at all times so that you can record your parts, both harmonies and solos, and practice them outside of regular rehearsal time.

Networking

Young actors need to be supportive of one another. The good and bad relationships you develop in your career will come back to help or hinder your progress. Theatre is a business of relationships and connections. Many theatre companies are started by frustrated actors who are not getting cast and branch out to become self-producers. The innovative and experimental work created at these theatres often becomes a part of the mainstay theatre scene. Your relationship to such actors becomes important

when one of them suddenly becomes the director or playwright of a hit show.

Your teachers, directors, and their peers are also important connections. The acting profession is actually quite a small industry, and cultivating friendships and professional relationships with those who have gone before can pay the dual dividends of increased knowledge of your craft for the present and unique opportunities in the future.

Besides the opportunities you might receive from your theatre connections, you will eventually have the opportunity to give back to others. This is perhaps even more important in a collaborative profession than in the business world. Join professional organizations. Work for free on occasion. Make outreach a part of your theatrical life—outreach to youth, to the aged, to those challenged or less fortunate. Volunteer to share what you've learned and the talent you've cultivated. All that you give, you will receive back, and all that you receive is a gift from those who have gone before in this very small and occasionally brutal business.

Performance Art

Another form of acting is performance art. Performance art is almost always interdisciplinary. Multimedia and mixed media compliment and enhance the theatrical aspects of the presentation, which is often called an *installation.*

During the late 1950s and into the 1960s, performance art was developed as a defiant alternative to more traditional theatrical events. Music was often improvised, slide projection was commonplace, and the performer would express him or herself in an abstract or absurd manner. Some of the best known early performance artists were John Cage and Yoko Ono. John Cage still has a tremendous influence in the field of classical music, and one of his performance art pieces is still ongoing. This piece adds a brick per year to play a specific pedal note on a German organ. This musical piece will take over 1000 years to complete. Other examples of performance art installations could include:

- Creating a living room in which the artist simply goes about daily life in front of the viewing public.
- Reading from classical plays or literature while dance is going on in response to the reading.
- Musicians improvising while a theatrical artist responds with poetry.

Performance art is all about concept. There is usually no director—the artist fulfills that function. As a result, performance art sometimes has a random or unplanned feel. Although it may appear spontaneous and simple, creating an interesting, multidisciplined environment is easily as difficult as creating an evening of good theatre. The art in both cases is dependent upon content, thought, audience response, timeliness, relevance, and creativity. Being involved in performance art gives the theatre actor a wonderful opportunity to be exposed to new and exciting artists and art forms.

Physical Warm-ups

There is not a sport in the world that doesn't require the athlete to warm up. While theatre is not a sport, it is a very physical process. Most educational and training theatre ensembles will have a group warm-up. Sometimes this is led by the director, at other times by one of the company members. Professional actors are expected to warm up on their own rather than taking up paid rehearsal time.

Because the tools of the acting trade are voice, body, and imagination, all three should be exercised during a warm up. You can develop your own warm-up routines, but you should also be open to learning them from other actors and even other disciplines. Remember to warm up the voice along with the body. Vocal warm-ups can include tongue twisters, over-enunciation, experimenting with your lines from the play, and singing vocalizations. Physical warm-ups should include the entire body, starting slowly and increasing in intensity. Your mental warm-up should include at least a little improvisation, even if it's only by talking with yourself or your character in the mirror. Meditation and guided imagery are other types of mental warm-ups that help clear the mind in preparation for its use onstage.

Radio

Before television, there was radio. The Golden Age of Radio featured nearly as many comedies, news shows, adventure programs, serials, soap operas, and musical revues as there are on television today. Some of the great stars and stories of early television began their careers on the radio, including Jack Benny, Burns and Allen, and *The Lone Ranger.* With the advent of television as the principal media in the American household, radio has become predominantly a vehicle for music, sports, news, and talk or opinion shows. Radio is generally not as lucrative as television for the actor. Jobs include disc jockey, sportscaster, news or weather forecaster, talk radio personality, and voice-over actors for advertising commercials.

Each of these requires extensive use of the voice. Actors with very unique and distinct voices tend to find work on radio most easily. A quick wit and improvisational ability also contribute to success in this field.

In recent years there has been a resurgence of interest in radio, and many stations are now broadcasting "made-for-radio" comedy, mystery, adventure, and variety shows. One of the most successful of these is *A Prairie Home Companion,* featuring the wit, wisdom, and storytelling of Garrison Keillor.

Most universities with a television and film department provide courses in radio work, and many of these universities allow students to get hands-on experience by working with the university's local FM or AM radio station.

Readers Theatre

Readers Theatre is just that—an opportunity to read a play without memorization. This allows a play to reach an audience in a shorter time period, allows actors to gain valuable experience getting to know plays, and allows audiences to engage their imaginations and discover new material.

Readers Theatre is used for educational purposes, for new play development, and for pure entertainment. In this medium, the level of blocking or movement is up to the director and/or cast members. Much of Readers Theatre is done with actors seated on stools with their scripts on music stands. Words rather than actions are the stars of the show. Performance in this genre is therefore dependent upon a clear commitment by the actor to the vocal work involved in creating a character or characters. (It is possible to reduce a ten-character play to a reading by four or five actors through the doubling of parts.)

Readers Theatre usually, but not always, has a director who also serves as a producer, assigning roles, guiding rehearsals, and planning the evening's reading. Either the director or a stage manager reads any stage directions in the script. Following are ways to stage these performances:

Platform Readings are done with a clear distinction between audience and actors. The actors sit in front of the audience on a bare stage.

Monodrama is the reading of a play or selections from a play by a single actor. Clarity of character and the ability to quickly shift from one voice to the next are essential to maintaining interest during this sort of presentation. Monodrama is also defined as "memorized work that is written for or by a single actor, such as a one-man or one-woman show." Historical figures are often the subjects of monodramas. A prime example is Hal Holbrook's *Evening with Mark Twain.*

Choral Readings involve more than one person reading at the same time. Choral reading is often done to great effect at large events. Actors on one side of the room might read a poem by an American poet such as Walt Whitman, while those on the other side might read excerpts from the daily news in a "call and response" manner. In choral reading, the actors must be keenly sensitive to one another and to the rhythms of the work being read. Choral reading is hard but can be very effective. Many people are familiar with choral reading through their own religious institutions.

There is a profound unity of purpose achieved through choral reading, which is why it is so prevalent in religion and also why the chorus was such an important part of early Greek theatre.

Group Readings One of the most entertaining ways to learn about theatre is to start a play-reading group. The group meets and chooses plays, then reads them, taking turns or choosing roles, sections, or otherwise dividing the material. Group readings are done mostly for the entertainment, education, and artistic development of the group doing the reading.

Chamber Theatre Chamber theatre takes its name from chamber music. Usually smaller than fully-staged theatre, Chamber Theatre often involves some staging. Actors may still carry scripts, but they do the work "on their feet."

Rehearsals

Rehearsals can be both the most exciting and most challenging part of the theatrical process. As an actor, the time you are not on stage may move very slowly. Be sure to use your time wisely. Study your lines and make sure you are ready for your entrances.

There are several types of rehearsals, each with a specific purpose.

Blocking Rehearsals are used to work out stage movement. Actors carry their scripts, carefully writing down stage directions. Nothing frustrates a director, assistant director, or stage manager more than having to go through blocking a second or third time for an actor who was either inattentive or who didn't write down what he or she was to do the first time the direction was given. A pencil and eraser are the best tools for this job, since the second time through, things may change. The director may see a better way to play or stage a scene, and in the case of a new play, the playwright may change a line or even an entire scene.

Working and Polishing Rehearsals follow blocking rehearsals and can be the most fun for both actor and director. When the rehearsal period is long enough, this is the time for exploration and discovery. The play is analyzed, subjected to experimentation, developed, dissected, and put back together.

Technical Rehearsals are not about the actor. During a technical rehearsal, the actor takes a backseat to the sound, lights, stage management, cues, and other elements that will allow the production to shine in its full theatricality. Actor discipline is extremely important during tech rehearsals. The actor must be prepared to start and stop, wait, wait, and probably wait some more—and yet be able to start again with full emotion and clear purpose the moment the rehearsal continues. Some technical rehearsals go "cue by cue," meaning that large chunks of dialogue during which there are no sound or light cues may be skipped. Again, the actor must be ready for this and give a clear and precise performance of the cues so that the technicians can recognize their cues and be prepared to do their part to support the production.

Dress Rehearsals are often difficult for actors. Added to performances that seemed "set" are the sudden distractions of unfamiliar clothing and makeup. This can be especially difficult for a *period* (not contemporary) play that requires elaborate costumes and/or complex makeup. Concentration becomes the most important skill an actor can use during this time—that and a positive attitude. "Make it an acting problem," is one of the favorite responses of a costumer, stage manager, or director to actor complaints about wigs that don't feel right or clothes that seem too big or appear unflattering. Actors need to remind themselves that costumes and makeup are similar to personal props. There are often discoveries to be made about characters based on the vision the costume designer and director had when wardrobes were planned. If the fabric of a costume is especially reflective or shiny, that character may also shine and reflect. If a costume flows, then the actor wearing it should give it every opportunity to do so. If costumes include accessories such as kerchiefs, lace, monocle, glasses, pocket watch, or pockets, characters should find ways to use them.

Making these discoveries when first wearing the costume is part of what makes the dress rehearsal feel so different. An experienced director knows that during a dress rehearsal some of the old work will be left behind as characters catch up with their costumes.

Final Rehearsal All elements of the production should be in place during the final rehearsal. Even though every actor will continue to make some new discoveries during the run of a show, the expectation of the production team is that at the final rehearsal they can see how the production will appear to the audience. This rehearsal is their final opportunity to give notes and to tweak the show before the public adds the most important dimension of response.

Previews In professional theatres with long runs, the final rehearsal is often followed by a series of preview rehearsals, which are actually performances of the show in front of an audience. These are especially important for new plays and are always done for shows that plan to move to a major theatre on Broadway, or even onto one of the many strong regional theatre stages. Previews give the production team time to make changes based on how the audience reacts to the material. Comedy can be clarified, timing cleaned up, and dramatic moments crafted for the maximum possible effect.

Press Night is the last preview or first performance depending on the theatre involved. Press night is when the critics are invited in to review the play. Major commercial theatre projects often live and die by the success of their previews and press nights.

Script

Actors create their own working script in a variety of manners. Many actors photocopy the script onto pages that can be put in a notebook. Some actors, like directors, prefer to have the script copied on only one side of each sheet, so the back becomes available for notes. These can be notes on staging and blocking, character notes, or notes received from the director during the course of the show. The actor traditionally highlights his or her lines so that they are easy to find during working rehearsals and for purposes of memorization. The notebook also provides a good place to keep rehearsal schedules and other handouts the actor receives from the stage manager, assistant director, director, producer, and other members of the production team.

Storytelling

Storytellers practice their craft by performing at various venues on the professional storytelling circuit. They may also belong to professional organizations and/or take part in national competitions. In addition, storytellers are in high demand in the world of theatre for youth.

A good storyteller uses the same tools as an actor—voice, body, and imagination. A storyteller combines a strong narrative voice that sets the scene and strong character voices that propel the story through dialogue. The storyteller is really multiple actors in one, creating each character and building the story through the combination of character and dramatic action. Storytellers who create their own stories must work much like playwrights, creating a story structure that includes conflict, rising action, crisis, and climax.

Storytellers usually tell more than one story during a session, and these should have some variety so that the entire session shows a dramatic build and a rhythmic ebb and flow. The strongest stories are usually saved for last.

Television

Next to the movie industry, television provides the most lucrative possibilities for the young actor. Since more "product" is created for television, there are more opportunities for acting jobs.

Most television programs are designed to appeal to the broadest possible audience. For this reason, some actors feel they compromise their "art" when they work in television. Such actors must weigh the relative values of great art with a full refrigerator. Some television shows, made-for-TV movies, and even series are works by important artists and exhibit great artistry.

On the other hand, there is no doubt that some programming is sensationalistic and driven solely by ratings—the industry's determination of what people are watching most frequently. Television reflects the mass culture of our country, while theatre generally reflects the cultural life of artists and their vision. This is not meant to be judgmental. People enjoy comedy, sports, news, and sentimental stories, and the industry is able to provide such fare. The comparison is similar to discussing the relative values of a newspaper and a novel. Fewer people will read the novel, but it may have a longer lasting effect on the aesthetic (artistic) history and strength of a culture.

Most television programming can be grouped into the following categories:

Children's Programming Since the 1950s with its *Captain Kangaroo* and Saturday morning cartoons, television has produced fare for children. In the early years, most programming was commercially driven by sponsors of breakfast cereals and toys. Since then, however, the advent of public television has opened the door for shows with educational as well as entertainment value. Programs such as *Sesame Street* and *Mister Rogers' Neighborhood* play an important role in the national education process.

Dramatic Series Television dramas range from action adventure, such as *ER*, to police and courtroom series, such as *Law and Order.* Drama series and sitcoms (situation comedies) usually include a stock (regular) cast of characters and many featured roles around whom each week's drama revolves. Dramatic series tend to choose topical themes and reflect the world as it is. For this reason, most series last anywhere from two to six seasons before the taste of the public and the nature of current events bring new work forward.

Educational and Informational Television Public television and channels such as the History Channel and the Discovery Channel have done much to make historical and factual events entertaining and available to the general public.

Reality TV Reality TV has always been a part of television programming. Early shows such as *The Dating Game, This Is Your Life,* and *Candid Camera* all dealt with reality-based incidents. Currently, however, reality-type programs dominate TV fare. The onslaught of such offerings is due in part to recent strikes by the actors' and writers' unions. Without scripts or actors, producers and networks looked for other ways to fill the holes in their schedules. The result was the development of reality programming such as *Survivor, Fear Factor,* and *The Bachelor.* Networks were delighted to discover that such shows drew large audiences (and thus, sponsors) and, for the most part, avoided the need for expensive professional talent. In fact, the acting industry has suffered because of the popularity of such shows. The artistic value of reality television is an easy target, but the fact that such shows remain popular is a strong statement about the current cultural climate in America.

Science Fiction From the movie houses of the 1930s, serialized adventures of *Flash Gordon* and *Superman* quickly made their way to the small screen. These were followed by such shows as *The Twilight Zone, Alfred Hitchcock Presents,* and *Star Trek.* Recent science fiction series have included further editions of *Star Trek* and newer, edgier shows such as *The X-Files* and *Blade.*

Situation Comedies (sitcoms) From *I Love Lucy, The Beverly Hillbillies,* and *All in the Family* to *Seinfeld, Friends,* and *The Simpsons,* the sitcom is one of the mainstays of television. In historical derivation, the sitcom most resembles commedia dell'arte—comedy based on larger-than-life stock characters in situations that reflect our lives and allow us to laugh at our own mistakes and weaknesses.

Soap Operas Soap operas are the melodramas of today's media. Viewers thrive on the sensationalistic surrealism of characters suffering even more than people do in real life. *Days of Our Lives, The Guiding Light,* and others have evolved and kept their audiences for decades by airing hyper-dramatic situations and the difficulties of both rich and poor.

Sporting Events Some of the highest ratings go to the industry that also consumes the most entertainment dollars—professional sporting events. The NFL, NBA, and collegiate athletics take up a good portion of airtime on commercial channels. These events also provide jobs for those who wish to work in the industry either on camera or behind the scenes.

Voice

Caring for and cultivating the voice take up much of the training time of the professional actor. Without clear diction and a strong instrument, an actor cannot hope to have a successful career in this very competitive business. Some actors and actresses are born with a particularly powerful or unique voice, but others may still aspire to success through diligent work and training.

Actors must develop vocal control of the following elements:

Accents Accents may seem easy, but they are very hard to do correctly. In some comedies, actors will "fake" an accent, having fun with the sound of "pretend" British, French, or German. This is fine for burlesque or broader comedy, but it is not acceptable when trying to create a real character. Some plays, and certainly many movie and television production companies, hire phonetic or diction experts as accent coaches. Actors without such resources can purchase tapes and guides for different dialects and accents. Nothing shouts "amateur" more than a bad accent, and nothing can enrich a play more than a well-researched one. Some actors and actresses have a talent or an "ear" for accents; for others, diction and accents are just another part of the hard work that is the discipline of the professional actor.

Emphasis and Subordination Some words are more important than others, as are some phrases. Your director might ask you to "point" a portion of your speech so that a crucial piece of information is not missed. On the other hand, some speeches or parts of lines are less important and can be "thrown away." This can be done to move quickly through material or even for comic intent.

Where the emphasis in a line is placed, will also have a definite impact on what the line means. Sometimes the playwright will underline or boldface a word or phrase to help make it clear where he or she is going with the line. Note how the emphasis of different words changes the meaning in the following sentences.

I'll take the money to town.
I'll **take** the money to town.
I'll take the **money** to town.
I'll take the money to **town**.

Final Consonants Some beginning actors drop the ends of individual words, not truly finishing consonants. "Give me the hat back, won't you, Fred?" might become "Gimme eh ha ba, on u, Fre?"

Practice speaking your lines, making sure that every consonant is crisp and clear. This may feel unnatural at first, but the more it becomes second nature to you, the easier it will be to command an audience with the clarity of your voice and line delivery.

Pause and Rate Attention to pauses and speaking rates can make vocal acting stronger and more natural sounding.

Pauses are an important part of speaking. On the positive side, a pause creates emphasis. The audience will literally hold its collective breath waiting to hear what you say next. On the negative side, too long a pause can indicate that you've forgotten your next line! Although long pauses occur naturally during real conversation, in the theatre, it often appears like a missed cue or a late entrance. If an actor leaves too many long pauses in between sentences or before starting his or her line, the scene will begin to drag.

Rate of delivery is also important. The actor needs to speak clearly and concisely at a pace that allows the audience to follow what's said but not become bored. Picking up cues does not always mean speaking faster—it can mean to speak sooner, one line after the other.

The opposite problem to dragging is rushing. Some actors learn their lines so well that they rattle them off without giving them full meaning. In more declamatory styles, including certain passages of Shakespeare, the actor can actually slow down and play with the poetry of the language. Most of the time, however, it is important to speak naturally but at a reasonable rate of speed.

Swallowing Words Beginning actors who lack experience with breath control, may swallow words—often at the end of sentences. An actor might have a line such as "I'm off and I won't be back until sunrise." If the actor swallows the end of the line it might sound like "I'm off and I won't be b--k t-l s--rse." Although difficult to show on paper, it is easy to spot when an actor rushes the end of a line, dropping pitch and volume while increasing rate.

Part **Two** Directing and Producing

The Director

Even though the director controls the production and develops its artistic vision, he or she is first and foremost the principal collaborator. A good director establishes unity of purpose through a spirit of cooperation and respect. Below are aspects of the director's work.

Choosing the Play There are several factors that guide the choice of a play. Some of these are artistic and some are practical.

- **Artistic Preference** The director may choose a play based on his or her passion for the specific play or playwright. The director may feel a period piece must be presented because only contemporary plays were done during the previous season. The director may want to explore the unique worlds of David Mamet or Maria Irene Fornes. The director might be committed to new works and may even hold a contest for new plays or select a new play from one of the many play development workshops across the country. Or, the director may simply choose a play because he or she has always wanted to direct it.

- **Box Office** The box office is a big and not always artistic factor in choosing a play. Even in educational theatre, filling the house can make a difference in the ongoing success of the program. Sometimes a theatre can support experimental or edgy work that brings in a smaller audience as long as they are willing to do one or two "box-office hits." Musicals and plays such as *West Side Story, The Odd Couple, Into the Woods, Oliver, A Christmas Carol, My Fair Lady, Camelot,* and many others are almost sure to fill the house.

- **Performance Space** The three main types of performance space are:

  1 **Proscenium** The proscenium is the classic theatre framed by the *proscenium arch*—the well-defined sides and top that border the front of the stage. Most proscenium stages have a main front curtain and then a playing area with *wings* (areas on the sides of the stage for the exit and entrance of actors and scenery). The proscenium stage establishes the "fourth wall" through which the audience watches the production.

  2 **Thrust** A thrust stage is any configuration in which the stage is built out so that the audience surrounds it on three sides.

  3 **Arena** Arena staging is theatre-in-the-round with the audience on all sides of the actors. This is the most intimate of theatre settings, but it presents obvious challenges to actors, the design team, and the director.

After analyzing a script, the producer and the director may decide that they want to present the play in the intimate space of an arena or thrust stage. On the other hand, when doing a production with a large cast and complex sets, they may opt for a full proscenium theatre.

Even when there is only one choice of space, it can sometimes be reconfigured. High schools with full proscenium stages may seat the audience on the stage in order to present theatre-in-the-round or three-quarter-round.

The choice of space may also be a financial one. If producing a big budget Broadway musical, the theatre must have enough seats to guarantee the income necessary to meet expenses.

The director may also choose a play based on the strengths of available talent. If he or she has a very strong African-American actor who is ready for a large role, the director may chose to showcase that actor by doing *Othello.* If the director has a large number of very talented singers who are strong physical actors, he or she may decide on a show such as *Sweeny Todd* or *Candide.* If the company has its own rock band, the director might consider *Rent* or *Grease* with the band onstage during the performance.

The size of the cast is also a criterion. High school producers may need to use thirty to fifty people and so may have to choose a large musical or Shakespearean production. Most schools have more female actors than male, so a director might look for plays such as *Steel Magnolias* that feature strong female casts.

Developing the Artistic Vision As the director reads and analyzes a script, he or she begins to develop an aesthetic vision. Sometimes this is a concept, such as setting *Romeo and Juliet* during the Civil War. Sometimes the vision is more technical, such as doing *The Glass Menagerie* in the round with as few set pieces and props as possible.

Along with the artistic vision, the director must also consider functional aspects of the script, such as:

- What acting areas are required?
- How many different locations are needed?
- How many entrances and exits occur?
- What levels might be used for various settings?
- What special effects or technical needs are required?

The director shares his or her initial vision and set of requirements with the production team members and then listens to input from them. Their ideas will help to shape, fulfill, and even add to the director's vision. In subsequent design meetings, the designers for costumes, sets, makeup, and lights will bring in sketches, plots, models, and renderings and share them with the rest of the team.

Planning the Blocking and Stage Composition As a director works with the actors, he or she moves them around the stage forming stage "pictures," or arrangements. Stage pictures show the relative power and importance of the characters. Audience focus will always go to the actor in the strongest position. Center stage and downstage right are the most dominant positions. Movement and stage pictures are dictated by issues of appropriateness, feasibility, genre, and intent.

- **Appropriateness** Moving actors around merely for the sake of movement will read as unnatural and unrealistic. In fact, moving people around as a means of holding the audience's interest does just the opposite. The movement becomes diluted and unimportant. All movement should relate to the content of the scene and be appropriate to the motivation of and relationships among the characters.

- **Feasibility** Actors must not be asked to do something that makes them uncomfortable or puts them in danger. An elderly actor can not suddenly spring across the room. An unskilled actor should not be asked to participate in stage combat or swordplay.

- **Genre** A director responds to genre and style when blocking movement patterns. Classical theatre may require adherence to a different set of rules than modern drama. Melodrama is often very stylized, comedy very broad, and drama very reserved. Sometimes the best movement is no movement at all.

- **Intent** What is the director trying to say with the movement and stage pictures he or she creates? How do these elements reflect relationships among characters as well as the mood and theme of the play?

The blocking developed by the director should be flexible. Actors bring to a production varying amounts of experience as well as their own character research and motivation. Often, after the initial blocking session, the actor may feel that his or her character would move in a manner other than the director has indicated. All such ideas should be explored. Although the final decision remains with the director, actors often provide new and interesting ways to block scenes based on their characters' motivations and impulses.

The Producer

In professional terms, a producer has both the best and worst of all possible jobs. The producer has the greatest possibility of realizing profit and recognition for artistic success as well as the greatest financial risk. Producers are often idea people who provide the backing and backbone for a production. Some are very hands-on, helping to decide which directors, designers, or actors to hire as well as choosing the play. A producer in high school theatre is often the drama teacher and occasionally a fine arts administrator or even the bookkeeper. The producer in a community or not-for-profit theatre setting is often the board of directors. In community theatre, if the production is profitable there will be money to fund the next production and perhaps increase production values as the theatre becomes more successful.

The producer is the money person in professional theatre, gathering the funding to get the show on its feet. Since theatre receives all money on the "back end" (revenue comes only after the production money has been spent), the producer is also the risk-taker. If the show should flop, the producer is the one left holding the bag. Everyone else gets paid for the work done. If the show makes a profit, so does the producer. The following people report to the producer:

The Business Manager The business manager in a high school production may be the school's treasurer or financial officer. In a small theatre, the producer often handles the business manager's duties, which include:

- Working with the producer and director to create a budget.
- Maintaining, updating, and reporting on the budget.
- Collecting and banking receipts.
- Making sure the play does not go over budget.
- Getting approval from the director or producer to go over budget.
- Authorizing and tracking expenses.
- Paying bills.
- Handling the payroll of contract labor and employees.
- Overseeing the box office.

The House Manager The house manager is responsible for the seating and comfort of the audience. He or she sees that the auditorium is a comfortable temperature, that the doors are open early for audience seating at each performance, and that programs are available for distribution. The house manager also supervises the ushers by helping them become familiar with the seating arrangements. Ushers hand out programs and escort audience members to their seats.

Publicity, Ticket, and Program Personnel Members of these crews design and procure printed materials such as posters, ads, and tickets; create advertising campaigns; sell paid advertising for programs; arrange for cast photos; write and place announcements about the show on the radio or in newspapers; distribute flyers; arrange for reviewers; sell tickets; and so forth.

The Production Team

One of the most critical jobs of the producer and director is to bring together an effective production team. In schools, this team may consist of both students and professionals. Students who have a considerable amount of technical experience can often be stage managers and, when given training and the benefit of experience, can even serve as costume or set designers.

Some or all of the following personnel may be part of the production team. Their roles will be discussed further in Parts Three through Eight of this handbook.

- **Choreographer** Plans and teaches all dance and stylized movement for a production.
- **Costume Designer** Designs, supervises, and/or builds the costumes.
- **Fight Choreographer** Plans fight and swordplay scenes and teaches fight techniques.
- **Music Director** If the production has live music, a musical director contacts, hires, trains, and conducts the musicians and works with the singers and sound designer.
- **Set Designer** Designs and supervises set construction and painting.
- **Sound Designer** Designs the soundscape for the show, including sound effects and incidental music.
- **Stage Manager** The stage manager is the unsung hero in theatre. In a good production, the director and stage manager seek to be invisible, allowing the actors and ultimately the play to take center stage. The director technically finishes his or her job on opening night. From that point on, the stage manager is responsible for everything that happens, both on and off the stage. A partial list of the stage manager's duties includes:

- Attending all production meetings.
- Preparing the prompt book.
- Posting the auditions, callbacks, and casting notices.
- Assisting in the selection of crew members.
- Preparing the cast and crew contact sheets.
- Setting up, posting, and updating the rehearsal schedule.
- Marking the ground plan on the stage or rehearsal area floor.
- Keeping track of time during breaks.
- Coordinating all tech and dress rehearsals.
- Calling light, sound, and music cues during the show.

A stage manager usually highlights cues in the prompt book since they are his or her "lines" for running the show. A stage manager also usually writes in a "warn" or "ready" cue so that when calling the show, the lighting and sound operators can be alerted before the cue actually runs. For example, the stage manager would call "Ready lights cue 1," "Ready sound cue 2," "Go cue 1," "Go cue 2," and so on. Sound cues and light cues are often written in different colors so that they are easy to spot.

A positive attitude from all members of the production team will create a positive attitude from the cast and crews serving under them.

The Prompt Book

The prompt book is the place where the director breaks the script down into units, names the units, indicates cues, and pre-plans the blocking. As blocking is given and/or changed and cues are added, the assistant director or stage manager keeps the book up to date. The prompt book should be easy to work with and functional for the duration of the rehearsal and production process. Usually, each page of the script is duplicated on three-hole-punched notebook paper. (The script should already have been paid for so there is no danger of copyright infringement.) In addition, some directors put a copy of the ground plan between each page of the script so that they can visualize the playing area and mark blocking and stage pictures.

The prompt book becomes the most comprehensive record of an individual production. When they are first produced, many plays contain few or no stage directions. In such cases, the prompt book notations become part of the manuscript when the play is published. Many directors and theatres keep copies of their prompt books in case they decide to repeat a production.

The Script

When choosing a script, it is important to consider what type of play you wish to live with as a producer or director. Producers generally choose plays based on box office receipts and profitability. Directors more often choose what appeals to them artistically. The best producer/director teams find a convergence of these two visions. When preparing to choose a script, the team must look at both genre and style.

The Comedy Genre Comedy can be broken down into several categories. *Low comedy* is physical and exaggerated and includes burlesque and farce. *Middle comedy* relies more on situations and mental aerobics than on the physical. Romantic comedy and parody fall into this group.

High comedy is intellectual in form, often mocking the upper classes. This group includes satire and comedy of manners.

The Dramatic Genre Drama includes the most classical form of Greek tragedy, but also refers to many other types of plays dealing with serious or realistic subjects, but not necessarily with the unhappy ending of tragedy. Drama can deal with social issues, family situations, or historical events. Categories include classic and Shakespearean tragedy, melodrama, psychological and social drama, and fantasy.

Experimental Style *Avant garde* or experimental theatre are catchall expressions that encompass whatever is current, new, and exciting in off-Broadway, off-off-Broadway, or street theatre. Once a style is accepted, it is no longer experimental.

Historical Style The style of a script can be defined in historical terms. Major historical styles include: *commedia dell'arte,* Elizabethan, Restoration, romanticism, realism, expressionism, theatre of the absurd, theatre of involvement, and transformational theatre.

Presentational Style When the "fourth wall" is broken, and an actor speaks directly to the audience, the style is called *presentational.*

Representational Style
Representational plays are those in which the actors seem unaware of an audience, The audience watches as though through a "fourth wall."

Post Production
This term has two different meanings. One is theatrical and the other is for film and video work.

In Theatre The show is over. Now what? You *strike*–which means all the company members help take apart and put away sets, props, costumes, etc., and return the theatre to a state of readiness for the next production. The stage manager runs the strike and is usually responsible for putting together a strike duty sheet that everyone follows. In professional companies, each group of workers has its own strike duties. Actors clean up their areas and return their props and costumes. Set crews take apart and store the set; costume crews clean and store the costumes; props crews return or put away props. In most nonprofessional theatres, strike involves everyone who participated in the production.

In Television and Film Post production has a completely different meaning in film and television. In these areas, post production is everything that happens to a film after the footage has been shot and the actors' work is over. Post production includes the following tasks:

- Edit and review the *dailies* and *rushes* (film from each day of shooting).
- Edit the video/film.
- Add sound effects and music.
- Add special effects.
- Create a rough cut for the director's approval.
- Add credits.
- Make and screen the final cut of the film.
- Distribute and promote the film.

Part **Three** Costumes

Costume Crew

The size of the costume crew for a particular show varies based on the production values of the theatre and the scale of the play being produced. The crew works with the costume designer prior to production week and under the stage manager from that point on. Crew members assist with:

- Organizing available costumes.
- Measuring actors.
- Finding, buying, renting, and borrowing costumes.
- *Building* (making) costumes: sewing, painting, gluing, etc.
- Creating and updating the costume plot and acquisitions list.
- Fitting and altering costumes.
- Serving as "dressers" for actors or actresses who have fast changes.
- Washing, repairing, ironing, and maintaining costumes.
- Keeping the dressing rooms clean.
- Returning any borrowed items after the show closes.

The costume crew *call* (the time to be at the theatre) is usually fifteen minutes to one-half hour before the actor call. Some members of the crew may be able to leave once everyone is dressed, but other crew members will stay for the entire show in order to be available for any emergency sewing or repair. The crew also does a check at the end of each performance to determine laundry and repair needs.

Costume Design

Before working on a costume plan, the costume designer will analyze the play to answer the following questions:

- When does the play take place (period)?
- How many characters are there?
- Who are the characters?
- How are their clothes described?
- Are they rich? poor?
- Over what period of time does the play take place?
- Do characters need to change clothes?
- Are there any special needs, i.e. accommodating a body mic or including pockets, bows, or other things mentioned in the script?

At the first production meeting, the costume designer will listen to the producer and director's vision for the show. Next, the designer will create costume *renderings,* sketches of characters in costume that enable the team to visualize the designer's concept. *Swatches* (small pieces of fabric selected for the costume) often accompany renderings. With the director's approval, the designer begins to supervise the gathering and building of the costumes.

Costume Considerations The creativity of costuming should follow some practical considerations in addition to the artistic concept for the play.

- **Action** What will the actor be doing in this costume: dancing, fighting, loving, falling, running?

- **Changeability** How easy is the costume to put on and take off, especially if the actor has fast changes, wears multiple costumes for different scenes, or plays multiple characters?

- **Comfort** Will the actor be able to work during the entire performance without worrying about the costume?

- **Durability** How well will the costume hold up? (Consider the fabric as well as the assembly.)

- **Historical Accuracy** Does the costume look as though it is truly from the play's historical period?

- **Coordinated Effect** How will all the costumes look with each other?

Costume Efficiency

- Look for ways to layer costumes. Does each change have to be full, or can a change be effected by adding or removing pieces of clothing?

- Plan for an actor's fast changes by having a member of the costume crew waiting in the wings to help.

- Use Velcro™ instead of buttons and snaps.

- Use reversible clothing. This is a quick way to create more than one look for the same actor.

Costume Plot

The costume designer will track all characters through the entire play, noting what each one will wear in any given scene as well as any changes the character might need to make. This costume plot allows the designer to make a clear list of all needed costumes. He or she then determines which are already available in the school or company's costume shop, which need to be borrowed, rented, or purchased, and which may be altered or built.

Decoration

Fabrics and trims can help create a period look. Gold braid, lace, velvet capes, "jeweled" clasps, leather or faux leather fabric, burlap, felt, and other specialty fabrics can transform a simple garment into anything from a peasant girl's dress to a Roman soldier's tunic and cape. Trims can be sewn on or applied with a hot glue gun. Some decorations are painted on with fabric paint or markers. Stenciling or sponging the material can create other effects.

"Distressing"

Often a costume needs to appear well worn, or *distressed.* This can be done by using sandpaper or a wire brush on the elbows, knees, collars, cuffs, and hems of the garment. Stretching clothing until it is baggy and out of shape also adds to the effect. Fabric can also be distressed by simply putting it on the ground and walking on it!

Dyeing

At one time or another, every costume department will find it necessary to dye fabric. Dyes such as Rit™ and Tintex™ are available in fabric stores, as well as grocery and discount department stores. For the deepest shades, you may have to use a unified aniline dye or a disperse dye available from theatrical supply houses. Costumes that need to be the same color should be dyed at the same time. Different batches seem to take to the dye in different ways. Wash all dyed material in cold water or have it dry-cleaned.

Measurements

The important measurements for women and men differ. You should create a standard measurement chart for both genders. Make and date charts for each actor and keep them on file. An actor who does a show two months later may not need a new chart. A year later, however, the actor might have different measurements. Although hair and eye color are not true "measurements," they are often helpful to the costumer in terms of matching costume color to a particular actor and should be added to the chart. Whenever possible, measurements should be taken by persons of the same sex as the actor—especially in school settings.

Patterns

When building costumes, it is often useful to begin with a commercial pattern. These are available in various sizes at any fabric store. Although some "period" patterns are available, you may have to adjust a contemporary pattern to achieve the look you need. Wedding dresses and formal wear often lend themselves to adaptation. Features such as sleeves, vest lengths, hemlines, and necklines can be modified to achieve the necessary silhouette.

Sewing

Sewing is simply a matter of creating a seam—which is a line of stitches that joins two or more pieces of fabric. It is necessary to leave some fabric free between the edge of the fabric and the seam—this is called the seam allowance—which is traditionally 5/8" wide. Whether stitching by hand or using a machine, use pins to hold the fabric in place while stitching along the seam allowance. To be an effective machine sewer, you have to learn to sew a straight line and keep a steady, medium speed to avoid fabric bunching up. Finish your seams by trimming the seam allowance with pinking shears to create a zigzag cut. This will keep the edges from fraying.

Wardrobe Room

Sometimes called a *costume room* or *costume shop,* the wardrobe room, depending on size, may be used for both the building and storage of costumes. A wardrobe room that is used for building costumes should have the following tools and supplies available:

- **Measuring Tools** Flexible measuring tape, sewing gauge for hems, measurement charts.
- **Marking Tools** Tracing paper and tracing wheel for moving markings from pattern to fabric; chalk for marking fabric during fittings.
- **Cutting Tools** Scissors and pinking shears.
- **Seam Ripper** For taking stitches out.
- **Long Cutting Table**
- **Fitting Equipment** Dress form or dressmaker's dummy.
- **Full-length Mirror**
- **Sewing Machine**
- **Steam Iron, Ironing Board, and Portable Steamer**
- **Storage Bins** For fabrics, scraps, accessories, patterns, and sewing notions.
- **Movable Clothes Rack**
- **Hot Glue Gun and Glue Sticks**
- **Notions** Needles, fasteners, thimbles, pins, snaps, hooks and eyes, Velcro™, buttons, etc.

Part Four Lighting

Color Effects

Besides its use for illumination, lighting provides design opportunities through the effect of color—including the gel color of the lights and the effects these have on objects being lighted. In addition, certain colors have an emotional effect on the audience. These colors have traditionally been associated with the following qualities:

- Yellow = joyful, youthful, cowardly
- Orange = exhilarating, lively, wealthy
- Red = bloody, passionate, angry, strong, warlike
- Pink = romantic, fantastic
- White = innocent, truthful, virginal, peaceful, pure
- Blue = calm, spiritual, formal, cold, depressing
- Purple = mystical, royal, mournful
- Soft Green = soothing, waterlike, tranquil
- Green = young, natural, springlike, jealous
- Gray = neutral, serious, cloudy, negative
- Brown = poor, earth-bound, peasantlike
- Black = tragic, deathly, somber, eerie

When beginning to plan a lighting design, it is important to know what happens when one color is placed over another. See page 294 of this text for an illustration of the effect of colored lights on a color wheel. While the lighting designer can work ahead of time with the set and costume designers to plan for effect, final adjustments cannot be made until tech rehearsals when the actors can be seen in costume and makeup under lights.

Light Crew

The light crew usually consists of the lighting designer, several technicians, one or more followspot operators (if necessary), and a dimmer board operator. The light crew:

- Maintains the lighting instruments.
- Hangs the instruments according to the plot.
- Gels and focuses the lighting instruments.
- Makes adjustments during technical rehearsals.
- Strikes (takes down) and stores the lights when the production closes.

Hanging and Focusing The light crew works under the supervision of the lighting designer to hang the lights according to the light plot. Lights are hung on the proper battens, which usually have different names. The battens are sometimes called *rails* and are numbered or labeled according to their position.

- **Balcony Rail** is a beam or batten at balcony level.
- **House Rail #1** might be over the house, but closer to the stage than the balcony rail.
- **First Electric** is a rail or batten with plugs, usually found just behind the proscenium.
- **Second Electric** is the next upstage batten.
- **Third Electric** is further upstage.

Most electrical rails can be lowered for the initial hanging of the lights. Preliminary focus may be done at this time. Because it is difficult to focus lights exactly until they are in place, ladders are still used to focus the lights when the electrics are raised back up above the stage. Once all the lights are hung and focused and the lighting designer approves the look, the gels are inserted.

The lighting crew then works with the director, stage manager, and lighting designer to do a *dry tech* of the production. The dry tech is simply an opportunity to run through the show from one light cue to the next to make sure that all the cues are in order and that the lighting looks as good as possible without actors or costumes to illuminate. This is a troubleshooting rehearsal during which the lighting designer and director may choose to add or subtract cues.

Most theatres built or renovated after 1993 have computerized light boards. These make the world of lighting much easier. Each light that is plugged in is patched through the computer into a dimmer. Dimmers can then be combined and levels set to create specific looks for each cue. Once programmed, the intensity and duration of each cue can be changed with just the touch of a few buttons.

Older theatres may work from manual dimmers and a manual patch board. A manual patch board has a number for each lighting plug that corresponds to another numbered plug in the light booth which is then plugged into a specific dimmer. These dimmer controls can then be combined on submasters (several of the dimmers put together) and brought up and down (raised and lowered in intensity).

Really old theatres may simply have a way to bring the lights up and down. The potential level of sophistication in your lighting plot will be directly proportional to the quality of the lighting system your school or theatre can provide.

Running the Show A running crew will usually consist of a lightboard operator, one or two followspot operators, a backstage lighting operator or, if necessary, a specials operator. *Specials* are windows, sunlight, lamps, special effects moments, or emphasis lighting.

Followspots are used more frequently in musicals than in any other form of theatre. Usually one followspot is enough to accentuate a singer during a solo. A second followspot is sometimes used to bathe the singer in light or to light two singers during a duet. Most followspots have color wheels so that they can illuminate the singers in a variety of colors that enhance costume, mood, and setting.

Homemade Lights

A drama department on a limited budget can make adequate spotlights for mounting on a teaser batten. Purchase 150-watt PAR-38 spots and screw them into clamp-on swivel sockets that can be mounted on a batten. (To be safe, use wire as well as clamps to attach the spots to the batten.) By using swivel sockets, you can adjust the lamps to any angle. Reflector spots are available in several colors, or you can use a clear lamp and attach spring tension holders that house special glass color filters. For greater color diversity, buy clear lamps and make frames for holding gelatin or plastic. Cut each frame from a large tin can or from sheet aluminum available at the lumberyard or at a metal shop. Fold the frame double, place the gelatin between the frames, and close them with brads at the top. Then wire the frame to the socket with a coat hanger or other heavy-duty wire, allowing space for ventilation between the lamp and the gel. Without such ventilation, the heat will burn or melt the gelatin.

Portable Lighting Systems Many rock bands use small portable lighting systems consisting of PARs mounted on a folding light stand. Most theatrical lighting companies make the stands, or "trees," for such lights and also sell small dimmer packs. These packs can either be plugged directly into a wall outlet or the lights themselves can be plugged in and then controlled from the dimmer board with microphone-type cable. A lighting system such as this usually consists of four lights per tree and most school "gymnatoriums" and multipurpose rooms can support two such trees. These lights can be gelled to provide color.

Lighting Design

The lighting designer must prepare for a production in the same way every other member of the production design team does—by first analyzing the script. The lighting designer looks for answers to the following questions:

- What scenes happen at night? during the day?
- What sources of light are mentioned (lamps, windows, etc.)?
- What sort of day is it? rainy? sunny? foggy? stormy?
- What season is it?
- What is the theme of the play?
- How does the mood change throughout the play?
- What areas must be well-lighted?

After hearing from the director and the other designers, the lighting designer will have new elements to consider:

- What "specials" are needed? (As you know, specials are specific lights used for monologues or to accentuate a certain speech or action. In *Macbeth,* the lighting of the dagger that hangs in midair is an example of a special.)
- What color choices have been made by the director, costumer, and/or set designer, and how may lights accentuate or contrast with those choices?

The Lighting Plan With input from the script, the director, and the other designers, the lighting designer develops a basic lighting plan. The plan shows which instruments will light specific parts of the stage. Each area should be covered by a minimum of two instruments, one from each side. Usually these are a contrast of warm and cool colors to provide depth. A third light can provide a front wash or fill in a color designed to give emotional power to the scene.

As a rule of thumb, lighting designers break the proscenium stage into six areas that must be lighted: upstage left, center, and right and downstage left, center, and right. Lighting instruments are then assigned to these areas. Additional instruments may be added to provide sidelighting, backlighting, color, and additional wash. After these playing areas have been covered, the lighting designer adds instruments to cover the specials. The complete lighting plan is shown visually in a diagram called the *light plot,* which is illustrated on page 240 of this text.

The Hanging Plot This is the compilation of the lighting plot with the instrument list. It provides an organized method of showing which instrument has to go to which position and be placed into which specific circuit or dimmer. The hanging plot is used by the light crew to hang, focus, and gel the lights for the production.

Part Five Makeup

The Makeup Crew

This crew will vary in size depending on the production. For a simple, realistic play, the crew could consist of one or two crew members whose duties will include:

- Ordering, buying, or otherwise supplying all nonpersonal makeup and special effects items (such as crepe hair, nose putty, and spirit gum).

- Setting up the makeup room in advance of makeup call.

- Making sure that all actors have their makeup charts and/or sketches.

- Assisting actors with makeup.

- Cleaning up the makeup area.

- Performing emergency re-application of makeup during the production.

- Striking and restocking makeup at the end of the production.

Makeup Design

The bigger the budget of the theatre, the more likely it is that there will be a makeup designer. Makeup is an intensely personal thing, however, and should be learned by the actor, who is usually expected to be able to do simple "street" makeup. Actors are also expected to provide their own basic makeup kit.

Like other members of the production team, makeup designers begin with an analysis of the script, looking for the theme of the play as well as the following:

- How many characters are there?

- When does the play take place?

- What style of makeup was prevalent during this time period?

- How old are the characters?

- What special features or attributes are mentioned in the script? (i.e., age, scars, coloration, significant features)

Character Makeup Sketches At the first production meeting, the makeup designer will listen to the director's overall production vision and will then begin to work on a plot for each character based on the expectations of the director and the requirements of the script. The designer may decide to sketch out how some characters should look. This is especially important if there are clowns, elves, or other fantastical characters.

Unusual Makeup Designs In fantasy productions such as *The Wiz, Cats,* or *The Lion King* and in many children's theatre productions, it is essential to create a sketch and a plan for animal or creature makeup. These designs can be suggestive or realistic. Suggestive makeup might include feathers, mop heads, fake teeth, and so on. Realistic makeup can be created using crepe hair, latex, and a life mask of the actor's face.

Life Masks A life mask can be made from plaster bandage strips one-inch wide and six- to eight-inches long. Apply petroleum jelly to the actor's face, then put the bandages on one at a time. Leave breathing holes and cover the eyes with waxed paper. When two to three layers have covered the face, use a blow dryer for fifteen to twenty minutes to set the mask. Remove the mask and allow it to dry.

Part Six   Props

Prop is an abbreviation of the word *property.* A prop is the "property" of the actor. As such, directors will often say that every actor is responsible for making sure his or her props are available when going on stage. However, props are ultimately the responsibility of a props master, or if the theatre is small, the set designer with help from the stage manager. Props are most closely related to set design, as they are part of the visual aspect of the play.

Consumable Props such as food items must be handled carefully. Remember to consider what actors have to do or say after eating or drinking a certain prop. If their mouths are filled with something dry, there must be water available on stage as well. Make sure whatever you prepare is fresh and kept covered and sanitary. Avoid using something for a prop that will tempt cast or crew members to help themselves. Instead, try to find items that are not particularly desirable but still achieve the effect and look you need.

Making or Finding Props Although it is always preferable to use the real thing, most theatre budgets don't allow the purchase of antiques or even replicas of certain items. The props master's job is to create, borrow, purchase, or otherwise dress the set and provide the actors with working and then final props. Many things can be made quite easily from wood, carved Styrofoam covered with plaster, or papier-mâché. The set crew and set designer can help with particularly difficult or large props to make sure they are in the same style as the set.

The Props Crew Again, depending on the scope of the show and the number of students/actors/volunteers involved, the props crew can be just the props master (who may also be the stage manager), or a complete crew. In small productions, props may be handled by the stage crew under the direction of the stage manager. Along with making or procuring props, the props crew is responsible for:

- Setting up the props table.
- Checking the prop list before and after every scene, act, and performance.
- Re-supplying and making consumable props for each show.
- Assisting the actors with finding props and returning them to the table.
- Striking the props at the end of the production and returning those that were borrowed.

The Prop Table is one of the most important backstage locations. Set up and designed by the props master and/or stage manager, the table will often have a location outlined and labeled for each prop. Actors are responsible for picking up their props from the table before making an entrance and returning them to the table if they exit the stage with a prop.

Part
Seven Sets

The Crew

The stage crew works directly for the stage manager and may be responsible for:

- Building and painting scenery.
- Making and painting props.
- Organizing props with the props crew.
- Erecting and bracing scenery.
- Shifting, flying, or rolling scenery in and out during the production.
- Placing props and setting the stage between acts and scenes.
- Operating special effects such as smoke machines, flash pots, trapdoors, revolving stages, etc.
- Re-setting all scenery at the end of the performance.
- Sweeping the stage and backstage areas.

The stage crew customarily dresses in all black so that they will not be noticed when they change scenery in minimal lights or blackouts. The stage crew, like the stage manager, forms the backbone of successful theatre production.

Design

Pre-planning Before the process of design begins, there are several things the set designer must consider. These have to do more with the facility than with artistic considerations. Necessary information includes:

- **Aprons, Fly Loft, and Wings** Where is the storage area for what you build? Is there room to take scenery off and on the stage? Is there tracking? Is there fly space? Is it a full fly? Can you fly your scenery in and out? Is the system manual or automatic? Will the fly system make any noise when it operates?

- **Equipment** What does the theatre have in terms of construction equipment and supplies for building? How many pre-existing flats, drops, and scrims are there? What are the heights and widths of the flats? Is there a permanent cyclorama, or cyc, curtain?

- **The Shop** How big is the shop? When is it available? When can you work? What other shows are being built? What tools are there and are they all fully operational?

- **The Stage** Is there a revolving stage floor? Are there trapdoors? Are there pre-constructed permanent steps, ramps, thrusts, pits, or rakes that you must work around?

The answers to these questions help the designer prepare a plan and budget for the set. If existing equipment can be used, money will be saved, and perhaps spent instead on an interesting design choice that will further the artistry of the production.

Script Analysis The set designer will analyze the play for several specifics before beginning to map out a design. These include:

- What is the director's artistic vision for the play?
- What locations does the play call for?
- When does the play take place?

- What objects or areas are required by the play?
- What entrances and exits are suggested by the script? Are they necessary?
- What is the theme of the play?

Design Principles Keeping all these things in mind and based on the pre-design planning, the designer will develop a preliminary design concept based on the following principles of design:

- **Balance** There must be some balance from one side of the stage to the other. A large double door stage right might be balanced by a large chest of drawers or a stairway stage left. If everything is on one side of the stage, it "tips the boat." Most sets, however, exercise some asymmetrical or informal balance rather than perfect symmetry. (The exception is extreme stylization.)
- **Central Axis** There will be a focal point to the design, usually slightly off center. This can be the highest or lowest point on stage, the bulkiest or sparsest point of the set. This focal point will be balanced by the director's choice of how to populate the stage and space the actors. Actors effectively become part of the stage picture.
- **Line** Lines in columns, costume, draperies, and positioning or height of flats have a psychological and emotional effect on the audience. General principles of line include:

  Crooked lines = chaos, pain, conflict

  Curves and angles = intensity, danger, excitement

  Curved lines = wealth, expanse, comfort

  Diagonal lines = force, strife, conflict, or discord

  Horizontal lines = stability, calmness, peace

  Long vertical lines = dignity, hope, spirituality

- **Mass** Bulk and weight have a profound effect. Both can bring the play closer to audience members, making them feel closed in.
- **Proportion** The set will appear realistic if all elements are scaled to a six-foot-tall person. Nonrealistic sets can have people overshadowed by high peaks, tall buildings, or, when the person is more important than the background, placed in abstract settings such as pipe grids.
- **Shape** This is the outline provided by the set. The background can appear circular, triangular, pointed, or linear in order to create a sense of realism, impressionism, or expressionism as fits the genre of the play.

Final Design When the design concept is complete, the designer will create *renderings* (drawings) and a three-dimensional model of the set. Once this is accepted by the director, the designer puts together the working drawings so that the construction and stage crews can begin to build the sets. The stage manager often has input into the practicality of these working drawings and renderings.

Set Construction

Sets consist not only of backdrops and flats, but also things such as ramps, platforms, boxes, and stairs. Although muslin or canvas flats are more traditional, many contemporary theatres have shifted to lightweight lauan or plywood construction. However the set is created, it must be safe and stable as well as being functional and visually interesting.

Erecting Flats Sets are often built in pieces and then assembled on the set. They can be moved into place by stagehands who either lift one edge up and then tilt it into place or who "walk" the flat up by having one crew member place a foot against the bottom while another lifts the top and slowly walks it into place. Flats can also be flown into place by lifting them up on a flyline, swinging them to where they need to be, and lowering them into position. This method is called *floating* and is the most time-consuming but easiest on the stagehands.

Joining and Bracing Flats Once in place, flats can be joined by either lashing them together using cleat hooks and rope, or hinging them. Using loose pin hinges will allow for easy removal, especially if the set is designed for touring or repeat usage. When the flats are all in place, *dutchman* (muslin strips dipped in sizing) is applied to cover the seams. If flats are perfectly matched, a strip of masking tape can be substituted. In the case of plywood or lauan flats, a small amount of wood putty, caulking, or sheetrock mud between the flats can cover the seams.

Flats are kept upright with stage braces. Commercial, adjustable stage braces can be used that are anchored to the floor with screws. If there are restrictions against nails or screws, you can build a plywood floor plate with a rubber adhesive bottom and then attach the stage brace to that. Such a plate should be weighted with stage weights in order to make it sturdy and slip-proof. You can also use a simple triangular wooden bracing, called a *jack*.

This brace consists of three pieces of wood that form a triangle: one going up the back of the flat, one extending out at a right angle from the bottom of the flat, and a third on an angle connecting the first two. The jack should also be weighted with sandbags, or stage weights, or screwed into the floor with a foot iron.

Changing the Set Sets can be constructed in ways to make set changes go smoothly. Here are three useful methods:

- **Revolves** You must have a stage with a large, built-in revolve or build a round platform that will serve as a revolve. The revolve allows you to build up to three "looks" that can be revealed as the set is turned mechanically or by hand. Revolves give a very distinct and dramatic look, especially if the change occurs as an actor walks "into a scene."

- **Wagons** Platforms on wheels, from 4' x 8' to 8' x 16', can be preset in the wings, depending on available wing space. Called *wagons,* they can be furnished or "dressed" backstage during a prior scene. The same wagon can be used for multiple locations depending on what furniture, props, or flats are set on it and what scenic units may be flown in to join the wagon once it is in place. Many high-tech theatres have hydraulic wagons that can roll sets in from all sides as well as the back of the stage.

- **Jackknifing** This involves either two wagons on either side of the stage or simply braced scenery on sliders that are easy to move. One scene is simply pivoted out from right or left as the other scene is pivoted into place. When the scenery is in place, it is flush with the proscenium. When it is out of the way, it rests flat against the stage right or stage left side of backstage. The full set is pivoted so the previous set cannot be seen. This is best done in a blackout or when the main curtain is down as it is not as smooth a transition as a revolve and requires several stage crew members.

Set Painting

Base Coat All flats need a primer and a base coat of color. With some careful planning, you can change the color of the base coat to match the details of the set. For example, blue paint might be used where windows will be created, a brick-red color could be used for the fireplace, and beige for the rest of walls.

Kinds of Paint There are several types of paint that make scenic painting easy, including:

1 **Casein paints** These are used for professional scenery and will hold up outdoors or in dampness.

2 **Latex paint** This covers well, cleans up easily, and is cheap and readily available. Painting with latex on muslin may reduce the life of the flat as the paint tends to crack as the cloth absorbs it.

3 **Vinyl and acrylic-base scenic paints** These have pure colors and strong durability.

Texturing A painted set can look far more interesting if you use one of the following methods of texturing to add depth and dimension:

- **Dry brushing** Use a dry brush lightly coated with paint. Move it quickly back and forth. Change colors and do the same in a different direction.
- **Feather dusting** This quick-texturing technique involves dipping an inexpensive feather duster into paint, brushing off the excess, and pressing the duster against the flat. Turn the duster gently and you will get a different pattern each time it moves. This effect can look like leaves or brush.
- **Rag rolling** A rag or rolled-up piece of frayed burlap dipped in paint can be rolled over the base coat in order to make it look like plaster.
- **Spattering** Use two or more colors, one lighter and the other a shade darker than the base. Fill the brush with paint and remove the excess. Stand a short distance from the flat and strike the brush handle with a hand, a board, or other surface so that the paint spatters onto the flat. Spattering may take some practice.
- **Stippling** This is done using a sponge or crumpled rag pressed against the base coat. Stippling should create a random pattern—do not make it look uniform.

Production Design

Each production has its own look or style. The production design is a composite of the visions of the producer, the director, and all the principal designers. The best production designs are based on these four qualities:

1 **Informative** Lets us know something about the piece, such as time and place.

2 Expressive Shows us something about the theme and mood of the play.

3 Appropriate Fits the world of the play, based on elements taken from the play.

4 Usable The set must have levels and be flexible and dramatically dynamic.

The production design can also be concept-driven, for example, setting *Romeo and Juliet* during the Civil War with the Montagues as a rich Southern family and the Capulets as a poorer family from the North. This concept begins to rule all aspects of the production. During meetings, the production team may make variations on the original design, perhaps deciding to do costumes in traditional antebellum period style but setting all the action in the middle of a battlefield, representing the war that separates the two families. The production design is an element that emphasizes theatre as a collaborative art form. The set in this case still remains informative, expressive, appropriate, and usable.

Technical Considerations for Three Types of Theatre Spaces

	Scenery	Lights	Sound	Makeup
Proscenium	Has the most options—sets can be flown in, rolled in from sides, turned, and set while mid-drop is down. This is most flexible for large sets and period shows.	Front lights (side possible). Easy to accomplish. The audience is never "in the light." Flexible	Audience is at a distance, so sound must be clear. Floor or hanging mics often used. Need monitors. Most difficult to create sound in this space.	Most difficult because of space between actor and audience. All effects must read from a distance, but not seem unrealistic close up.
Thrust	Backdrops are possible, but most set pieces must be low because sightlines become a problem. Actors may be blocked by sets.	Light is from front. Side light is more difficult. Must be careful not to shine light on audience. Can do effects on back wall.	Actors are easier to amplify, closer to audience. Orchestra can be a problem; no pit. Floor mics helpful. Monitors helpful.	Less makeup needed, as audience is closer (except for special makeup).
Arena	Most difficult, but very freeing. No drops. Unit sets work best; must be small because of sightlines. Everything must be brought on in full view of audience.	Most difficult to light, but light is important to delineate areas. Lights from above and sides. Must be careful not to shine light in eyes of audience.	In a smaller theatre, less amplification is needed. Speakers can "surround" the audience for effect, or sound can come from above.	Little makeup needed, as audience is so close (with the exception of special makeup).

Part Eight   Sound

Sound Crew

The head of the sound crew usually runs the cues called by the stage manager. There may be more than one crew member if the sound is coming from multiple sources. The microphone mixer or board operator hooks up the wireless mics, sets the floor mics, and makes sure that they all have batteries and are turned on and off at the appropriate moments.

Guidelines

1 Be sure that the sound operator is in the house where the balance can actually be heard. Placing a sound operator in a booth with glass doors and expecting him or her to adjust sound based on what is heard through a headset is a recipe for disaster.

2 Replace the batteries in all cordless microphones every night. Make sure the actors know how to turn their microphones off and on and that they keep them on during the show so that all control is done by the soundboard operator.

3 Never leave a wireless microphone turned up after an actor leaves the stage.

4 Make sure there are monitors for musical productions. Singers may be off key if they cannot hear each other or the orchestra accompaniment.

5 Balance live music with the amplified voices. Orchestras in contemporary musicals are often slightly amplified so that the sound can be balanced and equalized between voices and instruments.

6 Don't touch the equalizers. These should not be used to increase amplification. The professionals who installed the equipment or who are hired to set up the sound design for a show will adjust the equalizers, which should then be left at those levels unless there is a serious problem with either feedback or highs and lows.

7 Every performance will be unique. The sound operator must be aware of where laugh lines are and how the audience might react. The operator should also watch carefully because actors may unexpectedly change positions and deliver their lines at different places on stage relative to fixed hanging or floor microphones. The sound operator's job is to follow the action with the microphone levels.

8 Make sure a sound check is done every night. Each actor should do a few lines and all microphones should be tested.

9 Sound operators must play the mics like musical instruments. They should know when a performer is going to enter, speak, and leave. The sound

operator should not be afraid to speak with actors about correcting anything that affects sound quality.

10 When touring, or even in an auditorium where additional sound is used, be sure to tape cords and cables down with gaffer's tape.

Sound Design

Like all other designers, the sound designer does an analysis of the play for meaning as well as needed sound effects and then begins to develop a *soundscape* for the production. The sound designer will attend the initial production meeting and amend the original concept to fit the over-all production design. At the next production meeting, the sound designer should have examples of music choices and important sound effects as well as a chart of microphone placement and wireless microphone usage.

Soundscape A soundscape is the "color palette" of the sound designer. It contains his or her interpretation of the overall feel of the production design. For example, in a recent production of *Frankenstein,* the powerful soundscape consisted of a combination of odd and organic laboratory sounds and industrial 1980s music

between scenes. The soundscape for *The Robber Bridegroom* might consist of bluegrass music with a few electronically altered versions of the same pieces threaded throughout the show.

Sound Recording and Construction

The sound crew gathers the sounds to be used in the play and puts them together in a logical and simple playback method. Occasional sounds like the crashing or breaking of glass can be constructed, but most of these sounds are available either on recordings or on many sound effects sources on the Internet. Today's digital technology makes it easy to compile sounds and use digital editing to create either a DAT or a CD that will have all the cues lined up one after the other so that sound operation is done by push-button control. Digital editing is so precise that the simplest changes can be made in tempo, pitch, and volume and a new CD burned or DAT made quickly from one rehearsal to the next. If your school or theatre does not have such technology, you can usually find a student or professional who has the necessary equipment and will be willing to help create a sound score for your production.

The Business of Theatre

Agents, Lawyers, and Managers

Agents Finding an agent is the "catch 22" of the acting industry. Often you can't be seen until you have an agent, and you can't get an agent until you've worked and been "seen." In the early days of your career, an agent can help you become "marketable." You still have to the do the essential work of proving yourself in auditions, but the agent can get you through the door for movies, television, and stage acting. And an agent will certainly help you in negotiations once success starts to come your way. Agents also represent writers and directors in both the film and television industries. Agents receive a percentage (generally ten percent) of every contract they negotiate for you.

Lawyers Entertainment lawyers serve a more specific function than agents do. They negotiate contracts and help protect the actor/director. Entertainment lawyers usually work for a fee rather than a percentage. Many very successful artists have both a lawyer and an agent. Don't worry about finding a good entertainment lawyer–when you are successful, they will find you.

Managers Some actors also find it helpful to have a manager. Managers are concerned with all aspects of an actor's career, often serving as counselor, friend, image consultant, and career guide. Like an agent, managers receive a percentage of what the actor earns.

Auditions

In larger cities, audition calls are listed in trade and industry magazines and newspapers. New York and Los Angeles have trade magazines such as *Backstage* and *Onstage,* as well as Web sites that list auditions. In other areas you may need to do some investigating to discover how and where auditions are held. Read the local newspapers and study the theatre scene where you are living. Attend shows and introduce yourself. If you see a theatre company that you like, ask them if and when they hold open auditions and always check listings and bulletin boards at local Actors' Equity Association offices.

Some auditions are open and others are exclusive. Exclusive auditions require you to have an agent set up the appointment. If you don't have an agent, the best thing to do is to attend every possible open audition that seems to fit your age and type. Don't waste the time of directors and producers by showing up for auditions where you clearly won't be cast. You may also hear about auditions for talent "showcases" or volunteer/ internship programs. Study all of these carefully. Doing some work for free in hopes that it may lead to money and publicity later is a gamble that sometimes pays big dividends. Too much free work can devalue you as an actor, but it is also a way to network and meet other people in the business.

"Foot-in-the-Door" Jobs

Below is a list of jobs that are not ones you left home to pursue. However, they all may help you make the connections you need to move up the industry ladder.

- *Box Office Worker* Sells tickets.

- *Drama Specialist* If you have some training, particularly college or university training, you might find work at a youth program or camp that needs a drama specialist. You may be expected to teach theatre, direct, or even act with young people ranging from the very privileged and experienced to at-risk students.

- *Dresser* Like a costume assistant, a dresser simply works backstage and helps a principal actor with quick costume changes.

- *Extra* Extras get paid next to nothing, but they do get screen time and once in a while are picked out for speaking roles or extra on-camera opportunities in a movie.

- *Food Service Provider* This can range from working in a concession stand to working a catering job for a company that provides meals for production personnel.

- *Grip* This term comes from simply "gripping" equipment—moving things on location, holding microphones, pulling cables, and otherwise assisting on a movie set.

- *Intern* An intern is sometimes paid a minimal amount but often works for free in order to learn some aspect of the trade. This is a good stepping stone; just don't get stuck.

- *Production Assistant* This is a catchall title that can include jobs as diverse as appointment book manager, errand runner, props collector, script-reader, or even tutor.

- *Receptionist* This person answers phones and greets visitors for directors, producers, or production companies.

- *Stagehand* Although these jobs are usually held for trained technical people, it is sometimes possible to get hired as a stagehand for a particular production. Technical theatre people probably have the easiest time finding work in the industry.

- *Stand-in* Most television and movie stars do not stand and wait while the camera angles are set and lights arranged. They have a stand-in of the approximate height, build, and hair color who "stands in" the position until it's time to do the scene. Although this can be very boring work, it puts your face in front of directors, camera people, and the actors on a regular basis.

Headshots, Portfolios, Demo Reels, and Resumes

Headshots When you go to an audition, you will be expected to bring a *headshot,* a photo of your head and shoulders. Most actors have at least one current headshot—as recent as two years for a young person and within five years for an adult. Some actors have several photos. They choose whichever one is most appropriate to the audition or job interview at hand.

Headshots will cost $100 and up, depending on the photographer. They should be done by a professional photographer who is experienced in this field. Your senior picture is *not* a headshot. Ask a fellow actor or a talent agent to recommend someone.

Once you've had your sitting, the photographer will give you contact sheets from which you will pick your favorite shot. Get help in choosing the image that will best serve you. If possible, ask a director and/or casting director who looks at headshots on a daily basis to help you. They can give you feedback on how your photo compares to other actors' and how well it reflects your appearance. Glamour shots that give a false impression can work against you. You then need prints made of your headshot. You can order 300 to 500 copies of your picture for under $100. Don't scrimp here. You need plenty of photos so that you are not afraid to leave a trail of them at auditions and with directors and theatre companies. Make this investment before you start trying to sell yourself as a performer.

A Portfolio A portfolio can be a very useful tool. Most directors, educators, and designers use a portfolio to show examples of their work when a "live" audition isn't appropriate. The portfolio consists of sketches, photographs, programs, drawings, and other documentation of your work. It is an excellent interview tool for actors looking for work with a company, though rarely is such evidence called for in an audition.

Demo Reels The *demo reel* is a film portfolio featuring clips from television or motion picture work you have done. As with headshots, ask other people in the industry to recommend professionals who can help you put together your demo reel.

Resumes You must have a resume. (See pages 553–554 of this handbook.) In fact, you might want to have multiples—each designed to showcase the aspect of your work most likely to get you a specific job.

For example, if you are auditioning for film, list your film and/or video credits first. If you are auditioning for a Shakespearean play, be sure to place prior Shakespeare credits early in the resume.

Location

Some actors are comfortable in New York, others in Los Angeles, and many at regional theatre centers in between such as Chicago, Minneapolis, Seattle, San Francisco, and so on. You need to find a place where you can make connections and have the least amount of fear. Of course, New York and Los Angeles are the biggest markets, but they are also the most competitive. In both regional and major urban markets there are many smaller theatre companies willing to work with new actors. You don't have to wait for the "big audition" to begin developing your craft.

Networking and Connecting

Networking is one of the greatest keys to success. You must do your best to know who is doing what sort of work in the business and try to find ways to get close to people who are having success. Sometimes this means working at a related job, such as becoming a paramedic for film or television sets or helping to organize extras for a casting director. Apprenticeships and opportunities to further others in the business can only help you later on.

Connecting is similar to networking but has more to do with consciously seeking out those who might help you. You need to be courteous and not pushy, but it never hurts to try making a connection with someone who might be able to help you. Often people who are successful in the business are very willing to serve as mentors to others. This may be the way they got their start, and successful people are often willing to share their expertise. Just remember when you become successful to help others along the way.

Organizations and Unions

Larger cities offer alumni groups from universities or colleges you might join. These groups provide a valuable service, allowing you to meet others who may work in the industry and who may have experiences to share. Join any such organizations that you can. It is also an excellent idea to join professional organizations such as TCG (Theatre Communications Group), ASSITEJ/USA (The United States Center for the Association of Theater for Children and Young People), or AATE (The American Alliance for Theatre and Education). You may also soon qualify for the various unions including AEA (Actors' Equity Association), SAG (Screen Actors' Guild), AFTRA (American Federation of Television and Radio Actors), IATSE (International Alliance of Theatrical Stage Employees), WGA (Writers Guild of America), or DGA (Dramatists Guild of America).

Joining a union will take money and time and is not always the best decision. Many companies have a certain number of union vs. nonunion jobs and young actors can price themselves out of the market by becoming union members too soon. On the other hand, the union provides a safety net in terms of pay scale and health insurance as well as connecting the young actor to others in the business. Certain large film or television roles may require actors to join

SAG or AFTRA, which may, by the time of this printing, be merged into one union. Consulting with friends or officers in the various unions is a great way to find out what you should do in your location with your particular skills.

Self-Esteem

While you are waiting for your career to take off, be sure you are also living your life to the fullest—doing things for other people as well as for yourself. You should always have a "fall-back" trade in case you become frustrated with your progress in the theatre. Don't base your self-esteem on what others think of your work or how often you get a role.

Stamina and Commitment

Theatre is a rough business. You must be fully committed to a career in theatre and aware that for most people success doesn't come overnight. Actors who are "discovered" are much less frequent occurrences than careers launched through determination and commitment. Try your best to not take things personally, to move past rejection, and to find things that satisfy your soul as you're making the journey. Also, remember that the journey itself is part of the career, even if it means living through many rejections and setbacks.

Finances and Taxes

Finances are difficult for a young actor. The best advice is to find a job that is flexible enough to allow you to audition and perform, but still lucrative enough to support you when theatre and acting jobs are not coming in. Remember that to make money, you must spend money—on headshots, resumes, training, makeup, travel to auditions, and so on. Waiting tables is the obvious parallel profession to acting, but there are other jobs that will allow you time to audition and work, including temp agency work, especially in the larger markets.

Some of your theatre earnings will likely be "contract" income rather than "employee" income. Remember that when you are hired on contract, you are responsible to the government for both income tax and the full amount of your Social Security tax. This is a tax that is matched by your employer when you are "employed" rather than "contracted." It is always easier to be an employee at tax time, but writers, designers, and directors are often contracted and must, therefore, take care of their own Social Security deductions. For this reason, you must keep very careful records of all your income and expenses. The costs each time you travel, do your hair for a specific role, spend money going to an audition, or take a director to lunch are deductible business expenses. If you have a reasonable amount of self-employment, it will probably be worthwhile for you to itemize your deductions rather than use the short tax form. A good accountant who is knowledgeable about the industry will be able to advise you on which form will be most advantageous for you and whether or not you need to pay quarterly tax estimates. Of course he or she will charge a fee, but remember that even this expense is tax-deductible.

A Theatrical Miscellany

Most Often Recommended Playwrights and Their Works

The following plays are those most often recommended by high schools, colleges, and universities.

Aeschylus *Orestia* (Greek, 458 B.C.) A triad of plays in which a son seeks revenge against his mother for the murder of his father. In the final play he is exonerated for killing his mother by a tribunal of Athenian judges and the goddess Athena.

Aeschylus has been called the Father of Tragedy. He wrote approximately 90 plays of which seven survive and won the City Dionysia drama competition thirteen times. He is credited with adding a second actor to the drama form of the day and reducing the chorus from fifty to twelve. One of his most important works is *Prometheus Bound*.

Aristophanes *Lysistrata* (Greek, 411 B.C.) In this comedy, the women of warring Athens and Sparta go on a marital strike until their men end their fighting. "Aristophanes made in this play a last appeal, half farcical, half serious, for peace." (Sir Paul Harvey)

Considered the finest comic writer of ancient Greece, his biting, bawdy satires such as *The Birds, The Frogs,* and *The Clouds* abound with humorous ideas and bold attacks.

Beckett, Samuel *Waiting for Godot* (Irish, 1952) A Theatre of the Absurd play in which two tramps sit endlessly waiting for someone named Godot, who never arrives. Other plays by Beckett include *Endgame* and *Proust*

Playwright, novelist, and poet, Samuel Beckett is best known for his darkly humorous, minimalist works. He was a founder of the "Theatre of the Absurd," which espoused the belief that the universe is chaotic and beyond human understanding. In 1969 he won the Nobel Prize for Literature.

Brecht, Bertolt *Mother Courage and Her Children* (German, 1941) In this antiwar play set during the Thirty Years War, Mother Courage moves her wagon from battlefront to battlefront peddling her wares. One by one her children are killed, even though she seeks to profit from war and not become personally involved in it. *The Caucasian Chalk Circle* is another oft-produced Brecht play.

Brecht developed what he called epic theatre in which he hoped to encourage audience members to think critically and to promote social reform through political action. To that end, he inserted many unconventional elements into his dramas such as narration, song, posters, projections, and letting lighting units and other backstage equipment be seen by the audience.

Chekhov, Anton *The Cherry Orchard* (Russian, 1904) The members of an aristocratic family are unwilling and unable to face the loss of their property. Their plight depicts the decline of the powerful Russian landowners following the end of the feudal system in 1861. Other dramatic works by Chekhov include *Uncle Vanya* and *The Sea Gull.*

Chekhov's mother, a gifted storyteller, has been credited with instilling in him the narrative skills that were employed to great effect in his classic short stories and dramas. He is known for his realistic dialogue and textured character development.

Euripides *Medea* (Greek, 431 B.C.) In this tragedy of vengeance, Medea is a passionate woman whose love turns to hate when her husband deserts her. It climaxes with her killing their two sons. Among his other best-known plays are *Electra* and *The Bacchae.*

The playwright, Euripides, is one of three great tragedians of Ancient Greece—the others being Aeschylus and Sophocles. When and how he began to write is uncertain, but it is known that he first entered the annual Athenian drama competition in 455 B.C. His role in the development of the tragedy form was the creation of strong female and slave characters. He also ridiculed Greek heroes in his plays and allowed audiences to see the inner motivations of his characters.

Goethe, Johann von *Faust Part 1* (German, 1808) This play's main character is the legendary scholar who sells his soul to the devil. In this poetic drama, Faust is attracted to a young peasant girl. The devil's plans for his soul are temporarily thwarted because Faust's lust for her turns to love.

Goethe's abundance of work spanned genres as well as subjects. Novelist, painter, minister of state, and scientist are but a few of the titles he claimed. Though he is best known for his literary contributions, his scientific discoveries were also praised by scholars. His work incorporates elements of the enlightenment, romanticism, and sensibility movements.

Ibsen, Henrik *A Doll's House* (Norwegian, 1879) In this drama, the main character slams the door and walks out on a marriage based on inequality. Her revolt against her marriage to a selfish, hypocritical man who treats her as a doll rather than as an individual gave impetus to the fight for women's rights. *Ghosts, Hedda Gabler,* and *The Wild Duck* are other important Ibsen works.

Ibsen challenged Victorian sensibilities through dramas that exposed the realities and hypocrisy behind staid and upright appearances. Audiences were shocked with his choice of subject matter, which ranged from the treatment of women to venereal disease to religion. In one of his most studied plays, *An Enemy of the People*, Ibsen pitted the individual against the crowd, challenging the idea that the majority is infallible.

Marlowe, Christopher *Doctor Faustus* (British, 1604) In this play, Faust is torn between his lust for knowledge as a means to power and his awareness of the sinfulness of his desires. Because the legend of Faust appears so frequently in the arts, the term *Faustian* has come to mean a willingness to sacrifice spiritual values in return for knowledge or power. Other dramas include *Tamburlaine the Great,* and *Edward II*.

Marlowe was a brilliant poet and dramatist. During his short life, though never breaking free of convention as Shakespeare would, he elevated the rigidly formatted style of his day to the level of serious art.

Miller, Arthur *Death of a Salesman* (American, 1949) A Pulitzer Prize-winning play in which a traveling salesman "riding on a smile and a shoeshine" realizes that his dreams will never be real and, unable to cope with the failures of his life, commits suicide. Other oft-produced Miller plays are *All My Sons* and *The Crucible*.

Miller viewed the common man as a worthy hero for dramatic tragedy. It was his concern for his characters combined with a strong social awareness that gained him critical acclaim. Along with stage plays,

Miller also wrote a screenplay, *The Misfits*, for his second wife, Marilyn Monroe.

Molière *The Misanthrope*, (French, 1666) Alceste, the leading character in this comedy, is admirable in hating the hypocrisy in his society. In his zeal for complete honesty, however, he succeeds in becoming a complete fool. Other famous plays include *Tartuffe, The School for Wives, The Physician in Spite of Himself,* and *The Miser*.

Molière is the pen name of Jean Baptiste Poquelin. He became famous for plays that mocked pretension, hypocrisy, greed, and depicted the follies of society. This often made him enemies, but his genius also won him many fans, including the King of France, Louis XIV. Molière is considered the greatest of all writers of French comedy and is still one of the standards by which comic artistry is judged.

O'Neill, Eugene *Desire Under the Elms* (American, 1924) A naturalistic drama about love, lust, and greed that contrasts a sensitive, emotional son with his severe, puritanical father. Other plays include *Long Day's Journey into Night, The Iceman Cometh, The Emperor Jones, Anna Christie, Strange Interlude,* and *Mourning Becomes Electra*.

After one year at Princeton University, O'Neill left school to pursue "life experience." Unfortunately for him, this experience included poverty, alcohol abuse, and attempted suicide. During treatment for tuberculosis, O'Neill began reading plays. Soon, he was writing them. His plays are largely psychological studies of men and women of his day. He is considered by many to be America's greatest dramatist. In 1936 he was awarded the Nobel Prize for Literature—the only American playwright to ever receive the award. He also won three Pulitzer Prizes for his work.

Shakespeare, William *Hamlet* (British, 1600) A great tragedy in which a prince is troubled by his inability to act to avenge the "murder most foul" of his father. Scholar William Hazlett says the play "abounds most in striking reflections on human life…." Many colleges urge students to read as much Shakespeare as possible—at least one tragedy, one comedy, and one history. Other much-loved titles include *Romeo and Juliet, Macbeth, A Midsummer Night's Dream, Twelfth Night, Othello, The Tempest, The Taming of the Shrew,* and *King Lear.*

Shakespeare was born and baptized in the town of Stratford-upon-Avon. His father was a prominent citizen who served as town chamberlain and mayor. William attended grammar school in Stratford, where he would have learned Latin— a requirement for a professional career—

and some Greek. In 1582 he married Anne Hathaway. The couple had three children—a daughter Susanna, and twins, Judith and Hamnet. Little is known about Shakespeare's life between 1585 and 1592. During that time he moved to London and became an actor and playwright. Several of his early plays were written during this time. Unlike many theatre people of his day, Shakespeare actually earned a good living. By 1599 he was part-owner of the Globe, one of the newest theatres in London. Such plays as *Othello, Hamlet,* and *King Lear* were first performed there.

In 1610 or 1611, Shakespeare moved back to the familiar surroundings of Stratford. He was almost fifty. Over the years he had acquired a comfortable estate where he continued to write. In 1613, his play *Henry VIII* premiered in dramatic fashion. The stage directions called for a cannon to be fired when King Henry came on stage. The explosion set the theatre on fire, and it burned to the ground.

Shakespeare died in 1616, having produced an unmatched body of work including 38 plays and more than 150 sonnets. His writing is more admired, studied, performed, translated, quoted, and enjoyed than any other author in history.

Shaw, George Bernard *Pygmalion* (British, 1913) A play in which a professor of phonetics interferes with the social order by teaching a Cockney girl to act and speak like a duchess. Other famous plays include *Arms and the Man, Man and Superman, Major Barbara,* and *Saint Joan.*

Shaw did not take education seriously until, at age twenty, he decided to become a writer. He then spent his days reading and his evenings at lectures, catching up on what he had missed. He also began to write novels, at which he failed completely. It was not until the mid-1880s that Shaw attempted to transmit Socialist ideas in brilliant and usually comic form. Shaw won the Nobel Prize for Literature in 1925.

Sophocles *Oedipus Rex* (Greek, 430 B.C.) The tragedy of a king who unwittingly has killed his father and married his mother. When he discovers what he has done, he blinds himself for "there is nothing beautiful left to see in this world." Other works by Sophocles include *Antigone* and *Electra.*

As a youth, Sophocles was known not only for his writing ability, but also for his music skills, athletic prowess, charm, and physical beauty. He was only twenty-seven when he beat the well-established Aeschylus in a major playwriting competition. Sophocles is considered one of the three great tragic playwrights of classical Athens, along with Aeschylus and Euripides. He is also credited with several dramatic innovations, including painted scenery and introducing a third actor to the stage (previously, only two were used).

Wilde, Oscar *The Importance of Being Earnest* (British, 1895) A worldly and cynical farce about a confusion of identities that ends happily when Earnest turns out to be a long-lost infant whose nurse had absentmindedly misplaced him. Other popular works by Wilde include *The Picture of Dorian Gray* and *Lady Windemere's Fan.*

Wilde was a brilliant student, graduating with honors from Oxford University. While still at school, he won the prestigious Newdigate Prize for his long poem *Ravenna.* After finishing school, Wilde pursued a literary career, producing a novel, poetry, plays, fairy tales, literary reviews, and critical studies. He became almost as famous for his flamboyance and witty conversation as for his writing. Wilde used his wit and brilliance to craft plays about the society of his day, creating a new form of comedy for the English theatre. These social comedies were to be his greatest successes. In 1895, Wilde was convicted of deviant behavior and sentenced to two years in prison. After his release, he spent the rest of his life in Paris.

Wilder, Thornton *Our Town* (American, 1938) In this Pulitzer Prize-winning play the stage manager speaks directly to the audience from a set bare of props. The play tells the story of two families as they experience daily life, love, marriage, and death.

Wilder's plays and novels usually maintain that true beauty and meaning are found in ordinary experience. He is considered a serious and highly original dramatist who often employed nonrealistic theatrical techniques. Wilder won two Pulitzer Prizes: one for his novel *The Bridge of San Luis Rey* and another for *Our Town. The Skin of Our Teeth* and *The Matchmaker* are other often-produced Wilder plays.

Williams, Tennessee *The Glass Menagerie* (American, 1945) The mother in this play dwells on the past and longs to find "a gentleman caller" for her crippled daughter, who has withdrawn into the world of her glass animals. As in many of Williams's plays, the characters live in a world of unfulfilled dreams.

Williams's plays are filled with dramatic tension. Neurotic, desperate individuals were his specialty, but Williams's poetic realism got inside the hearts and heads of these characters. Other important works include *A Streetcar Named Desire* and *Cat on a Hot Tin Roof.*

An Extended Reading List

Auburn, David *Proof*

Albee, Edward *Who's Afraid of Virginia Woolf, Zoo Story, Three Tall Women, A Delicate Balance*

Bolt, Robert *A Man for All Seasons*

Capek, Karel *R.U.R*

Chase, Mary *Harvey*

Congreve, William *The Way of the World*

Eliot, T.S. *Murder in the Cathedral*

Foote, Horton *The Young Man from Atlanta*

Fugard, Athol *"Master Harold"…and the Boys*

Gibson, William *The Miracle Worker*

Giradoux, Jean *The Madwoman of Chaillot*

Goldsmith, Oliver *She Stoops to Conquer*

Guare, John *Six Degrees of Separation; The House of Blue Leaves*

Hansberry, Lorraine *A Raisin in the Sun*

Hart, Moss and George S. Kaufman *You Can't Take It with You*

Hellman Lillian *The Little Foxes, Toys in the Attic*

Henley, Beth *Crimes of the Heart*

Hwang, David Henry *Golden Child*

Inge, William *Picnic*

Ionesco, Eugene *The Lesson*

Kushner, Tony *Angels in America*

Lawrence, Jerome and Robert E. Lee *Inherit the Wind*

MacLeish, Archibald *J.B.*

Mamet, David *Glengarry Glen Ross*

Marlowe, Christopher *Dr. Faustus*

McCullers, Carson *The Member of the Wedding*

O'Casey, Sean *Juno and the Paycock, The Plough and Stars*

Pinter, Harold *The Birthday Party, Betrayal, The Homecoming*

Pirandello, Luigi *Six Characters in Search of an Author*

Rostand, Edmond *Cyrano de Bergerac*

Sartre, Jean-Paul *No Exit*

Sheridan, Richard *The Rivals, School for Scandal*

Simon, Neil *The Sunshine Boys, Brighton Beach Memoirs, Lost in Yonkers, The Odd Couple, Fools*

Stoppard, Tom *Rosencrantz and Guildenstern Are Dead, Arcadia, The Real Thing*

Synge, John Millington *Playboy of the Western World*

Uhry, Alfred *Driving Miss Daisy, The Last Night of Ballyhoo*

Wilson, August *Fences, The Piano Lesson, Two Trains Running, Seven Guitars, Radio Golf*

Wilson, Lanford *Talley's Folly*

Zindel, Paul *The Effect of Gamma Rays on Man-in-the Moon Marigolds*

Top Ten High School Musicals and Dramas

Ever wonder what shows other schools are producing? Here are the top ten musicals and plays for 2007 as determined by the International Thespian Society which has an approximate membership of 3,600 high schools in the United States, Canada, and abroad. The Society's purpose is to honor student excellence in the dramatic arts. It is a division of the Educational Theatre Association. To learn more about these organizations go to www.edta.org.

Musicals

1. *Little Shop of Horrors* by Alan Menken and Howard Ashman
2. *Seussical: The Musical* by Stephen Flaherty and Lynn Abrams
3. *Thoroughly Modern Millie* by Richard Morris, Dick Scanlon, and Jeanine Tesori
4. *Beauty and the Beast* by Alan Menken, Howard Ashman, Tim Rice, and Linda Woolverton
5. *High School Musical* by David Simpatico and others
6. *Grease* by Jim Jacobs and Warren Casey
7. *Fiddler on the Roof* by Joseph Stein, Jerry Bock, and Sheldon Harnick
8. (tie) *Bye Bye Birdie* by Michael Stewart, Charles Strouse, and Lee Adams
8. (tie) *Oklahoma!* by Richard Rogers and Oscar Hammerstein
10. (tie) *Anything Goes* by Cole Porter, Guy Bolton, P.G. Wodehouse, Howard Lindsay, and Russel Crouse
10. (tie) *Guys and Dolls* by Frank Loesser, Jo Swerling, and Abe Burrows

Short Plays

1. *Check Please* by Jonathan Rand
2. *Check Please: Take 2* by Jonathan Rand
3. *The Actor's Nightmare* by Christopher Durang
4. *Sure Thing* by David Ives
5. *This Is a Test* by Stephen Gregg
6. (tie) *15 Reasons Not to Be in a Play* by Alan Haehnel
6. (tie) *Hard Candy* by Jonathan Rand
8. (tie) *The Least Offensive Play in the Whole Darn World* by Jonathan Rand
10. (tie) *Bang, Bang, You're Dead* by William Mastrosimone
10. (tie) *I Never Saw Another Butterfly* by Celeste Raspanti

Full-length Plays

1. (tie) *Arsenic and Old Lace* by Joseph Kesselring
1. (tie) *A Midsummer Night's Dream* by William Shakespeare
3. (tie) *The Importance of Being Earnest* by Oscar Wilde
3. (tie) *The Odd Couple* by Neil Simon
5. *You Can't Take It with You* by George S. Kaufman and Moss Hart
6. (tie) *The Diary of Anne Frank* by Frances Goodrich and Albert Hackett
6. (tie) *Our Town* by Thornton Wilder
8. *The Curious Savage* by John Patrick
9. *Noises Off* by Michael Frayn
10. *Fools* by Neil Simon

Top Ten Playwriting Tips

If playwriting is your thing, these tips can help you sharpen your craft.

TIP 1: Proper Format

Presenting your script properly is crucial. As a reader, it's easy to get turned off to a script that isn't formatted correctly and which makes reading more difficult. Page margins are usually 1" on the top, bottom, and on the right, but 1.5" on the left (because of hole punching/brads/binding). Manuscript format calls for the character name to be centered (or left indented at a consistent margin, either an extra 2.5" or 3") in CAPS, with dialogue on the next line running margin to margin. Stage directions go on their own line and in parentheses, indented an extra 2" on the left side (so basically 3.5" from the left edge of the paper). A common mistake is for writers to copy published script format by putting character names on the left, which is harder to read.

SPECIAL SOFTWARE NOTE:

If you can afford it, buy scriptwriting software such as Final Draft. You can use it for writing both plays and screenplays, and because it does all the formatting work for you, it leaves you time to be creative.

TIP 2: Don't Rush It Out

Why not send your "finished" script to a major theatre right away? Two reasons. First, you are competing with playwrights who are much more experienced than you are. And unlike film, which has a reputation for coveting youth, theatre doesn't have that reputation. Second, if you send out a script that's not ready, you potentially have a strike against you when it comes to getting that theatre to read your future work. They may remember you as the hack who sent them the lousy script.

TIP 3: Read Away Your Influences

Young writers are often unduly influenced by the style of their favorite playwrights. If you read Beckett plays, you may well incorporate his style into your own writing instead of developing your own voice. So after you read those Beckett plays, read Arthur Miller, then read August Wilson. Read Shakespeare, Tony Kushner, Edward Albee, Marsha Norman, David Mamet, Paula Vogel, Sarah Ruhl, and Anton Chekhov. Swirl all these different styles into the melting pot of your mind, and eventually, if you write enough, your own style will develop.

TIP 4: Write What You Know—Or Not

Many young writers are told, "Write what you know." Good advice, but sometimes what you don't know is so much more interesting. Playwright Jon Dorf says of one of his characters, "Ben is about a teenager living on the street in Harvard Square and looking for the woman he believes is his mother. Yes, I lived in Harvard Square in college and was a teenager at one time, but I've never been homeless, have two wonderful parents, etc.; Ben's life is not one I knew. So I read about it. I spent a term volunteering at a shelter for troubled teens. I kept my eyes open. But above all, I was truly, desperately interested in the world of my play and the people in it. It's that desperate interest that allows you to write what you don't know."

TIP 5: Just Get It on Paper!

A first draft isn't supposed to be perfect. Not even close. Don't worry—just keep going! Let the play go where it wants to go, because THE MOST IMPORTANT THING is finishing. The time to second-guess yourself is after you can safely type "Blackout. End of play."

TIP 6: Write Something Else

Finish a script? Start another one. Now. Writing a script is like giving birth, and the script is your baby, but no first (or second or third or . . .) draft is ever perfect. By writing something new, you make the new play your baby, and the first play becomes the older sibling, perhaps even a teenager. Now you have some distance to look at it critically. Also, if you're sending out a script to contests or theatres, writing something new definitely beats waiting for the mail to arrive every afternoon. And on that note, remember that responses to your submissions may range from weeks (this is extremely speedy) to months or even a year or two.

TIP 7: Give Every Character a Moment!

Actors want the chance to act. No one gets excited about playing the third tree on the left. So make sure to give every character at least one important moment

where the actor can shine. This is how you make actors want to do your play, even if their roles aren't the largest.

TIP 8: Stuff That Doesn't Play

Some things just don't seem to work on stage. You may be the genius who can pull them off, but there are some things you're probably better off avoiding. Here they are: People talking about how they feel rather than showing how they feel. Phone calls on stage. Chase scenes, especially car chases. Animals. Elaborate special effects. Stage directions that dictate characters' facial expressions (e.g., a dirty look—half the time you can't even see it from the audience). Inside jokes.

TIP 9: Stuck? Try Improv

Not sure where to go in a scene, or is it just not working? Actors are often a great source of ideas. Get a few actor friends together, set up the scene for them, and let them play it out, with you recording (either audio or video) what happens. Try it as many times as you like, changing some element of the set-up each time, so that you get to see different choices played out in front of you. They might hit on something useful.

TIP 10: Know Your Audience

A play with lots of humor about your particular high school teachers will only work at your high school, because no other audience will understand the jokes. If you are writing a play for children, leave out the four-letter words. If it's a touring show, don't write sets that can't be packed into a box at the end of the day. Writing for the high school market? Try to write more female roles than male roles, as schools usually have an abundance of women. Writing for professional theater? Keep your cast size down, because every actor who does a bit part still has to be paid.

—Courtesy of Jon Dorf, youngplaywrights101.com

Contest and Submission Opportunities for Young Playwrights

Depending on where you live, there are competitions for residents of the following areas. Submission deadlines are also indicated.

Alabama Alabama Shakespeare Festival, March 11

California California Young Playwrights Project, June 1

Chicago Pegasus Players, Connecticut 203-270-2951, March 27

Cuyahoga County Ohio, Dobama Theatre's Marilyn Bianchi Kids' Playwriting Festival, January 26

Delaware Delaware Theatre Company, Delaware Young Playwrights Festival

Florida Florida Stage, December 17; Florida Studio Theatre, March 15; Gorilla Theatre, Young Dramatists Project, February 18

Illinois Buntville Crew, 217-394-2772, May 31

Maryland CenterStage Young Playwrights Festival, February 17

New Jersey Playwrights Theatre of New Jersey, New Jersey Young Playwrights Contest, January 26; High School/Jr. High/Elementary, February 16; Waterfront Ensemble/New Jersey Dramatists, for ages 19 and under, February 1

New York City Write A Play! NYC School Playwriting Contest, April 1

Central Pennsylvania Lebanon Community Theater's Playwriting Contest, April 30

Western Pennsylvania City Theatre Company Young Playwright's Contest, April 15

Philadelphia Philadelphia Young Playwrights, May 16

San Francisco SF Young Playwrights Festival, December 16

Vermont Vermont Young Playwright's Project

Virginia Wayside Theatre's Young Playwright's Festival, limited to Shenendoah Valley area, Janurary 15

Washington, D.C. Arena Stage, April 8

The Midwest High School Playwriting Competition for residents of Illinois, Indiana, Iowa, Kansas, Kentucky, Michigan, Minnesota, Missouri, Nebraska, North Dakota, Ohio, South Dakota, or Wisconsin

Below are American competitions without geographical restrictions (annual deadlines, when known, are in parentheses).

Arlington Children's Theater Young Playwrights (September 1)

Baker's Plays (January 30)

Blank Theatre Young Playwrights Festival (March 15)

Fledgling Films (ongoing for production in July) is soliciting teen and preteen written plays and screenplays, to be produced as short films at the Fledgling Films Summer Institute. Accepting national and international submissions, with a strong preference toward works written primarily in English. Writers receive a small honorarium, an invitation to be involved in the filming process, and a copy of the finished film. Ideal script/play is 10–30 pages in length. Submit to: Fledgling Films, 949 Somers Road, Barnet, Vermont 05821, USA. Send SASE for return of materials. Contact Carrie Sterr, csterr@sover.net or 802-592-3190 with questions.

Geva Theatre (Rochester, NY) sponsors a Young Writers Festival

New South Festival (sponsored by Atlanta's Horizon Theatre) accepts submissions for one-act plays by student writers

Orange Tree Theatre Company, based in Ithaca (NY), is a company that is run by teens for teens

Princeton University Ten-Minute Play Contest (March 1, open to high school juniors only)

Scholastic Writing Awards (Deadlines vary according to region)

Syracuse Stage is open to all, though it really makes the best sense if you live in upstate New York (February 14)

TADA!, a very good children's theater company in New York, sponsors a contest for playwrights 19 and under (January 4)

VSA Playwright Discovery Program (April 15, for writers 21 and under, for plays dealing with some aspect of disability)

Young Playwrights Festival National Playwriting Contest (December 1)

Remember, deadlines can change from year to year, and contests sometimes get discontinued—so confirm the information on each specific competition before submitting.

—Courtesy of Jon Dorf, youngplaywrights101.com

Theatrical Superstitions

Actors and other stage personnel have a long list of superstitions that guide how they act, what they say, and what they do when they are in the theatre. Here are some of the most common beliefs.

Break a Leg Actors never wish other actors "good luck" (unless, of course, they actually want to wish them *bad* luck). Instead they say: "break a leg which turns out to be a good thing." Exactly how, when, or why this tradition came into being is a mystery, but here are some of the more popular explanations.

1 In ancient Greece people stomped their feet instead of clapping their hands to show appreciation for actors and plays. Stomping long and hard enough might metaphorically or even actually result in a broken leg.

2 In Shakespeare's era "break" could also mean "bend." So bending the leg to take many bows could also happily be referred to as "breaking" a leg.

3 Another possible origin for this superstition comes from the idea that mischievous sprites who inhabit the theatre could overhear stage folks asking for good luck and might perversely grant the opposite. To trick these evil spirits, actors asked each other to "break a leg" instead of wishing them good fortune.

The Scottish Play Next to "break a leg," the most widely held theatrical superstition involves Shakespeare's play *Macbeth*. Theatre people never refer to this play by its name. Rather, they simply call it "the Scottish play." The genesis of this belief is unclear. However, many famous actors have suffered serious accidents while performing in a production of *Macbeth,* which reinforces the superstition. In truth, the dim lighting and extensive stage combat with broad swords makes the show accident-prone by its very nature. In addition, the show calls for witchcraft and witches as important plot elements—features that some believe serve as dangerous invitations to the powers of evil.

In order to dispel any possible bad spirits, those who hear or say "Macbeth" must immediately utter, "Angels and Ministers of grace defend us!" Then the perpetrator must exit the theatre and perform a ritual similar to that of "break a leg" above.

The Ghost Light Every professional and most amateur theatres have a ghost light— a light onstage that is never turned off. Its purpose is to help the first and last person in and out of the theatre, and to keep evil spirits away.

Other Superstitions

- No whistling in the theatre.
- Never say the last line of a new play until opening night.
- The theatre should be dark one night a week (usually Monday) so that ghosts can perform their own plays.
- Don't use real money or jewelry on stage.
- A bad dress rehearsal portends a successful opening night.
- No peacock feathers on stage.
- Sleeping with a script under the pillow will help with memorization of lines.
- Never put hats or shoes on dressing room tables or chairs.

Drama Across the Curriculum

Don't ever think that your work in theatre class is limited to theatrical productions. Much of what you have learned can be extremely useful in other classes.

In general, your work with breathing, posture, movement, and managing stage fright can all give you added self-confidence when you make presentations, do demonstrations, and even answer questions in your other classes.

Specific ways in which drama can help you make successful presentations can be found on the Additional Projects page of each chapter, as listed below. These activities can also serve as springboards for new project and presentation ideas.

CURRICULUM	PAGE NUMBER	ACTIVITY
LANGUAGE ARTS	72	3
	109	1
	130	4
	162	2,3
	177	2
	380	1,5
	393	1,2,4
	415	3
SOCIAL STUDIES	148	4
	162	4
	380	6
	492	1
SCIENCE	249	4
	297	5
MUSIC	328	1, 2, 3
	341	2
ART	194	3
	229	1, 2, 3, 4, 5
	249	2
	276	4
	309	1, 3
	341	1
	364	5

accent the sound and patterns of speech from a specific region

acetone (ASS•ih•tohn) a solvent similar to nail polish remover used to remove spirit gum

act the main sections of a play

active listening using what you hear to build meaning

adapt to change a text from one form to another

adrenaline a hormone that produces the feel of sudden increased energy

amphitheater a round structure arranged around an open space with tiered seating

amplifier a device that provides the power supply to sound equipment

antagonist a main character who opposes the protagonist

apron the stage floor between the front edge of the stage and front curtain

archetype (AR•kih•typ) a character who represents a certain type or idea

arena stage staging in the center of a room with the audience sitting on all sides of the playing area; also called *theatre-in-the-round*

articulation clearly pronouncing words

artistic selectivity selecting the minimal amount of information needed to portray a character while still communicating necessary ideas and emotions

aside words spoken by a character to the audience rather than to the other characters who supposedly do not hear the speech

audible able to be heard

audience participation when the audience takes part in the action of the play

auditions tryouts for a part in a play

auditorium the part of a theatre where the audience sits

auditors the people conducting auditions

avant garde (ah•vahn•GARD) experimental new work; unorthodox

backdrop or drop a painted curtain without fullness, hung from a batten

backlot at a motion picture studio, an outdoor lot where sets are created to simulate a location

backstage the area behind the scenery not visible to the audience

barn door an accessory for Fresnel lighting instruments that houses moveable flaps to control the light beam

base foundation color used for stage makeup

batten a horizontal pipe suspended over the stage, from which scenery, lights, or curtains are hung; also called a *rail*

bit part a role with very few lines

blackout when all stage lights go off simultaneously

blocking the director's planned movement for the characters

body language using expressions and body movement to communicate rather than words

body mic a small microphone that can be hidden in the performer's clothing or hair

book the written script for a musical

border lights long, narrow, metal enclosures that house a row of lamps and reflectors; also called *strip lights*

box office 1. where tickets are purchased for theatrical events 2. the amount taken in for ticket sales

box set a set representing the walls of a room, sometimes with a ceiling

build 1. to make a costume from scratch 2. the increase of vocal intensity toward a climactic point

Bunraku (bun•RAH•koo) traditional Japanese puppetry

burlesque (bur•LESK) physical comedy that uses exaggeration that is directed at a person, custom, artifact, or event

business detailed bits of action such as knitting, setting the table, etc., as distinguished from broad stage movement; also called *stage business*

business manager the person in charge of finance, publicity, ticket sales, programs, and other business relating to a theatrical production

call posted announcement of rehearsals, etc., placed on the call-board near stage entrance

callback a second audition at which only those actors under serious consideration for roles are called in

cameo a one-scene part

casting the process of selecting actors for various roles

catharsis (kuh•THAR•sis) emotional purging or an uplifting release that the audience feels during a play, particularly at the end of a tragedy

CD-R (compact disk, recordable) a compact disk used for recording and playing back sound

character a role that an actor portrays in a play

character makeup makeup that changes an actor's appearance drastically

character role a role in which character traits and appearance differ from that of the actor

cheating out playing a bit toward the audience while conversing with others on stage

choreographer the person responsible for designing a show's dance numbers

chorus 1. In Greek drama, a group of actors who speak in unison and comment on the action of the play 2. the singers in a musical other than the principal performers

climax the high point of the play at which the protagonist makes an irrevocable decision; also called the *turning point*

closed audition an audition open only to union members or those represented by an agent

close-up a camera shot that shows only an actor(s) head

clown white white makeup often used by mimes

cold reading when an actor auditions for a role without having read the script

collodion (kuh•LOH•dee•un) a clear, thick liquid used on the skin to make scars

comedy a play that ends happily and arouses laughter through humorous treatment of an aspect of life

comedy of manners comedy that originated in the later 1600s which makes fun of upper-class pretentiousness and the attitudes of the wealthy

commedia dell'arte (kuh•MAY•dee•uh del•AR•tay) improvised comedy featuring stock characters that began in Renaissance Italy

conflict the dramatic opposition of the protagonist with society, with his or her peers, or with him- or herself

console the lighting control panel; also called a *dimmer board panel*

continuity in film or television, the matching of visual elements from take to take and from scene to scene

costume designer person in charge of designing or otherwise obtaining costumes for a show

costume parade when actors walk onstage in full costume for the purpose of determining comfort, utility, movement, and proper lighting

costume plot a list of every character and his or her costume for each scene

costume shop the place where costumes are built and stored

counter-cross moving in the opposite direction—and out of the way—of another actor who is moving across the stage

counterweight system a system that uses lines, cables, and weights to raise and lower the battens that hold scenery, drops, and lights

crash box a heavy box filled with glass or broken shards, used for sound effects

creme foundation a makeup foundation with an oil base

crepe hair artificial hair made of wool used for making beards and mustaches

crinolines full, stiff underskirts

crisis an event that occurs just when it seems things could either resolve or worsen; the crisis leads to the climax

cross an actor's move from one side of the stage to another

cross light when two spotlights are placed on opposite sides of the stage at a 45-degree angle to minimize shadows on an actor's face

cue 1. the last words or action of one actor that immediately precede another actor's speech **2.** signal for light changes, curtain, etc.

curtain set a set that uses the cyclorama at the back of the stage to act as a wall or drapery

cut 1. delete **2.** a command to stop action and dialogue

cyc or cyclorama (sy•kluh•RAH•mah) a curtain or wall at the back and sides of the stage

DAT (digital audiotape) a small tape used for recording and playing back sound

dead zone an area of the stage without adequate lighting

decorative props details on stage such as paintings, newspapers, or window curtains; also called *set dressing*

demographic an advertising term meaning a group of people

denouement (day•noo•MAH) the outcome of the main problem in a drama

deus ex machina (DAY•us eks MAH•kih•nah) literally, "god in the machine"; a mechanical crane used to lower and raise gods in ancient Greek theatre

development the creation of a script and the plan by which the film will be produced

dialogue conversation among characters

diaphragm (DY•uh•fram) the muscle below the rib cage

diction the style, dialect, rhythm, and words of the characters

digital audio software computer software that allows the user to mix sounds

dimmer board a lighting control panel

dimmers controls that change the level of lighting intensity

director the person who interprets a play, casts, blocks, and helps actors develop their characters

discovery space in Elizabethan theatres, the space located between two doors at the back of the stage used for small interior settings

dissolve in film and TV, when one shot is faded out and another is faded in

double cast selecting two actors for each role; the casts then split the performances

downstage the area of the stage closest to the audience

dramatic criticism the act of reviewing a dramatic work

dramaturg a person who performs a variety of tasks to assist with the production of a play, including reading and evaluating scripts, researching historical and societal issues, and sharing pertinent information with the director and cast

dress rehearsals the final rehearsals before opening night run without stopping; actors are in full makeup and costume and all production elements are in place

dress the stage keep the stage picture balanced

drop a canvas or muslin curtain that forms part of the scenery

dry tech a rehearsal run without actors in order to check technical cues

dual role the actor's two realities onstage—the actor-as-character and the actor-as-actor

dutchman thin strips of muslin used to cover the gap between flats

elevation sketch a drawing that shows how the stage will look from the perspective of the audience

ellipsoidal (ih•lip•SOY•dul) reflector spotlight a spotlight with an ellipsoidal reflector, usually hung from the auditorium ceiling to light downstage acting areas; also called a *Leko*

emoting expressing emotions

empathy emotional feedback between performer and audience

ensemble a group of actors working together to create an artistic whole rather than stressing individual players

epic a long narrative poem that tells the story of a legendary hero

epic theatre a drama in which the audience is encouraged to think critically about political and social issues; theatricality overrides realism

equalizer a device on the sound board that balances high, medium, and low frequencies to achieve a desired blend of sounds

etiquette appropriate conduct

exposition information that gives you an idea about what has happened before the play began and what is happening as the play begins

external traits characteristics that make up physical appearance, such as posture, gestures, mannerisms, voice, and clothing

farce a physical comedy that exaggerates situations until they are hardly believable

final cut the finished film

flats pieces of canvas stretched over wooden frames that are painted and linked together to create scenery such as walls and doorways

floodlights lights that illuminate broad areas of the stage

floor plan a diagram that shows the walls, doors, windows, furniture, and other important architectural details on the stage drawn to scale

fly space the area above the stage where scenery, drops, and lights are hung when not in use

foil a character whose personal attributes contrast sharply with the main character or protagonist

followspots spotlights that produce strong beams of light that follow an actor onstage

foundation makeup the color of one's skin

fourth wall the imaginary wall through which the audience views the play

Fresnel (fruh•NEL) a spotlight with a step-lens that throws an efficient and soft beam, usually hung from the teaser batten to light upstage areas

full back/full front facing completely away from or completely toward the audience

gelatins (gels) transparent color sheets inserted into a frame in front of a spotlight or floodlight

genre a type or classification of literature

gestures movements of separate parts of the body such as waving an arm or shrugging a shoulder

gobo a template of thin metal inserted into an ellipsoidal reflector spotlight to create a light pattern on stage

Goethe's (GUR•tuz) principles three criteria posed by German philosopher Goethe used to critique a work of art: **1.** What was the artist trying to do? **2.** How well did the artist accomplish it? **3.** Was it worth doing?

going up forgetting one's lines during a rehearsal or performance

grand drape the front curtain on a proscenium stage, usually made of a heavy, luxurious fabric

greasepaint heavy, oil-based theatrical makeup

greenroom a room where actors relax before and after performances

grid or gridiron the framework high over the stage that supports the curtain and scenery riggings

groundlings (in Elizabethan times) tradespeople and lower class citizens who stood in the pit around the stage to watch a performance

ground plan a diagram drawn to scale that shows the walls, doors, windows, furniture, and other important architectural details of the stage

hand props items handled and/or carried on stage by actors during the show, such as letters, books, guns, dishes, and so forth

hanging plot the plan created by the lighting designer that shows where the crew should hang the lighting instruments

high comedy comedy such as satire or comedy of manners that makes fun of political situations, cultural habits, and accepted social standards

holding for laughs waiting for audience laughter to diminish before continuing dialogue

hot spot a place where too much light hits a small area of the stage

house another name for auditorium; the place where the audience sits

house lights auditorium lights used before and after the play and during intermission

house manager the person who oversees the box office, supervises the ushers, and attends to conditions in the auditorium

illusion of the first time the actor's ability to perform in a show over and over while making it appear that the dialogue and situations are happening for the first time

impressionistic relying on colors and lines to create mood and setting rather than on realistic representations

improvisation an impromptu scene where the actors make up the dialogue and action

inciting incident the first event that suggests the situation of the drama will change; the event to which all other actions in the play can be traced

inflection variety of vocal pitch

ingenue (AHN•juh•nu) a young female lead character, often the love interest in the play

installation a presentation of performance art

instrument the term used to refer to a stage light

internal traits the characteristics that make up personality, such as family circumstances, environment, occupation, level of education, interests, and so on

interplay interaction between characters

Kabuki (kuh•BOO•kee) stylized Japanese drama which originated in the 1600s

kill eliminate; for example, "kill the noise" means to be quiet

Kyogen (ky•O•gen) a short Japanese comedy performed without music and masks

lamp the bulb for a lighting instrument

larynx (LAR•inks) the part of the throat that contains the vocal cords

lavalier (lah•vuh•LEER) mic See *body mic*

left the left side of the stage from the actor's perspective when facing the audience; also called *stage left*

legitimate theatre originally evolved from England's Licensing Act of 1737, in which plays could only be performed in two specific playhouses, today the term refers to all live play performances (as opposed to film)

Leko (LEE•ko) another name for an ellipisoidal reflector spotlight

lighting designer the person responsible for creating a lighting plan for a theatrical production

light plot a plan showing the position of lighting instruments

low comedy comedy that is physical and sometimes vulgar; it includes outlandish behavior and oddly harmless violence

makeup cosmetics, false hair, and other products that an actor uses to change his or her appearance

makeup designer the person responsible for creating makeup designs for a production

makeup morgue a collection of portrait pictures or photos used as a reference when creating a character's makeup

mansions small platforms or stations where scenes of plays were performed, and viewers moved from place to place to view the entire story

masques extravagant entertainments held at court that included dance, song, and recitation

master gesture a distinctive gesture used to establish a character's personality

melodrama an overly dramatic play that focuses more on cliff-hanging action and intense emotions than on character development or real problems

Method acting an acting approach that calls on the actor to use personal experience and sense memory to develop a character

middlebrow comedy comedy based on plot and sentimental situations; often used in romantic and situation comedies

mime an actor who communicates through movements of the body and face, but does not speak; a more formal and disciplined version of panto-mime

minidisk a small disk for use in digital recording

minimal set a set made of two- or three-fold flats that create walls or hide furniture; also called the *profile set*

miracle play a drama depicting the lives of the saints

mixer See *sound board*

modified authenticity the idea that a costume does not have to replicate a historical design exactly, but rather give the impression of that design

monologue a long speech by one character

morality play a drama that teaches right from wrong

motivation a specific reason for saying or doing something; to show a character's desires through voice and movement

multimedia using more than one medium onstage, including TV, film, dance, etc.

muscular memory when you know the role so well that your actions become effortless and appear completely natural

musical a dramatic production accompanied by song and dance

music director the person who directs the actors, singers, and often the orchestra in a musical

musical comedy a comedic drama featuring song and dance

mystery play a drama based on a Bible story

neoclassicism with regard to drama, a form of writing in which playwrights were to observe classical influences and adapt them to their work

Noh traditional Japanese theatre in which the story is communicated through poetry, dance, and music

nose putty a pliable substance used in a character's makeup to build a false nose, chin, or forehead

objectives goals

observation recognizing a fact or event

obstacle anything that gets in the way of an objective

off book having a part memorized so that a script is no longer needed

offstage any part of the stage that the audience cannot see

onstage any part of the stage that is visible to the audience

open stance when an actor faces the audience; full front

outcome result

pan **1.** to review negatively **2.** to move a film or TV camera from left to right or vice versa

pancake makeup makeup that is pressed into a hard round cake and applied with a wet sponge

pantomime telling a story or presenting an idea through bodily movement and expression rather than words

parody imitate in a humorous way

passion play a drama depicting scenes from Christ's life, especially the days of his suffering and resurrection

PBS Public Broadcasting Service, a group of television stations that specializes in educational and arts programming; partly funded by government money and private donations

Peking Opera Chinese drama that features chanting, singing, and musical accompaniment

performance art unstructured dramatic events in which movement, music, improvisation, and games are presented, often with the purpose of making a political statement

periaktoi (pair•ee•AK•toy) the Greek word for a triangle of flats that can be revolved for scenery changes; also called a *prism set*

permanent set a set that remains in place throughout the production

pilot the first episode of a television show that introduces a potential new series

pinking shears a kind of scissors that cuts a zigzag edge, used to prevent fabrics from unraveling

pitch **1.** the relative highness or lowness of a voice **2.** to present a plan or idea in hopes of convincing others to invest in or accept it

pliable **1.** adaptable to varying conditions **2.** flexible

plot the story of a play from beginning to end

poetry slam a competitive poetry reading in which poets present short, original poems that are judged by the audience

postproduction the phase of filmmaking when the film editor does most of his or her work including mixing the sound tape with film images and arranging and cutting scenes to make the final cut

preproduction the phase of filmmaking that must be completed before the film can be shot

presentational a style of play in which the actor may speak directly to the audience

principals actors in major roles

prism set See *periaktoi*

producer a person who secures financial backing for a play or film, chooses the director, and oversees the day-to-day business of the production

production the phase of filmmaking in which the movie is shot

production numbers elaborate song-and-dance sequences in which most of the cast takes part

profile facing sideways to the audience so that they only see one side of your body

project to increase voice or actions so they will carry to the audience

prompt book a book (usually a three-ring binder) that contains the script annotated with the director's ideas about details such as movement, as well as technical cues for lights, sound, etc.

props or properties set furnishings including furniture, pictures, ornaments, drapes, and so on. See *hand props* and *set props*

props master the person in charge of obtaining and organizing all of the props for a play

props plot a list of props needed for each scene

prop table a backstage location where hand props are kept

proscenium stage a stage with a permanent framed opening through which the audience sees the play

protagonist the main character with whom audience empathy lies

public domain a work that belongs to the public; royalty-free

pull to retrieve costumes or props from storage

quarter turn a 90-degree turn

quick study one who can memorize a part rapidly

rail **1.** the top or bottom board of a flat **2.** another term for *batten*

raked stage a slanted stage, where upstage is slightly higher than downstage

rate the speed at which one speaks

rave review a very positive review

Readers Theatre a form of drama in which actors are seated and read aloud from scripts

realism a type of literature that depicts life objectively and accurately

realistic play a play that imitates real life

reality TV a form of television programming in which nonprofessional participants speak and act as they would in real life

recall to remember a fact or event so as to re-create it

regional accent the sound of speech from a particular region

rehearsal a session where the play is practiced in preparation for performance

rendering a colored drawing of a set or costume

repertory a group of plays presented in rotation over a period of time by the same company of actors

representational a theatrical style, in which the actors are "unaware" that the audience is watching

resolution the end of a plot when the conflict is resolved

resonance a rich, warm vocal tone

Restoration comedy See *comedy of manners*

rhetorical involving speech (rather than action)

right the stage area to the actor's right as he or she faces the audience; also called *stage right*

role a part in a play

romanticism a literary, artistic, and philosophical movement of the late 18th and early 19th centuries that emphasized the imagination and emotions

rough cut the "first draft" of a film that has been roughly edited

roundels colored glass disks used in border lights

royalties the fees paid to the rights holder of a play, other literature, or music in order to use or perform it

rule of three the belief that pratfalls, accidents, and misunderstandings designed to make the audience laugh are only funny three times in a row

run through a rehearsal without interruption

rushes or dailies in film, the unedited footage shot each day

satire comedy that ridicules the foolish behavior of certain people

scenario an outline of a play

scene a part or division of an act of a play

scenery the background pieces such as flats and drops that create the play's setting

scene shop the place where scenery and props are constructed

scoring a role 1. marking the script with notes on blocking and delivery 2. analyzing the script as an aid to character development

screenplay a script for a film

scrim a loose-weave curtain on a batten used for "visions," "flashbacks," and so on, opaque when lighted from the front, transparent when the set behind it is lighted

script a printed copy of the play

sense memory tapping into memories in order to recapture an experience

set the scenery used onstage

set designer the person in charge of creating a plan for the set(s) of a production

set dressing anything on stage that adds to the visual representation, including actors

set piece a three-dimensional scenery piece that stands by itself, such as a rock or tree

set props items used to dress the set, such as furniture, carpets, and lighting fixtures

shooting script a version of the script for a film in which each shot is tracked by number and type of shot

sightlines imaginary lines indicating visibility of stage areas from different areas of the house

sitcoms situation comedies

skene (SKEE•nee) in ancient theatres, a building behind the stage used by the actors

social drama a play that focuses on serious, real-life problems of ordinary people

soliloquies speeches in which one actor speaks aloud, revealing his or her inner thoughts

sound board a device that controls sound sources and allows them to be manipulated and balanced; also called a *mixer*

sound designer the person responsible for planning the sound for a show

soundscape the sound designer's artistic vision for a production's sound

soundstage the location in a studio where a film is shot

spectacle everything the audience sees, including scenery, costuming, dance, pantomime, and swordplay

spiking marking the rehearsal area with masking tape to show the positions of furniture, doors, etc.

spill light leakage from stage lights

spirit gum an adhesive used for applying items such as a false beard or nose putty

spotlight a generic term for several types of lighting instruments

stage business See *business*

staged reading the reading of a drama in which actors use manuscripts and rough blocking

stage fright feeling nervous before a performance

stage left/stage right See *left, right*

stage manager the person who directs the backstage crews and runs the show once it goes into performance

stakes the consequences that result from an outcome

stealing the scene taking audience attention away from the proper focal point

step on to cut off or interrupt another character by speaking over his or her lines

stiles the vertical boards that make up the sides of a flat

stippling adding color and texture to a surface by dabbing it lightly with a paint-filled sponge or rag

stock character a character with a set of recognizable traits, such as the young lover, the irate father, the clever servant, and so on—often seen in *commedia dell'arte* productions

storyboard a series of rough drawings depicting the chronological sequence of a film, TV show, or ad

straight makeup makeup that enhances natural features and coloring

strike 1. to remove something from the set; 2. to take down set and props after the show's final performance

strip lights See *border lights*

subtext information that is implied in the dialogue but not stated

supporting roles roles that support a leading role

suspend disbelief the ability of a viewer to accept what he or she sees and hears as real

swatch a small sample of fabric

symbol an object that is used to represent an abstract concept or principle

syndication when a television program that has already aired on a network is sold to other stations

tableau a visual effect in which actors create a picture by standing in a frozen position

tag line the final line of a play or scene

tape 1. a cassette or videotape 2. to record on tape

target audience the group of people to whom advertisers believe a television show or film is most relevant

teaser the overhead curtain that masks the first batten of lights and adjusts the height of the proscenium opening

teaser batten a batten that is hung behind a teaser curtain

technical acting an acting approach that calls on the actor to use learned techniques for movement, speech, and character development rather than emotions and sense memory

theatre-in-the-round See *arena stage*

theatre of the absurd a type of drama based on the idea that life is meaningless and that searching for order only brings about confusion and conflict

theme the underlying message or meaning of a play or other piece of literature

thespian an actor

three-quarter turn a 270-degree turn

thrust stage a stage that juts into the audience area, with the audience usually sitting around its three sides

timing to move and say one's lines at the most effective moment

tiring house in an Elizabethan theatre, the backstage area where actors would go to change costumes

tormentors side curtains or flats that adjust the proscenium width

tragedy a drama in which a protagonist struggles against some force, usually making an ennobling sacrifice before going down in defeat (usually death)

tragic flaw a weakness of character that ultimately causes the protagonist's destruction

trailer a preview that provides publicity for a film's release

transmitter a device that sends a signal from the microphone to the receiver

trapdoor an opening in the stage floor that allows actors to enter and exit

travesty a humorous imitation

trilogy three related works of literature

trim decorative items such as buttons, lace, ribbon, jewelry, etc.

tryouts auditions for parts in a play

turning point See *climax*

typecasting casting someone over and over again in the same type of role

understudy an actor who learns a role in case a lead actor cannot perform

unit set a set made of several pieces that can be rearranged to produce more than one scene

unity a balance in the variety and kinds of movement in a play

upstage the stage area farthest away from the audience, toward the backstage wall

upstaging drawing the audience's attention to yourself when it should be focused on another character

vaudeville (VAWD•vil) a variety show featuring many acts, including trained animals, singers, acrobats, dancers, and comedians

villain a despicable character, especially in a melodrama

visualize to picture in one's mind

vocalizing singing without words

voice-over the voice of an unseen narrator

volume the relative loudness of a voice

wagon stage platforms on which scenery is placed and rolled onto the stage

walk-on a part in which the actor walks on and off stage without having any lines to say

warn to notify that a cue is approaching

wings offstage to right and left of the acting area

Wooden O's round or octagonal theatres, such as Shakespeare's Globe, with two or three tiers of thatched roof galleries on three sides of an open court

working script a script-in-progress that will change as a film is made

work lights white lights used solely for rehearsal

Excerpt from *Spinning Into Butter: A Play* by Rebecca Gilman. Copyright ©2000 by Rebecca Gilman. Reprinted by permission of Faber and Faber, Inc., an affiliate of Farrar, Straus and Giroux, LLC.

Excerpt from *A Star Ain't Nothin' but a Hole in Heaven* by Judi Ann Mason. Copyright ©1977 by Judi Ann Mason. Reprinted by permission of the author.

Excerpt from *A Waitress in Yellowstone* by David Mamet. Copyright ©1984 by David Mamet. Reprinted by permission of Grove/Atlantic, Inc.

Excerpt from *Weebjob* from *War Cries, Plays by Diane Glancy* by Diane Glancy. Copyright (c)1997 by Diane Glancy. Originally published by Holy Cow Press, Duluth, MN. Reprinted by permission of the author.

Excerpt from *You Can't Take It With You* by Moss Hart and George S. Kaufman. Copyright 1937 by Moss Hart and George S. Kaufman. Copyright renewed ©1964 by Anne Kaufman Schneider and Catherine Carlisle Hart. Reprinted by permission of Dramatists Play Service, Inc. Caution: The reprinting of *You Can't Take It With You* included in this volume is reprinted by permission of the author and Dramatists Play Service, Inc. The amateur performance rights in this play are controlled exclusively by Dramatists Play Service, Inc. 440 Park Avenue South, New York, NY 10016. No professional or non-professional production of the play may be given without obtaining in advance, the written permission of the Dramatists Play Service, Inc., and paying the requisite fee. Inquiries regarding all other rights should be addressed to Anne Kaufman Schneider 26 E. 63rd Street., New York, NY 10011.

Image Credits

Cover photos: top, left to right: Richard Feldman/Theatre Pix; © Donald Cooper/Photostage; Reuters NewMedia Inc./CORBIS; bottom: Richard Feldman/Theatre Pix

3: © Robbie Jack/CORBIS; 4–5: © David Turnley/CORBIS; 12–13: © Donald Cooper/Photostage; 13: Photofest; 17: Photofest; 18: © Bettmann/CORBIS; 19: © Bettmann/CORBIS; 20–21: © Reuters NewMedia Inc./CORBIS; 27: © Steve Prezant/CORBIS; 28: © Franz-Marc Frei/CORBIS; 29: Corel; 30 top: © Charles & Josette Lenars/CORBIS; 30 bottom: © Michael S. Yamashita/CORBIS; 31: © Michael S. Yamashita/CORBIS; 32–33: Michael Brosilow; 38 left: © Leonard de Selva/CORBIS; 38 right: Michael Brosilow; 39: Michael Brosilow; 43: © Robbie Jack/CORBIS; 44–45: © Robbie Jack/CORBIS; 48: Corel; 49: Burdette Parks, Roundlake Studios; 52: Corel; 53 top: © Neal Preston/CORBIS; 53 bottom: MICHAEL HALSBAND/Landov; 54–55: Chris Bennion/Theatre Pix; 62–63: © The Newark Museum / Art Resource, NY; 63: Des Moines Community Playhouse; 64–65: © Robbie Jack/CORBIS; 66: Corel; 67: © Robbie Jack/CORBIS; 71: © Roger Ressmeyer/CORBIS; 73: © HOWARD JACQUELINE/CORBIS SYGMA; 74: Connie Verkade; 75: © 2002 David Polenberg; 76–77: Michael Brosilow; 79: © Robbie Jack/CORBIS; 80: Donald Cooper, Photostage; 84: Lisa Ebright; 85 top: Jeffery St. Mary Sunrise Foundation, photograph by Jeffery St. Mary; 85 bottom: Lisa Ebright; 87: Burdette Parks, Roundlake Studios; 89: © Robbie Jack/CORBIS; 90–91: © Robbie Jack/CORBIS; 93: Michael Brosilow; 95: Michael Brosilow; 97: Library of Congress; 98: © FOGEL FRANCOIS/CORBIS SYGMA; 99: CBS/Landov; 100–101: Kevin Berne; 102 top: Western Michigan University; 104: Utah Shakespearean Festival; 106: College of Southern Idaho; 107: © Robbie Jack/CORBIS; 110: ArtToday; 111 top: © Bettmann/CORBIS; 111 bottom: © Robbie Jack/CORBIS; 112–113: Corel; 114: Joan Marcus/Bloomberg News/Landov; 115: Burdette Parks, Roundlake Studios; 119: City of Westminster Archive Centre, London, UK/Bridgeman Art Library; 121 top: THE KOBAL COLLECTION / CASTLE ROCK ENTERTAINMENT; 121 bottom: THE KOBAL COLLECTION / RENAISSANCE FILMS/BBC/CURZON FILMS; 122–123: © CORBIS; 123: © Bettmann/CORBIS; 124–125: Corel; 125: Des Moines Community Playhouse; 126: © Robbie Jack/CORBIS; 127: THE KOBAL COLLECTION / ODYSSEY; 131: AP Photo/E Pablo Kosmicki; 132: © Leonard de Selva/CORBIS; 133 left: © Robbie Jack/CORBIS; 133 right: AP Photo/File; 135: Corel; 137: RAFAEL PEREZ/Reuters/Landov ; 138–139: AP Photo/Alan Solomon; 140: Richard Feldman; 147: A. Vincent Scarano; 149: AP Photo/Tina Fineberg; 150 top: ArtToday; 150 bottom: © Robbie Jack/CORBIS; 151: AP Photo/Kenneth Lambert; 152–153: © Micheline Pelletier/CORBIS SYGMA; 163 left: THE KOBAL COLLECTION / MARAT SADE/UNITED ARTISTS; 163 right: © Colita/CORBIS; 164: © Lindsay Hebberd/CORBIS; 165 top: © Jacques M. Chenet/CORBIS; 165 bottom: AP Photo/Ted S. Warren; 167: © Robbie Jack/CORBIS; 179: Western Michigan University; 180: The Harvard Theatre Collection, The Houghton Library; 181: Richard Feldman; 182–183: The Flying Karamazov Brothers; 186 top: Corel; 187: Burdette Parks, Roundlake Studios; 194: © Francis G. Mayer/CORBIS; 195: Richard Feldman; 196 top: Corel; 196–197: Western Michigan University; 199: Digital Vision; 201: Neo Futurists; 205: Burdette Parks, Roundlake Studios; 206: © Roger Wood/CORBIS; 207: Michael Rubottom; 210–211: Donald Cooper/Photostage; 212–213: Clive Barda/ArenaPAL; 213: Wayne Kischer; 221: Corel; 224 bottom: Richard Feldman; 226: Richard Feldman; 229: G.W. Mercier; 230: North Wind Archives; 231: Tallahassee Little Theatre, Susan Stripling photography; 232–233: Richard Feldman; 234 top to bottom: Strand; Strand; Guy Currier, Altman Lighting;Lighting

626 Acknowledgments

Innovation; Strand; Oasis Stage Werks; 235 top to bottom: University of Indianapolis; PLC Collection; PLC Collection; PLC Collection; DHA Lighting Limited; PLC Collection; 236: Corel; 237: Western Michigan University; 238: Goodman Theatre, Eric Y. Exit; 242: Wallace Photography; 245: Corel; 250: © Historical Picture Archive/CORBIS; 251 right: Beinecke Rare Book and Manuscript Library, Yale University; 251 left: Richard Feldman; 253: © Robbie Jack/CORBIS; 254–255: Liquid Library; 256: Michael Brosilow; 257: Art Today; 261: THE KOBAL COLLECTION / COLUMBIA; 263 left: THE KOBAL COLLECTION; 263 right: Michael Brosilow; 265: © Robbie Jack/CORBIS; 269: © RAAB SHANNA/CORBIS SYGMA; 274 top: Nan Zabriskie; 274 bottom: ©1996 Liz Lauren; 277: © MAIMAN RICK/CORBIS SYGMA; 278: The Devonshire Collection, Chatsworth. Reproduced by permission of the Duke of Devonshire and the Chatsworth Settlement Trustees.; 279 top: Mummenschanz; 279 bottom: © CORBIS SYGMA; 280–281: © Robbie Jack/CORBIS; 281: Des Moines Community Playhouse; 282: CBS-TV / THE KOBAL COLLECTION; 298: Cynthia Clampitt; 299 top: Western Michigan University; 299 bottom: Goodman Theatre; 300–301: Corel; 302: Corel; 305: Corel; 310 left: Photos.com; 310 right: ArenaPAL; 311: Henrietta Butler/ArenaPAL; 315: AP Photo/ Denis Doyle; 316: © Kelly-Mooney Photography/CORBIS; 317: Michael Le Poer Trench/ArenaPAL; 318: Carol Rosegg/ ArenaPAL; 319: Colin Willoughby/ArenaPAL; 320: THE KOBAL COLLECTION / MIRAMAX / JAMES, DAVID; 329: AP Photo/ Stephen Chernin; 330: © Liu Liqun/CORBIS; 331: Michael Le Poer Trench/ArenaPAL; 332: AP Photo/Robert Spencer; 333: © DICKINSON TIM/CORBIS SYGMA; 334: © Michael S. Yamashita/CORBIS; 334: AP Photo/Anat Givon; 335 left: Robert Strickland; 335 right: Corel; 341: AP Photo/Harry Cabluck; 342: © Michael S. Yamashita/CORBIS; 343: Bread and Puppet Theatre Headquarters; 344: THE KOBAL COLLECTION / MGM/MAIDEN/NEW REGENCY / ARONOWITZ, MYLES; 352: © Bettmann/CORBIS; 353 top: T. Charles Erickson; 353 bottom: THE KOBAL COLLECTION / TOUCHSTONE/UNIVERSAL; 355: THE KOBAL COLLECTION / 20TH CENTURY FOX/PARAMOUNT / WALLACE, MERIE W.; 356: THE KOBAL COLLECTION / 20TH CENTURY FOX / NITKE, BARBARA; 358: THE KOBAL COLLECTION / CINEMA CENTER; 365 left: THE KOBAL COLLECTION / UNIVERSAL; 365 right: © Reuters NewMedia Inc./CORBIS; 366: © Bettmann/CORBIS; 367: THE KOBAL COLLECTION / IFC FILMS / GIRAUD, SOPHIE; 368–369: THE KOBAL COLLECTION / WARNER BROS TV/BRIGHT/ KAUFFMAN/CRANE PRO; 369: © Bettmann/CORBIS; 370: THE KOBAL COLLECTION; 371 top: THE KOBAL COLLECTION / CBS-TV; 371 bottom: THE KOBAL COLLECTION / DARREN STAR PRODUCTIONS /

BLANKENHORN, CRAIG; 372: THE KOBAL COLLECTION / CTW/JIM HENSON PROD; 373: © Reuters NewMedia Inc./ CORBIS; 375: © Reuters NewMedia Inc./CORBIS; 381: AP Photo/Bob Galbraith; 382: THE KOBAL COLLECTION / ABC-TV; 383: © William Burlingham/The Actors Gymnasium; 385: © David Butow/CORBIS SABA; 387: The Advertising Archive Ltd.; 394: © Bettmann/CORBIS; 395: Richard Feldman; 399: © Bettmann/CORBIS; 400–401: Corel; 401: Kati Wilson, Loyola Marymount University Costume Design student and costume designer for JB; 403: Art Today; 404: © Robbie Jack/ CORBIS; 405 middle: Art Today. 406: © AFP/CORBIS; 408: Art Today; 409: © Bettmann/CORBIS; 410: © Marc Garanger/ CORBIS; 412: Cynthia Clampitt; 413: © Burstein Collection/ CORBIS; 416–417: AP Photo/Diether Endlicher; 419: Michael Brosilow; 420: © Lindsay Hebberd/CORBIS; 423: Burdette Parks, Roundlake Studios; 424: Utah Shakespearean Festival; 425: Andrea Pistolesi/Getty Images; 426: Art Today; 431: © Robbie Jack/CORBIS; 435: AP Photo/Luca Bruno; 436, 437: © Bettmann/CORBIS; 438: Michal Daniel; 441: Nigel Norrington/ArenaPAL; 442–443: Pete Jones/ArenaPAL; 459: © ELBAZ SOPHIE/CORBIS SYGMA

Mike Aspengren Illustrations: 56, 58, 65 top, 102, 145, 184, 185, 186 bottom, 188, 189, 190, 214, 215, 217, 218, 219, 222, 223, 224 top, 225, 240, 241, 262, 285, 294, 405 left and right,

William Burlingham Photographs: back cover, 6, 7, 22, 23, 24, 25, 35, 37, 46, 57, 61, 69, 94, 143, 154, 156, 160–161, 169, 172, 193, 228, 258, 259, 266, 267, 268, 283, 284, 286, 287, 289, 290, 291, 292, 293, 304–305, 309

The editors wish to thank the playwrights, publishers, and agents who have allowed their copyrighted materials to be used in this book. Every effort has been made to contact all copyright holders. If we have omitted anyone, please let us know and we will include a suitable acknowledgment in subsequent editions.